Las Vegas

timeout.com/las-vegas

Time Out Digital Ltd
Universal House
251 Tottenham Court Road
London W1T 7AB
United Kingdom
Tel: +44 (0)20 7813 3000
Fax: +44 (0)20 7813 6001
Email: guides@timeout.com
www.timeout.com

Published by Time Out Digital Ltd, a wholly owned subsidiary of Time Out Group Ltd.
Time Out and the Time Out logo are trademarks of Time Out Group Ltd.

10 9 8 7 6 5 4 3 2 1

This edition first published in Great Britain in 2013 by Ebury Publishing.
A Random House Group Company
20 Vauxhall Bridge Road, London SW1V 2SA

Random House Australia Pty Ltd 20 Alfred Street, Milsons Point, Sydney, New South Wales 2061, Australia

Random House New Zealand Ltd 18 Poland Road, Glenfield, Auckland 10, New Zealand

Random House South Africa (Pty) Ltd Isle of Houghton, Corner Boundary Road & Carse O'Gowrie, Houghton 2198, South Africa

Random House UK Limited Reg. No. 954009

Distributed in the US and Latin America by Publishers Group West (1-510-809-3700)

For further distribution details, see www.timeout.com.

ISBN (UK): 978-1-84670-398-0

A CIP catalogue record for this book is available from the British Library.

Printed and bound by Butler Tanner & Dennis, Frome, Somerset.

The Random House Group Limited supports the Forest Stewardship Council® (FSC®), the leading international forest-certification organisation. Our books carrying the FSC label are printed on FSC®-certified paper. FSC is the only forest-certification scheme supported by the leading environmental organisations, including Greenpeace. Our paper procurement policy can be found at www.randomhouse.co.uk/environment.

MIX
Paper from
responsible sources
FSC® C023561

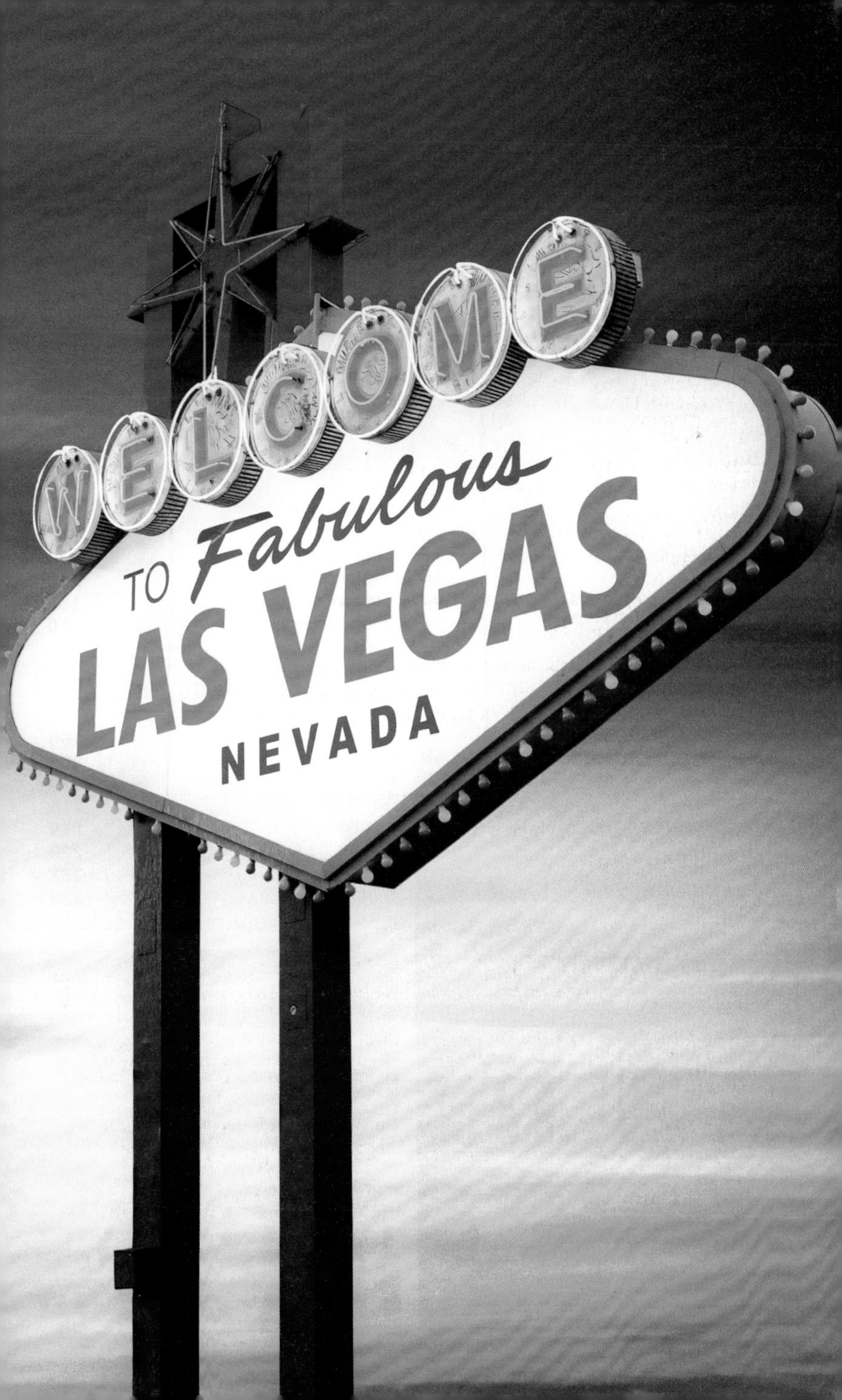
WELCOME
TO Fabulous
LAS VEGAS
NEVADA

Contents

Introduction

Anyone who has visited Las Vegas will be happy to tell you what this place is all about. Maybe Vegas is their shopping mecca, or the place to see many varieties of entertainment literally across the street from one another. Maybe it's their club-hopping paradise and the place to party all night long, or perhaps they just like lounging by the pool. They might return for the limitless dining options or because they have high hopes of hitting the jackpot, even though they always leave with substantially less money than they had upon arrival.

But if you've only dreamed of visiting Las Vegas, you'll have your own sort of image of the place in mind. Maybe it's Vegas in its nascent entertainment days, when the Rat Pack ruled and its visitors and citizens adhered to a certain style, or the Mob-fuelled time of a town run by organised crime, or the kitschy and debauched vision of Hunter S Thompson, or the swinging singles of *Swingers* (still very much playing itself out at nightclubs – and daylife parties – up and down the Strip).

But regardless of whether you're here for the first time or the tenth, you have felt its magnetic pull. You want to come to Las Vegas because it offers you something you can't get or be at home. Las Vegas is the most mythologised city in America and, perhaps, the world. We make up stories about what it is and what it offers, which is very easy to do in a city that is so often shedding its skin and growing a new one.

From its earliest days, Las Vegas evolved as a respite, a place to rest between 'here' and 'there'. Around that idea grew its promises of diversion: gambling, liquor and women in its frontier days; world-class dining, high-end shopping and Cirque du Soleil in its current incarnation. That idea is still current today. In fact, whether people will admit it or not, it is the gasoline that fuels our engine. We are a tourist town, and to be anything less than proud of that fact would be a disservice.

With that in mind, this guide to Las Vegas is, then, by its very nature incomplete. To give due space to everything on offer here would take volumes. But we have done our best to hit the high notes. From some of the best and newest restaurants, like Rx Boiler Room, to recently unveiled shows, such as *Million Dollar Quartet,* to fun activities for thrill-seekers and families alike, we've included everything we could. Undoubtedly, by the next edition – even by the time you read this – there will be more. Because that's just the way Vegas rolls.
Todd Peterson, Editor

About the Guide

GETTING AROUND

The back of the book contains street maps of Las Vegas, as well as overview maps of the city and its surroundings. The maps start on page 278; on them are marked the locations of hotels and casinos (**❶**), restaurants and buffets (**❶**), and bars and lounges (**❶**). Many businesses listed in this guide are located in the areas we've mapped; the grid-square references in the listings refer to these maps.

THE ESSENTIALS

For practical information, including visas, disabled access, emergency numbers, lost property, useful websites and local transport, please see the Essential Information. It begins on page 290.

THE LISTINGS

Addresses, phone numbers, websites, transport information, hours and prices are all included in our listings, as are selected other facilities. All were checked and correct at press time. However, business owners can alter their arrangements at any time, and fluctuating economic conditions can cause prices to change rapidly.

The very best venues in the city, the must-sees and must-dos in every category, have been marked with a red star (★). In the Explore chapters, we've also marked venues with free admission with a FREE symbol.

PHONE NUMBERS

The area code for Las Vegas is 702. You don't need to use the code when calling from within Las Vegas: simply dial the seven-digit number as listed in this guide.

From outside the US, dial your country's international access code (00 from the UK) or a '+' symbol, followed by the US country code (1), 702 for Las Vegas, followed by the seven-digit number as listed in this guide. So, to reach the Bellagio, dial +1-702 693 7111. For more on phones, including mobile-phone use, see page 268.

FEEDBACK

We welcome feedback on this guide, both on the venues we've included and on any other locations that you'd like to see featured in future editions. Please email us at guides@timeout.com.

Time Out Guides

Founded in 1968, Time Out has grown from humble beginnings into the leading resource for anyone wanting to know what's happening in the world's greatest cities. Alongside our influential weeklies in London, New York and Chicago, we publish more than 20 magazines in cities as varied as Beijing and Beirut; a range of travel books, with the City Guides now joined by the newer Shortlist series; and an information-packed website. The company remains proudly independent, still owned by Tony Elliott four decades after he launched *Time Out London*.

Written by local experts and illustrated with original photography, our books also retain their independence. No business has been featured because it has advertised, and all restaurants and bars are visited and reviewed anonymously.

ABOUT THE EDITOR

Todd Peterson moved to Las Vegas in the late 1990s, working as an entertainment writer. He later relocated to New York, where he wrote for publications including People.com, *Rolling Stone* and *GQ*, before returning to Las Vegas with his family in 2012. Besides writing and editing, he runs the travel website FreeVacation.com.

A full list of the book's contributors can be found on page 11.

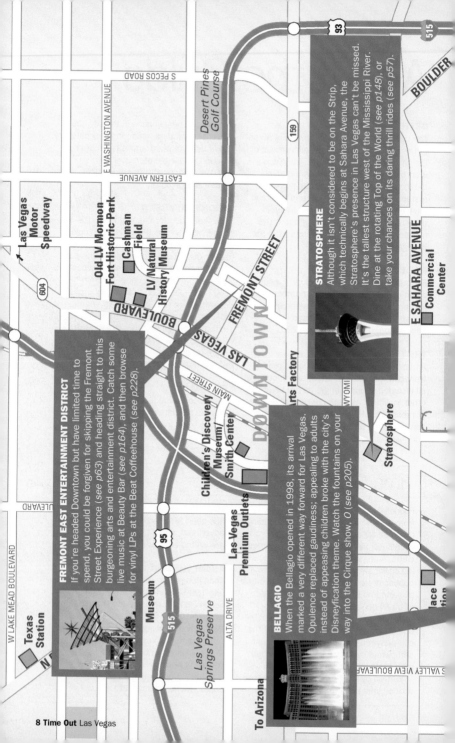

FREMONT EAST ENTERTAINMENT DISTRICT

If you're headed Downtown but have limited time to spend, you could be forgiven for skipping the Fremont Street Experience (see p63) and heading straight to this burgeoning arts and entertainment district. Catch some live music at Beauty Bar (see p164), and then browse for vinyl LPs at the Beat Coffeehouse (see p228).

BELLAGIO

When the Bellagio opened in 1998, its arrival marked a very different way forward for Las Vegas. Opulence replaced gaudiness; appealing to adults instead of appeasing children broke with the city's Disneyfication theme. Watch the fountains on your way into the Cirque show, *O* (see p205).

STRATOSPHERE

Although it isn't considered to be on the Strip, which technically begins at Sahara Avenue, the Stratosphere's presence in Las Vegas can't be missed. It's the tallest structure west of the Mississippi River. Dine at the rotating Top of the World (see p148), or take your chances on its daring thrill rides (see p57).

W LAKE MEAD BOULEVARD

Texas Station

W WASHINGTON AVENUE

E WASHINGTON AVENUE

S PECOS ROAD

EASTERN AVENUE

Desert Pines Golf Course

Las Vegas Motor Speedway

Old LV Mormon Fort Historic Park

Cashman Field

LV Natural History Museum

FREMONT STREET

LAS VEGAS BOULEVARD

DOWNTOWN

MAIN STREET

Arts Factory

Children's Discovery Museum / Smith Center

Las Vegas Premium Outlets

Museum

Las Vegas Springs Preserve

ALTA DRIVE

To Arizona

Stratosphere

E SAHARA AVENUE

Commercial Center

WYOMI

S VALLEY VIEW BOULEVARD

BOULDER

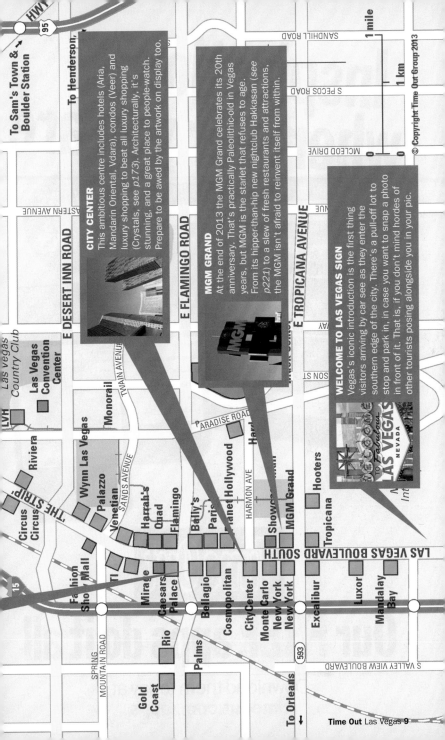

CITY CENTER

This ambitious centre includes hotels (Aria, Mandarin Oriental, Vdara), condos (Veer) and luxury shopping to beat all luxury shopping (Crystals, see p173). Architecturally, it's stunning, and a great place to people-watch. Prepare to be awed by the artwork on display too.

MGM GRAND

At the end of 2013 the MGM Grand celebrates its 20th anniversary. That's practically Paleolithic-old in Vegas years, but MGM is the starlet that refuses to age. From its hipper-than-hip new nightclub Hakkasan (see p221) to a slew of fresh restaurants and attractions, the MGM isn't afraid to reinvent itself from within.

WELCOME TO LAS VEGAS SIGN

Vegas's iconic introduction is the first thing visitors arriving by car see as they enter the city. There's a pull-off lot to stop and park in, in case you want to snap a photo in front of it. That is, if you don't mind hordes of other tourists posing alongside you in your pic.

To Sam's Town & Boulder Station

To Henderson

E DESERT INN ROAD

E FLAMINGO ROAD

E TROPICANA AVENUE

SANDHILL ROAD

S PECOS ROAD

MCLEOD DRIVE

EASTERN AVENUE

Las Vegas Country Club

Las Vegas Convention Center

LVH

Riviera

Monorail

TWAIN AVENUE

SANDS AVENUE

Wynn Las Vegas

Palazzo

Venetian

Harrah's

Flamingo

Bally's

Paris

PARADISE ROAD

Planet Hollywood

HARMON AVE

Showcase Mall

MGM Grand

Hooters

Tropicana

LAS VEGAS BOULEVARD SOUTH

Circus Circus

'THE STRIP'

Fashion Show Mall

TI

Mirage

Caesars Palace

Bellagio

Cosmopolitan

CityCenter

Monte Carlo

New York New York

Excalibur

Luxor

Mandalay Bay

15

SPRING MOUNTAIN ROAD

Rio

Palms

Gold Coast

593

S VALLEY VIEW BOULEVARD

To Orleans

HWY 95

To Hendersor

1 mile

1 km

© Copyright Time Out Group 2013

TimeOut Las Vegas

Editorial
Editor Todd Peterson
Consultant Editor Lisa Ritchie
Deputy Editor Ros Sales
Fact checkers Camille Cannon, Genevie Durano
Proofreader Marion Moisy
Indexer Ros Sales

Editorial Director Sarah Guy
Management Accountant Margaret Wright

Design
Senior Designer Kei Ishimaru
Designer Darryl Bell
Group Commercial Senior Designer Jason Tansley

Picture Desk
Picture Editor Jael Marschner
Picture Researcher Ben Rowe
Freelance Picture Researcher Isidora O'Neill

Advertising
Sales Director St John Betteridge
Advertising Sales Melissa Keller, Christy Stewart

Marketing
Senior Publishing Brand Manager Luthfa Begum
Head of Circulation Dan Collins

Production
Production Controller Katie Mulhern-Bhudia

Time Out Group
Chairman & Founder Tony Elliott
Chief Executive Officer Aksel Van der Wal
Editor-in-Chief Tim Arthur
UK Chief Commercial Officer David Pepper
Group IT Director Simon Chappell
Group Marketing Director Carolyn Sims

Contributors
This guide was updated, with additional writing throughout, by Todd Peterson. **Introduction** Todd Peterson.
Las Vegas Today Todd Peterson. **Gambling** Deke Castleman. **Diary** Beverly Bryan. **Casinos & Hotels** Will Fulford-Jones, Phil Hagen, Amy Schmidt (*Lavish Loos* Joe Brown; *Getting Personal* Todd Peterson). **Sightseeing** Todd Peterson, Will Fulford-Jones, CM Buford, Dayvid Figler, Emily Richmond, Deke Castleman. **Restaurants & Buffets** Todd Peterson, Will Fulford-Jones, Phil Hagen, Al Mancini, James P Reza, Amy Schmidt (*Sin City's Sweet Tooth* Joe Brown). **Bars & Lounges** Kate Silver. **Shopping** Amy Schmidt, Erika Pope (*Tattoo You* Joe Brown; *Rejuvenation Stations* Genevie Durano). **Casino Entertainment** Will Fulford-Jones, Julie Seabaugh. **Children** Phil Hagen (*Get Your Hops Up* Todd Peterson). **Film** Mike Prevatt (*Essential Las Vegas Films* Todd Peterson). **Gay & Lesbian** Mike Prevatt (*Massive Attack* Todd Peterson). **Nightlife** PJ Perez (*We Love the Daylife* Joe Brown; *Essential Vegas Albums* Todd Peterson). **Sports & Fitness** Kate Silver (*Get Your Motor Runnin'* Todd Peterson). **Performing Arts** David Surratt, PJ Perez. **Weddings** Beverly Bryan, Renée Battle. **Escapes & Excursions** Will Fulford-Jones. **History** Will-Fulford Jones. **Architecture** Phil Hagen.

Maps john@jsgraphics.co.uk

Cover photograph Slot Machines by Westend61/SuperStock
Back cover photography Shutterstock, Songquan Deng, Erik Kabik/erikkabik.com

Photography pages 3, 6, 12/13, 25, 41, 44/45, 46, 53, 56, 57, 59, 98, 101, 233, 242/243, 244, 247, 249, 252, 256, 259, 262, 265, 267, 268, 277, 283, 286, 289, 290/291, 310/311 Shutterstock; 8 (bottom left), 66, 102 (top), 119, 120, 122, 127, 129, 174 (bottom), 176, 232 Jeffrey J Coleman/Shutterstock.com; 8 (bottom right), 55, 76/77 Andrew Zarivny/Shutterstock.com; 18, 164 (top) Mona Shield Payne; 28, 32, 37, 52, 64, 67, 69, 74, 84 (bottom), 96 (top), 130, 134, 139, 140, 146, 152, 155, 158, 159, 163, 165, 167, 180, 186, 193, 208, 209, 212, 215, 217, 218, 228, 236241, 255 Jonathan Perugia; 38 Action Sports Photography/Shutterstock.com; 39, 42, 43, 81, 90 (bottom), 92, 97, 113, 121 Kobby Dagan/Shutterstock.com; 49 Spirit of America/Shutterstock.com; 50 Lowe R. Llaguno/Shutterstock.com; 63, 84 (top) Jorg Hackemann/Shutterstock.com; 68 James Mattil/ Shutterstock.com; 87 Greg Anderson Photography; 93 Songquan Deng/Shutterstock.com; 94 Las Vegas Convention and Visitors Authority; 95 Eugene Buchko/Shutterstock.com; 96 (bottom) Gary Paul Lewis; 99 David Drebin/Shutterstock.com; 102 (bottom) Reed Kaestner Photography; 105 O'Gara/Bissell Photography; 114 Erik Kabib; 125 Foto Tehnik; 135 Thomas Schauer; 160 Scott Frances; 174 (top), 175, 179 Ritu Manoj Jethani/Shutterstock.com; 194/195 Geri Kodey; 196 Tomasz Rossa; 201 (top) Anthony Morgan/Alamy; 202, 203, 220 Denise Truscello; 213 REX/Everett Collection; 219, 225 Danny Mahoney; 229 Steve Hall; 235 Hannah Maule-Ffinch; 261 Jorg Hackemann; 264 REX/Keystone USA-ZUMA; 270/271 Matt Carbone; 272 Getty Images/ Time & Life Pictures Creative; 281 Alamy.

The following images were provided by the featured establishments: pages 14, 40, 61, 78, 80, 82, 83, 85, 88, 89, 90 (top), 107, 108, 111, 112, 115, 117, 126, 132, 133, 136, 137, 138, 141, 143, 144, 151, 157, 161, 162, 164 (bottom), 168, 170, 177, 178, 184, 187, 188, 191, 198, 199, 200, 201 (bottom), 205, 206, 207, 210, 221, 222, 224, 227, 231, 238, 284.

In Focus

Las Vegas Today

Making and remaking the Entertainment Capital of the World.

TEXT: TODD PETERSON

You don't have to live in Las Vegas very long before you will overhear – or participate in – some variation of a conversation that goes like this: 'Our friends (or relatives) from Cleveland (or Des Moines or New York or Tokyo) just came to visit. They couldn't believe our neighbourhood. They had no idea what Las Vegas was like. They thought we lived in the back of a casino or something'. It's a familiar refrain among locals: once people learn you live here, they can't wait to visit. Relatives you never knew you had and friends you hadn't realised cared so much about you will extend invitations for you to host them. Such is life when you live in a town that everyone wants to visit – whether they'll admit it or not.

PERCEPTION VS REALITY

To people who do not live here, Las Vegas is the Strip and vice versa. Its nicknames – like 'Sin City' and 'the Entertainment Capital of the World', or, perhaps less endearingly, 'the City of Lost Wages' (a local favourite) – are emblematic not of a town with real and regular folks, but rather of a destination where people go to be amused and, often, misbehave. Locals may scoff at the notion that this city is one big playground. But when it comes right down to it, there is more than a grain of truth to it.

That isn't to imply that living in Las Vegas is a vacation or anything like that. But the perception of Las Vegas and the Strip being one and the same has some resonance. For one thing, the Strip is the engine that drives much of the state of Nevada. (And by 'Strip', we mean all hotels and casinos, whether they're located properly on the Strip or not. But more on that in a minute.)

Gaming, entertainment, tourism: these industries contribute mightily to Las Vegas and the rest of Nevada. Not only are these fields huge employers locally and statewide, but their contributions to government coffers keep taxes low and eliminate the need for a state income tax. This has made Las Vegas an attractive place to live. At least until the latter part of the last decade.

By now, the too-often-told story of the worldwide economic crisis would rather be forgotten by those who survived it – and, financially, many people didn't – but its effects are still much in evidence. In Las Vegas, the residential real estate market tanked and home prices dived by more than 50 per cent in many parts of the city. With that, credit for construction and business loans dried up, and Las Vegas, which appeared to be on the precipice of another major expansion, ground to a halt.

THE BUMP IN THE ROAD

At the end of 2008, Steve Wynn opened Encore, his companion property to Wynn Las Vegas, just as banks were closing and it seemed the US financial sector might implode. The long-awaited CityCenter, which had been announced in 2004, limped along until its completion in 2009. Its mix of high-end hotel rooms (Aria and Mandarin Oriental), extravagant shopping (Crystals), and pricey condos (Veer) couldn't have come on the market at a worse time. In December 2010, the Cosmopolitan opened as well, but other projects weren't so lucky.

The Fontainebleau, then under construction on the northern end of the Strip, ran into one problem after another when investors couldn't obtain financing to continue building. Today, the hotel's glass shell sits empty at 68 storeys – its future uncertain – after being purchased for pennies on the dollar. Likewise, the Echelon, which was to be built on the site of the old Stardust, was started in 2007 before its parent company, Boyd Gaming, shut the project down in 2008. In early 2013 the site was sold to an Asian gaming company, which announced plans to build a new mega-resort on it.

These unfinished projects have been the subject of much debate locally. Despite bright spots elsewhere – CityCenter, Cosmopolitan – empty buildings like Fontainebleau remind Las Vegans that something is wrong with the machine, like smoke pouring from under the hood.

However, locals had elsewhere to look as construction resumed apace. On the Strip, the Imperial Palace underwent a makeover and emerged as the Quad in the summer of 2013, a rebranding intended to appeal to a younger, hipper clientele. Next to the Quad, building continued on Caesars Entertainment's open-air mall, the Linq. When complete, this dining, shopping and entertainment district will house the world's largest Ferris wheel, the High Roller, topping out at 550 feet.

Slated to open in late 2013, the Linq is also interesting for its air of permanence. Like other structures built since the turn of the century, the new sky-high towers look as if they're here for good. There is more permanence to construction now than at any time in Vegas's past. You don't, for example, implode an Aria when the crowds start to thin.

These new visions of the city are, it seems, being built to last. To a certain degree, then, we're stuck with what's

IN FOCUS

going up – not that that's a bad thing, but it also indicates a change in how this city is and will be perceived. An eyesore like the Excalibur wouldn't (mercifully) stand a chance in today's Las Vegas.

REMAKING OF A CITY

As Las Vegas slowly recovers from the recession, one part of the city is marching full-speed ahead in a major shift that could have even longer ranging implications – culturally, economically, and maybe even architecturally – than what is being built on the Strip. Although you wouldn't know it today, Las Vegas's origins began in the Downtown area. Long, long before there was a 'Strip', the area of Las Vegas was staked out around the Downtown blocks, specifically 110 acres between what are now the north–south avenues of Stewart and Garces, and the east–west boundaries between Main and 5th Streets.

As the fortunes of Las Vegas rose and fell, Downtown tended towards the latter. Despite being a rich and integral part of the city, Downtown was quickly overshadowed by the Strip. The area's regression into also-ran hotel-casinos and increasingly destitute neighbourhoods marched on year after year, as all eyes were on the Strip. For decades, Downtown was a place seldom mentioned in the national press. Many locals weren't all that proud of it either.

In the early 1990s, some of the hotel-casino owners in the area decided to do something about the downward slide. Fremont Street, between Main Street and Las Vegas Boulevard, was closed to cars. An electronic canopy was installed over the street, permanently lighting it, while adding graphics and music. And so, in 1995, the Fremont Street Experience was born. Even by Vegas standards (and an upgrade in 2004) the FSE is something of a monstrosity. The blocks-long screen blasts visual images from dusk until late into the night, and while some Downtown casinos would say it's helped attract visitors to the area, nearly as many hotel-casinos have closed as have stayed open here. Others are on life-support. On either side of the street are entrances to a

number of once-prominent but long-since-struggling Downtown properties, including Binion's, the original Las Vegas home of poker, and now just a casino; the recently renovated and renamed D, formerly Fitzgeralds; Golden Nugget, the classiest joint in the area; and Vegas's oldest original hotel-casino, the Golden Gate. Scattered among them are souvenir shops and kiosks, as well as some newer eateries and bars fighting an uphill battle for respectability. Much of the time, the area under the FSE resembles an open-air keg party run amok. It is, then, the very antithesis of a Bellagio or an Aria, and it's certainly not very Cosmopolitan.

Aside from this, there has been an even greater problem facing Downtown; one that affects the entire city, not just the Strip's or the Downtown casino's bottom line. And that problem has been that there is not actually a 'downtown' there. A downtown is typically associated with a prominent business district or some sort of cultural centre. Las Vegas's has neither. In fact, aside from the Strip – which might be fine for visitors, but not for locals – there is no 'heart of the city'. It's a city of roughly two million people, without a pulse of its own.

Like any metropolitan area, Las Vegas has certain names associated with it. Here, people tend to think of entertainers, Sinatra or Elvis perhaps. Or maybe Mob figures associated with Vegas's ascension: Bugsy Siegel, Meyer Lansky. There are others too, maybe not as recognisable, but even more important: former senator Pat McCarran or current Senate Majority leader Harry Reid. In business, there are many: Steve Wynn, Kirk Kerkorian and Bob Stupak. And now, there's a new name: Tony Hsieh.

THE BEGINNING

Online shoe retailer Zappos.com relocated from San Francisco to Las Vegas in 2004, Tony Hsieh, the company CEO, continued to build the online empire, and by 2009 he was making inroads in Las Vegas's Downtown area too.

By then, the Fremont East Entertainment District east of FSE had already taken hold, and new bars and businesses were slowly gaining traction. Hsieh most certainly recognised a good idea when he saw it. Shortly thereafter, he hammered out a deal with the city to relocate Zappos' headquarters into the old City Hall building. In collaboration with other partners and developers, the Downtown Project was born. The plans Hsieh has outlined for the redevelopment of Downtown are not just some cosmetic makeover. The Project has purchased a huge amount of land and property, some of which is already being built on. Hsieh's ambitious plans include not just those for his own business, but also solid infrastructure such as schools and live-work spaces.

But Hsieh isn't the only person who has had grand designs for the reinvention of Downtown. Former mayor Oscar Goodman, whose wife Carolyn now occupies the job, has long been a champion of Downtown. Before Hsieh arrived, Goodman was already envisioning a Downtown that wasn't there, and if not for Goodman, recent projects such as the stunning new Smith Center for the Performing Arts and the remaking of Symphony Park might never have happened.

Despite Hsieh's and Goodman's well-intentioned plans, changes to Downtown are not without their critics. The issues that arise in the face of such a massive undertaking, such as the displacement of businesses and low-income housing, are legitimate concerns. Still, the potential that remains for Vegas is quite clearly a once-in-a-generation shift. If proponents of a new Downtown succeed, in five to ten years' time this could be a radically different city.

GREEN, GREEN VEGAS

However, Las Vegas's future depends not just upon the Strip's engine or the remaking of Downtown. Like a gambler in over his head, there is more at stake. This city needs a comprehensive change in how we view our surroundings. This became evident in late in June 2013. The city awoke to a heatwave that continued for days, with temperatures hitting 115 degrees fahrenheit and higher. Even though this desert valley normally gets hot in the summer, these temperatures moved beyond that, resulting in some of the hottest weather in nearly a decade. No

sooner had it cooled off just a bit, before lightning ignited fire in Carpenter Canyon, north-west of Las Vegas near the Mount Charleston area. The fire raged for the better part of two weeks, Las Vegas's light-filled skies blurry and hazy with smoke for days. By the time the fire was extinguished, nearly 30,000 acres of the nearby Spring Mountains had been scorched.

In the weeks that followed, flood warnings were issued for areas that had been burned. Rapid rainfall could lead to runoff, which would wash down the mountainsides. Whether there was a direct causal link between the previously blistering temperatures and Mother Nature's furious fire didn't matter. Although very few officials publicly admitted it, even the chance of fire combined with hotter than normal temperatures portends a much graver danger facing the entire US – indeed, the world. Catastrophic weather continues to be a problem across the country, and although the western US is no stranger to forest fires, such crippling high temperatures, when combined with fires man- or nature-made, remain a huge threat.

Unfortunately, Las Vegans overall have been slow to respond to environmental issues such as climate change. Conservation measures such as water regulation have more or less been thrust on the population, and it's likely more will follow out of necessity. In some ways this is understandable. In such an arid climate, it's difficult for the average citizen to understand why huge properties, golf courses and the like get a pass when John Q Public has to cut back on his water usage or recycle his disposables. There are, however, bright spots. Recent additions to the Strip, most notably CityCenter, most of whose properties were LEED-certified upon opening, offer a welcome model. It's one all forward-thinking companies would do well to adopt, as we march forwards into making and remaking a new Las Vegas.

Las Vegas – despite perceptions – is not like any other city. We depend on industries other cities would never count on. But the opportunity exists to be much, much more than that. We are seeing that opportunity open before us. Whether we will seize the reins remains to be seen.

IN FOCUS

Gambling

Place your bets.

TEXT: DEKE CASTLEMAN

The old and oft-told joke runs that no one in Las Vegas ever got rich through gambling except the owners of the casinos. For many people, it's a gag that's a lot funnier at the start of their trip than it is at the end. Gambling built Las Vegas, and the fact that the city is still expanding at record speed is proof enough that the novelty of the pastime is as bright as it's ever been. This may open your eyes to just how bright: in 2010, Nevada casinos took in $10.4 billion in gaming revenues.

Sorry to shatter your dreams, then, but if you're thinking that you'll walk away from Las Vegas set up for life, you'd best think again. However, if all you're after is a little fun, having filed your gambling budget under 'entertainment' and prepared yourself for manageable losses, you're in the right place. And you'll certainly have more fun if you know a little about the games you're playing. While the games staged by the casinos aren't especially complicated, a little knowledge will help your money last a good deal longer than it otherwise might. Indeed, play your cards right and you may even end up ahead. But don't bet on it.

HOW CASINOS MAKE MONEY

Before learning how to play the games, it's wise to get acquainted with the casinos' angles on them. There are four ways for the casinos to generate gaming revenue: the house edge, favourable rules, commissions and dumb players.

● The house edge is the difference between the true odds of an event occurring and the odds used for payouts. For example, in double-zero roulette, there are 38 possible winning numbers. If the casino paid true odds, it would pay off a winning number at 37:1 (for a total of $38, including your $1 bet). Instead, the casino pays off a winning number at 35:1. Calculating the house edge from this scenario is simple.

First, imagine placing a $1 bet on every possible number in double-zero roulette, a total wager of $38. No matter which number wins, you'll receive a payout of $36: winnings of $35 at the 35:1 payoff, plus your original $1 bet. The difference between the true-odds payout and the actual payout is $2, money that goes directly into the house's coffers. To calculate the house edge, simply divide the money kept by the house (2) by the money that the house would have paid on true odds (38). This calculation shows a house edge of 5.26 per cent, which means that the house expects to keep 5.26¢ of each dollar bet at a roulette table.

The house edge varies from game to game, and even within each game. Casinos love it when gamblers keep playing for hour after hour, because the house edge grinds its little takes from every dollar wagered. The law of averages favours the casino.

● The rules for casino games are structured to favour the house. The best example is blackjack, where the dealer gets to play his hand last. Should a player bust beforehand, the dealer wins by default. Even if the dealer ends up busting later, the player loses and the house wins.

● Commissions are collected by the house in a few table games. In poker, the house serves as dealer but doesn't play a hand. Instead, the house takes a percentage of every pot (a sum of money that's called the 'rake') or charges players a flat fee of $5 to $7 per half-hour of play. In baccarat, the house takes five per cent of all winnings from bank bets.

● Be they drunk, superstitious, careless or ill-informed, dumb gamblers are a boundless source of funds for the smart house. Why else do casinos offer gamblers free drinks? Alcohol is wonderful for loosening inhibitions, such as the inhibition against losing next month's rent, but it also causes sensible players to make stupid mistakes. An example: although the house edge in blackjack has been calculated at around two per cent, casinos expect a win (or 'hold') of 15 to 20 per cent of the total amount of money brought to the table (the 'drop'), due entirely to the incompetence of the players.

BETTING LIMITS AND MINIMUMS

At every table game, there's a sign detailing the minimum (and often maximum) allowable bet. At blackjack, it might be $5 to $500. Casinos expect players to bet towards the low end of the limit. This separates players by class, so a big player seeking a speedy $500-a-hand game doesn't have to endure poky play from a piker betting five bucks each time. High rollers can bet at higher-than-posted limits if the house is willing to 'fade' (cover) them. In roulette, the minimum means the sum total of all bets that an individual gambler can place in one round; in other words, if the table has a $5 minimum, you can cover it with five $1 bets. But in blackjack, if you play two hands at once, you must bet the minimum on each.

ETIQUETTE

Before you lay down your money, always note the minimum-bet requirement, usually posted on a sign in the far left corner. If you don't want to embarrass yourself, don't toss out a red ($5) chip on a $100-minimum table. Similarly, don't put a quarter into a dollar slot or video poker machine; the coin will pass through the thing and clank into the hopper, alerting the other players that you're a novice. That said, most machines no longer accept coins; only bills and cashout tickets will pass muster.

Table games have strict rules about when players can touch chips or cards, rules that exist to discourage cheats. Many blackjack games are dealt face up and players never touch the cards. Once you make a bet, never touch the chips you've laid down; if you're 'splitting' or doubling down in blackjack, push out a new pile of chips but don't touch the original bet. This rule is to discourage 'past posting', a scam by which cheats sneak more chips on to their bet after peeking at their cards.

Only handle dice with one hand. The pit bosses, the dealers and the other players will all get very nervous if you touch the dice with two hands, or make a fist around them with one hand so

---

The Gambler's Lexicon

The language of Las Vegas.

ante a small bet that players must place into the pot before a hand of poker is dealt.

bankroll your total gambling budget.

Black Book a list, kept by the State Gaming Control Board, of people barred from casinos due to cheating or a link to organised crime.

boxman casino executive who acts as the umpire in a game of craps.

bust a blackjack hand exceeding 21.

buy in exchange cash for casino chips.

cage the cashier, where chips and tokens are converted into cash and credit is established.

carousel a group of slots that are often connected to a joint progressive jackpot.

change colour swapping chips for ones of a higher or lower denomination.

checks another word for chips.

chips tokens issued by casinos and used, instead of cash, for table games.

colour up exchange small denomination chips for larger denomination chips.

comps 'complimentaries'; anything from free cocktails to 'RFB' (room, food and beverage). Their value is calculated by the gambler's average bet, multiplied by the time spent playing, multiplied by the house edge. To qualify, you must be a rated player or belong to a players club.

credit line amount of credit a gambler is allowed.

croupier casino employee who controls the action in baccarat and roulette.

drop total funds, including chips, cash and markers, gambled at a table or a machine.

edge see *house edge*.

European wheel a roulette wheel with a single '0' position, which gives players better odds. Most wheels in Vegas have '0' and '00'.

even money a bet that pays back an amount equal to the bet itself. In other words, if you win on a $5 bet, you receive your $5 stake plus a $5 win.

eye in the sky casino surveillance systems.

face cards jacks, queens and kings; also known as 'pictures' or 'paint'.

funbook a booklet of vouchers (meal deals and the like) or match-play coupons (valid in conjunction with cash).

George dealer-speak for a good tipper.

grind joint a casino with low table minimums and low-denomination slot machines.

high roller gambler who bets at least $100 per hand on a table game, and plays $5 slots.

hit in blackjack, to take another card.

hole card the blackjack dealer's face-down card.

house edge the percentage difference (retained by the casino) between the true odds and the actual payout.

inside bet in roulette, betting on a single number or small combination of numbers.

juice power and influence; who you know.

IN FOCUS

they can't be seen. Blow on them, shake them and turn them so your favourite numbers are up, but don't hide them for a second. That's how dice cheats use sleight of hand to get loaded dice into a game of craps.

All told, it's best for novice gamblers to stand back at first and watch the action; after a few minutes, you'll get the hang of the procedures. If you need to be corrected, the dealer will do so gently and unobtrusively. And don't worry if it happens: the other players at the tables have all been corrected at one time or another. They didn't step up to a crap table for the first time knowing everything about the game.

You must be 21 to gamble. If you're under 21 and start winning (or hit a jackpot that requires you to sign tax

layout diagram on the playing table that marks the area of the game.
loose a term used to describe a slot machine that pays out frequently. Casinos compete in claiming that their slots are the loosest.
low roller gambler who bets at low-minimum slot machines, usually in grind joints.
marker IOU signed by a rated player to obtain chips and paid off with chips or cash.
natural in blackjack, a two-card total of 21; in baccarat, a two-card total of eight or nine.
outside bet in roulette, betting outside the single-number layout: on black or red; on odds or evens; on the first, second or third 12 numbers as a group etc.
pit area behind the gaming tables reserved for casino employees.
pit boss casino executive who oversees the gambling action from inside the pit.
players club clubs for slots and video-poker players by which members accrue points as they play; these can then later be redeemed against meals, gifts, cash and other perks.
pot the bets accumulated while playing a hand of poker.
progressive a slot or video-poker machine on which the jackpot increases as more coins are played. A linked progressive is a group of machines that are networked to share their jackpot.

push in blackjack, where the dealer and player(s) have the same un-busted hand. No money changes hands.
rated player player whose gambling is assessed by the casino and is thus eligible for comps.
shill casino employee who plays at empty tables (with house money) to encourage visitors to join the action.
shoe container for decks of cards from which card games are often dealt.
shooter the player who throws the dice in a game of craps.
stand in blackjack, to refuse another card.
stiff someone who doesn't tip, one of the worst insults in Las Vegas; also refers to blackjack hands totalling 12-16.
tight used to describe a slot machine that is perceived to pay out infrequently.
toke a tip for a casino employee, often given in the form of a bet on their behalf.
true odds real chances of winning on any game as opposed to the money actually paid out by the casino.
underlay a bet that's higher than strict probability suggests is wise.
up card the blackjack dealer's face-up card.
vigorish also 'vig'; *see house edge.*
whale big-money gambler prepared to wager at least $5,000 a hand at high-stakes games.

IN FOCUS

forms), your chips or jackpot will be confiscated and you'll be tossed out of the casino faster than you can say, 'But…'. You may even be turned over to a Gaming Control Board agent. The lower your age and the higher your bet, the bigger the trouble.

Most casinos subscribe to the old tradition that cameras are unwelcome, and it's wise to leave your SLRs and camcorders in your room, your car or your backpack. If you're discreet, or even if you ask permission, you can sometimes get away with taking photographs in casinos, particularly at the Excalibur and Harrah's. On the other hand, wherever you go in a casino (except the toilets), you'll be watched by eye-in-the-sky cameras and taped for posterity. Nowhere on earth is Big Brother busier than in a casino; make sure you behave accordingly.

MONEY, MONEY, MONEY

To play table games, you'll need chips. However, in some games, you can throw down a bill for your first plays; in blackjack, for example, it's usually fine to play with cash, though any winnings will be paid as chips. You can buy chips at the table in a process called a buy in; you can also buy chips at the cage. Chips can only be redeemed at the cage.

Chips are like currency in the casino within which they're issued. However, due to problems with counterfeiting, casinos rarely honour each others' chips for gambling unless they're under the same ownership. It's sometimes possible to exchange sub-$100 denominations from other casinos for house chips at the cage.

Most modern slot and video-poker machines have bill slots that change greenbacks into credits. If you don't want to use it, or if you only have bills in denominations not accepted by the machine, press the 'Change' button. This activates a light on top of the machine, which summons a roving cashier.

Most casinos are converting to cashless machines (also known as 'ticket in/ticket out', or TITO). You play the machines by putting a regular bill in the slot; however, when you're ready to cash out, the machine dispenses not cash but a ticket detailing your total credits. You can either take the ticket and feed it into another machine, or redeem it for cash at the cage. Be very careful with the tickets, and be sure to redeem them before leaving the casino: some expire in 30 days. And don't leave a TITO machine for even a moment: someone will almost certainly press the 'Cash Out' button, grab the ticket and run.

LEARNING TO GAMBLE

If you want to study before arriving, you'll find hundreds of books on everything from baccarat to video poker. For recommendations, *see pp301-302* though you're generally safe with anything published by Huntington Press (3665 S Procyon Avenue, Las Vegas, NV 89103, www.huntingtonpress.com). There are lots of software programmes available, as well as a slew of instructive websites (*see p302*). The **Gamblers Book Club** and the **Gamblers General Store** are both excellent resources.

Many of the large casinos offer free hands-on lessons at table games. The instructors, usually informative and personable sorts, will take you through the playing procedures and etiquette one step at a time, but they almost certainly won't warn you about sucker games and bets: after all, they're paid by the casino. Lessons are usually held in the late morning during the week, when the casino is at its quietest; some are followed by open low-minimum 'live' games for punters who want to celebrate their new-found skills under casino conditions.

When you're ready to join a game, first stand back and watch the action for a while in order to pick up the rhythms and routines. (However, don't stand too long behind blackjack tables, as most bosses will suspect you of 'back counting' the deck in order to slip in a bet at the most advantageous time.) Choose a table with the lowest possible minimum, so that you're not risking $100, $25 or even $10 a hand at a game you're playing for the first time. Downtown casinos and locals' casinos tend to have lower minimums than the casinos on the Strip.

MAKING THE MOST OF IT

There are plenty of ways to make the most of your money, many of them set up by casinos in an attempt to draw customers. Most popular among them are the casinos' players clubs: they cost nothing to join, and the points you accrue on them can be redeemed for rooms, food and even cash.

Always ask for 'comps' when you play table games. As soon as you make a bet, call over a floorman and ask: 'How long do I have to play to get a buffet comp?' He or she will look at your bet and tell you. Play for as long as he or she indicates, then head off and eat yourself silly. And look for coupons in 'funbooks', free coupon booklets handed out in front of many casinos. Two-for-one, three-for-two and seven-for-five coupons on even-money bets give gamblers a huge edge over the house at blackjack, craps and the like.

While the casinos can help you make your money last, you can also help yourself. Play slowly, for one thing: you're better off exposing your bankroll to the house edge for 50 hands an hour at a busy table than 100 hands an hour playing one-on-one against the dealer, or pulling the handle on a slot machine for 400 spins an hour rather than running at double-time by hitting the spin button like a lunatic.

To ensure you have gambling funds for your whole trip, it's a good idea to divide your money into 'session' portions. Lost an entire portion quickly? End of session. Don't dig into your remaining bankroll until it's time for the next session. Always keep an eye on your coins, cash, tickets and chips; watch for 'rail thieves' when you're at the crap table; and ensure back-to-back slot machines have a plastic or metal guard between them to prevent 'reach through' thievery.

TIP TALK

Las Vegas is a town that runs on tips. This goes particularly for casino dealers, who are paid little more than the minimum wage. Every shift of dealers combines and divides their tips, which make up the bulk of their pay. Giving tips (or 'tokes', as dealers call them, short for tokens of appreciation) is smart, as a happy dealer is your friend. Dealers can assist players in a number of ways: they can slow down the pace of the game (extremely useful when you're playing for comps), create a sociable atmosphere, and even deal a little deeper in the deck, critical for card counters.

You can toke the dealer as you leave the table. However, while they appreciate the tip, it won't gain you any help while you're playing. A better method is to toke immediately after a big win; this way, the dealer knows you're thinking of him or her and could start to help you. Don't bother toking if the dealer is rude, creepy or uncooperative. In fact, don't even play there: just get up and move on to another table.

The best way to show your appreciation is to place a bet for the dealer alongside your own wager. If you win, the toke is paid off at regular odds and the dealer takes the winnings. If you lose, the house wins the toke, but the dealer will still appreciate the gesture. In blackjack, you can place a chip outside the line surrounding your wager circle, but if this toke bet wins, it has to be scooped up by the dealer right away. Alternatively, if you're riding a hot streak, place the dealer's toke next to your bet within your wager circle. If you win, you can let the toke ride (continue to the next deal): it's yours until you give it to the dealer. Just tell the dealer the extra bet is a toke. Note, though, that some dealers resent it if you let their tokes ride, and have a take-the-money-and-run attitude.

Baccarat

Long viewed as an obscure, weirdly ritualised game for high rollers, baccarat ('ba-cuh-rah') is a table game with a small house edge. It is currently the hottest trending game in town. In 2010, gamblers bet nearly $11 billion on baccarat – more than a third of the total wagered on table games that year.

Up to 15 players sit around the layout and bet on BANK, PLAYER or TIE. Dealers lay out two hands of two cards each, titled

PLAYER and BANK. The object is for each hand to total as close to nine as possible. Face cards and tens count as zero and any total over nine is reduced by eliminating the first digit (for instance, 15 is valued as five). Players have no control over whether to 'draw' or 'stand'. Dealers follow a strict set of rules to determine if they must 'hit' either hand with a third card.

If PLAYER or BANK bets win, the house pays at even money. Since the rules determine that BANK wins slightly more often, the house retains a five per cent commission on all BANK winnings. Even with the commission, the house holds only a 1.17 per cent edge on BANK bets and 1.36 per cent on PLAYER bets. (The TIE bet should be avoided. It pays off at eight to one, but since the true odds are about 9.5:1, the house edge equates to a whopping 14 per cent.)

The rhythm of baccarat is leisurely and the mood subdued. In fact, it's rarely necessary for players to speak. Baccarat pits are usually secluded behind velvet ropes or in high-limit rooms, which often come complete with small buffets that lend an air of exclusivity. However, if you can handle the minimum (often $100), you're welcome to join the action. Casinos catering to low-end gamblers tend to ignore baccarat, but high-end casinos hold it dear for good reason: it's very profitable. The Mirage has estimated that as much as ten per cent of its annual revenue comes from baccarat.

MINI BACCARAT
Mini baccarat is a low-stakes version of the game played in the main pit, usually near the blackjack tables. It's a good introduction: the rules are the same but the bets are lower. As it attracts fewer players, the pace of the game is faster.

Bingo

It might not be posh, but bingo is a gambling stalwart in Vegas, especially in neighbourhood casinos: the game is played in the same way as it is all over the world. The house edge is slightly better than the similar keno, though it's hard to pin it down to a precise figure since so much depends on the variety of the game and its payout. The one advantage bingo has over keno is that bingo numbers are called until a player wins. By contrast, a million keno games can go by without anyone hitting the big jackpot.

Blackjack (21)

Blackjack is by far the most popular table game in the casinos. The reasons are obvious: it's easy to play, the basic strategy slims the house edge to nearly zero, and dozens of books claim the house can be beaten with card counting.

THE BASICS
After placing their bets, everyone at the table is dealt two cards. Single- and double-deck blackjack (games played with either one deck, or two decks shuffled together) are dealt from the dealer's hand; for multiple-deck blackjack, the decks are combined and placed in a 'shoe', from which the dealer pulls cards. Face cards count as ten; aces can count as one or 11. (A hand in which an ace is counted as 11 is known as a 'soft' hand; for example, an ace and a six is called 'soft 17'.) Each player competes against the dealer's hand by trying to get as close as possible to a total of 21 without exceeding it (or 'busting'). The game moves clockwise around the table; the player sitting on the right as he or she faces the dealer is the first to play. The first of the dealer's cards is dealt face up (the 'up card'), with the second dealt face down (the 'hole card').

First, check your cards. If you want an extra card, ask to 'hit'; when satisfied with your total, you 'stand'. After all players have stood or busted, the dealer reveals his or her hole card and plays the hand according to fixed rules: he or she must hit totals of 16 or less and must stand on 17 or above. (The rules vary if the dealer has soft 17, with some casinos requiring dealers to hit and others to stand; the players' edge is increased by 0.2 per cent for the latter.)

Once the dealer has stood or busted, the hands are compared; players who beat the dealer are paid off at even money. Ties between the house and player are a 'push' and no money changes hands; dealers indicate a push by knocking gently on the layout. If a player is dealt an ace and a ten-value card, it's considered a natural blackjack (also known as a 'snapper'); unless the dealer's up card is an ace or a ten, indicating a possible blackjack, the player is immediately paid at 3:2. Watch out for games (often single-deck or low-limit) where naturals pay only 6:5; *see p35* **Sucker Bets**.

ETIQUETTE

With the crucial exception of the dealer's hole card, almost all multi-deck blackjack games are dealt with the cards face up. In these games, players never touch the cards, but instead indicate hit or stand

Blackjack Strategy

Make the numbers add up.

Dealer's up card

	2	3	4	5	6	7	8	9	10	A
If you have a total of										
2-8	H	H	H	H	H	H	H	H	H	H
9	H	D	D	D	D	H	H	H	H	H
10	D	D	D	D	D	D	D	D	H	H
11	D	D	D	D	D	D	D	D	D	D
12	H	H	S	S	S	H	H	H	H	H
13-16	S	S	S	S	S	H	H	H	H	H
17-20	S	S	S	S	S	S	S	S	S	S

Dealer's up card

	2	3	4	5	6	7	8	9	10	A
If you have an ace										
A+2	H	H	D	D	D	H	H	H	H	H
A+3	H	H	D	D	D	H	H	H	H	H
A+4	H	H	D	D	D	H	H	H	H	H
A+5	H	H	D	D	D	H	H	H	H	H
A+6	D	D	D	D	D	H	H	H	H	H
A+7	S	D	D	D	D	S	S	H	H	S
A+8	S	S	S	S	S	S	S	S	S	S
A+9	S	S	S	S	S	S	S	S	S	S

H=hit; **S**=stand; **D**=double down; **Sp**=split

Dealer's up card

	2	3	4	5	6	7	8	9	10	A
If you have a pair										
2s	Sp	Sp	Sp	Sp	Sp	Sp	H	H	H	H
3s	Sp	Sp	Sp	Sp	Sp	Sp	H	H	H	H
4s	H	H	H	H	H	H	H	H	H	H
5s	D	D	D	D	D	D	D	D	H	H
6s	Sp	Sp	Sp	Sp	Sp	H	H	H	H	H
7s	Sp	Sp	Sp	Sp	Sp	Sp	H	H	H	H
8s	Sp	Sp	Sp	Sp	Sp	Sp	Sp	Sp	Sp	Sp
9s	Sp	Sp	Sp	Sp	Sp	S	Sp	Sp	S	S
10s	S	S	S	S	S	S	S	S	S	S
As	Sp	Sp	Sp	Sp	Sp	Sp	Sp	Sp	Sp	Sp

Players should consider 'surrendering':
• with hard 13-16 against dealer's A
• with hard 14-16 against dealer's 10
• with hard 15-16 against dealer's 9
But if all that's too much to memorise, at least remember the following five golden rules:
• stand on 17-21, but always hit soft 17
• stand on 12-16 against dealer's 2 to 6, but hit on 12-16 against dealer's 7 to A
• always split 8s and aces, but never split the 'F's, (4s, 5s and face cards)
• double down on 10s and 11s against the dealer's 2 to 9
• never take insurance

IN FOCUS

with hand motions. This reduces the potential for misunderstandings, and also makes it easier for disputed plays to be reviewed on security videos. For a hit, players hold one hand palm down above the felt and brush their fingers toward them. To stand, players hold their hand the same way, but with the fingers straight outward, and move it right and left.

Single- and double-deck games are almost always dealt face down, and players hold their own cards. Always hold them with one hand; it makes the dealer and the eye nervous if you use both. Hitting is indicated by scratching the cards towards you on the layout, while standing is indicated by sliding the cards face down under the chips.

Though blackjack sets each player's hand against the dealer's, most players view the game as everyone against the dealer. Their goal is to make the dealer bust, which means payoffs for all players still in the game. These folks don't take kindly to people playing stupidly ('splitting' tens or hitting a 14, say, against a dealer's six), especially if the offending party sits in the last seat on the left (known as 'third base'), since they feel those cards should have gone to the dealer. In truth, it doesn't really matter, since on average, a player's good decisions cancel the bad decisions. However, many gamers focus only on the bad decisions, which is why novices shouldn't sit at third base.

BETTING

There are four ways in which players can alter their bets after the cards have been dealt: 'doubling down', 'splitting', 'insurance' and 'surrender'. Splitting and doubling down aggressively are the secrets to winning at basic strategy blackjack, as they give players the chance to press their bets when they're holding a strong starting hand.

● When a player 'doubles down', he or she makes another bet equal to the original and receives one (only one) more card. It's the choice move when you've got a total of nine, ten or 11 and the dealer shows a weak card such as

a six. You can double down only if you haven't already taken a hit.

● 'Splitting' is an option when players are dealt two cards of the same value. An additional bet equal to the original bet is put out and the cards are split, with each played as a separate hand. It's to the player's advantage to double down or split each of the post-split hands, though some casinos limit what you can do. Check the strategy chart (see p25) for more advice.

● 'Insurance' is a side bet offered when the dealer has a possible blackjack (in other words, when the dealer is showing an ace or ten-value card). An insurance bet is limited to 50 per cent of the original bet and is lost if the dealer doesn't have a blackjack. If he or she does have a blackjack, insurance pays at 2:1, making the whole bet into a push.

Despite the word's connotations, insurance is a sucker bet. Unless you're a card counter and can calculate the odds of a blackjack, there's no reason to take insurance, even if you're holding a natural 21. If you're holding a natural and the dealer is calling for insurance bets, you can take even money on your bet. If you don't take even money and the dealer has a two-card 21, it's a push. If the dealer doesn't have 21, your natural is paid at 3:2 (again, don't play 6:5 games; see p35 **Sucker Bets**).

● 'Surrender' is an obscure but useful rule that's not in effect everywhere. It permits players to fold and sacrifice half their bet as long as they haven't played their hand. This is an excellent way to drop out and minimise losses when dealt weak cards. If used correctly, it increases the player's edge by 0.2 per cent.

CARD COUNTING

Card counting is a technique whereby a player visually tracks exposed cards and mentally keeps a running total to determine if the deck is positive or negative. In the simplest count, the ten-value cards and aces are valued at –1, while cards numbered two to seven take a value of +1; the eights and nines have no value. If the running total is positive, players have an advantage and should raise their bets.

IN FOCUS

Does it work? Yes, but only if you devote weeks of practice, are cool under the pressures of casino play, and develop camouflage skills so that the house doesn't know you're counting. Although card counting isn't against the law, casinos frown upon it, and 'back off' (forbid card counters from playing blackjack) or 'bar' (kick them out of the casino) any player that they suspect of using the practice. Counting cards is a gruelling discipline at which most fail. However, successful card counters, especially high-stakes players, are among the few gamblers who beat the casinos at their own game.

If you're not among the few people who have perfected this dark art, it's best to stick to basic strategy. At its simplest level, this entails memorising a chart that contains the answer to every decision in blackjack, based on your first two cards and the dealer's up card. You can usually bring the chart to the table and check it as you play, as long as you don't slow down the game. For the chart, *see p35*.

Craps

Fast, furious and enormously confusing, craps is an action-filled dice game that terrifies most novices. It can also be hugely exciting: if you hear a roar of excitement while wandering through a casino, it's probably coming from a craps table. The players cheer, curse and scream; dice and chips fly across the table; and everybody roots for different numbers. Fortunes can be won and lost in minutes, which is why craps is worshipped by a subculture. It's confounding, but by sticking to a few smart bets, players can enjoy a boisterous game with a house edge as low as one per cent, and occasionally lower.

THE BASICS

Craps is played on a large table surrounded by a low, padded wall, with a rail for chips on top and, outside, a shelf for the ever-present drinks. The game is staffed by between one and four casino employees, and there's room for 12 to 14 players to belly up to the table.

The layout is divided into three sections. The two at each end are identical, but in the centre is an area reserved for special wagers known as 'proposition bets'. A game starts with dice being offered to a new shooter by the 'stickman', the dealer located mid-table who's holding the stick. This first roll of the dice is known as the 'come out roll'. (Each player will be offered the dice at some point, though it's common to refuse.) The shooter must throw two dice in such a way that they bounce off the table's far wall.

Basically, players bet on which numbers the shooters will throw, and in what order they will appear. The shooter must place a bet before his or her first throw, and traditionally chooses PASS (*see below*). Those betting with the shooter are known as 'right bettors' while those betting against the shooter are called 'wrong bettors'.

BETTING

There are four basic wagers known as 'line bets' marked on the layout: PASS, DON'T PASS, COME and DON'T COME (the DON'T bets are for wrong bettors). Players bet on the PASS or DON'T PASS lines. If the dice show seven (statistically the most likely roll) or 11 on the come out roll, PASS bettors win at even odds and DON'T PASS bettors lose. If the shooter throws a total of two or three, DON'T PASS wins and PASS loses. If the dice show 12, PASS bettors lose and it's a 'push' (or tie) for DON'T PASS bettors. Rolling two, three or 12 is known as 'crapping out'. If any other number is thrown (four, five, six, eight, nine or ten), that number becomes the 'point'.

Once a point is established, the shooter keeps rolling, attempting to repeat the point before rolling a seven (known as 'sevening out'). In this context, the point and seven are the only numbers that count: all PASS and DON'T PASS bets ride until the 'point' is hit or the shooter sevens out. If the shooter hits the point, PASS bettors win and DON'T PASS bettors lose. If the shooter tosses a seven, DON'T PASS bettors win, PASS bettors lose and the shooter relinquishes control of the dice. The shortest roll a shooter can have is two throws, hitting a point on the come out roll followed by a seven; in this situation, wrong bettors win. But if he or she avoids 'sevening out', the shooter can roll forever, and right bettors can rack up big bucks. Every time the 'point' is hit, the whole game is reset and the next throw is a fresh 'come out roll'. However, all the side bets, such as COME bets, remain in play.

COME and DON'T COME bets represent an optional second layer of betting that runs concurrently to the original layer. They're similar to PASS and DON'T PASS bets, with the same set of outcomes (an immediate win, lose or 'push', or the establishment of a 'point'), but they can only be made on throws subsequent to the come out roll. For instance, say the shooter establishes a point of four; on the next roll, you make a COME bet. (If you want, you can enter the game with a COME/DON'T COME bet at any time during a hand without having previously made a PASS or DON'T PASS bet.) The next roll is nine, so nine becomes your 'point'. If that throw had yielded seven or 11, you would have won, and the DON'T COME bets would have lost. If the dice had totalled two, three or 12, your COME bet would have lost. And if the shooter had hit his number, the COME bets would have ridden, awaiting the seven or a repeat of the come point.

TAKING THE ODDS

If a player sticks to the four 'line' bets outlined above, the house edge is only about 1.4 per cent. But even that tiny amount can be further reduced with the use of the 'odds' bet, a wager where the house holds an edge of, believe it or not, zero. Unsurprisingly, these are the only such wagers in the casino, which is doubtless the reason why the layout of a crap table doesn't mention them at all.

Once a point is established, any player with a line bet can back up that wager with an 'odds' bet, placing the bet behind the original 'line' bet on the craps layout. This allows players to increase their bet midstream. In a game with single odds, the maximum odds bet equals the line bet.

Craps.

That alone slashes the house edge from about 1.4 per cent to 0.85 per cent. Some casinos offer double odds, triple odds, 10x or even 100x odds, all of which reduce the house edge even further. A few offer different odds on specified points. Anyone making line bets in craps should take, at the very least, single odds on every bet made. It's worth attending a lesson to learn how to make the most of this tactic.

THE REST OF THE TABLE

Smart players stick to line and odds bets, but action junkies need more. For them, the table offers another world of wagers, none of which is worthwhile. Granted, some bets offer an edge only slightly worse than line bets. But most of the one-roll proposition bets are simply horrific.

For instance, the ANY 7 proposition bet has a stunning house edge of 16.67 per cent, the worst edge of any game wager apart from keno and the Money Wheel. Don't waste time on it. Instead, stick to right and wrong betting with line bets pressed with odds and you'll get more than enough action. A straightforward odds-effective play is to bet the minimum stake on PASS and bet the same amount on two COME bets, taking odds on both (double or triple, if they're offered and you can afford it).

Keno

This lottery offshoot is the worst bet in the casino, with an appalling house edge of 25 to 40 per cent. You might as well climb to the top of the Stratosphere and throw your money into the wind. At least you'll have a nice view.

IN FOCUS

As with an old-style lottery or bingo, keno involves a ticket (or 'blank') containing 80 numbers, on which players circle as many as 15 or 20 numbers. When the game starts, 20 numbers are selected at random (ping-pong balls are blown from a 'goose' into a pair of 'arms') and displayed on screens around the casino. If your numbers are picked, you win. If not, you lose. (Get used to the second option.) The greater the proportion of your numbers picked, the higher the payback. Remember that, if by some remote chance you win at keno, you must claim your money before the next game begins or you will forfeit your winnings.

There are many variations of keno, but none makes the edge even remotely acceptable. Worst of all, payouts for keno in no way reflect the true odds of your bet, since they're capped at an arbitrary figure. For instance, your chances of selecting nine numbers and hitting all of them are 1,380,700:1. Your payout for such a feat? Usually no more than $250,000 on a $2 bet. Here's another fun fact: if two players hit the big jackpot at the same time, they have to split the cash. The only way to win at keno is never to play it.

Money Wheel (or Big Six)

It makes sense to be wary of a game that's been imported to casinos from the morally challenged world of carnivals. That's the case with the Money Wheel (aka Big Six), the grandchild of spin-the-wheel games loved by carnies everywhere.

The game is simple. A large, ornate wheel is mounted vertically a few feet above the floor. On it are 54 evenly spaced slots. Two show joker or house symbols; the other 52 are divided into $1, $2, $5, $10 and $20 denominations. There are usually 24 $1 slots and only two $20 slots. A layout in front of the wheel has squares matching those denominations. Players put cash or chips on the squares of their choice, and the wheel spins. When it stops, bettors who selected the correct denomination win,

with the payoff determined by the dollar value of the winning slot. A $20 symbol pays off at 20:1; a $1 symbol pays off at even money. House or joker symbols pay off at 40:1, sometimes 45:1. As you might guess, the casino holds a serious edge, ranging from 11 per cent for a bet on the $1 symbol to 25.9 per cent on the joker. Don't be a sucker.

Poker

From the casino's point of view, poker isn't a good bet. In poker, gamblers bet against each other, not the house. A casino employee merely deals, acting as the cashier. The house's income is limited to a percentage taken from each pot, or a seat rental of $5 or $7 per half-hour. This small take is the main reason why many casinos opted out of the game in the 1990s.

However, thanks to the explosion in the popularity of poker over the past decade, many casinos have got right back into it. The entire state of Nevada had 701 poker tables in 2005; in 2010, Las Vegas alone had a total of 920 tables. Another telling statistic: in 2002, 631 players competed in the $10,000-buy-in World Series of Poker, the granddaddy of all gambling tournaments, with the winner taking home a first-place prize of $1.1 million. In 2010, the main event drew a record 7,319 entrants. And it's a younger crowd too: in the 2010 WSOP, only one player at the final table was older than 30; the 2011 winner, Canadian Jonathan Duhamel, was just 22 when he beat his 24-year-old competitor and took home the $8.9 million kitty. Blame television, which has cottoned on to the camera-friendliness of the game to dramatic effect. TV networks such as ESPN, Fox and even NBC televised poker tournaments, celebrity matches, one-on-one showdowns and even dramas based on the game during the height of its popularity. Online poker was growing at an amazing rate – a whole new generation of poker players were training on their computers for the big games and tournaments – until April 2011 when the US government charged the operators of several popular poker websites with a litany of crimes, effectively barring American players. Only recently have some Las Vegas casinos begun operating online games. However, while poker arrived as a national pastime, it still has a way to go before overtaking blackjack as the biggest-grossing table game in town. Whereas poker netted casinos $161 million in 2006, the same year saw blackjack yield an astonishing $1.38 billion.

PLAYING IN VEGAS

To join a poker game in a Las Vegas casino, just sit in an empty seat and buy in (which usually costs ten times the minimum or maximum bet, depending on the game) with chips or cash. If there's no space at any of the tables, put your name on a waiting list. The traditional rules that everyone knows are in effect for poker in Las Vegas: the most popular games are Texas hold 'em and certain variations of Omaha.

In Texas hold 'em, each player is dealt two cards face down, before five common cards are pitched face up on to the layout for the table. The first three common cards appear together (this is called the 'flop'), followed by the fourth card (the 'turn') and the fifth card (the 'river'). Players determine their best five-card hand from the seven cards available to them.

In seven-card stud, players get two cards face down and one face up, followed by three cards face up and a final card face

IN FOCUS

Be Popular at Poker

The lowdown on poker table etiquette.

DO...

Know the rules If you don't know how to play, attend a poker class at a casino and learn the basics, or learn at one of the many free poker websites. When in doubt at a game, ask the dealer, not the other players.

Be ready Pay attention. When it's your turn to act, do so with alacrity. A surefire way to raise the hackles of other players is to drag down the game with long deliberations. But don't jump the gun, either. Always wait until it's your turn before acting.

Handle your chips properly Stack your chips in such a way that other players and the dealer can tell what you're betting. 'Splashing' chips into the pot is rude and disruptive. Also, push your chips out in one move; 'stringing' your bets a few at a time is a bad move.

Ask for comps All players get free drinks. You can swipe your player's card to track your time; you usually get about a dollar in comp value for every hour. However, not all casinos use this system; be sure to ask how to get food comps and room discounts for your play.

DON'T...

Be an asshole Most of the problems that crop up at a poker table are due to bad or uncouth behaviour. Don't use foul language. Don't abuse other players. Don't hit on other players. Don't throw temper tantrums. Lose graciously and win graciously.

Blurt Don't be the peanut gallery at the table. Speculating on hand possibilities or, worse, talking about cards you just mucked can lead to all kinds of unfair advantages and recriminations. Likewise, after you've mucked your hand, stay out of it. You can inadvertently provide too much information to players still in the hand by reacting to the community cards.

Eat at the table or smoke at a non-smoking table The main problem with bringing food to a poker table is that the cards get greasy. And lighting up in a non-smoking area is one of the easiest ways to get beaten up in a poker game, either verbally or physically. Even at smoking tables, there's no smoking at the seat on either side of the dealer.

down. Again, players then put together the best hand from their own seven cards.

Both Omaha and Texas hold 'em have numerous rounds of betting and raising, so for all but the lowest-stakes games, a hefty bankroll is crucial. For games with betting limits, posted signs indicate the smallest and largest bet allowable (usually in the form '$5/$10'). In a limit game, you'll need a bankroll of at least 20 times the maximum bet. There are also pot-limit games, which means raises can go as high as the pot, and no-limit games, in which raises can go as high as the largest bankroll on the table. In all games, no matter the stakes, players are not allowed to bring more money to the table once a hand is dealt. If a player goes 'all in', betting all his or her money, and he or she can't match another player's raise, a side pot is formed for those who wish to continue betting. The all-in player is limited to playing for the main pot.

Explaining poker strategy here is impossible. Besides the complexities of the game itself, much of poker is psychological. Reading other players and bluffing are a huge part of the process; if you didn't know this already, you'll learn the first time you sit down in a card room. If you're not a seasoned poker player, be very careful of high-stakes games, which can be populated by sharks (sometimes operating in teams). They've learned the main casino secret: it's easy to take money from amateur gamblers. If you're a novice, stick to low-stakes games, which are usually straightforward and friendly.

LET IT RIDE

Let it Ride offers the unusual feature of allowing players to take back two thirds of their wager. Players bet three equal amounts and are dealt three cards face down. Two common cards are then dealt, also face down. At this point, players can pull back one of their bets by signalling to the dealer (don't touch your chips). When the first common card is turned over, players can withdraw their second bet. The final common card is then shown and payouts are made according to a fixed schedule, ranging from even money for a pair of tens or better to 1,000:1 for

a royal flush. As you might guess, the payouts are way below true odds. For instance, the odds against drawing a flush are 508:1, but the payout is eight to one. Overall, the house holds about a four per cent edge, if players make all the right decisions.

The biggest lure of Let it Ride is that players compete against the cards, not each other, so it's more appealing to amateurs. Also, the option to withdraw two thirds of the bet gives players the illusion that their money is lasting longer than it might in other games. However, don't be fooled: the house edge grinds down almost everyone in the end. And since it's basically five-card stud, it can be a long time between winning hands.

PAI GOW POKER

Pai gow poker – not to be confused with pai gow, a Chinese game that utilises tiles – is played with a 53-card deck, a standard deck plus a wild joker. Players get seven cards, which they assemble into a five-card hand and a two-card hand. The five-card hand must score higher than the two-card hand. The object is to beat both the banker's hands. The banker wins all hands that tie; if a player wins only one hand, it's a push. The house or any player can be the banker. Winning hands are paid at even money, minus a five per cent commission.

If it sounds intimidating, don't worry; the dealer will help you arrange your cards in such a way as to maximise your two hands. Once you've watched a few hands, it's easy to get the hang of it. Pai gow poker is a lot slower – and friendlier – than blackjack or mini baccarat, so it's a good game to play if you want to relax, socialise, or play as few hands as possible in a given period of time (more comps, less risk).

Roulette

Roulette doesn't have much of a fan club in the US. That's partly due to the calm nature of the game: Americans want action and speed when they gamble, and roulette gives them neither. Another reason is a subtle but crucial change in the US version. In Europe, roulette wheels typically have 36 numbered slots and one zero slot. On most American wheels, there are two zero slots (marked as zero and double zero). That change alone nearly doubles the house edge to 5.26 per cent, compared to 2.7 per cent on single-zero wheels.

Roulette is simple to play. The wheel is mounted horizontally and a matching table layout serves as the betting area. All numbers are coloured red or black except for the zero and double zero, which are green. Players place their chips on the layout, before a ball is launched on to a spinning wheel. The ball comes to rest in a slot, and the winners are paid off at set odds. To minimise confusion about who made which bet, each player receives individually coloured 'wheel' chips when they buy in; these chips can only be used at the roulette table.

The easiest wager is a straight-up bet, where the player drops a chip on a single number. (Apparently, 17 is the most popular, due both to its central location and to the fact that James Bond bets it in the movies.) If the ball settles on your number, the bet will be paid off at 35:1. You can also make bets on groups of numbers: on lines separating numbers, on rows of numbers, or in special areas denoting odd or even, red or black and so on. In this way, a single bet covers anywhere from two to 18 numbers. Needless to say, the more numbers covered by the wager, the lower the payoff. For instance, betting odd or even pays even money.

The variety of wagers makes roulette an interesting game, especially if you like the languid pace. However, the odds are tough. Your best bet is to find a casino with a single-zero wheel – these come and go on occasion – and try to look elegant while losing.

Slot Machines

Slot machines were once shunned by 'real' gamblers, patronised only by their bored wives and girlfriends or first-time casino-goers who knew nothing more about gambling than how to drop coins

into a slot. How times have changed. These days, they're the most popular and profitable part of the entire casino industry, so much so that some smaller casinos offer nothing but slots and video poker (*see p36*). Slot machines on the Strip collected $3.5 billion in 2010.

Novice gamblers prefer slots because there's little to learn and no pressure from dealers or other players. Put in money, pull the handle (or, more often nowadays, press the spin button) and in a few seconds, you're either a winner or a loser. Simple. What's more, jackpots can reach millions of dollars. But there is a downside, and a big one. Slots give the house an edge varying from two to 25 per cent, often making them one of the worst bets in the casino. And your chance of hitting a million-dollar jackpot is… well, what's the tiniest unit of measurement you can imagine? Smaller than that. Way smaller.

The basic slot machine in Las Vegas accepts a maximum of either two or three coins; however, some take four or five, some just one, and a new breed of slot machines is now able to take hundreds of coins, including pennies. Each coin beyond the minimum increases the payout proportionally (twice as much for two coins, triple for three) should a winning combination appear. In most cases, the winnings on betting the maximum number of coins are exponentially higher; almost always, the posted jackpot can only be won by betting the maximum number of coins on the winning pull/spin. What's

Slot machines.

more, many machines have multiple pay lines; on these machines, an added pay line is activated each time another coin is wagered. Always check the pay tables at the top of the machine.

Modern slots usually have a coin counter that displays your credits. Instead of coins crashing into the stainless-steel bin, wins are registered as credits. There's usually a bill changer on the machine: players can simply slide in a $20 bill, for example, and $20 worth of credits appear on the counter. Bets are made by pulling a handle or pressing a 'Spin' button. When you're done, hit the 'Cash Out' button and one of two things will happen. In older machines, coins equal to the unused credits will drop into the bin; the casino provides plastic cups to carry coins to other machines or the cashier. However, most slots these days are 'coinless'; when you hit 'Cash Out', you'll receive a voucher that can be redeemed at a ticket machine, a change booth or the cage, or fed into another slot machine and used as credits.

Slots fall into two categories: non-progressive (aka regular) and progressive. Regular slots have fixed payouts, which are posted on the front of the machine. Progressive slots offer a fixed payout schedule, but also offer the chance to hit a huge jackpot. This jackpot, funded by a percentage of every coin wagered, grows continuously until somebody wins it. A meter above the machines displays a running total of the current jackpot.

Many progressive slots are linked to form a system that feeds the jackpot. These machines might be from one carousel in a single casino, with a jackpot that resets at $1,000 and grows from there, or spread across casinos state-wide, yielding multi-million-dollar jackpots. With literally hundreds of machines in the system, jackpots can reach astronomical levels. The Megabucks linked progressive, for example, consists of more than 700 machines; the world record slot jackpot of nearly $40 million was hit in March 2003 at the Excalibur by a 25-year-old computer programmer. Though rare, these payouts are well publicised, not least because they make excellent bait.

NEW SLOTS

A few years ago, video machines with oversized screens, multiple games and other gimmicks were all the rage. Today, a new generation of slots is being developed. New machines are more interactive and look a lot like video poker; on these slots, you'll be able to make choices about which symbols to hold or discard, based on a certain internal and intuitive logic. Pop culture themes are still big: some of the most popular slots in town are based on hit movies and TV shows such as *The Hangover* and *Sex and the City*. Enhanced by digital bonus features and video pop-ups, slots are more fun to play today than they were even ten years ago, when they were still primarily 'one-armed bandits'; table-game players derisively referred to them as the 'idiot pull'.

However, these machines still won't line your pockets. Slot (and video poker) machines now account for upwards of 65 per cent of total casino revenues, which means they take in twice as much revenue as all other casino games combined. Of the $12.6 billion won by Nevada casinos in 2006, $8.3 billion – just under 66 per cent – came from slots and video poker.

HOW SLOTS WORK

Modern slots are controlled by a random number generator, a computer chip that churns out strings of numbers regardless of whether the game is being played. Pulling the handle (or pressing the spin button) on a machine releases the reels and selects one of these numbers. Each number corresponds to a certain set of symbols on the reels, which determines the outcome. The force of the pull has nothing to do with the point at which the reels stop rotating.

Regulating the payout amounts to computer science. By adjusting the random number generator, a slot technician can make a machine tighter or looser. In the old days, slots often had a built-in edge of 20 to 30 per cent, but the players flocked to the machines with the higher returns. Casinos did the sums and realised it was better to get five per cent of a lot than 30 per cent of nothing; hence, most Vegas slots now return

IN FOCUS

between 92 and 95 per cent of the drop (less on nickel machines), leaving the house edge at between five and eight per cent. In 2006, $138 billion was bet on slots and video poker in Nevada; the casinos' win of $8.3 billion equates to an overall hold of six per cent.

Certain casinos boldly advertise 98 or 99 per cent payouts, but the small print is crucial. In such circumstances, the payout is usually 'up to 99 per cent', which could mean that a single machine on the floor might be set at 98 or 99 per cent, if that. Short of running 2,000 to 5,000 plays through similar machines and comparing payouts, there's no way to find out which slots are set tight or loose. Payout percentages are supposedly verified by the state Gaming Control Board, but it rarely checks unless a casino advertises something truly absurd.

The real advantage for the house comes with the constant repetition of slot plays. For instance, say that a player with $50 starts betting $1 per pull on a quarter machine, via four 25¢ bets per pull. Sometimes the player wins and those winnings are reinvested: the drop might only be $50, but if they're playing at a reasonable speed, they could end up giving the casino $240 of action every hour. The six per cent edge is enough for a slot machine to retain about $14 an hour (six per cent of $240), a hold equal to more than a quarter of the original bankroll. With a little less luck, that money could vanish even faster. And over time, even an edge of half of one per cent grinds down players, which is why so many of them stumble away from machines empty-handed. That and the fact that the payout percentage factors in the big and seldom-won jackpots.

SLOT TIPS

Slot jockeys say non-progressive machines are looser (the technical term for this is 'hit frequency') than progressive machines, though payouts are smaller (again, the technical term is 'average payback'). Non-progressive machines that give smaller top payouts are reportedly looser than those that give large top payouts. Similarly, among progressive machines, those with smaller jackpots hit more often. In fact, the amount of your bet that goes to the progressive jackpot is an indication of payout frequency. According to one executive, if the amount is less than one per cent, the progressive machine is likely to have more non-jackpot winners. If three to five per cent of every bet goes towards the progressive jackpot, the game is seriously weighted towards fewer large payouts.

It gets more complicated. Machines with high hit frequencies pay out small amounts. Those with low hit frequencies pay out less frequently overall, but when they do pay out, each return is higher. And there's no correlation between hit frequency and average payback: hit frequency can be high while average payback is low and vice versa, or both can be low or high. Of course, none of this information is posted in a casino, so players are mostly flying blind. Some believe that slots placed near doorways and aisles are looser than others. And one casino executive has said that house machines, those with the casino's name and logo on them, are more generous than non-house-brand slots.

The only recommendation that makes any sense is that if you're going to play the slots for big money, bet the maximum number of coins on each pull. That way, if lightning strikes and you're a winner, you'll get the biggest payout possible. Avoid pumping cash into slots in non-casino locations such as convenience stores, which have a house edge one step below thievery. And, of course, never put a nickel into a slot machine without first having inserted your players club card into the reader. As long as you're playing the house's favourite game, you might as well get a bit of your play returned in the form of cashback or comps.

Slots can only pay out so many coins at any one time, so if you hit a monster jackpot, stay put and wait for an attendant to arrive. If you walk away, someone might claim your prize. The attendant will inform you of your tax obligations. US citizens need to fill out IRS paperwork on slot wins of more than $1,200; the tax situation varies for non-nationals.

IN FOCUS

PLAYERS CLUBS

Virtually every casino has a players club, the main aims of which are to keep track of a customer's slot and video poker play, and to retain customer loyalty by providing rewards in the form of points that can be redeemed for hard cash or merchandise. Many clubs offer introductory gifts such as free buffets, bonus points, rebates on losses or other perks to get your name on the dotted line.

All players clubs issue their members with an ID card, which should be inserted into the slot or video poker machine to allow the machine's computer to track the amount of play. Points awarded by the computer are then redeemable for cash or for comps in the casino's restaurants and at the shows. Members also qualify for discounts in the resort's shops, for reduced room rates, and for tickets to parties, barbecues and special tournaments.

Players club benefits change frequently. You can get an idea of what the various clubs are offering by checking out the *Las Vegas Advisor*, or the 'Best Bets' section of the Friday edition of the *Las Vegas Review-Journal* newspaper. All it takes to join a players club are a picture ID and a few minutes at the slot booth. Some casinos even have roving recruiters who'll sign you up at the machine. Membership is always free.

Sports betting

Thanks in no small part to Frank 'Lefty' Rosenthal, the casino executive whose life was dramatised in the movie *Casino*, betting on sports in Vegas is now a cult all of its own. Almost every casino has a sports book, at which money is gambled on countless aspects of the outcomes of

---

Sucker Bets

You gotta know when to hold…

Just when you think you know the rules, Las Vegas changes the games. Take blackjack, for example. Many gamblers know that a blackjack game dealt from a single deck offers savvy players the best chance to win. Now, however, many casinos have made a seemingly minor change to the single-deck rules, hoping players won't notice that it's no longer the best version of 21, but quite easily the worst.

A few years ago, single-deck blackjack was only available in the high-roller salons, with most of the low-limit games dealt from four or even six decks. In the last few years, however, single-deck tables have become more common than fake breasts at Mandalay Bay. This should be good news for gamblers. However, in the process, the payoff for natural 21s has been lowered in many casinos from 3:2 to 6:5; in other words, hitting a blackjack on a $10 bet will win you only $12 where it used to net $15. Doesn't

sound like much of a difference? Think again. The rule change is so bad that the casino's profit is several times higher than at the city's worst six-deck shoe game, and up to eight times more than at a regular single-deck game.

Keen-eyed Europeans will also notice that the odds have been shifted out of their favour on the roulette wheel. In many European casinos, the wheel has only a single green '0'. However, in the US, there's also a double zero ('00') on the wheel; that one extra green spot tips the house edge from 2.7 per cent to 5.26 per cent. Check before you play.

Finally, avoid almost anything called a 'side bet', extra bets beyond the basic wager at table games. They include jackpots for making certain hands at Let it Ride and three-card poker, or being dealt your first two cards of the same suit at blackjack. Don't waste your money: the casinos aren't charities, so there's no reason to give until it hurts.

pro sports and college games. They're lively places on big game days; even if you're not betting, they're often good places to watch the action. Whatever sports wagers you make and wherever you make them, remember that cellphones and two-way communicators are prohibited in or near the sports books, a policy that's strictly and universally enforced.

Glance up at the vast boards and you might think that sports betting here is tough to understand. It's not, but it is hard to beat the system and come away rich.

THE MONEY LINE

Most of the sports on which you can bet (baseball, boxing, football, hockey, basketball) offer 'money lines', which lay the odds on the favourite or take the odds on the underdog. Take the following baseball-related example:

| Boston Red Sox | + | 145 |
| New York Yankees | – | 160 |

This means that you must bet $16 on the Yankees to win $10 (plus your stake back). However, you need bet only $10 on the Red Sox to win $14.50. The favourite team is always the one with the '–' prefix, with the underdog denoted by '+'. (Unlike in European sports, the home team is always listed second.)

OTHER BETS

There's a large variety of bets in the Vegas sports books. Here, though, are examples of two of the more common ones. Both of them even the odds so that punters can make a 'straight bet', which here means putting up $11 to win $10 (plus your $11 stake back). In team games, one popular bet is on the margin of victory, or the 'point spread'. Take, for example, these odds for the 2007 Super Bowl.

| Indianapolis Colts | –7 |
| Chicago Bears | |

This means that the Colts were favoured to beat the Bears by seven points. Everyone favouring the Colts on the point spread was betting on them to win by more than seven points, while everyone

favouring the Bears was betting on either a Bears victory or a Colts win by fewer than seven points. The game ended Colts 29, Bears 17. The Colts won the game and also covered the point spread, meaning that everyone who bet on them won. If the Colts had beaten the Bears by exactly seven points, it would have been a push, and all money would have been refunded.

Another popular bet is to gamble on the total number of points scored in any given game. The casino advertises the total number of points they think will be scored in the game, and gamblers decide if they think the actual number will be higher or lower. This is known as the 'over/under'; like the point spread, this pays off at 10:11 odds. As above, if the outcome matches the casino's prediction, it's a push, and all bets are refunded.

Video Poker

This electronic cousin of live poker enjoys a huge following in Las Vegas. Although a video-poker machine resembles a slot machine and is typically located on the slot floor, it is an entirely different beast. Make no mistake about it: video poker is a game not of chance but of skill. If played perfectly, the house edge can often be flattened to zero or even pushed into the negative, which means a return to players of more than 100 per cent. Casinos can only afford to operate their machines in this way because perfect play is the province of the merest handful of experts, those people who use powerful computer programmes to work out strategies that are accurate to within ten thousandths of a percentage point.

A video-poker screen displays a five-card hand of draw poker, with every deal coming from a freshly shuffled 52-card deck. Buttons allow the player to hold or replace the dealt cards. After the draw, the game pays off according to a payout schedule listed on the screen. A pair of aces might pay even money, while a royal flush usually pays out at a rate of 4,000:1. Most basic poker rules are in effect as far as hand rankings go (minus 'kickers', or unpaired or unsuited high

Video poker.

brethren. For instance, in JoB, the full-pay version returns 9:1 on a full house and 6:1 on a flush; it's called a '9/6' machine. On the short-pay version, it's sliced to 8/5, 7/5 or even 6/5. The only reason to play a short-pay version of JoB would be if it was connected to a progressive jackpot or paid off on a pair of tens or better. However, 8/5 Bonus, with extra payouts for four-of-a-kind, is a different animal, as are Double Bonus, Double Double Bonus, Triple Bonus and Double Triple Bonus variations. Then there's Joker Poker, plus many different varieties of Deuces Wild.

Video-poker players should consult the books and reports on the market that detail proper play for sample video-poker hands. There are excellent computer programmes available that tutor players in strategies. Casinos don't mind if you refer to strategy charts while playing, but they draw the line at laptops. Since it's impossible to absorb the tactics for all the possible variations at once, we recommend you study and master strategy for JoB, then, as you feel more comfortable, move on to more complex and rewarding games such as the full-pay Deuces Wild and Double Bonus varieties.

The latest varieties of machine to become all the rage in Las Vegas are multi-play machines, such as Triple-Play, Five-Play, Ten-Play, 50-Play and even 100-Play. Here, three, five, ten, 50 or 100 hands of video poker are dealt at the same time from the equivalent number of decks, requiring three, five, ten, 50, or 100 times the bet. The twist is that only the cards in the bottom hand are displayed on the deal. When you hold cards from the hand, the held cards appear in all the upper hands; when you draw, all the hands' cards are filled in around the held cards.

In Spin Poker, when you discard cards, the open spots spin like slot reels. Heads Up Poker, meanwhile, combines live poker with video poker. You're dealt five cards and you bet the hand. The machine responds by calling, raising or folding (and sometimes bluffing). You play out the video-poker hand, but you still have the live hand to be resolved.

cards, on all but one or two variations), but the psychological angle is jettisoned. You're playing against a machine that doesn't respond to bluffing, so the quality of your hand is everything.

There's no way to summarise basic strategy for video poker, partly because it's extremely complex and partly because the game comes in so many different varieties. Each variety of video poker has own unique characteristics such as wild cards and bonus options, giving rise to different pay tables and different strategies. You can buy video-poker strategy cards (Huntington Press produces a good set), which allow you to make the right decision on every hand; in essence, you'll be playing computer-perfect strategy.

The most basic variation of video poker is 'Jacks or Better' (JoB), which plays most like five-card stud (no wild cards) and pays out on pairs of jacks or better. The strategies for JoB are pretty much intuitive for anyone who already knows how to play poker, but some rules have to be learned: for example, you never hold a kicker (a high-value card to be held along with a pair); you never draw to a four-card inside straight (for example, you're holding 3, 4, 6, 7 and you're looking for a 5); and you always go for a royal flush if you hold four of the cards required for it, even if it means sacrificing a flush, a pair or a straight in the process.

As with slots, it's wise to play the maximum number of coins, as this greatly increases the top payout for a royal flush. Another tip: be sure to play 'full-pay' games as opposed to their 'short-pay'

IN FOCUS

Diary

Las Vegas is all about celebration.

Las Vegas has a habit of attracting the kind of parties that don't happen anywhere else. As the spiritual home of gambling, it's obvious that the city should host the World Series of Poker, while a town that revels in the nickname Sin City is a natural location for the Fetish & Fantasy Halloween Ball. Still, that doesn't explain the presence of a Renaissance fair, several rodeo competitions, and innumerable events dominated by vintage cars, bikes and scooters.

For information on temporary attractions in town, check the free *Seven*, *Las Vegas Weekly* or *CityLife* weeklies.

IN FOCUS

SPRING

NASCAR Weekend
Las Vegas Motor Speedway *7000 N Las Vegas Boulevard, at Speedway Boulevard, North Las Vegas (644 4444 information, 1-800 644 4444 tickets, www.lvms.com).* **Tickets** $99-$245. **Date** early Mar.
One of the biggest auto-racing weekends of the year, the Vegas leg of NASCAR's appearance sees thousands of enthusiasts descend upon the city. Visitors should book accommodation well in advance. For details of other events at the Las Vegas Motor Speedway, *see p232.*

Monster Jam World Finals
Sam Boyd Stadium *7000 E Russell Road, at Boulder Highway, South-east Las Vegas (739 3267, www.monsterjam.com).* **Tickets** $80-$180. **Date** mid Mar.
Bring out your inner 13-year-old with this feast of automotive carnage, featuring an array of giant

---

THE BEST EVENTS

For tripping the light fantastic
Electric Daisy Carnival. *See p40.*

For avoiding all the bull
Professional Bull Riders Tour. *See p41.*

For playing your cards right
World Series of Poker. *See p40.*

---

trucks with enormous wheels; the 2013 champion, known as Grave Digger the Legend, was a 1,500-horsepower beast with 66in wheels. The pit party is also worth a look.

St Patrick's Day
Around Las Vegas. **Date** 17 Mar.
Vegas more than makes up for its lack of Irish heritage on St Patrick's Day. There's a parade in downtown Henderson and a three-day party at New York New York's Nine Fine Irishmen bar, which sprawls on to the casino's mini-Brooklyn Bridge. Elsewhere, Hennessey's Tavern on the Fremont Street Experience celebrates with music, drink and 'Irish nachos'.

Extreme Thing Festival
Desert Breeze Skate Park *8275 W Spring Mountain Road, at S Durango Drive, South-west Las Vegas (455 8200, www.extremething.com).* **Bus** 203. **Tickets** $17-$20. **Date** late Mar.
Extreme sports, such as skateboarding, BMX and wrestling championships feature here, along with extreme body modification, chiefly piercing and tattoos. And extreme music: punk, lots of it. Expect teenage aggression.

★ Viva Las Vegas
Orleans Hotel & Casino *4500 W Tropicana Avenue, at S Arville Street, South-west Las Vegas (1-562 496 4287, www.vivalasvegas.net).* **Bus** 103, 201. **Tickets** $30-$120. **Date** Easter weekend.
In order to dance to old-school rockabilly bands from all over the world, check out the burlesque competition and shop for the perfect 1950s cocktail dress at

the swap meet, you'll have to buy a ticket. However, the breathtaking hot-rod car show is worth the price of admission. Wear Sailor Jerry tattoos and Brylcreem to blend in.

UNLVino
Paris Las Vegas *3655 Las Vegas Boulevard South, at E Flamingo Road (946 7000, www. unlvino.com). Bus Deuce, 202.* **Tickets** $75-$100. **Map** p320 A7. **Date** mid Apr.
More than 100 international wine-growers participate in this fundraiser for UNLV. There are auctions of wine-themed art and vintage crates, but the real treat is chatting with the growers and sampling the wines. Designated drivers are thoughtfully provided.

Clark County Fair & Rodeo
Clark County Fairgrounds, on I-15, Logandale (1-888 876 3247, www.ccfair.com). **Admission** *Fair* $7-$9. *Rodeo* $19-$21. *Season pass* $21. Free under-5s. **Date** late Apr.
For a taste of hometown Southwestern life sans glitter, drive north for all kinds of ropin', ridin', country music and carnival fun.

Great Vegas Festival of Beer
Sunset Park *2601 E Sunset Road, at S Eastern Avenue, South-east Las Vegas (1-888 718 4253, www.greatvegasbeer.com).* **Tickets** $30-$40. **Date** late Apr.
Nevada and national breweries unite in displaying their boozy wares at this one-day event. Sample suds from locals such as Triple 7 Brewery, or national

craft beer-makers like Anchor and Goose Island. Enjoy your beer with a soundtrack from local and regional musicians, along with gastropub food from several eateries. Designated drivers are thoughtfully provided for a nominal fare.

Epicurean Affair
Location varies (878 2313, www.nvrestaurants. com). **Tickets** $105-$190. **Date** late Apr/ early May.
Local restaurants unveil their latest attempts to outdo each other in this industry festival of culinary hedonism. Expect a full-blown onslaught on the senses from exotic food, drink and spectacle.

Cinco de Mayo
Lorenzi Park, 3333 W Washington Avenue, at N Rancho Drive, North-west Las Vegas (229 6718). Bus 106, 208. **Map** p317 X1. **Date** weekend closest to 5 May.
The city's Mexican community comes together in a show of pride with all-day dancing, mariachi bands, fireworks and traditional cuisine. Festivities also take place at the Fremont Street Experience.

Helldorado Days
Various locations (870 1221, www.elks helldorado.com). **Date** mid May.
Instituted in 1935 to attract tourists to the area after the completion of the Hoover Dam, this revived celebration of Las Vegas's beginnings plays up the city's Western roots while also including golf and poker tournaments, trap-shooting contests, rodeos, art auctions, trail rides and a Downtown parade.

IN FOCUS

Helldorado Days.

SUMMER

Las Vegas Brews and Blues Festival
Las Vegas Springs Preserve *333 S Valley View Boulevard, at Meadows Lane, North-west Las Vegas (822 7770, www.vegasbrewsandblues.com). Bus 104, 207.* **Admission** $35-$40. **Date** early June.
Check out regional blues musicians while sampling some of the finest beer around. A portion of ticket sales usually goes to charity, and the entry fee includes a 'sampling mug' plus unlimited draughts of brew.

Vans Warped Tour
Location varies (www.vanswarpedtour.com). **Tickets** $30. **Date** mid/late June.
Record-breaking temperatures at the 2013 music tour didn't keep fans away, and not much else will either. The all-day event features tons of bands in a variety of styles – punk, hardcore, thrash – all of them loud, performing on multiple stages.

Electric Daisy Carnival
Las Vegas Motor Speedway *7000 N Las Vegas Boulevard, at Speedway Boulevard, North Las Vegas (www.electricdaisycarnival.com).* **Tickets** $289-$500. **Date** late June.
EDC has been a huge hit for Las Vegas since relocating here from LA in 2011. More than 110,000 people attended the three-day event in 2013, making entrance to and from the Speedway a nightmare. Electronic music fans could care less, as EDC draws some of the biggest names in the biz, with plenty of other psychedelic entertainment besides.

★ World Series of Poker
Rio *3700 W Flamingo Road, at S Valley View Boulevard, West of Strip (777 7777, www.wsop. com). Bus 202.* **Map** p317 X3. **Date** June-July.

It's a matter of conjecture whether the popularity of poker fuelled the popularity of this two-week tournament or vice versa. Either way, the WSOP is loved worldwide. In 2010, more than 7,000 competitors took part and $8.9 million was awarded to winner Jonathan Duhamel.

Black & White Party
Location varies (382 2326, www.afanlv.org). **Tickets** $35. **Date** late Aug/early Sept.
Affordable but still satisfyingly posh, the city's main AIDS fundraiser brings the community together with black-and-white costumes, food from the best chefs in town, and risqué amusements such as a spanking booth.

Las Vegas Pride
Various locations (1-866 930 3336, www.lasvegaspride.org). **Date** late Aug/early Sept.
Vegas's weeklong LGBT celebration begins with events ranging from pool parties to dinner and brunch gatherings, before culminating with a parade that just gets larger every year. Local celebrities such as Frank Marino turn out in force, as the parade winds through Downtown, and then hit various spots throughout the city for post-parade parties.

Las Vegas Harvest Festival
Cashman Center *850 Las Vegas Boulevard North, at E Washington Avenue, Downtown (1-415 447 3205, www.harvestfestival.com). Bus 113.* **Admission** $9; free under-12s. **Map** p317 Y1. **Date** early Sept.
Hundreds of artisans from across the country bring their hand-blown glass, silver jewellery and jars of chutney to this fair.

World Series of Poker.

Age of Chivalry Renaissance Festival.

AUTUMN

San Gennaro Feast

Location varies (286 4944, www.sangennaro feast.net). **Admission** $9. Additional $25 for carnival ride pass. **Date** Sept.

So popular it is staged three or four times a year, this Italian-American outdoor festival is mostly about the food, but it also includes carnival rides and a traditional procession.

Super Run

Henderson (643 0000, www.superrun.com). **Date** mid/late Sept.

The area's largest classic-car show takes over downtown Henderson for three days in September with hundreds of classic vehicles, from fully-built custom hot rods to a well-preserved hearse used when the Mob ran Vegas.

Greek Food Festival

St John the Baptist Greek Orthodox Church *5300 S El Camino Road, at E Hacienda Road, South-west Las Vegas (221 8245, www.lasvegas greekfestival.com). Bus 102.* **Admission** $7; free under-12s. **Date** late Sept.

One of Las Vegas's few true ethnic festivals. Enjoy three days of folk dancing, retsina and *souvlaki* with a boisterous crowd.

Las Vegas BikeFest

Cashman Center *850 Las Vegas Boulevard North, at E Washington Avenue, Downtown (1-866 245 3337, 450 7662, www.lasvegas bikefest.com). Bus 113.* **Tickets** $35-$70. **Map** p317 Y1. **Date** late Sept/early Oct.

Even non-bikers can enjoy the classic Harleys, the demo rides and 'Artistry in Iron' master-builder championships at this get-together for the black-leather set.

★ Life Is Beautiful Festival

Various locations (www.lifeisbeautifulfestival.com). **Tickets** $159.50-$349.50. **Date** late Oct.

This music/food/arts fest in Downtown Las Vegas was first held in 2013. Although the music was a huge draw – headliners included local-acts-turned-national-stars like the Killers and Imagine Dragons, as well as Kings of Leon, Beck and others – food proved popular as well, with top-rated chefs such as Hubert Keller, Michael Mina and Tom Colicchio participating. Capitalising on the popularity of First Fridays (*see p42* **Inside Track**), this Vegas feast shows there's more to Sin City than showgirls.

★ Fright Dome

Adventuredome at Circus Circus *2880 Las Vegas Boulevard, between Desert Inn Road & W Sahara Avenue (www.frightdome.com). Bus Deuce, 108.* **Tickets** $32.95-$89.95. **Map** p319 B5. **Date** Oct up to Halloween.

Colourful lasers, roaming characters, performances and several haunted houses. It's too scary for small kids – only 12-year-olds and older are allowed in.

Age of Chivalry Renaissance Festival

Sunset Park *2601 E Sunset Road, at S Eastern Avenue, South-east Las Vegas (1-800 745 3000 tickets, www.lvrenfair.com).* **Admission** *1 day* $10; $5 reductions. *3 days* $25; $10 reductions; free under-5s. **Date** mid Oct.

Chivalrous battles, costumed maidens and other displays of questionable historical accuracy. We recommend the roast turkey leg with a stein of mead.

Professional Bull Riders Tour

Thomas & Mack Center *4505 S Maryland Parkway, at E Tropicana Avenue, University District (1-719 242 2800 information, 1-800 745 3000 tickets, www.pbrnow.com). Bus 109, 201.* **Tickets** $18-$83. **Map** p317 Y3. **Date** late Oct.

Christmas

It isn't as prestigious as the National Finals Rodeo (*see below*), but this competition provides a more affordable chance to rub shoulders with the world's finest bull riders and their fans, and see some of the action up close.

Halloween
Around Las Vegas. **Date** 31 Oct.
Nearly every nightclub and bar hosts a fancy-dress party for Halloween, many overflowing with grown-ups playing naughty dress-up. The Fetish & Fantasy Ball, held in 2012 at the Hard Rock (*see p112*), reigns supreme for debauchery, dazzling costumes and Vegas-calibre spectacle.

Vegas Valley Book Festival
Various locations (www.vegasvalleybookfestival.org). **Tickets** free-$10. **Date** late Oct/early Nov.
Local authors, historians and poets get a chance to shine in this three-day celebration of bibliophilism that brings local literary heroes and such names as Chuck Palahniuk to town for readings, signings, debates and panel discussions.

INSIDE TRACK FIRST FRIDAY

One of the city's most popular festivals is its most regular. Held from 5pm to 11pm on the first Friday of every month in the Downtown 18b Arts District, First Friday (www.firstfridaylasvegas.com) is essentially a massive block party with an artistic bent. Local galleries and shops stay open late into the night; bands and DJs play on the specially erected stages; and there's tons of great street food and drinks on offer.

★ Rock 'n' Roll Las Vegas Marathon
Around Las Vegas (1-800 311 1255, www.run rocknroll.competitor.com). **Date** mid Nov.
Beginning in the afternoon, the marathon course starts near the Luxor (*see p98*) and has a rock 'n' roll theme, with bands playing along the route. If you're not cut out for going the full distance, there's always the half-marathon. (A new event, the half-of-the-half, was added in 2013.) If you want to run, register online; the earlier you do so, the cheaper the fee.

Motor Trend International Auto Show
Las Vegas Convention Center *3150 Paradise Road, at Convention Center Drive, East of Strip (892 0711, www.motortrendautoshows.com).* **Bus** SDX, 108. **Admission** $10; $7 reductions. **Map** p319 C5. **Date** late Nov.
A chance to see all the shiniest new models and prototypes from the world's automobile manufacturers before anyone else, though sadly you can't drive them away. Free parking is available at the Convention Center.

WINTER

National Finals Rodeo
Thomas & Mack Center *4505 S Maryland Parkway, at E Tropicana Avenue, University District (260 8605, www.nfrexperience.com).* **Bus** 109, 201. **Tickets** $75-$1,000. **Map** p317 Y3. **Date** early Dec.
Cowboys and girls from far and wide set Vegas ablaze for nine days as part of this massive annual event. Tickets are distributed by lottery a year beforehand, but you can watch proceedings on TV at the Gold Coast (*see p129*). Stock up on Western duds during the event, and then party at Sam's Town (*see p130*) after.

Christmas

Around Las Vegas. **Date** Dec.

The most spectacular festive event in the region is the annual Light the Night display in the cactus garden at Ethel M Chocolates in Henderson (*see p75*). The space is dotted with millions of lights, while carol-singers reel off all the festive favourites. Be sure to get yourself into the factory before 7pm for free chocolate samples.

Other events around the city bring good cheer in similar ways during December. A drive-through trail called A Gift of Lights winds through the whole of Sunset Park (E Sunset Road, at S Eastern Avenue, East Las Vegas). The Magical Forest at Opportunity Village (6300 W Oakey Boulevard, between S Jones Boulevard & S Torrey Pines Drive) contains a castle, giant candy canes, a forest of decorated trees and two million lights. And numerous watercraft sail around Lake Mead as part of the Parade of Lights.

New Year's Eve

Around Las Vegas. **Date** 31 Dec.

Las Vegas Boulevard and Fremont Street become absolutely rammed on New Year's Eve, a night filled with parties, one-hit celebrities, air displays, fireworks and general chaos. Room rates soar. To be honest, the whole thing is probably best avoided.

African American History Month

West Las Vegas Library *951 W Lake Mead Boulevard, at Concord Street, West Las Vegas (507 3980, www.lvccld.org). Bus 210, 214.* **Date** Feb.

The West Las Vegas Library houses a permanent collection of artefacts, photographs and documents relating to African American history in the West. During February, its theatre hosts a celebration of African American community and culture in the region, with spoken word, dance, theatre and music.

★ Chinese New Year Celebration & Asian Food Festival

Las Vegas Chinatown Plaza, 4255 Spring Mountain Road, between S Valley View & S Decatur boulevards, South-west Las Vegas (221 8448, www.lvchinatown.com). Bus 103, 104, 203. **Admission** $3; $1 reductions; free under-5s. **Date** late Jan/mid Feb.

The Chinese New Year celebrations in Vegas are actually pan-Asian; they also celebrate Japanese, Tahitian and Thai culture. Expect traditional lion and dragon dances and a feast of Eastern delicacies.

High Rollers Scooter Weekend

Various locations (www.lvscooterrally.com). **Date** mid Feb/early Mar.

Rockers on motorbikes had better steer clear: this weekend of mod rock and showing off is for sharp-looking multi-mirrored scooters and the aficionados who love them.

Chinese New Year

IN FOCUS

Explore

Las Vegas in 48 Hrs

Day 1 Walk the Walk

9AM It's longer than it looks, and often hotter than Hades, but every visitor should stroll the length of the Strip at least once, to get the measure of its absurdity. Start with the **Fabulous Las Vegas sign**, in the middle of Las Vegas Boulevard, near Mandalay Bay (*see p86*). Have an indoor and outdoor look at the oddest and somehow most fabulous of the Vegas casino buildings, the sci-fi-looking black glass pyramid that is the **Luxor** (*see p98*).

11AM Continuing north on the Strip, **New York New York** (*see p100*) is worth a peek, for its simulacrum of Manhattan's streetscapes and shops – if you're brave enough, make time for the rollercoaster, which goes careening skyward, offering an upside down view of the Strip. Push on north, to the magnificent heart of the Strip. The new **CityCenter** complex (*see p51*), is vast, but its main points of interest are the gorgeous **Aria** casino-hotel (*see p102*) and the high-end **Crystals** shopping centre (*see p173*). Go next door to the **Cosmopolitan** (*see p85*), the hippest hotel on the Strip. Head upwards to third floor, a people-watching haven ringed with restaurants; its time for lunch.

3PM Catch the monorail that connects CityCenter and the **Bellagio** (*see p82*); and make sure you're in a good viewing spot for one of the on-the-half-hour performances of the famous, fabulous fountains; also have a look at the scrumptious chocolate fountain – the world's largest – inside, at **Jean-Philippe Patisserie** (*see p82*). By now you will be ready for a rest.

7PM It's dinner time and you've got options. Head for the **Venetian** (*see p92*) and have an Italianesque bite by the famous *faux* canal, at **Valentino** (*see p147*) perhaps.

9PM Nighttime is the right time for exploring Downtown Las Vegas, which predates the Strip and is still buzzing with its own seedy grandeur. Poke around the **Golden Nugget** (*see 121*) and the **El Cortez** (*see p120*), then venture out to some fo the many up-and-coming bars and clubs dotting the Fremont East Entertainment District on the other side of Las Vegas Boulevard, like the **Griffin** (*see p165*) or **Beauty Bar** (*see p164*).

NAVIGATING THE CITY

Once you've made it to the fabled Las Vegas Strip – and to your casino-connected hotel room, the sparkling city is at your feet, made for enjoying by foot, by cab or hired car, bus or monorail.

A useful bus for tourists is the Deuce: the double-decker travels the length of Las Vegas Boulevard from the BTC in the north to just by I-215 in the south, stopping in front of all major casinos. Deuces are often busy, especially at night.

The Las Vegas Monorail is now running a reliable service along Paradise Road and then behind the Strip. However, it hasn't displaced the numerous hotel buses and monorails.

A car is recommended if you're staying away from the Strip or are keen to visit off-Strip attractions, and essential if you're planning to visit any out-of-town destinations. Most car-hire agencies are at or near the airport. Call around for the best rate, booking well in advance if

EXPLORE

Day 2 Away From the Strip

9AM You'll need a cab to explore these off-Strip highlights. Start the day with an only-in-Las Vegas experience that doesn't involve gambling – well, at least not with money. At **Vegas Indoor Skydiving** (*see p59*), you can free-fall in an indoor 21-foot vertical wind tunnel that generates air speeds of up to 130mph. After an hour of instruction, you get 15 minutes of flying time. This is best experienced before lunch…

11AM Head for another only-in-Vegas attraction – the **Atomic Testing Museum** (*see p59*). Relatively few know how near Vegas was to the Nevada Test Site, the US's principal on-continent nuclear weapons testing facility from 1951 to 1992. The story the museum tells is fascinating: how nuclear power came to represent the future, how it came to be something approaching a tourist attraction in this most carefully blasé of states and – most crucially, and in layman's terms – how it actually works.

12.30PM A quick spin to the west side of town, to visit **Las Vegas Springs Preserve** (*see p71*), an experiential ecological museum and a huge site given over to botanical gardens, nature trails and a number of conservation-oriented exhibits. While you're there, why not take time for lunch at the sustainability minded, on-site café, which has picnic-style dining with wonderful vistas of the desert and the city.

6PM Here's a more eccentric and entirely more urban jaunt: the gritty Commercial Center, where you can get a fantastic dinner at the internationally recognised Thai restaurant **Lotus of Siam** (*see p149*).

8PM Hightail it back to the Bellagio on the Strip, for the 10pm showing of Cirque du Soleil's *O* (*see p205*), Vegas's must-see show. Afterwards – assuming you have the energy – catch the city bus, the Deuce, down to the **MGM Grand** (*see p88*), where there's sure to be a raging scene at the hip new nightclub **Hakkasan** (*see p221*). Catch one of the resident DJs and dance into the small hours before retiring to your hotel, where you'll need to rest from your holiday.

EXPLORE

you're planning to visit over a holiday weekend or for a major convention.

There are taxi ranks outside most hotels, and restaurants and bars will be happy to call a cab for you. Technically you're not allowed to hail a cab from the street and most won't stop if you try but it's usually OK to approach an empty cab with its light on.

Limousines are a flashy and popular way to get around, and are available for hire outside hotels and at the airport.

SEEING THE SIGHTS

Many of Las Vegas's attractions – the majority of them on or near the Strip – are free or close-to-free for visitors and open seven days a week.

PACKAGE DEALS

Las Vegas is big on package deals for hotels, flights, dining and entertainment – see visitlasvegas.com or the Las Vegas Convention & Visitors Authority's business-related website, lvcva.com, for more.

The Strip

Vegas's beating heart.

When he built the tropical-themed, volcano-fronted Mirage in 1989, Steve Wynn lit the fuse on a renaissance that would see Las Vegas Boulevard virtually rebuilt within 15 years. The city awoke from a long dormancy – the years when it was popular with those slightly embarrassing friends of your parents – and began to deal in high-volume density. At first, families were the targets. As Wynn followed the volcano-fuelled Mirage with the pirate ships of Treasure Island, populist attractions began to spring up all along the Strip, effectively the stretch of Las Vegas Boulevard South between the classic 'Welcome' sign and Sahara Avenue.

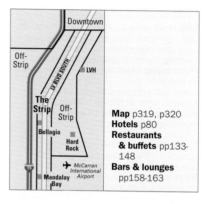

Map p319, p320
Hotels p80
Restaurants & buffets pp133-148
Bars & lounges pp158-163

THE STRIP REMADE

This new flashy style saw hotels fashioned after pyramids, castles and even a Disneyesque version of New York City. In 1998, Wynn steered the race in another direction, defining a new era of quality with the Bellagio. High-end travellers who previously had cared little about either gambling or rollercoasters discovered a city that now offered celebrity chefs and one-of-a-kind shows. By the time Wynn finished Wynn Las Vegas in 2005, resorts such as Mandalay Bay, the Venetian and Caesars Palace had already added boutique-style environs or were getting ready to do so, further upping the upmarket ante.

On the eve of the city's centennial in 2005, another new phase dawned. The Strip was now hip, beckoning twentysomethings – who couldn't care less about Wayne Newton or

prime-rib buffets – with an explosion of all-night dance clubs and swanky lounges. The latest wave of construction is reshaping the skyline with high-rise condos and mixed-use properties that will be virtual cities of their own. Glitzy high-rise hotel-casinos like the Cosmopolitan and Aria have dwarfed earlier giants like Bellagio, and old Vegas's neon has given way to brighter-than-bright LED screens. Hotels such as Mandarin Oriental and Vdara, neither of which offers gaming, have also shot skyward in the CityCenter complex. As Vegas goes vertical, it seems the entire ethos of the city is shifting as well.

RUSSELL ROAD TO TROPICANA AVENUE

As the tiny, neon-lit motor courts of the 1950s and '60s near Russell Road continue to perish under the wrecking ball, only the classic **Welcome to Fabulous Las Vegas** sign reminds visitors of the old California highway that once beckoned hot, thirsty drivers to get out of the heat. First-timers still brave the traffic to get a snap under this iconic landmark; you can purchase a miniature version, complete with flashing lights, at various gift shops along Las Vegas Boulevard. Facing the sign, the old Howard Hughes air terminal is behind you to the east (right), while the **Panevino** restaurant

INSIDE TRACK
HOTELS & CASINOS

For full details of the city's hotel-casino resorts, *see pp78-131.* The chapter covers every major casino in Vegas, detailing everything from its entertainment to its eating options, its guestrooms to its golf courses.

EXPLORE

(*see p143*) lies beyond the runways on Sunset Road, offering gorgeous views of the Strip and aircraft in transit. At your back, 300 miles away, is Los Angeles; in front of you lies the Strip, Las Vegas's *raison d'être*.

To the east is the **Little Church of the West** wedding chapel (*see p240*). Dating from 1942, it's the oldest building on the Strip, though with the caveat that it's been moved several times, most recently from the front lawn of the old Hacienda casino (imploded in 1996) to its current site. Across the Boulevard is the **Bali Hai Golf Club**

(*see p236*), one of only two golf courses on the Strip (the other is the guests-only facility at Wynn Las Vegas).

Just north, where the Hacienda once stood, is the South Seas-themed **Mandalay Bay** (*see p86*), effectively the beginning of the 21st-century Strip. The hotel's **Shark Reef** aquarium (*see p51*) is the best of the many animal-focused attractions in the city, but the resort is also home to a broad range of excellent eateries, the folk-art decorated **House of Blues** (*see p226*), the **Mandalay Place** mini-mall (*see p175*) and two other hotels,

Getting Your Bearings

Finding your way from the Strip.

The Las Vegas Valley is split into quarters by two intersecting freeways: I-15, coursing north–south through the centre of town on its way from Salt Lake City to LA, and US 95 (aka I-515), a north–south freeway that makes an east–west jink across the city. On a map, these roads approximate a twisted pinwheel shape, with a pivot just north-west of Downtown.

For street numbers, ground zero can be found at the junction of Fremont and Main streets in Downtown. From the Plaza at 1 S Main Street, numbers increase as you travel in any direction. Main Street ends at its intersection with Las Vegas Boulevard South; street addresses either east or west of the Main Street/Las Vegas Boulevard artery are tagged accordingly with 'E' or 'W'. North/south street delineations are based on an imaginary line from the eastern end of Charleston Boulevard, along Fremont Street in Downtown as far as Main Street, and then on to US 95 to the west.

Metropolitan Las Vegas is made up of four jurisdictions: Las Vegas, North Las Vegas, Henderson and unincorporated Clark County. Within and overlapping these jurisdictions are a number of areas and neighbourhoods, only some of which have widely recognised names. The Sights section of this guidebook has been divided into four chapters: **The Strip** (*see pp48-57*), the nickname for the stretch of Las Vegas Boulevard South between Russell Road in the south and Sahara Avenue in the north; **Off-Strip** (*see pp58-61*), loosely covering the streets immediately surrounding the Strip; **Downtown** (*see pp62-68*), centred on the junction of Fremont Street and Las Vegas Boulevard; and the **Rest of the City** (*see pp69-75*), covering everywhere else.

One mistake made by many visitors is not leaving the Strip. And that's understandable, given the hypnotic, wow-inducing glitz of the place. But there is a city beyond it – low on sights and arts, but with plenty of restaurants, bars and points of local interest worthy of your attention. Try to get out and see a couple.

The Strip.

EXPLORE

The Roller Coaster.

the tranquil **Four Seasons** (*see p109*) and the chic **Thehotel at Mandalay Bay** (*see p110*).

Next to Mandalay Bay is the unmistakable onyx pyramid of the **Luxor** (*see p98*), lights racing up its angles and exploding in a dramatic sky-bound beacon. An exhibition devoted to the *Titanic* proved popular enough to earn permanent residency at the Luxor. If it sounds a bit soft, head for **Bodies** (*see right*), which offers a peek at the human anatomy beneath the skin.

Just north of the Luxor lies the intersection of the Strip and Tropicana Avenue, home to more hotel rooms than you'll find in the whole of San Francisco. Here, crowds spill on to street corners and squeeze through pedestrian overpasses.

On the south-east corner of this ever-crazed junction are the white towers of the **Tropicana** (*see p104*). It was built in 1957 and was looking its age until 2011, when the new owners gave it a makeover with a South Beach vibe.

Across Tropicana Avenue to the north is the forever-expanding **MGM Grand** (*see p88*). The signature lion guarding the entrance is the nation's largest bronze sculpture. Inside, the exhibit **CSI: The Experience** (*see right*) is based on the hit TV franchise. The hotel also houses sprawling new nightclub **Hakkasan** (*see p221*).

Opposite the MGM Grand (and connected by an overhead skywalk) is the gloriously preposterous **New York New York** (*see p100*). Overhead runs the **Roller Coaster** (*see right*); inside, kids will enjoy the **Coney Island Emporium** (*see right*), while adults will be titillated by Cirque du Soleil's sexy **Zumanity** (*see p197*). Across a walkway to the south, completing the circle of casinos, looms

the medieval-themed **Excalibur** (*see p106*). It's still (somewhat) family-friendly but, in perhaps the most blatant symbol of the Strip's recent drift, has replaced its puppet show with a motorcycle-themed bar called Octane and added a male strip revue, *Thunder from Down Under*.

Bodies

Luxor *3900 Las Vegas Boulevard South, at W Hacienda Avenue (262 4400, www.luxor.com). Bus Deuce, 119, 201.* **Open** 10am-10pm daily (last entry 9pm). **Admission** $24-$32. **Map** p320 A8.

In the event that you've ever fancied dropping the best part of $30 in order to peek underneath the skin of dead strangers, this is the show for you. Having donated their remains to science, around 20 altruistic souls have been dissected, preserved and put on display for the edification of visitors to the Luxor. All things considered, the merchandise is in surprisingly good taste.

FREE Coney Island Emporium

New York New York *3790 Las Vegas Boulevard South, at W Tropicana Avenue (740 6969, www.newyorknewyork.com). Bus Deuce, 201.* **Open** 8am-midnight Mon-Thur, Sun; 8am-2am Fri, Sat. **Admission** free. **Map** p320 A8.

This arcade and family amusement centre attempts to recreate the atmosphere of the original Coney Island with more than 200 video and midway games, bumper cars, a prize counter and lots of sticky candyfloss (but, sadly, no freak show).

CSI: The Experience

MGM Grand *3799 Las Vegas Boulevard South, at E Tropicana Avenue (891 7777, www.mgmgrand. com). Bus Deuce, 201.* **Open** 9am-9pm daily (last entry 8pm). **Admission** $21-$28. **Map** p320 A8.

Fancy yourself as a forensic scientist? Well, here's your chance to put your skills to the test. This interactive adventure, inspired by the numerous TV programmes, casts you in the role of an investigator, charged with solving multiple murders through examining evidence, working with real scientists, and interpreting the clues.

★ Mob Attraction
Tropicana *3801 Las Vegas Boulevard South, at E Tropicana Avenue (739 2662, www.mob attraction.com).* Bus Deuce, 201. **Open** 10am-8pm daily. **Tickets** $18-$33. *4hr tour $98.50.* **Map** p320 A8.
Murders are solved across the street at MGM's CSI: The Experience; on the other side of the Strip to the west, the cadavers are examined at Luxor's Bodies. How did we get all these dead people? For the answer to that you'll have to check out the Tropicana's new adventure: Mob Attraction. Part historical collection, part interactive experience, it brings history to life with 3-D holograms of bad guys, Mafia paraphernalia, and lots of pictures and videos. Take the tour – recommended – for full immersion.

The Roller Coaster
New York New York *3790 Las Vegas Boulevard South, at W Tropicana Avenue (740 6969, www.newyorknewyork.com).* Bus Deuce, 201. **Open** 11am-11pm Mon-Thur, Sun; 10.30am-midnight Fri, Sat. **Tickets** $14. *All-day pass $25.* **Map** p320 A8.
Formerly known as the Manhattan Express, this scream-inducing ride now has a much simpler name. But one thing's the same: Gotham's never seen anything like it. The Coaster soars around skyscrapers and Lady Liberty, twisting, looping and diving at breakneck speeds. It features the first ever 'heartline roll', which creates the sensation a pilot feels when going through a barrel roll in an aeroplane. Try hard to smile in the last section: this is where the photos are taken.

★ Shark Reef
Mandalay Bay *3950 Las Vegas Boulevard South, at W Hacienda Avenue (632 4555, www.shark reef.com).* Bus Deuce, 119. **Open** 10am-10pm daily (last entry 9pm). **Admission** $12-$18; free under-4s. **Map** p320 A9.

A 'walk-through' aquarium, Shark Reef is filled with 100 species of underwater life, including rays, jellyfish, eels and, of course, 15 varieties of shark. A perfect complement to the South Seas-themed Mandalay Bay, the Shark Reef is an unexpected gem in a city lacking in the educational entertainment department.

Titanic: The Exhibition
Luxor *3900 Las Vegas Boulevard South, at W Hacienda Avenue (262 4400, www.luxor.com).* Bus Deuce, 119, 201. **Open** 10am-10pm daily (last entry 9pm). **Admission** $24-$32. **Map** p320 A8.
More than 3,000 bits and pieces recovered from the mother of all seafaring disasters are now on permanent display at the Luxor in this diverting show, which also affords visitors the chance to experience a simulation of the kind of weather experienced by the poor unfortunates on the night in question.

TROPICANA AVENUE TO HARMON AVENUE

A pleasant pedestrian boardwalk that morphs into a replica Brooklyn Bridge leads north on the eastern side of New York New York as far as the **Sporting House Bar & Grill**. As you stroll, note the classic 'Pepsi and Pete' sign on the wall of a replica brownstone building, challenging the Times Square-style giant neon Coke bottle on the Showcase Mall across the street. The mall houses the Strip's only cinema (the **UA Showcase 8**; *see p214*), **M&M's World** (*see p52*) and a variety of other stores.

Further on, and fronting the **Polo Towers** timeshare, sits the **Hawaiian Marketplace**. It's surprising that this jumble of shops, restaurants and a bird show has survived the wrecking ball, especially when you see what has happened across the road. The front of the **Monte Carlo** (*see p99*) is currently undergoing major renovations, but it's the activity directly north that has changed the face of Vegas.

Here sits **CityCenter**, the latest key development on the Strip. CityCenter is MGM Mirage's vast, ambitious hotel-casino-condo-retail-dining complex; a $9-billion, 68-acre complex – a city within the city, designed by eight international architects – featuring the twin towers of hotel-resort **Aria** (61 and 51 stories; *see p81*), two additional non-gaming hotels (**Vdara**, *see p111*, and **Mandarin Oriental**, *see p110*), condos (the gold-tinged Veer Towers, which tilt five degrees off-kilter in opposite directions), vast amounts of retail space in **Crystals** (*see p173*), theatres, restaurants, spas and a parking garage with room for 7,500 vehicles. It even has its own power plant and fire station, making CityCenter a semi-autonomous community in an

EXPLORE

unincorporated township (the Strip) within a larger, sprawling desert outpost that's struggling to address some far less flashy concerns of its own. But that's Vegas for you.

Next door is the **Cosmopolitan** (*see p85*), which debuted at the end of 2010. The choice of stylish international visitors (and locals, who took to the place immediately), Cosmo attracts a younger, more urbane crowd, who like to look at each other as much as they like to gamble – maybe more – and are well catered to by the resort's chic boutiques.

Crystals

CityCenter *3720 Las Vegas Boulevard South, at E Harmon Avenue (1-866 754 2489, 590 9299, www.crystalsatcitycenter.com). Bus Deuce.* **Open** 10am-11pm Mon-Thur, Sun; 10am-midnight Fri, Sat. **Map** p320 A7.

Outsparkling everything around it is Crystals, the ultraluxe shopping complex that fronts the CityCenter complex. With its elegant angles designed by architect Daniel Libeskind and its vast ceilings and pristine all-white settings, Crystals looks like a museum of shopping designed by a sci-fi art director. It features boutiques by Balenciaga, Dior, Pucci, Gucci, Fendi, Stella McCartney, Paul Smith and Tom Ford.

FREE M&M's World

Showcase Mall, 3785 Las Vegas Boulevard South, between E Tropicana & E Harmon avenues (740 2504). Bus Deuce, 201. **Open** 9am-midnight daily. **Admission** free. **Map** p320 A8.

A four-level chocolate-lover's paradise. Check out M&M Academy, an interactive entertainment showing visitors how these chocolate candies earn their trademark. The attraction includes a 3-D movie, and 'graduates' get a diploma. Yes, it's a bit over the top. But at least it's free. *Photo p50.*

HARMON AVENUE TO FLAMINGO ROAD

Planet Hollywood (*see p101*), which opened as the Aladdin in 2000, sits on the east side of the Strip at Harmon Avenue. The short-lived Aladdin was never one of the Strip's more popular casinos; the new owners judged that by getting rid of the ill-timed Baghdad motif, things would turn around. Alas, you won't find the Terminator dealing cards: unlike at the Planet Hollywood restaurants, the movie bric-a-brac is confined to the guestrooms, and the neutrally decorated casino lacks a specific theme. The hotel connects to the **Miracle Mile** mall (*see p175*).

To the north of Planet Hollywood is the spectacular (but small, in Vegas terms) **Paris Las Vegas** (*see p91*), complete with half-scale Eiffel Tower, grand fountains and sidewalk café (**Mon Ami Gabi**, *see p142*). From here,

Bellagio Fountains.

it's a skip north to the original 'Four Corners', where the Strip meets Flamingo Road. On the south-west corner of the street, at **Bally's** (*see p95*), a video screen competes with the bizarre tunnel entrance. To its north is the future site of Gansevoort Las Vegas (formerly Bill's Gamblin' Hall & Saloon), due to open in early 2014. These properties, however, are overshadowed by their neighbours across the Strip.

At the south-west corner of the Strip's intersection with Flamingo is the **Bellagio** (*see p82*), one of the most renowned properties in the city since its opening in 1998. The fountains that dance upon the large replica of Lake Como are among the best-loved attractions in Las Vegas, but there's plenty of note inside too: the **Gallery of Fine Art**, Cirque du Soleil's **O** (*see p205*) and the glass-domed Conservatory & Botanical Gardens, which lie beyond the lobby and are home to thousands of exotic plants and flowers.

With its striking blue-white lighting and huge fountains, the opulent and ever-expanding **Caesars Palace** (*see p83*) commands attention as the sole Strip casino to successfully mate the past with 21st-century Vegas. Little of Jay Sarno's Roman kitsch remains; the resort has successfully reinvented itself as an altogether more chic property. Just to the north of the main fountain is a small Brahma shrine, where visitors worship and leave offerings of fruit and flowers in exchange for good luck.

Near where Caesars meets the Mirage is the entrance to the Roman-themed **Forum Shops** (*see p174*), a vast atrium served by a spiral escalator and filled with luxury boutiques. The high-end shopping is conducted under an ever-changing 'sky' that's spelled by a Disney-like robot show. Animated statues come to life for a bizarre and very loud seven-minute revel with dancing water and laser lights.

FREE Bellagio Fountains

Bellagio *3600 Las Vegas Boulevard South, at W Flamingo Road (693 7111, www.bellagio.com).* *Bus Deuce, 202.* **Shows** 3pm-midnight Mon-Fri (every 30mins 3-7pm; every 15mins 7pm-midnight); noon-midnight Sat, Sun (every 30mins noon-7pm; every 15mins 7pm-midnight). **Admission** free. **Map** p320 A7.

The Bellagio's lake throws up entrancing fountain displays choreographed to music from Pavarotti to Sinatra (and, less appealingly, Lee Greenwood). The 1,200 water cannons, arranged in lines and circles, shoot water that dances and sways to the music, reaching as high as 240ft. The best seats are in the Bellagio restaurants, but you get a good view from the pavements out front, and from the top of the Eiffel Tower at Paris Las Vegas.

Bellagio Gallery of Fine Art

Bellagio *3600 Las Vegas Boulevard South, at W Flamingo Road (693 7871, www.bellagio.com).* *Bus Deuce, 202.* **Open** 10am-8pm daily (last entry 7.30pm). **Admission** $16; $13-$11 reductions; under-12s free. **Map** p320 A7.

The longest-standing gallery on the Strip stages a strong selection of shows; they're here on a temporary basis, but the last three have been in residence for a year apiece. Past exhibitions have included a wildly popular Monet collection leased from the Museum of Fine Arts, Boston; a showing of Ansel Adams photographs; and one devoted to Picasso's ceramics. A selection Andy Warhol's work, 'Warhol Out West', is on display through early 2014.

Eiffel Tower Experience

Paris Las Vegas *3655 Las Vegas Boulevard South, at E Flamingo Road (1-888 946 7000, www.parislasvegas.com).* *Bus Deuce, 202.* **Open** 9.30am-12.30am Mon-Fri; 9.30am-1am Sat, Sun. **Tickets** $7.50-$24.50. **Map** p320 A7.

OK, so it's only half the size of the original, but the Vegas Eiffel Tower gives visitors a great view of the Strip and the surrounding mountains, something you won't find in Paris. Take a lift to the 46th-floor observation deck; go at dusk to watch the Strip suddenly light up as if someone flicked a switch.

FLAMINGO ROAD TO SPRING MOUNTAIN ROAD

Wedged against the Gansevoort, the **Flamingo** (*see p96*) is one of the Strip's most historic properties, although nothing much remains of Bugsy Siegel's 1941 original. In its place is a lush pool area and winding pathways that take you past penguins, flamingos, mandarin ducks and koi fish swimming in ponds under three-storey-high waterfalls. If it weren't for the tennis courts, pool and spa, it could be a wildlife habitat, albeit the only one in the world with a plaque honouring a mobster.

This stretch of the Strip, covering the Flamingo, the recently rebranded **Quad** (formerly the Imperial Palace; *see p102*) and the altogether unremarkable **Harrah's** (*see p97*), is owned by Harrah's Entertainment, a mid-market corporation that's second only to MGM Mirage in terms of its influence in the city. Although the Imperial Palace is no more, part of its heart and soul remains in its **Auto Collections** (*see 54*), behind the hotel on top of the parking garage. And just past Harrah's, a 24-hour parade of hungry characters scoff food at Denny's, inside the small and independently owned **Casino Royale** (*see p105*), a worthwhile stop if you're slumming in homage to Hunter S Thompson's Vegas.

Back across the street, north of Caesars is a block-long tropical paradise that begins with the **Mirage** (*see p90*), which in 1989 became the Strip's first modern mega-resort. When it opened, it introduced the first large-scale free spectacle to Las Vegas: a 54-foot volcano right on the Strip. The revamped volcano is small, lacks a cinder dome and looks more like a granite wall than Mount Etna. However, the brief spectacle (every 15 minutes, 7pm-midnight daily), spewing fire and a piña colada scent into the palm trees, waterfalls and lagoon, is worth a look.

Inside the resort, pygmy sharks swim in an aquarium behind the registration desk. After looking tired for years, the Mirage got a much-needed shine with the arrival of Cirque du Soleil's much-heralded Beatles show **Love** (*see p204*),

EXPLORE

Eiffel Tower Experience.

in the mid noughties. After the show, fans can huddle at **Revolution** lounge (*see p161*) to decide if they liked it; if, that is, they don't fancy hitting any of the hotspots elsewhere: happening new nightclub **1 Oak** (*see p223*), and eateries **Stack** (*see p146*) and **Japonais** (*see p140*).

Just up from the Mirage sits **Treasure Island** (*see p104*), now marketing itself as **TI** in an attempt to shake off its family-oriented image. The resort fronts the Strip with a replica of an 18th-century village set on a lagoon, surrounded by cliffs, palm trees and nautical artefacts. The focus of attention, however, is the two fully rigged ships on which the Sirens of TI clash with a band of renegade pirates (every 90 minutes, 7-11.30pm daily). Formerly a family-friendly pantomime, the show received a crass revamp that tries to rebrand the property as a more adult resort. Regardless, it fills the pavement to capacity, as onlookers stare slack-jawed at the blazing cannons, toppling masts, exploding powder kegs and – key to the whole thing – heaving bosoms.

Opposite TI and the Mirage on the eastern side of the Strip, just north of Casino Royale, sits the **Venetian** (*see p92*), Sheldon Adelson's hugely successful reinterpretation of the city of canals, and next to it is Adelson's $1.8-billion addition, the **Palazzo**. Attractions at these properties include super-fashionable restaurant-club **Tao** (*see p147*), **Madame Tussauds** (*see right*), the highfalutin' **Grand Canal Shoppes** (*see p175*) and the **gondola rides**, with singing gondoliers who drag embarrassed tourists along the resort's canals.

Auto Collections at the Quad

Quad *3535 Las Vegas Boulevard South, between Sands Avenue & E Flamingo Road (794 3174, www.autocollections.com.com). Bus Deuce, 119, 202, 203.* **Open** 10am-6pm daily. **Admission** $11.95. **Map** p320 A6.

Sitting atop the fifth floor of the parking garage at the Quad are 200 rare and speciality cars (many of them for sale, at prices ranging from $50,000 to $2 million). Among them are a 1939 Chrysler Sedan that once belonged to Johnny Carson's father, in which Carson drove to his senior prom; JFK's 1962 Lincoln; various Rolls-Royces, and a room full of Duesenbergs.

Gondola rides

Venetian *Grand Canal Shoppes, 3355 Las Vegas Boulevard South, between Sands Avenue & E Flamingo Road (414 4300, www.venetian.com). Bus Deuce, 119, 203.* **Open** *Indoor* 10am-11pm Mon-Thur, Sun; 10am-midnight Fri, Sat. *Outdoor* 11am-10pm daily. **Tickets** $18.95 per person (gondola seats 4); $76.80 private 2-passenger gondola. **Map** p319, p320 A6.

Purchase your tickets at St Mark's Square, then take a ride along canals that weave through replica Venetian architecture. The wooden boats are authentic and the singing gondoliers are tuneful. However, despite the number of newly married couples that take the ride, the backdrop of gawking tourists will dampen any hopes of a romantic moment.

Madame Tussauds

3377 Las Vegas Boulevard South, between Sands Avenue & E Flamingo Road (862 7800, www.madametussauds.com). Bus Deuce, 119, 203. **Open** 10am-9pm Mon-Thur, Sun; 10am-10pm Fri, Sat. **Admission** $27.95; $17.95 reductions; free under-3s. **Map** p319, p320 A6.

The first US incarnation of London's all-conquering attraction contains more than 100 wax celebs in various settings and rendered with various degrees of accuracy (Cameron Diaz good, Shaquille O'Neal less impressive). The comparatively small attraction tones down the British history in favour of celebrity culture 'encounters': a photo opportunity to don a wedding dress and 'marry' George Clooney, for example, or a chance to sing in front of Simon Cowell. Hokey but fun.

Secret Garden & Dolphin Habitat

Mirage *3400 Las Vegas Boulevard South, between Spring Mountain & W Flamingo roads (791 7188, www.miragehabitat.com). Bus Deuce, 203.* **Open** 10am-7pm daily (last entry 6pm). **Admission** $19.95; $14.95 reductions; free under-3s. **Map** p319, p320 A6.

Marine mammals in the desert? Nothing's impossible in fabulous Las Vegas. Here, bottle-nosed dolphins frolic in a special habitat behind the Mirage. Adjacent to their home is the Secret Garden, a small but attractive zoo with Asian-themed architecture and some big-ticket animals: white tigers, white lions, golden tigers, black panthers and a snow leopard.

SPRING MOUNTAIN ROAD TO CONVENTION CENTER DRIVE

For 15 years, the stretch of the Strip north of Spring Mountain Road was old Vegas through and through, a parade of forgotten resorts and empty plots of land. A few of the old casinos remain, but it's mostly all-change around here, and has been since about 2005. In a nutshell, the difference between then and now is the difference between Sinatra's *Ocean's 11* and Clooney's *Ocean's Eleven*.

Naturally, Steve Wynn is at the centre of it all. It was Wynn who kickstarted the Vegas renaissance by building the Mirage in 1989. Then, 16 years later and a long stone's throw from its front door, he opened the $2.7-billion **Wynn Las Vegas** (*see p93*), a hyperreal return to the 'intimacy' of old Las Vegas. The resort sits on land formerly occupied by the Desert Inn, a Vegas classic that bit the dust just a few years earlier.

Gondola rides, Venetian.

In a reversal of the philosophy of streetside spectacle pioneered at the Mirage, Wynn Las Vegas is hidden from the Strip by a mountain. Behind it are a golf course, a lavish spa, top-end shops and even a Ferrari dealership; Wynn has never done things by halves. Right next to the resort, Wynn built a second building in a similar style to the first, though with even more lavish decor. **Encore** opened in 2008 and stands apart as a separate resort.

Directly across the road, the **Fashion Show Mall** (*see p177*) is further accelerating the redefinition of Vegas. The two 13-storey towers would dominate the landscape were it not for the **Cloud**, a 479-foot metal oval suspended between them. The Cloud serves as an outdoor projection screen, but it also provides much-needed shade for the de facto piazza and four rare (for Vegas) restaurants featuring outdoor seating facing the Wynn, including **Ra Sushi**, serving rock 'n' roll Japanese food. In coincidental but purposeful synergy with Wynn Las Vegas, the Fashion Show is a theme-free shopping centre (except for the runway shows every 30 minutes); before long, themed resorts will seem as dated as the old casinos did in 1989.

North of the Fashion Show sits what is one of the most expensive pieces of land in Las Vegas. For decades, the south-west corner of the Strip and Desert Inn Road was home to the New Frontier, built in 1942 (as the Last Frontier) and one of the first resorts on what was to become the Strip. The resort trod water for years, as rumours came and went about owner Phil Ruffin's plans for redevelopment. But then, after mapping out his ambition to build a Montreux-themed resort on the site, Ruffin abruptly sold up to New York-based developers El Ad Properties in May 2007, for a reported $1.2 billion. El Ad announced plans to build another resort on the site, and in late 2007 the New Frontier was imploded. El Ad's

plans were cancelled in 2011, and the lot – across from Wynn and Encore – sits vacant.

Across the Desert Inn Arterial, an east–west expressway that avoids both the Strip (by tunnelling under) and I-15 (by flying over), further changes are afoot. The plot of land on the western side of the street was home to the Stardust for nearly 50 years. Proving that nothing is sacred, the iconic resort was demolished in 2007 to make room for **Echelon Place**, a 90-acre, multi-hotel complex that was due to open in 2010 but now sits sadly unfinished on the Strip like a broken tooth, a sad reminder of the worldwide economic crisis.

The opposite side of the Strip is an altogether more sedate sight. Development here has yet to really take hold, leaving the Catholic **Guardian Angel Cathedral** (336 Guardian Angel Way, 410 8160) to go about its business in relative peace. The themed stained-glass windows here are one of the few places where you can still see old Vegas icons such as the Landmark Hotel. Rumour has it that the church accepts casino chips in its collection plate.

CONVENTION CENTER DRIVE TO SAHARA AVENUE

North of Convention Center Drive, the Strip quickly peters out into disrepair. A couple of scruffy strip malls sit adjacent to and opposite some creaking old casinos, though the most eye-catching features are the acres of empty lots and the clusters of construction work. The north Strip may be on the rise, but it has quite a way to travel before it reaches lift-off.

A fun little ode to the 1970s stubbornly survives in the shape of **Peppermill's Fireside Lounge** (*see p160*), though the lounge recently ruined its cosy, *Playboy*-like atmosphere by bolting flatscreen TVs on to every surface. The site next door was once home to the delightfully Googie-style La Concha Motel. But after innumerable plans for redevelopment fell by the wayside, the land is currently, stubbornly vacant, while the motel's old lobby has been moved Downtown by the Neon Museum (*see p64* **A Paean to Neon**).

It's back to blazing neon at the 50-year-old **Riviera** (*see p108*), where the façade and sign very nearly constitute overkill even by Vegas standards. You can skip the actual show, but don't miss the life-sized bronze statues promoting the **Crazy Girls** (*see p198*) just in front of the casino; punters rub their butts for a boozy photo-op. However, the Riv seems to be marking time while it awaits extinction, a refuge for the cost-conscious traveller but easily skipped by those not staying there.

Lucky the Clown still leers cheerfully over the Strip from the front of **Circus Circus** (*see p106*) across the road, though the original family fun palace is now showing its age. The casino under the pink-concrete big top stages free circus acts (11am-midnight daily) above the casino floor, while what was the Horse-a-Round Bar, now a family-friendly *gelato* stand, was immortalised in Hunter S Thompson's *Fear and Loathing in Las Vegas*. The cramped space and shabby decor lessen the spectacle; it's an odd experience watching a spangly trapeze artist fly overhead. While mom and pop gamble away the rent, kids whoop it up at **Adventuredome**, a popular indoor amusement park.

To the north of here sits Hilton Grand Vacation Suites, two timeshare towers. Across the road, construction stopped on a Las Vegas version of Miami's famous **Fontainebleau** in 2007. The property, which topped out at 68 storeys, went into bankruptcy, and was sold to investor Carl Icahn, who auctioned off furnishings intended for its interior in 2010. Today, speculation remains as to the unfinished hotel's fate, another forlorn monument to the financial crash.

Hidden Heights

The Wynn's mountain is one Vegas sight that conceals before it reveals.

The Mirage volcano, TI's *Sirens* pirate show and the Bellagio's dancing waters are the most popular free attractions on the Strip. All three were conceived by Steve Wynn, and were designed to lure passing visitors inside each resort. A decade later, though, Wynn reversed his previous policy of visibility. The volcano, the sexy pirates and the fountains all face the Strip. But at Wynn Las Vegas (*see p93*), visitors have to go inside the casino to find the signature attraction.

From outside the resort, visitors can see a small hill covered in trees: nearly 500 of them, some 65 feet tall and 60 years old (transplanted from the old Desert Inn golf course). Mount Wynn, however, isn't immediately obvious, either from here or inside the resort. To get the full effect, you'll need to take the spiral staircase down to the terraces at the SW Steakhouse or Lakeside Seafood; there's also a small outdoor bar and a tiny free-viewing platform.

The mountain consists of four environments that provide the backdrop for the row of restaurants and bars, each with its own distinct alfresco view. Eight waterfalls descend into the three-acre Lake of Dreams, with its 4,000-plus individually controlled and submerged LEDs. A freestanding 70-foot wall serves as the projection screen for a free light-and-sound show that plays every half hour starting at 9pm.

The mountain serves a second and perhaps equally important purpose. It blocks the lights and drowns out the sounds of the Strip, cocooning Wynn Las Vegas and providing the visual centrepiece for the whole property. Once, that is, you've figured out where to look.

INSIDE TRACK FRIGHTDOME

Prepared to be scared: in October, the **Adventuredome** (*see below*) transforms into the pleasantly creepy FrightDome, in time for Halloween.

There is, however, a large project brewing on the south-east corner of Las Vegas Boulevard and Sahara Avenue, formerly the site of the Sahara hotel. Instead of being imploded, as is so often the case with used-up Las Vegas hotels, the Sahara has been removed piece by piece to make way for **SLS Las Vegas**, a 1,700-room hotel-casino, scheduled to open in autumn 2014. Owned by the SBE Entertainment group, SLS – which stands for 'style, luxury and service' – is part of a rapidly expanding US chain.

For many, the Strip begins and ends right here at Sahara Avenue, although the Stratosphere's looming tower has pushed the unofficial boundary another half-mile north.

Adventuredome

Circus Circus *2880 Las Vegas Boulevard South, between W Sahara Avenue & Desert Inn Road (794 3939, www.adventuredome.com). Bus Deuce, 108.* **Open** 10am-midnight daily (subject to change). **Admission** *Unlimited rides* $27.95; $16.95 reductions. *Individual rides* $5-$8. **Map** p319 B5.
The five-acre park, climate-controlled under a pink plastic dome, is a scene Fred Flintstone would love: waterfalls, faux mountains and animated spitting dinosaurs stuck in fake tar pits. The rides are good, though hardly white-knuckle; the best is the double-loop, double-corkscrew rollercoaster, but it lasts a disappointingly brief 90 seconds. Tots will like the bumper cars, Ferris wheel and other small rides.

STRATOSPHERE AREA

The lot at the south-western corner of Sahara and the Strip is eye-catchingly vacant, while the much-rumoured redevelopment of the north-eastern plot has yet to occur. Diagonally opposite SLS Las Vegas, **Bonanza Gifts** (*see p187*) holds the fort at the intersection's north-western corner; claiming to be the world's largest gift shop, it sells a vast array of souvenirs, in a pleasantly kitschy time-travel to the Route 66 era. Just west is the pricey condo towers of Allure overlooking the Strip, and the classic **Golden Steer Steak House** (*see p150*).

Standing outside Bonanza, you'll be able to hear screams. Glance north, and you'll see why. At the top of the **Stratosphere** (*see p109*), the tallest building in Nevada, are four thrill rides: the **Big Shot**, which propels passengers vertically; **X-Scream**, which

dangles them over the edge of the tower; **Insanity: the Ride**, an inverted centrifuge that spins over the edge of the observation deck at a 70-degree angle; and the newer **SkyJump**, which lets intrepid (or crazy) souls plunge from the 108th storey in a harnessed free-fall.

The Stratosphere sits where Main Street and Paradise Road cross Las Vegas Boulevard and turn into each other by way of St Louis Avenue. As you approach it from the south, you'll see a string of downmarket motels; the old **Holiday House Motel** (no.2211, 732 2468) is notable for its animated neon sign and Palm Springs-like motor court design.

★ Big Shot, X-Scream, Insanity: the Ride & SkyJump

Stratosphere *2000 Las Vegas Boulevard South, at St Louis Avenue (380 7777, www.stratospherehotel.com). Bus Deuce, 108.* **Open** 10am-1am Mon-Thur, Sun; 10am-2am Fri, Sat. **Rides** *Single ride* $15. *3 rides* $33. *All-day pass* $34. *SkyJump* from $109.99. **Map** p319 C4.
If you're afraid of heights, stay away from the 1,150ft Stratosphere Tower. And even if you don't suffer from vertigo, you might want to steer clear of the resort's thrill rides. The Big Shot will rocket you 160ft up the tower's spindle at a force of four Gs; at the top, you'll experience a moment of weightlessness before free-falling back to the launch pad. X-Scream will propel you headfirst 27ft over the edge of the Tower and then leave you there to dangle. During Insanity, an arm will extend 64ft over the edge of the tower and spin you around at a terrifying rate. And SkyJump... Well, best save dinner for later.

Stratosphere.

Off-Strip

More casinos, of course, but activities and museums too.

You wouldn't expect to confuse Paradise Road for the Strip. Lined with an erratic hotchpotch of posh hotels and scruffy apartment blocks, convention facilities and adult clubs, strip malls and, er, more strip malls, Paradise is a low-key thoroughfare. However, as the Las Vegas Convention Center draws ever-increasing numbers of conventioneers, and the Strip attracts even more tourists, so the traffic along Paradise Road gets fiercer. It now resembles Las Vegas Boulevard in one crucial regard: if you're foolish enough to try driving down it in rush hour, you'll be waiting a while. During off-peak hours, though, locals swear by it as a timesaving way to avoid stop-start Strip-stalled traffic.

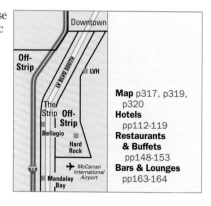

Map p317, p319, p320
Hotels
pp112-119
Restaurants & Buffets
pp148-153
Bars & Lounges
pp163-164

West of the Strip, the area between busy Las Vegas Boulevard and unremarkable Valley View Boulevard is bisected by I-15. Continuing north, Industrial Road is mostly notable for the parade of strip clubs that lines its western edge.

EAST OF THE STRIP

Running parallel to the Strip, **Paradise Road** has been the site of major development since 1969, when the Landmark and International casinos opened south of Sahara Avenue. The Landmark was erased a while ago (see *Mars Attacks!* to witness its real-life destruction), while the International was renamed the **Las Vegas Hilton** in 1971, the same year that it starred as the **Whyte House** in *Diamonds Are Forever*. Following its recent break with the Hilton chain, it's become the **Las Vegas Hotel** or LVH for short (*see p113*). The Hilton's showroom staged Elvis Presley's record-breaking run of 837 sell-outs in the 1970s, as well as sold-out runs of Liberace that same decade. Directly behind it is the exclusive **Las Vegas Country Club**.

Sprawling out from the south end of LVH and across Desert Inn Road, the **Las Vegas Convention Center** (*see p295*) has been more responsible than any one hotel for the huge growth in visitor numbers over the last decade. Seven million travellers arrive in the city for conventions each year, and many of them pass through this site to do business. The assortment of uncharismatic chain hotels nearby stands testament to its influence. At the intersection with Desert Inn Road, **Envy** steakhouse (*see p149*) serves hungry conventioneers; across the street is a shuttle to whisk patrons to the Wynn Las Vegas resort. Paradise Road, in fact, might aptly be renamed Steakhouse Alley, as it hosts, in addition to Envy, at least half a dozen steak purveyors, including Morton's, Del Frisco's Double Eagle and 35 Steaks + Martinis.

Further south, the road widens and the traffic eases. At Twain Avenue begins a collection of eateries known as 'restaurant row'. However, the stretch of Paradise between Flamingo and Tropicana holds more points of interest. On the eastern side lies a succession of strip malls that house a slew of excellent restaurants (try **Origin India**; *see p150*), dive bars (such as the **Double Down Saloon**; *see p163*) and gay hangouts (in the **Fruit Loop**; *see pp215-218*). East of all these businesses sits the campus of UNLV, which more or less backs on to Paradise Road.

EXPLORE

And on the western side of Paradise, at the junction with Harmon Avenue, is the **Hard Rock** hotel-casino (*see p112*), crammed with memorabilia, suntanned hipsters and cash-happy baby boomers. Despite competition from Palms – and, more recently, the Cosmopolitan – the Hard Rock is holding its own as a favoured resort for the young and restless, thanks to the renovated, state-of-the-art concert hall called the Joint, which opened with a pair of concerts by Vegas natives the Killers and none other than Sir Paul McCartney; and the weekly flesh-feast that is the Rehab pool party (Sundays in season; *see p223* **We Love the Daylife**). See if you can find the one-of-a-kind Sex Pistols-themed slot machine on the Hard Rock gaming floor.

South of Tropicana sits the vast **McCarran International Airport** (*see p292*) – the gleaming rows of slot machines in its lobby never cease to amaze the waves of fresh arrivals. McCarran is one of the world's most fascinating people-watching spots, as its population changes by the hour: it's variably and visibly overrun by black-clad retrobilly bikers, NASCAR fans, NBA stars, rodeo cowboys and, occasionally, hovering hordes of hookers waiting for their baggage.

Just south of McCarran on Sunset Road at Las Vegas Boulevard South, before it actually becomes 'the Strip', sits a more recent and triumphant development in the form of **Town Square** (*see p61*). This upscale (and always packed) shopping, dining and entertainment hub has rapidly become a favourite of both locals and tourists – a standalone destination apart from the shops on the Strip and the strip malls.

East on Tropicana is the **Atomic Testing Museum**, located on the Desert Research Institute campus. And to the west of Paradise, between Flamingo and Tropicana, sits a maze of small streets and empty lots, awaiting their inevitable redevelopment.

★ Atomic Testing Museum

755 E Flamingo Road, between Swenson Street & Paradise Road (794 5151, www.atomictesting museum.org). Bus 108, 202. **Open** 10am-5pm Mon-Sat; noon-5pm Sun. **Admission** $14-$20; $7-$17 reductions; free under-6s. **Map** p317 Y3.

From the city that once trotted out atomic pin-up girls in mushroom-cloud swimsuits for cheesy publicity stills comes a one-of-a-kind insight into the Nevada Test Site, the US's principal on-continent nuclear weapons testing facility from 1951 to 1992. The story it tells is fascinating: how nuclear power came to represent the future in the USA, how it came to be something approaching a tourist attraction in this most carefully blasé of states, and – most crucially, and in layman's terms – how it actually works.

An affiliate of the Smithsonian Institution, its headline exhibit is the motion simulator that endeavours to give visitors a taste of what it must have been like to sit in on one of the several hundred tests carried out at the site between 1951 and 1992. But the real keys to the museum's success are the clarity with which it tells its tale (chronologically, through a succession of themed rooms), and the eye-popping quality of the exhibits (some kitsch, some terrifying). The recent addition of an exhibit on Area 51 is intriguing or ridiculous: you decide.

Vegas Indoor Skydiving

200 Convention Center Drive, between Las Vegas Boulevard South & Paradise Road (1-877 545 8093, 731 4768, www.vegasindoorskydiving.com). Bus Deuce, 108. **Open** 9.45am-8pm daily. **Rates** $75. **Map** p319 B5.

Skydiving without an airplane? Well, sort of. You can free-fall in one of only three skydiving simulators in the world, an indoor 21ft vertical wind tunnel that generates air speeds of up to 120mph. After half an hour of instruction, you get 15 minutes of flying time shared with four others. Like it? Take a second go-round for $40.

WEST OF THE STRIP

In the area between busy Las Vegas Boulevard and unremarkable **Valley View Boulevard**, the I-15 carves a rift into a section of land that didn't offer much resistance to it. Wedged next to it and running parallel, Frank Sinatra Drive offers quicker, back-door access to many Strip hotels.

Atomic Testing Museum.

EXPLORE

Continuing north, **Industrial Road** itself is just as speedy, though it's the strip clubs along its western edge that are the draw for many.

Overpasses at Tropicana, Flamingo or Sahara take drivers across I-15 to Valley View Boulevard (which, incidentally, isn't continuous between Tropicana Boulevard and Flamingo Road). If you're heading this way from the Strip, Flamingo is the road to take: it's lined with a quartet of very different hotel-casinos, each with something to offer the visitor.

Head west on Tropicana to South Arville Street and you'll see a locals' favourite, the **Orleans** (see p127), which attracts lovers of country music and 1970s pop culture with its concerts; you'll also find such down-home American events as tractor pulls, rodeos and barbecue competitions at its Events Center. The Orleans' bowling alley and movie theatre are a strong draw for Vegas residents and visitors, as is its large and popular poker room.

On the northern side of Flamingo sits the **Rio** (see p115). Wickedly funny magicians Penn & Teller (see p202) have been holding court there in their own dedicated theatre for more than a decade. Just west of the Rio across Valley View is the **Gold Coast** (see p129), and beyond that, the **Palms** (see p114) on

Demolition City

Here today, gone tomorrow.

Will Self once compared the constant, inevitable and yet barely tangible regeneration of urban landscapes to an intruder entering one's house in the middle of the night and moving all the furniture by a couple of inches. You know something's changed, but you can't quite tell what, or how, or even when.

In Las Vegas, things are different: progress happens instantaneously yet takes forever. Structures are erased without ceremony or sentiment, the swing of a wrecking ball bouncing from building to building like dice cascading backwards from the wall of a craps table. And then begins the inexorably tedious yet painfully visible process of regenerating the space. What takes five minutes to destroy can take five years to rebuild, by which time everyone has lost interest.

The streets surrounding the Strip are filled with casualties that time hasn't managed to erase. Harrah's levelled the Bourbon Street casino (formerly at 120 E Flamingo Road) in 2006, but its sidewalk remains lined with stars that together comprise a cheap-as-chips jazz Walk of Fame. South of the Strip and closed since 2006, the crumbling Klondike (5191 Las Vegas Boulevard S) is the first casino most visitors see as they drive from the airport into the city. And then there are the high-profile casualties on the Strip itself: the Stardust, erased in 2007; the Algiers, a memory since 2004; even the El Rancho, built in 1941 as the first resort on what became the Strip but closed since 1960.

These hotel-casinos were all demolished to make way for something better; their demise was brought about by real-estate moguls with the grandest of plans for their lots. Eight-figure sums were spent, but on nothing more than a crash, a bang and an 'And finally' item on the nightly news. The one thing they have in common? None of the plans have materialised quite as expected.

On the sites of the El Rancho and Algiers sits the unfinished and troublesome Fontainebleau, a monument to development dreams gone awry. When the Stardust was imploded it was to make way for the Echelon Place resort. Those plans were scrapped and the land was recently sold to an Asian gaming company.

Harrah's has been slow to announce plans for the Bourbon Street's plum site. For a change, though, there's still something in its way: the land surrounding the scruffy, unassuming Stage Door Casino (4000 Audrie St, 733 0124) across from the Bourbon Street lot is empty; the single-storey building is in the shadow of its skyscraping neighbours and the monorail that runs above it. But the owners have bucked a citywide trend and refused to sell to Harrah's, who own the vacant lots around it.

Inside, the Stage Door is like any blue-collar local bar late in the evening. Outside, the world wanders by, looking on with amusement at this mutinous holdout. The owners would make far more by selling up than they are by staying open, but pride is keeping them rooted to the spot. Once used to advertise some putatively terrific gambling schedule or food special, the building's frontage now reads, with insouciant defiance, 'We have 17 years left on our lease'.

EXPLORE

Dig This.

the southern side of Flamingo. The nightlife here is energising, with nightclubs such as **Moon** (*see p223*) competing with music venue the **Pearl** (*see p226*) and a slew of restaurants for the attentions of visitors.

Beyond the Rio, the Gold Coast and Palms, Valley View Boulevard continues north through a semi-residential, semi-industrial district. In recent years, a number of attractions – including **Battlefield Vegas** and **Dig This** – have taken advantage of this under-developed area. An easterly turn at Sahara leads past small strip malls ad infinitum until the train-themed casino **Palace Station** (*see p129*) just before I-15.

★ Battlefield Vegas

2771 Industrial Road, at Circus Circus Drive (566 1000, www.battlefieldvegas.com). Bus SX. **Open** 9.30am-7.30pm daily. **Rates** from $159. **Map** p319 B5.

Visitors to Las Vegas frequently 'misremember' key aspects of their stay: how much money they won (read: lost), how much they drank, how much they ate. At Battlefield Vegas, you can rewrite history on a much larger scale – say the World War II Battle of Iwo Jima or 1944's D-Day landings at the Normandy beaches. At this shooting range/simulated-adventure outpost, you get armed to the teeth and ready for, well, battle. Choose from one of 15 or so 'experiences' that recreate historical battles, let you act out your Mob fantasies (the Badda Bing), or cast you as a modern-day special-ops soldier (Seal Team VI). Or just head over to the facility and blow off some machine gun rounds.

Dig This

3012 S Rancho Drive, between Meade Avenue & W Sirius Avenue (222 4344, www.digthis vegas.com). Bus 119. **Open** 10am-3.30pm daily. **Rates** from $249. **Map** p319 A5.

Ever feel like you could move mountains? Now you can, literally. At Dig This, which has quickly become one of Vegas's top attractions, you can climb aboard a bulldozer or earth excavator and literally move the ground. Get a crash course in operating one of these machines, then try your hand at the controls in activities such as Bulldozer Teeter-Tooter or Excavator Basketball on an excavator. Carve trenches, pile up mounds of dirt, or stack 2,000lb tyres while testing your blue-collar skills.

Town Square

6605 Las Vegas Boulevard South, between I-15 & I-215 (269 5000, www.mytownsquare lasvegas.com). Bus SDX, 104, 117. **Open** 9am-10pm daily.

This upscale outdoor mall – an appealing aggregation of shopping, dining and entertainment, with its own home-design district – has become the go-to place for locals who can't be bothered with the Strip. Major outlets range from Apple to Whole Foods, and include an 18-screen cinema. It's a planned environment focused on walkability, though it's certainly no substitute for a real urban experience – Town Square's streets are kept eerily pristine, with piped-in music burbling merrily from the flowerbeds, and spray-misters keeping the would-be spenders cool on hot days. But it's good fun for the kids, who are kept busy at the Children's Park or on rides through the centre on the Town Square Train.

EXPLORE

Downtown

There's change afoot in Old Las Vegas.

North of the Strip, Downtown Las Vegas is another world. Sure, there's been a splash of paint here and an outrageously uninteresting electronic canopy there, but Downtown hadn't changed much in spirit for decades. For years it seemed to drift ever lower, and to many – both locals and visitors – it seemed as if it might forever be the graveyard of dreams. Existing in the Strip's shadow, Downtown was a place where plans for revitalisation were long articulated but never realised. Cheerleaders were waiting for years for *something* to happen, only to see their hopes fleeing further with each passing year.

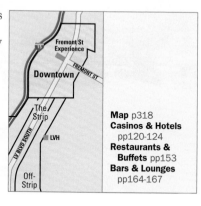

Map p318
Casinos & Hotels
  pp120-124
Restaurants &
  Buffets pp153
Bars & Lounges
  pp164-167

Imagine the local surprise, then, when a 21st-century Downtown began to sprout in 2006. Huge cranes and land-movers arrived, bringing steel beams, glass panes and concrete. With them came entrepreneurs armed with small-scale business plans and modest amounts of capital, who soon began seeing an uncharacteristically swift fruition of their notions. And then came the economic crash. So what happened next?

ONE HUNDRED YEARS OF HISTORY

Las Vegas began at what is now the core of Downtown. In May 1905, settlers and speculators gathered in front of a wooden railroad platform, land now occupied by the Plaza hotel, in order to bid on the 1,200 lots that constituted the original town site. Thus the city was seeded. In the 1930s and '40s, hotels and casinos dotted Fremont Street, then the city's main commercial drag. But the rise of the Strip and suburban expansion drew trade away from Downtown. Like an arid plant, Downtown first began to whither, and then began to die.

The construction of the Fremont Street Experience in 1995, which turned a five-block section of the road into a pedestrian-friendly gambling mall and covered it with a canopy that screens light and sound shows, succeeded in luring some tourists back to Glitter Gulch. Despite the later addition of some restored neon signs, some locals complained that it destroyed much of Fremont Street's character. Still, it was a stab at saving what was left of Downtown.

In implosion-friendly Las Vegas, where change happens fast and experiments are sometimes shelved before their natural expiry date, don't be too surprised if today's guidebook treasure is tomorrow's empty lot. Even so, there's never been a better time to discover Downtown, an amorphous amalgamation of things gone right and wrong. By turns sleazy and chic, downcast and upmarket, desperate and enthusiastic, it's a section of town in which constant and concerted efforts to make something incredible have failed only in specificity. Something wonderful *is* emerging, just not quite as originally intended.

GETTING THERE

If you're using public transport, you can reach Downtown from the Strip by catching the double-deckered Deuce bus. If you're driving, head north on I-15 and then east on US 93/95 (I-515), taking the Casino Center exit (the faster route); alternatively, drive north on the Strip and 4th Street (the more interesting route). The parking garages off Fremont Street are all safe

Fremont Street.

EXPLORE

places to park, though you may need to get your parking ticket validated inside one of the casinos or other local businesses to get free parking.

FREMONT STREET

Once the centre of Las Vegas and then a scruffy shadow of its former self, **Fremont Street** was originally seen as the focal point of efforts to save Downtown. Not so much so today. The old casinos remain, lining the stretch of Fremont west of Las Vegas Boulevard much as they have done for decades, though change is afoot both on Fremont and its surrounding areas.

The Fremont Street Experience

Many tourists think that Downtown begins and ends under the electronic canopy that covers Fremont Street between Las Vegas Boulevard and Main Street. It doesn't – in fact, it's easy to imagine a time in the not-so-distant future when the **Fremont Street Experience** might seem a relic of 'old Vegas' – but for convenience's sake, this stretch is the best starting and finishing point for an exploration of Downtown.

Inaugurated in 1995 and modified several times since, the five-block Fremont Street Experience was Downtown's attempt to drag a formerly desolate road into the 21st century. It's been a qualified success, but it's never quite drawn the crowds it was intended to muster. Sure, tourists come to this pedestrianised mall and in great numbers, particularly for the special free weekend events (concerts, car shows and the like). Still, the demographic

hasn't changed much since its debut; this remains mostly a blue-collar corner of Vegas's sprawling network of resorts.

The covered mall is dominated by a huge LED-studded canopy that flows 90 feet above it, flickering into action on the hour each night with intermittently entertaining sound and light shows. More interesting is **Vegas Vic**, the 40-foot neon cowboy who's been waving to visitors since 1951; sadly, he no longer calls out 'Howdy, Podner!' from a hidden speaker. Across the street, Vic's female counterpart Vegas Vicky kicks up her heels over the **Girls of Glitter Gulch** strip club, a long-standing embarrassment to a city desperate to make seedy Downtown into a respectable destination. A strip club ringed by casinos beneath a vintage neon sign that itself sits under a vainglorious 21st-century bibelot; it is at this corner that Downtown's attractions and distractions congeal into one.

At night, the FSE can become littered with crazy-eyed desperados, too-tanked hoochies and wide-mouthed tourists craning their necks to see every pixel of the jet fighter images soaring above them to some-or-other patriotic song. Overhead, the air is punctuated with screams of delight from riders flying down the length of the street on the recently installed ziplines that stretch from one end of the FSE to the other. But keep your focus at eye level: the street is a vital gathering spot for the keen people-watcher. Revellers imbibing ample alcohol; the schlock and kitsch of street performers; and the uninitiated – or merely curious – wandering around mouths agape

A Paeon to Neon

This city's all lit up.

If there's one piece of the past that lovers of Las Vegas miss above all others, it's the old-time signs. Just listen to Alan Hess, author of *Viva Las Vegas: After-Hours Architecture*, wax nostalgic about one of his favourites: the 15-storey, 40,000-bulb Aladdin sign from the 1960s: 'It was a full-blown fantasia, a dreamy mirage made real. The artistry that requires – to put that much steel and neon up in the desert sky and make it convincing, otherworldly, floating – is tremendous. It represented the ultimate achievement of that era of Las Vegas design. And it's an art that has not been recaptured in recent years.'

Discarding the past is itself a key part of Vegas history. The giant movie set known as the Strip constantly moves on to the next big idea without so much as a glance behind it. These days, though, the town's two-million-strong permanent community of non-tourists carries enough influence to preserve some of the neon left in the wake of the economic machine. The main voice of this movement is a non-profit project called the Neon Museum, set up 'to collect, preserve, study and exhibit neon signs and associated artefacts to inspire educational and cultural enrichment'.

One of the museum's first achievements was to refurbish the genie's lamp that once crowned the old Aladdin sign and install it at the corner of Fremont Street and Las Vegas Boulevard in 1996, 40 years after its original debut. Since then, the collection has expanded apace, and now includes everything from 1940s pieces to the decommissioned Stardust sign. Piece by piece, each sign is moved from its location to the museum on Las Vegas Boulevard, where it undergoes enough work to spruce it up without washing away its patina.

There are 11 old signs dotting Downtown, in the so-called 'outdoor galleries' on or just off Fremont Street. The old Hacienda horseman is riding high again, and the long-defunct Nevada Hotel continues to help light up the night, alongside smaller signs devoted to the Flame Restaurant, the Chief Hotel Court and the Anderson Dairy. The museum has also put several signs on display at the Old Las Vegas Mormon Fort Historic Park (*see p67*), including the shapely Arabesque 'A' from the Sahara.

The best, though, is the collection, the **Neon Museum** – aka 'The Boneyard' – (770 Las Vegas Boulevard N, 387 6366, www.neonmuseum.org), a three-acre park full of historic Vegas signage. The landmark lobby from the old La Concha Motel, one of the city's great Googie structures, has been rescued and moved up the boulevard to serve as the visitor centre, gallery and gift shop for the museum. Tours must be booked in advance, so call ahead first.

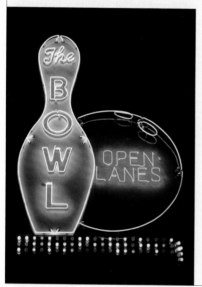

EXPLORE

make for a Hieronymus Bosch painting come to life. For now, the casinos still remain the main draw: partly for the gambling rules, more generous here than on the Strip, but mostly due to the low accommodation prices.

Once upon a time, Binion's Horseshoe was the Wild West home of outlaw gaming, the World Series of Poker and true no-frills, no-nonsense gambling. Scandal and debt gave rise to a sequence of ownership shuffles that resulted in it losing its family ownership, its 'Horseshoe' name, its magic and, finally, its hotel rooms in 2009. Only the casino remains (128 Fremont Street, www.binions.com). Across the street, the **Golden Nugget** (see p121) has changed hands a few times in recent years, but with a more attractive outcome. After a renovation brought swanky lounges, upscale restaurants and, most eye-catchingly, shark tanks in the new pool, the Nugget continues to bring a little glamour back to far-from-fancy Fremont.

Unchanged for many the years is the **Golden Gate** (see p124), the city's oldest hotel. Built in 1906 as the Hotel Nevada (room and board, $1 per day), the Golden Gate was later known for decades as the Sal Sagev (read it backwards). In 2012 the hotel began a series of renovations that chipped away some of its charm – the vintage lobby and piano bar were removed – but were designed to help it remain a player, however small, in Downtown.

Further nods to old Vegas can be found with the throwback elegance and overwrought decor of Hugo's Cellar at the **Four Queens** (see p123), and with the utterly basic interior of the **Fremont** (see p123), the archetypal Downtown grind joint. The **Plaza** (see p124), sitting at the end of Fremont, oversees them all, like a silent, towering patriarch. The newest entrant down here, the **D** (see p120), is an imposing figure too. In the space formerly occupied by Fitzgeralds hotel-casino, the D is attempting to mint its reputation as a hip and cool Downtown hotel with a nod to vintage Vegas in its retro casino.

Neon city

At the opposite end of the Fremont Street Experience to the Plaza, closer to Las Vegas Boulevard, the attractions are a little patchier. **Neonopolis**, an off-again, on-again multi-level dining, retail and entertainment centre, sits at the corner of Las Vegas Boulevard and Fremont. The mall-like space houses an eclectic collection of shops, eateries and clubs, including the world's largest LGBT nightclub, **Krave Massive** (see p217). Also here, on the ground level, is the **Heart Attack Grill** (450 Fremont Street, www.heartattackgrill.com), proudly serving its Quadruple Bypass Burger (nearly 10,000 calories!) and butterfat milkshakes. In

line with the centre's name, Neonopolis also displays numerous vintage neon signs in its courtyard area.

Several such signs can also be found on North 3rd Street between Fremont and Ogden Streets, a stretch that both complements and anticipates the changes further east (see below). The western side of 3rd Street has been taken over by a few businesses that pay homage in sorts to old Downtown: witness the steakhouse swank of **Triple George** (see p153) and the often-raucous **Hogs & Heifers** (see p165). Across from Neonopolis on Fremont are **Hennesseys** (www.hennesseyslasvegas.com), **Mickie Finnz** (see p153) and **Brass** (www.brassthelounge.com), three spots trying to draw a mix of tourists and locals with upscale bar food, local bands and gambling.

A recent addition to Fremont Street seems to be the demarcation line between one world and another. **SlotZilla**, a massive steel and concrete counterpoint to the Plaza, at the other end of Fremont Street Experience, is currently under construction. When finished (late 2013), this 'Zilla will be a 12-storey behemoth, featuring both upper and lower ziplines (replacing the former attraction). Whether SlotZilla becomes a welcome – and porous – attraction to Fremont Street, around which pedestrians flow between the FSE and emerging Fremont East district, or whether it becomes the end of the line for tourists on the FSE side and local hipsters on the other remains to be seen.

Fremont East

Across Las Vegas Boulevard, Fremont Street is a different place. What was once a dark, desolate and often dangerous stretch is now a lively and welcoming 'hood in development – for a few blocks at least. The **Fremont East Entertainment District**, as it's called, is home to a number of popular bars and restaurants that are slowly expanding eastward. Above the street an illuminated sign reads 'Fremont East', with a martini glass and the word 'Vegas' lit above that. This stretch is becoming lined with bars, among them pioneers like **Griffin** (see p165) and **Beauty Bar** (see p164), both of which laid roots before this area was technically 'safe'. On the northern side of Fremont, at the intersection of 6th Street, is the **Beat Coffeehouse**, a coffeeshop/bar/music venue/record store. It shares is premises with the **Emergency Arts Center** (see p66). On the other side of 6th Street lies the **El Cortez** (see p120). These joints are supplemented by tasty eateries, including **Kabob Korner** (507 E Fremont St, 384 7722) and nearby **Eat** (see p153).

The Fremont East Entertainment District will have to make it on charm – and liquor –

EXPLORE

Fremont East.

alone: gambling will mostly be conspicuous by its absence, as Vegas aims to construct an urban core that bears comparison with the likes of San Diego. Local authorities have widened the streets, shuffled the urban blight down the way and given decent tax incentives to new businesses. Much of this is the result of work by the Downtown Project, a hugely ambitious undertaking initiated by Zappos.com, the internet shoe and accessories merchant, its CEO Tony Hsieh and his redevelopment team.

The Downtown Project has bought huge tracts of land along Fremont Street east of Las Vegas Boulevard all the way to S Maryland Parkway ten blocks away, as well as other parcels of Downtown land to the north and south of Fremont Street and in the 18b Arts District (see p68). Hsieh's group also purchased the old Las Vegas City Hall as the new headquarters for Zappos, as well as the former hotel-casino **Gold Spike** (at 4th Street & Ogden Avenue), which the Downtown Project converted into an after-hours hangout, without casino, for Downtowners. Although there's not much to see yet, work is currently under way along E Fremont Street, particularly on Container Park, a shopping and entertainment centre.

Further down Fremont Street, remnants of shabby old Downtown – a wonderworld of decrepitude and danger – are still visible, though many venues have been shuttered. In time, the redevelopment may pay off for those who have invested so much in reinvigorating the famous Glitter Gulch of yore. For now, though, it's still the up-and-coming part of town.

Emergency Arts Center

520 Fremont Street, at 6th Street, Downtown (www.emergencyartslv.com). Bus Deuce & all BTC-bound buses. **Open** *noon-5pm, 7pm-midnight*
Mon; noon-5pm Tue, Thur; noon-8pm Wed; noon-5pm, 6-9pm Fri; 10am-1pm Sat. **Map** p318 D2.
After the Las Vegas Art Museum fell victim to the recession, the Vegas arts scene seemed to go on life support. It was appropriate then that this arts centre located in an old medical building stepped in to spell relief. Emergency Arts not only resuscitated the scene, but also now provides the area's art heartbeat, providing affordable space for working artists of all stripes.

NORTH TO WASHINGTON AVENUE

Parallel to Fremont Street a couple of blocks north, **Stewart Avenue** is where Downtown winds down. The corner with Las Vegas Boulevard was home to the old City Hall, and until a couple of years ago, was where you'd find the happiest mayor/movie star/gin spokesman in the world: Oscar B Goodman. After his wife, Carolyn, was elected mayor, Goodman opened the steakhouse **Oscar's** – with the tagline 'Beef, Booze & Broads' – in the Plaza Hotel (see p124). Also on Stewart Avenue, at 3rd Street, is the new **Mob Museum**, dealing with Vegas's historic relationship with organised crime.

On 4th Street between Stewart and Ogden avenues, across from the (converted) Gold Spike sits the former Lady Luck hotel and casino. This long-closed property was swept up in the redevelopment craze, and rechristened the **Downtown Grand**. The new hotel-casino was originally slated to open in late 2013, although that is unlikely. Regardless, when opened, the Grand will likely provide another boost for the area.

To the north along Las Vegas Boulevard sit more remnants of the city's past. Beyond the overpass of I-515 sits the **Neon Museum** (*see p64* **A Paean to Neon**) and a couple of low-key attractions that have been designated, slightly optimistically, as the Cultural Corridor: one of the **City of Las Vegas Galleries**, with satisfying exhibitions from serious artists, in the Reed Whipple Cultural Center (821 Las Vegas Boulevard N, at E Washington Avenue). and the **Las Vegas Natural History Museum**.

Just to the east is **Cashman Field**, where the Las Vegas 51s, the Los Angeles Dodgers' AAA team, play baseball through the heat of summer (*see p232*). Also in the general area is the fascinating **Old Las Vegas Mormon Fort Historic Park** (*see right*). And those into old architecture should check the Biltmore Bungalows, which aren't bungalows at all. Located a block west of Las Vegas Boulevard on Bonanza Road, they were built to house the civilian workers stationed in Las Vegasto aid in the war effort, and remain a great representation of a mid-century, master-planned community.

Las Vegas Natural History Museum

900 Las Vegas Boulevard North, at E Washington Avenue (384 3466, www.lvnhm.org). Bus 113, 208. **Open** 9am-4pm daily. **Admission** $10; $5-$8 reductions. **Map** p318 E1.

This small, enthusiastically run museum doesn't offer much in the way of bells and whistles. The Marine Life Room features small sharks in a large tank, the Wild Nevada Room has exhibits on the flora and fauna of Nevada, and the Young Scientist Center has some interactive displays. However, the big draw is five roaring, robotic dinosaurs, among them a vast T-Rex.

Old Las Vegas Mormon Fort Historic Park.

★ Mob Museum

300 E Stewart Avenue, at N 3rd Street (229 2734, www.themobmuseum.org). Bus SDX & all BTC-bound buses. **Open** 10am-7pm Mon-Thur, Sun; 10am-8pm Fri, Sat. **Admission** $19.95; $13.95-$15.95 reductions. **Map** p318 D1.

Not to be confused with the other organised-crime exhibition at the Tropicana (*see p104*), this non-profit museum is sanctioned and supported by government grants. The idea, its creators say, was to build a museum detailing the true and very real impact the Mafia had on Las Vegas. Since opening on 14 February 2012 – the anniversary of Chicago's infamous 1929 Valentine's Day Massacre – the Mob Museum has been a huge hit. Get the lowdown on crime legends that include Lucky Luciano, Meyer Lanksy, Al Capone and others at the interactive attractions and displays.

Old Las Vegas Mormon Fort Historic Park

500 E Washington Avenue, at Las Vegas Boulevard North (486 3511, www.parks.nv.gov/olvmf.htm). Bus 113, 208. **Open** 8am-4.30pm Mon-Sat. **Admission** $1; free under-12s. **No credit cards. Map** p317 Y2.

Built by a group of Mormon missionaries in 1855 and then left to become part of the Las Vegas Ranch, this is Vegas's pioneer settlement site, the oldest Euro-American structure in the state and an example of what Vegas was like before the railroad. Though only remnants of the original structure remain, restoration and reconstruction have brought the compound back to life, and guides are on hand to answer questions.

WEST TO I-15

Some of the greatest changes to Downtown in recent years have taken place in the other direction from Fremont Street – to the west. This area, formerly a rundown rail yard, was slated to be a stadium in the late 1990s. That project never happened, and the city bought the land in 2000. Developers followed, eventually building the popular **Las Vegas Premium Outlets North** (875 South Grand Central Parkway) and the enormous **World Market Center** (495 S Grand Central Parkway, 599 9621, www.wmclv.com), which houses a variety of home and design shops, as well as seasonal exhibitions. Also just off Grand Central Parkway is the new home of the **Discovery Children's Museum**. All of which was exciting, but the icing on the cake was the unveiling of the **Smith Center for the Performing Arts** (*see p229*) in 2012.

Today, the once-decrepit industrial land is home to the beautiful 60-acre **Symphony Park** on which the Smith Center sits. A pedestrian bridge from Las Vegas's new City Hall on Main Street between Clark and Lewis avenues connects the Downtown area with Symphony Park on the other side of the rail tracks.

EXPLORE

★ Discovery Children's Museum

360 Promenade Place, at S Grand Central Parkway (382 3445, www.discoverykidslv.org). Bus SDX & all BTC-bound buses. **Open** *Summer* 10am-5pm Mon-Sat; noon-5pm Sun. *Autumn-spring* 9am-4pm Tue-Fri; 10am-5pm Sat; noon-5pm Sun. **Admission** $12. **Map** p318 C1.

This stimulating museum, similar to (though smaller than) the Exploratorium in San Francisco, features scientific exhibits involving the viewer as a part of the demonstration. Don't be put off by the name: this is the sort of place that many adults would visit by themselves if they thought they could. Creative exhibits include sections on water power, eco sustainability and patents, among others.

SOUTH TO OAKEY BOULEVARD

Las Vegas Boulevard grows less pleasant the farther south of Fremont you travel, but the stroll does at least begin with several points of interest. The **Lloyd George Federal Courthouse** (no.333) is a handsome steel-and-glass building that occasionally hosts cultural events during lunchtimes and less official protests on the streets outside.

Nearby, on Lewis Avenue, is the **Poets Bridge**, done out with a curious water feature, and a sidewalk engraved with quotes from 20 Nevadan poets. The bridge's main feature is a brass plaque on which is inscribed 'The Long Shot', written by New York writer (and former Las Vegas resident) Gregory Crosby. It's perhaps the best poem ever written about Las Vegas.

There's ancient history around these parts, though in Las Vegas, that means the 1930s at the earliest. Although most of residential Las Vegas is unimaginatively cast in the same faux-Mediterranean stucco, the area bounded by 6th Street, Bridger Avenue, 9th Street and Oakey Boulevard is a rare example of architectural diversity and small-town comfort: well-kept single-storey homes with large yards and wide driveways are typical. The list of 1940s and '50s buildings in the area is headed by the **Las Vegas Academy of the Arts** (*see p230*), the only piece of 1930s art deco architecture in the city.

On South 7th Street, just before Charleston Boulevard, sits a cluster of attractive, early 20th-century bungalows with plaster walls and wooden floors; the area is now known as 'Lawyer's Row', after the punk attorneys who've taken over the locale. South of Charleston, meanwhile, is the **John S Park** neighbourhood. Filled with 1940s bungalows and swankier dwellings from the '50s and '60s, it was the city's first official Historic District. Self-guided tours created by the City Historical Preservation Division are available from City Hall.

Back on Las Vegas Boulevard, the scene soon degenerates, the street lined with shady-looking storefronts and vintage motels that do most of their business either by the hour or by the month. Among the various buildings offering quickie marriages, the angels-on-crack painted ceiling of the 24-hour drive-through **Little White Wedding Chapel** (*see p240*) is worth a look. For the most part, the street isn't as dangerous as it looks, but nor is it an especially salubrious or attractive part of town.

The 18b Arts District & around

Walk south of Fremont Street along Main Street, and the pickings are slimmer than on Las Vegas Boulevard. Here you'll find old-fashioned eaterie **El Sombrero** (807 S Main Street, 382 9234) and the card-playing, chip-tossing paraphernalia of the **Gamblers General Store** (*see p197*).

When you reach Charleston Boulevard, you'll be on the edge of the **18b Arts District**, loosely bordered by Charleston, Las Vegas Boulevard, Wyoming Avenue and Commerce Street. The '18b' name comes from the original size of the area, which was 18 blocks. Today, many locals refer to the district simply as '18b'. The district is home to many galleries, studios and other creative businesses, as well as an array of shops and bars, all of which bring culture and edge to a once-downtrodden part of town. The Arts District is at its best on **First Friday** (*see p42*), a monthly block party when the streets come alive with festive cheer.

18b Arts District.

The Rest of the City

Life beyond the Strip.

Like Los Angeles, off-Strip Las Vegas is comprised of sprawling, extended suburbs made up of still-mushrooming residential developments, with the institutions and infrastructure that any large city requires scattered within their midst. Until the global economic collapse – it hit Las Vegas harder than just about anywhere else in the US – new estates seemed to spring up overnight, barely keeping pace with the 6,000-plus people who were migrating to Clark County every month through the 1990s until 2008, when growth flat-lined and the county experienced a net loss of residents.

Overall, interest in the areas apart from the Strip lie not in great beauty or a wealth of visitor attractions, but as a reassuringly benign refuge of normality, far from the sensory overload. For many Vegas residents, the Strip is 'the office', a glittering cubicle farm, 'the place Mommy and Daddy work'. Yet despite Vegas's well-earned reputation as a town devoid of coherent town planning, you will find glimpses of a rich history, pockets of character and a defiant civic identity, with surprisingly old and deep religious – mostly Mormon – roots.

MOTOR CITY

When you set out, keep in mind that the Vegas suburbs can be downright hostile to pedestrians (even before considering the glaring sun and melting desert heat.) The bus system is reliable and will get you to most places of note, but a car is necessary to explore the city properly. Leave plenty of time for delays caused by the new construction work. But fear not: it's hard o get lost in a flat city that's built on a network and that has, at its centre, the tallest observation tower west of the Mississippi.

The neighbourhoods in this chapter are arranged clockwise, starting in the south-west corner of town and finishing in the south-east.

SOUTH-WEST LAS VEGAS

Like the ever-expanding waistline of a chowhound at a buffet, the area surrounding Las Vegas grows as much in girth as it does in density. Nowhere is this truer than of south-west Las Vegas, which over the last two decades has burst its metaphorical seams. Fifteen years ago the southern edge was largely held in check by the I-215. Since then, Vegas has jumped its former boundaries to include areas like Enterprise and

Southern Highlands, west of the I-15 and south of the I-215. The interior section of this town (to the north-east) includes the ultra-posh and private residential developments of **Spanish Trail** and **Spanish Hills**, home to many of Las Vegas's notable figures. Take the I-215 ('the Beltway') west from the I-15 and exit north at Rainbow and you'll head through **Spring Valley**, one of the older Vegas locales. Stay on the Beltway, though, and out past Durango Drive it makes a sharp curve from an east–west axis and heads due north. Here the Beltway practically butts up against the mountains to the west. Still, that hasn't stopped development from springing up all around, right on into the foothills. Evidence of this is easily visible from the brand-new water amusement park **Wet 'n Wild**, off Durano in the far south-western corner of the city. But if you stay on the Beltway and continue far enough, just past Sahara Avenue, you'll be able to exit on W Charleston Boulevard, right at the **Red Rock Resort** (*see p126*).

★ Wet 'n' Wild

7055 S Fort Apache Road, at W Arby Avenue (979 1600, www.wetnwildlasvegas.com). Bus 201A. **Open** *June* 10am-8pm Mon-Thur, Sun;

10am-10pm Fri, Sat. *July, Aug* 10am-6pm Mon-Thur, Sun; 10am-10pm Fri, Sat. *Sept* 10am-6pm Sat, Sun. Times can vary; check website for other mths. **Admission** $24.99-$39.99.

Not to be confused with the former Strip attraction of the same name that closed a decade ago, this pool and waterslide park opened in summer 2013 and sold out its season passes within hours. Slides like Canyon Cliffs – which drop riders four storeys on a bed of water – and the popular three-person Rattler are just two of the nine slides currently in operation. There's also a 'lazy river' that carries riders along on inner tubes; Splash Island, a kids' area; and a wave pool. The park's operators own some 70 acres surrounding Wet 'n' Wild, and more attractions are in development. For families in particular, it's a brilliant way to beat the summer desert heat.

NORTH-WEST LAS VEGAS
Sahara Avenue

Like the majority of Las Vegas's east–west streets, Sahara Avenue west of the Strip yields little of interest. National chains and big-box warehouse stores dominate the landscape; there are few better examples than the four-cornered **Sahara-Decatur Pavilions** at the junction of Sahara and… well, you know. Chains make up most of the tenants, though there's fine Persian food at independent eatery and market **Habib's** (2575 S Decatur Boulevard, 870 0860). Continuing on, you'll pass countless car dealerships and fast food joints before reaching Rainbow Boulevard, surrounded by residential properties and heavy commercial development.

Farther west is Durango Drive, the beginning of the **Lakes** neighbourhood, where the waterside homes afford residents the chance to go boating and fishing. Lake East Drive features

---

INSIDE TRACK
SEGREGATED VEGAS AND THE MOULIN ROUGE

In the 1950s, when Vegas was called 'the Mississippi of the West', hotels forced African-American entertainers such as Nat King Cole and Sammy Davis Jr to flee the Strip after showtime. They sought refuge at the Moulin Rouge in the north-west corner of the city, and generated a legendary stint of after-hours shows. In 1960, five years after the Moulin Rouge opened, casino bosses signed an agreement that ended the city's racial segregation. Today, its site is a historic destination and its sign survives at the Neon Museum (*see p64*).

---

a walking trail through the surrounding parks, eventually dumping you out at Twain Avenue.

Sahara's western reaches are home to the beautiful **Sahara West Library** (no.9600). The cinema at neighbouring **Village Square** (*see p213*) is known for the indie film selections it regularly screens – one of the few venues in town that reliably shows anything other than the blockbusters of the week (although blockbusters take up most of the space). At the far-western end of Sahara Avenue, nestled at the base of the mountains, lies the **Red Rock Country Club** (2466 Grassy Spring Place, 360 3100), a desert golf community that gives new meaning to the word 'exclusive'.

Charleston Boulevard

Flat, wide and seemingly endless, Charleston cuts a broad swathe through the city, extending westwards right out to the foothills of the mountain from which it takes its name. It's more residential than Sahara, though not much more attractive. Still, there are occasional diversions, including, close to the Strip, the Charleston Heights Arts Center (800 S Brush Street, between W Charleston Boulevard & Evergreen Avenue), home to a theatre and one of the **City of Las Vegas Galleries** (*see p67*).

Along the way, Charleston defines the southern edge of **Summerlin**. This 'Westside' planned community incorporates homes (from $100,000 condos to multi-million-dollar mansions), parks, schools and businesses to create a regular prefab life; the infrastructure is magnificent, but the *Truman Show* effect is disconcerting. European visitors won't have trouble navigating the numerous roundabouts, but the wayward local motorists, unaccustomed to such complexity, seem to have more trouble.

At Rampart Boulevard, development has transformed what were once empty acres into a commercial area. To the north, **Boca Park Fashion Village** (no.750) features an array of fairly pedestrian shops such as Target and American Apparel and chain eateries like PF Chang's and Claim Jumper. Continuing north on Rampart, past Alta Drive, you'll find the new, upscale shops of **Tivoli Village** (*see p177*). Two resorts lie to the west of Rampart: the so-so **Suncoast** (*see p130*) and the smarter **JW Marriott Summerlin** (*see p125*), surrounded by the green, manicured fairways of several major golf courses.

Further west, across from the **Summerlin Town Center** mall at Charleston's intersection with Town Center Drive, sits **Red Rock Resort** (*see p126*), the first billion-dollar off-Strip casino-hotel. If you head still further west across the Beltway, you'll enter open country, and the gorgeous canyon from which the casino takes its name (*see p248*). Just past it, you'll find an agreeable taste of the Wild West at **Bonnie Springs Old Nevada** (*see p249*), an honest-to-goodness mining town back in the 1800s. Now it's an adorable tourist trap, with pony rides, a comically eclectic petting zoo, a tiny railroad train – and, of course, a saloon. Don't miss the general store, if only for the fun of spotting the 'Made in China' stickers on the bottom of nearly every souvenir.

Rancho Drive

Bordered by Oakey and Charleston boulevards, Rancho Drive and I-15, the **Scotch 80s** offers a different taste of old Vegas. Las Vegas mayor Carolyn Goodman and her husband, former mayor Oscar Goodman, are among those who live in this swanky neighbourhood of large-lot homes, built mostly in the 1950s and '60s, an 80-acre enclave just a dice roll from Downtown. The quiet labyrinth of tree-lined streets hides ranch-style estates and one-acre home sites, along with surprisingly lush gardens: underground water meant the area was once almost swampy. To the south-east of here are the **Glen Heather Estates**, smallish homes with a modernist bent; west lie the 1950s-vintage **McNeil Estates**, where young professionals are joining more established residents in a bid to restore the charming ranch-style homes.

If you continue north, you'll reach the corner of Rancho and Alta drives. Just north is **Rancho Circle**, perhaps the city's most exclusive old district. Slightly west of here, loosely bordered by US 95, Valley View Boulevard and Alta Drive, is the historic 180-acre **Las Vegas Springs Preserve**, recently reopened as a desert ecology-themed visitor attraction. And east of Rancho Drive at Tonopah Drive is **Binion Ranch**, the home of the legendary gambling family who launched – and, until 2004, owned – Binion's. Family patriarch Benny Binion once lived in this long-boarded-up block-and-timber ranch house; as recently as the 1990s, horses and cattle were still kept on the property.

To the west of Rancho Drive sits **Lorenzi Park** and the nearby **Nevada State Museum & Historical Society**. Further north leads you past the **Southern Nevada Zoological Park**; a turn west at Vegas Drive passes the palatial home of the elusive master illusionists Siegfried & Roy, who can still stir up the town when one or the other makes an appearance at a show opening on the Strip. It's on the north side; look for the white adobe walls and the wrought-iron gate bearing the initials S and R. Tiger Woods wannabes can try out their skills (golf only, please) at the **Las Vegas National Golf Club** (*see p233*) across the

road; budding Schumachers might prefer the **Las Vegas Mini Gran Prix** (*see p211*).

Rancho Drive continues in a north-westerly direction past the **Texas Station** (*see p131*), **Fiesta Rancho** (*see p129*) and **Santa Fe Station** casinos (*see p130*) en route to the outdoor attractions of **Floyd Lamb State Park** and **Mount Charleston** (*see p250*). Five years ago, much of this area was empty desert. Today, though, stucco has engulfed everything and shows no sign of abating.

★ **Las Vegas Springs Preserve**

333 S Valley View Boulevard, at Meadows Lane (822 7700, www.springspreserve.org). Bus 104, 207. **Open** 10am-6pm daily. **Admission** $18.95; $10.95 reductions; free under-5s. **Map** p317 X1.
Also known as Big Spring, this is where legendary Old West explorers Kit Carson and John Fremont parked their horses in the mid 1800s. Huge cottonwoods and natural scrub fill the area, surrounding an early 19th-century well house. The land has survived both fire and the threat of being paved over in the name of freeway expansion; it was restored as the Central Park of Las Vegas for the city's centennial in 2005 and opened to the public two years later as the Las Vegas Springs Preserve, a huge site given over to botanical gardens, nature trails and a number of museum exhibits. All in all, a very laudable endeavour, if heavy on the videogame-style educational exhibits aimed at youngsters. The sustainability minded Springs Café offers picnic-style dining with wonderful vistas. *Photo p74*.

Southern Nevada Zoological Park

1775 N Rancho Drive, between Vegas Drive & Lake Mead Boulevard (647 4685, www.lasvegaszoo.org). Bus 106. **Open** 9am-5pm daily. **Admission** $9; $7 reductions; free under-2s. **Map** p317 X1.
It'll never be confused with similar operations in the Bronx or San Diego, but Vegas's zoological park contains an interesting collection of reptiles and birds indigenous to the state of Nevada, as well as a variety of endangered cats and the last family of Barbary apes in the US. The park also has a coati exhibit, botanical displays of endangered palms and rare bamboos, plus a children's petting zoo.

NORTH LAS VEGAS

A working-class city that grew from the Nellis Air Force Base to the north-east, North Las Vegas has experienced a limited renaissance of late, a result of the growth in the valley as a whole. African American, Asian and Hispanic residents have moved in as Anglos have moved out, turning the area into a melting pot of ethnicities; new homes and shops have sprung up to fill land north of Craig Road (between Rancho Drive and I-15) in a pricey new development known informally as the

EXPLORE

THE WORLD CAN BE AN UNJUST AND TREACHEROUS PLACE, BUT THERE ARE THOSE WHO STRIVE TO MAKE IT SAFE FOR EVERYONE.

Operating in some of the world's most dangerous and oppressed countries, **Human Rights Watch** conducts rigorous investigations to bring those who have been targets of abuse to the world's attention. We use strategic advocacy to push people in power to end their repressive practices. And we work for as long as it takes to see that oppressors are held accountable for their crimes.

KNOWLEDGE IS POWER.
LEARN ABOUT LIFE-CHANGING EVENTS IN YOUR WORLD THAT DON'T ALWAYS MAKE THE HEADLINES AND HOW YOU CAN HELP EFFECT POSITIVE CHANGE.

Stay informed, visit HRW.org

HUMAN RIGHTS WATCH

Golden Triangle. The shiny new locale seems somewhat removed from its surroundings, but that's the price of progress.

Largely untouched by redevelopment, the older sections of North Las Vegas carry more urban flavour than does Las Vegas itself. To reach them, turn off either US 95 or Rancho Drive and head east along Craig Road, then turn north back towards Downtown along Las Vegas Boulevard North. En route, you'll pass **Jerry's Nugget** casino (no.1821, 399 3000, www.jerrysnugget.com), numerous ethnic eateries, the historic public **Forest Lawn Cemetery** and the **Las Vegas Paiute Indian Reservation** (1 Paiute Drive, 386 3926), which represents the original ten acres deeded to the Paiute by Helen Stewart back in the 1900s.

Planetarium

Community College of Southern Nevada, 3200 E Cheyenne Avenue, between N Pecos Road & N Van Der Meer Street (651 4759, www.csn.edu/ planetarium). Bus 110, 111. **Shows** 6pm, 7pm, 8pm Fri; 3.30pm, 6pm, 7pm, 8pm Sat. **Admission** $6; $4 reductions.
The small cinema here has a 360° screen. After the day's last performance, you also get the opportunity to scan the sky through the planetarium's telescopes (weather permitting).

EAST LAS VEGAS

Once characterised by ugly quick-build housing tracts and trailer parks, East Las Vegas has been unable to avoid the incursion of new development. Still, the once-posh **Commercial Center** (953 E Sahara Avenue, between S 6th Street & S Maryland Parkway) has resisted change. One of the city's older malls, it's a scruffy spot that's home to a couple of the city's best ethnic restaurant (**Lotus of Siam**; *see p149*), various gay bars, numerous Asian organisations (Korean Vegas Weekly, Filipinas Paralegal Services, and so on) and sundry other businesses. South on Maryland Parkway is the smarter **Boulevard Mall** (*see p176*); behind it is the modernist **Paradise Palms**, another old 'hood at the earliest stages of revival. Further down Maryland is the University District (*see right*).

East of here is Fremont Street, which runs into Downtown to the north-west and to the south-east, past Sahara Avenue, becomes Boulder Highway. Beyond that, Interstate 515 (which merges highways 93 and 95) demarcates what was once the eastern edge of the city. New development has since jumped this boundary, with the increasing expansion of **Sunrise Manor**. But, like much of Las Vegas, this development skipped the interior areas, leaving large tracts of land around Fremont Street

between Charleston Boulevard and Sahara Avenue desolate and under-developed. One site of note on this stretch, however, is the location of the former Green Shack (2524 Fremont Street). In continuous operation from the 1920s until 1999, the restaurant evoked decades of memories: construction workers building the Hoover Dam stopped here, as did politicos and gangsters. But despite protests from preservationists, the building was demolished in 2005 to make way for a banqueting hall that's yet to be built.

At the far north-eastern end of the valley, beyond Sunrise Manor, is Frenchman's Mountain, commonly known as **Sunrise Mountain**. Here, in the 1960s and '70s, the independently minded rich who had declined spots in the Scotch 80s built modern desert homes with pools and panoramic views of the city. Following their lead, there has been a lot more new housing development in this part of town.

Along **Boulder Highway** sit several locals' casinos. Catch a movie at **Boulder Station** (*see p128*); if you're here in December, don't miss the Christmas lights at **Sam's Town** (*see p130*). A turn west down Tropicana Avenue to Pecos Avenue will take you to the **Pinball Hall of Fame**.

FREE Pinball Hall of Fame

1610 E Tropicana Avenue, between S Maryland Parkway & S Eastern Avenue (596 2627, www.pinballmuseum.org). Bus 201. **Open** 11am-11pm Mon-Thur, 11am-midnight Fri, Sat. **Admission** free. **Map** p317 Y3.
More than 100 pinball machines spanning seven decades are on show in this unique museum – a true attraction in a city of replicated ones. Over the years, owner Tim Arnold has assembled a vast array of machines from Gottlieb, Bally, Williams and other oddball manufacturers. Descriptions of each machine's attributed and historic values have been attached to them. Best of all, Arnold invites all comers to play his machines.

THE UNIVERSITY DISTRICT

Bounded roughly by Flamingo Road, Paradise Road, Tropicana Avenue and Eastern Avenue, the University District is an enclave of normality and casual sophistication a mere skip from the Strip. Most businesses of note are on Maryland Parkway, with the rest of the area given over to apartments.

The University of Las Vegas, aka **UNLV** (4505 S Maryland Parkway, 895 3011), runs along S Maryland Parkway, where the stunning **Lied Library** (*see p297*) and a beautiful desert garden compete for visitors' attention. The university also has many walking paths and trees, a tranquil refuge from the summer sun.

Las Vegas Springs Preserve.
See p71.

The **Marjorie Barrick Museum** and the neighbouring **Donna Beam Fine Art Gallery**, both on campus, stage shows by student and professional artists; the former also houses a permanent natural history exhibition.

Local businesses reflect the presence of the university, which is to say that prices are keen. **Paymon's Mediterranean Café & Market** (*see p155*), a local lunch favourite, is adjoined at the corner of Maryland and Flamingo by the restaurant's **Hookah Lounge** (*see p168*), a Bedouin-styled cocktail bar. Across the way is the used-clothing superstore **Buffalo Exchange** (*see p182*); further up Maryland are two shopping centres filled with pizza joints, coffeehouses, bars including the **Freakin' Frog** (*see p168*), and even a tattoo studio: the **Pussykat Tattoo Parlor** (*see p190*) is one of the best in town, in a town with more tattoo shops than most.

FREE Marjorie Barrick Museum

4505 S Maryland Parkway, at E Tropicana Avenue (895 3381, http://barrickmuseum.unlv. edu). Bus 109, 201. **Open** 10am-5pm Mon-Wed, Fri; 10am-8pm Thur; noon-5pm Sat. **Admission** free. Suggested contribution $5; $2 reductions. **No credit cards. Map** p333 Y3.
Technically UNLV's natural history museum, the Barrick has fine permanent displays on ancient and modern Vegas, including a wonderful collection of folk-art masks. It's also one of the city's finest art exhibition spaces: a number of excellent shows have graced its rooms, drawing from UNLV's art faculty and regional sources. It's a must for any gallery crawl; call or check the website for details of current shows.

HENDERSON & GREEN VALLEY

The history of Henderson and Green Valley is a tale of a city within a city. Henderson itself was founded in 1941 as a company town for workers at the then-new Basic Magnesium Plant. North-west of Henderson across I-515 (US 95), Green Valley is technically part of the city of Henderson, and contains the vast majority of its visitor attractions. If you've time, spend a few hours down here, especially if you're en route to Boulder City and the Hoover Dam.

Henderson

Thanks to its origins, Henderson garnered a reputation as an industrial city, one that it retains to some extent, even though it was, for a time in the booming early 2000s, the fastest growing suburban area in America. The city has kept its original downtown, centred on Water Street. It's currently undergoing a revitalisation spearheaded by the city government, which is making an active effort to attract galleries and pedestrian-friendly shops. The purchase of land by loft developers is a sign that the area may soon soar skywards. The **City of Lights Gallery** (no.26, 3 E Army Street, 260 0300, www.citylightsartgallery.com) is attempting to lead the way in the creation of the arts district. On the western side of I-515 lies the **Acacia Demonstration Gardens** (50 Casa Del Fuego Street, 267 4000), where you can explore gardens and wetlands dedicated to animal habitats.

Elsewhere, less sophisticated pockets of original tract houses, mobile home parks and low-rent apartments survive, and are unkindly referred to as 'Hendertucky'. Even so, the area's not without appeal. Manufacturing continues at **Ethel M Chocolates**, which offers tours to the public – the chocolate factory's Christmas display, which lights up an acre of ground containing 300 species of cactus and other desert plants is not to be missed. And not far from here, the **Clark County Heritage Museum** is also worth a look.

Clark County Heritage Museum

1830 S Boulder Highway, at Equestrian Drive (455 7955, www.co.clark.nv.us). Bus HDX. **Open** 9am-4.30pm daily. **Admission** $2; $1 reductions. Long before Las Vegas was a resort destination, it was just another western railroad town. Here you'll find an assortment of exhibits relating to southern Nevada's past: a re-created city street featuring historic area homes with period furnishings, a 'timeline' mural and a 1918 Union Pacific steam engine.

FREE Ethel M Chocolates

2 Cactus Garden Drive, between Sunset Way & Mountain Vista Street (435 2655, www.ethelm.com). Bus 217. **Open** 8.30am-6pm daily. **Admission** free. Chocolate producer Ethel M offers self-guided factory tours complete with samples. To offset any feelings of overindulgence, it also has an environmentally aware cactus garden and a fascinating 'living machine', showing how plants can recycle wastewater. Here during the holidays? Check out the gardens, bedecked with millions of lights.

▶ *For more on Christmas/winter holiday celebrations in Vegas, see p43.*

Green Valley

Green Valley was established in the late 1970s as the valley's first planned community. Its design, and its eventual success, proved massively influential across the whole region; developments such as Summerlin wouldn't have happened without it.

The presence of homes in all price ranges has drawn all kinds of people: ethnic eateries, creative businesses and cultural events thrive here, creating a sense of community synergy of which others in the metropolis are envious. Take the Biosphere at Vanderburg Elementary School, for example, a large rainforest habitat complete with a waterfall, plants, fish and even free-roaming lizards. The $1.2 million cost of building it was covered by private donations and proceeds from campus fundraisers.

The high-tone **Green Valley Ranch** casino resort (*see p125*) is the subdivision's best accomplishment, its fine restaurants (especially Hank's steakhouse, named after Green Valley founder and local legend Hank Greenspun), bars, day spa, comfortable casino, concert venue and multiplex cinema all drawing

visitors and locals. In summer, the resort's outdoor pool area, which flaunts bocce courts and a design by Michael Czyz, hosts shows at its amphitheatre.

Next door is the **District**, an open-air esplanade of upscale restaurants and shops; among the latter is **Flea Bag's Barkery & Bow-tique** (2225 Village Walk Drive, Ste 173, 914 8805, www.fleabagsonline.com), selling gourmet pet biscuits (named after favourite customers) and Juicy Couture pet carriers. Across from here is the **Henderson Pavilion** (200 S Green Valley Parkway), an outdoor performing arts facility that hosts an annual Shakespeare in the Park event. And south on Green Valley Parkway is **Anthem**, an over-the-top country club that introduces the absurdist notion of gated communities within gated communities.

In the older section of Green Valley, the **Green Valley Town Center** reveals the area's community focus. This area is home to **Barley's Casino & Brewing Company** (4500 E Sunset Road, 458 2739), a microbrewery and casino. Also new here is the centre's movie theatre, reopened as the **Galaxy Luxury+ Theatre** (*see p214*), a film house that offers moviegoers recliners and booze. Further attractions lie along Sunset Road: to the east is **Sunset Station** (*see p130*), a neighbourhood casino with a fabulous, Gaudi-inspired bar, while a spin westbound will lead you past the huge **Sunset Park** (at 2601 E Sunset Road, 455 8200), which contains picnic sites, grills and games courts, and hosts **Age of Chivalry** (www.lvrenfair.com) each fall, with medieval guilds practising their jousts in public most weekend evenings.

LAKE LAS VEGAS

While Las Vegas grew, failed, grew, stagnated and grew again during the last century, the land that now holds **Lake Las Vegas** remained isolated and undeveloped. Eventually, it was settled not by Spanish traders, indomitable frontiersmen or stop-at-nothing prospectors, but by one Ronald F Boeddeker, a developer who envisioned a body of water surrounded by Mediterranean-style development, with golf courses, hotels, gaming, restaurants and boutiques alongside homes. Construction began here in the 1990s.

Lake Las Vegas is now a resort community in a desert setting, with opulent homes surrounding a vast man-made lake that empties into Lake Mead. The **Hilton Lake Las Vegas** (*see p131*) offers the Strip's Four Seasons serious competition in the ultra-luxe, casino-free hotels sector; adjoining it is the **Montelago Village**, a twee lakeside spot with boutiques, restaurants and a wine bar. In the summer, bring a blanket and watch as musicians take to the marina.

EXPLORE

Consume

Casinos & Hotels

Full-blown fantasies or cutting-edge design.

Seven decades ago, Vegas was framed around Downtown, a raffish cluster of buildings that provided little more than lairy gaming arenas and a few scruffy bedrooms. In the 1940s, a number of large resorts opened several miles away on a deserted highway, spurring a boom that saw the city reinvent itself as a swanky resort town. Then, after a decade of the doldrums, in 1989, Steve Wynn opened the **Mirage** (*see p90*) and inspired a regeneration of Las Vegas Boulevard. In 2005, Wynn returned with **Wynn Las Vegas** (*see p93*), raising the bar once again for aspiring casino

operators and prompting yet more improvement works among his rivals. Fast-forward another five years, and the Strip is transformed again, with the appearance of **CityCenter**, a city within a city rising from the middle of the Strip, dominating the skyline and changing the gravitational centre of the city. Not as colossal, but perhaps as important in what it means for how the 'next Vegas' will play out is the **Cosmopolitan** casino-resort (*see p85*), squeezed in next to CityCenter, with an unusual vertical, rather than horizontal, orientation – the main people-watching action is on the third floor.

CONSUME

ALL CHANGE

The industry is always building something new: a 1,000-room tower, a 4,000-seat theatre, a 100-unit shopping mall. The latest Strip trend is the construction or expansion of already existing resort pools – including **Mandalay Bay**'s (*see p86*) newly built Daylight pool/nightclub – following the success of the scandalous Rehab pool parties at the **Hard Rock** (*see p112*). The casino moguls have cannily capitalised on the daylight hours with a concept called 'daylife', turning the de rigueur pools into money fountains with spa-like accoutrements and massive pool parties and poolside concerts.

Hotel-casinos that don't expand are quick to change; it's a case of adapt or die. If you've not been to Vegas for four or five years, the changes will be noticeable. But even if you were here six months ago, you'll still see something new.

> ❶ Red numbers in this chapter correspond to the location of each hotel as marked on the street maps. *See pp317-320.*

STAYING IN LAS VEGAS

Though you could plump for an alternative – a motel, a hostel, even an RV park – the majority of visitors to Las Vegas stay where the action is: a hotel-casino. These often-vast complexes, which line the Strip and clutter Downtown, are where most tourists spend upwards of 90 per cent of their time. All have casinos, restaurants, bars and assorted entertainments, alongside other amenities that range from the predictable (pools, malls) to the truly exceptional (zoos, rollercoasters). And all, of course, have guestrooms, from the 100 or so offered at the **Golden Gate** (*see p124*) to the 6,000-plus at the **MGM Grand** (*see p88*).

Visitors to Las Vegas once spent very little time in their gaming-subsidised guestrooms, which is why rooms in hotel-casinos built before 1989 are smallish. But during the 1990s, casino moguls realised the value of providing guests with a nice place to sleep: rooms in newer hotel-casinos are brighter and more capacious. Wireless internet, phones and, at many places, use of an iPad or other tablet device, along with TVs (with cable) and air-conditioning are standard in rooms within Las Vegas hotel-casinos, which all offer free parking. Beyond that, it's a crapshoot.

WHERE TO STAY

Most visitors stay on the three-mile stretch of Las Vegas Boulevard South that runs from the Mandalay Bay resort north to Sahara Avenue (and usually includes the Stratosphere a few blocks north) – aka the Strip. Most never leave it. The Strip is where you'll find almost all the city's most glamorous, upscale and eye-catching resorts, as well as a number of its best bargains. If you want to stay on the Strip, remember it's a long (and, in summer, debilitating) hike from one end to the other. It's not enough simply to stay at a property with a Las Vegas Boulevard South address; the street number is also crucial.

The range of properties on the Strip is not as huge as it was a half-decade ago: most historic mid-century hotels and motels have been levelled in the name of progress. However, there's still variety. Note that while some hotel amenities are off-limits to non-guests, many others are open to everyone (bars, restaurants, clubs, shows). Access to spas (see ppp190-191), varies by hotel; most are open to the public, but a few limit access to their own guests.

There are, of course, hotels in other parts of town. A handful of big resorts are located just off the Strip, chief among them the **Hard Rock** (see p112) and the **Palms** (see p114). Downtown, the hub of Las Vegas until the 1950s, can't compete with the Strip in the glamour stakes – although recent expansions, like the **D** (see p120), may change that – but you'll find bargains galore. Near the Convention Center sit hotels aimed squarely at the business traveller, including **LVH** (formerly the Hilton; see p113). And although the Station casinos are chiefly frequented by locals, a few of them – principally **Red Rock Resort** (see p126) and **Green Valley Ranch** (see p125 – are well worth investigating.

RATES AND RESERVATIONS

Las Vegas has more rooms than anywhere in the world: roughly 150,000 and counting, with the numbers still rising. And eight out of ten of the world's largest hotels are here. However, with up to 40 million visitors a year, it needs them. Some weeks, bargains abound in even the poshest properties; at other times, you'll need to book way ahead if you want to avoid sleeping in your car.

Rates fluctuate wildly depending on the date and what convention or event happens to be in town: the same room can quadruple in price from one night to the next. You'll often find exceptional deals midweek and/or during off-season, when $200 rooms can go for a quarter

of their rack rate, even at the ritziest places – it's worth asking (and asking again) if there are any special rates or discounts that can be applied. There's no consistency, though: at weekends, prices skyrocket, and a two-night minimum is in effect almost everywhere. Steer clear of major conventions, too; for a full list, see www.lvcva.com.

For one night in a double room, expect to pay $40-$100 in a budget hotel-casino, $70-$200 in a mid-range operation, and $150 and up in a first-class property. In addition to these basic rates, rooms are subject to hotel tax (12 per cent on the Strip, 13 per cent elsewhere). You can book either by phone or online with almost every property in the city.

PLAYING IN LAS VEGAS

Depending on the time and location, the action on Vegas's casino floors can be fast and furious, as slot players hammer 'spin' buttons, blackjack players celebrate 21s and craps players whoop it up in the dice pit. The scene is played out to the soundtrack of clinking glasses, rattling chips and the electronic arpeggios of slot machines. It's overwhelming.

Still, with the nationwide spread of gambling, the experience has been dumbed down from the high-rolling James Bond image, and there's little required etiquette: common sense and common courtesy should see you through. Any outfit will do, from shorts to a dinner jacket, though you may want to carry a watch (clocks are conspicuous by their absence) and a sweater (the air-con is always cranked to the max).

Playing in Las Vegas is no longer just about gambling: casino attractions have evolved with the times. The circus acts at **Circus Circus** (see p106) and the volcano at the **Mirage** (see p90) remain, but resorts have also embraced adulthood. Nightclubs are all the rage, though you'll need to win big at the tables if you want to really enjoy yourself within their swanky confines.

ABOUT THIS CHAPTER

This section is divided geographically, with each area subdivided into hotel-casinos and non-casino properties. The majority of the hotels are either right on the **Strip** or very close to it

Aria.

(a loose area that we call **Off-Strip**), and range from the incomparably luxurious to the hopelessly dissolute. In **Downtown** Las Vegas, the properties are smaller, older and cheaper. Casinos in the **Rest of the City** appeal more to locals than visitors, but compensate for their lack of frills with a full array of gambling and good-value eating options.

LISTINGS INFORMATION

The address we've given for each casino is its main entrance. Arrive here on foot or in a car – especially for valet parking (for hotels that offer it). However, many casinos have entrances at the side and/or around the back, and these can be essential if you don't want to spend hours stuck in traffic driving along the choked-up Strip.

Most hotel-casino reviews have four headings: **Accommodation**, a survey of the guestrooms; **Eating & drinking**, where you'll find details on each hotel's bars and restaurants (many of these are also reviewed elsewhere; follow the cross-references for fuller critiques); **Entertainment**, detailing the main shows and lounges (again, follow the cross-references for more information); and **Games**, which provides an overview of the gambling facilities. Reviews of non-casino hotels are shorter for one key reason: there's less to review.

At the end of each review, we have detailed the property's key amenities and the specific range of gambling it offers. Bear in mind that table minimums are subject to change and can rise at night.

For reviews of some restaurants mentioned here, *see p132-157* **Restaurants**. For shows, *see p196-207* **Casino Entertainment**. For clubs, *see p219-228* **Nightlife**. For **bars** and **lounges**, *see p158-169*.

The Strip

Almost two thirds of the hotel rooms in Las Vegas are on the Strip, the stretch of Las Vegas Boulevard between the 'Welcome to Fabulous Las Vegas' sign and Sahara Avenue. Furthest south are **Mandalay Bay** (plus the **Four Seasons Las Vegas** and **Thehotel at Mandalay Bay**) and the **Luxor**. A little north, at the junction of Tropicana Avenue, sit four large casinos: the **Tropicana**, the **Excalibur**, **New York New York** and the **MGM Grand**. The **Monte Carlo** is just north of NYNY, next to the massive resort complex that is **CityCenter** (*see p51*).

The centre of the Strip has the biggest cluster of hotel-casinos: **Planet Hollywood** and **Paris Las Vegas** are followed to the north by **Bally's**, the **Bellagio**, **Caesars Palace** and the new Gansevoort Las Vegas (under construction at time of writing and scheduled to open in early 2014), all at the junction with Flamingo Road; it's the liveliest corner of the city. Slightly further north, past the **Flamingo**, the **Quad** (formerly Imperial Palace), **Harrah's**, **Casino Royale** and the **Venetian**, is the intersection of Spring Mountain Road and Sands Avenue, home to the **Mirage**, **TI (Treasure Island)**, the Fashion Show Mall, the **Wynn Las Vegas** and **Encore**. North of here is **Trump International**, **Circus Circus** and the **Riviera**.

dows above the lobby check-in stations is a sculpture of the Colorado River, made of (reclaimed) silver by world-renowned designer Maya Lin, who conceived of the Vietnam Veterans Memorial in Washington DC. Look past Lin's sculpture and you'll see a giant, curvy Henry Moore bronze; the parking area features an illuminated art piece with illuminating aphorisms by Jenny Holzer.

Along with the scores of entertainment options, including restaurants, bars, clubs, shops, a candy store and a Cirque du Soleil theatre, Aria also offers a state-of-the-art convention centre, 38 meeting rooms, four ballrooms with theatrical stages – and, when your mind wanders away from the convention at hand, a three-storey, 400ft window – a glass curtain – overlooking the pool.

Accommodation
In the top ten of the largest hotels in the world, Aria has 4,004 rooms, more than 500 of which are suites – and some of those are Sky Suites or rooftop Sky Villas, accessed by private elevator. The rooms are scaled from 520 to 2,000sq ft; the Sky Villas soar up to 7,000sq ft. Every room features a central-console touchscreen system that automatically opens and closes curtains, adjusts or turns off lights and electronics, and regulates the temperature when a guest enters or leaves the room. Bathrooms are stylish and spacious, with double sinks and enough counter space to comfortably suit two preparing for a night (or day) out, along with a separate WC, enclosed shower and sunken tub.

Eating & drinking
Aria offers a startling array of restaurant choices, many of which joined the ranks of the city's best upon opening. Fine-dining options include Barmasa, Javier's, Julian Serrano, Sage, Jean Georges Steakhouse, Sirio Ristorante, Michael Mina's American Fish and Blossom. More casual options include Lemongrass, pizza joint Five50, Aria Café and, of course, a stylish buffet with international flavours.

Entertainment
One of the central features of Aria – well, it's on the second floor – is Cirque du Soleil's international hit *Zarkana*, which replaced *Viva Elvis* in late 2012. Featuring music by Elton John protégé Nick Littlemore, *Zarkana* is the story of a resurrected circus led by the ringmaster, Zark. A little bit spooky, somewhat surreal and totally spectacular, the show offers all the aerial acrobatics you expect from a Cirque production and an enchanting score to boot.

Gambling
Aria contains the only gambling space within the CityCenter complex, and its casino is a contemporary beauty, with 150,000sq ft of space. The expected table games and slots are surrounded at the fringes by restaurants, shops and cafés – and natural light

HOTEL-CASINOS
Expensive

★ Aria
CityCenter, 3730 Las Vegas Boulevard South, at E Harmon Avenue, Las Vegas, NV 89158 (reservations 1-866 359 7757, front desk & casino 590 7757, www.arialasvegas.com). Bus Deuce/self-parking Las Vegas Boulevard South/valet parking Las Vegas Boulevard South or W Flamingo Road. **Rooms** 4,004. **Map** p320 A8 ❶

One of the newest and most strikingly beautiful buildings in Las Vegas, Aria is also the tallest and largest structure in the CityCenter complex. The casino-hotel-resort, which opened in December 2009 as a joint venture between MGM Resorts International and Infinity World Development of Dubai, is a pair of 61-storey curved glass-and-steel towers joined at the centre. Its other attributes are equally high-flown: Aria is an AAA five-diamond hotel, with a scale and level of amenities that makes it a destination in its own right.

Sustainability is on everyone's minds, and particularly in resource-challenged Las Vegas. Described as perhaps 'the most technologically advanced hotel ever built', Aria exemplifies the trend, with its efficient, gorgeous, incorporation of energy-saving ingenuity into the design of the hotel, including smart rooms that 'automatically turn off lights, regulate temperature and even shut curtains when a guest leaves the room'.

Aside from its height and techno-superiority, another element that makes Aria so spectacular is its dedication to artwork, to be found everywhere from the parking garage and exterior fountains to the lobby and interior spaces. Spanning the vast win-

CONSUME

CONSUME

makes its way on to the floor via windows and sky-lights, an unheard-of development in Vegas.

Amenities Bars (10). Business centre. Concierge. Disabled-adapted rooms. Gym. Internet (Wi-Fi, $15). No-smoking floors. Pool (outdoor). Restaurants (16). Room service. Spa. TV: pay movies.

Games Baccarat ($100-$15,000); Big Six; blackjack ($10-$10,000); Caribbean stud; craps (3x, 4x, 5x; from $5); casino war; Let it Ride; mini baccarat ($25-$15,000); pai gow poker; pai gow tiles; poker (24 tables); roulette (single & double zero); three-card poker.

Bellagio

3600 Las Vegas Boulevard South, at W Flamingo Road, Las Vegas, NV 89109 (reservations 1-888 987 6667, front desk & casino 693 7111, www. bellagio.com). Bus Deuce, 202/self-parking Las Vegas Boulevard South/valet parking Las Vegas Boulevard South or W Flamingo Road. **Rooms** 3,933. **Map** p320 A7 ❷

Since the Spa Tower opened at the Bellagio in 2005, the property seems to have paused for a breather. Sure, it's added the Adam Tihany-designed Club Privé, a high-limit gambling lounge that spotlights unbelievably rare spirits and world-class cigars. Granted, it's redone the poker room, and all 2,500 rooms in the main tower received a $70-million makeover in 2011. Otherwise, though, why tamper with a winning formula?

The Bellagio continues to evoke a supersized, all-American Italian villa, complete with an eight-acre lake fronting the Strip, a lush garden conservatory that changes with the holidays and an elegant pool area that's been reimagined as a formal Italian garden. It remains the archetypal playground for the well-heeled adult, with high-minded, grown-up entertainment in the form of posh restaurants, a tiny but tony promenade of boutiques, and Cirque du Soleil's most sophisticated show. The expanded spa in the Spa Tower features a salon, a fitness centre and even a one-chair barbershop; it's a lavish perk available only to guests, as is access to the renowned Shadow Creek golf course. But the most eye-catching attraction is the signature fountain, which, in the afternoons and evenings, shoots water into the air, synchronised to a variety of different soundtracks. The sidewalk on the Strip in front of the hotel offers superb views, as do the Bellagio's lakefront restaurants and bars.

Accommodation

The 3,933 rooms are large and beautifully furnished. The beds all have Serta mattresses, and the spacious, marble-floored bathrooms come with deep-soaking tubs and private-label toiletries. Wireless internet, flatscreen TVs, electronic curtains and well-stocked minibars are standard. The Presidential suites atop the Spa Tower are ultra-modern; and the nine luxury villas, outfitted with gold fixtures,

Lalique crystal accents, butler service, gyms, steam rooms, kitchens and private pools, are open to any-one willing to fork out $6,000 a night. The hotel's TV network simulcasts the fountain show music, so you can listen in your room as you watch the water.

Eating & drinking

The Bellagio has Vegas's best collection of superstar chefs under one roof. The roster starts with Julian Serrano's French/Mediterranean Picasso, decorated with paintings by the eponymous artist. Lovers of steak head for Prime, Jean-Georges Vongerichten's superior chophouse, while those after seafood seek out Michael Mina. For Italian, try Todd English's Olives, with its splendid view of the fountain show, or the circus-themed Circo; the latter is overseen by Manhattan restaurateur Sirio Maccioni, who also owns the more formal Le Cirque next door. In the Spa Tower, you'll find the serene Sensi, which serves Asian, Italian, grilled and seafood delicacies, and Pâtisserie Jean-Philippe, where a towering tri-coloured chocolate fountain (milk, white and dark) hints at the sweet sensations held within. The glitterati enjoy the upscale comfort food at Fix, while those looking for casual fare can check out the 24-hour Café Bellagio. The best drinks are served at Petrossian (see p160), named several times as one of America's best hotel bars by the hospitality industry's Santé magazine.

Entertainment

A cast of dancers, musicians, clowns, acrobats, divers, swimmers and aerialists takes to the watery stage in O, a breathtaking spectacle from Cirque du Soleil. Afterwards, retire to the stately Lily Bar and Lounge to watch the action on the casino floor

from a distance. For late-night fun, check out the pretty crowds sipping pricey martinis at the Bank or gyrating at Hyde.

Gambling

The Bellagio's casino draws celebs such as Ben Affleck and Drew Barrymore, but its ostentatious luxury verges on vulgar: the upholstery, carpets and striped canopies are a clash of colours and patterns. As you might expect, table limits are higher than at most Strip properties: minimums are often $25-$50 and it's difficult to find even $10 blackjack. Still, the race and sports book is one of the most comfortable in town, and the poker room has replaced Binion's as the mecca for pros, sharks and big-time players.

Amenities *Bars (7). Business centre. Concierge. Disabled-adapted rooms. Gym. Internet (Wi-Fi). No-smoking floors. Pools (outdoor, 5). Restaurants (19). Room service. Spa. TV: pay movies.*
Games *Baccarat ($100-$15,000); Big Six; blackjack ($10-$10,000); Caribbean stud; craps (3x, 4x, 5x; from $5); casino war; Let it Ride; mini baccarat ($25-$15,000); pai gow poker; pai gow tiles; poker (40 tables); roulette (single & double zero); three-card poker; slots.*

Caesars Palace

3570 Las Vegas Boulevard South, at W Flamingo Road, Las Vegas, NV 89109 (reservations 1-866 227 5938, front desk & casino 731 7110, www.caesarspalace.com). Bus Deuce, 202/self-parking & valet parking Las Vegas Boulevard South or S Industrial Road. **Rooms** 3,349. **Map** p320 A7 ❸
When it was announced in 2005 that the powerful Harrah's group was set to take over Caesars Palace, many Vegas observers feared that the chain would denude the place of all of its sass and turn it into Just Another Strip Resort. It didn't happen. While Aria is perhaps the epitome of new Vegas luxury, Caesars remains an icon of classic Sin City decadence, a meld of affluence, kitsch and glamour that continues to be a compelling sight almost five decades after its 1966 opening.

The resort remains a monument of sorts to ancient Greece and Rome, with miles of gold decor, marble columns, arches and colonnades, manicured gardens and copies of Greek and Roman statuary. These days, though, it's more about elegance than the kind of camp instilled in it by legendary founder Jay Sarno, at least in theory. It's an enormous place, spread over a bewildering, labyrinthine casino floor and up into a variety of different towers.

Key to Caesars' continuing allure is the 4.5-acre Garden of the Gods pool area, a San Simeon-like peach with four mosaic pools, marble statuary, fountains and mini-throne lifeguard stands. A section of it, by the Venus pool, is set aside for topless sunbathing. While the pool draws a crowd only in summer, the ever-expanding Forum Shops (*see p174*) pulls visitors year-round. Fashioned, in true Vegas style, after an ancient Roman streetscape, the mall contains an unmatched range of shops, many of them not found anywhere else in the city. Other selling points include the luxurious Qua Baths & Spa and the Venus salon; guests also get access to Cascata, the resort's golf course in Boulder City. *Photo p84.*

Accommodation

You'd expect some variety in a hotel this huge, and so it proves. The standard rooms are expansive and well maintained, if not especially inspiring. If you've got a little cash, it's worth splashing for the 'Deluxe'

CONSUME

Bellagio.

Caesars Palace. See p83.

rooms in the Augustus and Palace Towers, upgraded with high-tech facilities and stylishly modern design. The suites are fancier still: some have circular beds, in-room saunas, wet bars, living/dining rooms, home theatres, wine grottoes, and even steam and workout rooms. And the newly opened Nobu Hotel (see p117 **Getting Personal**) within Caesars redefines luxury.

Eating & drinking

Top of the tree are high-end French spot Restaurant Guy Savoy, New York-import Rao's, featuring some of Vegas's best Italian food, and chef Nobu Matsuhisa's namesake Nobu. If you're looking for something late at night – or any other time – try chef Michael Richard's Central, which offers American comfort food with a French twist. Other options include the Japanese-oriented Hyakumi; the Empress Court, for upscale Chinese; the Gordon Ramsay Pub & Grill; and Serendipity 3 for a sweet treat.

There are also a number of excellent eateries in the Forum Shops, among them Joe's Seafood, Prime Steak & Stone Crab, surf 'n' turf specialists the Palm and Il Mulino New York. Alternatives include Sushi Roku, straightforward Italian eaterie Trevi, and Wolfgang Puck's trend-setting Spago. For casual fare, try Cafe Della Spiga.

Entertainment

Elton John makes appearances with his hits-packed Million Dollar Piano show throughout the year, and Shania Twain started a two-year residency at the Colosseum in December 2012. Other semi-regular headliners include comic Jerry Seinfeld, Celine Dion and Rod Stewart. The acro-cabaret of Absinthe is another popular attraction.

The most notable nightlife option, and one of the most fashionable in the entire city, is the perpetually celeb-packed Pure, a gigantic nightclub overlooking the Strip that features four clubs within one. Elsewhere, the Shadow Bar offers bartenders with flair and silhouetted beauties bumping and grinding behind backlit scrims; for old-time Caesars Palace kitsch, there's the enduring Cleopatra's Barge. In summer, there's the Venus Pool Club. Also on site are the Seahorse Lounge, serving high-end cocktails in a room dominated by a giant aquarium, the 24-hour Galleria Bar, and Numb, which specialises in frozen drinks, on the casino floor.

Gambling

Few casinos offer the limits or the atmosphere of Caesars; when there's a big fight in town, limits on the main floor can go through the roof. The sports book is one of the liveliest spots to watch the action, and accepts some of the biggest bets. You get a good view of the baccarat pit, an intimate nook where huge wagers are common. And for the boldest of slot players, the $500 machine, with a $1 million jackpot, uses gold-plated tokens. (Caveat: it pays a winning spin of only two $500 coins; for every other payback, the machine locks and an attendant hand-pays, for tax-paperwork purposes.) The high-limit slots are in the Palace Casino near the main entrance; blackjack pits and slots in the Forum Casino offer slightly lower limits.

Amenities *Bars (7). Business centre. Concierge. Disabled-adapted rooms. Gym. Internet (Wi-Fi, $11.99). No-smoking floors. Pools (outdoor). Restaurants (10). Room service. Spa. TV: pay movies.*

Games *Baccarat ($100-$15,000); Big Six; blackjack ($5-$10,000); Caribbean stud; casino war; craps (3x, 4x, 5x; from $10); keno; Let it Ride; mini baccarat ($25-$5,000); pai gow poker; pai gow tiles; poker (62 tables); roulette (single zero & double zero); Spanish 21; three-card poker.*

★ Cosmopolitan

3708 Las Vegas Boulevard South, between W Harmon Ave & W Flamingo Road, Las Vegas, NV 89109 (reservations 1-855 455 1055, front desk & casino 698 7000, www.cosmopolitanlasvegas.com). Bus Deuce/self-parking Las Vegas Boulevard South/valet parking Las Vegas Boulevard South or W Flamingo Road.
Rooms 2,995. **Map** p320 A7 ❹

Like Aria, its next-door neighbour on the Strip, the Cosmopolitan is a luxury resort hotel and casino made up of two high-rise towers. But perhaps because of its unusual vertical orientation – the action plays out on three floors, instead of the usual sprawling single floor – the Cosmopolitan almost instantly became the new favourite of hip visitors and, most unusually, Vegas locals, who typically shun the Strip in favour of closer-to-home casinos and entertainment. Its third floor, which is also atypical in that it doesn't have any gaming or cocktail waitressing, has become the place to see dressed-up cosmopolitans, observed from a comfy perch on the witty assortment of mid-mod furnishings positioned mid-floor.

Built on what used to be the parking lot for the tiny Jockey Club timeshare, the $3.9 billion hotel, designed by Arquitectonica, has 2,995 rooms and

Cosmopolitan.

300,000sq ft of stylish retail and restaurant space. The emphasis on high design and contemporary style makes the gambling action seem almost secondary – which may end up posing a bit of a problem for the Cosmo's owners. But for the moment, they're enjoying the buzz and the kudos of owning the most electrically current of the city's casinos.

Accommodation

Rooms at the Cosmopolitan are outfitted to make you feel as if you are at home – if home was within the pages of a high-end interiors magazine. Stylish and stylised, yes, but comfort was a guiding principal of designing Cosmo's rooms and suites, which come standard-equipped with HD plasma screen TVs, high speed internet, minibar and unusually luxurious bathrooms with marble floors. A big plus: most of the rooms have sliding glass doors that open on to individual patios – this is highly unusual for Vegas, where the windows customarily do not open, for a variety of reasons.

Eating & drinking

Cosmopolitan has an internationally spiced collection of restaurants, including two by chef José Andrés – his signature tapas restaurant Jaleo, and China Poblano (see p137), which combines Mexican and Chinese cuisine. Other big food-world names with stakes in Cosmo include Blue Ribbon Sushi by Bruce and Eric Bromberg; Greek-food heaven Esitatorio Milos from Costas Spililadis; and Scott Conant's Italian eatery Scarpetta, where the signature spaghetti is out of this world (Conant also helms wine bar D.O.G.C.); and Comme Ça from David Myers. Carnivores will delight in STK and high-end burger joint Holsteins, or grab breakfast (and other meals) all day long at the Henry.

Entertainment

Upon opening, Cosmopolitan's 62,000sq ft Marquee club became the most buzzed-about new space in Las Vegas. The indoor-outdoor venue, which accommodates the increasingly popular 'daylife' concept of clubbing and concerts by the pool, features a multimillion-dollar sound stage and coliseum-style seating surrounding a dancefloor, which itself is decorated with four-story LED screens and projection walls that display light and image shows. The club is now solidly on the circuit of visiting international house music DJs, and the Marquee stage attracts an unusual array of up-to-the-moment artists. Similarly, Cosmo's Boulevard Pool, which overlooks the Strip, has become a happening music venue as well, hosting Set Your Life to Music, a weeknight concert series that brings in an eclectic array of artists – in addition to a two-week-long spring concert series and various movie nights.

Gambling

As mentioned before, the glitter and glam of the constantly moving crowd can distract from the action

and attraction of the casino floor, but that doesn't mean it's not equipped to be a serious player on the Strip. In addition to its relatively intimate race and sports book, the 100,000sq ft casino (featuring cabanas!) offers nearly 1,500 state-of-the-art slot machines, plus baccarat, blackjack, roulette, and several varieties of poker and pai gow.

Amenities *Bars (5). Business centre. Concierge. Disabled-adapted rooms. Gym. Internet (Wi-Fi). No-smoking floors. Pools (outdoor). Restaurants (19). Room service. Spa. TV: pay movies.*
Games *Baccarat ($100-$15,000); blackjack ($10-$10,000); craps (3x, 4x, 5x; from $5); Crazy 4 poker; fortune pai gow poker; Let it Ride; roulette; slots; three-card poker; Ultimate Texas poker.*

★ Mandalay Bay

3950 Las Vegas Boulevard South, at W Hacienda Avenue, Las Vegas, NV 89119 (reservations 1-877 632 7800, front desk & casino 632 7777, www.mandalaybay.com). Bus Deuce, 119/self-parking & valet parking W Hacienda Avenue. **Rooms** 2,791. **Map** p320 A9 ❺

Not only do the suits at MGM Mirage know not to mess with a good thing, they also know how to make it better. There's no finer example of this skill than the South Seas island-themed Mandalay Bay, one of the Strip's most luxurious resorts. At its heart has always been an 11-acre water park with a sandy beach, a wave pool, a lazy river, two additional pools and a jogging track set in lush green foliage, plus the Moorea Beach Club, a limited-access retreat that transforms into a sultry hotspot with its 'Toptional' beach. But a $30-million expansion added a three-storey, climate-controlled, glass-fronted casino on the sand, where guests can enjoy beachside gambling, casual dining or sun worshipping. Book one of the decked-out Villas Soleil, where you and 15 pals can take advantage of your own wet bar, MP3 player, flatscreen TV and private third-level pool.

The interior is just as impressive. Since opening 14 years ago – an eternity in Las Vegas time – Mandalay Bay has lost none of its appeal. An understated oasis of water features, lush foliage, huge aquariums and island architecture, it encompasses a sensuous spa, a classy collection of restaurants, a pair of wedding chapels, several theatres and the kid-friendly Shark Reef aquarium (see p51). Mandalay Place, a nice sky-bridge mall that connects the hotel with the Luxor, contains a number of upscale boutiques and restaurants, a chic barber and Minus5 Ice Lounge, where – you guessed it – the temperature is a constant 5° below Celsius.

If all this doesn't work for you, there are two other hotels accessible from Mandalay Bay. A corridor off the lobby leads to the Four Seasons (see p109), which has its rooms on floors 35 to 39 but is run as a separate operation. Meanwhile, Thehotel at Mandalay Bay (see p110) is an all-suite, casino-free tower that eschews the island theme entirely.

Accommodation

All 2,791 guestrooms and suites at Mandalay Bay were remodelled a few years ago with a contemporary look and additional amenities: lofty pillow-top beds with triple sheeting, 42in plasma-screen TVs, iPod docks and high-speed internet access. Bathrooms come with 15in LCD TVs and giant tubs. Larger suites command excellent views of the Strip or the surrounding mountains and come with wet bars.

Eating & drinking

Mandalay Bay is unusual among the major resorts on the Strip in that it locates many of its eateries in a 'restaurant row' away from the casino, so you can dine without seeing – or, just as crucially, hearing – so much as a single slot machine. The top spot on the block is Michael Mina's Stripsteak, the first steakhouse by a chef previously known for his seafood. Other noteworthy spots include Hubert Keller's Fleur, whose menu spans the globe; two Charlie Palmer restaurants, Aureole and Charlie Palmer Steak; Wolfgang Puck's signature Trattoria del Lupo; and Rick Moonen's new Rx Boiler Room. Border Grill offers tasty Mexican fare in a casual setting, while Red Square – fronted by the huge statue of a headless Lenin – boasts caviar and vodka galore. Sample the sushi at Mizuya, or get your comfort-food fix at the always-open Citizens Kitchen and Bar.

You'll have to venture into the casino to sample the Cajun cooking at House of Blues, upstairs from the music venue. Try Sunday's soul-stirring Gospel Brunch or, if you can, the super-exclusive Foundation Room, which serves dinner to members and VIPs

Mandalay Bay.

MGM Grand.

CONSUME

amid luxury furnishings on the top floor. Ringing the casino are the nice 24-hour Raffles Café and the Noodle Shop. At Mandalay Place, meat-lovers can have theirs with lettuce and tomato at the Burger Bar; grab a drink at Ri Ra Irish Pub; or nurse a headache with the Hangover Special at Hussong's Cantina.

Entertainment

The 12,000-seat Mandalay Bay Events Center has a schedule of boxing events and concerts, but a better choice is the more acoustically reliable House of Blues. When the weather's warm, the hotel also produces the Beach Concert series. But the big, new draw is Cirque du Soleil's latest show *Michael Jackson One* (see p205), which opened to stellar reviews in June 2013.

Cirque is making itself felt elsewhere at Mandalay Bay, particularly in the recently opened Light nightclub – a smallish but impressive nightspot that it operates, which features Cirque performers crawling across walls and ceiling. By contrast, the newly constructed Daylight pool/club stands south of the hotel itself and adjacent to the Strip. The 50,000sq ft venue hosts a variety of DJs, and guests can reserve a cabana or – for the high rollers – one of the two private bungalows on either side of the stage.

Gambling

The 135,000sq ft casino is airier than many, with 2,400 machines (including nickel video slots that take up to 45 or 90 coins), but you have to hunt for good video-poker machines. Table games – 122 of them – include blackjack, roulette, craps, Let it Ride, Caribbean stud, pai gow poker and mini baccarat. You'll also find a poker room where you can get your fix of seven-card

stud and Texas or Omaha hold 'em. The race and sports book has 17 large screens, enough seating for some 300 sports fans, a bar and a good deli.
Amenities *Bars (10). Business centre. Concierge. Disabled-adapted rooms. Gym. Internet ($11.99). No-smoking floors. Pools (outdoor). Restaurants (21). Room service. Spa. TV: pay movies.*
Games *Baccarat ($100-$15,000); blackjack ($10-$15,000); craps (3x, 4x, 5x; from $10); keno; Let it Ride; mini baccarat ($25-$15,000); pai gow poker; pai gow tiles; poker (10 tables); roulette (single & double zero); three-card poker.*

★ MGM Grand

3799 Las Vegas Boulevard South, at E Tropicana Avenue, Las Vegas, NV 89109 (reservations 1-877 880 0880, front desk & casino 891 7777, www.mgmgrand.com). Bus Deuce, 201/self-parking Las Vegas Boulevard South, Koval Avenue or E Tropicana Avenue/valet parking E Tropicana Avenue. **Rooms** 6,852. **Map** p320 A8 ❻
There is a spa here, of course. Not to mention a pool, a convention centre and a kid-friendly animal attraction (the popular Lion Habitat). However, the MGM Grand really comes alive after dark, when this immense resort is at its vibrant, buzzing best.

For a time, the largest hotel on earth aimed itself squarely at families. When Vegas fashion started to move back towards the adult market, the MGM was by no means quickest to react. However, it's since thrown itself into the grown-up market with commitment and smarts, building an unlikely but deserved reputation as one of the liveliest resorts on the Strip. Billing itself as 'Maximum Vegas' takes the point a bit far, but there's little doubt that the

MGM balances the needs of cash-happy big spenders, easygoing middle Americans and youthful club kids as well as any resort in the city does.

Accommodation

The 5,044 rooms (including 751 increasingly plush suites) in the main building are mostly done out with art deco-styled furnishings, designed to evoke backlot bungalows from Hollywood's glamour age. They manage it pretty well, too, though you suspect Clark Gable and Louise Brooks would sooner be down the street at the Wynn. A fourth-floor guest services desk functions as an additional concierge, a massive plus in this huge hotel.

However, the real luxury is elsewhere on the lot. First to arrive was the Mansion, which contains 29 handsomely appointed and even more handsomely priced villas. In 2005, the hotel added 51 Skylofts, vast, chic two-storey suites designed by Tony Chi that remain among the town's more fashionable temporary addresses. And then there's the Signature, a luxurious condo-hotel development with three 576-suite towers. Rooms have jacuzzi tubs and balconies; guests also get access to private pool areas, among other perks. Brand new on the scene are a handful of Stay Well rooms, complete with vitamin C shower water, aromatherapy and EMF protection. Only in Las Vegas…

Eating & drinking

Quietly, steadily and with great savvy, the MGM Grand has grown to house the best and most varied range of restaurants in the city. Many casinos make the 'something for everyone' claim about their eating options; the MGM comes closer than any to fulfilling the brief.

You can't move for all the celebrity chefs, or at least the assistants who quietly do their bidding. The flagship operation is Joël Robuchon, devised by the notoriously inventive French chef; those diners unable to stretch to the $425 16-course tasting menu may prefer the fractionally more casual L'Atelier de Joël Robuchon. Among other high-end options are Tom Colicchio's Craftsteak, where the focus is on meat, fish and fowl from small farms; Fiamma, an Italian trattoria imported from New York; Japanese restaurant Shibuya and the all-Chinese Pearl. Michael Mina's Pub 1842 is the latest addition to the all-star cast.

Other big names with a toe in the MGM's restaurant pool include Cajun specialist Emeril Lagasse (Emeril's) and Wolfgang Puck (at the laid-back Wolfgang Puck Bar & Grill), both of which are very good options. Diego deals in excellent Mexican food, while there's more casual fare at the Rainforest Café, Colicchio's 'Wichcraft, the Stage Deli and the Grand Wok & Sushi Bar, which shares a kitchen with the 24-hour coffeeshop. The buffet is one of the best on the Strip.

Like its nightclubs Studio 54, Tabú and the just-opened Hakkasan – which also serves dinner – the MGM's bars tend towards the hipper end of the scale. The splashiest is Centrifuge, with a large central bar upon which dancers sometimes do their thang. Zuri, a cigar bar of sorts, and the open-plan Rouge are more sophisticated haunts, while the West Wing is a good place to cool your heels.

Entertainment

The entertainment options at the MGM are led – as is fast becoming customary in Las Vegas casinos – by Cirque du Soleil. The fourth Cirque production to launch in the city, *Kà* is a spectacular, high-concept piece of dramatic fluff that plays in a vast theatre accessible towards the rear of the main casino floor.

The 740-seat Hollywood Theatre hosts perhaps half a dozen acts on regular rotation for runs of anywhere from a week to a month. Ticket prices are high, but you're paying a premium for the privilege of seeing such big names as David Copperfield and Tom Jones in intimate confines. Intimacy isn't a word generally associated with the 16,800-seat MGM Grand Garden Arena, which stages a mix of concerts (from Black Sabbath to Justin Timberlake to Lil Wayne) and sporting events (boxing, ultimate fighting).

The nightlife here is strong and relentlessly fashionable, and the opening of the much-ballyhooed dining nightclub Hakkasan will cement the MGM's reputation as the place to be, with DJs in residency including Deadmau5, Tiesto, Calvin Harris and Steve Aoki for starters.

Gambling

The MGM has four gaming areas (Entertainment, Hollywood, Monte Carlo and Sports) in which you'll find all the games, including Spanish 21. It's the largest casino in Las Vegas and boasts hundreds of

CONSUME

Mirage

tables. Table minimums can go down to $10 on weekdays, but most are higher; in the pit, you'll find $25 minimums and $15,000 maximums. There's also a large race and sports book with floor-to-ceiling screens, one of the best poker rooms in town, and 3,700 slots, from a nickel to $500.

Amenities *Bars (7). Business centre. Concierge. Disabled-adapted rooms. Gym. Internet (Wi-Fi $11.99). No-smoking floors. Pool (outdoor). Restaurants (18). Room service. Spa. TV: pay movies.*

Games *Baccarat ($100-$15,000); blackjack ($10-$10,000); casino war; craps (3x, 4x, 5x; from $5); Crazy 4 poker; keno; Let it Ride; mini baccarat ($25-$15,000); pai gow poker; pai gow tiles; poker (22 tables); roulette (single zero & double zero); three-card poker.*

Mirage

3400 Las Vegas Boulevard South, between Spring Mountain & W Flamingo roads, Las Vegas, NV 89109 (reservations 1-800 374 9000, front desk & casino 791 7111, www.mirage.com). Bus Deuce, 203/self-parking Spring Mountain

Road/valet parking Las Vegas Boulevard South.
Rooms 3,044. **Map** p320 A6 ⑦

With its Polynesian village decor, lush landscaping, lagoon-like pool and waterfalls, the $650-million Mirage set the standard for modern resorts when Steve Wynn opened it in 1989. But in much the same way that the likes of the Tropicana and the Flamingo were left standing at the gate when the Mirage welcomed its first guests, so the Mirage was in turn overtaken by its sassier competitors, who shrewdly realised that there was money to be made from a younger, more fashionable generation. The owners have pepped things up no end over the past few years, though. Dining options have vastly improved, nightclubs and lounges aimed squarely at the under-30s rather than the over-40s have opened, and Christmas-camp Siegfried & Roy have been replaced with a vibrant Beatles-based show. The Mirage might not look like a different resort, but it certainly feels like one.

For all that, many of the old favourites remain. The mocked-up volcano at the front is no more realistic than it ever was, but its hourly shows (evenings only) remain a draw. Also still here are the 100ft rainforest atrium filled with fresh and faux palm trees and orchids, the much-imitated 20,000-gallon aquarium behind the registration desk, and the Secret Garden & Dolphin Habitat (*see p54*). And do make time to stop by the gorgeous pool area, which comprises a series of blue lagoons, inlets and waterfalls, plus two islands exotically landscaped with various palm trees and tropical flowers.

Accommodation

Decor in the rooms is on the conservative side, with tasteful splashes of colours in cranberries, greens and browns. Rooms are as comfortable as you'd expect – this was the hotel that launched the super-sizing of Vegas after all – and very well appointed, with 42in TVs and iPod/MP3 docks. The suites are spacious and nicely done as well, and often surprisingly affordable.

Eating & drinking

Dining options at the Mirage are undergoing a revitalisation. The Samba Brazilian Steakhouse; Italian favourite Onda; fine-dining Chinese restaurant Fin; Japonais, imported via Chicago and New York; and the swanky Stack, all remain. But steak lovers will be pleased with the brand-new Tom Colicchio's Steak House and its flame-roasted meats. Likewise, *Iron Chef America* star Masaharu Morimoto is slated to open Morimoto, a Japanese eaterie, in 2014. Casual choices include California Pizza Kitchen and New York's Carnegie Deli.

Entertainment

The big show at the Mirage is one of the biggest and best in the city: *Love*, Cirque du Soleil's surprisingly successful reinvention of the Beatles' back catalogue. Ventriloquist Terry Fator, an early winner of the *America's Got Talent* TV competition, has replaced the late, beloved impressionist Danny Gans. The Aces of Comedy series features some of the funniest names in the biz, including Daniel Tosh, Lewis Black and Seth Meyers.

The nightlife here has exploded of late, particularly with the 2013 New Year's Eve opening of 1 Oak, which has become a hotspot overnight, drawing DJs, hip hoppers and movie stars galore. The Cirque-designed Revolution Lounge, with its novel interactive tables and speciality cocktails, is a welcome place for a post-Love drink too. Cigar/mojito joint Rhumbar faces the Strip, and is a fun place to down a couple of Spanish Trampolines while watching the crowd meander by.

Gambling

The Mirage has nearly 100 blackjack tables, most dealt from six-deck shoes. Minimums are high: $10 for 21, craps and roulette; $15 for mini baccarat; $100 for baccarat. You can find a good game of poker at any hour; since many players are tourists, the action, on both the low- and high-limit tables, is plentiful. For a break, check out the high-limit slots. If you're polite, and it's not too busy, an attendant might offer you some freshly sliced fruit, normally reserved for players who insert $100 tokens five at a time (their generosity truly knows no bounds). The Red, White & Blue slot offers a $1 million jackpot.

Amenities *Bars (5). Business centre. Concierge. Disabled-adapted rooms. Gym. Internet (Wi-Fi $12.99). No-smoking floors. Pools (outdoor). Restaurants (14). Room service. Spa. TV: pay movies.*

Games *Baccarat ($100-$15,000); Big Six; blackjack ($10-$10,000); craps (3x, 4x, 5x; from $10); Crazy 4 poker; keno; Let it Ride; mini baccarat ($15-$15,000); Mississippi Stud; pai gow poker; pai gow tiles; poker (20 tables); roulette (single zero & double zero); three-card poker; Ultimate Texas hold 'em.*

Paris Las Vegas

3655 Las Vegas Boulevard South, at E Flamingo Road, Las Vegas, NV 89109 (reservations 1-877 796 2096, front desk & casino 946 7000, www. parislasvegas.com). Bus Deuce, 202/self-parking & valet parking Las Vegas Boulevard South or Audrie Street. **Rooms** 2,915. **Map** p320 A7 ❽

What happens when the City of Lights collides with the City of Light? Versions of Paris's greatest monuments cut down to size, all-you-can-eat crêpes at the buffet, reasonably polite waiters, ancient Rome across the street… and, of course, the lights never go out. If only the real Paris could be so accommodating. Even the French love Las Vegas.

To say that this huge resort in the heart of the Strip is one of the town's most eye-catching is to do its effervescent absurdity a rank injustice. Its reproductions of Parisian landmarks start with the 34-storey hotel tower modelled after the Hôtel de Ville, and also take in the Louvre, the Paris Opéra, the Arc de Triomphe and, of course, the half-scale replica of the Eiffel Tower, built using Gustav Eiffel's original plans, that plunges into the casino. The theming continues within, with French-themed restaurants, shops and even – though you'll need to look closely – the casino. It may seem rather sub-Disney at first glance, but it's by no means all haw-hee-haw cliché: you can also get a massage in a mock-Balinese spa, sun yourself by the rooftop pool, or take in a show by American Idol winner Taylor Hicks, who is holding a yearlong residency at Paris.

Accommodation

The smallish guestrooms are comfortable, prim and stately, decorated in rich Regency style; some are furnished with canopied beds and armoires, and workspace and internet connections are standard. The spacious marble bathrooms are outfitted with vanities, a make-up mirror and soaking tubs.

Eating & drinking

Paris Las Vegas doesn't do too badly at living up to its theme city's culinary reputation, albeit without the breadth of styles you'll find at the Venetian or Bellagio. Along with JJ's Boulangerie and La Creperie, serving sandwiches and delicious sweet and savoury crêpes, and the quaint Le Village Buffet, which features regional cuisine from five French provinces, the hotel has the Eiffel Tower Restaurant, located on the tower's 11th floor, and the bustling Mon Ami Gabi, a streetside brasserie serving classics such as *steak frites*. New on the scene is Gordon Ramsay Steak, a delicious if pricey place to get your beef (and seafood and pork) fix. Le Provençal offers upscale French-Italian fare, while Le Café Ile St Louis is a comfortable spot from which to watch the crowds. But most ridiculous of all? Le Burger Brasserie, putatively a French take on American classics (see the $777 Kobe beef/Maine lobster burger). Hmm…

Entertainment

If Paris Las Vegas's strolling mimes leave you unenthusiastic, there are a variety of other ways to spend the night wisely (or otherwise). Aside from current musical headliner Taylor Hicks, the Tony-winning musical *Jersey Boys* has found a new home in Paris. If we all ignore hypnotist Anthony Cools, who performs six shows a week, perhaps he'll go away. Chateau Nightclub and Gardens occupies two storeys, in which old-world France meets new. Downstairs, there's dance music under sparkly lights among the shady faux trees of Le Cabaret. And there are decidedly non-French duelling piano sing-alongs in Napoleon's (*see p160*), a champagne and cigar bar.

Gambling

Three of the Eiffel Tower's four legs plunge into the Paris casino, which is smaller, noisier and more energetically crowded than most. The 100 table games and 2,000-plus slot machines are not as budget-friendly as they used to be, though there are still plenty of 25¢ slots. The race and sports book has big TVs and 'parimutuel' betting on horse racing. Theming is rampant, from Monet-influenced carpets and Paris Métro-style wrought-iron canopies above the games to security guards in gendarme uniforms. Check out the LeRoy Neiman paintings in the high-limit pit.

Amenities *Bars (6). Business centre. Concierge. Disabled-adapted rooms. Gym. Internet ($10.99). No-smoking floors. Pool (outdoor). Restaurants (11). Room service. Spa. TV: pay movies.*
Games *Baccarat ($100-$15,000); blackjack ($5-$10,000); craps (3x, 4x, 5x; from $5); Let it Ride; mini baccarat ($15-$5,000); þai gow poker; þai gow tiles; roulette (single zero & double zero); three-card poker.*

Venetian & Palazzo

3355 Las Vegas Boulevard South, between Sands Avenue & E Flamingo Road, Las Vegas, NV 89109 (reservations 1-866 659 9643, front desk & casino 414 1000, www.venetian.com). Bus Deuce, 119, 203/self-parking & valet parking Las Vegas Boulevard South or Koval Lane. **Rooms** Venetian 4,049. *Palazzo* 3,025. **Map** p319, p320 B6 ⑨
Sheldon Adelson's Venetian manages the neat trick of recreating the city of canals in the desert. To-scale replicas of the Rialto Bridge, the Doge's Palace and the Campanile are rendered with affection, and the singing gondoliers and itinerant 'street' performers in St Mark's Square perform with gusto and a wink. It's less tacky than you might expect.

Attractions here are, perhaps with the exception of the adjacent Madame Tussaud's (see p54), pretty good. The Grand Canal Shoppes (see p175) is a meandering mall with flowing canals and faux façades that curve around to St Mark's Square. Another key draw is the Canyon Ranch SpaClub, which offers a full range of spa services along with movement and wellness classes, a climbing wall and a café. The resort connects to the Sands Expo (see p295); indeed, the Venetian pulls in much of its business from conventioneers, especially midweek.

The adjacent Palazzo has an upper-crust Beverly Hills feel. The resort features a new mall, the Shoppes at Palazzo (see p170), connected to the Venetian via the Grand Canal Shoppes and anchored by Barneys department store.

Accommodation

The standard suites (there are no regular rooms) at the Venetian are far larger than the Vegas norm – 650sq ft and up. The sumptuously appointed suites underwent renovations during 2007, no doubt to keep them on a par with the Palazzo's. The 12-storey Venezia Tower atop the car park has rooms that are similar to those in the original tower, but with some extra amenities (private elevators, complimentary newspaper delivery, access to the secluded Italian-style pool garden and arboretum). For more exclusivity, the tower's top five floors contain an old world drawing-room-style lounge and speciality baths.

Eating & drinking

Where to begin? The Venetian's restaurant roster reads like a Who's Who of top chefs. Thomas Keller (of French Laundry fame) oversees stellar brasserie Bouchon; Wolfgang Puck and Emeril Lagasse respectively run the San Francisco-style café Postrio and the Cajun Delmonico Steakhouse; Joachim Splichal's Pinot Brasserie brings a lighter taste of French cuisine; and Tom Moloney's Aquaknox serves Californian cuisine. This being ersatz Venice, there's plenty of Italian food: Piero Selvaggio's dual rooms Valentino and the Grill at Valentino; Zeffirino, a Genoan-style seafood restaurant with a fan club that includes Pavarotti; and Canaletto. Newer arrivals include Tao, an Asian bistro related to the fashionable New York restaurant-club; Mario Batali's B&B Ristorante and Otto Enoteca Pizzeria; and Daniele Dotto's intimate Casanova. Less pricey options (it's all relative) include Noodle Asia for pan-Asian noodle dishes, Hong Kong dim sum and vegetarian specialities; the excellent 24-hour Grand Lux Café; and Taqueria Cañonita.

Entertainment

The Venetian has expanded its nighttime entertainment options with the musical Rock of Ages, as well as Smokey Robinson's Motown tribute Human Nature. Other headliners feature a rotating roster of venerable comedians, including Joan Rivers, Tim Allen and David Spade, among others.

After numerous attempts at starting a nightclub scene stalled at the gates, the Venetian finally hit the bull's-eye with Tao, a pan-Asian boîte, nightclub and rooftop lounge that entertains thousands at weekends. For more lounge and less club, check out the sizzling minimalist V Bar (see p162).

Gambling

In the casino, the 140 table games include blackjack, craps, Caribbean stud, Let it Ride and pai gow. The casino's 2,600 slots are weighted toward reel games, with a large mix of $1 machines. For the player with pull, there are high-denomination machines – $5, $25 and $100 – in the casino's high-limit salon, which also includes a baccarat pit and 12 table games (with blackjack starting at $10,000 a hand).

Amenities Bars (3). Business centre. Concierge. Disabled-adapted rooms. Gym. Internet ($10). No-smoking floors. Pools (outdoor). Restaurants (18). Room service. Spa. TV: DVD (selected rooms)/pay movies.

Games Baccarat ($100-$15,000); mini baccarat ($25-$10,000); Big Six; blackjack ($10-$5,000); Caribbean stud; craps (3x, 4x, 5x; from $10); keno; Let it Ride; pai gow poker; pai gow tiles; poker (59 tables); roulette (double zero). Gambling lessons (craps 11am, 5pm Mon-Fri; roulette noon Mon-Fri; blackjack 12.15pm Mon-Fri).

Wynn Las Vegas & Encore

3131 Las Vegas Boulevard South, between E Desert Inn Road & Sands Avenue, NV 89109 (reservations 1-888 320 9966, front desk & casino 770 7000, www.wynnlasvegas.com).

Venetian & Palazzo.

CONSUME

Wynn Las Vegas & Encore. *See p93.*

CONSUME

Bus Deuce, 108, 203/self-parking & valet parking Las Vegas Boulevard South or (Tower Suites) Spring Mountain Road. **Rooms** *Wynn Las Vegas* 2,716. *Encore* 2,034. **Map** p319, p320 B6 ⑩

Before he'd even finished building his namesake hotel, Steve Wynn was, true to form, already planning an addition to it. However, Encore has since morphed into rather more than a mere addendum: it's another full-scale resort, complete with restaurants, bars and nightclubs. Wynn, after all, can't let himself be outdone by fellow mogul Sheldon Adelson and his neighbouring Palazzo (*see p92*). But in the meantime, Wynn Las Vegas has more than enough diversions to keep visitors busy.

Known as the man who brought Vegas entertainment curbside, Wynn went against his own convention and designed this resort from the inside out. Luxury is everywhere, as you'd expect from a casino that cost somewhere in the region of $2.7 billion. On the far side of the faux mountain (*see p56* **Hidden Heights**), the Lake of Dreams fuses light, water, horticulture and architecture into a multimedia experience. The garden-themed Spa at Wynn houses 45 treatment rooms, a beauty salon and a fitness centre, while the 18-hole golf course (designed by Tom Fazio) is overlooked by 36 fairway villas.

The exclusivity extends to the Wynn Esplanade mall (*see p176*), where you'll find the crème de la crème of high-end fashion designers, including Louis Vuitton, Christian Dior, Oscar de la Renta and Brioni. If you can't fathom the thought of a hire car, there's also Penske Wynn Ferrari Maserati, Nevada's only factory-authorised Ferrari and Maserati dealership. There are several notable works of art hanging in the hotel's common areas.

Accommodation

The large and lavish (naturally) guestrooms offer floor-to-ceiling windows, signature Wynn beds with 320-thread-count European linens, a seating area with a sofa and ottomans, a dining table and chairs, flatscreen LCD TVs, spacious bath areas and bedside drapery controls. The suites set a new Vegas standard: some have their own massage rooms, VIP check-in areas, private pools and dining rooms. Don't even get us started on the villas.

Eating & drinking

Wynn and Encore have a variety of award-winning restaurants, including signature spots such as David Walzog's SW Steakhouse, Tableau, Bartolotta Ristorante di Mare and Encore's ultrasexy new Asian hotspot Andrea's. For more casual Italian-American, try Allegro; Asian bistro Red 8; the poolside Terrace Pointe Café; or the sumptuous Buffet. Parasol Up and Parasol Down (for both, *see p160*), the hotel's lobby bars, offer everything from tea to cocktails.

Entertainment

Erstwhile Cirque du Soleil producer Franco Dragone was called on to design *Le Rêve*, named after the Picasso masterpiece that was initially the inspiration for the hotel itself. It has been continually revamped since opening night, but it still includes the same aerial acrobatics for which Dragone is known. Garth Brooks holds court in occasional close-up shows at the intimate Encore theatre. Wynn has jumped on the DJ bandwagon, with super-seductive nightclubs XS and Surrender, both of which feature plenty of flesh and thumping soundtracks. Tryst, located under a 90ft waterfall, is also a popular spot.

Gambling

As you might expect, the action at Wynn is both sophisticated and decidedly pricey. Blackjack minimums start at $15, with a few single-deck games that pay the reduced 6:5 for naturals; hotel guests can also play 21 poolside at the Cabana Bar. Craps minimums are similar to blackjack. A single-zero roulette wheel is usually open in the high-limit room, though the minimums are high. The slots run the gamut from pennies to a $5,000 machine. Amazingly, Wynn has tried to attract local video-poker players with full-pay machines at higher denominations (very rare), though the schedules change unexpectedly; check the *Las Vegas Advisor* for their comings and goings. The keno lounge is one of the most comfortable in town.

Amenities *Bars (6). Business centre. Concierge. Disabled-adapted rooms. Gym. Internet ($11.95; Wi-Fi in lobby). No-smoking floors. Pool (outdoor). Restaurants (18). Room service. Spa. TV: DVD (suites only)/pay movies.*

Games *Baccarat ($100-$15,000); Big Six; blackjack ($15-$10,000); craps (3x, 4x, 5x; from $10); Let it Ride; mini baccarat ($50-$10,000); pai gow poker; pai gow tiles; poker (26 tables); roulette (single & double zero); three-card poker.*

Moderate

Bally's

3645 Las Vegas Boulevard South, at E Flamingo Road, Las Vegas, NV 89109 (reservations 1-877 603 4390, front desk & casino 967 4111, www.ballyslasvegas.com). Bus Deuce, 202/self-parking & valet parking Las Vegas Boulevard South or E Flamingo Road. **Rooms** 2,814. **Map** p320 A7 ⓫

A classic, Dan Tanna-esque *Vega$* experience can still be had at the grande dame of the Strip's Famous Four Corners. Though now owned by Harrah's, Bally's has stayed true to its Hollywood roots, albeit probably because management simply hasn't got around to renovating yet. The garish eight miles of ostentatious looping neon, part of a multimillion-dollar 'grand entry' that delivers tourists to the hotel's elegant *porte cochère*, is pretty ugly, but Bally's retains its classic appeal inside. Amenities include an oversized, heated pool with private cabanas; eight floodlit tennis courts next to a pro shop, where you can sign up for lessons (it's one of the last hotels on the Strip with tennis courts); a full-service health club; and access to the Caesars-owned Cascata golf course. The Bally Avenue Shops house one-off boutiques.

Accommodation

The good-sized standard rooms are decorated with a West Coast casual elegance of bright velvet couches offset by muted earth tones. Of the 2,814 rooms, 265 are suites: the one- and two-bedroom Grand Suites, each with a huge jetted tub and wet bar, are slightly more contemporary. The 22nd Club offers access to private concierge services, free breakfast and evening cocktails with gorgeous Strip views.

Eating & drinking

The restaurant selection is like the rest of the resort: a throwback to old-school subtlety. Bally's Steakhouse does grilled beef and seafood right; while those looking for an Asian twist can check out Sea:

Bally's.

CONSUME

The Thai Experience or Ichiban Sushi. There are also lots of casual spots for sushi, ice-cream, sandwiches and Italian fast food, plus cocktails at the sport-and-slots bar Sully's and the Mexican-slanted Tequila Bar. Amid this, there is one surprise: Sunday's Sterling Brunch, a spectacular linen-and-champers buffet for which booking is necessary.

Entertainment

For an old-school Vegas show experience, *Jubilee!* is just the ticket: beautiful showgirls reprising world-famous production numbers with lavish sets and spectacular choreography (topless on the late run). A rotating line-up of local acts plays the Indigo Lounge, and Drai's After Hours – after losing its home at Bill's Gamblin' Hall – moved here, marking Bally's foray into the nightclub arena.

Flamingo.

Gambling

The casino is a large, rectangular space, an inviting atmosphere of soft lighting and art deco accents with 65 table games and 2,100 slot machines. Among them are 'champagne' $1,000 slots, with a top payout of a cool mil. Not surprisingly, you'll find all the latest creations from machine-maker Bally, including laser-disc versions of craps, roulette and blackjack; all are excellent practice tools before heading to the actual tables. The buy-ins at the tables start at $10 with an occasional $5 single-deck 6:5 21 game, though many players wager far more than the minimum. The video poker is pretty pitiful, but the sports book, on the lower level, is as classy and technically advanced as those at the Bellagio and the Hilton, and it's only crowded on big-game days.

Amenities *Bars (5). Business centre. Disabled-adapted rooms. Gym. Internet ($10.99). No-smoking floors. Pool (outdoor). Restaurants (12). Room service. Spa. TV: pay movies.*

Games *Baccarat ($100-$15,000); blackjack ($5-$3,000); Caribbean stud; craps (3x, 4x, 5x; from $5); keno; Let it Ride; mini baccarat ($15-$5,000); pai gow poker; pai gow tiles; poker (9 tables); roulette (double zero); three-card poker.*

Flamingo

3555 Las Vegas Boulevard South, at E Flamingo Road, Las Vegas, NV 89109 (reservations 1-888 902 9929, front desk & casino 733 3111, www.flamingolasvegas.com). Bus Deuce, 202/self-parking & valet parking Las Vegas Boulevard South or Audrie Street. **Rooms** 3,626. **Map** p320 A7 ⑫

The Flamingo is the Strip's sleeping giant. Its location at the heart of the action couldn't be better; and thanks to its beginnings under Bugsy Siegel, its name is virtually legendary. But while its competitors at Caesars and the Bellagio across the street are raising their game in an attempt to draw new crowds, the Harrah's-owned Flamingo seems content to coast along in third gear, happy to milk a gradually ageing clientele who apparently aren't interested in what the competition might be able to offer them.

Behind the signature pink neon sign, the resort is huge, with six guestroom towers. Hidden between them is the resort's centrepiece: a lush 15-acre tropical pool area with waterslides, waterfalls and jungle-like foliage enveloping four distinct pools (including Bugsy's oval-shaped original). Also outdoors are four tennis courts and an assortment of wildlife, including (yes) flamingos. So far so good, then, but the interior of the Flamingo is markedly less impressive, wedged some time in the 1980s and unable or unwilling to escape. The new Go guestrooms are a sign that change may be on the horizon, but it's going to be a long and difficult job.

Accommodation

The standard rooms at the Flamingo are smallish, fairly basic and profoundly old-fashioned, despite a

Harrah's.

relatively recent renovation. All of which makes the new Go guestrooms a bit of a surprise. Designed in a more modern style and done out with flatscreen TVs, iPod-friendly hi-fis and wireless access, they're more inviting than you'd expect from either the other rooms or, for that matter, the rest of the resort.

Note that while room rates at all Vegas properties vary from night to night, the differentials at the Flamingo are spectacular even by local standards. Guestrooms can be ridiculously cheap during the week and outrageously expensive at weekends.

Eating & drinking

The gastronomic revolution that's enlivened Vegas vacations over the last decade or so has yet to reach the Flamingo. Aside from a 24-hour coffeeshop and the inevitable buffet, visitors can choose from Mexican (Carlos 'n Charlie's), steaks and seafood (Center Cut Steakhouse), or sushi and shabu-shabu (popular chain Hamada of Japan). None disgrace their surroundings, but when your signature restaurant is Jimmy Buffet's Margaritaville, a theme bar-restaurant decorated in colours loud enough to blind from 50 paces, perhaps a rethink is in order.

Entertainment

Ageless Osmond siblings Donny and Marie seem to have found a home in the Flamingo's showroom for the early show, which is just about the perfect speed for the time-trapped resort. George Wallace (the comedian, not the late segregationist governor of Alabama), a reliably funny man who seems to have found a gig for life, holds down the late slot. The 30-year-old Legends in Concert also recently moved here, for all your ersatz Elvis and bad Britney Spears impersonations. Late at night its theatre is home to burlesque shows.

Gambling

The casino area, though a bit claustrophobic and loud, offers you a real chance to survive: crap and blackjack minimums are a reasonable $5 outside

prime time. The addition of the 15,000sq ft Margaritaville Casino in 2011 helped, though, with 22 additional table games and 220 slots. You'll also find a lively card room, a keno parlour, and a race and sports book.

Amenities *Bars (5). Business centre. Disabled-adapted rooms. Gym. Internet ($10.99, web TV $9.99). No-smoking floors. Pools (outdoor). Restaurants (9). Room service. Spa. TV: pay movies.*

Games *Blackjack ($5-$3,000); Caribbean stud; craps (3x, 4x, 5x; from $5); keno; Let it Ride; mini baccarat ($10-$5,000); pai gow poker; poker (11 tables); roulette (double zero); three-card poker.*

Harrah's

3475 Las Vegas Boulevard South, between Sands Avenue & E Flamingo Road, Las Vegas, NV 89109 (reservations 1-800 214 9110, front desk & casino 369 5000, www.harrahslasvegas.com). Bus Deuce, 202/self-parking & valet parking Koval Lane. **Rooms** 2,667. **Map** p320 A6 ⑱

This middle-of-the-road, middle-of-the-Strip resort might not have the same cachet as many of its neighbours, Caesars Palace and the Venetian among them, but its parent company is one of the most powerful in town. The acquisition in 2005 of the former Imperial Palace (now the Quad), which sits between Harrah's and sibling property the Flamingo, might have been the catalyst for recent change. The 35-year-old resort still plays the tired Mardi Gras theme, but fresh entertainment options, new eateries and just-renovated guestrooms have injected the property with a little spirit.

Accommodation

The guestrooms and suites in Harrah's three towers are comfortable and festive. The standard rooms are on the small side and short on amenities, but many offer decent views on the action on the Strip. Others, however, have minibars, and some have jetted tubs. The deluxe rooms have updated decor and amenities.

Luxor.

Eating & drinking

Although most of the restaurants here are suitable for casual or smart-casual diners, the recent addition of Ruth's Chris Steak House stepped up Harrah's dining game. Rock 'n' roll chef Kerry Simon opened KGB: Kerry's Gourmet Burgers – one of the first 'name' chefs to come to Harrah's. Ming's Table offers a smattering of Asian options, from pad thai to tuna rolls to kung-pao chicken. Your next best bets are the Oyster Bar, the buffet Flavors or the Café at Harrah's.

Entertainment

The musical *Million Dollar Quartet* – which recounts the Sun Records recording session of Elvis, Johnny Cash, Jerry Lee Lewis and Carl Perkins one night in 1956 – features a soundtrack popularised by those artists. The family-friendly afternoon magic show delivered by the hugely likeable Mac King is also popular. The solo comedy *Defending the Caveman* plays at the famous Improv, with other fresh comedians each week. And you can listen to live country music in Toby Keith's I Love This Bar & Grill (*see p159*).

Gambling

Harrah's has a wide selection of table games, including action-packed craps tables and a variety of 21 options. Most blackjack games are dealt from the shoe, but higher limits – at least $25 minimum – are dealt from hand-held decks. Beware the single decks, which have lower limits but pay a measly 6:5 for naturals. Occasionally, gracious pit bosses will bring out the European single-zero roulette wheel for high rollers. For lively action, take a seat in the cosily compact poker room; the race and sports book offers booths and table seating.

Amenities *Bars (7). Business centre. Disabled-adapted rooms. Gym. Internet ($11.95). No-smoking floors. Pool (outdoor). Restaurants (8). Room service. Spa. TV: pay movies.*

Games *Baccarat ($25-$10,000); blackjack ($10-$5,000); craps (3x, 4x, 5x; from $5); keno; Let it Ride; mini baccarat ($15-$5,000); pai gow poker; poker (12 tables); roulette (double zero); three-card poker.*

Luxor

3900 Las Vegas Boulevard South, at W Hacienda Avenue, Las Vegas, NV 89119 (reservations 1-877 386 4658, front desk & casino 262 4102, www.luxor.com). Bus Deuce, 119, 201/self-parking & valet parking Reno Avenue. **Rooms** 4,407.
Map p320 A9 ⑩

Second only to New York New York in terms of the absurdity of its exterior, the Luxor impresses on scale long before you've set foot inside it. While some casinos limit theming to the interiors, leaving the buildings as smart but not altogether memorable towers, the 30-storey glass pyramid housing much of the Luxor makes one hell of a first impression. At night, a high-intensity light shoots skywards from the top; visible in space, it's also a beacon to swarms of insects and bats during warmer months.

The homage to ancient Egypt continues inside, but to a far lesser extent than it did when the casino opened in 1993. The campiest elements of the theming evaporated years ago, but even more Egyptiana was mummified during a renovation that began in 2006. The theming around the pool has been toned down, and most of the hotel's Egyptian-slanted bars and restaurants have gone. Elsewhere the Luxor is diversifying too: the popular human-autopsy show *Bodies* is bringing in, well, bodies, and bars like Savile Row are aimed squarely at younger guests.

Accommodation

Only around half of the hotel's 4,407 guestrooms are actually located in the pyramid. These Strip-fronted rooms offer great views and are accessed by special elevators called 'inclinators', which rise, like enclosed ski lifts, at an angle of 39°. However, there are compensations if you don't get hooked up with a pyramid room: the guestrooms in the towers, just behind the pyramid, are larger.

Eating & drinking

The eating options here are best described as reliable. Tender Steak & Seafood and More the Buffet both have good reputations and are probably the best bets in the casino. Also making a name for itself is T&T (Tacos & Tequila), while Public House is a good place to put some late-chow on top of that alcohol. Elsewhere, the Backstage Deli apes New York Jewish food as only a casino in Nevada can, while Rice & Company offers dinner, sushi, drinks and dessert.

Entertainment

Masked hip hop troupe Jabbawockeez recently moved into a newly built theatre here, with their show *Prism*. Prop comic Carrot Top also headlines, along with magician Criss Angel's show, *Believe*, produced in partnership with Cirque du Soleil. The underdressed dancers of the *Fantasy* revue (*see p98*) provide late-night entertainment, or you can go the other way and see *Menopause the Musical*. Überhip Los Angeles club LAX also has an outpost inside the casino.

Gambling

The massive casino, decorated with hieroglyphics and 'ancient' artefacts, is filled with the latest high-tech slot and video-poker machines. Expect $10 minimums at blackjack and craps, higher on weekends. For poker players, the card room offers weekend action so lively that Cleopatra herself would have been impressed. Take a few minutes to walk the perimeter of the circular casino and get your bearings; if you can't identify landmarks, you'll wind up going in circles.
Amenities *Bars (3). Business centre. Concierge. Disabled-adapted rooms. Gym. Internet (Wi-Fi*
$11.99). No-smoking floors. Pool (outdoor). Restaurants (6). Room service. Spa. TV: pay movies.
Games *Blackjack ($10-$10,000); craps (3x, 4x, 5x; from $5); keno; Let it Ride; mini baccarat ($15-$5,000); poker (10 tables); roulette (double zero); three-card poker. Gambling lessons (blackjack, craps, roulette noon daily).*

Monte Carlo

3770 Las Vegas Boulevard South, between W Harmon & W Tropicana avenues, Las Vegas, NV 89109 (reservations 1-888 529 4828, front desk & casino 730 7777, www.montecarlo.com). Bus Deuce, 201/self-parking & valet parking Rue de Monte Carlo. **Rooms** 2,992. **Map** p320 A8 ⑮

Modelled after the Place du Casino in (of course) Monte Carlo, this handsome but low-key resort is an appealing mid-range option. The many attractive features, including its tasteful exterior architecture, is on course to get much better as a new plaza fronting the Strip is now under construction connecting the Monte Carlo and sister property New York New York. And while it could seem that this $344-million resort might be on the same page as, say, the $1.6-billion Bellagio, the truth is that it appeals to those after an approximation of high style at low prices.

Next to its neighbours, the Monte Carlo may not stand out, but that may change with the addition of a joint arena behind the Monte Carlo and NYNY. Construction of the 20,000-capacity venue is scheduled to be complete in 2016. Meanwhile, Monte Carlo's lack of flash and filigree is just what its admirers like about the hotel. The casino floor is about as mellow as they come, thanks to the bright lighting and high ceilings, and the rooms are simple and familiar. Elsewhere, however, the Monte Carlo is on the move. In the entertainment department, recently adding the Blue Man Group (*see p204*) – one of the best performances in Las Vegas.

Monte Carlo.

CONSUME

Accommodation

The Monte Carlo's tri-tower set-up contains 2,992 rooms, including 224 suites. The standard rooms are comfortable, with vaguely old-world feel, and conservative in style. Suites include Italian marble baths and plenty of room to stretch out. The decor gets progressively more opulent the further up the price scale you climb; if you've got the change, spring for a room in Hotel 32, the property's boutique option.

Eating & drinking

The Monte Carlo's signature eaterie is André's, the sole Strip location of André Rochat's venerable former Downtown establishment. The 5,000sq ft Brand Steakhouse has been making a name for itself (serving a 120oz slab of meat intended for six people has helped), and Diablo's Cantina is an excellent choice for Mexican and speciality drinks like the Twisted Sister (served by the pitcher – buyer beware). D.Vino is upscale and elegant Italian, and those looking for something more laid-back can visit Dragon Noodle, the Pub, or, of course, the buffet.

Entertainment

Once a place you stayed at and went elsewhere to see shows, the Monte Carlo and its neighbour to the north, New York New York, are creating venues guests at other hotels come to. For the Monte Carlo, the reason is Blue Man Group, which moved here with a revamped show in 2012. One of the liveliest and most interactive shows on the Strip, Blue Man is guaranteed to have you on your feet by the end of its performance. The Ignite Lounge is a good place to sit back and watch Blue Man's pre-show procession, to say nothing of the sexy (female) dancers atop the platforms in the Party Pit. Hop across the way to Minus5 Ice Lounge if you're getting overheated.

Gambling

There are plenty of $5 blackjack tables, many 5¢ opportunities among the 2,200 slots, and a bright, casual atmosphere. Players appreciate the details: stools with backs at every machine, wide walkways throughout the casino and even single-zero roulette. The Monte Carlo attracts brisk traffic from neighbouring casinos, but the tables never seem crowded. Players stand a better chance of landing a one-on-one blackjack game with the dealer than at most Strip resorts.

Amenities Bars (11). Business centre. Concierge. Disabled-adapted rooms. Gym. Internet ($11.99). No-smoking floors. Pool (outdoor). Restaurants (9). Room service. Spa.

Games Baccarat ($25-$15,000); blackjack ($5-$3,000); craps (3x, 4x, 5x; from $5); Crazy 4 poker; keno; Let it Ride; mini baccarat ($10-$5,000); pai gow poker; poker (8 tables); roulette (double zero); three-card poker. Gambling lessons (craps 11am daily).

New York New York

3790 Las Vegas Boulevard South, at W Tropicana Avenue, Las Vegas, NV 89109 (reservations 1-866 815 4365, front desk & casino 740 6969, www.newyorknewyork.com). Bus Deuce, 201/self-parking Las Vegas Boulevard South or W Tropicana Avenue/ valet parking W Tropicana Avenue. **Rooms** 2,024. **Map** p320 A8 ⑯

So good they named it twice? Well, yes, as it goes. The most audacious, preposterous example of hotel theming in Las Vegas – and, for that matter, perhaps even the world – remains a thrilling success more than 15 years after it welcomed its first guests. Built at a cost of $485 million, it's been called the largest piece of pop art in the world.

A mini-New York Harbor, complete with tugboats, a scaled-down Brooklyn Bridge and a giant Statue of Liberty, loom over the Tropicana/Strip intersection. Above it, the resort's skyline includes a dozen of the Big Apple's most famous landmarks, among them the Empire State Building, the Chrysler Building and the New Yorker Hotel but not the World Trade Center; the hotel was themed after 1950s New York, long before the twin towers were built. Inside, along with representations of Times Square, Central Park, Greenwich Village and Wall Street, you'll find every New York cliché in the book: a Broadway subway station, graffitied mailboxes, steam rising from manhole covers... It sounds silly, but it's tremendous fun, and seems to inspire visitors to act as if they were out on the East Coast: it has energy like no other casino floor in town.

The resort's greatest trick, one that New York City has yet to achieve, is to balance the needs of adult visitors with those of its younger guests. Grown-ups will enjoy the nightlife here, not to mention Cirque du Soleil's adult-oriented show *Zumanity* (*see p197*), but there's plenty for the young 'uns. The Coney Island Emporium (*see p50*) is nirvana for kids and wannabe-kids-again, a mix of old-fashioned midway games, high-tech interactive videos and virtual-reality rollercoasters. The hotel's real rollercoaster, the Roller Coaster (*see p51*), twists, turns and rolls around and above the property. The pool and spa are, alas, real let downs: a replica of the famous Vertical Club would have been fitting or, perhaps, the Central Park Reservoir.

Accommodation

NYNY's rooms are concealed behind (but not in) an assortment of towers and skyscrapers. The rooms are done fairly nicely, in art deco-styled woods with black accents, and are maintained to a high standard. Although they're pretty small, they're bargains in comparison to some of their Strip competitors, especially during the week. Check when you make your booking that the Manhattan Express doesn't rumble by your window, or you'll be continually disturbed by the squeals of riders.

New York New York.

Eating & drinking

The restaurants aren't matches for those in the city on which they're modelled. But if they lack subtlety (and they do), they're at least a vibrant bunch. The smartest by far is Gallagher's Steakhouse, a Big Apple import; there's also competent Italian at Il Fornaio; reasonable Mexican at Gonzalez y Gonzalez; and serviceable Chinese at Chin-Chin. Nine Fine Irishmen is a rather hokey but locally popular Irish pub, while Coyote Ugly is a happening – if clichéd – drinking hole. A food court fashioned after Greenwich Village (cobblestone streets, a subway station, apartment buildings) contains burgers, pizzas and fried fish, though no knishes. However, the best eating option is the most straightforward: America, a 24-hour diner that delivers average-to-excellent renditions of dishes from all over the 50 states.

Entertainment

NYNY's leading show is Cirque du Soleil's *Zumanity*, an intriguing but only partly successful attempt at mixing Cirque's ever-dazzling acrobatics with the sexiness of the Strip-standard adult revue. Duelling piano players lead boozy sing-alongathons all night, every night at the Bar at Times Square; while Pour 24 is named for the number of beers on tap, not to mention the hours that it's open.

Gambling

The capacious casino is modelled on Central Park, without the muggers but with twice the crowds. Minimums for blackjack (practically all six-deck shoes) and craps are $10; it's $5 for roulette. The range of slots is one of the best on the Strip. Dim sum hors d'oeuvres are served in the Asian-styled Dragon Pit, with saké, plum wine, Asian beer and teas.

Amenities *Bars (8). Business centre. Concierge. Disabled-adapted rooms. Gym. Internet ($11.99). No-smoking floors. Pool (outdoor). Restaurants (11). Room service. Spa.*
Games *Blackjack ($5-$5,000); Big Six; craps (3x, 4x, 5x; from $10); Crazy 4 poker; Let it Ride; mini baccarat ($10-$5,000); roulette (double zero); Texas hold'em bonus; three-card poker.*

Planet Hollywood

3667 Las Vegas Boulevard South, between E Harmon Avenue & E Flamingo Road, Las Vegas, NV 89109 (reservations 1-866 919 7472, front desk & casino 785 5555, www. planethollywoodresort.com). Bus Deuce, 202/ self-parking & valet parking E Harmon Avenue.
Rooms 2,600. **Map** p320 A7 ⓐ

The Aladdin rubbed its magic lamp for the last time in spring 2007 and out popped Planet Hollywood, a hipper casino version of the restaurant chain. Amenities include the Planet Hollywood Spa by Mandara, which promises to ready guests for their 15 minutes of fame; the adjacent Miracle Mile Shops (*see p175*), a vast galleria of stores – some familiar and some less so; eateries/watering holes (erstwhile rocker Sammy Hagar's Cabo Wabo; PBR Rock Bar); and a modernised theatre. *Photo p102.*

Accommodation

Planet Hollywood's 2,600 movie-themed rooms and suites are done out in what is known as 'Hollywood hip' decor: contemporary shades of rich chocolate and royal purple, Googie-esque carpets and amenities such as high-definition plasma TVs. Overall, the rooms are spacious and well kept, with most providing nice views of the Strip (to the West) or the Mountains (to the east).

CONSUME

CONSUME

Planet Hollywood. *See p101.*

Eating & drinking

The dining scene features a serviceable if not entirely imaginative line-up, including the Japanese-Californian fusion cuisine of Koi, already a haven for Hollywood's A-list; Yolos, a Mexican eaterie complete with margarita fountain; and the Glazier family's Strip House, a sexy steakhouse that's anything but traditional. Smaller bites are served at the Earl of Sandwich, Pink's is famous for its hot dogs; P.F. Chang's is, well, P.F. Chang's – modern Chinese for diners who don't want to think too hard – and Planet Dailies is a high-energy coffeeshop. Gordon Ramsay BurGR has become the go-to place for meat; and the Spice Market Buffet is still one of the best in town.

Entertainment

It's adults-only with *Peepshow*, that old Vegas staple, the topless review. Renowned hypnotist Marshall Sylver recently returned to the showroom for an extended stay; and Sin City Comedy hosts an ever-changing line-up of fresh, new jokers. Planet Hollywood comes alive at a number of clubs after dark. The Gallery Nightclub is popular if overpriced, and TV correspondents from gossip-news show *Extra* mix and mingle with celebrities and regular folk in the Extra Lounge. Britney Spears is rumoured to be starting a two-year residency at PH soon too.

Gambling

In previous years Planet Hollywood's casino underwent a number of renovations. It seems to have finally hit a groove, and its race and sports book is one of the most comfortable around, with 33 plasma TVs and a VIP lounge.

Amenities *Bars (5). Business centre. Concierge. Disabled-adapted rooms. Gym. Internet (Wi-Fi $11.99). No-smoking floors. Pool (outdoor). Restaurants (9). Room service. Spa. TV: pay movies*
Games *Baccarat ($100-$15,000); blackjack ($5-$3,000); craps (3x, 4x, 5x; from $5); keno; Let it Ride; mini baccarat ($25-$5,000); pai gow poker; poker (11 tables); roulette (double zero).*

Quad

3535 Las Vegas Boulevard South, between Sands Avenue & E Flamingo Road, Las Vegas, NV 89109 (reservations 1-800 351 7400, front desk & casino 794 3311, www.thequadlv.com). Bus Deuce, 119, 202, 203/self-parking & valet parking Las Vegas Boulevard South. **Rooms** *2,640.* **Map** *p320 A6* **⑬**
The name might not ring a bell, but the Quad is anything but a newcomer. Formerly the Imperial Palace, it's the latest on the Strip to receive a major update and rebranding. After Harrah's purchased the Imperial Palace in 2005, speculation was rife as to what would become of it – sandwiched as it is between its new owner's eponymous casino-hotel and the Flamingo (also owned by Harrah's). The property, which will abut Caesars Entertainment's still-under-construction open-air mall the Linq, is poised to become a hot destination.

Although many of the familiar attractions from the Imperial Palace remain, including the popular Auto Collection (*see p54*) and – amazingly – Frank Marino's well-past-its-prime show *Divas*, it's hard not to imagine that when the Linq opens the Quad, given its location, won't aim for a hipper, more urbane crowd.

Accommodation

The IP's guestrooms were small – some very small – and the Quad's will remain so. Still, the prices are often incredibly affordable, particularly during the middle of the week, making the Quad an especially good bet if you don't plan to spend too much time in your room. If you need to stretch out, you'll probably want to invest in one of the suites.

Eating & drinking

Changes are afoot when it comes to dining. While the options are limited, they're improving, though all remain strictly on the casual side. Locals' favourite Hash House A Go Go (billed as 'twisted farm food') opened an outpost here, and Ginseng 3 features Korean-Japanese-Chinese fusion. Quesadilla's menu is no surprise, nor is the Emperor's Buffet. But perhaps the most eagerly awaited arrival is celebrity chef Guy Fieri's yet-to-be-named restaurant, which will sit at the front of the Quad.

Entertainment

America's Got Talent alums Recycled Percussion make for a family-friendly show, and for reasons unknown, the aforementioned *Divas* still plays nightly. Juggler and physical comedian Jeff Civillico works the showroom by day, but one can't help think the Quad is just biding its time with this roster of acts.

Gambling

This part of the Strip is always packed, and so is the Quad's casino. Recent renovations have provided a much-needed revamp to IP's former down-on-its-luck appearance. More work will follow, eventually increasing the casino to 65,000sq ft. For now, traffic may be a little stunted due to all the construction outside. Rest assured, that will change, as this end of the Strip increasingly tries to improve its odds among a younger clientele.

Amenities *Bars (1). Business centre. Concierge. Disabled-adapted rooms. Gym. Internet (Wi-Fi $9.99). No-smoking floors. Pool (outdoor). Restaurants (6). Room service. Spa. TV: pay movies.*
Games *Big Six; blackjack ($10-$500); craps (3x, 4x, 5x; from $3); keno; Let it Ride; pai gow poker; poker (5 tables); roulette (double zero); Texas hold 'em bonus; three-card poker.*

Lavish Loos

When you've got to go… you might as well go in luxury.

When nature calls, you have to answer. But in Vegas, where they've extended extravagance to even the humblest of rooms, you can choose to go in style. If you opt for the fantasy facilities at certain hotel-casinos and nightclubs, it may be the best part of your night.

The chandelier-lit ladies' room at Vanity nightclub at the **Hard Rock Hotel & Casino** (*see p112*) stuns with sheer scale – at 2,000 square feet, it's more lounge than loo. Instead of sharing a mirror, patrons can preen at individual vanity tables. Of course there are attendants to touch up hair and makeup and even fetch pricey cocktails – you could end up spending the whole evening here.

Men are not left out of the fun of the lavish lav. Decked out with faux-snakeskin wallpaper, the men's room at Vanity sports TV monitors mounted over the urinals; at the Mix Lounge at **Thehotel at Mandalay Bay** (*see p110*), a strip of windows runs above the urinals, so gents can take in the view as they're relieving themselves, while women can sit and monitor action on the

Strip out of the floor-to-ceiling windows in their stalls. In addition to the many flatscreens hung on the walls in the bar, TVs are even built into the stalls of both the men's and women's restrooms at the Sporting House Bar & Grill at **New York New York** (*see p100*), so fans won't miss a play. And for guys at **Main Street Station** (*see p122*), the urinals are embedded in a graffiti-covered segment of the actual Berlin Wall, while the elegant women's room at Flirt Lounge in the **Rio** (*see p115*) – the post-Chippendales show gathering spot – sports purple on purple on purple couches and curtains, and is nicknamed the Gossip Pit.

None of these can match the over-the-top opulence you'll find in many of the hotel room WCs throughout Vegas, however. Bathrooms at the **Palazzo** (*see p92*) are large enough to host a small party; while the light-and-dark marble design of those at **Mandarin Oriental** (*see p110*) include a deep standalone tub. Even the bathrooms at Downtown's **Golden Nugget** (*see p121*) get in on the act, with wood and marble decor and countertop TVs.

CONSUME

TI (Treasure Island)

3300 Las Vegas Boulevard South, at Spring Mountain Road, Las Vegas, NV 89109 (reservations 1-800 288 7206, front desk & casino 894 7111, www.treasureisland.com). Bus Deuce, 203/self-parking & valet parking Las Vegas Boulevard South or Spring Mountain Road. **Rooms** 2,885. **Map** p320 A6 ⑲

Once an object lesson in what happens when you slavishly follow focus groups rather than your own commercial instincts, Treasure Island struggled with an identity crisis for years: 'We're Pirates of the Caribbean! No, we're Robinson Crusoe! We're for families! No, adults!' And while it would have been difficult to jettison the entire pirate theme without a complete makeover, rebranding the campy water battle with scantily clad women and a less-than-child-friendly name – *Sirens of TI* – has underscored Treasure Island's intention to play to a more adult market.

On many levels it seems to be working. Weekend nights bring in a decidedly twentysomething crowd, and the new line-up of restaurants is worlds better than what went before. For those who think not of gimlets but of golf when they hear the word 'club', the hotel offers package deals to the Bear's Best course, designed by Jack Nicklaus. The pool is a good one, and surprisingly unheralded in the city. And though TI has little shopping on its own property, a pedestrian bridge provides easy access to the adjacent Fashion Show Mall (*see p177*).

Accommodation

The 2,885 rooms in TI's 36-storey Y-shaped tower are good enough for the price, decorated in appealing shades and without any undue ornamentation. Many have decent views of the Mirage volcano and the *Sirens* show below. The 220 suites are spacious, with living rooms, wet bars, two baths, jacuzzis and impressive TVs; they're a good deal if you feel like splashing out but not breaking the bank.

Eating & drinking

One does not stay at TI for the fine dining options, of which there are few. Phil's Italian Steakhouse is by far the classiest, but its not a destination eaterie. The Seafood Shack offers fresh catches of the day, but beyond that the fare is pedestrian at best. Senor Frog's and Gilley's BBQ draw raucous crowds, but they're not there for the food specifically. The Coffee Shop & Pho Vietnamese is one of the places on the Strip focusing strictly on Vietnamese cuisine, but for a quick, gut-busting meal you might just wanna grab an oversized hot dog from Little Richie's.

Entertainment

Twenty years after Cirque du Soleil's Las Vegas debut, its flagship production *Mystère* is still good G-rated fun, even if the rest of TI is less so. In addition to the aforementioned *Sirens of TI*, the hotel still manages to attract an impressive roster of comedians, including notables like Bill Cosby and rising stars such as Whitney Cummings. As far as nightclubs and hip 'n' happening scenes go… well, forget about that at TI. Yes, Senor Frog's is packed on Saturday nights and a different crowd altogether frequents Gilley's, but here you can leave your pretensions at home (or in your hotel room).

Gambling

In the ever-crowded casino, you'll find all the usual games, as well as a race and sports book, but you're the one who's likely to be on the down side. Here, as at the Mirage, table limits are high and six-deck shoes are the rule, but you can still find a few video-poker machines here with good payback percentages.

Amenities *Bars (5). Business centre. Concierge. Disabled-adapted rooms. Gym. Internet (Wi-Fi $11.99). No-smoking floors. Pool (outdoor). Restaurants (11). Room service. Spa.*
Games *Baccarat ($100-$15,000); Big Six; blackjack ($5-$15,000); casino war; craps (3x, 4x, 5x; from $5); keno; Let it Ride; mini baccarat ($25-$10,000); pai gow poker; pai gow tiles; poker (7 tables); roulette (single and double zero); three-card poker.*

★ Tropicana

3801 Las Vegas Boulevard South, at E Tropicana Avenue, Las Vegas, NV 89109 (reservations 1-800 462 8767, front desk & casino 739 2222, www.troplv.com). Bus Deuce, 201/self-parking & valet parking Las Vegas Boulevard South, E Tropicana Avenue or Reno Avenue. **Rooms** 1,600. **Map** p320 A8 ⑳

Recently renovated, with a fresh, South Beach Miami-themed look and feel, the Tropicana was at the heart of the biggest bidding war in casino history when, in 2006, Columbia Sussex (owner of various Westin, Sheraton and Marriott hotels) paid $2.75 billion for the rights to redevelop the 50-year-old 'Tiffany of the Strip'. Problems continued for the property over the next several years until a court put the matter to rest. In 2012, the Trop partnered with DoubleTree Hilton for a complete $200 million overhaul. It's been worth the wait. Long-time fans of the venerable hotel-casino might not recognise it, but newcomers will be pleasantly surprised by the upgrade.

Accommodation

The standard Club Deluxe rooms aren't especially large, but the remodelling has rendered them modern and comfortable. Plus, they have views of the Trop's gorgeous pool. All the rooms now have a chic, sleek feel, with amenities that include wireless internet connects, 42in TVs, iPod/MP3 docking stations and in-room safes.

Eating & drinking

Biscayne Steak, Sea & Wine, a reinterpretation of the classic Las Vegas steakhouse, serves up a colossal shrimp cocktail and tasty prime rib. Other choices include Bacio for classic Italian cuisine, the Beach Café and the South Beach Food Court, with a Starbucks outpost.

Entertainment

The Tropicana hosts a rather eclectic range of diversions. The Laugh Factory is a reputable comedy venue, with two shows daily, while various live performers rotate through the Tropicana Lounge. But two new options are generating the biggest buzz: the first is Mob Attraction (*see p51*), an interactive 3D experience chronicling Las Vegas's organised-crime history. The other is the brand-new Bagatelle Beach, a Mediterranean-style pool and day club, adjacent to the Trop. Bagatelle features two (smallish) pools, white-sand beaches, cabanas and volleyball/soccer playing areas.

Gambling

The recent renovations expanded the casino to 50,000sq ft – a welcome addition that includes a new high-limit area and a significantly larger race and sports book. Thankfully, they didn't get rid of the swim-up blackjack.

Amenities *Bars (3). Business centre. Disabled-adapted rooms. Gym. Internet. No-smoking floors. Pool (indoor/outdoor). Restaurants (4). Room service. Spa. TV: pay movies.*
Games *Big Six; blackjack ($5-$3,000); craps (3x, 4x, 5x; from $5); keno; Let it Ride; pai gow poker; poker (6 tables); roulette (double zero); three-card poker.*

Budget

Casino Royale

3411 Las Vegas Boulevard South, between Sands Avenue & E Flamingo Road, Las Vegas, NV 89109 (reservations 1-800 854 7666, front desk & casino 737 3500, www.casinoroyalehotel.com). Bus Deuce, 202, 203/self-parking Las Vegas Boulevard South/no valet parking. **Rooms** 152.
Map p320 A6 ㉑

Virtually the forgotten resort on the Strip, this independently operated, 152-room casino has nothing to do with the James Bond movie of the same name. Rather, it's a truly basic little casino-hotel that survives despite being surrounded by the city's major players. Favoured by budget travellers after cheap minimums and even cheaper drinks, it's a cheery place without much charisma but with plenty of value – and a great location.

Accommodation

As you might expect from the cut-price room rates, the rooms here aren't anything special: they're basically motel-standard, though the handy mid-Strip location goes some way to make up for the lack of facilities.

Eating & drinking

The Outback Steakhouse and Denny's are the closest things to signature restaurants here. The most notable feature of the bar is the dollar beers it offers around the clock, and a Fat Tuesday's recently opened on the premises. There's also a food court with Subway, a pizza joint and a hot-dog place. Finish your meal with a sweet stop at Ben & Jerry's.

CONSUME

Tropicana.

CONSUME

Entertainment

You'll have to make your own here.

Gambling

There's not much to say about this place, though the minimums are low and it's the only casino on the Strip to offer 100x odds for craps, reducing the house edge to a mere 0.02%.

Amenities *Bars (2). Business centre. Disabled-adapted rooms. No-smoking floors. Pool (outdoor). Restaurants (3).*

Games *Blackjack ($5-$1,000); craps (20x; from $3); keno; roulette (double zero); three-card poker.*

Circus Circus

2880 Las Vegas Boulevard South, between Desert Inn Road & W Sahara Avenue, Las Vegas, NV 89109 (reservations 1-877 434 9175, front desk & casino 734 0410, www.circuscircus.com). Bus Deuce, 108/self-parking S Industrial Road/valet parking Las Vegas Boulevard South or S Industrial Road. **Rooms** 3,767. **Map** p319 B5 ㉒

When MGM Mirage purchased additional plots of land bordering Circus Circus, many in town muttered that it must be just a matter of time before Lucky the Laughing Clown was asked to fold up his Big Top and beat it. After all, he's been luring tourists into this garish casino for more than 40 years – a lifetime by Vegas standards – and not much has changed. Sure, MGM Mirage could ask performers from Cirque du Soleil to perform on the stage above the casino, and the carnie-style area that hosts the daily circus performers could be transformed into a futuristic arcade. But then there's a risk that the place would end up unrecognisable from its famous turn in *Fear and Loathing in Las Vegas*, and who wants that?

Accommodation

After several expansions, there are now 3,767 remodelled rooms, recently redone in earthier colours – a welcome update to the garishness that distinguished them previously. While not huge, the standard rooms are decent sized, and Wi-Fi and plasma TVs are now part of the package. Ask for a south-facing room in the Skyrise Tower for the best view of the Strip. Other amenities include pools and the 399-space Circusland RV Park.

Eating & drinking

Given Circus Circus's somewhat out-of-the-way location, it's not easy to hop across the street to another property. Thankfully, the Steak House (*see p146*) is a surprisingly high-quality dining room (winning Zagat's award for Las Vegas's top steak house in 2011). As far as upscale eateries go, that's about it. But Blue Iguana Mexican Express isn't bad for a quick bite, and Rock & Rita's offers a tasty take on American favourites at prices that can't be beaten. The Circus Buffet is mediocre, but its cheapness ensures its popularity.

Entertainment

Circus Circus never had a showroom; it no longer even has the G-string-clad pony girls, who used to ride plastic ponies on a ceiling-hung track, tossing balloons at the kiddies. But the midway and circus acts remain: acrobats, trapeze artists and magicians perform every half-hour (11am-midnight). The 19 rides and attractions at the Adventuredome (*see p57*) include Nickelodeon's Spongebob SquarePants 4-D thrill ride, a rollercoaster, a carousel and hot-air balloons. For Halloween, the Adventuredome turns into a mega-haunted house for the month of October.

Gambling

Connected by walkways and a monorail, three of the casinos offer the same gaming options, while a fourth is devoted to slots. The race book is located near the back of the resort, in the Skyways Tower area. A five-dollar bill is enough to get you started at most tables; it might take all day to find someone risking more than $10.

Amenities *Bars (5). Business centre. Disabled-adapted rooms. Gym. No-smoking floors. Pool (outdoor). Restaurants (8). Spa.*

Games *Blackjack ($3-$3,000); craps (2x; from $3); keno; Let it Ride; poker (5 tables); roulette (double zero). Gambling lessons (blackjack, craps, poker, roulette 10.30am Mon-Fri).*

Excalibur

3850 Las Vegas Boulevard South, at W Tropicana Avenue, Las Vegas, NV 89109 (reservations 1-877 750 5464, front desk & casino 597 7777, www.excalibur.com). Bus Deuce, 201/self-parking & valet parking W Tropicana Avenue. **Rooms** 3,991. **Map** p320 A8 ㉓

The jury's still out on whether or not this caricature of a castle will become the next generation's Circus Circus. MGM Mirage has been busy transforming the Polynesian-tilted Mirage (*see p90*) into a hipper version of its former self, leaving Excalibur on its own. However, there have been a few changes of note, in particular the addition of dining and entertainment options that eschew the family-friendly theme: the silly Dick's Last Resort restaurant, a music revue by the Australian Bee Gees and a male strip show (also from Australia. Go figure). Identity crisis, anyone? *Photo p108.*

Accommodation

Housed in two towers behind the castle façade, the small rooms have none of the elegance of the hotel's adjacent sister resorts, the Luxor and Mandalay Bay. But a handful of spacious Parlor Suites have guest bathrooms, dining and living areas; with bold colours, dark wood furniture and wrought-iron fixtures, your surroundings could be worse.

Eating & drinking

The pickings are slim here. While the Steakhouse at Camelot serves decent cuts at a wallet-friendly price,

Circus Circus.

that's about as good as it gets. Buca di Beppo offers serviceable Italian, and at biker-themed Octane, bartenders serve up such cocktails as Blood, Sweat & Gears and Tailpipe Wind. Dick's Last Resort is a playfully tacky watering hole that serves massive cocktails and finger foods by the bucket. There's also the requisite buffet and a food court.

Entertainment
The medieval (and still child-friendly) orientation extends into the night with the entertaining *Tournament of Kings*, which features jousting, pyrotechnics and a surprisingly decent dinner. The Fun Dungeon keeps children busy with midway games and an arcade. The hilarious male revue *Thunder from Down Under* provides adult-oriented fare, while the Australian Bee Gees are still – somehow – 'Stayin' Alive'.

Gambling
Neon knights slay neon dragons in the casino, one of the few in town where photography is allowed. Visitors are surrounded by images of playing-card kings and queens, but the table games are affordable for any commoner. Thousands of slots jam the joint; video poker is scarcer. When you're done throwing coins in machines, toss a few in the moat for good luck: they'll be donated to local charities.
Amenities *Bars (4). Disabled-adapted rooms. Gym. Internet ($10.95). No-smoking floors. Pool (outdoor). Restaurants (6). Spa.*
Games *Big Six; blackjack ($5-$2,000); craps (3x, 4x, 5x; from $5); Crazy 4 Poker; keno; Let it Ride; poker (10 tables); roulette (double zero); Texas Hold 'em bonus; three-card poker.*

Hooters
115 E Tropicana Avenue, between Las Vegas Boulevard South & Koval Lane, Las Vegas, NV 89109 (reservations 1-866 584 6687, front desk & casino 739 9000, www.hooterscasinohotel.com). Bus Deuce, 201/self-parking & valet parking E Tropicana Avenue. **Rooms** 696. **Map** p320 B6 ㉔
How does the hotel version of Hooters differ from the restaurants familiar across middle America? Simple: instead of a handful of hot female service-industry workers in skimpy orange outfits, here there are dozens (200, if you're counting). At the bar, at the blackjack table, by the pool… even at the hotel's very own Hooters restaurant. If you (or your spouse) don't appreciate this amenity, stay somewhere else.

Accommodation
There are 696 rooms (including 17 suites); the standard ones are comfortable and the hotel recently began renovating all of them. The two tropical-themed pools are inviting (cabanas too!) and open around the clock.

Eating & drinking
Cuisine here begins and ends with chicken wings at its eponymous restaurant, of course, but in between are a couple of fun surprises. Pete & Shorty's offers real Midwestern man cuisine (aka bar food), and the Mad Onion has 'upscale' dining and downscale prices. You can also grab something to go at the Bait Shoppe.

Entertainment
Hooters has recently reconfigured its nighttime line-up, bringing in the Prince tribute Purple Reign. Kevin Lepine's adult-themed hypnosis show, Unleashed, also plays nightly.

Gambling
Hooters has struggled since it opened, which either explains or is a direct result of its tight casino (perhaps both). The blackjack has terrible rules: dealer

CONSUME

hits soft 17, you can only double on 10 and 11, and all games pay 6:5 for naturals. Most tables have $10 or $25 minimums and some, mostly the ones in the Hooters Girls Fun Pit, are dealt by you know who. Beware of some of the video-poker schedules: they look typical, but some of the payouts are short. Craps isn't bad, with 3-5x odds and a field 12 paying triple. The players club returns a decent 1% for slot play and 0.5% for video poker, but only in comps: there's no cashback.

Amenities *Bars (3). Concierge. Disabled-adapted rooms. Gym. Internet ($12.95). No-smoking floors. Pools (outdoor). Restaurants (5). Room service. Spa. TV: pay movies.*

Games *Blackjack ($10-$2,000); craps (3x, 4x, 5x; from $10); keno; Let it Ride; pai gow poker; poker (3 tables); roulette (double zero); three-card poker.*

Riviera

2901 Las Vegas Boulevard South, between E Sahara Avenue & E Desert Inn Road, Las Vegas, NV 89109 (reservations 1-855 468 6748, front desk & casino 734 5110, www.rivierahotel.com). Bus Deuce, 108, 203/self-parking Riviera Boulevard or Paradise Road/valet parking Las Vegas Boulevard South. **Rooms** 2,100. **Map** p319 B5 ㉕

When the Riviera opened in 1955, Liberace headlined in its showroom. Though the original king of bling is long gone, the entertainment offerings at the Riv more than half a century later are just as camp. The first high-rise hotel on the Strip continues to thumb its nose at family-style entertainment, staying true to its roots as an adult playground. Other throwbacks include two tennis courts, an old-school pool (surrounded by hotel towers for too much shade) and guestrooms that haven't been dramatically upgraded for years. Still, there remains a market for this sort of hotel: unrepentantly old-fashioned, basic and – key to the entire operation's continued viability – cheap.

Accommodation

There are 2,100 rooms on five levels, two floors being all suites. The standard rooms are all in the original tower, while the deluxe rooms (better views) and suites are in the two newer towers. The newer tower rooms are smallish but not cramped, and decorated with dark wood furniture. Half the rooms have views over the pool; the rest face the surrounding mountains. Don't expect much in the way of luxury, though recent renovations have made some improvements.

Eating & drinking

As at most middlebrow resorts, the attraction here isn't the food. There's R Steak & Seafood, a buffet, a café and a food court. And Queen Victoria Pub has lots of beers and burgers. Hey, at least you won't starve.

Excalibur. *See p106.*

Entertainment

The Riv's signature show, the topless fandango *Crazy Girls*, has been in residence five minutes short of forever (well, more than 25 years). Jan Rouven's magic show, Illusions, has been positively received, while the Riviera Comedy Club features new comedians every week.

Gambling

The gaming area is an L-shaped expanse of red and mock gold with an elevated lounge and bar in the centre (your best bet for a meeting place that everyone can find). Minimums at the tables are not as low as the surroundings would suggest: $5-$10 blackjack in a $2 setting. The lowest limits and nickel slots are found in a part of the casino dubbed Nickel Town, a plausible nickname for the whole resort.

Amenities *Bars (2). Business centre. Disabled-adapted rooms. Gym. Internet (Wi-Fi $9.99). No-smoking floors. Pool (outdoor). Restaurants (4). Room service. Spa. TV: pay movies.*

Games *Blackjack ($5-$2,000); craps (3x, 4x, 5x; from $5); keno; Let it Ride; mini baccarat ($25-$2,000); pai gow poker; poker (6 tables); roulette (double zero); three-card poker.*

★ Stratosphere

2000 Las Vegas Boulevard South, at W St Louis Avenue, Las Vegas, NV 89104 (reservations 1-800 998 6937, front desk & casino 380 7777, www.stratospherehotel.com). Bus Deuce, 108/self-parking & valet parking Las Vegas Boulevard South. **Rooms** 2,444. **Map** p319 C4 ㉖

The Stratosphere strives to be a destination resort out of necessity: it's between the Strip and Fremont Street, essentially no-man's land. Its lure starts at its summit, with a variety of rides atop the highest freestanding observation tower in the US (1,149ft). There are indoor and outdoor observation decks, a revolving restaurant, and thrill rides with names such as Insanity (*see p57*). Down below are some 40 Tower Shops (not exactly the Fashion Show Mall), a remodelled casino and even a nightclub.

Accommodation

Guestrooms in the tower would be interesting, but all the Stratosphere's sleeping quarters are in separate buildings below. Some are in the original Vegas World mid-rise; a more recent tower brought the total to 2,444 rooms and suites. There are an overwhelming 13 different types of room, from the smallish standard rooms to the massive 'premier suites'. On the eighth floor, there's a big pool and recreation deck.

Eating & drinking

Eating options run from the pricey Top of the World, which rotates once every 90 minutes, to a sandwich joint. Among those in the middle are Fellini's Ristorante, with decent Italian and steak; Roxy's, which has a 1950s diner motif and rock 'n' roll

singing waiters; and the new McCall's Heartland Grill, the best bang for your buck. Level 107 Lounge, 107 stories above the Strip, offers stunning views of the Vegas Valley.

Entertainment

The Stratosphere has upped its game over the past few years. Swing singer and local favourite Frankie Moreno holds court with his ten-piece band most of the week, and the new show, *Pin Up*, which isn't quite as risqué as it sounds, stars Playmate Clair Sinclair. If you're looking for thrills away from the showroom or casino floor, there's an indoor/outdoor observation deck on the tower, plus four ridiculously terrifying rides (*see p57*).

Gambling

The casino area is spacious and comfortable, if not particularly noteworthy. The layout approximates a series of circles, which looks good but seriously complicates any attempt to get directly from one end of the complex to the other. The emphasis is on liberal machines and table-game gimmicks, which go some way to improve players' odds. The Stratosphere advertises a 98% return on more than 150 $1 dollar slots, a 100% return on some video-poker machines and 10x odds on craps, as well as double-exposure blackjack and crapless craps (with a bunch of cockamamie rules that aren't player-friendly).

Amenities *Bars (4). Business centre. Concierge. Disabled-adapted rooms. Gym. Internet (Wi-Fi in some rooms $9.95). No-smoking floors. Pools (outdoor). Restaurants (6). Room service. Spa. TV: pay movies.*

Games *Big Six; blackjack ($5-$3,000); craps (10x; from $5); Let it Ride; pai gow poker; poker (16 tables); three-card poker.*

NON-CASINO HOTELS

Expensive

Four Seasons

3960 Las Vegas Boulevard South, at W Hacienda Drive, Las Vegas, NV 89119 (reservations 1-800 819 5053, front desk 632 5000, www.four seasons.com/lasvegas). Bus Deuce, 119/no self-parking/valet parking Las Vegas Boulevard South. **Rooms** 424. **Map** p320 A9 ㉗

The first boutique hotel (that's 'boutique' in Las Vegas terms) to open on the Strip remains its most popular. It has its own private driveway, entrance, lobby, valet and crack concierge staff, as well as an award-winning spa, landscaped gardens surrounding a secluded pool, restaurants and lounges. The twist is that the 424 rooms and suites are located in the Mandalay Bay resort, though private elevators whisk guests to their quarters. Guests may use Mandalay Bay's facilities, as well as those within Thehotel at Mandalay Bay (*see p110*).

CONSUME

The guestrooms are spacious and luxurious, especially the large marble bathrooms with sunken jacuzzis. Extra points are garnered for superior service: complimentary cocktails greet guests upon arrival, and repeat visitors have room keys waiting for them at valet, while families will find rooms child-proofed and stocked with age-appropriate amenities (nappies for babies, PlayStations for older children). Joggers get chilled water and towels after exercising. Dining options include Charlie Palmer Steak (*see p137*) and the popular Verandah Café (*see p147*), which features Italian-influenced American fare.

Amenities *Bars (3). Business centre. Concierge. Disabled-adapted rooms. Gym. Internet. No-smoking floors. Pool (outdoor). Restaurants (2). Room service. Spa. TV: DVD/pay movies.*

★ Mandarin Oriental

CityCenter, 3752 Las Vegas Boulevard South, at E Harmon Avenue, Las Vegas, NV 89109 (reservations 1-800 526 6566, front desk 590 8888, www.mandarinoriental.com/lasvegas). Bus Deuce/no self-parking/valet parking Las Vegas Boulevard South. **Rooms** 392.
Map p320 A7 ㉓

Luxury is the keyword at Vegas's Mandarin Oriental. Along with the first US restaurant by star chef Pierre Gagnaire, 27,000sq ft is devoted exclusively to a spa and salon. One unusual attribute is that its breathtaking Sky Lobby is located on the 23rd of its 47 floors.

Accommodation

The Mandarin Oriental's 392 guestrooms and suites range from 500sq ft to a spacious 3,100sq ft, with views of the Strip and the surrounding mountains. The hotel is LEED Gold certified, and the rooms are graced with electronic controls that conserve energy while controlling room temperature, curtains, lighting and the entertainment systems, which include a 42in flatscreen HD TV, and another TV in the bathroom. That the bedding and linens are luxe goes without saying.

Eating & drinking

The hotel immediately made its mark on the Vegas fine-dining scene with the arrival of Twist by chef Pierre Gagnaire. The first US restaurant by the Michelin-starred chef, Twist offers classic French cuisine, with a modern, well, twist. The Mandarin Oriental also hosts MOzen Bistro, with its pan-Asian cuisine, and the Pool Café, on the eighth-floor deck. The Tea Lounge, off the lobby on the 23rd floor, has a serene view of a city in constant motion.

Amenities *Bars (2). Business centre. Concierge. Disabled-adapted rooms. Gym. Internet (Wi-Fi). No-smoking floors. Pools (2 outdoor; 2 indoor lap pools). Restaurants (4). Room service. Spa. TV: pay movies.*

★ Thehotel at Mandalay Bay

3950 Las Vegas Boulevard South, at W Hacienda Avenue, Las Vegas, NV 89119 (reservations 1-877 632 7800, front desk 632 7777, www.mandalaybay.com). Bus Deuce, 119/self-parking & valet parking W Hacienda Avenue. **Rooms** 1,117.
Map p320 A9 ㉙

The rather clumsy name of this property has reputedly caused cab drivers no end of confusion, to the point where a change has been rumoured. The hotel itself, though, needs no such alterations. Located around the back of Mandalay Bay (follow the signs carefully), Thehotel has filled a gap in the market that most major cities have plugged with a W. Which is to say that it's chic without being too high fashion, and a big hit with hipsters in their late twenties while being careful not to exclude everyone else.

The rooms here are all suites, decorated in rich colours and furnished with chairs and beds that manage to be both stylish and extremely comfortable. The restaurants, shows and gaming at Mandalay Bay are just a corridor away, but the handsome hotel lobby is slot-free. Atop the hotel tower is Alain Ducasse's ultra-posh restaurant Mix, and its attached lounge. The Bathhouse spa is also excellent. The whole place doesn't feel like Vegas, which, for many guests, is part of the appeal. Recommended.

Amenities *Bar. Business centre. Concierge. Disabled-adapted rooms. Gym. Internet. No-smoking floors. Pools (outdoor). Restaurants (2). Room service. Spa. TV: pay movies.*

Trump International

2000 Fashion Show Drive, between Spring Mountain & E Desert Inn roads, Las Vegas, NV 89109 (reservations 1-866 939 8786, front desk 982 0000, www.trumphotelcollection.com/las-vegas). Bus 119, 203/no self-parking/valet parking Fashion Show Drive. **Rooms** 1,282.
Map p319 A5 ㉚

A joint venture between 'the Donald' and Phil Ruffin, Trump's first Vegas property – instantly recognisable with its gilding – is as posh as its sister properties in New York and Florida. When Donald Trump revealed his plans to build a condo-hotel tower here on *The Apprentice*, the condos were all reserved within three weeks. It was no surprise when, in a subsequent episode, he announced plans to build a second, 64-storey tower a little further down the line.

The 1,282 spacious guestrooms feature floor-to-ceiling windows, whirlpool tubs, plasma TVs (in the bathrooms too) and, of course, lots and lots of marble. There's a predictably top-notch restaurant, DJT, and a poolside eatery H2(EAU), with lighter fare and a full bar. And speaking of the pool, it's as luxurious as you'd imagine with excellent city views. *Photo p112.*

CONSUME

Amenities *Business centre. Concierge. Disabled-adapted rooms. Gym. Internet (Wi-Fi). No-smoking rooms. Pool (outdoor). Restaurants (2). Spa. TV: pay movies.*

Vdara

CityCenter, 2600 W Harmon Avenue, at Las Vegas Boulevard South, Las Vegas, NV 89158 (reservations 1-866 745 7767, front desk 590 2111, www.vdara.com). Bus Deuce/no self-parking/valet parking W Harmon Avenue. **Rooms** 1,495. **Map** p320 A7 ⓷

Vdara calls itself 'a non-gaming, non-smoking, eco-friendly, all-suite boutique', and as part of the CityCenter complex that has changed the Strip's very centre of gravity, it exemplifies an all-new Vegas, and an entirely new way of thinking about the city, and its accommodation. With no casino, no shows or attractions, and only a couple of dining establishments focusing mostly on lighter fare, it's a distinctly serene and relaxing environment, at the racing heart of the Strip. If the peace gets too much, guests cam ise the walkways that connect Vdara to siblings Aria (*see p81*) and Bellagio (*see p82*).

Its curvilinear 57-storey tower houses 1,495 suites. Along with being eco-conscious – the hotel has the world's first fleet of stretch limos powered by clean-burning compressed natural gas – Vdara is very art-aware: pieces from CityCenter's fine-art collection are showcased, including works by Frank Stella and Maya Lin, among others. *Photo p113.*

Accommodation

Vdara's gentle arc-shaped structure complements the curves of its next-door neighbour, Aria. The open-plan suites, which range from 582 to 1,750sq ft, include fully equipped kitchens and high-tech media hubs, and are sold as private residences; owners have the option to lease their units as hotel rooms when they are not in residence.

Amenities *Business centre. Concierge. Disabled-adapted rooms. Gym. Internet (Wi-Fi). No smoking. Pools (outdoor). Room service. Spa. TV: pay movies.*

Mandarin Oriental.

CONSUME

Trump International. *See p110.*

CONSUME

Off-Strip

HOTEL-CASINOS
Expensive

★ Hard Rock
4455 Paradise Road, at E Harmon Avenue, Las Vegas, NV 89169 (reservations 1-800 473 7625, front desk & casino 693 5000, www.hardrock hotel.com). Bus 108/self-parking Paradise Road/ valet parking E Harmon Avenue. **Rooms** 670. **Map** p320 C7 🔞

The exact point at which rock 'n' roll sold its soul is a mystery, but you can bet the Hard Rock took a healthy cut. The image of Sid Vicious adorns slot machines, Bob Dylan's lyrics line the elevators, and a notice reminds guests that smart dress is required, a rule that would bar more or less every one of the casino's icons. Still, despite its blazingly middle-American appropriation of rock imagery, the Hard Rock has been an unqualified success since its 1995 opening. The golf-shooting, Dockers-wearing baby-boomer brigade is here in force midweek, but on weekends, the hotel draws a crowd of boisterous fun-seekers, A-list glitterati and local hipsters.

The Palms may have stolen some of its thunder over the past few years, particularly on the nightlife front, but the Hard Rock remains a premier party place. The casino design (circular, with a bar in the middle) is a beauty and means the place always feels buzzing even when it's half-empty. Out back, the pool scene is even hotter: sandy beaches, waterfalls and swim-up black-jack. Amenities include the Reliquary Spa, electric purple limos and SUVs for guests, some terrific restaurants and the coolest sundries boutique in town: selling everything from liquor to lube, it embodies the concept of the convenience store. *Photo p114.*

Accommodation
The casino itself may be like a zoo, but the upstairs guestrooms are remarkably peaceful and minimalist, with mod space-age-y furnishings that are part-*Jetsons,* part-I Ching. And, thanks largely to the fact that the Hard Rock isn't that old, they're also very spacious. Most rooms have been decorated with museum-quality photos of rock stars, and some of the suites – Stones Suite; Sex & Pistols Suite – take the music theme to the max.

Eating & drinking
The Hard Rock really excels with its eating options. Nobu offers the city's best sushi, while 35 Steaks + Martinis is meat and booze par excellence. The new Culinary Dropout also has lots of drink too, plus a creative menu ranging from meatloaf to jambalaya. Hard Rock mainstay the Pink Taco specialises in gentrified Mexican cooking, while also boasting a kinetic early-evening bar scene, and Mr Lucky's is the city's coolest coffeeshop. New on the scene is Fu, with everything from Asian tapas to wok-fried noodles.

Entertainment
When it opened nearly 20 years ago, the 3,000-capacity Joint helped bust any lingering music-industry stigma about playing Vegas, and it remains one of the strongest music venues in the city. Its 2009 expansion added room for another 1,000 bodies, and what it lost in intimacy it gained in elbowroom – depending on who's playing. In 2012, the Hard Rock opened Vinyl, a mid-sized venue (650 capacity) to cater to bands and fans that don't fill the Joint. You'll find a trendy and inviting sports lounge in the Ainsworth, and the nightclub Vanity opens for special events.

HR was the property that launched the 'daylife' craze, with its scandalous Rehab pool party. Rehab just celebrated its 10th birthday and shows no signs of slowing down despite its advanced age (in Vegas years). Rehab parties now fall on Sunday to be followed by – thankfully – Relax Mondays. But, truth be told, the pool is almost always in full swing, weather permitting. There have since followed legions of imitators, but Hard Rock did it first.

Gambling

A mid 1990s beast it may be, but this is still a hip and extremely popular gambling den. The casino remains small by Vegas standards: only some 800 slots and video-poker machines, and 76 tables. The main floor is one big circle, with an outer hardwood walkway and an elevated bar in the centre. Dealers are encouraged to be friendly and enthusiastic; some will even give you a high-five if you hit a natural blackjack, a stunt that would give the pit boss a heart attack anywhere else.

Amenities *Bars (7). Concierge. Disabled-adapted rooms. Gym. Internet. No-smoking rooms. Pool (outdoor). Restaurants (8). Room service. Spa. TV: pay movies.*

Games *Baccarat ($100-$3,000); Big Six; blackjack ($10-$5,000); craps (3x, 4x, 5x; from $5); Let it Ride; mini baccarat ($5-$2,000); pai gow poker; roulette (double zero); three-card poker.*

Moderate

LVH (Las Vegas Hotel)

3000 Paradise Road, between E Sahara Avenue & E Desert Inn Road, Las Vegas, NV 89109 (reservations 1-888 732 7117, front desk & casino 732 5111, www.thelvh.com). Bus SDX, 108/self-parking Paradise Road or Joe W Brown Drive/valet parking Paradise Road. **Rooms** 3,000. **Map** p319 C5 ⑬

Formerly the Las Vegas Hilton (and originally called the International, and later the Las Vegas Hotel and Casino), the LVH underwent a reboot when the property parted ways with the Hilton chain in 2012. The hotel has a rich history: it was here that Elvis performed his record-setting sold-out Vegas shows, and Liberace played to a packed house twice weekly in the 1970s.

Given that LVH is next door to Vegas's Convention Center, it still has the biggest stake in Vegas's convention business. So it should come as no surprise that LVH is as self-sufficient as resorts come. There are 3,000 rooms, a smörgåsbord of fine restaurants, and an endless list of amenities – a full-service spa, a rec deck with tennis courts, wedding facilities (where Elvis himself got married), golf, shopping and pretty much everything else you'd need while in Vegas.

Accommodation

Just east of the Strip, LVH is perfect for those who want to be close to, but not in the middle of, the bustle. (The on-site monorail station can connect you to that in a hurry.) Standard rooms come in a variety of levels, from Classic to Premium to Superior. There is also a Business Class room for conventioneers. A selection of suites is available as well, running in size from 440sq ft to more than 1,400sq ft.

Eating & drinking

At the top of the food chain, teppanyaki eatery Benihana has an impressive 'Japanese village' setting, though the food is costly. Other upscale establishments include TJ's Steakhouse and Teru Sushi. There's a slew of less formal restaurants too, including 888 Noodle Bar, Burger Bistro, Paradise Café, the Buffet, and rocker-turned-restaurateur Vince Neil's Tatuado Restaurant & Café. There's a variety of quick-bite delis and cafés too.

Entertainment

The 1,700-seat showroom hosts a rotating cast of performers, while Shimmer Cabaret features comedy and smaller shows. For a lounge vibe, hit up Tempo for dancing and music from the 1970s to the '90s and beyond.

Vdara. *See p110.*

Gambling

The 95,000sq-ft casino offers a wide variety of slot and video-poker machines. Its race and sports book seats 350 people and can become quite crowded during big games. You'll find most of the traditional table games here, as well as some – like casino war – that are fast disappearing from other floors.

Amenities *Bars (8). Business centre. Disabled-adapted rooms. Gym. Internet (Wi-Fi $10). No-smoking floors. Pool (outdoor). Restaurants (13). Room service. Spa. TV: pay movies.*
Games *Baccarat ($100-$2,000); Big Six; blackjack ($5-$2,000); casino war; craps (3x, 4x, 5x; from $5); keno; pai gow poker; roulette (double zero); three-card poker; Ultimate Texas Hold 'em.*

★ Palms

4321 W Flamingo Road, at S Valley View Boulevard, Las Vegas, NV 89103 (reservations 1-866 942 7770, front desk & casino 942 7777, www.palms.com). Bus 104, 202/self-parking W Flamingo Road, S Arville Street or S Valley View Boulevard/valet parking W Flamingo Road. **Rooms** *798.* **Map** *p317 X3* 34

Ever since MTV's *Real World* took over a floor at the Palms, owner George Maloof has shown a Midas touch for keeping up with everybody from twentysomething hipsters to blue-rinse daytime gamblers. At night, the Palms attracts a Who's Who of Hollywood players and sports stars with nightclubs, a concert hall, chic restaurants, a tattoo parlour, 'bachelor suites' replete with dancer poles and some rooms with giant beds (Maloof and his brother own the Sacramento Kings basketball team). But the magic also works on locals, who appreciate the movie theatre, food court, slots-driven casino and quality service. Connected to the hotel via a moving walkway called the SkyTube is Palms Place, a condo-hotel and spa.

Accommodation

The rooms at the Palms aren't gigantic, but many compensate by having great views – and you get to curl up on the same type of bed as you would find at the luxury Four Seasons. Two floors of Fantasy Suites include a Hugh Hefner Sky Villa with balcony pool; the Hardwood Suite, a vast playpen with a jacuzzi and a half-court basketball court; the Kingpin Suite, with a pool table and a bowling lane; and an Erotic Suite, with a circular, eight-foot rotating bed with mirrored ceiling. The 'What happens in Vegas' line has surely been uttered more here than anywhere else.

Eating & drinking

Up in the penthouse of the original tower is Alizé, André Rochat's third French restaurant. From Chicago comes N9ne, a steakhouse, champagne/caviar bar and celebrity hangout; the folks behind it also run Nove, an extravagant hotspot decked out in crystal chandeliers, purple leather and croc-

Hard Rock. *See p112.*

odile skin. Heraea, one of the newer additions, is a sports bar/lounge/restaurant designed to appeal to women – or those who aren't sports fans, anyway. Simon has sushi and burgers, while 24 Seven Café offers pretty much what you'd expect. There's also a buffet and food court.

Entertainment

For a time, the Palms was the place to be seen clubbing. Though the competition has stiffened in recent years, places like Moon, with its retractable roof, remain popular, as does Ghostbar, on the 55th floor of the Palms Ivory Tower. Other happening venues include the massive club Rain, as well as Scarlet and Rojo Lounge. High rollers can hit the Mint, where table minimums start at $100.

Elsewhere, Pearl, an intimate concert hall, gives the House of Blues and the Joint serious competition, and the Palms three pools are usually filled with beautiful, sculpted bodies.

Gambling

Underpinned by a classy hardwood floor, the casino includes 2,400 slots, 55 table games (many with $10 minimums), and a race and sports book. A survey conducted just after the casino opened found the slots to be the loosest in Las Vegas; judging from the video poker, this relative generosity lives on.
Amenities *Bars (9). Business centre. Concierge. Disabled-adapted rooms. Gym. Internet (Wi-Fi $11.99). No-smoking floors. Pools (outdoor). Restaurants (9). Room service. Spa. TV: DVD/pay movies.*
Games *Baccarat ($100-$10,000); blackjack ($10-$5,000); craps (3x, 4x, 5x; from $5); Let it Ride; mini baccarat ($10-$5,000); pai gow poker; poker (10 tables); roulette (double zero); three-card poker.*

CONSUME

Rio

3700 W Flamingo Road, at S Valley View Boulevard, Las Vegas, NV 89103 (reservations 1-866 746 7671, front desk & casino 777 7777, www. riolasvegas.com). Bus 202/self-parking & valet parking W Flamingo Road, S Valley View Boulevard or Viking Street. **Rooms** *2,563.* **Map** p317 X3 ③⑤

The Rio is another identity crisis in progress. In a bid to appeal to a younger audience, the Rio has quietly been dispensing with its all-ages Mardi Gras-themed Masquerade Show in the Sky, a free and noisy parade that seemed to wind through the place non-stop. In its place, hints of a naughtier celebration remain: like the VooDoo Rooftop Nightclub and VooDoo Beach, the Rio's answer to daytime pool parties. As the Rio remains relatively disconnected from the rest of the Strip, it also attempts to keep its guests happy with attractions like golf packages at nearby courses including Cascata and Rio Secco, and a handful of decent if not spectacular shops. During the summer months the Rio practically bursts at the seams when it hosts the World Series of Poker.

Accommodation

Rio bills itself as an 'all-suites' hotel, and the rooms do offer a pretty good rate of return on size versus dollar. The comfortable mini-suites feature floor-to-ceiling windows, big televisions and fridges, and give you 600sq ft in which to stretch out. The full suites, measuring 1,600sq ft, come with better sound systems and wet bars.

Eating & drinking

The range of options is wide and appealing. At the top, literally (it's on the 50th floor), is the VooDoo Steakhouse. Buzios Seafood and Italian restaurant Martorano's are excellent choices as well. If you're looking for more laid-back options, there's the Royal India Bistro, casual Chinese dining at KJ Dim Sum & Seafood, or burgers at the All-American Bar and Grille. Poke around and you'll find other cafés, bars and delis.

Entertainment

The postmodern comedic magic of Penn & Teller is the rock of the Rio; the entrenched Chippendales put on exactly the kind of show that you'd expect. A Michael Jackson tribute, *MJ Live*, also plays nightly, though it'll be interesting to see how long it'll hang on with Cirque's new Michael Jackson show on the Strip. And speaking of tributes, *The Rat Pack Is Back* celebrates Vegas's golden era in the Crown Theater.

Gambling

The casino is huge, sprawling for two blocks, and the predominant colours are green ($25) and black ($100): at weekends, it's hard to find $10-minimum blackjack. Smaller-stakes gamblers should aim for the lower-limit tables in the outlying areas of the casino or, better yet, walk across the street to the Gold Coast. Poker is plentiful, but it's a tough room filled with locals.

Amenities *Bars (9). Business centre. Concierge. Disabled-adapted rooms. Gym. Internet ($12.95, Wi-Fi in convention area). No-smoking floors. Pool (outdoor). Restaurants (11). Room service. Spa. TV: pay movies.*

Games *Asia poker; baccarat ($100-$15,000); blackjack ($15-$10,000); craps (3x, 4x, 5x; from $5); keno; Let it Ride; pai gow poker; poker (8 tables); roulette (double zero).*

CONSUME

Westin Las Vegas

160 E Flamingo Road, at Koval Lane, Las Vegas, NV 89109 (reservations 1-866 837 4215, front desk & casino 836 5900, www. westinvegas.com). Bus 119, 202/self-parking & valet parking E Flamingo Road. **Rooms** *826.* **Map** p320 B7 ⑯

The first Westin-branded hotel in Las Vegas is a low-key resort, which is just how the majority of its guests like it. There is a small casino here – called the Casuarina – and even (though you'll need to look to find it) a cosy little showroom. But the Westin is aimed less at holidaymakers and more at the business traveller who wants to get some work done but also wants the bright lights of the Strip within easy reach. There's a good deal of meeting space, and rooms contain all the amenities a laptop-toting workaholic could want. But it's also a comfortable place to stop for a while: the service is solid, the pool area is relaxing, and the Hibiscus spa has 15 treatment rooms and a full-service salon.

Accommodation
The rooms here are everything you'd expect from a Westin property, which is to say that they're comfortable, handsome (in a discreet way), immaculately maintained and well equipped for the business traveller. The Heavenly Beds live up to their names.

Eating & drinking
Suede, the hotel's sole restaurant, offers comfort food 24/7; there's also a Starbucks on site.

Entertainment
There is a showroom here, but no single show seems to stick around for very long.

Gambling
The gambling feels like an afterthought, with just over 250 machines and eight table games. However, the Westin is one of the few non-smoking casino areas in the city.
Amenities *Bar. Business centre. Concierge. Disabled-adapted rooms. Gym. Internet ($9.95). No-smoking floors. Pool (outdoor). Restaurants (2). Room service. Spa. TV: pay movies.*
Games *Blackjack ($5-$500); craps (2x; from $5); roulette (double zero).*

NON-CASINO HOTELS

Expensive

Platinum
211 E Flamingo Road, at Koval Lane, Las Vegas, NV 89169 (reservations 1-877 211 9211, front desk 365 5000, www.theplatinumhotel.com). Bus 119, 202/no self-parking/valet parking E Flamingo Road. **Rooms** *255.* **Map** p320 B7 ㉟

The second condo-hotel to open in Las Vegas (the first was the Residences at the MGM Grand), this impressive property sits within a five-minute walk of the Strip. It's conveniently close, but the location also allows it to retain a welcome sense of distance. Free of both gambling and smoking, the Platinum is a refuge from the madness mere metres away: perfect for the residents who snapped up many of its 255 suites and now live here part-time, but also great for visitors keen on retaining their sanity while those all around are losing theirs. It's a well-run operation, free of bustle but retaining a certain urban style in its restaurant, relaxed ground-floor bar and fabulously appointed spa. And the suites themselves are both spacious (the bathrooms in some suites are bigger than guestrooms at a couple of hotels in town) and handsome, done out with high-spec amenities and comfy beds. The cannily designed indoor-outdoor pool on the fifth floor is another nice touch in a property that's quietly full of them.
Amenities *Bar. Disabled-adapted rooms. Gym. Internet ($12.99). No-smoking rooms. Pool (indoor/outdoor). Restaurant. Room service. Spa. TV: pay movies.*

Renaissance
3400 Paradise Road, between E Desert Inn Road & E Twain Avenue, Las Vegas, NV 89169 (reservations 1-800 750 0980, front desk 784 5700, www.renaissancelasvegas.com). Bus 108, 203/self-parking & valet parking Paradise Road. **Rooms** *548.* **Map** p319 C6 ㊳

This 15-storey, 548-room Marriott hotel south of the Las Vegas Convention Center seems all about business, with a list of amenities that includes the highest-tech wireless internet service, ergonomic desk chairs and even 'Exhibitor Suites'. The hotel has a sophisticated executive level with a lounge, a pool area, spa service, inviting beds and flatscreen televisions in every room. The Renaissance has neither nightclub nor casino. Still, there is one type of sin on site: Envy, a Richard Chamberlain steakhouse that serves a variety of rich comfort foods, from a Kobe filet mignon to truffle mac and cheese, with wines from a 1,500-bottle cellar. Escaping work is easy, with a monorail station nearby and the Strip a block away.
Amenities *Bars (1). Concierge. Disabled-adapted rooms. Gym. Internet (Wi-Fi $12.95). No-smoking hotel. Pool (outdoor). Restaurants (3). Room service. Spa. TV: pay movies.*

Moderate

Alexis Park
375 E Harmon Avenue, between Koval Lane & Paradise Road, Las Vegas, NV 89169 (reservations 1-800 582 2228, front desk 796 3300, www.alexispark.com). Bus 108, 203/ self-parking E Harmon Avenue/no valet parking. **Rooms** *495.* **Map** p320 C8 ㊴

Built as an apartment complex and later transformed into an all-suites hotel, the gaming-free,

Getting Personal

When it comes to hotel openings, small is the new big.

Las Vegas is notorious as a city of excess. Back in the 20th century, bigger was always better, and anything new had to out-size whatever had gone before. But times have changed. These days, small is the new big, and while mega-resorts are still the bread and butter of the city, an influx of new hotels with a more intimate, personal feel has little or nothing to do with the 'more is better' mindset.

These 'boutique' properties – and bear in mind that 'boutique' in Vegas terms can still be pretty sizeable – are popping up all over the city. First came the **Four Seasons** at Mandalay Bay (located on floors 35-39; *see p109*). Now an old-timer by Vegas standards, this was one of the original places where visitors could enjoy a high-class stay removed from the *Sturm und Drang* of the casino floor, and the round-the-clock revelry that characterised most properties. Four Seasons guests arrive at a separate – and un-Vegas-like – entrance, from where they're whisked away to their room. Business travellers enjoy amenities ranging from private meeting rooms to secretarial services; families have access to a quiet and private hotel pool, much unlike the general-admission pools surrounded by marauding hordes at other hotels, and all guests can keep fit in the Four Seasons private exercise facility, with state-of-the-art equipment you won't find just anywhere.

It's nearly impossible to build such hotels as standalone properties on the Strip. For one thing, most of the land is already claimed by the large concerns; plus, the competition is formidable. Hence the solution from the large resorts – think MGM Grand with nearly 7,000 rooms or the more than 3,000 rooms at Caesars Palace – of carving out a 'space within a space', often on a selection of floors, to separate those wanting a 'boutique' experience from the riff raff who prefer their Vegas vacations traditional-style: loud, garish and marked by excess.

Consider the newly opened **Nobu Hotel** in Caesars Palace (*see p83*), which has 'only' 181 rooms, but they range in size from 1,000sq ft to 4,350sq ft. Guests at Nobu are treated to an in-room menu from the namesake restaurant, as well as priority reservations in the restaurant, a private concierge and ahead-of-the-line access to

Pure nightclub, among other things. Naturally, it all comes with a price tag to match.

But not all boutiques are expensive. Staying at either the 64-room **Artisan Hotel** (*see p118*) or 150-room **Rumor** (*see p118*) isn't likely to break the bank, and the **MGM Grand** (*see p88*) has a range of Signature rooms with extra amenities, including priority concierge service and a private pool, that are highly affordable.

Despite the above-mentioned difficulties in opening a smaller hotel on the Strip, construction is under way on the **Gansevoort Las Vegas** (opening in 2014), a 188-room intimate resort that will sit on the desirable intersection of Las Vegas Boulevard S and Flamingo Road. Although the Gansevoort will be dwarfed by its neighbours – the Flamingo to the north has more than 3,500 rooms and across the Strip is Caesars Palace – the hotel is already touting its, well, relative smallness, from its Parisian-styled rooms to its access to the upscale rooftop nightclub Drai's.

This new-style Vegas is also making its presence felt among large newcomers to the Strip: specifically the **SLS**, which is currently going up on the site of the old Sahara on the northern end of the Strip. Although it will house more than 1,600 rooms, SLS – whose name stands for 'style, luxury and service' – is declaring it'll bring unique, individual style to the city, from its Philippe Starck-designed interior to its own brand of clubs, eateries and shops.

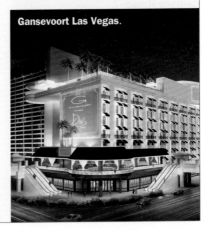

Gansevoort Las Vegas.

Mediterranean-style Alexis is a surprisingly sedate operation. The two-storey buildings, situated along winding pathways, house nearly 500 well-appointed suites, ranging in size from 450sq ft to 1,275sq ft and offering a host of unexpected amenities (gas fireplaces, large bathrooms and, in some cases, upstairs lofts). But the main selling point? It's right by the Hard Rock (see p112).

Amenities *Bar. Business centre. Disabled-adapted rooms. Gym. Internet (Wi-Fi $5). No-smoking rooms. Pools (outdoor). Restaurant. Room service. Spa. TV: pay movies.*

Artisan

1501 W Sahara Avenue, at Highland Drive, Las Vegas, NV 89102 (reservations 1-800 554 4092, front desk 214 4000, www.the artisanhotel.com). Bus SX, 108/self-parking W Sahara Avenue/no valet parking. **Rooms** 64. **Map** p319 B4 ⓐ

This boutique hotel, housed rather unexpectedly in a former Travelodge in the shadow of I-15, shares a trait with most Strip resorts: it has a theme. The old-world European decor is inspired by art and artists; paintings, a mix of pieces by local artists and reproductions of iconic works by the likes of Rembrandt and Van Gogh, cover virtually every inch of wall space in the public areas, and even decorate the ceilings. The theme continues in the Artisan Lounge, a late-night hotspot frequented by local hipsters, and in the hotel's dining room. The 64 individually decorated guestrooms and suites are priced a little highly for the location, but they're likeable enough and a good option if you fancy steering clear of the Strip.

Amenities *Bar. Business centre. Concierge. Disabled-adapted rooms. Gym. Internet (Wi-Fi free). No-smoking floors. Pools (outdoor). Restaurant. Room service. Spa. TV: pay movies.*

Carriage House

105 E Harmon Avenue, between Las Vegas Boulevard South & Koval Lane, Las Vegas, NV 89109 (reservations 1-800 221 2301 ext 280, front desk 798 1020, www.carriagehouse lasvegas.com). Bus Deuce, 119/self-parking E Harmon Avenue or Audrie Street/no valet parking. **Rooms** 155. **Map** p320 B8 ⓐ

Located next door to Grand Chateau, a new time-share resort owned and operated by Marriott, the Carriage House is often overlooked by visitors. However, the moderately priced rooms are a great value for the location, the best of any hotel not actually on Las Vegas Boulevard South. The rooms and suites are kept in decent shape; even the smallest ones have kitchenettes. Outside, there's a tennis court, a heated pool and a simple sun deck.

Amenities *Business centre. Concierge. Disabled-adapted rooms. Internet (Wi-Fi, free). No-smoking floors. Pool (outdoor). TV: DVD/pay movies.*

Comfort Inn

4350 Paradise Road, between E Flamingo Road & E Harmon Avenue, Las Vegas, NV 89169 (reservations 1-877 424 6423, front desk 938 2000, www.comfortinn.com). Bus 108/self-parking Paradise Road/no valet parking. **Rooms** 199. **Map** p320 C7 ⓐ

In truth, this outpost of the ubiquitous national chain isn't anything special. However, it's a useful standby in the event that the rest of the town is booked solid or running at often ridiculously high weekend prices: the rates here never seem to change by more than ten bucks a night, regardless of the time of year or the time of week. The hotel offers a similar range of amenities to those delivered by Comfort Inns throughout the South-west, including an outdoor pool, a very basic breakfast, and an assortment of kitchen utilities (microwave, coffeemaker) that no one ever seems to use. Still, it's kept in fair condition and the location is terrific for hipsters: it's opposite the Hard Rock and close to the Double Down Saloon.

Amenities *Disabled-adapted rooms. Gym. Internet (Wi-Fi, free). No-smoking floors. Pool (outdoor). TV: pay movies.*

Courtyard Las Vegas Convention Center

3275 Paradise Road, at E Desert Inn Road, Las Vegas, NV 89169 (reservations 1-800 661 1064, front desk 791 3600, www.marriott.com). Bus 108, 203/self-parking Paradise Road/no valet parking. **Rooms** 149. **Map** p319 C5 ⓐ

While Las Vegas's status as the world's most ridiculous resort town grabs headlines, it's worth stressing that the city is also the convention capital of the US, welcoming millions of business travellers each year alongside all the leisure traffic. This outpost of Marriott's Courtyard chain is tilted squarely at those here for work purposes, and particularly at those who've flown in to attend an event at the Las Vegas Convention Center, opposite the property. All rooms have workspaces and internet access, and decor that won't offer any distractions from the job at hand. It's one of several such chain-tied business hotels within walking distance of the LVCC; others include the immediately adjacent Residence Inn (3225 Paradise Road, 796 9300, www.marriott.com) and a tidy, well-equipped branch of the popular Embassy Suites hotel group (3600 Paradise Road, 893 8000, www.embassysuites.com).

Amenities *Bar. Business centre. Disabled-adapted rooms. Gym. Internet (Wi-Fi $9.95). No-smoking floors. Pool (outdoor). Restaurant. TV: pay movies.*

★ Rumor

455 E Harmon Avenue, at Paradise Road, Las Vegas, NV 89169 (reservations 1-877 997 8667, front desk 369 5400, www.rumorvegas.com). Bus 108/self-parking Paradise Road/valet parking E Harmon Avenue. **Rooms** 150. **Map** p320 C8 ⓐ

This new boutique hotel, directly across Harmon Avenue from the Hard Rock, is the latest player in Vegas's burgeoning trend for smaller hotels. Located three blocks from the Strip, Rumor is ideally positioned for visitors looking to avoid the mayhem of larger properties but wanting to stay close to the action. The all-suite rooms are done out in bold colours: reds, blues, purples, with ultra-comfy furniture, flatscreen TVs, and soaking tubs. The on-site restaurant, Addiction, serves a varied menu from polenta to pulled pork, and is also highly affordable. Rumor also boasts a decent pool area, with DJs spinning some nights.

Amenities *Bar. Concierge. Disabled-adapted rooms. Gym. Internet (Wi-Fi, free). No-smoking floors. Pool (outdoor). Restaurant. Room service. TV: pay movies.*

Budget

Aruba Hotel

1215 Las Vegas Boulevard South, at E Charleston Boulevard, Las Vegas, NV 89104 (reservations 1-866 383 3150, front desk 383 3100, www. arubalasvegas.com). Bus Deuce, 206/self-parking Las Vegas Boulevard South/no valet parking.
Rooms 94. Map p319 C3 ⑮

The slightly shady stretch of Las Vegas Boulevard South between the Stratosphere and Charleston

The D. See p120.

Boulevard is lined with old motels. Many of them are pretty sketchy places, as you'd expect given the signs out front advertising hourly rates and free adult movies, but a few stand out from the crowd. The Holiday Motel (2205 Las Vegas Boulevard South) is a pretty scruffy place, but its animated vintage neon sign is one of the most handsome in town. And up the road, the Aruba at least makes an effort to elevate itself above its surroundings. This is still a pretty basic and thin-walled motel, sure, and the location, well… But a recent refurbishment has spruced it up a lot, with the management tilting at a vintage Vegas vibe, and the regular events in the Thunderbird Lounge (swing night on Fridays, occasional bands on Saturdays) are a nice touch.

Amenities *Bar. Disabled-adapted rooms. Gym. No-smoking rooms. Pool (outdoor). Restaurant. Room service. Spa. TV.*

Budget Suites

3655 W Tropicana Avenue, between S Valley View Boulevard & I-15, Las Vegas, NV 89103 (reservations 1-866 877 2000, front desk 739 1000, www.budgetsuites.com). Bus 201/self-parking Paradise Road/no valet parking.
Rooms 480. Map p317 X3 ⑯

Budget Suites is perfect for visitors planning on staying in Las Vegas for an extended period and requiring some self-catering facilities. The daily rates are nothing special, but a one-bed apartment can be rented for around $250 a week, with further discounts for monthly rentals. Each secure 220- to 300-unit complex is made up of basic mini-suites, all with their own kitchen and bathroom. Maid service is available, but you can save on the expense by bringing your own linen and towels. There are four locations dotted around Las Vegas, but this is the closest to the Strip.

Amenities *Disabled-adapted rooms. Pool (outdoor).*

Sin City Hostel

1208 Las Vegas Boulevard South, at E Charleston Boulevard, Las Vegas, NV 89104 (reservations & front desk 868 0222, www.sin cityhostel.com). Bus Deuce, 206/self-parking Las Vegas Boulevard South/no valet parking.
Map p319 C3 ⑰

The lack of youth hostels in Vegas is easily explained by the fact that you can get a room in a Downtown casino for $30 or so. Still, despite its location in the Naked City neighbourhood, the Sin City Hostel has built up a nice reputation. The dorms are relatively cosy, and there are semi-private doubles. Amenities include free laundry facilities, an internet terminal and a jacuzzi pool. Guests must produce a student ID or proof of international travel at check-in.

Amenities *Disabled-adapted rooms. No-smoking rooms.*

CONSUME

Downtown

In 1906, people were gambling in what is now Downtown Vegas. The sawdust joints and casinos with wooden boardwalks and floors attracted railroad workers, ranchers and the like. For classic Vegas, you should head here, where what's left of the neon turns night into day, and casinos offer fewer sideshows to distract from gambling. The house rules at the casinos are often more liberal than on the Strip and minimum bets tend to be lower. However, poor attitudes on the casino floors, a result of poorer management, leaves Downtown gambling a sad shadow of its former self.

HOTEL-CASINOS

Moderate

The D
301 E Fremont Street, at S 3rd Street, Las Vegas, NV 89101 (reservations 1-800 274 5825, front desk & casino 388 2400, www.thed.com). Bus Deuce & all BTC-bound buses/self-parking S 3rd Street/valet parking S 4th Street. **Rooms** 638.
Map p318 D1 ◆

The D, formerly the Irish-themed Fitzgeralds, is a reboot of a tired old property. Hoping to ride the wave of Downtown's semi-resurgence, the D – so-named for 'Downtown' – seems mostly aimed at younger travellers attracted to Downtown's attempt to reinvent itself, and those without the bankroll for pricey Strip digs. Whether it'll be successful or not is another story, since it will depend largely on how the area evolves. While a lot of folks are betting on Downtown's comeback, and there's no doubt about its increasing appeal to a local younger crowd, capturing the tourist trade is a different matter altogether. Following a $15-million renovation, the updated rooms are appealing, but the casino seems to be hedging its bets as it opts for a 'vintage Vegas' feel – and time will tell if this gamble works. Yes, things are happening Downtown, but it's still hard to feel grown up with the Fremont Street Experience right outside your door. *Photo p119.*

Accommodation
For anyone who has stayed at Fitzgeralds, the revamp of this 34-storey hotel is a major improvement. It's still a far cry from, well, just about anything on the Strip, but given the D's surroundings you could do worse. Much, much worse.

Eating & drinking
Andiamo, an Italian steakhouse, is really the only choice for any sort of fine dining here, and since its recent opening it has garnered rave reviews. It features an impressive selection of pastas, steaks and seafood, and a good wine list. Beyond that, there's D Grill, with

typical café food, and American Coney Island, a glorified hot dog stand. Oh, and McDonald's.

Entertainment
The D's casino is a throwback to old Vegas, and so is its entertainment. Unfortunately, in this case that's not a compliment. Currently hosting a musical variety show, a dinner/murder-mystery performance, a cut-rate comedic magician and a topless revue, when it comes to entertainment the 'd' might as well stand for 'directionless'. If you're planning on seeing one of these, make sure you hit one of the D's three bars first.

Gambling
Will the retro focus of the D's two-storey casino create enough excitement to keep gamblers out of the other Downtown grind joints? Only time will tell, but for those who take their playing seriously there's not much to recommend here – unless you're a fan of Sigma Derby, the simulated horseracing game. Like we said…
Amenities *Bars (3). Business centre. Disabled-adapted rooms. No-smoking rooms. Pool (outdoor). Restaurants (3).*
Games *Blackjack ($5-$500); craps (3x, 4x, 5x; from $3); keno; roulette (double zero).*

★ El Cortez
600 E Fremont Street, at N 6th Street, Las Vegas, NV 89101 (reservations 1-800 634 6703, front

El Cortez.

Golden Nugget.

CONSUME

desk & casino 385 5200, www.elcortezhotelcasino. com). Bus Deuce & all BTC-bound buses/self-parking E Ogden Avenue/valet parking N 6th Street. **Rooms** 364. **Map** p318 D2 ⓭

The owners pumped $20 million into the old El Cortez a few years ago, replacing smoke-saturated carpeting, widening the casino aisles, installing new table games, adding a wine cellar, revamping the valet entrance and remodelling the rooms. But the historic building's Spanish-style architecture is still intact, and so is another Vegas relic: Jackie Gaughan, who bought the property way back in 1963. Now in his 90s, Gaughan no longer owns the property, having sold his remaining interest in 2008. But he still resides in a penthouse apartment atop the hotel. He frequently walks the casino floor, and occasionally sits down at low-limit poker games here.

Accommodation
While not particularly amazing, the rooms have been remodelled and are considerably nicer than they were a few years back. The Ogden House, across the street, has been renovated in an attractive modern design and renamed the Cabana Suites. Recommended if you're staying Downtown.

Entertainment
If karaoke is your thing, you're in luck. There's also an Elvis tribute show. Other than that, you'll have to make your own fun here, though there are many, many bars nearby.

Eating & drinking
The Flame Steakhouse consistently earns high marks from diners and won't break the bank. You won't find any 'name' chefs working out of its kitchen, but you will get a good piece of meat at a great price. Café Cortez is the place to go for casual dining, and the hotel also offers 'El Cortez Gambling Gourmet', by which food is brought right to the gaming table so you can keep on (hopefully) winning without breaking stride.

Gambling
Boasting slots '41%' looser than the Strip, El Cortez is the place to go if you're short on cash and high on hope. Here you can also still find coin-operated slots, an all-but-extinct animal everywhere else in Las Vegas. Craps minimums go as low as $3, but 10x odds are continuous. Test your luck at roulette for a measly 25 cents. The poker room also has one of the last seven-card stud games you'll find in Vegas outside tournaments.

Amenities *Bars (3). Disabled-adapted rooms. No-smoking rooms. Restaurants (2).*
Games *Blackjack ($3-$500); craps (10x; from $3); keno; mini baccarat ($5-$1,000); poker (3 tables); roulette (double zero).*

Golden Nugget
129 E Fremont Street, at S Casino Center Boulevard, Las Vegas, NV 89101 (reservations 1-800 634 3454, front desk & casino 385 7111, www.goldennugget.com). Bus Deuce & all BTC-bound buses/self-parking E 1st Street/valet parking S Casino Center Boulevard. **Rooms** 2,419. **Map** p318 C1 ⓰

Following the improvements over the last decade, the Nugget has consolidated its position as the best casino on Fremont Street. The refurbishments have been dramatic, and almost entirely for the better. The casino floor now feels almost grand, complete

Four Queens.

CONSUME

with a new poker room and the city's most handsome sports book. A slew of new restaurants have revitalised what had become a fairly tired catering programme. And then there's the fabulous pool area, complete with private cabanas, its own lounge (the Dive Bar) and water slides running through a central shark tank. Well, why not?

Accommodation

While not exactly swanky, the lodgings here are pretty decent, and better than those found at most other Downtown properties. The four hotel towers contain a total of 2,419 rooms, a number of plush suites (some of which are spread over two levels). The suites atop the spa tower are in a more modern style, the ones atop the original tower positively old-Vegas opulence.

Eating & drinking

Key to dining at the Golden Nugget is the branch of Vic & Anthony's – an award-winning steakhouse that shouldn't be missed. Other solid bets are Lillie's Noodle House and the Italian-slanted Grotto. The Carson Street Café has been overhauled, but continues to serve a range of casual American classics, and the buffet rightly retains its reputation as the neighbourhood's finest. But perhaps the most dramatic additions are the Nugget's drinking establishments, which include Rush Lounge, Ice Bar and the brand-new Bar 46, among others.

Entertainment

The Nugget's 600-seater is currently home to impressionist Geordie Brown. Guest headliners add a little variety, the Fremont Street Experience is right outside and, of course, there are the sharks.

Gambling

The Nugget's elegant marble lobby may seem out of place on Fremont Street, and the high minimums (mostly $10 for craps and blackjack) in the nicely renovated casino are unusual for Downtown. There's a segregated pit for players with larger bankrolls who want to play baccarat and blackjack without the hoi polloi; it's the only high-limit pit Downtown. However, there are also good selections of slot and video-poker machines from low to high denominations. The sports book was relocated to where the buffet used to be; it's now full-scale.

Amenities *Bars (6). Business centre. Concierge. Disabled-adapted rooms. Gym. Internet (Wi-Fi $11.99). No-smoking floors. Pool (outdoor). Restaurants (8). Room service. Spa. TV: pay movies.*

Games *Blackjack ($5-$2,500); craps (3x, 4x, 5x; from $5); keno; Let it Ride; mini baccarat ($5-$2,500); pai gow poker; poker (13 tables); roulette (double zero); three-card poker. Gambling lessons (blackjack, craps, poker, roulette; 10am daily).*

Main Street Station

200 N Main Street, at E Stewart Avenue, Las Vegas, NV 89101 (reservations 1-800 713 8933, front desk & casino 387 1896, www.mainstreet casino.com). Bus Deuce & all BTC-bound buses/ self-parking & valet parking N Main Street.
Rooms 406. **Map** p318 C1 ㉛

Main Street Station used to be the nicest Downtown casino not called the Golden Nugget, but now it has the D to contend with. Themed as a fin-de-siècle delight (check out the gas lamps that front the property), the casino is filled with antiques of all kinds, not all of them Victorian. Teddy Roosevelt's Pullman car is here, now a chic smoking lounge; a carved oak fireplace from Prestwick Castle in Scotland and a set of doors from an old London bank are also on display. Chunks of the Berlin Wall sit in the men's room. Go ahead and pee on it. Accessible yet smart, upscale (for Downtown) yet fun, this isn't the most charismatic property, but it's likeable all the same.

Accommodation
The 406 guestrooms are comfortable, if rather basic, but the prices are beyond fair. Upgrade to a Deluxe and still pay much less than you would on the Strip.

Eating & drinking
The choices are limited but good. The Pullman Grille, its name a nod to a railway theme that's delivered in fairly tasteful fashion, deals in surf and turf favourites. It's fine, but the Triple 7 Brew Pub remains a better bet, the well-above-average burgers and sandwiches acting as perfect stomach lining for the tasty beers brewed on site. Many locals swear by the Garden Court Buffet: the room is beautiful, the selections are excellent and the prices ($10.99 for dinner) are most definitely right.

Entertainment
Nothing, really.

Gambling
Main Street offers a good selection of slots and video poker, three-card poker and low limits at the tables; $5 single- and double-deck blackjack dominates, and the craps tables offer 20x odds. An illuminated sign over the roulette area depicts a single-zero wheel, but the wheel itself contains two zeros.
Amenities *Bar. Disabled-adapted rooms. No-smoking rooms. Restaurants (3). Room service.*
Games *Blackjack ($5-$1,000); craps (20x; from $5); keno; Let it Ride; pai gow poker; roulette (double zero); three-card poker.*

Budget

Four Queens
202 E Fremont Street, at S Casino Center Boulevard, Las Vegas, NV 89101 (reservations 1-800 634 6045, front desk & casino 385 4011, www.fourqueens.com). Bus Deuce & all BTC-bound buses/self-parking E Carson Avenue/valet parking S 3rd Street. **Rooms** 690.
Map p318 D1 ⑫
Pushing 50, the Four Queens are still ladies in waiting – specifically, waiting for a genuine Fremont resurgence. But for visitors who like their gambling vacations cheap and to the point, this is a prime location for a taste of Vegas past.

Accommodation
The hotel's 690 guestrooms (including 45 suites) have been remodelled, but keep your hopes down. Still, the flatscreen TVs are a nice touch.

Eating & drinking
The best of Downtown's bunch might be Hugo's Cellar, a romantic, quintessentially old-school restaurant: long-stem roses handed out at the door, salad cart, steak and lobster, and, of course, the flaming tableside cherries jubilee. Magnolia's Veranda is a standard Downtown 24-hour café (complete with the standard prime-rib dinner), while the Chicago Brewery features microbrews, pizza and a cigar lounge.

Entertainment
The Canyon Club, run by House of Blues expats, is a 600-capacity venue, but don't expect anything all that entertaining.

Gambling
Cramped and crowded, for some reason the Four Queens packs 'em in nightly. It's not that the gambling here is any stronger than next door or across the street, though the beers are better thanks to the presence of a brewpub. The roulette chips are dollars, with a $5 minimum. A $5 toke to the cocktail waitresses earns a huge smile and frequent service.
Amenities *Bars (3). Disabled-adapted rooms. No-smoking rooms. Restaurants (3).*
Games *Blackjack ($5-$500); craps (5x; from $5); Let it Ride; keno; pai gow poker; roulette (double zero); three-card poker.*

Fremont
200 E Fremont Street, at N Casino Center Boulevard, Las Vegas, NV 89101 (reservations 1-800 634 6182, front desk & casino 385 3232, www.fremontcasino.com). Bus Deuce & all BTC-bound buses/self-parking & valet parking N Casino Center Boulevard or E Ogden Avenue.
Rooms 447. **Map** p318 D1 ⑬
Most of the original charm has disappeared from the Fremont after a half-century, and a tropical-island motif has moved in – along with a large Hawaiian clientele. The famous block-long neon sign still holds its own, except when outshone by the Fremont Street Experience that runs above it.

Accommodation
The hotel's 447 guestrooms (including 23 suites) are modern, and feature floral patterns in hues of emerald and burgundy.

Eating & drinking
The Fremont courts visitors from the Pacific Rim, hence the surprising Second Street Grill: an unexpectedly upscale and risk-taking fusion-focused dining room, it delights discerning visitors with dishes like miso glazed rock cod (with soba noodles and baby bok choy) and mahi mahi. The Paradise Buffet and Café offers American and Chinese specialities in 'a rainforest setting', and Lanai Express is an Asian fast-food joint. There's also a Tony Roma's, reputedly the most successful in the nation.

CONSUME

CONSUME

Entertainment
Nothing doing here.

Gambling
This is a nondescript grind joint in the middle of Grind Central with nothing much to recommend it, but also nothing much to criticise. There's usually a slot or slot-club promotion going on; if you're in the neighbourhood, enquire at the slot-club booth.
Amenities Bars (4). No-smoking rooms. Pool (outdoor). Restaurants (4).
Games Blackjack ($5-$1,000); craps (2x; from $5); Let it Ride; keno; pai gow poker; roulette (double zero); three-card poker.

Golden Gate
1 Fremont Street, at S Main Street, Las Vegas, NV 89101 (reservations 1-800 426 1906, front desk & casino 385 1906, www.goldengatecasino.com). Bus Deuce & all BTC-bound buses/self-parking & valet parking S Main Street. **Rooms** 122. **Map** p318 C1 **54**

Being the oldest and smallest of anything aren't normally facts about which a Vegas property brags, but the Golden Gate manages to pull it off. Having celebrated its 100th birthday in 2006 (it's been known as the Golden Gate only since 1955; it was opened as the Hotel Nevada), this 122-room property appears positively quaint alongside the flashy Golden Nugget, the enormous brash Plaza and the garish Fremont Street Experience. A $12-million renovation in 2012 added 14 suites and two penthouses, and scrapped the hotel's vintage lobby and piano bar.

Accommodation
Golden Gate's recent renovation has produced rooms that are considerably nicer if small; many original 10ft-by-10ft bedrooms remain. The new suites are more spacious, naturally, and recommended if you plan on spending any time in your room at all.

Eating & drinking
Once Las Vegas's signature 'dish', the shrimp cocktail originated at the Golden Gate. Today, Du-par's Restaurant and Bakery reportedly serves about 30 tons of shrimp cocktail per year. A favourite among locals and out-of-towners, Du-Par's is probably the only eaterie attached to a casino at which you'll still find a 'blue plate special'. The pies are amazing too.

Entertainment
The piano player is gone, but, hey, there are dancing casino dealers!

Gambling
An old-time, no-frills, family-owned casino navigated by a multitude of wheelchair-required small ramps. The carpet's worn, the tables and machines are packed like sardines, and the bosses brook no nonsense. From the far dice-table closest to the deli, you can make a dash for the famous shrimp cocktail between rolls. The

comps here are liberal: play $10 blackjack for an hour and ask for the coffeeshop for two.
Amenities Bars (3). No-smoking rooms. Restaurant.
Games Blackjack ($3-$300); craps (10x; from $3); Let it Ride; roulette (double zero); three-card poker.

Plaza
1 Main Street, at E Fremont Street, Las Vegas, NV 89101 (reservations 1-800 634 6575, front desk & casino 386 2110, www.plazahotelcasino.com). Bus Deuce & all BTC-bound buses/self-parking & valet parking S Main Street. **Rooms** 1,003. **Map** p318 C1 **55**

This iconic Downtown spot, which stands at the head of Fremont Street, originally opened as the Union Plaza in 1971, on the site of an old railroad depot. In 2011, the Plaza was thoroughly renovated – to the tune of $35 million – and the rooms (and casino) vastly improved. Even after all that, the prices are still right, and the rooftop swimming pool is an appealing extra.

Accommodation
The Plaza can usually be relied upon to deliver some of Downtown's cheapest rooms. The renovations added flatscreen TVs and internet access to the rooms, as well as much-welcomed comfier bedding.

Eating & drinking
Along with the upgraded rooms came Oscar's Steakhouse, a project of former Las Vegas mayor Oscar Goodman (his wife, Carolyn Goodman, was elected in 2011). It's not over-the-top fancy (hey, it's the Plaza), but the place has a nice vibe. The steaks are very good and overall it marks a welcome addition to a hotel that needed a proper eaterie. If you're looking for something other than steak, there's also Hash House A Go Go (great for breakfast), and Island Sushi and Hawaiian Grill. You'll also find a pizza joint and food court on the premises.

Entertainment
Unfortunately, the Plaza improvements didn't do anything for its entertainers. Tired comedian Louie Anderson is still working out his childhood issues here and a music revue, the Phat Pack (go figure), plays the showroom. Hey, look! The Fremont Street Experience is over there...

Gambling
You'll find 600 slot machines here, and in the pit there are the usual assortment of table games. (Also, bingo!) The race and sports book is decent, with 75 screens, and it's also next to the bar in case the game doesn't go your way.
Amenities Bars (5). Disabled-adapted rooms. Gym. No-smoking rooms. Pool (outdoor). Restaurants (5).
Games Bingo; blackjack ($5-$500); craps (5x; from $5); keno; roulette (double zero); three-card poker.

The Rest of the City

HOTEL-CASINOS
Expensive

★ Green Valley Ranch

2300 Paseo Verde Drive, at S Green Valley Parkway, Henderson, NV 89052 (reservations 1-866 782 9487, front desk & casino 617 7777, www.greenvalleyranch.com). Bus 111/self-parking & valet parking S Green Valley Parkway or Paseo Verde Parkway. **Rooms** 490.

Green Valley Ranch was a gem right out of the box in 2001, and it hasn't stopped polishing itself since. In its third expansion, the former boutique-style resort with the Argentinian cattle baron motif has doubled its guestroom capacity, improved the gambling options, and added a 500-seat entertainment lounge. Amenities already in place before the renovation included District, a main-street-style shopping mall (*see p177*), a great mix of restaurants and one of the hottest pool areas in town.

Accommodation

The guestrooms are done out with old-world decor, supplemented by goose-down pillows and fluffy robes. The huge penthouse suite comes complete with a baby grand, a dining table for ten, his and hers baths, a full kitchen and numerous plasma screens. There's a cutting-edge spa out back, part of the eight-acre Whiskey Beach area; rent a cabana and order bottle service at the private pool called the Pond.

Eating & drinking

The gaming area is lined with dining options, including a couple of Asian places (China Spice and Sushi+Sake), upscale Italian at Terra Verde, and a re-creation of vintage Vegas at Hank's, with 'fine steaks and martinis'. Still hungry? You need the Feast Around the World Buffet, a local favourite. Also, the Grand Café's midnight to 6am specials can't be beaten.

Entertainment

Quinns Irish Pub is the main place for live music, although the Grand Events Center hosts occasional shows. Drop Bar has DJs and drinks, and the brand-new Sip is a classy place to grab a drink. Inside there's a 500-seat entertainment lounge and a ten-screen cinema, and next to the hotel is the District shopping mall, with around 50 shops and restaurants.

Gambling

With 2,200 slots and video-poker machines, there's pretty much a game for everyone who wants to play. Overall, the casino is expansive, and rarely feels crowded. The pit, which surrounds the Drop Bar, is a bit cramped, however. A recent renovation brought a new 22-table poker room and a state-of-the-art sports book. Mini baccarat starts at $10 a hand.
Amenities *Bars (12). Business centre. Disabled-adapted rooms. Gym. Internet ($12.99). No-smoking rooms. Pools (outdoor). Restaurants (14). Room service. Spa. TV: pay movies.*
Games *Blackjack ($5-$5,000); craps (3x, 4x, 5x; from $10); keno; mini baccarat ($10-$1,000); pai gow poker; roulette (double zero).*

JW Marriott Summerlin

221 N Rampart Boulevard, at Summerlin Parkway, Las Vegas, NV 89145 (reservations 1-877 869 8777, front desk & casino 869 7777, www.jwlasvegasresort.com). Bus 207, 208, 209/self-parking & valet parking N Rampart Boulevard. **Rooms** 548.

This expansive Spanish-style spa and golf resort is not your typical Marriott. The resort sits on 54 acres in Summerlin, just outside Las Vegas, and boasts truly awe-inspiring views of nearby Red Rock Canyon. On site are a beautiful waterfall pool, a splendid spa, a full-service beauty salon, a fully equipped fitness centre, several restaurants and clubs, and a few shops. JW is also a hit with golfers, both for its TPC Las Vegas packages (the course is right down the street) and its proximity to other Las Vegas courses. A complimentary shuttle provides access to the Strip.

Accommodation

Divvied up between two towers, the resort's spacious rooms are more luxurious than anything you'd usually encounter at a Marriott. All rooms feature over-sized raindrop showers and separate whirlpool baths.

Golden Gate

CONSUME

Eating & drinking

Local celebrity chef Gustav Mauler has carved a neat niche for himself with the Italian trattoria Spiedini. Shizen offers sushi and teppanyaki, while a lively crowd enjoys bangers 'n' mash and top-shelf Irish whiskey at JC Wooloughan Irish Pub. Fine-dining options include Ceres, which serves breakfast against gorgeous views of the resort's waterfalls; the intimate Carmel Room, with fine continental cuisine served with Mediterranean flair; and, in season, light fare poolside at the Waterside Grille.

Entertainment

There's Celtic folk and rock in JC Wooloughan.

Gambling

Rampart casino, inside JW Marriott, is among Las Vegas's most expansive and luxurious, with a stunning, palm-painted backlit dome over the pit. The table and slot chairs are extremely swish, helping to make this a hugely comfortable place. There's a story behind it all: the casino was originally designed to attract affluent visitors, but it turned out that few were willing to take the $50 cab ride from the Strip and the place went bankrupt. The new owners hired a veteran management group that instead targeted affluent Summerlin locals with unexpectedly low minimums and decent slot-club benefits.

Amenities *Bars (4). Business centre. Concierge. Disabled-adapted rooms. Gym. Internet ($9.95). No-smoking floors. Pools (outdoor). Restaurants (8). Room service. Spa. TV: pay movies.*

Games *Baccarat ($100-$5,000); blackjack ($5-$5,000); craps (10x; from $5); Crazy 4 poker; keno; mini baccarat ($5-$500); pai gow poker; roulette (double zero).*

★ Red Rock Resort

11011 W Charleston Boulevard, at I-215, Las Vegas, NV 89135 (reservations 1-866 767 7773, front desk & casino 797 7777, www.redrocklasvegas.com). Bus SX/self-parking & valet parking W Charleston Boulevard. **Rooms** 815.

Like Green Valley Ranch, Red Rock Resort is located in an affluent suburb. And, like its sister property in Green Valley, this is a luxe destination. But the comparisons between Red Rock and its sibling end there. This billion-dollar operation pays homage to the classic resort architecture of the early 1950s and '60s as well as the natural landscape that surrounds it. The rusty red and tan exterior mimics the colours of the nearby mountain range, while floor-to-ceiling glass walls afford spectacular views. There's even an Adventure Spa that takes full advantage of the desert surroundings by offering horseback riding, guided hikes and mountain biking. For pure relaxation, head to the Red Rock Spa.

Gold-leaf ceilings, Swarovski-crystal chandeliers and crocodile-leather wall panels are just a few of the more luxurious elements that set Red Rock apart from other neighbourhood casinos; indeed, the steakhouse and its trendy clubs and bars mirror the Strip's hipster aesthetic. The centrepiece is the palm tree-lined, circular Sandbar Pool, complete with a 'beach', with 19 private cabanas, six wading pools and, best of all, blackjack.

Accommodation

The guestrooms are fashionably outfitted with modern furniture and accessories that don't sacrifice comfort for style. Slip into the plush robe and slippers, plug in your iPod and pour yourself a drink from the self-service martini bar. The villa suite features a private patio complete with its own bar, a ten-person whirlpool spa and views of the beach area.

Red Rock Resort.

Orleans.

Eating & drinking
The choice here is wide and appealing. T-Bones Chophouse is an elegant steakhouse with a great wine list, while the authentic Italian dishes of Terra Rossa are divine. Hachi serves sushi and Japanese fusion dishes in a plush setting, while LBS's burgers and fries are terrific (as are the shakes – especially the ones with alcohol). Yard House offers American cuisine done right, and there's also a Pink's Hot Dogs and buffet. In the heart of the casino, you'll find the Lucky Bar, home to those red patent-leather crocodile panels as well as an awe-inspiring crystal chandelier. The Onyx Lounge specialises in signature martinis, while the Sandbar serves cool poolside libations.

Entertainment
A roster of bands keeps the Rocks Lounge jumping, usually for a very low or no cover charge. In warm months, the Sandbar hosts occasional poolside shows. There's also a 16-screen multiplex with private viewing boxes and a 72-lane bowling alley.

Gambling
The name of the game here is machines: there are more than 3,200 of them, split evenly between slots and video poker. Table minimums are reasonable. **Amenities** Bars (8). Business centre. Concierge. Disabled-adapted rooms. Gym. Internet ($12.99). No-smoking rooms. Pools (outdoor). Restaurants (11). Spa.
Games Blackjack ($5-$5,000); craps (3x, 4x, 5x; from $5); keno; mini baccarat ($5-$10,000); pai gow poker; poker (20 tables); roulette (double zero).

Moderate

Orleans
4500 W Tropicana Avenue, between S Decatur & S Valley View boulevards, Las Vegas, NV 89103 (reservations 1-800 675 3267, front desk & casino 365 7111, www.orleanscasino.com). Bus 103, 104, 201/self-parking & valet parking W Tropicana Avenue, Cameron Street or S Arville Street. **Rooms** 1,886. **Map** p317 X3 ⑤
The theme at the Orleans is more Disneyland than French Quarter. Still, the locals don't seem to mind,

mostly because the Vegas-style action is very real. Located very close to the Strip (and within a five-minute walk of the Palms), the Orleans is one of the few casinos at which locals and tourists happily mix in every part of the operation. The rooms aren't especially exciting, but they're kept in good condition and by no means offensively designed. In any case, it's hard to grumble at these prices.

The 11 restaurants run the casino-dining gamut, including steak and seafood (Canal Street), prime rib (Prime Rib Loft), buffet (French Market), Mexican (Coasta Cantina) and Koji's Chinese-Japanese fusion – right on down to a TGI Friday's.

Entertainment comes courtesy of the Orleans Arena, home of hockey's Wranglers and arena football's Gladiators; the Century Orleans 18 cinema (see p214); and the 70-lane bowling centre. You might occasionally find Bourbon Street-style jazz or modern rock in the 999-seat Orleans showroom, though country and nostalgic rock are the norms.

But the gambling is the main draw for locals, with the casino offering lively, low-limit action. The poker room is one of the best in town, with 'bad-beat jackpots' (awarded to the player who loses with a very big hand) and regular tournaments. The blackjack is mostly double-deckers that pay 3:2 for naturals. **Amenities** Bars (7). Business centre. Disabled-adapted rooms. Gym. Internet (Wi-Fi $10.95). No-smoking floors. Pool (outdoor). Restaurants (11). Spa.
Games Blackjack ($5-$2,000); craps (2x; from $5); keno; Let it Ride; mini baccarat ($5-$1,000); pai gow poker; poker (35 tables); roulette (double zero); three-card poker.

Silverton
3333 Blue Diamond Road, at I-15, Las Vegas, NV 89139 (reservations 1-866 722 4608, front desk & casino 263 7777, www.silvertoncasino.com). Bus 217/self-parking & valet parking Dean Martin Drive. **Rooms** 300.
Its location, just off I-15 several miles south of the Strip, doesn't flatter the Silverton. However, this is a surprisingly attractive property that, while by no means offering the Cosmopolitan or Aria much competition in the coolness or extravagance departments, is nonetheless smarter and more stylish than

CONSUME

you might expect. The rooms are decent if somewhat expensive for the location, and the casino offers the usual array of table games and slots.

Entertainment is by and large limited to shows from guitar bands that could politely be described as 'vintage'; the hotel even persuaded Hootie & the Blowfish to lend their name to the agreeably retro Shady Grove Lounge. Twin Creeks Steakhouse, the Sundance Grill's round-the-clock American classics and Seasons' all-you-can-eat buffet headline the eating options. Bonus: Just across I-15 is the Bootlegger Bistro (see p154).

The casino is surprisingly expansive and upscale, with 1,600 machines and 29 table games; the video poker is good enough to attract the pros.
Amenities Bars (5). Disabled-adapted rooms. Gym. Internet (Wi-Fi $10). No-smoking floors. Pool (outdoor). Restaurants (5). Room service. TV: pay movies.
Games Blackjack ($5-$2,000); craps (10x; from $5); keno; pai gow poker; roulette (double zero); three-card poker.

South Point
9777 Las Vegas Boulevard South, at E Silverado Ranch Boulevard, Las Vegas, NV 89183 (reservations 1-866 791 7626, front desk & casino 796 7111, www.southpointcasino.com). Bus 117/self-parking E Silverado Ranch Boulevard/valet parking Las Vegas Boulevard South. **Rooms** 2,163.
After effectively selling the Coast casino chain to Boyd Gaming in 2004, Michael Gaughan (son of legendary local casino operator Jackie) began working for his former competitors, watching as they spent more than $500 million building the South Coast casino on an isolated site several miles south of the Strip. When, after a year, it failed to achieve lift-off, Michael jumped in and bought the resort, first changing its name and then upgrading both its facilities and its image. It's an appealing place, its rooms decorated with attractive colours and without unnecessary ornamentation. Amenities include a 64-lane bowling alley, a 16-screen cinema and, right out of left field, a 4,400-seat equestrian arena. Michael's Gourmet Room headlines the dining options; there's also an Italian eaterie (Don Vito's), a steakhouse (the Silverado), an oyster bar (Big Sur) and the obligatory

buffet (the Garden). The big casino includes more than 2,500 machines and 60 table games, along with a race and sports book. A shuttle runs to and from the southern end of the Strip.
Amenities Bars (10). Business centre. Disabled-adapted rooms. Gym. Internet (Wi-Fi $10.99). No-smoking floors. Pools (outdoor). Restaurants (12). Room service. Spa. TV: pay movies.
Games Bingo; blackjack ($5-$2,000); craps (2x; from $5); keno; mini baccarat ($5-$5,000); pai gow poker; poker (22 tables); roulette (double zero); three-card poker.

Budget

Arizona Charlie's Boulder
4575 Boulder Highway, at E Twain Avenue, Las Vegas, NV 89121 (reservations 1-888 236 9066, front desk & casino 951 5800, www.arizona charliesboulder.com). Bus BHX/self-parking & valet parking S Decatur Boulevard. **Rooms** 300.
Arizona Charlie's Boulder is a no-frills, 300-room bunkhouse for serious players who need a place to drop. The theme is the Yukon gold rush, though you won't notice: the interior design is little more than a floor, a ceiling and rows of machines. Food options include the Yukon Grille, a low-price steakhouse, but the surest bet at Charlie's is still the Sourdough Café, where you can grab a generous meal any time of the day, usually for less than $10 a head. There's also a buffet. The Palace Grand Lounge hosts a range of lounge acts. The blackjack games here are decent, with typical low minimums, as is some of the video poker. Another outpost, Arizona Charlie's Decatur (740 S Decatur Blvd, 1-800 342 2695, 258 5200, www.arizonacharliesdecatur.com) can be found in north-west Las Vegas.
Amenities Bars (3). Disabled-adapted rooms. No-smoking floors. Pool (outdoor). Restaurants (4). TV: pay movies.
Games Bingo; blackjack ($3-$1,000); craps (10x; from $5); keno; roulette (double zero).

Boulder Station
4111 Boulder Highway, at E Desert Inn Road, Las Vegas, NV 89121 (reservations 1-800 683 7777, front desk & casino 432 7777, www.boulder station.com). Bus BHX, 203/self-parking & valet parking Boulder Highway. **Rooms** 300.
This Victorian-styled Station casino on the Boulder Strip is mostly a locals' joint. The Railhead hosts a stable of mostly forgettable acts on the cheap, but there are plenty of family-friendly amenities, such as an 11-screen movie theatre and a Kids Quest childcare centre. There are decent dining options too: the Feast Gourmet Buffet is popular, as is the Broiler. The casino is typical for the Station chain, though the minimums in this part of town seem to run a little lower, with some $3 tables scattered about, 10x odds at craps and 50¢ roulette chips. The newest machines seem to show up here first.

CONSUME (side tab)

INSIDE TRACK JOIN THE CLUB

If you're planning to gamble in one casino or group of casinos (all Harrah's properties, for example), it's worth signing up for the casino's players' club. You'll be issued a card, which you can use in machines or at tables. Give the card to the dealer or plug it into the machine before you play, and earn points back towards freebies. The more you play, the more points you earn. Ask a cashier or floor person where to sign up.

Fiesta Rancho.

Amenities *Bars (5). Disabled-adapted rooms. Internet ($9.99). No-smoking floors. Pool (outdoor). Restaurants (6). Room service.* **Games** *Bingo; blackjack ($3-$1,000); craps (10x; from $2); keno; Let it Ride; mini baccarat ($5-$1,000); pai gow poker; poker (11 tables); roulette (double zero); three-card poker.*

Fiesta Rancho

2400 N Rancho Drive, at W Lake Mead Boulevard, Las Vegas, NV 89032 (reservations 1-800 678 2846, front desk & casino 631 7000, www.fiestarancho.com). Bus 106, 210/self-parking N Rancho Drive, W Lake Mead Boulevard or Carey Avenue/valet parking W Lake Mead Boulevard. **Rooms** 100.

The slot-club at the Fiesta Rancho is known for regular triple-points days and no-hassle food comps. There's also a 300-seat bingo room and a drive-up sports-betting window, where you don't even have to get out of the car to lay some money down. Besides the gaming, it's the party-style atmosphere that draws visitors here. A variety of acts play Club Tequila, where the emphasis is on Latin music; the obligatory Mexican food comes courtesy of Garduno's huge menu and the Blue Agave Steakhouse. Escape the desert heat in the outdoor swimming pool or the NHL-size ice arena. For visitors arriving at the other end of the city, there's Fiesta Henderson (also much closer to McCarran airport) in the south-east (777 W Lake Mead Pkwy, Henderson, NV; 1-888 899 7770, 558-7000, www.fiestahenderson.com).

Amenities *Bars (3). Disabled-adapted rooms. Internet ($9.99). No-smoking rooms. Pool (outdoor). Restaurants (3). Room service. Spa. TV: pay movies.* **Games** *Bingo; blackjack ($5-$1,000); craps (10x; from $2); keno; mini baccarat; pai gow poker; poker; roulette (double zero).*

Gold Coast

4000 W Flamingo Road, at S Valley View Boulevard, Las Vegas, NV 89103 (reservations 1-800 331 5334, front desk & casino 367 7111, www.goldcoastcasino.com). Bus 104, 202/self-parking & valet parking S Valley View Boulevard, W Flamingo Road or Wynn Road. **Rooms** 711. **Map** p317 X3 ⑤⑦

Boyd Gaming took hold of Coast Casinos in 2004, and for years it has relied on its proven formula for success. Locals love the GC's machines and the players' club, both of which often take top honours in the *Las Vegas Review-Journal*'s 'Best of Vegas' survey. There's plenty of $5 blackjack, $5 pai gow and $1 roulette for low rollers, one of the city's bigger bingo rooms (eight sessions daily) plus a 70-lane bowling alley. The 711 rooms have been upgraded with the seemingly mandatory 32in LCD TVs. For food, choose from the Cortez Room, a mid-priced steakhouse; the all-Asian Ping Pang Pong; the Java Vegas coffeeshop; or the buffet, rated highly by locals. The one new addition is a noodle bar called Noodle Exchange. *Photo p130.*

Amenities *Bars (4). Business centre. Concierge. Disabled-adapted rooms. Gym. Internet ($10.99). No-smoking floors. Pool (outdoor). Restaurants (6). Room service. TV: pay movies.* **Games** *Bingo; blackjack ($5-$2,000); craps (2x; from $2); keno; mini baccarat ($10-$1,000); pai gow poker; roulette (double zero).*

Palace Station

2411 W Sahara Avenue, at N Rancho Drive, Las Vegas, NV 89102 (reservations 1-800 634 3101, front desk & casino 367 2411, www.palacestation.com). Bus SX, 119/self-parking & valet parking W Sahara Avenue, N Rancho Drive or Teddy Drive. **Rooms** 1,028. **Map** p319 A4 ⑤⑧

The original Station casino has been a locals favourite for more than 30 years, thanks largely to its popular gaming promotion. You'll find 1,600 slot and video-poker machines here, along with 45 gaming tables, a 300-seat bingo room, poker room, keno lounge, and a race and sports book. The hotel draws its share of tourists too, due to its close proximity to the Strip and cheap rooms. Several of the restaurants offer fine neighbourhood fare: the Feast Gourmet Buffet; steaks and seafood in the Broiler; and a food court. Jack's, an Irish pub, has live music. The rooms and suites range from economy courtyard to deluxe tower rooms.

Amenities *Bars (4). Business centre. Disabled-adapted rooms. Gym. Internet (Wi-Fi, $9.99). No-smoking rooms. Pool (outdoor). Restaurants (6). Room service. TV: pay movies.*

CONSUME

Games *Bingo; blackjack ($5-$3,000); craps (3x, 4x, 5x, 10x; from $5); keno; Let it Ride; mini baccarat ($10-$1,000); pai gow poker; poker (9 tables); roulette (double zero).*

Sam's Town

5111 Boulder Highway, at E Flamingo Road, Las Vegas, NV 89122 (reservations 1-800 897 8696, front desk & casino 456 7777, www.samstown lv.com). Bus BHX, 115, 202/self-parking & valet parking Boulder Highway, E Flamingo Road or Nellis Boulevard. **Rooms** *646.*

If you like Old West-style casinos, this is your place. Though gunfire is kept to a minimum, the theme is nonetheless prevalent, from the saloon-style bars to Roxy's, the rowdy dance hall. There's even a quality western store (Sheplers). Elsewhere, modern amenities include a 24-hour bowling centre, an 18-screen movie theatre and Sam's Town Live!, a 1,100-seat venue that stages a variety of country and pop concerts. In the middle of all this is Mystic Falls Park, a ten-storey atrium whose indoor nature walk (with trees and chirping birds) gets interrupted four times daily by the Sunset Stampede, a laser light and water show. Check out the TV sets over the tables in some of the pits, and bet up to 20x odds at the crap tables. There are thousands of video-poker machines, though few, if any, are full pay.

Amenities *Bars (6). Disabled-adapted rooms. Internet (Wi-Fi $10). No-smoking rooms. Pool (outdoor). Restaurants (4). TV: pay movies.*
Games *Bingo; blackjack ($5-$3,000); craps (20x, from $5); keno; Let it Ride; pai gow poker; poker (9 tables); roulette (double zero).*

Santa Fe Station

4949 N Rancho Drive, at US 95 (junction 90A), Las Vegas, NV 89130 (reservations 1-866 767 7770, front desk & casino 658 4900, www.santa festation.com). Bus 101, 106, 219/self-parking & valet parking N Rancho Drive or Lone Mountain Road. **Rooms** *200.*

Santa Fe staples include a 432-seat bingo room, a wide variety of slots, bowling alley, showroom, dancehall and a multiplex. Locals enjoy good Mexican fare at Cabo (great margaritas!); other options include the endlessly popular Feast Buffet and unexpectedly impressive Charcoal Room for steak and seafood. Santa Fe also operates a Kids Quest childcare and entertainment centre. The smallish casino has low-limit table games, though with no competition nearby, the rules are not altogether favourable. The video poker is typical for Station: there are a few 99% machines, but the rest lower. There is also a 24-hour poker room and a sports book.

Amenities *Bars (6). Business centre. Disabled-adapted rooms. Gym. Internet ($9.99). No-smoking rooms. Pool (outdoor). Restaurants (4). Room service. TV: pay movies.*

Gold Coast. *See p129.*

Games *Blackjack ($5-$1,000); craps (10x; from $5); Let it Ride; pai gow poker; poker (14 tables); roulette (double zero); three-card poker.*

Suncoast

9090 Alta Drive, at N Rampart Boulevard, Las Vegas, NV 89145 (reservations 1-877 677 7111, front desk & casino 636 7111, www.suncoast casino.com). Bus 206/self-parking & valet parking Alta Drive & Rampart Avenue. **Rooms** *388.*

This Coast Casino shares the qualities of its siblings but with one major difference: it's in Summerlin, and thus surrounded by 81 holes of world-class golf, and an assortment of upper-scale shopping and dining options. Stay on site, though, and you'll find a large and player-friendly casino floor with a progressive players' club that plies regulars with comps. The 500-seat showroom features a variety of headliners, and there's a 64-lane bowling alley and 16-screen movie theatre. Beef lovers should head to SC Prime Steakhouse, and Salvatore's serves upscale Italian. Coasta Cantina has decent Mexican, and there's a standard buffet and coffeeshop. The resort offers a childcare centre as well.

Amenities *Bars (6). Disabled-adapted rooms. Gym. Internet (Wi-Fi $11). No-smoking rooms. Pool (outdoor). Restaurants (8). Room service. TV: pay movies.*
Games *Baccarat ($15-$2,500); bingo; blackjack ($5-$2,000); craps (2x; from $5); keno; Let it Ride; pai gow poker; poker (10 tables); roulette (double zero); three-card poker.*

Sunset Station

1301 W Sunset Road, between N Stephanie Street & I-515, Henderson, NV 89014 (reservations 1-888 786 7389, front desk & casino 547 7777, www.sunsetstation.com). Bus 115, 212/self-parking & valet parking Stephanie Street, W Sunset Road, Marks Street or Warm Springs Road. **Rooms** *457.*

Slot-clubbing locals keep every inch of the capacious Sunset Station casino buzzing. The usual table games, with $5-$10 minimums (and 10x odds at craps), are situated under a stained-glass ceiling, with a wide ranges of slots and video-poker machines. There are plenty of other ways to spend your money too. A 13-screen Regal Cinema (*see p214*), childcare centre and bowling centre cater for adults and children; grown-ups may prefer the live music at Club Madrid. But the restaurants are the steady draws, with cuisine that ranges from Chinese to go at Panda Express to the smarter Sonoma Cellar Steakhouse. In between, there's the worth-the-wait Feast Buffet, plus mojitos and margaritas at Viva Salsa. And don't miss the gaudy Gaudi Bar in the centre of the action.

Amenities *Bars (11). Disabled-adapted rooms. Internet ($9.99). No-smoking rooms. Pool (outdoor). Restaurants (8). Room service.*
Games *Bingo; blackjack ($5-$5,000); craps (10x; from $2); keno; Let it Ride; mini baccarat ($5-$1,000); pai gow poker; poker (8 tables); roulette (double zero); three-card poker.*

Texas Station

2101 Texas Star Lane, at N Rancho Drive, between W Lake Mead Boulevard & Vegas Drive, North Las Vegas, NV 89130 (reservations 1-800 654 8888, front desk & casino 631 1000, www.texasstation. com). Bus 106, 210/self-parking N Rancho Drive/ valet parking W Lake Mead Boulevard or N Rancho Drive. **Rooms** 200. **Map** p317 X1 ⑳

Bigger is better in this Lone Star-themed hotel, which features a 60-lane bowling centre, 18-screen movie theatre, and 1,700-plus slot and video-poker machines. In the poker room, the game of choice is, inevitably, Texas hold 'em. And where would Texas be without a steakhouse? The award-winning Austins is a fine example of what a steakhouse should be: prime steaks dry-aged for 21 days, hand-cut and then marinated in their secret sauce. Surprisingly, there are only 200 rooms, making the hotel side of this casino almost boutique by Vegas standards. Texas also has a Kids Quest childcare and entertainment centre.

Amenities *Bars (9). Disabled-adapted rooms. Internet ($10.99). No-smoking rooms. Pool (outdoor). Restaurants (5). Room service. TV: pay movies.*
Games *Bingo; blackjack ($5-$1,000); craps (10x; from $5); keno; Let it Ride; pai gow poker; poker (8 tables); roulette (double zero); three-card poker.*

NON-CASINO HOTELS

Expensive

Hilton Lake Las Vegas

1610 Lake Las Vegas Parkway, off E Lake Mead Parkway, Henderson, NV 89011 (reservations 1-800 241 3333, front desk 567 4700, www. hilton.com). No bus/self-parking & valet parking Lake Las Vegas Parkway. **Rooms** 349.

Despite its idyllic if isolated location within the Lake Las Vegas community, roughly 20 miles south-east of the Strip, this luxurious resort has had a tough time keeping its rooms filled. In 2013, for the third time in ten years, the hotel changed hands, ending up with the Hilton chain. Perhaps it's because this beautiful location doesn't really feel much like Las Vegas. Key to this, of course, is the lack of an in-house casino: gamblers can wander next door to the Casino Montelago (898 7777, www.casinomonte-lago.com), but there's no gaming on-site. The hotel, however, offers all the luxury you could want: the rooms are handsome but not flashy, with plush beds and chairs, generous bathrooms and most conceivable amenities (minibars, internet access and so on). Firenze, the lobby bar, delivers worthwhile cocktails and decent sandwiches. Medici Café serves a winning range of Mediterranean-influenced American dishes for breakfast and lunch. The luxury extends to the hotel's capacious spa, regarded as one of the city's best. Nearby amenities include the Falls and Reflection Bay golf courses, which essentially adjoin the hotel, and Montelago Village, a sort of upscale Italianate theme park dotted with boutiques, restaurants and bars.

Amenities *Bars (2). Business centre. Concierge. Disabled-adapted rooms. Gym. Internet (Wi-Fi; included in $25 resort fee). No-smoking floors. Pools (outdoor). Restaurants (3). Room service. Spa. TV: pay movies.*

Westin Lake Las Vegas

101 Montelago Boulevard, off Lake Las Vegas Parkway, Henderson, NV 89011 (reservations 1-866 716 8137, front desk 567 6000, www. westinlakelasvegas.com). No bus/self-parking & valet parking Lake Las Vegas Parkway. **Rooms** 493.

Despite changing hands (it used to be a Hyatt, then a Loews), this Lake Las Vegas property still has a Moroccan theme and most of the same amenities. But upgraded rooms and resurfaced pools have given the hotel a facelift, as has the removal of the small casino, now a venue primarily for weddings and meetings. As for food, Marssa serves Pacific Rim cuisine and sushi, and Rick's Café offers American cuisine with a Mediterranean flair. The Arabesque Lounge has beautiful views of the lake and mountains; for outdoor dining, try the SandsaBar Grill. Along with hiking, biking and bird watching, the major sports are on a 320-acre private man-made lake (sailing, canoeing, kayaking, fishing), and three golf courses. There's also a white-sand beach and sports area, as well as nearby golf. Check out the resort's Fit-cation Package if you want to go home looking better than when you arrived.

Amenities *Bars (2). Business centre. Concierge. Disabled-adapted rooms. Gym. Internet (Wi-Fi $9.95). No-smoking floors. Pool (outdoor). Restaurants (4). Room service. Spa. TV: pay movies.*

CONSUME

Restaurants & Buffets

A culinary turnaround reflects the new, sophisticated Vegas.

Nowhere in Las Vegas is the power of cash more evident than in its array of restaurants. For years, food here was designed purely to provide stomach lining for drinkers and fuel for gamblers. The sole aim of catering crews was to get diners in and out of their restaurants as quickly as possible, sending them back to the gambling tables where the real profits were to be made. The choice of cuisine didn't extend far beyond all-you-can-eat buffets, 24-hour coffeeshops and, for the rich visitor, swanky steakhouses. These days all that has changed as big-name chefs vie for customers.

THE VEGAS RESTAURANT SCENE

Since the arrival in 1992 of Wolfgang Puck, the first star chef to open a restaurant in the city, Las Vegas's dining scene has been turned on its head. The range of restaurants in the casinos is broader than ever, catering to more or less every taste and budget. The casino moguls have spent millions luring the world's best chefs to the city, forking over even more cash on spectacular interior design and fresh ingredients, flown in from around the country every day of the year. The buffets and all-night eateries remain, but many of them have been upgraded and are virtually unrecognisable from days of yore.

Despite all the welcome improvements, things aren't perfect. Many of the star chefs who've lent the weight of their names and/or reputations to restaurants in the city don't cook here, though that doesn't stop them from setting extremely high prices. There's still plenty of mediocrity: overpriced steakhouses, inauthentic Chinese eateries, dreary breakfast bars and the like. And a few of the town's high-end, big-name restaurants coast along on autopilot after an initial marketing blitz, when reputations are made and trends are set. But many others sustain a high standard. Indeed, the smart restaurateurs are aware that even in a resort town such as this, word-of-mouth is a powerful tool, especially now that foodie blogs and restaurant review apps mean that everyone can be a critic.

Away from the Strip, things are less consistent but often impressive. Carnivores are well served by a fine array of steakhouses and barbecue joints; many excellent but low-key, high-value Asian restaurants sit tucked away in unlikely strip-mall locations; and there's even a plethora of Middle Eastern eateries. Follow the recommendations in this chapter, and you can't go wrong.

PRACTICALITIES

The ebb and flow of visitors through Las Vegas is so unpredictable that making reservations, while not always necessary, is nonetheless recommended for all major Strip restaurants, especially those at the higher end of the scale. Weekends are busy, but many eateries do a brisk trade during the week thanks to the influx of conventioneers. Aside from some special Sunday feeds (such as the **Sterling Brunch** at Bally's; *see p157*), casino buffets don't accept reservations; prepare to queue at busy

---

❶ Blue numbers in this chapter correspond to the location of each restaurant as marked on the street maps. *See pp317-320.*

---

times. Away from the Strip, you'd do well to book for Friday and Saturday nights.

Vegas is a pretty casual town – that shlump in cargo shorts and flip-flops might be a billionaire – and only a few restaurants enforce a dress code that moves much beyond an insistence on shoes and a shirt. You should be all right if you employ common sense: you can get away with almost anything at the **Burger Bar** (see p136), but men would do well to wear a jacket when dining at **Picasso** (see p143). If in doubt, it's always advisable to ask staff when you make your reservation.

Restaurants

THE STRIP

America
New York New York *3790 Las Vegas Boulevard South, at W Tropicana Avenue (740 6451, www. newyorknewyork.com). Bus Deuce, 201.* **Open** 24hrs daily. **Main courses** $12-$27. **Map** p320 A8 ❶ **American & steakhouses**
Like the casino in which it's housed, America is terrific fun. In both, a simple concept is executed with wonderfully playful enthusiasm. The all-purpose menu offers innumerable dishes from across the country, many of them inspired by a particular corner of the US: chicken quesadillas by way of Albuquerque, for example, or Philadelphia cheese steaks. It's not really about the authenticity, mind; this is just good, solid cooking served with an exclamation mark, a wide smile and a heartfelt 'have a nice day!'

American Fish.

THE BEST RESTAURANTS

For a Jules Verne-inspired meal
Rx Boiler Room (see p145).

For a taste of new Downtown
Las Vegas
Eat. or **Triple George** (for both, see p153).

For a hunka hunka red meat
Steak House (see p146) or **Cut** (see p138).

For unusual culinary combinations
China Poblano (see p137) or **Simon** (see p152).

For too much, too many
Bacchanal or **Carnival World Buffet** (for both, see p156).

American Fish
Aria, CityCenter *3746 Las Vegas Boulevard South, at W Harmon Avenue (877 230 2742, www.arialasvegas.com). Bus Deuce.* **Open** 5-10.30pm daily. **Main courses** $37-$74. **Map** p320 A7 ❷ **Seafood**
Chef Michael Mina's take on the classic seafood restaurant takes sustainability – in the ingredients and in the decor, made from reclaimed materials – as its mission. Mina creates fresh and saltwater fish dishes with another unique touch: the cooking water itself is drawn from various oceans and lakes. The menu also features several fine cuts of steak.

André's
Monte Carlo *3770 Las Vegas Boulevard South, between W Harmon & W Tropicana avenues (798 7151, www.andrelv.com). Bus Deuce, 201.* **Open** 11am-2.30pm, 4-10pm Mon-Fri; 11am-2.30pm, 4pm-midnight Sat, Sun. **Main courses** $25-$72. **Map** p320 A8 ❸ **French**
This former Downtown institution relocated to the Monte Carlo a few years back, but nothing was lost in translation. Local legend and chef André Rochat's take on haute French cuisine is revealed in interpretations such as peppercorn-crusted filet of beef and pan-seared duck breast, though the menu changes seasonally. Enjoy with a sip from Rochat's world-class wine cellar: 1,500 bottles are listed.

Andrea's
Encore Las Vegas *3131 Las Vegas Boulevard South, between E Desert Inn Road & Sands Avenue (770 5340, www.wynnlasvegas.com). Bus Deuce, 108, 203.* **Open** 6-10.30pm Mon-Thur, Sun; 6pm-2am Fri, Sat. **Main courses** $21-$89. **Map** p319 B5 ❹ **Pan-Asian**
The new Andrea's, which opened at the end of 2012, has quickly become a place to see and be seen. But

the reviews are in and the verdict is that this spot isn't just about the ambience. Yes, the expansive dining room is fashionably smart and DJs provide a late-night soundtrack, but the menu is an Asian-food aficionado's delight. Countless sushi combinations, shrimp pad Thai, dim sum, kimchee – Andrea's has it covered.

Aquaknox

Venetian *3355 Las Vegas Boulevard South, between Sands Avenue & E Flamingo Road (414 3772, www.aquaknox.net). Bus Deuce, 119, 203.* **Open** noon-3pm, 5.30-11pm Mon-Thur, Sun; noon-3pm, 5.30-11.30pm Fri, Sat. **Main courses** *Lunch* $9-$29. *Dinner* $32-$52. **Map** p319 B6 ❺ **Seafood**
The prevalence of so many excellent seafood restaurants in this desert resort town remains baffling to outsiders, and understandably so. But Aquaknox stands as solid proof that with a little expense and

a good deal of effort, it's possible to conjure up excellent fish out of next to nothing. Served in a sleek room that nods constantly to the cuisine's watery theme, Tom Moloney's food lets its fresh ingredients do the work. Good idea.

L'Atelier de Joël Robuchon

MGM Grand *3799 Las Vegas Boulevard South, at E Tropicana Avenue (891 7358, www.mgm grand.com). Bus Deuce, 201.* **Open** 5-11pm daily. **Main courses** $41-$97. **Map** p320 A8 ❻ **French**
This workshop-style dining room, right next door to Robuchon's signature restaurant (*see p141*), features a few tables and a counter at which you can sit and watch some of the world's best dishes (they're simpler and cheaper than at the other place) being prepared. Push the boat out and go for the seasonal discovery tasting menu; it's worth the $159 price tag.

A Wine Romance

Las Vegas's relationship with wine is a new one, but it's getting stronger.

Not that long ago, Las Vegas's reputation for wine could be summed up in one imaginary but by no means implausible conversation.
Waiter: 'Red or white'?
Diner: 'Yes'.

While there are still some restaurants in which that conversation continues to take place, the wine in many restaurants is much better, much more expensive and much more likely to complement that Kobe beef steak. And it will be expertly selected and uncorked at the table by somebody whose sole responsibility is to select and uncork wines.

These days, every restaurant worth its salt in Las Vegas has a sommelier, if not a full-on director of wine. It's hardly surprising, given the number of vintages on offer. **Alizé** (*see p150*) at the Palms has a 65-page wine menu; and wine director William Sherer at **Aureole** (*see p135*) has filled a wine tower so high (four storeys) and mighty (55,000 bottles) that it has a computer tablet for a menu and 'wine angels' who rope up in search of your choice.

For all the changes, which began with the improvement of the town's dining in the early 1990s, Las Vegas's wealth actually stems more from the beer-drinking legions of middle-American visitors than from the wine-consuming elite. So why the demand for sommeliers? Jaime Smith, a former wine director at MGM Grand who now works at Las Vegas mega-distributor Southern Wine & Spirits, has a theory. 'As opposed to large metro areas where, generally speaking, the public is in tune with wine and seeking it out, here people come to turn their brains off. They need someone to help them decide.'

Aureole.

Aureole

Mandalay Bay *3950 Las Vegas Boulevard South, at W Hacienda Avenue (632 7200, www.aureole lv.com). Bus Deuce, 119.* **Open** 5.30-10.30pm daily. **Main courses** $29-$70. **Tasting menu** $85. **Map** p320 A9 **7** American & steakhouses
Where else can you dine within sight of a four-storey, 4,500-bottle wine tower, up and down which float harnessed wine angels, fetching your choice? The food, orchestrated by Charlie Palmer, is a delight, with seasonal American dishes with a French twist, including Alaskan halibut with a vegetable fricassée and blue cheese crusted filet mignon. Megan Bringas's ethereal sweets make breaking your diet well worthwhile.
▶ *For the Charlie Palmer Steakhouse, see p137.*

Barmasa

Aria, CityCenter *3730 Las Vegas Boulevard South, at E Harmon Avenue (877 230 2742, www.arialasvegas.com). Bus Deuce.* **Open** 5-11pm daily. **Main courses** $18-$78. **Map** p320 A7 **8** Japanese
Entering this austere room with its darkened vaulted ceiling, one feels instantly at ease – it's like joining a sophisticated nighttime picnic in an urban backyard. The first Las Vegas restaurant by star chef Masa Takayama is heaven for fans of Japanese cuisine. Takayama prepares the finest in fresh fish – only those that have been out of Japan's coastal waters 24 hours or less will do. Inside Barmasa is a teppan eatery, Tetsu, the first of its kind by Masa.

Bartolotta Ristorante di Mare

Wynn Las Vegas *3131 Las Vegas Boulevard South, between E Desert Inn Road & Sands Avenue (770 3305, www.wynnlasvegas.com). Bus Deuce, 108, 203.* **Open** 5.30-10pm daily. **Main courses** $35-$100. **Set menu** $150-$180. **Map** p319, p320 B6 **9** Seafood
If you're lucky, you'll land a table with a view of the water outside at this posh, but by no means flashy, eatery within the Wynn resort – all the better to get you in the right frame of mind for Paul Bartolotta's cultured take on the Mediterranean seafood tradition. (That said, the menu also features pasta and a few meat options.) The high prices mean it's probably one best saved for those really special occasions.

Border Grill

Mandalay Bay *3950 Las Vegas Boulevard South, at W Hacienda Avenue (632 7200, www.bordergrill.com). Bus Deuce, 119.* **Open** 11am-10pm Mon-Thur; 11am-11pm Fri; 10am-11pm Sat; 10am-10pm Sun. **Main courses** $22-$36. **Map** p320 A9 **10** Mexican
Chefs Mary Sue Milliken and Susan Feniger, formerly of TV's *Too Hot Tamales*, offer an interesting take on Mexican food in this laid-back joint. 'Modern Mexican cuisine', according to them, is earthy, light and healthy – not the spicy, dairy-laden dishes most familiar in the US. Their classic dishes bear this out

China Poblano. See p137.

– the quesadillas are a great call – and the Sunday brunch, served until 3pm, should not be missed.

Botero

Encore *3121 Las Vegas Boulevard South, at Sands Avenue (770 3463, www.wynnlas vegas.com). Bus Deuce, 108, 203.* **Open** 6-10pm daily. **Main courses** $31-$100. **Map** p320 A7 **11** American & steakhouses
The voluptuous flavours and atmosphere of chef Mark LoRusso's contemporary cosmopolitan dinner-only steakhouse are inspired by the artwork of the restaurant's namesake, Colombian artist Fernando Botero – several of his sculptures are featured on the poolside premises. It's a steakhouse, yes, but LoRusso has an unforgettable way with seafood too, as evidenced by his Dungeness crab *agnolotti* and *brazino* with niçoise vegetables.

Bouchon

Venetian *3355 Las Vegas Boulevard South, between Sands Avenue & E Flamingo Road (414 6200, www.bouchonbistro.com/lasvegas). Bus Deuce, 119, 203.* **Open** 7am-1pm, 5-10pm daily. *Brunch* 8am-2pm Sat, Sun. *Oyster bar* 3-10pm daily. **Main courses** *Breakfast & lunch* $8-$25. *Dinner* $19-$48. **Map** p319, p320 B6 **12** French

Le Cirque.

Inside this bistro and oyster bar, the much-heralded Thomas Keller serves authentic French country fare modelled after the cuisine served in the original *bouchons* of Lyon. Indoors or on poolside seating in the gardens, indulge in Bouchon french toast for breakfast, served bread-pudding style with warm layers of brioche, custard and fresh fruit with maple syrup; or, for dinner, try the *truite amandine*, pan-roasted trout with almonds, brown butter and green beans.

★ Burger Bar

Mandalay Bay *3950 Las Vegas Boulevard South, at W Hacienda Avenue (632 9364, www.burger-bar. com). Bus Deuce, 119.* **Open** 11am-11pm Mon-Thur, Sun; 11am-1am Fri, Sat. **Main courses** $9-$60. **Map** p320 A9 ⓭ **American & steakhouses**

You'll never go back to McDonald's again, once you've had the burgers at this chic hamburger haven. Start with your choice of various beefs, buffalo or lamb; then build on it with toppings from 'the farm' (bacon, for example), 'the garden' (sliced cucumber), 'the pantry' and more. Wash it down with a salted caramel martini or a milkshake designed to your specifications. Ironically, it took a Frenchman to reinvent this most American of meals: it's the brainchild of Hubert Keller, the chef behind Fleur (*see p139*).

INSIDE TRACK
TIPS ON TIPPING

Tipping is a way of life in the US and workers in service industries rely on gratuities. Restaurant waiting staff should get 15-20 per cent, as should bartenders. At buffets, it depends on the place and price. For casino-style buffets, a couple bucks is good for the bus and drink staff, while high-end brunches – **Sterling Brunch** (*see p157*), for example – should be treated the same as regular wait staff at 15 to 20 per cent.

BurGR

Planet Hollywood *3667 Las Vegas Boulevard South, between E Harmon Avenue & E Flamingo Road (785 5555, www.gordonramsay.com). Bus Deuce, 202.* **Open** 11am-midnight Mon-Thur, Sun; 11am-2am Fri, Sat. **Main courses** $12-$15. **Map** p320 A7 ⓮ **American & steakhouses**

BurGR, a play on Gordon Ramsay's initials, is the latest addition from the fiery *Hell's Kitchen* chef to the Las Vegas culinary map. Four-star dining it isn't, but watch as the meat handlers sear mouthwatering patties on a 30ft open grill right in front of you. Choose from a number of delicious burger options, like the Uber Cheese Burger or the Farm Burger with duck-breast bacon.

Carnegie Deli

Mirage *3400 Las Vegas Boulevard South, between Spring Mountain & W Flamingo roads (791 7310, www.mirage.com). Bus Deuce, 203.* **Open** 24hrs daily. **Main courses** $14-$30. **Map** p319, p320 A6 ⓯ **Jewish**

Las Vegas has long delighted in bringing the world to its doorstep and reconstituting it for a theme-park crowd, a trend that reached its absolute apogee with the arrival of this Manhattan institution. Gone are the wisecracking staff and gigantic sandwiches; in their place are polite servers and surprisingly expensive (yet still sizeable) meals. It's not bad, but anyone who's been to the original may feel let down.

★ Central

Caesars Palace *3570 Las Vegas Boulevard South, at W Flamingo Road (650 5921, www. centrallv.com). Bus Deuce, 202.* **Open** 24hrs daily. **Main courses** $14-$65. **Map** p320 A7 ⓰ **American**

One of the newer entries into the casual/comfortable eaterie category is Central at Caesars Palace. Chef Michel Richard's second such restaurant (the first opened in Washington, DC) is an around-the-clock diner serving California-cool cuisine with an inevitable *soupçon* of French flavour. The 300-seat restaurant, directly off Caesars lobby, is sleek, airy and modern – the perfect place to grab a casual bite and watch the crowds walk by.

Charlie Palmer Steak

Four Seasons *3960 Las Vegas Boulevard South, at W Hacienda Drive (632 5120, www.charliepalmersteak.com). Bus Deuce, 119.* **Open** 5.30-10.30pm Mon-Sat. **Main courses** $28-$72. **Map** p320 A9 ⓱
American & steakhouses

Every upscale steakhouse chain in America has an outpost in Vegas. However, Charlie Palmer (who is also at the helm of Mandalay Bay's Aureole; *see p135*) stays a cut above the rest by offering ever-changing variations on the staple steak-spuds-seafood fare, thanks to resident chef de cuisine Stephen Blandino. There are classic cuts to please even the most jaded of palates, like an 18oz bone-in ribeye, plus Megan Bringas's fantastic desserts.

★ China Poblano

Cosmopolitan *3708 Las Vegas Boulevard South, at W Harmon Avenue (698 7900, www.chinapoblano.com). Bus Deuce.* **Open** 11.30am-11.30pm Mon-Thur; 10am-11.30pm Fri-Sun. **Main courses** $10-$20. **Map** p320 A7 ⓲ Chinese & Mexican

Hands down, China Poblano at the Cosmopolitan offers the most unlikely menu pairings you'll find. You may ask yourself where Chinese and Mexican cuisines intersect, but you'll have to visit China Poblano to get that answer. The important thing is that it does work, and fantastically well. With a variety of small-plate meals from Viva China tacos to the fabulous Shrimp Mojo, each dish is an unexpected, and exciting, combination. *Photo p135.*

Le Cirque

Bellagio *3600 Las Vegas Boulevard South, at W Flamingo Road (693 8865, www.bellagio.com). Bus Deuce, 202.* **Open** 5.30-10pm Tue-Sun. **Set menus** $72-$135. **Map** p320 A7 ⓳ French

This Vegas version of the New York institution is overseen by Mario Maccioni, who grew up playing and working in his father Sirio's original. Chefs come and go; some of the best in the world have passed through the kitchens of Le Cirque's various locations. But the unparalleled French cuisine and world-class service never change, and this incarnation has one attribute that none of the New York locations could ever boast: views of the Bellagio's elegant Lake Como.

Comme Ça

Cosmopolitan *3708 Las Vegas Boulevard South, at W Harmon Avenue (698 7910, www.commeca restaurant.com). Bus Deuce.* **Open** 5.30-11pm Mon-Thur; noon-11pm Fri-Sun. **Main courses** *Lunch* $16-$27. *Dinner* $26-$52. **Map** p320 A7 ⓴ French

With a rotating daily menu and classic dishes including *truite amandine* and steak Diane, at first glance this LA import might seem like any other French-style bistro. But chef David Myers – who earned his culinary chops with legends Charlie Trotter and Daniel Boulud – elevates such Gallic standbys.

★ Country Club

Wynn Las Vegas *3131 Las Vegas Boulevard South, between E Desert Inn Road & Sands Avenue (770 3463, www.wynnlasvegas.com). Bus Deuce, 108, 203.* **Open** 11.30am-3pm Mon, Tue, Sun; 11.30am-3pm, 5.30-10pm Wed-Sat. **Main courses** *Lunch* $18-$26. *Dinner* $35-$72. **Map** p320 B6 ㉑ American & steakhouses

Country Club.

Diego.

This upscale eaterie in Steve Wynn's eponymous property – supposedly the casino mogul's favourite – exudes high-stakes clubhouse chic with his take on an upmarket golf club, at prices that won't chew up your greens fees. Chef Carlos Guia delivers an American-flavoured, Cajun-influenced menu with a ton of terrific dishes, including recommended plates like Chef Carlos's Gumbo and creole-spiced Colorado bison rib-eye. Some of the tables overlook the hotel's own golf course. A jazz brunch is served on Sundays.

Craftsteak

MGM Grand *3799 Las Vegas Boulevard South, at E Tropicana Avenue (891 7318, www.craft restaurant.com). Bus Deuce, 201.* **Open** 5.30-10pm Mon-Thur, Sun; 5.30-10.30pm Fri, Sat. **Main courses** $36-$260. **Map** p320 A8 ㉒ **American & steakhouses**
The selection of meats (grass-fed veal, lamb shank, filet mignon, braised short ribs) is impressive, but the sides and the quiet invention shown in the kitchen distinguish Tom Colicchio's Craftsteak from more run-of-the-mill casino steakhouses. Ingredients come from small family farms and other below-the-radar sources, and you can tell. It's all served in a cultured, if slightly noisy, atmosphere.

★ Cut

Palazzo *3355 Las Vegas Boulevard South, between Sands Avenue & E Flamingo Road (607 6300, www.wolfgangpuck.com). Bus Deuce, 119, 203.* **Open** 5.30-10pm Mon-Thur, Sun; 5.30-11pm Fri, Sat. **Main courses** $36-$165 **Map** p320 B6 ㉓ **American & steakhouses**
Wolfgang Puck, the man responsible for revolutionizing Las Vegas visitors' eating expectations (with Spago), opened this classic steakhouse in the Palazzo in 2008. Since then, Cut has demonstrated that it's a slice above many other steak joints. For one thing,

that's all you find here: meat, meat and more glorious meat. Go for the 100% pure wagyu rib-eye if you can; but you won't go wrong with any of the other options either.

Delmonico Steakhouse

Venetian *3355 Las Vegas Boulevard South, between Sands Avenue & E Flamingo Road (414 3737, www.emerilsrestaurants.com). Bus Deuce, 119, 203.* **Open** 11am-2pm, 5.30-10pm Mon-Thur, Sun; 11am-2pm, 5.30-10.30pm Fri, Sat. **Main courses** *Lunch* $14-$52. *Dinner* $36-$52 **Map** p320 B6 ㉔ **American & steakhouses**
Looking for a slight twist on the typical steak and seafood eaterie? We've got just the place for you. Emeril Lagasse's signature Cajun spin separates Delmonico's from the rest of the pack. Try the New York strip steak with seared foie gras and a side of New Orleans-style creamed spinach. Then pinch yourself just to make sure you're not down on the bayou.

Diego

MGM Grand *3799 Las Vegas Boulevard South, at E Tropicana Avenue (891 3200, www.mgm grand.com). Bus Deuce, 201.* **Open** 5.30-10pm Mon-Fri, Sun; 5-10pm Sat. **Main courses** $25-$40. **Map** p320 A8 ㉕ **Mexican**
The experience at MGM's lively *cocina* starts as soon as you see the bold colours and backlit tequila-bottle

Fix.

tower. Traditional Mexican recipes are exemplified and often modernised; Oaxacan *carne asada* (mesquite-grilled, chile-marinated beef), Yucatan-style braised pork, cactus and tequila salsa, and so on. Start with the crab tostadas and, if you want to keep your meal simple, grab the 'enchilada style' burrito.

Eiffel Tower Restaurant
Paris Las Vegas *3655 Las Vegas Boulevard South, at E Flamingo Road (948 6937, www.eiffeltowerrestaurant.com). Bus Deuce, 202.* **Open** 11.30am-2pm Mon-Fri; 10am-2pm Fri, Sat; 5-10.15pm Mon-Thur, Sun; 5-10.45pm Fri, Sat. **Main courses** Lunch $18-$32. Dinner $32-$69. **Map** p320 A7 ㉘ **French**
In recent years, the food at Eiffel Tower Restaurant – lamb, foie gras, steaks – which is to say high-class French dishes with subtle twists, has steadily improved to rival its stunning location. Eleven floors above the Strip in the Eiffel Tower (with great views of the Bellagio's fountains) and designed with a beautifully modern sophistication, it's a stunner. The prices reflect this state of affairs, but then what else would you expect?

Estiatorio Milos
Cosmopolitan *3708 Las Vegas Boulevard South, at W Harmon Avenue (698 7930, www.milos.ca). Bus Deuce.* **Open** noon-2.30pm, 5.30-11pm Mon-Thur, Sun; noon-2.30pm, 5.30pm-midnight Fri, Sat. **Main courses** Lunch $22-$34. Dinner $24-$68. **Map** p320 A7 ㉗ **Greek & Mediterranean**
Montreal-based restaurateur Costas Spiliadis has been turning out fresh-off-the-hook seafood for 35 years. He arrived on Vegas's dining scene after establishing locations in New York, Athens and Miami. This intimate eaterie offers signature dishes including octopus, *carabineros* prawns (a large, deep-sea variety), and a raw-fish bar that will leave you wanting more.

Fiamma
MGM Grand *3799 Las Vegas Boulevard South, at E Tropicana Avenue (891 7600, www.fiamma lasvegas.com). Bus Deuce, 201.* **Open** 5.30-10pm Mon, Sun; 5.30-10.30pm Tue-Thur; 5.30-11pm Fri, Sat. **Main courses** $21-$39. **Map** p320 A8 ㉘ **Italian**
Stephen Hanson remodelled the once-proud Olio into this beautiful if oversized trattoria, a sister to his Fiamma Osteria in New York's Soho. A favourite for its cosy, trendy bar scene, Fiamma also dishes up Italian faves, such as lobster gnocchi and short rib raviolini, as well as a few chophouse-style steak, seafood and poultry dishes. Save room for dessert: the chocolate-y Torta al Cioccolato is heaven.

Fin
Mirage *3400 Las Vegas Boulevard South, between Spring Mountain & W Flamingo Roads (791 7337, www.mirage.com). Bus Deuce, 203.*

Fleur.

Open 11am-2pm, 5-11pm daily. **Main courses** *Lunch* $13-$22. *Dinner* $14-$295. **Map** p319, p320 A6 ㉙ **Chinese**
The menu isn't anything out of the ordinary; there's nothing on here to frighten the horses. But Chi Choi's renditions of Chinese classics, some slightly adapted for the modern world, are nonetheless very good, and the space in which they're served is sublime and cultured. There are options suitable for most wallets.

Fix
Bellagio *3600 Las Vegas Boulevard South, at W Flamingo Road (693 8300, www.fixlasvegas.com). Bus Deuce, 202.* **Open** 5-11pm Mon-Thur, Sun; 5pm-1am Fri, Sat. **Main courses** $28-$125. **Map** p320 A7 ㉚ **American & steakhouses**
The idea at Fix, one of the sexy Light Group eateries in town, is to bring you the 'scene and the cuisine': rather than sequestering its cast of primped diners, it opens its classy, undulating interior design to the casino so everyone can smell the wood-fired surf 'n' turf. We suggest a lounge seat, an espresso martini and small plates of crab cake bites.

Fleur
Mandalay Bay *3950 Las Vegas Boulevard South, at W Hacienda Avenue (632 9400, www.hubert keller.com). Bus Deuce, 119.* **Open** 11am-10.30pm daily. **Main courses** $12-$95. **Map** p320 A9 ㉛ **Modern European**
Fleur by Hubert Keller features 30ft walls of cultured stone, a floral sculpture, semi-private cabana tables and, in the wine loft, a private dining area. The real selling point, however, remains Hubert Keller's dedicated culinary experimentation. With small-plate dishes from every corner of the world, Fleur truly is an epicurean delight. Where else can you pair ahi tuna tacos with mozzarella flatbread and slow roasted salmon miso? Where else would you want to?

Japonais.

Gallagher's Steakhouse

New York New York *3790 Las Vegas Boulevard South, at W Tropicana Avenue (894 7111, www.gilleyslasvegas.com/bbq). Bus Deuce, 201.* **Open** 4-11pm Mon-Thur, Sun; 4pm-midnight Fri, Sat. **Main courses** $28-$50. **Map** p320 A8 ⊕ American & steakhouses

If you're weary of roaming the streets of the Big Apple looking for a surf 'n' turf place, then… you must be in the wrong place. New York is on the other side of the country. But if you're roaming Vegas's New York New York, then Gallagher's is just the place. Slabs of steak beckon from the window of the faux-cobblestone streets, and you'd be wise to answer. Simple, straightforward and just what you need for another few hours of navigating the Central Park-themed casino.

Gilley's

TI (Treasure Island) *3300 Las Vegas Boulevard South, at Spring Mountain Road (894 7111, www.gilleyslasvegas.com/bbq). Bus Deuce, 203.* **Open** 11am-midnight daily. **Main courses** $9-$35. **Map** p329 A6 ⊕ American & steakhouses

Had your fill of of sceney restaurants? Feed your face BBQ-style at Gilley's. There's nothing upscale about this restaurant/watering hole in Treasure Island; it's a rowdy and rollicking dancehall that serves heaping platters of meat-and-potato meals, slathered in sauce. If you have a hearty appetite, try the Ten Gallon Platter, which includes ribs, pulled pork, hot links and chicken – but don't blame us in the morning.

Gordon Ramsay Steak

Paris Las Vegas *3655 Las Vegas Boulevard South, at E Flamingo Road (877 346 4642, www.parislasvegas.com). Bus Deuce, 202.* **Open** 4.30-10.30pm daily. **Main courses** $48-$105. Set menu $145. **Map** p320 A7 ⊕ American & steakhouses

When celeb chef Gordon Ramsay opened his steakhouse in Paris Las Vegas in 2012, the joint bade *au revoir* to the classical French theme. This hip, modern steakhouse is in marked contrast to the rest of the hotel. No matter, Ramsay's meat joint is fantastic (if loud) fun, and his food shines too. Definitely not the place for a romantic evening, but if you like your meat, well, meaty, you'll be right at home here.

Jaleo

Cosmopolitan *3708 Las Vegas Boulevard South, at W Harmon Avenue (698 7950, www.jaleo.com). Bus Deuce.* **Open** 5-11pm Mon-Thur, Sun; 5pm-midnight Fri, Sat. **Main courses** $16-$72. **Map** p320 A7 ⊕ **Tapas**

It's loud and fun, and a visit to José Andrés' tapas restaurant can feel like sitting alfresco at a streetside café in Madrid. Jaleo is located on the third floor of the Cosmopolitan – that's the prime people-watching area of the city's hippest casino – and diners share small plates like bacon-wrapped dates, fried eggplant with honey and *jamon* Serrano with sangria and *flan*, and watch the unsurpassable parade of hyped-up humanity.

Japonais

Mirage *3400 Las Vegas Boulevard South, between Spring Mountain & W Flamingo roads (792 7979, www.japonaislasvegas.com). Bus Deuce, 203.* **Open** 5-10pm Mon-Thur, Sun; 5-11pm Fri, Sat. **Main courses** $25-$65. **Map** p319, p320 A6 ⊕ **Japanese**

Chef Jun Ichikawa offers only the most traditional styles of sushi, shunning fusion cuisine and American-style rolls. Not sure where to begin? Try the tasting menu, which pairs toro tartare, sea urchin, squid, and monkfish foie gras, wrapped in fluke and octopus. *Robata* (Japanese charcoal grill) is also a speciality. Take time to check out the lounge, located under the Mirage's domed atrium, and order a Floating Orchid. You (probably) won't regret it.

Jean Georges Steakhouse

Aria, CityCenter *3730 Las Vegas Boulevard South, at E Harmon Avenue (877 230 2742,*

www.arialasvegas.com). Bus Deuce. **Open** 5-10.30pm daily. **Main courses** $26-$65. **Map** p320 A7 ❸
Steak & seafood
Named for chef Jean-Georges Vongerichten and, well, steak, this entry brings some contemporary, international angles and curves to the traditional steak and seafood house. Starters include spring pea soup, exquisitely presented platters of oysters, and retro shrimp cocktail. The meal culminates with perhaps a Chilean sea bass with miso-yuzu glaze, a 10oz New York strip steak, or – for the big eater – a 36oz porterhouse, which you can dress with house-made hot sauce or soy-miso butter.

Joël Robuchon
MGM Grand *3799 Las Vegas Boulevard South, at E Tropicana Avenue (891 7925, www.mgm grand.com). Bus Deuce, 201.* **Open** 5.30-10pm Mon-Thur, Sun; 5.30-10.30pm Fri, Sat. **Main courses** $125-$325. **Set menus** $195 5 courses; $250 6 courses; $425 16 courses. **Map** p320 A8 ❸ **French**
The only US fine dining restaurant by the so-called 'Chef of the Century' has a lot to live up to. But what goes on in the kitchen, from Robuchon's famous *pommes purées* to dishes such as braised beef cheeks, is even more spectacular than the five-room space, which feels like a 1930s Parisian mansion. It comes at a price, of course. But once you're here, you might as well dig deep for the exquisite tasting menus.

Joe's Seafood, Prime Steak & Stone Crab
Caesars Palace (Forum Shops) *3500 Las Vegas Boulevard South, at W Flamingo Road (792 9222, www.joes.net). Bus Deuce, 202.* **Open** 11.30am-10pm Mon-Thur, Sun; 11.30am-11pm Fri, Sat. **Main courses** $20-$58. **Map** p320 A7 ❸
Seafood

When it opened a few years back, Joe's impressed many with its fresh-daily seafood, bone-in steaks and gracious service. Since then, more pricey seafood and steak joints of higher pedigree have elevated local expectations. Still, Joe's represents rare value in the field of upscale Vegas dining, and is one of the gems in the Forum Shops.

Julian Serrano
Aria, CityCenter *3730 Las Vegas Boulevard South, at E Harmon Avenue (877 230 2742, www.arialasvegas.com). Bus Deuce.* **Open** 11.30am-11.30pm daily. **Main courses** $20-$38. **Map** p320 A7 ❹ **Spanish**
Serrano serves up Spanish cuisine at its sexiest at his colourful new tapas restaurant at CityCenter's Aria. Lobster gazpacho, stuffed bacon-wrapped dates, Iberian pork shoulder and divine risotto and paella. The Spanish sandwiches are one of the best deals in the city for the quality and flavour, all under $20. The menu also offers a wide variety of vegetarian and vegan meals.

Mastro's Ocean Club
Crystals, CityCenter *3720 Las Vegas Boulevard South, at W Harmon Avenue (798 7115, www. mastrosrestaurants.com). Bus Deuce.* **Open** 5-11pm daily. **Main courses** $20-$38. **Map** p319, p320 A7 ❹ **American & steakhouses**
Cantilevered out over the austere white environs of the high-end Crystals shopping centre, Mastro's is a restaurant within a sculpture – from the outside it looks like a Jules Verne rendering of a sailing/starship; inside feels warm, inviting and classically comfortable. The menu is substantial surf 'n' turf, with fantastic steaks and grilled lobster tails – don't miss the lobster mashed-potatoes.
▶ *For shopping at Crystals, see p173.*

CONSUME

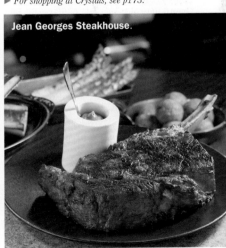

Jean Georges Steakhouse.

CONSUME

Mesa Grill

Caesars Palace *3570 Las Vegas Boulevard South, at W Flamingo Road (731 7731, www.mesagrill.com). Bus Deuce, 202.* **Open** 11am-2.30pm, 5-11pm Mon-Fri; 10.30am-3pm, 5-11pm Sat, Sun. **Main courses** *Brunch* $16-$26. *Lunch* $15-$24. *Dinner* $30-$52. **Map** p320 A7 ❷ **American & steakhouses**

Rather like Bobby Flay, the celebrity chef behind this popular restaurant, the Mesa Grill is a little on the brash side. The room itself is dazzling in all the best ways, a flourish-packed riot of colour and energy. But the nuevo-American food, like Flay, could do with a little more subtlety. The likes of pork tenderloin with sweet potato tamale and crushed pecan butter are fine, some dishes can read better than they taste.

Michael Mina

Bellagio *3600 Las Vegas Boulevard South, at W Flamingo Road (693 7223, www.michael mina.net). Bus Deuce, 202.* **Open** 5.30-10pm Mon, Tue, Thur, Sun; 5.30-10.15pm Fri, Sat. **Main courses** $41-$110. **Set menus** $65-$115. **Map** p320 A7 ❸ **Seafood**

Michael Mina's flagship restaurant in Vegas may have changed its name (it was formerly Aqua), but it still delivers what is considered by many to be the best seafood anywhere on the Strip. His caviar parfait is legendary, but the ever-changing menu also features such deep-sea delights as Maine lobster pot pie and medallions of ahi tuna. Mina's steaks are fantastic as well.

Mix

Thehotel at Mandalay Bay *3950 Las Vegas Boulevard South, at W Hacienda Avenue (632 7200, www.mandalaybay.com). Bus Deuce, 119.* **Open** 6-10pm Mon-Thur, Sun; 6-10.30pm Fri, Sat. **Main courses** $28-$69. **Map** p320 A9 ❹ **French**

From the glorious 43rd floor Strip location to the consistently high marks from diners, culinary legend Alain Ducasse's Vegas eaterie has hit the right note. Now under the helm of chef Bruno Riou (who trained under Ducasse for a decade), food is classic steak and seafood with a French touch, and both service and preparation are top shelf. Want the view without the meal? Check out the lounge next door.

Mon Ami Gabi

Paris Las Vegas *3655 Las Vegas Boulevard South, at E Flamingo Road (944 4224, www.monamigabi.com). Bus Deuce, 202.* **Open** 7am-11pm Mon-Thur, Sun; 7am-midnight Fri, Sat. **Main courses** $12-$40. **Map** p320 A7 ❺ **French**

Chicago-based Lettuce Entertain You Enterprises (ouch!) is responsible for, among others, the Eiffel Tower Restaurant (*see p139*) and this spot on the ground floor. While the Eiffel is decidedly upscale, Mon Ami Gabi wears its French theming more casually. As such, it's enjoyable. Breakfast and

lunch specialities run from classic quiche lorraine to a tuna melt, while we recommend the filet mignon merlot (with a red wine reduction) for dinner. It's a people-watching paradise, too, especially from the alfresco bit.

Nobu

Caesars Palace *3570 Las Vegas Boulevard South, at W Flamingo Road (785 6628, www.caesarspalace.com). Bus Deuce, 202.* **Open** 5-11pm Mon-Thur; 5pm-midnight Fri; 11am-3pm, 5pm-midnight Sat; 11am-3pm, 5-11pm Sun. **Main courses** *Lunch* $12-$55. *Dinner* $22-$64. **Map** p320 A7 ❻ **Japanese**

This iconic New York sushi haven, by chef Nobu Matsuhisa, is attached to the brand-new boutique Nobu Hotel within Caesars Palace (*see p117*). It's the largest Nobu restaurant in the country, and the first to offer *teppanyaki* in addition to its huge sushi selection. Its opulence – both the restaurant's and the hotel's – is second to none, with a menu to match. It's not the first Nobu in Vegas (the original is at the Hard Rock Hotel), but this outpost will be the one by which the others are judged.

Noodles

Bellagio *3600 Las Vegas Boulevard South, at W Flamingo Road (693 8865, www.bellagio.com). Bus Deuce, 202.* **Open** 11am-2am daily. *Dim sum* 11am-3pm Fri-Sun. **Main courses** $18-$94. **Map** p320 A7 ❼ **Pan-Asian**

A gem showcasing the subtle, modern elegance of Tony Chi's pan-Asian dishes, Noodles is everything its name implies: rice noodles, egg noodles, vermicelli and more. Enjoy the urban diner feel, the late hours, the selection of dim sum (available Friday to Sunday), traditional dishes like *kung pao* shrimp, and, of course, the rest of the hot and chilled noodle dishes from across Asia.

Olives

Bellagio *3600 Las Vegas Boulevard South, at W Flamingo Road (693 8865, www.toddenglish.com). Bus Deuce, 202.* **Open** 11am-2.45pm, 5-10.30pm daily. **Main courses** *Lunch* $17-$32. *Dinner* $29-$55. **Map** p320 A7 ❽ **American & steakhouses**

Classy but casual, delicious but affordable, Todd English's Las Vegas establishment overlooking the Bellagio lake has grown into a trustworthy dining institution. Boston-based English (the original Olives is in Charlestown, MA) keeps his 'interpretive Mediterranean' cuisine alive and well with such innovations as butternut squash tortellini and an incredible take on the lobster roll.

Pampas

Planet Hollywood *3663 Las Vegas Boulevard South, between E Harmon Avenue & E Flamingo Road (737 4748, www.pampasusa.com). Bus Deuce, 202.* **Open** 11.30am-10.30pm Mon-Thur,

Sun; 11.30am-11.30pm Fri, Sat. **Main courses** *Lunch* $11-$29. *Dinner* $27-$50. **Map** p320 A7 ㊾ **Brazilian**

This Brazilian *churrascaria rodizio* restaurant is an all-you-can-eat establishment where various barbecued meats are paraded from table to table on large skewers, and sliced right there and then for hungry diners. Not an ideal venue for vegetarians, perhaps (although vegetarian *rodizios* are available), but carnivores will be licking their lips with delight at the very idea.

Panevino

246 Via Antonia Avenue, at S Gillespie Street (222 2400, www.panevinolasvegas.com). Bus Deuce. **Open** 11am-10pm Mon-Fri; 5-10pm Sat. **Main courses** *Lunch* $15-$34. *Dinner* $19-$48. **Map** p317 X4 ㊿ **Italian**

The number-one reason to eat at Panevino is the panoramic view, offered through architecturally enhanced windows that run the length of the restaurant and frame the action at McCarran International Airport and the Strip beyond. The food, though, comes a close second: the menu has plenty of interesting offerings, including risottos, pastas, pizzas and seafood.

Pearl

MGM Grand *3799 Las Vegas Boulevard South, at E Tropicana Avenue (891 7380, www.mgmgrand.com). Bus Deuce, 201.* **Open** 5.30-10pm Mon, Thur, Sun; 5.30-10.30pm Fri, Sat. **Main courses** $18-$50. **Map** p320 A8 (51) **Chinese**

A quiet, time-honoured winner on the Strip's upscale restaurant scene, Pearl offers a fresh take on classic Chinese cuisine from Canton and Shanghai provinces, with dishes that rotate to reflect the changing of the seasons. There are also plenty of memorable touches off the menu, including an exotic-tea cart and an elegant contemporary room designed by Tony Chi.

Phil's Italian Steak House

(TI) Treasure Island *3300 Las Vegas Boulevard South, at Spring Mountain Road (894 7351, www.treasureisland.com). Bus Deuce, 203.* **Open** 5-10pm daily. **Main courses** $19-$65. **Map** p320 A6 (52) **Italian & steakhouses**

This Treasure Island dining room doesn't win many 'best-of' awards, but that may be because of the rather low profile it keeps. In truth, the oversized room at TI may not serve the best steak you've ever had, but it's certainly worth visiting if you want a good slice of meat that won't dent your wallet. The same is true for Phil's Italian dishes like the *osso bucco* or the *risotto aragosta*.

Picasso

Bellagio *3600 Las Vegas Boulevard South, at W Flamingo Road (693 8865, www.bellagio.com). Bus Deuce, 202.* **Open** 5.30-9.30pm daily. **Set menus** $75-$115. **Map** p320 A7 (53) **French**

When your room is lined with $20 million of Picasso paintings, you have to work pretty hard to make an impression. But Julian Serrano usually manages to do it. Unlike a lot of celebrity chefs with high-profile restaurants in Vegas, Serrano actually cooks at Picasso, building two crisp, daisy-fresh and wonderfully uncomplicated French-slanted menus nightly. Service is a treat and the wine list is stellar.

Pink's

Planet Hollywood *3667 Las Vegas Boulevard South, between E Harmon Avenue & E Flamingo Road (405 4711, www.pinkshollywood.com). Bus Deuce, 202.* **Open** 10.30am-midnight Mon-Thur, Sun; 10.30am-3am Fri, Sat. **Main courses** $6-$9. **Map** p320 A7 (54) **American & steakhouses**

You're unlikely to catch the great and the good of Hollywood here, as you might if you spend enough time hanging around by the 70-year-old LA original. However, if you're in the mood for a diet-busting dog

topped with all manner of greasy gloop, there's really nowhere else in town for such superior junk food.

Pinot Brasserie

Venetian *3355 Las Vegas Boulevard South, between Sands Avenue & E Flamingo Road (414 8888, www.venetian.com). Bus Deuce, 119, 203.* **Open** 11.30am-3pm, 5-9pm Mon-Thur, Sun; 11.30am-3pm, 5-10pm Fri, Sat. **Main courses** *Lunch* $16-$32. *Dinner* $29-$47. **Map** p319, p320 B6 ⑮ **French**

Joachim Splichal gives his French cuisine a lighter touch, with pastas, seafood, steak and wild game. The homey decor is *très rustique*, with copper pots, leather club chairs and paintings depicting wildlife frolicking in the French countryside. An individual cheese menu offers diners a sampling of five types (out of 30) for $22. The bistro also has a large rotisserie and oyster bar.

Postrio

Venetian *3355 Las Vegas Boulevard South, between Sands Avenue & E Flamingo Road (796 1110, www.wolfgangpuck.com). Bus Deuce, 119, 203.* **Open** 11am-10.30pm Mon-Thur, Sun; 11am-11pm Fri, Sat. **Main courses** *Lunch* $9-$28. *Dinner* $16-$50. **Map** p319, p320 B6 ⑯ **American & steakhouses**

The most intimate – and, some say, best – restaurant in Wolfgang Puck's Vegas collection, Postrio blends San Francisco and Venice to achieve a romantic atmosphere. Food fuses Mediterranean and Asian influences; seasonal specials include pan-roasted 'Hong Kong style' Scottish salmon with stir fry vegetables, and seafood curry in a coconut broth. The desserts are a must: try the warm chocolate beignets with caramel espresso ice-cream.

Prime

Bellagio *3600 Las Vegas Boulevard South, at W Flamingo Road (693 7223, www.bellagio.com). Bus Deuce, 202.* **Open** 5-10pm daily. **Main courses** $25-$48. **Map** p320 A7 ⑰ **American & steakhouses**

Prime indeed. In fact, one could go further: first class, superior and pre-eminent pretty much sum up Jean-Georges Vongerichten's steakhouse, where the striking setting comes with a perfect view of the Bellagio's fountains. There's magic on the plate, too: steaks are the highlights, but don't overlook the parmesan-crusted chicken, seared ahi tuna or wood-grilled veal chop. And start with the bacon-wrapped shrimp. You can thank us later.

★ Rao's

Caesars Palace *3570 Las Vegas Boulevard South, at W Flamingo Road (731 7267, www. caesarspalace.com). Bus Deuce, 202.* **Open** 5-10.30pm Mon, Tue, 11am-3pm, 5-10.30pm Wed-Sun. **Main courses** *Lunch* $14-$28. *Dinner* $18-$57. **Map** p320 A7 ⑱ **Italian**

The original Rao's has been operating in New York City for more than 115 years, and is known as one of the toughest reservations in the Big Apple. The

Sensi.

Caesars Palace spinoff is a lot easier to access, although you'll still need to book in advance. And the food is well worth the wait: classic Italian recipes that have been fine-tuned by the same family for more than a century. One of the house specialities is spaghetti alla bolognese, but everything on the menu is sure to please.

Red 8

Wynn Las Vegas *3131 Las Vegas Boulevard South, between E Desert Inn Road & Sands Avenue (770 3380, www.wynnlasvegas.com). Bus Deuce, 108, 203.* **Open** 11.30am-midnight Mon-Thur, Sun; 11am-1am Fri, Sat. **Main courses** $17-$50. **Map** p320 B6 ⑩ **Pan-Asian**
Many of the restaurants at Wynn set the sky as their limit when pricing their dishes, but this pleasingly simple Asian bistro keeps things so affordable that even the riff-raff can eat here. Stick with the noodle dishes and you won't be disappointed.

Restaurant Guy Savoy

Caesars Palace *3570 Las Vegas Boulevard South, at W Flamingo Road (731 7286, www. caesarspalace.com). Bus Deuce, 202.* **Open** 5.30-9.30pm Wed-Sun. **Main courses** $60-$180. **Set menus** $258 9 courses; $348 13 courses. **Map** p320 A7 ⑩ **French**
Managed by Guy's son Franck Savoy, with Mathieu Chartron presiding over the kitchen, this is among the most expensive dining rooms in Vegas. However, it's worth every penny, providing a level of culinary sophistication rarely glimpsed here. Highlights include artichoke and black truffle soup served with toasted mushroom brioche, and guinea hen cooked inside a pig's bladder to preserve the moisture. If you have the cash, try the 13-course innovation-inspiration menu.

★ Rx Boiler Room

Mandalay Bay *3930 Las Vegas Boulevard South, at W Hacienda Avenue (632 9300, www.rm seafood.com). Bus Deuce, 119.* **Open** 11.30am-11pm daily. **Main courses** $25-$35. **Map** p320 A9 ⑩ **American & steakhouses**
Rick Moonen moved to Vegas from New York to ensure that everything at his restaurant, RM Seafood, lived up to its initials. But after a multiyear run, the two-storey eaterie dedicated to 'delicious, sustainable seafood', closed its doors to make way for Moonen's Rx Boiler Room (the 'Rx' is pronounced 'Rick's'), a comfort-food spot with a steampunk design and a casual dining atmosphere.

★ Sage

Aria, CityCenter *3730 Las Vegas Boulevard South, at E Harmon Avenue (590 8690, www.arialasvegas.com). Bus Deuce.* **Open** 5-11pm Mon-Sat. **Main courses** $39-$54. **Set menus** $89-$120. **Map** p320 A7 ⑩ **American & steakhouses**

Easily one of the best newer places in which to eat in Las Vegas, Sage is a testament to the idea that great food does not have to be complicated. Chef Shawn McClain strives for simplicity in dishes such as Kobe skirt steak and organic chicken, and the result is a memorable meal that satisfies. For pre- (or post-) dinner cocktails, check out Sage's absinthe menu, with 11 varieties, as well.

Sensi

Bellagio *3600 Las Vegas Boulevard South, at W Flamingo Road (693 8865, www.bellagio.com). Bus Deuce, 202.* **Open** 5.30-10pm daily. **Main courses** $32-$55. **Map** p320 A7 ⑩ **Pan-Asian & Italian**
Japanese firm Super Potato designed this culinary theatre to complement Martin Heierling's world cuisine, a combination of Italian and Asian influences, grilled dishes and seafood classics. Four glass-enclosed kitchens in the middle of the room provide an interactive stage: watch curries plunge into a red-hot tandoori oven on the Asian stage; spot focaccias with vacherin cheese and black truffles slipped into a wood-fire oven in the Italian corner; and see Blue Point oysters shucked in the raw section.

SHe by Morton's

Crystals, CityCenter *3720 Las Vegas Boulevard South, at W Harmon Avenue (254 2376, www. she-lv.com). Bus Deuce.* **Open** 5.30-11pm Mon-Thur, Sun; 5.30pm-midnight Fri, Sat. **Main courses** $30-$96. **Map** p320 A7 ⑩ **American & steakhouses**
One of many celebrity owned restaurants in Las Vegas, SHe – its patron is *Desperate Housewives* star Eva Longoria – has had a tough run. Originally opened as a steakhouse/nightclub, the club portion closed within a month. Whether SHe the eaterie will thrive remains to be seen. Tucked into the entrance of the Crystals shopping centre, a *Housewives* hangout if there ever was one, the candlelit restaurant infuses a classic steakhouse with Latin flair.

Shibuya

MGM Grand *3799 Las Vegas Boulevard South, at E Tropicana Avenue (891 7800, www.mgm grand.com). Bus Deuce, 201.* **Open** 5-10pm Mon-Thur, Sun; 5-10.30pm Fri, Sat. **Main courses** $40-$90. **Map** p320 A8 ⑩ **Japanese**
Shibuya is really three beautiful restaurants in one: a 50ft marble sushi bar; a collection of *teppanyaki* (table cooking) grills under hot pink stainless steel canopies; and a pair of modern rooms where guests can indulge in a French spin on modern Japanese cuisine. Guests in any section are free to order from the various menus, and everything is easily shared.

Sinatra

Encore *3121 Las Vegas Boulevard South, at E Desert Inn Road (770 3463, www.wynnlasvegas. com). Bus Deuce, 108, 203.* **Open** 5.30-10pm

CONSUME

Stripsteak.

Mon-Thur, Sun; 5.30-10.30pm Fri, Sat. **Main courses** $27-$55. **Map** p320 A7 ⑥⑥ Italian
Inspired, of course, by the Chairman of the Board himself, this dinner-only Italian restaurant is subtly decorated with Ol' Blue Eyes memorabilia – including the Oscar Sinatra won for his role in *From Here to Eternity* – and transports visitors back to an earlier moment in Vegas history. Start with the signature Sinatra Smash cocktail and move on to the lobster risotto, osso bucco 'My Way' and veal milanese.

Social House
Crystals, CityCenter *3720 Las Vegas Boulevard South, at W Harmon Avenue (736 1122, www. crystalsatcitycenter.com/social-house). Bus Deuce.* **Open** noon-11pm Mon-Thur, Sun; noon-midnight Fri, Sat. **Main courses** *Lunch* $20-$26. *Dinner* $22-$125. **Map** p320 A7 ⑥⑦ Pan-Asian
This eatery in Crystals, the high-end shopping mecca at CityCenter, recently rebranded itself as an Asian-food destination, tagging itself as a place for 'sushi, sake and socialising'. Chef John Lee has helped to remake the beautiful venue into an A-list hotspot. In addition to its seemingly endless sushi and sake selections, Social House also serves a wide variety of teas and small-plate samplings.

Spago
Caesars Palace (Forum Shops) *3500 Las Vegas Boulevard South, at W Flamingo Road (369 6300, www.wolfgangpuck.com). Bus Deuce, 202.* **Open** *Café* 11.30am-11pm Mon-Thur, Sun; 11.30am-midnight Fri, Sat. *Restaurant* 5.30-10pm daily. **Main courses** *Lunch* $12-$38. *Dinner* $18-$72. **Map** p320 A7 ⑥⑧ American & steakhouses
The Wolfgang Puck eatery that reinvented Vegas dining in 1992, Spago has managed to stay smart with tourists and power-lunchers by regularly reinventing itself. And although Spago may have its detractors (as does anything in Las Vegas that's more than five years old), it still manages to turn out quality food. Options in the formal dining room include seasonal specialities (lobster, truffles) and

organic vegetarian offerings; in the indoor patio café, there are signature salads, pizzas and sandwiches.

Stack
Mirage *3400 Las Vegas Boulevard South, between Spring Mountain & W Flamingo roads (693 8300, www.stacklasvegas.com). Bus Deuce, 203.* **Open** 5-10pm Mon, Wed, Thur, Sun; 5-10.30pm Tue; 5-11pm Fri, Sat. **Main courses** $29-$62. **Map** p319, p320 A6 ⑥⑨ American & steakhouses
The name refers to the design by the Graft Lab of Berlin, in which the mahogany walls resemble geological strata, something like the mouth of a canyon, beckoning you. It will lure you in; the American-style cuisine (giant steaks, Kobe burgers, whipped potatoes and comfort desserts such as jelly-filled doughnut holes) will make you glad you stayed.

★ Steak House
Circus Circus *2880 Las Vegas Boulevard South, between W Sahara Avenue & Desert Inn Road (794 3767, www.circuscircus.com). Bus Deuce, 108.* **Open** 4-10pm Mon-Fri, Sun; 4-11pm Sat. **Main courses** $40-$77. **Map** p319 B5 ⑦⓿ American & steakhouses
Feel like you wouldn't be caught dead dining at an eatery that's presided over by Lucky the Clown? Then you'll never know what you're missing. True, the surroundings here neuter some of the sophistication, but this is still an excellent choice if you've a yen for a large lump of cow. The steaks here are aged for 21 days and then mesquite-grilled – order rare or you'll miss out on some of the flavour. What's more, the prices are well below those of other beef emporia along the Strip. A Vegas legend of sorts.

Stripsteak
Mandalay Bay *3950 Las Vegas Boulevard South, at W Hacienda Avenue (632 7414, www.michael mina.net). Bus Deuce, 119.* **Open** 5.30-10.30pm daily. **Main courses** $29-$105. **Map** p320 A9 ⑦① American & steakhouses

Star chef Michael Mina's first steakhouse has proved to be a hit-or-miss experience. Some diners call it the best steak and service they've ever had; others proclaim it 'terrible'. The food isn't bad, but at prices this high ($25 for a waygu burger; $59 for a 10oz filet mignon), it needs to be dazzling. It's rarely quite that good. The slow-poached prime rib is the best bet, but that said, do try one of the supreme desserts. The open-plan restaurant area can get pretty loud when it's busy, which is reasonably often.

Sushi Roku

Caesars Palace (Forum Shops) *3500 Las Vegas Boulevard South, at W Flamingo Road (733 7373, www.sushiroku.com). Bus Deuce, 202.* **Open** noon-10pm Mon-Thur, Sun; noon-11pm Fri, Sat. **Main courses** *Lunch* $12-$29. *Dinner* $25-$55. **Map** p320 A7 **72 Japanese**
As if Las Vegas wasn't enough like LA, in slinks this Santa Monica/Hollywood hotspot, all dressed up and ready for some celebrity action. With similar prices to Nobu (*see p142*) but less of the cachet, Sushi Roku proves that getting super-fresh fish in the desert isn't cheap. Fanatics are split on whether it's worth the price tag, but anyone worth their $500 jeans knows that the Strip views and loungey bar scene are draws equal to the sensational sashimi.

Tableau

Wynn Las Vegas *3131 Las Vegas Boulevard South, between E Desert Inn Road & Sands Avenue (770 3330, www.wynnlasvegas.com). Bus Deuce, 108, 203.* **Open** 7am-2.30pm daily. **Main courses** *Breakfast & brunch* $16-$33. *Lunch* $14-$28. **Map** p319, p320 B6 **73**
American & steakhouses
If breakfast is the most important meal of the day, then the second-most important must be lunch. Either way, Tableau has you covered. Start your day with Tableau's lobster and shrimp frittata, or the white chocolate and orange French toast. Finding a morning meal in Vegas as delicious as those served at Tableau is a treat. If the morning scene isn't your thing, lunch starts at 11.30am. Grab a poolside table if you can.

Tao

Venetian *3355 Las Vegas Boulevard South, between Sands Avenue & E Flamingo Road (388 8338, www.taorestaurantlv.com). Bus Deuce, 119, 203.* **Open** 5pm-midnight Mon-Thur, Sun; 5pm-1am Fri, Sat. **Main courses** $20-$88. **Map** p319, p320 B6 **74 Pan-Asian**
This ever-fashionable NYC import is best known these days as a nightclub and lounge (*see p224*) that attracts the beautiful people and microcelebs with money to burn. However, the pan-Asian food – spanning extensive sushi options and small plates, up to a Kobe ribeye in cilantro butter – is also pretty good, especially when paired with one of the club's speciality drinks.

Trevi

Caesars Palace (Forum Shops) *3500 Las Vegas Boulevard South, at W Flamingo Road (735 4663, www.trevi-italian.com). Bus Deuce, 202.* **Open** 11am-11pm Mon-Thur, Sun; 11am-midnight Fri, Sat. **Main courses** $14-$33. **Map** p320 A7 **75 Italian**
For the most part, Caesars and the adjacent Forum Shops wear their theming lightly. One notable exception is this Italian eatery, named for the fountain and located right by its Vegas replica. Trevi replaced the long-serving Bertolini's, and previous visitors may not notice a great deal of difference in the menu of Italian comfort food. But this is still a reliable option; and next to its competitors in the Forum Shops, it's pretty fairly priced.

Valentino

Venetian *3355 Las Vegas Boulevard South, between Sands Avenue & E Flamingo Road (414 3000, www.venetian.com). Bus Deuce, 119, 203.* **Open** 5.30-10pm daily. **Main courses** $28-$52. **Map** p319, p320 B6 **76 Italian**
Piero Selvaggio's companion restaurant to his LA original, delivered by executive chef Luciano Pellegrini, is authentic in every regard. The food is plenty impressive, whether you order *pollo al mattone* (young chicken in a succulent lemon caper sauce), veal or baked Mediterranean bass. Accompany your choice with one of the Italian cocktails and finish with tiramisu or flan – all delivered in a room that stays on the right side of the line separating handsome from gauche.

Verandah Café

Four Seasons *3960 Las Vegas Boulevard South, at W Hacienda Drive (632 7200, www.mandalaybay.com). Bus Deuce, 119.* **Open** 6.30am-10pm Mon-Fri; 7am-10pm Sat, Sun. **Main courses** *Breakfast/brunch* $14-$28. *Lunch* $15-$26. *Dinner* $15-$39. **Map** p320 A9 **77 American & steakhouses**
Outfitted in everything from suits to tennis shorts, rock stars, real-estate magnates and other sundry types find this comfortable California country club-styled spot irresistible. The under-promoted yet popular Sunday brunch is an all-you-can-savour treat, putting other buffets to shame at a price that says it should. A poolside dining area (request when booking) spirits you away to Santa Barbara for bellinis and blintzes.

► *For more buffets, see p156.*

Wing Lei

Wynn Las Vegas *3131 Las Vegas Boulevard South, between E Desert Inn Road & Sands Avenue (770 3388, www.wynnlasvegas.com). Bus Deuce, 108, 203.* **Open** 5.30-10pm daily. **Main courses** $28-$88. **Map** p319, p320 B6 **78 Chinese**
As if naming your casino after yourself wasn't outlandish enough, Steve Wynn has also lent his identity

CONSUME

to this super-smart restaurant: Wing translates as 'Wynn' in Chinese. Happily, the mogul's vanity doesn't extend to taking charge of the kitchen. Expect cultured Chinese food in a predictably luxurious environment in this Michelin-starred restaurant.

Wolfgang Puck Bar & Grill
MGM Grand *3799 Las Vegas Boulevard South, at E Tropicana Avenue (891 3000, www.wolfgang puck.com). Bus Deuce, 201.* **Open** 11.30am-10.30pm Mon-Thur, Sun; 11.30am-11.30pm Fri, Sat. **Main courses** $20-$39. **Map** p320 A8 ❼
American & steakhouses
Styled after a California beach bungalow, and a very modish one at that, this Puck outpost offers a contemporary take on Californian cuisine. Signature dishes include truffled potato chips with blue cheese, crispy chicken milanese and Puck pizzas; every bite is delicious and perfectly suited to a lazy lunch or dinner.

Stratosphere Area

Florida Café
Howard Johnson *1401 S Las Vegas Boulevard South, at W Charleston Boulevard (385 3013, www.floridacafecuban.com). Bus Deuce, 108.* **Open** 7am-10pm daily. **Main courses** $8-$17. **Map** p319 C3 ❺⓿ **Latin American**
A rather scruffy-looking motel at the wrong end of Las Vegas Boulevard provides the unlikely setting for the most popular Cuban restaurant in Las Vegas. This isn't subtle food, by any means, and nor is it especially healthy. But don't let that stop you – as comfort cooking goes, it's just exotic enough to stand out from the pack. Try a Cuban sandwich if you're not absolutely ravenous.

Thai Original BBQ
1424 S 3rd Street, at Las Vegas Boulevard South (383 1128, www.thaioriginalbbqlv.com). Bus Deuce. **Open** 11am-10pm daily. **Main courses** $8-$12. **Map** p319 C3 ❻⓿ **Thai**
Despite its gritty locale, Thai Original BBQ remains one of the best Thai eateries in town. The friendly and helpful service makes choosing from the large menu of specialities simple; the hearty portions of such classics as pad thai are worth the trip. Highlights include papaya salad, excellent satay, and rich and spicy beef noodle soup.

★ Top of the World
Stratosphere *2000 Las Vegas Boulevard South, at W St Louis Avenue (380 7711, www.topoftheworldlv.com). Bus Deuce, 108.* **Open** 11am-3.30pm, 4-11pm Mon-Fri; 11am-3.30pm, 4-11.30pm Sat, Sun. **Main courses** Lunch $25-$45. Dinner $40-$79. **Map** p319 C4 ❻⓶ **American & steakhouses**
The views are the main selling point of this restaurant at the top of the Stratosphere, and with good

---

INSIDE TRACK RED, RED MEAT

It seems burgers are all the rage these days with Gordon Ramsay's popular new **BurGR** (*see p137*), as well as super-tasty meat sandwiches from **LBS** at Red Rock Resort (*see p126*) and **Holsteins** at the Cosmo (*see p85*). But if you're looking to pay top dollar for a slab of ground beef between two buns, head to Hubert Keller's **Fleur** (*see p139*) at Mandalay Bay, where you can nosh on the world's most expensive: the Fleur Burger 5000 – a Wagyu beef burger with foie gras and truffles, served with a 1995 bottle of Chateau Petrus – a bargain at $5,000.

---

reason: they're spectacular, especially on a clear night. However, the food is better than it needs to be – a brisk, cultured mix of American and French-influenced classics. Prices are almost as high as the restaurant itself; you can just stop by for a drink if the food is out of budgetary range.

OFF-STRIP
East of the Strip

Culinary Dropout
Hard Rock *4455 Paradise Road, at E Harmon Avenue (552 8100, www.hardrockhotel.com). Bus 108.* **Open** 11am-midnight Mon-Thur; 11am-2am Fri; 9am-2am Sat; 9am-midnight Sun. **Main courses** $12-$32. **Map** p320 C7 ❻⓷ **American & steakhouses**
This new addition to the Hard Rock's impressive dining roster is not your typical pub fare. Yes, Culinary Dropout is a great place to knock back a few brews – crafts, draughts, cans, or even wine if you prefer – but it also has an unusual assortment of dishes to pave the way for those drinks. Try the jambalaya, fried chicken or rainbow trout in this casual and inviting eatery.

Envy
Renaissance *3400 Paradise Road, between E Desert Inn Road & E Twain Avenue (784 5700, www.envysteakhouse.com). Bus 108, 203.* **Open** 6.30-11am, 5-10pm daily. **Main courses** Breakfast $14-$19. Dinner $30-$90. **Map** p319 C6 ❻⓸ **American & steakhouses**
Plenty of big deals are hammered out at this modern steakhouse during convention season. House specialities include a Tuscan veal chop and a surf 'n' turf dish with a filet mignon – try it with one of the signature sauces like the spicy chipotle-gorgonzola. Enjoy your meal with one of the 1,500 bottles of wine housed in a candlelit, walk-in cellar and wine wall.

Firefly

3824 Paradise Road, at E Twain Avenue (369 3971, www.fireflylv.com). Bus 108, 203. **Open** 11.30am-2am daily. **Main courses** $12-$20. *Tapas* $4-$10. **Map** p320 C6 ⑥ **Tapas**

This popular tapas bar is populated by a parade of pretty locals almost every night of the week. Music (downtempo to Latin house) competes with sangria-fuelled chatter, as small plates – scrumptious bacon-wrapped dates, mushroom tarts, shrimp ceviche – emerge from the busy kitchen. Can't make it here? Try one of the other locations: 9560 W Sahara Ave (834 3814) or 11261 S Eastern Ave (in Henderson, 778 1400).

Fogo de Chão

360 E Flamingo Road, between Paradise Road & Howard Hughes Parkway (431 4500, www.fogodechao.com). Bus 108, 202. **Open** 11.30am-2pm, 5-10pm Mon-Thur; 11am-2pm, 5-10.30pm Fri; 4.30-10.30pm Sat; 4-9pm Sun. **Main courses** $32-$64. **Map** p320 C3 ⑥ **Brazilian & steakhouses**

This authentic *churrascaria* – the original was opened in Porto Alegre, Brazil, in 1979 – has steadily been making inroads in the US for years. Its recent addition to Las Vegas has proven popular with visitors and locals, both for its outstanding food and for its service. Try house specialities like Frango (bacon-wrapped chicken) or Beef Ancho. Meat on a stick – how can you go wrong?

Gandhi

4080 Paradise Road, at E Flamingo Road (734 0094, www.gandhicuisine.com). Bus 108, 202. **Open** 11am-10.30pm daily. *Buffet* 11am-2.30pm daily. **Main courses** *Lunch buffet* $12. *Dinner* $13-$26. **Map** 336 C7 ⑦ **Indian**

Good northern and southern Indian cuisine, including a fine selection of vegetarian dishes, are combined at this longtime local favourite. The all-you-can-eat lunch buffet is nice and spicy, and stars such dishes as chicken pakora, *keema naan* (stuffed bread with minced lamb) and chicken tikka masala for next to nothing.

Komol

Commercial Center, 953 E Sahara Avenue, between S 6th Street & S Maryland Parkway (731 6542, www.komolrestaurant.com). Bus SX, 109. **Open** 11am-10pm Mon-Sat; noon-10pm Sun. **Main courses** $7-$21. **Map** p317 Y2 ⑥ **Thai**

Despite its location in the run-down Commercial Center, where it competes with the nationally renowned Lotus of Siam and a pair of nationally infamous sex clubs, Komol remains hugely popular for its authentic rendering of Thai cuisine, vast range of vegetarian and vegan options, plus 1950s Americana such as egg foo young, all at bargain prices. Specify the degree of heat you'd like, and the kitchen will try to comply.

Lawry's The Prime Rib

4043 Howard Hughes Parkway, at E Flamingo Road (893 2223, www.lawrysonline.com). Bus 108, 202. **Open** 11.30am-2pm, 5-10pm Mon-Thur; 11.30am-2pm, 5-11pm Fri; 5-11pm Sat; 5-10pm Sun. **Main courses** *Lunch* $17-$26. *Dinner* $37-$59. **Map** p320 B7 ⑥ **American & steakhouses**

With a name like 'The Prime Rib', there's little question about what to expect on the menu at Lawry's. But if that's what you're craving, you won't find a much better choice in Las Vegas. This outpost just a couple of blocks off the Strip has been serving delicious slabs of red meat for more than 15 years, and still the crowds keep coming back. If it ain't broke…

★ Lotus of Siam

Commercial Center, 953 E Sahara Avenue, between S 6th Street & S Maryland Parkway (735 3033, www.lotusofsiamlv.com). Bus SX, 109. **Open** 11.30am-2.30pm, 5.30-10pm Mon-Fri; 5.30-10pm Sat, Sun. **Main courses** *Lunch buffet* $9. *Dinner* $9-$35. **Map** p317 Y2 ⑥ **Thai**

Lauded by food bloggers and critics, Lotus of Siam was rated the best Thai restaurant in the US by now-defunct culinary bible, *Gourmet* magazine. We might not go that far, but it is certainly a rare and unexpected treat in an otherwise unprepossessing strip mall. Saipin Chutima puts her specialities on the huge and easy-to-read menu, and isn't afraid to make her food spicy. However, many diners opt for the excellent and super-cheap lunch buffet.

Mr Lucky's 24/7

Hard Rock *4455 Paradise Road, at E Harmon Avenue (693 5592, www.hardrockhotel.com). Bus 108.* **Open** 24hrs daily. **Main courses** $10-$26. **Map** p320 C7 ⑥ **American & steakhouses**

This round-the-clock staple of dining in the Hard Rock has grown with the hotel. Recently renovated with a more up-to-date look, Lucky's still offers the crowd-pleasing plates that have kept hungry guests coming back for nearly two decades, dishing out burgers, sandwiches and breakfast classics (try the *huevos rancheros*) to a disparate pre- and post-party crowd. Great people-watching too.

Nobu

Hard Rock *4455 Paradise Road, at E Harmon Avenue (693 5090, www.hardrockhotel.com). Bus 108.* **Open** 6-10.30pm Mon-Thur, Sun; 5-11pm Fri, Sat. **Main courses** $11-$80. **Set menus** $150-$200. **Map** p320 C7 ⑥ **Japanese**

Plenty of imitators have emerged in recent years, trying to replicate chef Nobu Matsuhisa's Japanese fusion cuisine and ultra-hip room. But Nobu remains the original, one reason why it will probably never lose its credibility or its appeal. Big prices and little slices follow the leads of its New York and London brethren. If you can, indulge in the chef's *omakase* tasting menu.

Origin India

*4480 Paradise Road, at E Harmon Avenue
(734 6342, www.originindiarestaurant.com).
Bus 108.* **Open** 11.30am-11.30pm daily. **Main
courses** *Lunch buffet* $12. *Dinner* $16-$33.
Map p320 C7 ㉝ **Indian**

Having reigned unchallenged for years, Gandhi (*see
p149*) now has some genuine competition for the title
of Vegas's best Indian eaterie. The low-lit swank of
Origin India differentiates it from Vegas's other
Indian restaurants, but the pleasingly spicy food is
also a class apart, with classics such as *saag gosht*
(lamb with spinach) and a creamy chicken *makhani*
rendered in technicolour brilliance.

Pamplemousse

*400 E Sahara Avenue, at Paradise Road (733
2066, www.pamplemousserestaurant.com). Bus
SX, 108.* **Open** 5-10pm Tue-Sun. **Main courses**
$24-$38. **Map** p319 C4 ㉞ **French**

Along with André's (*see p133*) and the Bootlegger (*see
p154*), Georges La Forge's eaterie is one of a very few
non-casino old Vegas classics, having served country-
style French fare to such regulars as Wayne Newton
and Robin Leach for decades. The camp-classic eaterie,
whose name was suggested by Bobby Darin, isn't on
the radar for many visitors, but if you want to see
Vegas as it was, this is one place to do so.

Pink Taco

Hard Rock *4455 Paradise Road, at E Harmon
Avenue (693 5525, www.hardrockhotel.com).
Bus 108.* **Open** 11am-10pm Mon-Thur, Sun;
11am-close Fri, Sat. **Main courses** $14-$21.
Map p320 C7 ㉟ **Latin American**

Only the Hard Rock could get away with giving a
restaurant a name that was such a jaw-dropping
double entendre. Happily, though, this Mexican
eaterie transcends its moniker. The menu doesn't
hold any surprises, at least not if you stick to the
favourites (burritos, enchiladas). Hit the Pink Taco
during its buzzing happy hour for Mexican-style
sliders or mini taco appetisers.

★ 35 Steaks + Martinis

Hard Rock *4455 Paradise Road, at E Harmon
Avenue (693 5500, www.hardrockhotel.com). Bus
108.* **Open** 5-10pm Mon-Thur, Sun; 5-11pm Fri,
Sat. **Main courses** $28-$100. **Map** p320 C7 ㊱
American & steakhouses

The Hard Rock has struggled with steakhouses
since its original meaterie, AJ's Steakhouse, closed
in 2009. The short-lived Rare 120 quickly flamed out,
but the outlook is much better for 35 Steaks (partly
named for Elvis's birth year, 1935). Following in AJ's
footsteps is no easy task, but since opening in 2011,
35 Steaks is hitting all the right notes. There are
plenty of steaks, naturally, and other tasty options
including chicken or sea bass, but save room for
the 'King' of desserts – caramelised bananas and
peanut-butter ice cream (bacon optional).

West of the Strip

Alizé

Palms *4321 W Flamingo Road, at S Valley View
Boulevard (951 7000, www.alizelv.com). Bus 104,
202.* **Open** 5.30-10pm daily. **Main courses** $47-
$85. **Map** p317 X3 ㊲ **French**

Up on the 56th floor of Palms, venerated local André
Rochat has hired chef Mark Purdy to produce his
classics and deliver some fresh takes on French cuisine. Many of the dishes, such as lobster thermidor
and foie gras terrine, taste as great – in a grand, old-
style fashion – as they sound. It comes at a price, but
Rochat, who's been cooking foie gras in Vegas since
Dan Tanna was around, is the business.

Golden Steer Steak House

*308 W Sahara Avenue, between Las Vegas
Boulevard South & S Industrial Road (384 4470,
www.goldensteersteakhouselasvegas.com). Bus SX.*
Open 4.30-10.30pm daily. **Main courses** $40-$55.
Map p319 B4 ㊳ **American & steakhouses**

The enormous (and, yes, golden) steer that signposts
this old-school steak place on Sahara Avenue also
advertises its decor. Discreet it certainly is not: think
updated bordello crossed with an Old West saloon
and you're almost there. But the steaks are classic:
large, juicy and perfectly grilled. Sinatra and Dino
both ate here; four-plus decades later, it remains vintage Vegas at its most unreconstructed.

★ Heraea

Palms *4321 W Flamingo Road, at S Valley View
Boulevard (701 0201, www.palms.com). Bus 104,
202.* **Open** 11am-10pm Mon, Sun; 11am-11pm Tue-
Thur; 10am-midnight Fri, Sat. **Main courses** $17-
$34. **Map** p317 X3 ㊴ **American & steakhouses**

This recent addition to the Palms' eating establishments is a new twist on an old trick. Part sports
bar/part steakhouse (sort of), Heraea – named for the
goddess Hera's women's Olympic games – is
intended to be the kind of place guys can bring their
gals while they watch the Big Game. Sleek and inviting, it mostly works on that level, but it also works
in many other ways. Try the Kobe sliders while sipping a speciality cocktail.

Kabuto

*5040 W Spring Mountain Road, at S Decatur
Boulevard (676 1044, www.kabutolv.com). Bus
103, 203.* **Open** 6-11pm Mon-Sat. **Main courses**
$48-$95. **Japanese**

If you've ever bought sushi rolls at a grocery store,
Kabuto many not be the place for you. In fact, this
traditional *edomae* sushi house takes care to point
out what it does *not* serve: namely, *maki* and *hako*
sushi. Make no mistake, the subtle raw-fish delicacies served here – nigiri sushi and sashimi – appeal
to a refined palate, and have prices to match. Once
you've tried it, however, you may have a tough time
enjoying a California roll.

CONSUME

Sin City's Sweet Tooth

Get your fix of sugar on the Strip.

Las Vegas is justifiably known as a place to indulge cravings and vices: it's identified internationally as the place to drink, smoke, gamble and make sexytime, anytime. From all over the world, people come here to indulge their dream of excess, to forget the bitter and taste the sweet.

And pay attention to that last part – because Sin City has an unspoken vice, which is actually an open secret: Vegas has a raging sweet tooth. Often called an adult Disneyland, the Strip is more like Candy Land, a 21-and-over Willy Wonka factory where everyone has a golden ticket. It's forever been candy-coloured, but in the past decade the Strip has been sugarcoated and dipped in chocolate, with sprinkles on top.

We're not talking your humble McDonald's sundaes either. Like all the other human desires that have been tarted up here, candy has been Vegasised, from the bedazzled $25 'couture' lollipops at outposts of the **Sugar Factory** (*see p185*) at Paris (as well as MGM Grand, Mirage and Planet Hollywood) – a favourite of the Kardashian klan and the *Jersey Shore* gang – to the chocolate pastries at **Payard** at Caesars Palace (*see p83*) and the carefully tended Zen gardens of *gelato* and frozen yoghurt emporiums at just about every casino. At **Serendipity 3**, a tasty and extravagant ice-cream parlour fronting Caesars Palace, specialities of the house include an $11 frozen hot chocolate, a deep-dried Oreos and ice-cream sundae, and the Golden Opulence sundae – a $1,000 concoction topped with edible gold leaf – that you have to order 48 hours in advance.

One of the most crowded spots at the always-crowded Bellagio (*see p82*) is the **Jean-Philippe Patisserie**, where people gather to gawk at the world's largest chocolate fountain. It's no accident that there's also an outpost of this high-end cake shop at the very heart of the Aria casino (*see p81*) at CityCenter, where the sweet stuff is laid out erotically, like lingerie or jewels.

New locations to get your sugar fix are popping up all the time: the Forum Shops (*see p174*) recently opened a spot for bald chocolate magnate, **Max Brenner**, while new at the MGM Grand (*see p88*) is **Corner Cakes**, a round-the-clock pastry/coffee/candy store that will satisfy your cravings at any hour of the day or night.

Perhaps the enduring appeal of sugar on the Strip is that winning is its own reward; for those who lose, candy offers instant comfort and solace – orally administered – when the big prize didn't pay out as planned. You may leave Las Vegas with any and all manner of mementos – but you're almost certain to go home with a jacked-up glycaemic index and sticky fingers for souvenirs.

Serendipity 3.

CONSUME

CONSUME

N9ne

Palms *4321 W Flamingo Road, at S Valley View Boulevard (933 9900, www.palms.com). Bus 104, 202.* **Open** 5-10pm Mon-Thur, Sun; 5.30-11pm Fri, Sat. **Main courses** $28-$72. **Map** p317 X3 ⓿
American & steakhouses
Superb steak and seafood? Absolutely. A quiet spot for a date? Absolutely not. A busy bar scene, a DJ, busy lighting and acoustics seemingly designed to force diners to yell make N9ne feel like a nightclub – and that's intentional. The appetisers and sides are well-executed complements to the mains, and the flaming s'mores dessert is a show unto itself. A Saturday booking requires an A-list name or months of planning.

Nove Italiano

Palms *4321 W Flamingo Road, at S Valley View Boulevard (942 6800, www.palms.com). Bus 104, 202.* **Open** 6-10pm Tue-Thur; 6-11pm Fri, Sat. **Main courses** $22-$54. **Map** p317 X3 ⓿ **Italian**
This expensive sister to N9ne (*see above*) sits atop the Palms' super-luxury Fantasy Tower and boasts one of the best views in town, along with beautiful modern decor. The steaks are mediocre and the service is steeped with attitude. But for all that, the only complaint you'll hear about the Nove spaghetti, prepared with lobster, shrimp, crab, scallop, calamari and basil, will relate to its $43 price tag.

Raku

5030 W Spring Mountain Road, at S Decatur Boulevard (367 3511, www.raku-grill.com). Bus 103, 203. **Open** 6pm-3am Mon-Sat. **Main courses** $22-$44. **Set menu** $75-$100. **Japanese**

Owner and chef Mitsuo Endo has taken Las Vegas's Asian food scene by storm since opening Raku in 2008. That's no small feat in city that boasts so much variety in Asian cuisine – particularly along this stretch of road. But Endo's multiple-award-winning eaterie continues to be a favourite among all comers. Order from the *robata* grill if you want, but spring for the *omakase* menu if you can.

Simon

Palms *4321 W Flamingo Road, at S Valley View Boulevard (942 3292, www.palms.com). Bus 104, 202.* **Open** 7am-11pm daily. **Main courses** $25-$56. **Map** p317 X3 ⓿ **American & Pan-Asian**
Acclaimed rock 'n' roll chef Kerry Simon's eponymous new eaterie at Palms has a little something for everyone. There's a sushi bar, wood-baked pizzas (the beef carpaccio is best), and main courses ranging from meatloaf to steaks (with a side of Tuscan fries), never mind the breakfast options. Is it a little schizophrenic? Sure. But if anyone can pull it off, put your money on Simon.

DOWNTOWN

Chicago Joe's

820 S 4th Street, between Gass & Hoover avenues (382 5637, www.chicagojoesrestaurant.com). Bus Deuce & all BTC-bound buses. **Open** 11am-10pm Tue-Fri; 5-10pm Sat. **Main courses** $10-$39. **Map** p318 C2 ⓿ **Italian**
The kind of no-frills, fair-prices locals' favourite that everyone loves, CJ's – located in a tiny 1932 brick house – has lasted 30 years, thanks to its solid southern Italian cooking and American regional specialities (like Chicago spicy lobster), and its homey, authentic but quirky setting. Joe's is far removed from the $50 pasta joints on the Strip, and that's the whole point.

Nove Italiano.

Doña Maria's

910 Las Vegas Boulevard South, at E Charleston Boulevard (382 6538, www.donamariatamales. com). Bus Deuce, 206. **Open** 8am-10pm daily. **Main courses** *Lunch* $9-$13. *Dinner* $13-$16. **Map** p318 C3 ⓤ **Mexican**

The prices are good and the location is central, but Doña Maria's is very popular with the city's large Mexican community for one reason above all others: the loud and occasionally boisterous place offers some of Vegas's best Mexican food. The tamales (spicy chopped meat and ground corn, served in a corn husk) are the real draw, but the *tortas* (sandwiches) and fiery salsas help keep the place busy.

Du-Par's

Golden Gate *1 Fremont Street, at S Main Street (366 9378, www.du-pars.com). Bus Deuce & all BTC-bound buses.* **Open** 24hrs daily. **Main courses** $8-$18. **Map** p318 C1 ⓤ **American & steakhouses**

Go for the pancakes, stay for the shrimp cocktail. This seemingly timeless diner – the Golden Gate's only eaterie – is nationally renowned for its pancakes (really!). But in the future it'll probably be remembered more as the home of the shrimp cocktail, which was introduced to Las Vegas here. Whatever meal you come here for, you can be sure it won't break the bank.

★ Eat.

707 Carson Avenue, at S 7th Street (534 1515, www.eatdtlv.com). Bus Deuce, 208 & all BTC-bound buses. **Open** 8am-3pm daily. **Main courses** $9-$13. **Map** p318 D2 ⓤ **American & steakhouses**

Despite naming her restaurant in a manner guaranteed to be overlooked by anyone searching for food on the internet, owner/chef Natalie Young (who did previous stints at Mr Lucky's, *see p149*, among others) has one thing going for her: she produces damn good comfort food at reasonable prices. Choices like a truffled egg sandwich (breakfast) or a shrimp po'boy (lunch) ensure that the place won't be mistaken for a old greasy spoon. And that's a good thing.

Hugo's Cellar

Four Queens *202 E Fremont Street, at S Casino Center Boulevard (385 4011, www.hugoscellar. com). Bus Deuce & all BTC-bound buses.* **Open** 5.30-11pm daily. **Main courses** $30-$52. **Map** p318 D1 ⓤ **American & steakhouses**

Hugo's is one of Vegas's original fine-dining establishments, and its old traditions are still good ones: pampering wait staff, a tableside visit from the famous salad cart, a solid wine list and a rose for the lady. The menu is vintage Vegas gourmet rather than fusion, heavy on the meat and seafood (steak and lobster are the stars), and just what you'd expect for dessert (cherries jubilee, bananas Foster).

Mickie Finnz Fish House

425 E Fremont Street, at Las Vegas Boulevard South (382 4204, www.mickiefinnzlasvegas.com). Bus Deuce & all BTC-bound buses. **Open** 11am-2am daily. **Main courses** $9-$15. **Map** p318 D1 ⓤ **American & steakhouses**

Part of a Fremont Street triple (alongside Irish pub Hennesseys and upscale lounge Brass), this vaguely tiki spot is perfect for the laid-back Downtown crowd. Don't let the name trick you into thinking seafood is the main menu staple: although the grilled fish tacos really are delicious, the menu also offers a large selection of bar food and snacks (nachos, burgers, pizzas) intended to lay a good foundation for the drinking later on.

Triple George

201 N 3rd Street, at E Ogden Avenue (384 2761, www.triplegeorgegrill.com). Bus Deuce & all BTC-bound buses. **Open** 11am-10pm Mon-Thur, Sun; 11am-11pm Fri, Sat. **Main courses** *Lunch* $9-$27. *Dinner* $13-$37. **Map** p318 D1 ⓤ **American & steakhouses**

A lunchtime haven for business suits but an evening haunt for more casually clad Downtowners, this subtly chic art deco room was conceived as a San Francisco-style chophouse, with a central wooden bar surrounded by several private dining enclosures. The steaks, seafood and chops are all good, but it's the salads and house-made soups that are the highlight here. A valiant, upmarket addition to the area.

Vic & Anthony's

Golden Nugget *129 E Fremont Street, at S Casino Center Boulevard (386 8399, www. vicandanthonys.com). Bus Deuce & all BTC-bound buses.* **Open** 5-11pm daily. **Main courses** $26-$46. **Map** p318 C1 ⓤ **American & steakhouses**

Modelling itself as a classic Vegas steakhouse, with a live Maine lobster tank, masculine decor and attentive service, Vic & Anthony's manages to make a meal in a new restaurant feel like a step back in time. Start off with a strong cocktail and a tray of fresh blue point oysters, then move on to various seafood dishes, grain-fed beef, or lamb and veal chops. A smart start to a vintage Vegas weekender.

THE REST OF THE CITY

Agave

10820 W Charleston Boulevard, between I-215 & S Town Center Drive, Summerlin (214 3500, www.agavelasvegas.com). Bus SX. **Open** 24hrs daily. **Main courses** $11-$26. **Latin American**

This 24-hour cantina has emerged from its honeymoon period as a gathering place more than a restaurant. The menu reflects the adventurous decor, which offers a central Mexican vibe via imported Guadalajaran fixtures. Dishes such as goat tacos and

CONSUME

a *chile relleno* stuffed with rock shrimp complement the numerous tequilas. The secluded patio is a wonderful spot to while away a happy hour.

Bootlegger Bistro

7700 Las Vegas Boulevard South, at Blue Diamond Road, South of Strip (736 4939, www.bootleggerlasvegas.com). Bus 117, 217. **Open** 24hrs daily. **Main courses** *Breakfast* $6-$14. *Lunch* $10-$23. *Dinner* $12-$35. Italian

This operation comes with a flamboyance that's two parts Italian, one part Las Vegan and three parts pure showbiz. There's a full menu here, Italian staples such as you'd expect. But the entertainment is the key: lounge acts with patter as old as the city itself. That said, it all makes perfect sense. A 24-hour classic.

Casa di Amore

2850 E Tropicana Avenue, at S Eastern Avenue, East Las Vegas (433 4967, www.casadiamore.com). Bus 110, 201. **Open** 5pm-5am Mon, Wed-Sun. **Main courses** $21-$42. **Map** p317 Z3 ⑪ Italian

The vibe in this cosy, clubby Amer-Italian spot is overwhelmingly '60s Vegas. The Rat Pack atmosphere and extended hours draw old-school Las Vegans more or less around the clock for classic pizzas, authentic recipes (baked clams, chicken pasta soup) and seafood; however, it's at its busiest after-hours on weekends, when musicians entertain the crowds.

Hash House a-Go Go

6800 W Sahara Avenue, at S Rainbow Boulevard, West Las Vegas (804 4646, www.hashhouseagogo.com). Bus SX, 101. **Open** 7.30am-2.30pm, 5-10pm daily. **Main courses** $12-$27. American & steakhouses

'Twisted farm food', advertises the menu, which sounds like an altogether less appetising prospect than the excellent comfort cooking that's actually served at this capacious roadhouse. The dinners (chicken and biscuits, meat loaf) are great if pricey, and the lunches (sandwiches, burgers as big as your head) also impress. But to see the Hash House at its best, come for the phenomenal breakfasts and weekend brunches, which'll fill even the emptiest of stomachs.

Hedary's

7365 W Sahara Avenue, at S Buffalo Drive, West Las Vegas (873 9041, www.hedarys.com). Bus SX. **Open** 11am-10pm Tue-Thur; 11am-11pm Fri, Sat. **Main courses** $9-$25. Middle Eastern

This comfortable outpost of the Lebanese Hedary family's Texas original offers fabulous, fresh renditions of falafel, houmous, tabouleh, kibbeh and more, along with good kebabs from the grill. For vegetarians, the tasting meze offers a never-ending supply of incredibly good small plates.

★ Lindo Michoacan

2655 E Desert Inn Road, between S Eastern Avenue & S Pecos Road, East Las Vegas (735 6828, www.lindomichoacan.com). Bus 110, 111, 203. **Open** 10.30am-11pm Mon-Thur; 10.30am-midnight Fri; 9am-midnight Sat; 9am-11pm Sun. **Main courses** $9-$39. **Map** p317 Z3 ⑫ Mexican

Las Vegas's favourite neighbourhood Mexican, Lindo is housed in a colourful, bigger-than-it-looks building on Desert Inn Road, and is busy at virtually all times of day. The lunch specials are good value, but dinner is more enjoyable, with the menu of standards brought to life by an atmosphere that's never less than lively. There are two other Lindos in the city, one on the west side (10082 W Flamingo Road, 838 9990) and one in Henderson (645 Carnegie Street, 837 6828).

M&M's Soul Food

3923 W Charleston Boulevard, at S Valley View Boulevard, West Las Vegas (453 7685, www.mmsoulfoodcafe.com). Bus 104, 206. **Open** 7am-8pm daily. **Main courses** $6-$20. American & steakhouses

Comfort food doesn't get much heartier than the soul food dished up here. It's a pretty basic room; indeed, it feels a tad dreary after dark. But the food is fabulous: chicken, short ribs and other goodies dished up a variety of ways with an array of moreish sides (try the yams and the macaroni cheese). Get there in good time, mind: it closes early.

Marché Bacchus

2620 Regatta Drive, at Breakwater Drive, Summerlin (804 8008, www.marchebacchus.com). No bus. **Open** 11am-9.30pm Mon-Thur; 11am-10pm Fri, Sat; 10am-9.30pm Sun. **Main courses** *Lunch* $12-$18. *Dinner* $19-$39. French

This French bistro and wine shop tucked in the north-west corner of the city has been steadily increasing its profile over the last few years. Husband and wife team Jeff and Rhonda Wyatt purchased the shop in 2007 and promptly set out to create a spot everyone would know about. In 2011 they hired celeb chef Alex Stratta and things really took off. Reserve a table on the expansive lakeside patio and try dishes such as maple leaf duck breast or lobster and corn *agnolotti*, paired with the perfect bottle from the shop.

Michael's

South Point *9777 Las Vegas Boulevard South, at E Silverado Ranch Boulevard, South of the Strip (796 7111, www.southpointcasino.com). Bus 117.* **Open** 5.30-10pm daily. **Main courses** $48-$76. American & steakhouses

Formerly located on the Strip in Barbary Coast (later Bill's Gamblin' Hall), Michael's found a new home when namesake Michael Gaughan opened South Point. It's the sort of fancy-pants eaterie that doesn't

Lindo Michoacan.

print prices on the menu, rendering some diners speechless when the tab arrives. Still, the food is consistently ranked among Vegas's finest and the setting – despite the cowboy-hoedown aura of South Point – is truly old school.

Montesano's

9905 S Eastern Avenue, between Ione Road & St Rose Parkway, South-east Las Vegas (876 0348, www.montesanos.com). Bus 110. **Open** *11am-9pm Mon-Sat.* **Main courses** *$7-$20.* **Map** *p317 X2* Italian

It might feel like a kitschy pop-culture joint, but this longtime family-run establishment is an authentic slice of Brooklyn in Vegas that's been around for more than two decades. Folks line up daily for fresh-baked bread, decadent desserts and tasty takeaway, or sit down in the dining room for eggplant *parmigiana* and gnocchi with pink cream sauce, which competes with an extensive and original selection of pizzas.

Paymon's Mediterranean Café & Market

4147 S Maryland Parkway, at E Flamingo Road, University District (731 6030, www. paymons.com). Bus 109, 202. **Open** *11am-1am daily.* **Main courses** *$9-$21.* **Map** *p317 Y3* ⑭ Middle Eastern

Long before the idea caught on, Paymon Raouf was serving the kind of ethnic food that the college crowd adores. Even now, when so many Middle Eastern restaurants have opened in Vegas, the Med still wins out, simply because its kebabs and salads are better than anyone else's. Next door's Hookah Lounge is an effective companion. There's a second location on the west side (8380 W Sahara Avenue, 804 0293).

Table 34

600 E Warm Springs Road, between Bermuda & Paradise roads, South-east Las Vegas (263 0034, www.table34lasvegas.com). Bus 217. **Open** *11am-2.30pm Mon; 11am-2.30pm, 5-9.30pm Tue-Fri; 5-9.30pm Sat.* **Main courses** *Lunch* $10-$18. *Dinner* $14-$32. American & steakhouses

The comfortably modern decor serves as a palate cleanser for Puckish pizza (chef Wes Kendrick is a Wolfgang protégé), home-made soups and New American mains such as braised pot roast, and mac and cheese with smoked ham and English peas. It's all surprisingly affordable.

Terra Rosa

Red Rock *11011 W Charleston Boulevard, at I-215, West Las Vegas (797 7531, www.redrock lasvegas.com). Bus SX.* **Open** *noon-10pm Mon-Thur, Sun; noon-11pm Fri, Sat.* **Main courses** $12-$46. Italian

Red Rock's signature Italian restaurant is too nice a room to suffer the indignity of shorts and T-shirts, and yet it does. A Tuscan menu (with some Italian-American choices) treats guests to house-made pasta, fresh fish specialities and the ubiquitous wood-fired pizza. Want something lighter? Dress well, snag a seat at the tiny bar and take a wine flight (from the 1,500-bottle wine room) with antipasto.

Todd's Unique Dining

4350 E Sunset Road, between N Green Valley Parkway and Mountain Vista Street, South-east Las Vegas (259 8633, www.toddsunique.com). Bus 212. **Open** *4.30-10pm Mon-Sat.* **Main courses** $22-$36. American & steakhouses

Owner and chef Todd Clore has been plugging away at his neighbourhood eatery for nearly ten years. Clore, formerly chef de cuisine for the Sterling Brunch at Bally's, set out to open a place where he could do it his way – which has turned out to be appealing to locals and those visitors willing to make the trek from the Strip. Dishes like skirt steak 'on fire' and whitefish in rock-shrimp butter make for a unique meal.

Vintner Grill

10100 W Charleston Boulevard, at Hualapai Way, Summerlin (214 5590, www.vglasvegas.com). Bus SX. **Open** *11am-10pm Mon-Thur; 11am-11pm Fri; 4-11pm Sat; 4-10pm Sun.* **Main courses** $12-$40. American & steakhouses

The Corrigan family elevates the neighbourhood dining experience with this well-hidden New American bistro. With a dramatic interior design reminiscent of old Hollywood, and a large patio area segmented into cosy dining nooks, Vintner almost overnight became the hottest table for well-heeled Summerlin folks. Could it be the Mediterranean-influenced menu (lamb *osso bucco*, wood-fired pizza)? The comfortable lounge? The sexy crowd? Yes, yes and yes.

Zaba's Mexican Grill

3318 E Flamingo Road, at S Pecos Road, East Las Vegas (435 9222, www.zabas.com). Bus 111, 202. **Open** *10.30am-9.30pm Mon-Fri; 11am-9.30pm Sat; 11am-8pm Sun.* **Main courses** $6-$9. **Map** *p317 Z3* ⑮ Mexican

¡Aye-aye-aye! Part of the ever-growing trend of burrito and taco chains, Zaba's is as fresh as *salsa fresca*, with tender grilled meats and delectable guacamole. The decor is stark but the selections are miles away from fast food, despite the speed with which they're prepared. Five other locations are scattered throughout the city. *¡Muy delicioso!*

Buffets

The idea of the buffet started in the 1940s at the original El Rancho. Looking to keep customers in his casino after the show, Beldon Katleman dreamed up the Midnight Chuckwagon Buffet, promising 'all you can eat for a dollar'. His idea of treating guests to a feast for a small price was soon copied and expanded upon by other hotels: why not offer it all day long?

Casino buffets typically serve breakfast, lunch and dinner, with many also offering an extended brunch at weekends. The cost can vary widely, from as little as $8 for breakfast to upwards of $50 or more per person. Prices are lower in the locals' casinos away from the Strip; kids often eat for less (generally half-price). But whatever the price and time, all buffets work in the same way: you pay your money at the start and then stuff yourself silly from a range of at least 50 food selections, featuring everything from salads to cakes.

However, a few rules do apply to all buffets. Eat as much as you want while you're there, but don't take anything away with you. Health codes oblige you to take a new plate every time you return; leave your plates and a small tip on the table, to be picked up by the staff. And to avoid queueing, arrive early for breakfast, late for lunch and early for dinner.

In addition to the buffets detailed below, other hotel buffets are notable, whether by dint of luxury (**Country Club** at **Wynn**; *p93*), bounty and display (**Aria**, *see p81*, and **Bellagio**, *see p82*), size (**Circus Circus**, *see p106*, serves up to 10,000 diners a day), price (**Palace Station**, *see p129*, is among the best of the cheaper options) or quality of food (the **Mirage**, *see p90*, and **Main Street Station**, *see p122*, offer decent spreads). Locals' casinos such as the **Suncoast** (*see p130*) and **Sunset Station** (*see p130*) offer ordinary food at ridiculously cheap prices. And for the best-kept buffet secret in town, visit the **Verandah Café** (*see p147*) at the Four Seasons for weekend brunch.

Bacchanal Buffet

Caesars Palace *3570 Las Vegas Boulevard South, at W Flamingo Road (731 7928, www.caesarspalace.com). Bus Deuce, 202.*
Buffets *Breakfast* 7-11am Mon-Fri. *Brunch* 8am-3pm Sat, Sun. *Lunch* 11am-3pm Mon-Fri. *Dinner* 3-10pm Sat, Sun. **Prices** $20-$25 breakfast; $30-$35 lunch; $40-$45 brunch/dinner. **Map** p320 A7 ⑯
Named the best buffet of 2013 by the *Las Vegas Review-Journal*, this spread at Caesars Palace is nothing short of amazing. With more than 500 different dishes prepared in nine different kitchens – each with a culinary theme of its own – Bacchanal shouldn't just offer a single meal. It should offer a weekly pass.

Buffet at Bellagio

Bellagio *3600 Las Vegas Boulevard South, at W Flamingo Road (693 7111, www.bellagio.com). Bus Deuce, 202.* **Buffets** *Breakfast* 7-11am Mon-Fri. *Brunch* 7am-3.30pm Sat, Sun. *Lunch* 11am-3.30pm Mon-Fri. *Dinner* 3.30-10pm daily. **Prices** $18 breakfast; $28-$38 brunch; $21 lunch; $32-$38 dinner. **Map** p320 A7 ⑰
The Buffet at Bellagio is very much like the rest of the hotel: smart yet approachable, stylish yet undemonstrative, expensive yet probably just about worth it. Usual buffet fare gets upgraded with extras such as venison, steamed clams and crab legs. Dinner on Friday and Saturday is gourmet, so expect to go all out.

Carnival World Buffet

Rio *3700 W Flamingo Road, at S Valley View Boulevard, West of Strip (777 7777, www.riolasvegas.com). Bus 202.* **Buffets** *Breakfast* 8-11am Mon-Fri; 8-10am Sat, Sun. *Brunch* 10am-3pm Sat, Sun. *Lunch* 11am-3pm Mon-Fri. *Dinner* 3-10pm daily. **Prices** $21-$24 breakfast; $31 brunch; $23 lunch; $31-$36 dinner. **Map** p317 X3 ⑱
A favourite among locals, the pioneering Carnival World Buffet journeys the planet for its food. It's an idea that several other casinos have since copied, but no one has yet topped the Rio's intercontinental spreads, which take in everything from sushi to barbecue ribs. Finish with a slice of one of the 70 varieties of house-made pies, cakes or pastries.

Golden Nugget Buffet

Golden Nugget *129 E Fremont Street, at S Casino Center Boulevard, Downtown (386 8221, www.goldennugget.com). Bus Deuce & all BTC-bound buses.* **Buffets** *Breakfast* 7-10.30am Mon-Fri. *Brunch* 8am-3.30pm Sat, Sun. *Lunch* 10.30am-3.30pm Mon-Fri. *Dinner* 3.30-10pm daily. **Prices** $11 breakfast; $19 brunch; $13 lunch; $19-$22 dinner. **Map** p318 C1 ⑲
Downtown's smartest buffet more than delivers the goods that its reputation demands of it. The room isn't particularly cosy, but the quality of the food more than compensates. The offerings are near the top of the Vegas food chain, especially the carvery and the excellent desserts.

Le Village Buffet

Paris Las Vegas *3655 Las Vegas Boulevard South, at E Flamingo Road (946 7000, www. parislasvegas.com). Bus Deuce, 202.* **Buffets** *Breakfast* 7-11am Mon-Fri; 7-10am Fri, Sat. *Brunch* 10am-3pm daily. *Lunch* 11am-3pm daily. *Dinner* 3-10pm Mon-Fri; 3-11pm Sat, Sun. **Prices** $22-$24 breakfast; $31 brunch; $25 lunch; $31-$34 dinner. **Map** p320 A7 ⓬⓪

The one French-themed casino in town really should offer a good buffet, and so it does. The 400-seat Le Village Buffet has stations representing five French provinces, and dishes up a variety of fine foods (it's especially good for meat-lovers). But go easy on starters and mains, so as to save room for the fresh pastries and desserts.

Sterling Brunch

Bally's *3645 Las Vegas Boulevard South, at E Flamingo Road (862 5138, www.ballyslas vegas.com). Bus Deuce, 202.* **Buffet** 9.30am-2.30pm Sun. **Prices** $40-$60. **Map** p320 A7 ⓬①

Not to be mistaken with déclassé feed-your-face experiences, Bally's Sunday-only Sterling Brunch is

the buffet's upscale sibling. Yes, you can have as much as you want, but think caviar and champagne; crab claws, sushi and sake; a lobster and cognac omelette. You'll pay for all this, sure. But there's a reason it's been running for 25 years.

★ Wicked Spoon

Cosmopolitan *3708 Las Vegas Boulevard South, between W Harmon Ave & W Flamingo Road (698 7000, www.cosmopolitanlas vegas.com). Bus Deuce.* **Buffets** *Brunch* 8am-2pm Mon-Fri; 8am-3pm Sat, Sun. *Dinner* 5-9pm Mon-Thur, Sun; 5-10pm Fri, Sat. **Prices** $24 brunch Mon-Fri; $33 brunch Sat, Sun; $38 dinner Mon-Thur, Sun; $41 dinner Fri, Sat. **Map** p320 A7 ⓬②

Perhaps one of the best-kept secrets in buffet dining, the Wicked Spoon serves up a spread unlike any other. This isn't a line up and heap it on your plate place. Here, you can sample a variety of items you're unlikely to find at other buffets: dim sum, miniature chicken pot pies, pork *chalupas* – all served on individual-sized plates and designed to mix and match.

Wicked Spoon.

CONSUME

Bars & Lounges

Drink with mermaids? Only in Vegas.

You're sporting a furry Russian hat to ward off the sub-zero temperatures. You're sipping banana-flavoured vodka. You're staring at a giant bronze head of Lenin. You're in the 'vodka locker' (read: freezer) of **Red Square**, a bar that, by taking its theme to the zenith of ridiculousness, is perfectly, archetypally Vegas.

The hallucinatory creativity that built a neon oasis in the desert has also been employed in the construction of the city's bars. The resorts are dotted with the kind of piano bars, meat markets and casual lounges you might expect to find. However, you can also sink beers with swimming mermaids, down bourbon from a Mason jar, and piss on the Berlin Wall. Should these gimmicks fail to inculcate a sense of wonder, a bacon martini may do the trick.

CONSUME

HOURS AND GAMBLING

Wherever you prefer to take your libations, one thing you won't hear very often is the phrase 'last call'. Liquor flows as freely at five in the morning as it does at five in the evening: many of the bars in town, including at least one in every casino, are open 24 hours a day, though it should be noted that you're just as likely to be refused service here as in other cities.

Although there are a few exceptions, among them the **Artisan** and the **Downtown Cocktail Room**, the bartops at most off-Strip, non-casino hangouts are lined with video poker machines. Indeed, many such bars are kept afloat as much by gambling revenue as by alcohol sales. If you're gambling, drinks are usually free with a minimal deposit (usually $10 to $20) into your nearest machine; always ensure that the bartender knows you're playing.

In addition to the bars listed below, small music venues such as the **Bunkhouse Saloon** also function as bars; *see p224-228*. A number of restaurants also have busy bars, among them **Aureole** (*see p135*), with its spectacular central wine tower. And keep an eye out for one of the more than 40 wallet-friendly, beer-centric PT's pubs in the city (www.pteglv.com).

---

❶ Green numbers in this chapter correspond to the location of each bar as marked on the street maps. *See pp317-320.*

THE LAW

You have to be 21 to consume or buy alcohol in Nevada. If you look less than 40, you'll regularly be required to produce photo ID, such as a driver's licence or passport. Las Vegas's drink-driving laws are as harsh and uncompromising as those of any major US city, and the cops don't let too many woozy fish swim by. So – as anywhere – it's best to leave the car behind: you can easily walk back and forth between bars either on the Strip or Downtown, and a taxi ride to and from most of the more distant joints will be cheap. Cabs are plentiful around the Strip; elsewhere, the bartender will be happy to call one for you. For the law on smoking, *see p298*.

THE STRIP

Aurora

Luxor *3900 Las Vegas Boulevard South, at W Hacienda Avenue (262 4591, www.luxor.com). Bus Deuce, 119, 201.* **Open** 24hrs daily. **Map** p320 A9 ❶

Who needs stargazing when you can enjoy the shimmering lights of the Aurora Borealis from the comfort of your bar stool? Duck into this lobby bar at the Luxor for a few of its speciality cocktails – named after Luxor attractions – like the Carrot Top (vodka, rum, grenadine and more) or Bodies (tequila, orange liqueur, OJ), and you may forget all about the night sky.

Centrifuge.

Bar at Times Square

New York New York *3790 Las Vegas Boulevard South, at W Tropicana Avenue (236 0374, www.newyorknewyork.com). Bus Deuce, 201.* Open 11am-2.30am daily. **Map** p320 A8 ②

Bellowing voices pour from this packed bar, where duelling pianos provide the upbeat entertainment. Sure, there's beer behind the emotion, but there's also a lot of genuine fun being had. The musicians can and will play anything if you've got the money to tip 'em. The best of the city's piano bars.

Centrifuge

MGM Grand *3799 Las Vegas Boulevard South, at E Tropicana Avenue (891 7777, www.mgm grand.com). Bus Deuce, 201.* Open 3pm-6am daily. **Map** p320 A8 ③

Having dramatically remade its restaurants, the MGM then turned its attention to its bars. Along with Rouge, the Centrifuge is the most eye-catching, a circular bar near the front of the casino with TV screens, dancing girls and excellent cocktails. It's more expensive than it should be, but still worth a look nonetheless.

Chandelier

Cosmopolitan *3708 Las Vegas Boulevard South, at W Harmon Avenue (698 7979, www.cosmopolitanlasvegas.com). Bus Deuce.* Open 24hrs daily. **Map** p320 A7 ④

The Chandelier is at the centre of the new Vegas bar scene – and a three-storey chandelier is at the centre of this gorgeous, multi-level bar. You'll be surrounded by sparkle, and dazzled by your fellow cocktailers as you sip a Fire-Breathing Dragon – or ask your bartender to come up with something to commemorate the moment.

Gold

Aria, CityCenter *3730 Las Vegas Boulevard South, at W Harmon Avenue (693 8300, www. arialasvegas.com). Bus Deuce.* Open 5pm-4am Tue-Sat. **Map** p317 Y3 ⑤

Next to Aria's Cirque du Soleil theatre, Gold is an inspired, 1950s-themed collaboration between Cirque and the Light Group. This gleaming 'ultra-lounge' is comfy and swanky, and tends to get busier as the evening wears on. With all the gold-dipped tones – even the bartenders and servers seem golden – you might leave feeling the Midas touch. *Photo p160.*

I Love this Bar & Grill

Harrah's *3475 Las Vegas Boulevard South, between Sands Avenue & E Flamingo Road (369 5000, www.harrahslasvegas.com). Bus Deuce, 202.* Open 11.30am-2am Mon-Thur, Sun; 11.30am-3am Fri, Sat. **Map** p320 A6 ⑥

Boot-scoot your way on down here for a cold domestic and some Southern-fried fun and food. Named after his hit single 'I Love this Bar', Toby Keith's place is tinged with country. But even those repelled by cowboy boots might find it's their kind of place, since it doesn't smash you over the ten-gallon hat with its theme.

Jimmy Buffet's Margaritaville

Flamingo *3555 Las Vegas Boulevard South, at E Flamingo Road (733 3302, www.margaritaville lasvegas.com). Bus Deuce, 202.* Open 8am-2am Mon-Thur, Sun; 8am-3am Fri, Sat. **Map** p320 A7 ⑦

CONSUME

THE BEST BARS

To travel the world
Pub 1842. *See p161.*

To evoke the ghost of Vegas past
Atomic Liquors. *See p164.*

To get your sophistication on
Vesper. *See p162.*

To feel pretty in
Beauty Bar. *See p164.*

Gold. *See p159.*

You've heard of Deadheads, right? Well, here you'll find their ornithological equivalent: parrotheads, men dressed in khaki shorts and floral shirts with parrots perched on their heads, united in their devotion to the self-described 'gulf and western' music of Jimmy Buffet. The ambience is not for the faint of heart or the sophisticated of taste.

Lily
Bellagio *3600 Las Vegas Boulevard South, at W Flamingo Road (693 8300, www.lilylv.com). Bus Deuce, 202.* **Open** 5pm-4am daily. **Map** p320 A7 ⑧

With stone tabletops (imported from Spain, no less), leather couches and mirrored walls, Lily seems less like a lounge than a private club. And that, naturally, comes at a price: seasonal cocktails costing $15 and up are the norm. As the night wears on and the crowds thicken, the swanky couches are reserved for parties willing to pony up $300 or more for bottle service.

Napoleon's
Paris Las Vegas *3655 Las Vegas Boulevard South, at E Flamingo Road (946 7000, www.parislasvegas.com). Bus Deuce, 202.* **Open** 4pm-2am Mon-Thur, Sun; 2pm-3am Fri, Sat. **Map** p320 A7 ⑨

There are 100 varieties of champagne on offer at this longstanding hangout within the Paris resort. They're a better choice than the rather over-inventive cocktails, and certainly more authentic than the obligatory duelling pianists, who work their way through Parisian classics such as, er, 'Goodbye Yellow Brick Road' and 'Living on a Prayer' at 9pm nightly.

Parasol Up/Parasol Down
Wynn Las Vegas *3131 Las Vegas Boulevard South, between E Desert Inn Road & Sands Avenue (248 3463, www.wynnlasvegas.com). Bus Deuce, 108, 203.* **Open** *Parasol Up* 11am-4am Mon-Thur, Sun; 11am-5am Fri, Sat. *Parasol Down* 11am-2am daily. **Map** p319 B6 ⑩

Whether you're Up or Down, there's a Parasol cocktail for you. These two pricey, Euro-chichi hangouts overlooking the waterfall – which is lit up by projected images and colours – have more charm than standard casino bars, and are full of the sort of beautiful, wealthy people who like to hang out at this most chichi of resorts.

★ PBR Rock Bar & Grill
Planet Hollywood *Las Vegas Boulevard South, between E Harmon Avenue & E Flamingo Road (750 1685, www.pbrrockbar.com). Bus Deuce, 202.* **Open** 8am-midnight daily. **Map** p320 A7 ⑪

Scantily clad, buxom cowgirls – check. Mechanical bull – check. Pabst Blue Ribbon – check. Therein lies pretty much everything you need to know about PBR Rock Bar, located in PH's Miracle Mile Shops right on the Strip. If beer's not your thing, try one of the cocktails like the Hoedown Throwdown (Southern Comfort, vodka, and so on) served in a handled Mason jar. Toss back a couple and get ready for the bull.

★ Peppermill's Fireside Lounge
2985 Las Vegas Boulevard South, at Convention Center Drive (735 4177, www.peppermilllasvegas.com). Bus Deuce, 203. **Open** 24hrs daily. **Map** p319 B5 ⑫

Known for the seats around the combination firepit-fountain and for the luxuriant dresses worn by the bosomy waitresses, this place is old Vegas at its best. Or, at least, it was, until they put flatscreen TVs on every available surface and ruined the vintage feel. Still, the drinks are impressive; try a Scorpion, which will arrive in a glass that's bigger than your head.

Petrossian
Bellagio *3600 Las Vegas Boulevard South, at W Flamingo Road (693 7111, www.bellagio.com). Bus Deuce, 202.* **Open** 24hrs daily. **Map** p320 A7 ⑬

If you like to drink to the sounds of tinkling ivories, but you want something a little more refined than the duelling pianos at Bar at Times Square, Petrossian might be right up your alley. Named one of the best hotel bars in the US premier hotel-industry magazine *Santé*, this upscale lounge features pianists throughout the day and an afternoon tea service beginning at 1pm. Also, liquor.

★ Pub 1842

MGM Grand *3799 Las Vegas Boulevard South, at E Tropicana Avenue (891 7777, www.mgm grand.com). Bus Deuce, 201.* **Open** 11.30am-midnight Mon-Thur, Sun; 11.30am-1am Fri, Sat. **Map** p320 A8 ⑭

So named for the year that pilsner beer was first brewed, this new gastropub from chef Michael Mina is heavy on both the beer and the food. Mina's hand is evident in bar bites like lobster corn dogs and Korean BBQ salmon burger, but you can just go for the beer too: more than 60 varieties are available. Get an $18 'beer wheel', with eight different brews – after fortifying yourself with the 1842 Burger first.

Red Square

Mandalay Bay *3950 Las Vegas Boulevard South, at W Hacienda Avenue (632 7407, www.redsquarelasvegas.com). Bus Deuce, 119.* **Open** 4-10.30pm Mon-Thur, Sun; 4-11pm Fri, Sat. **Map** p320 A9 ⑮

The vodkas here are so good that they made Lenin lose his head. Well, that's the only rational explanation for the enormous decapitated statue of the father of the Soviet Union over the entrance, though you can always ask the barman what happened to Vlad's missing body part (it's in the walk-in 'vodka locker', on ice). The food here is fine and the drinks are strong.

Revolution

Mirage *3400 Las Vegas Boulevard South, between Spring Mountain & W Flamingo Roads (693 8300, www.mirage.com). Bus Deuce, 203.* **Open** 10pm-4am Mon, Tue, Thur-Sun. *Abbey Road* noon-4am daily. **Map** p319, p320 A6 ⑯

Pub 1842.

Todd English PUB

RAW BAR

If you want to drink to a Beatles soundtrack, arrive early, before the band is ditched in favour of more contemporary sounds. That aside, the Fab Four theme of this spot is generally carried out pretty well, with subtle and not-so-subtle nods to their classic songs (crystals hanging from the ceiling, portholes behind the bar). Interactive tabletops, like giant Etch-a-Sketches, are a highlight. For a more low-key spot, try the Abbey Road Bar just in front of Revolution.

Shadow Bar
Caesars Palace *3570 Las Vegas Boulevard South, at W Flamingo Road (731 7110, www. caesarspalace.com). Bus Deuce, 202.* **Open** 4pm-2am Mon-Thur; 2pm-3am Fri, Sat; 2pm-2am Sun. **Map** p320 A7 ⑰
Question: how do you get naked women to shake, writhe and strut their stuff without showing any flesh? Answer: shadow play. This saucy spot continues Las Vegas's hesitating shimmy towards bringing strip clubs to the Strip without any actual stripping. The ladies concerned, silhouetted on screens, play up what comes naturally (or, possibly, surgically), while expensive drinks add a haughty note to proceedings.

Todd English PUB
CityCenter *3720 Las Vegas Boulevard S, at W Harmon Avenue (489 8080, www. toddenglishpub.com). Bus Deuce.* **Open** 11am-2am Mon-Fri; 9.30am-2am Sat, Sun. **Map** p320 A7 ⑱
Celebrity chef Todd English's gastropub – in the CityCenter complex, cosied right up to the enormous Aria casino-hotel – established itself on arrival as one of the most comfortable, personable and delicious bars in a town full of bars. The array of beers on tap – there are more than 30, including a smart selection of craft beers and seasonals – is matched by English's witty touch on saloon fare.

V Bar
Venetian *3555 Las Vegas Boulevard South, between Sands Avenue & E Flamingo Road (414 3200, www.venetian.com). Bus Deuce, 119, 203.* **Open** 5pm-2am Mon-Wed, Sun; 5pm-3am Thur-Sat. **Map** p319 B6 ⑲
Brought to you by the creators of the Big Apple's Lotus and LA's Sunset Room, V Bar is as basic, simple and understated as its name. The young, attractive and affluent clientele put on a show for lesser mortals peeking in through small slits in the wall-length frosted-glass windows. Dress smart-casual unless you want to join them on the outside.

★ VDKA
Encore *3121 Las Vegas Boulevard South, at E Desert Inn Road (770 7000, www.wynnlasvegas. com). Bus Deuce, 108, 203.* **Open** 6pm-2am daily. **Map** p319 B5 ⑳
So many vodkas, so little time. This new bar, adjacent to Asian eatery Andrea's, offers some 150 different flavours – think bacon, think peanut butter – in a variety of concoctions that range from delicious (blood orange cosmopolitan) to very nearly demented (sugar cookie martini). But, hey, feel free to pick your own poison.

★ Vesper
Cosmopolitan *3708 Las Vegas Boulevard South, at W Harmon Avenue (698 7000, www.cosmopolitanlasvegas.com). Bus Deuce.* **Open** 24hrs daily. **Map** p320 A7 ㉑
Inspired by the James Bond cocktail of the same name, Vesper is an oasis amid the otherwise thrumming activity of the Cosmopolitan. This isn't to say it's quiet; situated away from the casino near the hotel's lobby, Vesper is often buzzing, but with a more sophisticated – *cosmopolitan*, if you will – vibe. The drinks, prepared by serious alcohol artisans, are amazing if pricey. But what a way to spend your money.

View Bar
Aria, CityCenter *3730 Las Vegas Boulevard South, at W Harmon Avenue (590 7111, www.arialasvegas.com). Bus Deuce.* **Open** 2pm-2am daily. **Map** p320 A7 ㉒
Aria at CityCenter is one of the best sights in the city – and its lobby bar, called View Bar – is one of the best spots for people-watching, centrally located as it is in the airy lobby, across from the check-in stations. But you're paying – and quite dearly – for the views: cocktails run from $15 to $20. Kick back and make them last while you watch the beautiful people stroll by.

OFF-STRIP
East of the Strip

★ Double Down Saloon
Paradise Plaza, 4640 Paradise Road, between E Harmon & E Tropicana avenues (791 5775, www.doubledownsaloon.com). Bus 108. **Open** 24hrs daily. **Map** p320 C8 ㉓

No head for drink? Then hand over $20 for puke insurance: if you barf, staff will clean up. Otherwise, you're on your own at this darkly chaotic bar. 'The Happiest Place on Earth', they bill it, and with good reason: the music is loud, whether from the impeccably punkish jukebox or the regular bands, and the vibe is welcoming. Specialities include Ass Juice and bacon martinis (no one's ever had two). Beers are a better bet.

Piero's
355 Convention Center Drive, between Paradise Road & Debbie Reynolds Drive (369 2305, www.pieroscuisine.com). Bus SDX, 108. **Open** 5.30-10pm daily. **Map** p319 B5 ㉔
The lounge at this renowned Las Vegas Italian eaterie is worth a visit if for nothing more than the history lesson. Yes, scenes from the movie *Casino* were shot here; yes, local celebrities like Jerry Lewis, Steve Lawrence and Eydie Gorme dine here – to say nothing of former presidents, A-list film stars and sports heroes. And check out those monkey paintings.

Shaken, Stirred and Just About Everything Else
Cocktails the Vegas way.

Throughout its history, Las Vegas has taken other people's ideas and twisted them into something altogether different. Alcoholically speaking, this tendency has borne fruit in many of the city's bars, which are constantly regenerating their cocktail menus to include an array of only-in-Vegas beverages. There's only one Onomatopoeia in town, and it's at the **Downtown Cocktail Room** (*see p165*). In fact, this comfy gin joint's drinks menu boasts a lot of one-of-a-kinds, such as the Clever Genever and the Orthodox Caveman, all of them rated on a helpful and taste-friendly scale of 1 ('easy/very approachable') to 5 ('advanced palate').

Vegas's cocktail revival began when Steve Wynn hired the best cocktail guy in the business, Tony Abou-Ganim – aka 'the Modern Mixologist' – to help him open the Bellagio in 1998. Abou-Ganim worked with chefs to create cocktail lists while also teaching bartenders about spirits: how to mix them, how to serve them and how to tell their stories.

These days, a bar is behind the times if it doesn't rotate its cocktail menu seasonally, draw ingredients fresh from organic farms, or employ at least one master mixologist who's trying to outdo the guy at the next resort. Fancy, house-invented drinks are the rage up and down the Strip, as well as Downtown. The **Wynn** (*see p160*) has held up its end with signature drinks like the Dream, a champagne cocktail served in a flute, while the nightclubs here and at sister resort **Encore** bear risqué names (and ingredients) like the Ménage a Trois at Tryst, combining Hennessy, champagne and 150-year-old Grand Marnier – as well as flakes of gold and gold syrup, and a $3,000 price tag.

If you're just looking for something different in the alcohol department without taking out a second mortgage, creative drinks menus abound off the Strip as well as on. At **Herbs & Rye** (*see p168*), you won't find a drink called Herbs & Rye on the menu, but order one anyway. You can thank us later.

Downtown Cocktail Room.

CONSUME

Beauty Bar.

West of the Strip

Artisan Lounge

Artisan *1501 W Sahara Avenue, at Highland Drive (214 4000, www.theartisanhotel.com). Bus SX, 119.* **Open** 24hrs daily. **Map** p319 B4 ⓭

Gold-framed prints and paintings cover the walls and ceiling here, almost to the point of absurdity; there are even empty frames suspended in the air, and statues interspersed with shelves full of books. Somehow, it all works. A unique amalgam of lodge, bar and gallery, the Artisan is arty Vegas's living room away from home. Thanks to the lack of gambling, it's also one of the quietest lounges in town.

Ghostbar

Palms *4321 W Flamingo Road, at S Valley View Boulevard (942 7777, www.palms.com). Bus 104, 202.* **Open** 8pm-2am daily. **Map** p317 X3 ⓭

Suspended 55 floors above the city (check out the see-through patio with a view all the way to the ground) and decked out in blues and space-age silvers, Ghostbar is a dramatic spot. Enter via the private elevator (and prepare to pay the private cover charge), and try to get here before the glamorous masses: it starts to get busy from 11pm.

★ Money Plays

4755 W Flamingo Road, between S Decatur Boulevard & Cameron Street (368 1828, www.moneyplayslv.com). Bus 104, 202. **Open** 24hrs daily.

Not particularly fancy, not particularly sophisticated, Money Plays isn't the type of bar that's trying to muscle in on the casino-hotel business. Instead, it's just a good ole locals' hangout, just down the street from Palms. Plenty of great beers on tap, darts, shuffleboard, and occasionally live music. Curious as to the type of bars Vegas residents frequent? Try this one.

DOWNTOWN

★ Atomic Liquors

917 E Fremont Street, between S 9th & S 10th streets (349 2283, www.atomiclasvegas.com). Bus BHX. **Open** 24hrs daily. **Map** p318 D2 ⓭

The oldest surviving freestanding bar according to local lore, Atomic Liquors reopened under new ownership after a two-year hiatus. Once a restaurant and later, in the 1950s, a viewing point for the bomb tests conducted in the desert, Atomic toughed it out for many years while Downtown faded away. This stretch of Fremont has greatly improved, so here's to drinking at the Atomic again!

★ Beauty Bar

517 E Fremont Street, at Las Vegas Boulevard South (598 1965, www.thebeautybar.com). Bus Deuce & all BTC-bound buses. **Open** 9pm-2am daily. **Map** p318 D2 ⓭

The 'martinis and manicures' concept featured on *Sex and the City* was made famous by the New York version of this chain; a shame, then, that cosmetology laws forbid full manicures here. The 1950s decor was salvaged from the Capri Salon of Beauty in Trenton, NJ, with lighting from the old Algiers hotel in Vegas; it's matched by themed cocktails, such as the Platinum Blonde, the Prell and the Red Head. Bands and DJs entertain more or less nightly.

Commonwealth

525 E Fremont Street, at Las Vegas Boulevard South (445 6400, www.commonwealthlv.com). Bus Deuce & all BTC-bound buses. **Open** 6pm-2am Wed-Fri; 8pm-2am Sat, Sun. **Map** p318 D2 ⓭

Part speakeasy, part garden gathering-spot, part gleaming hipster hangout, Commonwealth is among the latest in new bars to bet on the revitalisation of Downtown's Fremont Street. With live music on the

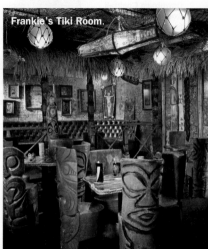

Frankie's Tiki Room.

Crown & Anchor. See p167.

rooftop and an 'invite-only' lounge, Commonwealth may turn out to be the new face of Las Vegas's long-forgotten neighbourhood.

Dino's
1516 Las Vegas Boulevard South, at W Utah Avenue (382 3894, www.dinoslv.com). Bus Deuce, 108. **Open** 24hrs daily. **Map** p319 C3 ⓾
The sign on the side, advertising this as 'The last neighbourhood bar in Las Vegas' is hyperbole. Still, this local dive offers an upbeat mix of hipsters, freaks, drunks and, on the karaoke nights hosted by Elton John doppelgänger Danny G (Thur-Sat), off-key crooners and wannabes. Bar regulars compete to join the Drunk of the Month Club.

★ Downtown Cocktail Room
111 Las Vegas Boulevard South, at E Fremont Street (880 3696, www.thedowntownlv.com). Bus Deuce & all BTC-bound buses. **Open** 4pm-2am Mon-Fri; 7pm-2am Sat. **Map** p318 D2 ③①
Despite its name, this chic, upscale bar will make you forget you're Downtown; or, at least, Downtown Las Vegas. Done out in deep, sexy reds and sheer curtains you can close for added nook privacy, this understated lounge will put you in the mood to leave with a date even if you didn't come in with one. DJs entertain nightly, though the music is generally pitched at conversation-friendly levels.

Frankie's Tiki Room
1712 W Charleston Boulevard, at Shadow Lane (385 3110, www.frankiestikiroom.com). Bus 119, 206, 207. **Open** 24hrs daily. **Map** p319 B3 ③②
Once your eyes get acclimatised to the dimness, the decor and details of this newish variation on the classic tiki lounge begin to emerge: a jukebox stuffed with surf-rock, Hawaii-themed movies on the screens, and, of course, neon-hued tropical drinks, served in fanciful, Vegas-themed ceramic tumblers designed by tiki artists (you can buy them as souvenirs).

★ Griffin
511 E Fremont Street, at Las Vegas Boulevard South (382 0577). Bus Deuce & all BTC-bound buses. **Open** 5pm-3am Mon-Fri; 7pm-3am Sat; 8pm-3am Sun. **Map** p318 D2 ③③
This putatively Brit-styled joint is the place to go medieval. Windowless, with an eerie but romantic glow fed by candlelight and fireplaces, the Griffin doubles as an after-work beer pub and a late-night indie-rockin' haunt. Tattooed hotties pull Stellas while a dollar stirs T-Rex and the Smiths from the juke.

Hogs & Heifers
201 N 3rd Street, at E Ogden Avenue (676 1457, www.hogsandheifers.com). Bus Deuce & all BTC-bound buses. **Open** 1pm-4am daily. **Map** p318 D1 ③④
'Is that the sound you make when he takes you from behind?' yells a classy maven in boots from her roost on top of the bar. To some onlookers, Hogs & Heifers isn't pretty or fun; still, those onlookers seem to fall in the minority. The schtick here can get fairly raunchy, so stay away if you take easy offence. Arrive on your Harley if you're fixin' to fit right in.

Huntridge Tavern
1116 E Charleston Boulevard, at S Maryland Parkway (384 7377). Bus 108, 109, 206. **Open** 24hrs daily. **Map** p318 D3 ③⑤
For decades, this hangout has been everything a dive bar should be: of low estate without being seedy, intriguing without being dangerous, careworn without being ugly. Presumably, the fiftysomethings who warm the stools here do go home to their families every once in a while. Still, with brews this cheap, you couldn't blame them if they just stayed put.

Rush Lounge
Golden Nugget *129 E Fremont Street, at S Casino Center Boulevard (386 8221,www.golden nugget.com). Bus Deuce & all BTC-bound buses.* **Open** 6pm-2am Mon-Thur, Sun; 6pm-4am Fri,Sat. **Map** p318 C1 ③⑥

Before 2007, 'contemporary' wasn't an adjective that applied to the Golden Nugget casino. Now, however, it's just about the most accurate description for its upscale Rush Lounge, swathed in sexy reds, browns and horizontal stripes. A rare find among Downtown casinos, not least because it prefers table games to video poker.

Triple 7 Brew Pub

Main Street Station *200 N Main Street, at E Stewart Avenue (387 1896, www.mainstreet casino.com). Bus Deuce & all BTC-bound buses.* **Open** 11am-7am daily. **Map** p318 C1 ⓷⓻

The Triple 7 serves fair beer and above-par bar food, and has an unbeatable $2.50-a-drink happy hour. But the real reason to visit this microbrewery is to gawk at the multi-million-dollar collection of antiques and collectibles, which even extends to the restroom: gents are able to express their opinion on communism by relieving themselves on a portion of the Berlin Wall.

Vanguard Lounge

516 E Fremont Street, at Las Vegas Boulevard South (868 7800, www.vanguardlv.com). Bus Deuce & all BTC-bound buses. **Open** 3pm-2am Mon-Fri; 6pm-2am Sat. **Map** p318 D2 ⓷⓼

This cosy little bar is another on the forefront of East Fremont Street's rebranding from danger zone to a hip and happenin' hood. Enjoy the extensive wine list or grab one of the speciality cocktails – like the Juneau You Want It – either inside or on Vanguard's sidewalk seating. DJs perform nightly, from 9pm to close.

THE REST OF THE CITY

★ Champagnes Café

3557 S Maryland Parkway, between E Desert Inn Road & E Twain Avenue, East Las Vegas (737 1699, www.champagnescafe.blogspot.com). Bus 109, 203. **Open** 24hrs daily. **Map** p317 Y3 ⓷⓽

With velvety flock wallpaper, Frank and Dino on the jukebox, and a shrine (a martini, a coffee cup and a cigarette) dedicated to former manager Marty, this vintage bar is a Dom Pérignon '53 among Vegas saloons. Hipsters, barflies and discerning locals head here at all hours for cheap drinks; many find it hard to leave.

Crown & Anchor Pub

1350 E Tropicana Avenue, at S Maryland Parkway, University District (739 8676, www.crownandanchorlv.com). Bus 109, 201. **Open** 24hrs daily. **Map** p317 Y3 ⓸⓪

The British-themed Crown & Anchor manages the feat, difficult in this town, of being a freestanding, independent pub, separate from a casino or strip mall. Collegiate types and football-shirted expats head here to down pints of Boddingtons, tuck into fish and chips and bash away hopefully at Thursday's quiz night. A newer second location recently opened across town (4755 Spring Mountain Road, between S Decatur Boulevard & S Arville Street, 876 4733). *Photo p165.*

Davy's Locker

1149 E Desert Inn Road, at S Maryland Parkway Avenue, East Las Vegas (735 0001, www.davys lockerlv.com). Bus 109, 203. **Open** 24hrs daily. **No credit cards. Map** p317 Y3 ⓸⓵

Sadly, the interior of this long-standing fixture can't match the sign out front, a truly evocative old glory that's surely destined for the Neon Museum if the bar ever closes. After more than four decades, though, it seems pretty firmly ensconced, a calm, slightly divey little wellspring of cheap drinks and melancholy on a forlorn stretch of Desert Inn Road.

★ Dispensary Lounge

2451 E Tropicana Avenue, at S Eastern Avenue, East Las Vegas (458 6343, www.thedispensary lounge.com). Bus 110, 201. **Open** 24hrs daily. **Map** p317 Z3 ⓸⓶

Freakin' Frog.
See p168.

CONSUME

You can look at the waterwheel, you can listen to the waterwheel, but you certainly can't touch it. Sort of like the waitresses. The Dispensary is a throwback to old Vegas, complete with shag carpets, fake plants and leotard-clad serving staff who become more boisterous and less balanced as the night wears on (well, you try wearing high heels on a shag carpet). A dark, quiet answer to a bright and frenetic city.

Drop Bar

Green Valley Ranch *2300 Paseo Verde Drive, at S Green Valley Parkway, Henderson (617 7777, www.greenvalleyranchresort.com). Bus 111.* **Open** 24hrs daily.

It's easy to be tricked into feeling that you're not old enough to be lounging with a glass of pinot noir on the frightfully white bar stools and leather couches at Drop. By contrasting the whites with deep, dark floors and walls, the designers have achieved a seriously sexy look, with sheer curtains providing separation from the lively casino. A luxurious place to celebrate a win or to lick your wounds.

Freakin' Frog

4700 S Maryland Parkway, at E Tropicana Avenue, University District (217 6794, www. freakinfrog.com). Bus 109, 201. **Open** 2pm-4am daily. **Map** p317 Y3 ④③

Despite its irritatin' name, the Frog is a locals' favourite, and not just because of the 400-strong beer selection. Located across the road from UNLV, this is about as close as Vegas gets to a college bar. Order some fried mac 'n' cheese triangles or a corn dog to accompany your discussion of Peruvian beer versus, say, Colt 45 (both of which are stocked). There's a whiskey bar upstairs. *Photo p167.*

Herbs & Rye

3713 W Sahara Avenue, at S Valley View Boulevard, West Las Vegas (982 8036, www. herbsandrye.com). Bus SX, 104. **Open** 5pm-3am Mon-Sat. **Map** p317 X3 ④④

Mixologists reign at the bar of this Italian/tapas restaurant, which aspires to a 1920s speakeasy feel. The bartenders focus on quality, tradition and innovation – the cocktail menu is arranged according to the history of spirits. Ask for a Bee's Knees – a '20s-era nectar of gin, honey and lemon.

Hookah Lounge

Paymon's Mediterranean Café & Market, 4147 S Maryland Parkway, at E Flamingo Road, University District (731 6030, www.hookahlounge.com). Bus 109, 202. **Open** 11am-1am daily.

In this dark and ornate haven – a stark contrast to the adjoining Mediterranean Café – you'll be served by a hookah jockey dispensing cocktails and water pipes. Flavours range from floral to fruity, but we recommend Turkish pistachio. Take a couple of puffs and then pass it on. There's food and herbal smoke before 9pm; afterwards, the kitchen closes and the real tobacco is brought out.

★ Mermaid Bar & Lounge

Silverton *3333 Blue Diamond Road, at I-15, South Las Vegas (263 7777, www.silverton casino.com). Bus 217.* **Open** 11am-1am daily.

While you're sitting and sipping your Shark Attack and gazing into the 117,000-gallon aquarium, it might occur to you to wonder: where are the mermaids? Don't fret: they, and their companion mermen, will be along in a while, diving in on the hour in the evenings (except Tue) and performing underwater versions of *Swan Lake*. Cheap drinks and jellyfish tanks add to the eccentric appeal.

Carnaval Court.

INSIDE TRACK DRINK FREELY

Liquor and Las Vegas: the two have long been synonymous. Sit down at a slot machine or table game and before long a cocktail waitress will appear to take your drink order – no charge. Any establishment that offers gambling makes a better return from it than from the liquor, which is sure to loosen your inhibitions – and wallet. But be careful: a couple of beers could cost you $40 or more in a tabletop video poker machine.

Lounges

Many visitors to Vegas leave town arguing that a number of the big shows staged in Strip casinos really aren't strong enough to merit an admission charge. But as long as people are willing to pay $55 to see a Joan Rivers impersonator or drop $30 to hear an impressionist, the casinos will be more than happy to take the money and run.

Conversely, few visitors make the case that the resorts should start charging for the free entertainment offered in their lounges. Traditionally, Vegas lounges have been reserved for acts on their way up or down the showbiz ladder: Louis Prima revived his career in the now-shuttered Sahara's Casbah Lounge, and others have made their name by playing Vegas lounges for little more than a tip and a wink. These days, though, many of the musicians who provide a soundtrack to the drunken gambling are of a rather lower grade.

There's a limit to the number of classic rock covers any sane person can stomach, and many visitors will have a similarly low tolerance for the too-smooth jazzers and *American Idol* wannabes who try out a little bit too hard to catch the eyes and ears of passing punters. Even so, pleasant musical surprises aren't as rare as you might expect, and even the worst rendition of 'Don't Stop Believin'' can get the head nodding and the nostalgia flowing after a liberal infusion of vodka.

THE STRIP

Le Cabaret

Paris Las Vegas *3655 Las Vegas Boulevard South, at E Flamingo Road (946 7000, www. parislasvegas.com). Bus Deuce, 202.* **Open** 9pm-1am Mon-Thur, Sun; 9pm-2am Fri, Sat. **Map** p320 A7 **45**
Le Cabaret has more character than most antiseptic casino lounges. With its faux shady trees and sparkling lights, you'll almost feel like you're doin'

the 'Neutron Dance' in gay Paree. Or, at least, you will after the eighth drink of the evening.

Carnaval Court

Harrah's *3475 Las Vegas Boulevard South, between Sands Avenue & E Flamingo Road (369 5000, www.harrahslasvegas.com). Bus Deuce, 202.* **Open** 11am-3am daily. **Map** p320 A6 **46**
At this outlandish outdoor bar, the show-off entertainment comes as much from the bartenders as the musicians: it's not uncommon to see a barkeep pouring shots into the upturned mouths of waiting patrons, like baby birds begging to be fed. Indeed.

Indigo Lounge

Bally's *3645 Las Vegas Boulevard South, at E Flamingo Road (1-877 603 4390, www.ballys lasvegas.com). Bus Deuce, 202.* **Open** 9pm-2am Mon-Fri, Sun; 9pm-3am Sat. **Map** p320 A7 **47**
Right next to the Bally's/Paris Las Vegas walkway, this casual, high-energy lounge features a scattering of pop, dance, Motown and R&B acts. Comfy chairs and a surprisingly good roster of decent musicians make this an excellent place to cool your heels.

Mizuya Lounge

Mandalay Bay *3950 Las Vegas Boulevard South, at W Hacienda Avenue (632 4760, www.mandalaybay.com). Bus Deuce, 119.* **Open** 11am-3am Mon-Thur; 11am-4am Fri; 9am-4am Sat; 9am-3am Sun. **Map** p320 A9 **48**
Dance bands play at Mandalay Bay's largest music lounge and sushi bar, beyond restaurant row, and draw energetic crowds nightly. A mellower vibe can be found in the casino's Orchid Lounge.

THE REST OF THE CITY

Bourbon Street Cabaret

Orleans *4500 W Tropicana Avenue, between S Decatur & S Valley View Boulevards, West of Strip (365 7111, www.orleanscasino.com). Bus 103, 104, 201.* **Open** 6pm-3am Tue-Sun. **Map** p317 X4 **49**
Local bands play a mix of rock, pop, Latin and disco in this small lounge six nights a week. It's styled like a French Quarter courtyard and adorned with wrought-iron decorations, with grand pianos suspended overhead. There's usually a two-drink minimum in effect.

Rock's Lounge

Red Rock Resort *11011 W Charleston Boulevard, at I-215, West Las Vegas (797 7777, www.redrocklasvegas.com). Bus SX.* **Open** varies.
Fake smoke pours out of the lounge of this swanky neighbourhood casino, a thick haze that either beckons or repels you from the cheese-o-rama of acts like Zowie Bowie (no relation) and various Dave Matthews Band wannabes.

Shops & Services

Never mind the gambling, where's the mall?

Taking in a show? Check. Dining at a star-studded restaurant? Check. Rolling the dice or doubling down? Check. But... buying a pair of Manolos? Really? Yes, it's true. Though few predicted it 20 years ago, the way in which tourists now enjoy Vegas has changed dramatically since the Forum Shops opened at Caesars Palace in 1992. According to the Las Vegas Convention & Visitors Authority, more than half of the city's 40 million visitors spend time shopping. The key is in the old something-for-everyone cliché: there's Nike Golf for the weekend duffer, Prada and Tom Ford for the label hound, and the Gap for just about everybody else.

CONSUME

THE SHOPS

Change in the Vegas shopping scene has been rapid and dramatic. The 2004 opening of the cool, urban **Mandalay Place** (*see p175*) was followed by dramatic renovations and expansion at the **Fashion Show Mall** (*see p177*), the christening of a new wing at the **Forum Shops** (*see p174*), the unveiling of the **Wynn Esplanade**'s (*see p176*) selection of super-smart stores, and the 2007 remodelling (and renaming) of the **Miracle Mile Shops** (*see p175*). Off Strip, the **Las Vegas Premium Outlets** (*see p178*) in Downtown has been a huge success; also Downtown, the **Holsum Design Center** (241 W Charleston Boulevard, at Grand Central Parkway) has brought small local businesses into focus.

THE BEST SHOPS

For looking, but not touching
Crystals. See p173.

For stretching your dollar
Las Vegas Premium Outlets. See p178.

For the night you'll never mention again
Love Jones. See p183.

For T-shirts no one will wear
Bonanza Gifts. See p187.

Further south on Las Vegas Boulevard, the **Town Square** mall (*see p177*) has 150 stores, 12 restaurants, a buzzy, locals-heavy club scene and a multiplex with an IMAX theatre. While the aforementioned Las Vegas Premium Outlets also has about 150 stores.

So go ahead, shop till you drop – if you do, your hotel room is often just an elevator ride away: many of the newest, highest-end malls are built right into the casino resorts.

The **Grand Canal Shoppes** at the Venetian and Palazzo (*see p175*) is now home to Barneys, Las Vegas's first branch of the department store favoured by New York's funky fashion elite.

And now, outshining them all is **Crystals** (*see p173*), the ultra-luxe shopping complex that fronts the new **CityCenter** complex on the Strip, with its elegant angles designed by architect Daniel Libeskind. With its vast ceilings and pristine all-white settings, Crystals looks like a museum of shopping designed by a sci-fi art director, and it features boutiques by Balenciaga, Dior, Pucci, Gucci and Fendi, Stella McCartney, Paul Smith and Tom Ford.

Right next door there's the even newer **Cosmopolitan** (*see p173*), the choice of the international hipoisie (and locals, who took to the place immediately). Its collection of boutiques will get you kitted out to be noticed. And soon there will be even more options. Scheduled to open in late 2013, the **Linq** (www.caesars.com/thelinq) will be an outdoor retail-dining-entertainment complex located on the central

Where to Shop

Where to find what you want.

THE STRIP

Most shoppers remain confined to the Strip, and not without good reason: the majority of the town's more interesting and popular malls are found on it. The shopping complex **Crystals** (*see p173*) is beyond high-end, but the **Forum Shops** (*see p174*) remains one of the most popular destinations.

DOWNTOWN

Unless you're hunting for cheap T-shirts or other knick-knacks to commemorate your stay, you won't find much on Fremont Street, which is devoid of decent shops. However, the **Arts District** is crammed with vintage stores and galleries, and the **Las**

Vegas Premium Outlets (*see p178*) is perfect for those with champagne tastes and beer budgets.

THE REST OF THE CITY

The **Town Square** outdoor shopping/dining/entertainment complex (*see p177*), south of the Strip, is a favourite among locals, and many tourists find it worth their while to make the quick trip too. **Tivoli Village** (*see p177*), in the north-west, is great for strolling and dining, as is the **District** (*see p177*) in the opposite corner of the valley. Otherwise, the malls are plentiful and the best of Vegas's independent retailers are in strip malls or stand-alone buildings around the city. It really does pay to travel.

Strip between the Quad and the Flamingo. The open-air mall will house a variety of shopping and eating establishments, but its most defining feature will be the High Roller, which, when completed, will be the world's largest observational wheel at 550 feet tall.

If all this sounds too serious, rest assured that good taste hasn't completely taken over Vegas. You'll still be able to find all the kitschy knick-knacks you could possibly want in the town's many souvenir stores. Certainly, **Bonanza Gifts** (*see p187*), which declares itself the 'World's Largest Gift Shop', isn't getting any smaller...

SERVICE WITH A SMILE?

It may come as a surprise, but service is not always a strong point here. Attendants can range from wonderfully helpful to downright rude at shops right next to one another; it might seem rather odd in a city so completely based on pleasing its visitors, until you work out that this is just about the only major service industry in town where the professionals stand no chance of being tipped handsomely for their work.

General

DEPARTMENT STORES

The following stores stock a broad range of products, from fashion to homewares. In addition, the numerous branches of **Target** (www.target.com) in Vegas offer trendy designer labels (Isaac Mizrahi, Liz Lange, Mossimo) at

discount prices. And be sure to look out for **Barneys New York**; the Big Apple's most fashionable export has opened a branch in the Venetian's new Shoppes at the Palazzo.

Dillard's

Fashion Show Mall, 3200 Las Vegas Boulevard South, at Spring Mountain Road (733 2008, www.dillards.com). Bus Deuce, 203. **Open** 10am-9pm Mon-Sat; noon-6pm Sun. **Map** p320 B6.
The American west's equivalent of Marks & Spencer has excellent beauty aisles, a good selection of women's shoes, and a great range of men's suits at decent prices. By the same token, there's not much to quicken the pulse.
Other locations throughout the city.

Macy's

Fashion Show Mall, 3200 Las Vegas Boulevard South, at Spring Mountain Road (731 5111, www.macys.com). Bus Deuce, 203. **Open** 10am-9pm Mon-Thur; 9am-10pm Fri; 9am-11pm Sat; 11am-7pm Sun; (hours subject to change). **Map** p319, p320 B6.
The king of department stores, Macy's offers a variety of quality merchandise at competitive prices. Clothing, strong on both men's and women's lines, ranges from classic (Ralph Lauren) to hip (Ben Sherman) to utilitarian.
Other locations throughout the city.

Neiman Marcus

Fashion Show Mall, 3200 Las Vegas Boulevard South, at Spring Mountain Road (731 3636, www.neimanmarcus.com). Bus Deuce, 203. **Open** 10am-8pm Mon-Sat; noon-7pm Sun. **Map** p319, p320 B6.

The world's best designers are on display at this upmarket department store, among them the cat-walk-friendly likes of Prada, Manolo Blahnik, Escada, Missoni and Chanel. It also has a good range of accessories, make-up, lingerie and perfumes, and a fantastic homewares selection. It's nicknamed 'Needless Mark-Up' for a reason, but there are dis-counted goods down at the Fashion Outlets of Las Vegas in Primm (874 2100; *see p178*).

Nordstrom

Fashion Show Mall, 3200 Las Vegas Boulevard South, at Spring Mountain Road (862 2525, www. nordstrom.com). Bus Deuce, 203. **Open** 10am-9pm Mon-Sat; 11am-7pm Sun. **Map** p319, p320 B6.

Those who swear by Nordstrom agree that it's a good place for style-conscious people of any age to find great stuff at reasonable prices and with excel-lent service. Both the men's and women's shoe departments are worth a look. Harking back to the days when shopping used to be an 'experience', Nordy's even treats its customers to piano music and a fine café. Those of lesser means should try its Henderson outlet.

Other locations Nordstrom Rack, 579 N Stephanie Street, at W Sunset Road, Henderson (948 2121).

Saks Fifth Avenue

Fashion Show Mall, 3200 Las Vegas Boulevard South, at Spring Mountain Road (733 8300, www.saksfifthavenue.com). Bus Deuce, 203. **Open** 10am-8pm Mon-Wed, Sat; 10am-9pm Thur, Fri; noon-7pm Sun. **Map** p319, p320 B6.

For those with discriminating taste and a heavy-weight bank account, a trip to Saks is like a visit to church: you go once a week to pay homage and hear the word. The men's and women's apparel sections are especially strong (Marc Jacobs, Dolce & Gabbana, Hugo Boss).

▶ *If you've got the taste but not the money, check out Off 5th, Saks's outlet store at the Las Vegas Outlet Center (7400 Las Vegas Boulevard South, at Warm Springs Road, 263 7692).*

MALLS
Casino malls

Casino malls tend to attract the high-end brands and big-name chains, rather than any discount outlets. For designer labels, head to the brand-new **Crystals** (Balenciaga, Dior, Pucci, Gucci and Fendi, Stella McCartney, Paul Smith and Tom Ford), the **Wynn Esplanade** (Chanel, Cartier, Manolo Blahnik), **Via Bellagio** (Prada, Armani, Tiffany) and the **Forum Shops** (Marc Jacobs, DKNY, Carolina Herrera). The latter also houses a number of high-street staples (Gap, Banana Republic), as does Planet Hollywood's **Miracle Mile Shops**.

Le Boulevard

Paris Las Vegas *3655 Las Vegas Boulevard South, at E Flamingo Road (946 7000, www. parislasvegas.com).* Bus Deuce, 202. **Open** 9am-11pm daily. **Map** p320 A7.

Just about every shop in this small but divine mall (it's basically an extended hallway) comes with a strong but delightful French influence. Les Eléments has collectibles and gifts designed to warm the heart (and home) of even the most ardent Francophile, while La Cave has cheeses, pâtés and wine. Get your French news at Presse, or take home a souvenir from 24-hour gift shop (Le Journal) where you can pur-chase everything from a Paris Las Vegas T-shirt to Diet Coke and cigarettes.

★ Cosmopolitan

CityCenter *3708 Las Vegas Boulevard South, between E Harmon Avenue & E Flamingo Road (698 7000, www.cosmopolitanlasvegas.com).* Bus Deuce. **Open** 10am-11pm daily. **Map** p320 A7.

The Cosmopolitan set out to be different from any-where else in Las Vegas, and it has achieved this goal with style, sophistication and wit. The choice of the international and hip, as well as chic locals, Cosmo attracts a younger, more urbane crowd. The vertical layout (three storeys, centred around a chan-delier that even Liberace himself couldn't have envi-sioned) is studded with unusual shopping options, including Amsterdam's outré, avant-garde Droog assemblage of conceptual furniture. You'll also find an outpost of the UK's AllSaints Spitalfields, the Beckley luxury boutique, the discerning Stitched menswear collections, and Skins 6/2 Cosmetics, which sells potions with 'retail theater'. Once you have your look together, grab a cocktail and head for the third floor, an endless people-watching parade, with an amusing collection of mid-century modern furniture for striking a pose upon.

Crystals at CityCenter

CityCenter *3720 Las Vegas Boulevard South, at E Harmon Avenue (590 9299, www.crystals atcitycenter.com).* Bus Deuce. **Open** 10am-11pm Mon-Thur, Sun; 10am-midnight Fri, Sat. **Map** p320 A7.

Hollywood should stage the Academy Awards at the new Crystals shopping centre at the CityCenter com-plex. God knows it's big enough, with its soaring ceilings and vast expanses of white stone. And all the designer labels favoured by celebrities and socialites are in place: Balenciaga, Dior, Pucci, Gucci and Fendi; Stella McCartney, Paul Smith and Tom Ford; as well as jewellers-to-the-stars Bulgari, Cartier, Tiffany, Van Cleef and Arpels, Mikimoto and Harry Winston. Between bouts of browsing and buying, there are restaurants by Wolfgang Puck and Todd English (his PUB is a fantastically fun casual saloon), the pan-Asian Social Club and the lavish, retro-futuristic Mastro's Ocean Club, which perches over the fabulous fray. Since precious few can afford

CONSUME

Crystals. *See p173.*

the baubles on display, there's often plenty of room inside the boutiques, where it's often 'look but don't touch'. But the biggest draw at Crystals, its water-themed public art, is definitely look and touch: one work features giant obelisks of ice that emerge and then slowly melt, creating fantastic shapes and textures via heat, wind, and the touch of thousands of tourists; another offers rainbow-hued whirlwinds within Plexiglas cylinders.

▶ For more art in Las Vegas, see pp186-187.

★ Forum Shops

Caesars Palace *3500 Las Vegas Boulevard South, at E Flamingo Road (893 4800, www.caesars.com). Bus Deuce, 202.* **Open** 10am-11pm Mon-Thur, Sun; 10am-midnight Fri, Sat. **Map** p320 A7.

Sure, it might be trying too hard with the faux-Roman vibe – classical pillars, statues, huge replica of the Trevi Fountain – but with more than 160 boutiques and shops under its trompe l'oeil, always-

twilit Italian sky, the Forum Shops rakes in a whopping $1,300 in sales per square foot each year, the nation's highest per-square-foot revenue. And that's a lot of square feet – the Forum Shops recently added 175,000 square feet and additional levels that extend the mall to the Strip. It's far and away the best of the casino malls; you could spend your entire visit here.

In the main mall, mid-range chains (Banana Republic, Gap, Abercrombie & Fitch, Diesel) punctuate the serious designer line-up: Elie Tahari, Christian Dior, Valentino, Ermenegildo Zegna, John Varvatos, et al. Accessorise your outfit at Cartier, David Yurman, Christian Louboutin, De Beers, Inglot or Tiffany & Co. But the real jewels are the refined shops that front directly on to the Strip. Spiral escalators and marble floors help create a swanky setting for tenants such as fashion powerhouses Kate Spade, Marc Jacobs, Pucci, Thomas Pink and Carolina Herrera. There are attractions at either end of the mall: statues come to life at one extremity, with Atlantis rising from the waves at the other. When your feet or credit cards are exhausted, head for the Qua Baths & Spa or pop by Numb Bar for a frozen cocktail.

Grand Canal Shoppes

Venetian & Palazzo *3377 Las Vegas Boulevard South, between Sands Avenue & E Flamingo Road (414 4500, www.grandcanalshoppes.com). Bus Deuce, 119, 203.* **Open** 10am-11pm Mon-Thur, Sun; 10am-midnight Fri, Sat. **Map** p320 A6.

The Grand Canal Shoppes felt like a second-rate Forum Shops when it opened in 1999. In places, that's what it still resembles. The walkways are narrow and cramped, but the smaller space does at least give a reasonable impression of an intimate city streetscape – and it's studded with cafés, such as the Grand Lux and a Venice-by-way-of-Brooklyn import, Grimaldi's Pizzeria. With its faux-alfresco feel, the outpost of Wolfgang Puck's Postrio here is one of the most pleasant places in the city to dine; and Asian bistro Tao becomes one of the city's hottest clubs at night. Let's not overlook the novelty of browsing shops along one of Vegas's wonders: a Venetian canal, paddled by singing gondoliers. Oh, then there are the shops, of course: Barneys New York, Coach, Jimmy Choo, Cartier, BCBG/Max Azria and Burberry are among the best of the generally high-end retailers. If it all becomes a bit too much, there's an on-site oxygen bar called Breath. And the Grand Canal may be the only mall with its own branch of the Madame Tussauds wax museum. *Photo p176.*

► *For a review of Postrio, see p144. For Tao, see p147.*

Mandalay Place

Mandalay Bay *3950 Las Vegas Boulevard South, at W Hacienda Avenue (632 9333, www.mandalaybay.com). Bus Deuce, 119.* **Open** 10am-11pm daily. **Map** p320 A9.

What separates this smallish retail experience from other Strip malls is its vow to 'break the chains': it leases its stores only to companies otherwise absent from Vegas. It's a savvy move, and one that brought the city its first Urban Outfitters (which has since also opened in the Miracle Mile Shops); an outpost of Frederick's of Hollywood lingerie; unusual art offerings, including the Art of Music and Peter Lik Gallery. The handful of great boutiques includes Nora Blue, Elton's Men Store and Le Paradis; other highlights include the Las Vegas Sock Market, and sweet spot Lick, for all your candy – bacon-flavoured included – needs. For nibbles, try Rick Moonen's new steampunk-inspired Rx Boiler Room (Moonen is TV-famous from his appearances on the *Top Chef* reality show). The Burger Bar (*see p136*) continues to be popular, with its baroque twists (foie gras!) on the humble hamburger. And when you need to chill out, pop into the Minus5 Ice Lounge, an all-ice cocktail bar – where you'll be outfitted with a parka and gloves before you sip your vodka from an ice goblet. The mall is located on a bridge that connects Mandalay Bay to the Luxor, and is accessible from either resort. *Photo p177.*

Miracle Mile Shops

Planet Hollywood *3663 Las Vegas Boulevard South, between E Harmon Avenue & E Flamingo Road (866 0703, www.miraclemileshopslv.com). Bus Deuce, 202.* **Open** 10am-11pm Mon-Thur, Sun; 10am-midnight Fri, Sat. **Map** p320 A7.

Formerly the Desert Passage, this 1.2-mile loop-mall recently underwent a multi-million-dollar makeover, transforming it from a Moroccan-style market into a contemporary urban centre. The Hollywood-style facelift added trendier, younger labels to attract the kind of hipsters usually found hanging at the Palms or the Hard Rock, among them Lucky Brand, H&M, Bettie Page, Swarovski, Quiksilver, Marciano and

Forum Shops.

CONSUME

Urban Outfitters. What makes it stand out are the scores of eating options – grab a sandwich at Ocean One or party late at PBR Rock Bar & Grill (*see p160*) – and entertainment venues studded throughout the mall, plus a free hourly 'thunderstorm' show that brings everyone to a halt. *Photo p178.*

Via Bellagio

Bellagio *3600 Las Vegas Boulevard South, at W Flamingo Road (693 7111, www.bellagio.com). Bus Deuce, 202.* **Open** 10am-midnight daily. **Map** p320 A7.

In line with its upmarket image, the Bellagio's small mall contains a dozen of the smartest designer names this side of Wynn Las Vegas. Long-standing tenants such as Tiffany & Co, Prada, Gucci, Chanel, Dior, Giorgio Armani and Hermès have been joined of late by the likes of Fendi and Bottega Veneta. If your wallet can't cope, at least pop in to enjoy the location: the venue is a shrine to materialism, with daylight streaming through the vaulted glass ceilings on to opulent walkways and tidy storefronts. The food is a cut above regular mall fodder too: try Todd English's Olives, a Mediterranean bistro overlooking the lake, with a marvellous view of the hourly Bellagio fountain show.

Wynn Esplanade

Wynn Las Vegas *3131 Las Vegas Boulevard South, between E Desert Inn Road & Sands Avenue (770 7000, www.wynnlasvegas.com). Bus Deuce, 108, 203.* **Open** 10am-11pm daily. **Map** p319, p320 B6.

Steve Wynn took Oscar de la Renta on a personal tour of the then under-construction Wynn Las Vegas in an attempt to convince the couturier that it would be the finest resort in town. It worked. De la Renta located his signature shop inside the Wynn Esplanade, as have Alexander McQueen, Jaeger-LeCoultre, Hermès, Brioni, Manolo Blahnik (the second signature store in the US) and Piaget, to name but a few. There's also the requisite collection of designer labels, among them Chanel, Dior and Louis Vuitton, and the mustn't-miss Ferrari-Maserati showroom and logo gift shop ($10 admission required – unless you're buying a car).

Non-casino malls

Even without its casino malls, Vegas caters efficiently and effectively for shoppers. The revamped **Fashion Show Mall** leads the way, supplemented by the more prosaic **Boulevard Mall** and other less notable developments.

In addition, Las Vegas now has its very own 'lifestyle centres', open-air complexes that 'serve as multi-purpose leisure-time destinations' (according to the International Council of Shopping Centers). The best is **Town Square** out on Las Vegas Boulevard South near the aiport. The **District**, in Green Valley, is also superb, as are the new shops at **Tivoli Village** in Summerlin. Others include **Rampart Commons** (1055 S Rampart Boulevard, at W Charleston Boulevard, Summerlin) and the nearby **Boca Park Fashion Village** (750 S Rampart Boulevard, at Alta Drive, Summerlin).

Boulevard Mall

3528 S Maryland Parkway, at E Desert Inn Road, East Las Vegas (735 8268, www.boulevardmall. com). Bus 109, 203. **Open** 10am-9pm Mon-Sat; 11am-6pm Sun. **Map** p317 Y3.

Grand Canal Shoppes. See p175.

Mandalay Place. *See p175.*

A bastion of the Las Vegas shopping scene and the first mall of its type to open in the city; it's centrally located, reasonably priced and loaded with familiar favourites such as Sears, Marshall's, Macy's and JC Penney. When you're weighed down with bags and nearing collapse, head to the food court for cheap international cuisine.

The District
Green Valley Ranch *2240 Village Walk Drive, at S Green Valley Parkway, Henderson (564 8595, www.thedistrictatgvr.com). Bus 111.* **Open** 10am-8pm Mon-Thur; 10am-9pm Fri, Sat; 11am-7pm Sun.
Highlights at the open-air District, across the street from the lush Green Valley Ranch casino-resort in Henderson, include REI, Anthropologie, Coldwater Creek and Francesca's Collections, a sweet little accessories and gift shop. Eateries, among them Lucille's Smokehouse Bar-B-Que, Elephant Bar, the splendid King's Fish House, the high-energy burger joint Al's Garage and the deliciously authentic Settebello Pizzeria Napoletana, are an important part of the mix. The District crossed over Green Valley Parkway to include the city's second Whole Foods Market, its first West Elm furniture showcase and chic women's boutique Loft.

Fashion Show Mall
3200 Las Vegas Boulevard South, at Spring Mountain Road (369 8382, www.thefashion show.com). Bus Deuce, 203. **Open** 10am-9pm Mon-Sat; 11am-7pm Sun. **Map** p319, p320 B6.
True to its name, the Fashion Show Mall offers live runway shows every Friday through Sunday, from noon to 6pm on the hour, with models showcasing styles from the scores of retailers within the mall's vast compound. A $1-billion expansion of the Fashion Show Mall included the addition of the Cloud, an amazing image projection screen/sunshade that hovers over the front of the shopping centre and broadcasts to the Strip. However, it's the line-up of shops that's the real eye-catcher. The mall has nearly doubled in size; original tenants such as Macy's, Neiman Marcus and Saks Fifth Avenue have been joined by anchor tenants including Dillard's and Nordstrom, and speciality shops such as Pandora, Apple, Puma, True Religion and Zara. The range of restaurants is also fine: try Ra Sushi and Capital Grille. *Photo p179.*

★ Tivoli Village
440 S Rampart Boulevard, at Alta Drive, Summerlin (570 7400, www.tivolivillagelv.com). Bus 114. **Open** 10am-8pm Mon-Thur; 10am-9pm Fri, Sat; 11am-6pm Sun.
Rampart Boulevard in Summerlin, located in the north-eastern area of Las Vegas, was already rife with malls before the first phase of Tivoli Village opened in 2011: Boca Park Fashion Village lies on the other side of Alta Drive, and just up the road from that is the popular and dependable Rampart Commons. No matter to Tivoli's developers, who painstakingly worked through the economic slump to build and open this classy and luxurious European-themed shopping centre. But this open-air market has little in common with its neighbours up the road, opting, instead, for more of a 'lifestyle' experience than a shopping expedition. Accessorise your home, at Ethan Allen; your wardrobe, at Republic of Couture; or your dog, at Shaggy Chic; then complete your afternoon with a meal at Poppy Den. You're welcome.

★ Town Square
6605 Las Vegas Boulevard South, at the intersection of I-15 & I-215, South of Strip (269 5000, www.mytownsquarelasvegas.com). Bus SDX, 104, 117. **Open** 9am-9pm Mon-Sat; 10am-6pm Sun.
Though it's somewhat off the Strip – a mile and a half south of Mandalay Bay – this addition to the city's shopping and entertainment scene is worth the cab ride. Vegas locals often opt for the stylised street scene and less-overwhelming outdoor plaza of Town Square over the Strip: shopping options

CONSUME

Miracle Mile Shops. *See p175.*

CONSUME

include just about everything you'd want, from Abercrombie & Fitch and Armani Exchange to White House/Black Market to a design district. There are a host of dining choices, the best of which may be the outdoor patio at Brio; you'll also find a Whole Foods Market, a consistently packed Apple store, an 18-screen state-of-the-digital-art multiplex, and a cluster of busy and buzzy clubs, including Blue Martini, Double Helix Wine & Whiskey Lounge, Yard House and New York-Irish import McFadden's Saloon.

Discount malls

For brand-name bargains, you can't beat a discount mall, where stores sell last season's stock at a fraction of its original price. Vegas has two of its own (*see below*), but there are more bargains south of the city: the **Fashion Outlets of Las Vegas** mall in Primm (32100 Las Vegas Boulevard South, 874 1400, www.fashionoutletlasvegas.com) houses over 100 stores, among them big-names such as **Coach** and **DKNY**.

Swap meets, at which new and used goods are hawked at bargain rates, are also worth a look. The **Broadacres Open Air Swap Meet** (2960 Las Vegas Boulevard North, at N Pecos Road, North Las Vegas, 642 3777, www.broadacres mec.com) and the **Fantastic Indoor Swap Meet** (1717 S Decatur Boulevard, at W Oakey Boulevard, South-west Las Vegas, 877 0087, www.fantasticindoorswapmeet.com) are both open Friday to Sunday.

★ Las Vegas Premium Outlets South
7400 Las Vegas Boulevard South, at E Warm Springs Road, South of Strip (896 5599, www. premiumoutlets.com). Bus SDX, 117, 217.
Open 10am-9pm Mon-Sat; 10am-8pm Sun.
This is the southern – and closer to the Strip – version of the outlet mall of the same name near Downtown. The long-established shopping centre has decent bargains from Calvin Klein, Off 5th, Nike, Adidas, Calvin Klein, Hugo Boss and much, much more – 140 stores in all. **Las Vegas Premium Outlets North** (875 S Grand Central Parkway, 474 7500) has more of the same with an additional ten stores. Goods may be less expensive than at the regular retail outlets, but with all these choices it's easy to blow your budget here too. *Photo p180.*

Specialist
BOOKS & MAGAZINES

Reading is not a priority in Las Vegas (whatever reading goes on takes place by the pool), and independent bookstores have had even more of a hard time of it than in other cities. There are branches of book chain **Barnes & Noble** in the outer-lying areas of Las Vegas (8915 W Charleston Boulevard, 242 1987; 2191 N Rainbow Boulevard, 631 1775; and 567 N Stephanie Street, Henderson, 434 1533, www.barnesandnoble.com).

Specialist

Gamblers Book Club

5473 Eastern Avenue South, near McCarran International Airport, between E Hacienda Avenue and E Russell Road (382 7555, www.gamblers book.com). Bus 110. **Open** 9am-7pm Mon-Fri; 9am-6pm Sat. **Map** p318 D3.

The Gamblers Book Club is supposedly the world's largest distributor of gambling books, be they coffee-table tomes, industry histories or tips on beating the system. It usually stocks a good selection of bargain books; so if you want to save your money for the tables, get your betting tips here first. If you don't just want to read about gambling, there are also cards, chips and gambling-related software for sale.

Used & antiquarian

Bauman Rare Books

Venetian & Palazzo *3327 Las Vegas Boulevard South, between Sands Avenue & E Flamingo Road (948 1617, www.baumanrarebooks.com).* Bus Deuce, 119, 203. **Open** 10am-11pm Mon-Thur, Sun; 10am-midnight Fri, Sat. **Map** p320 A6.

Need a breath of civilisation and civility? Step into the hushed, luxe halls of this antiquarian purveyor of vintage volumes, modelled after Bauman's famous Madison Avenue shop – but, for the high-roller with a taste for rare books, open 13 hours a day (or more), seven days a week. The 2,300sq-ft gallery has offered desirable documents and books, including first editions of Chaucer, Joyce and Twain.

Dead Poet Books

937 S Rainbow Boulevard, between W Charleston Boulevard & Alta Drive, West Las Vegas (227 4070). Bus 101, 206. **Open** 10am-6pm Mon-Sat.

You'll find a charming hotchpotch of antiquarian books here on almost every topic; specialities include metaphysical cookbooks (yes, really), military histories and first editions.

CHILDREN
Fashion

Gap Kids and **BabyGap** can both be found in the Miracle Mile Shops (862 4042; *see p175*); check www.gap.com for other locations. **Las Vegas Premium Outlets North** (*see p178*) also has a whole slew of children's stores, among them **OshKosh B'Gosh** (221 1400), **Disney** (386 2944), **Carter's** (386 3082) and **Stride Rite Keds Sperry** (388 2055).

Janie & Jack

Fashion Show Mall *3200 Las Vegas Boulevard South, at Spring Mountain Road (892 9571, www.janieandjack.com).* Bus Deuce, 203. **Open** 10am-9pm Mon-Sat; 11am-7pm Sun. **Map** p320 B6.

CONSUME

Fashion Show Mall. *See p177.*

Las Vegas Premium Outlets.
See p178.

This precious addition to the Gymboree family relies on a sugarcoated colour palette to dress up its sweet ensembles for babies and toddlers. Personalised baby gifts include embroidered fleece blankets. There's a second location in the District near Green Valley Ranch (2240 Village Walk Drive, 492 0379).

★ Kidrobot

Cosmopolitan *3708 Las Vegas Boulevard South, between W Harmon Avenue & W Flamingo Road (698 7670, www.kidrobot.com). Bus Deuce.* **Open** 10am-11pm daily. **Map** p320 A7.

Looking for something a little more stylish for your child than overalls? Toy designer Paul Budnitz's Kidrobot outpost at the Cosmopolitan has smart shirts and hoodies for the kids – plus some pretty awesome toys to boot. Get junior a T-shirt and then pick out some collectibles for yourself.

Toys

Build-a-Bear Workshop

Fashion Show Mall *3200 Las Vegas Boulevard South, at Spring Mountain Road (388 2574, www. buildabear.com). Bus Deuce, 203.* **Open** 10am-9pm Mon-Sat; 11am-7pm Sun. **Map** p319 A7.

An individual teddy bear makes a cute gift for the one you love, or indulge the kids by letting them pick out their own gift. Choose your bear's fur and eye colour, costume (the range is huge) and stuffing type, and watch as teddy experts assemble the fluffy creature. It's a real treat for the young and the young at heart.

ELECTRONICS & PHOTOGRAPHY

General

Best Buy (3820 S Maryland Parkway, at E Flamingo Road, 732 8283, www.bestbuy.com), a national chain dealing in audio, visual and computing kits of every stripe, has stores

throughout the city. For troubleshooting, it also offers a **Geek Squad** (1-800 433 5778), available 24 hours a day for any computer-related emergencies (in store or call-out).

For affordable, non-digital film processing, head to one of the myriad branches of chain drugstores at **Walgreens** (*see p189*) or **Smith's** (*see p185*).

Fry's Electronics

6845 Las Vegas Boulevard South, at I-215, South of Strip (932 1400, www.frys.com). Bus SDX, 104, 117, 217. **Open** 8am-9pm Mon-Fri; 9am-9pm Sat; 9am-7pm Sun.

This San Jose-based retailer is best known for outfitting Silicon Valley's dot-commers during the boom. This branch stays true to Fry's not-so-humble roots, but also caters to those who merely want high-quality computing, audio and video equipment – most of it at very competitive prices.

Sahara Camera Center

2600 W Sahara Avenue, at S Rancho Drive, West of Strip (457 3333, www.saharacamera center.com). Bus SX, 119. **Open** 9am-6pm Mon-Thur; 10am-5pm Fri; 10am-4pm Sat. **Map** p319 A4.

Claiming to be 'Nevada's largest full-service camera store', the Sahara Camera Centre pretty much has – and does – it all, with rentals and repairs, quality new and used equipment, knowledgeable staff and one-hour photo processing. Prices are fair.

Specialist

For hi-fi buffs, the Fashion Show Mall (*see p177*) houses branches of audio-visual high-flyer **Bang & Olufsen** (701 9100) and the **Apple store** (577 9740; also at Town Square, south of the Strip). You'll find the latest Sony technology at **Sony Style** (697 5420) in the Forum Shops at Caesars.

FASHION

Las Vegas's wild and unexpected growth as a shopping destination has benefited one industry above all others: fashion. Every major chain is represented here, and a good many designer labels have also shown up to claim their stake. Some savvy European shoppers now come to Las Vegas instead of New York for a chance to restock their wardrobes at US prices. However, the city does still lack its own fashion scene: there aren't many local designers working here, just plenty of very well-dressed Las Vegans.

There's a lot more to shopping in Vegas than the stores mentioned below, and the vast malls can make for an overwhelming experience. To get the most out of your limited shopping time, check out the malls' websites for a little pre-trip browsing and planning.

Designer

Most international design houses have stores in Vegas, which are to be found in the casino malls. **Via Bellagio** (see p176) offers **Prada** (866 6886) and **Giorgio Armani** (893 8327), while the **Wynn Esplanade** (see p176) features **Oscar de La Renta** (770 3487), **Brioni** (770 3440) and **Dior Homme** (735 1345). Across at the **Grand Canal Shoppes** in the Venetian (see p175), you'll find British brand **Burberry** (382 1911).

Dolce & Gabbana (892 0880) and classic London shirt maker **Thomas Pink** (696 1713) reside at the **Forum Shops** (see p174), which also offers menswear from the likes of **Brooks Brothers** (369 0705) and **Hugo Boss** (696 9444). And the **Grand Canal Shoppes** have a few stores that you won't find elsewhere, most notably **Barneys New York** (692 4200) and **Cole Haan** (369 2381).

C Level

Boca Park Fashion Village *750 S Rampart Boulevard, at W Charleston Boulevard, Summerlin (933 6867). Bus 206.* **Open** 11am-7pm Mon-Sat; 11am-6pm Sun.
Budding socialites visit this two-storey loft space to keep up with owner Edith Castillo's well-edited, ever-changing collection of established and emerging designer labels (for both men and women), including pieces from Heather Hawkins, Eugenia Kim and Rachel Pally.

Intermix

Caesars Palace (Forum Shops) *3500 Las Vegas Boulevard South, at E Flamingo Road (731 1922, www.intermixonline.com). Bus Deuce, 202.* **Open** 10am-11pm Mon-Wed, Sun; 10am-midnight Fri, Sat. **Map** p320 A7.

The Keledjian brothers stock a mix of European and American designer womenswear in this growing chain of eclectic boutiques. They prefer to help customers mix and match pieces (hence the name) from different collections by designers such as Chloé, Stella McCartney, Ronny Kobo and Missoni, rather than buy a whole look from one collection.

★ John Varvatos

Caesars Palace (Forum Shops) *3500 Las Vegas Boulevard South, at E Flamingo Road (939 0922, www.johnvarvatos.com). Bus Deuce, 202.* **Open** 10am-11pm Mon-Thur, Sun; 10am-midnight Fri, Sat. **Map** p320 A7.

This men's lifestyle collection has been going since 2000, finding bad-boy credibility by using the likes of Chris Cornell, Iggy Pop and, most recently, Willie Nelson to front its ad campaigns. Shop here for eclectic tailored suits, funky sportswear, accessories and great boots.

Mojitos Resort Wear

Wynn Las Vegas (Esplanade) *3131 Las Vegas Boulevard South, between E Desert Inn Road & Sands Avenue (770 3545, www.wynnlasvegas.com). Bus Deuce, 203.* **Open** 9am-9pm Mon-Thur, Sun; 9am-11pm Fri, Sat. **Map** p319, p320 B6.

This high-end boutique caters to vacationing jet-setters with designer labels for men, women and kids. Get outfitted for your stay at Wynn in brands like Burberry, Zenga, Ted Baker and more.

Scoop NYC

Caesars Palace (Forum Shops) *3500 Las Vegas Boulevard South, at E Flamingo Road (734 0026, www.scoopnyc.com). Bus Deuce, 202.* **Open** 10am-11pm Mon-Thur, Sun; 10am-midnight Fri, Sat. **Map** p320 A7.

This NY-based boutique chain has been hugely successful with its 'ultimate closet' concept, allowing hip shoppers (men, women and children) to find everything they need under one roof. Prices vary, with clothes, accessories and shoes from the likes of Rag & Bone, Marc Jacobs and Helmut Lang.

General

Miracle Mile (see p175) has a good range of trendy stores for those on a budget, among them **Urban Outfitters** (733 0058), **H&M** (369 1195) and **Chico's** (732 2816), while the **Grand Canal Shoppes** (see p175) include branches of **Kenneth Cole** (836 1916) and **Ann Taylor** (731 0655).

However, as is often the case, the **Forum Shops** (see p174) comes out on top by a long way. Stores here include the pick of the US chains, among them **Abercrombie & Fitch** (731 0712) and perennial favourite **Banana Republic** (650 5623), alongside chic accessible designer labels such as **DKNY** (650 9670).

CONSUME

The **Fashion Show Mall** (*see p177*) mixes upscale with casual in a similar way to the Forum Shops, and with almost as much success. Among those present are **Quiksilver** (734 1313) and femme favourite **Bebe** (892 8083), plus the trendier likes of **Lucky Brand** (369 4116), **Diesel** (696 1055) and the youthful brand **True Religion** (791 5670). Don't forget the town's discount malls : you'll find over 150 different labels at the two **Las Vegas Premium Outlets** (*see p178*), among them **Tommy Hilfiger** (382 1630), **Calvin Klein** (366 9898) and **Timberland** (386 3045).

Francesca's Collections

Green Valley Ranch (District) *2240 Village Walk Drive, at S Green Valley Parkway, Henderson (435 3288, www.francescas.com). Bus 111.* **Open** 10am-9pm Mon-Sat; 11am-7pm Sun.
Stocked with a treasure trove of trendy street fashions, girly baubles, glittering hair accessories and playful gifts, Francesca's is the perfect place to pick up that last-minute gift for the girls back home, at very affordable prices.
Other locations throughout the city.

Lacoste

Caesars Palace (Forum Shops) *3500 Las Vegas Boulevard, at E Flamingo Road (791 7616, www.lacoste-usa.com). Bus Deuce, 202.* **Open** 10am-11pm Mon-Thur, Sun; 10am-midnight Fri, Sat. **Map** p320 A7.
The polo shirt, created by French tennis champion René Lacoste in the 1930s, bears the crocodile logo that comes from his nickname. There are cheaper goodies in its store at Las Vegas Premium Outlets.
Other locations Fashion Show Mall (*see p177*; 796 6676).

Suite 160

Mandalay Bay (Mandalay Place) *3930 Las Vegas Boulevard South, at W Hacienda Avenue (304 2513, www.suite160.com). Bus Deuce, 119.* **Open** 10am-7pm Mon-Sat; 1-6pm Sun.
The street-chic brainchild of former skateboarder Jeffrey Brown. Look for old-school favourites like Adidas and Nike, plus new urban lines by (among others) LeBron.

Ted Baker

Caesars Palace (Forum Shops) *3500 Las Vegas Boulevard South, at E Flamingo Road (369 4755, www.tedbaker-london.com). Bus Deuce, 202.* **Open** 10am-11pm Mon-Thur, Sun; 10am-midnight Fri, Sat. **Map** p320 A7.
This London-based label – there is no 'Ted Baker' per se – stocks well-cut, tidy but fun apparel for men and women. Their collection of shirts, suits and traditional (but quirky) gentlemen's accessories particularly stands out.

Used & vintage

Buffalo Exchange

4110 S Maryland Parkway, at E Flamingo Road, University District (791 3960, www.buffalo exchange.com). Bus 109, 202. **Open** 10am-8pm Mon-Sat; 11am-7pm Sun. **Map** p317 Y3.
For first-rate second-hand clothes, this countrywide vintage chain is more popular than ever, especially with students at nearby UNLV. Its prices range from budget to middling; pieces from shop clearances round out the stock.

FASHION ACCESSORIES & SERVICES

Clothing hire

Al Phillips (*see below*) also hires out men's formalwear. For details on weddings in Vegas, *see p238-241*.

David's Bridal

2600 W Sahara Avenue, at S Rancho Drive, West of Strip (367 4779, www.davidsbridal.com). Bus SX, 119. **Open** 11am-9pm Mon-Fri; 10am-7pm Sat; noon-6pm Sun. **Map** p319 A4.
Off-the-rack gowns at reasonable prices in a variety of styles are this store's speciality. There are also tons of accessories, including frocks for the bridal party and dyeable shoes.

I&A Formalwear

4850 W Flamingo Road, at S Decatur Boulevard, West Las Vegas (1-877 246 6060, www.iaformal wear.com). Bus 103, 203. **Open** 9am-6pm Mon-Fri; 9am-5pm Sat. **Map** p318 Z2
The biggest range of designer tuxedos (Ralph Lauren, Oscar de la Renta, Christian Dior) in Las Vegas.

Williams Costume Company

1226 S 3rd Street, at E Colorado Avenue, Downtown (1-866 330 9824, www.williams costumeco.net). Bus Deuce, 105, 108, 206. **Open** 10am-5.30pm Mon-Sat. **Map** p319 C3.
The only place in town that carries sufficient ancient Egyptian, Renaissance gentry and Elvis costumes to dress the bride, groom and all the guests in your chosen theme.

Cleaning & repairs

Al Phillips (www.alphillips-thecleaner.com) has locations all over Vegas, and they will pick up and deliver your items. All branches provide dry-cleaning, laundry and repairs, and hire men's formalwear.

Cora's Coin Laundry

1097 E Tropicana Avenue, at S Maryland Parkway, University District (736 6181).

Bus 109, 201. **Open** 8am-8pm daily.
No credit cards. **Map** p317 Y3.
Just two miles off the Strip, Cora's is popular with
UNLV folk, offering self-service or drop-off laundry,
dry-cleaning and – of course – video poker.

Shoe Lab
*3900 Paradise Road, between Sands Avenue
& E Flamingo Road, East of Strip (791 0341,
www.shoelabworld.com). Bus 108.* **Open** 10am-
6pm Mon-Fri. **Map** p319 C5.
The Shoe Lab can work miracles on any broken shoe
or damaged handbag. It also sells leather care accessories such as polish, brushes and shoe trees.

Jewellery

Hit the jackpot? Vegas is the place to flash
your cash on blinging baubles. Blow your
winnings, or simply max out the credit cards
at any number of fine jewllery stores. Pick
up a tiara from **Tiffany & Co** (697 5400)
at **Via Bellagio** (*see p176*), or indulge your
loved one with a string of diamonds by
Fred Leighton (693 7050). Or trip the
light fantastic with understated luxury at
David Yurman (794 4545) or invest in a
future family heirloom from **Cartier** (418
3904), both to be found at the **Forum Shops**
(*see p174*). Smaller spenders might prefer
the pirate's treasures of **Jewelers of Las
Vegas** (2400 Western Avenue, at W Sahara
Avenue, West of Strip, 382 1234, www.the
jewelers.com). Some of the shops listed under
Luggage (*see p183*) also carry jewellery and
fashion accessories.

Chrome Hearts
Caesars Palace (Forum Shops) *3500 Las
Vegas Boulevard South, at E Flamingo Road
(893 9949, www.chromehearts.com). Bus Deuce,
202.* **Open** 10am-11pm Mon-Thur, Sun; 10am-
midnight Fri, Sat. **Map** p320 A7.
Free your inner-rock wild side at this fine silver and
leather shop. Its signature handcrafted silver jewellery is adorned with skulls, crossbones, crucifixes
and flames, but the store also sells some of the softest
and most stylish leather jackets, trousers and coats
money can buy.

Lingerie & underwear

Agent Provocateur
Caesars Palace (Forum Shops) *3500 Las
Vegas Boulevard South, at E Flamingo Road
(696 7171, www.agentprovocateur.com). Bus
Deuce, 202.* **Open** 10am-11pm Mon-Thur,
Sun; 10am-midnight Fri, Sat. **Map** p320 A7.
The smarties behind the Agent Provocateur brand
know that there's something rather empowering
about wearing fine lingerie, whether or not you share

it. Look for some of the most titillating and trashy
yet tasteful creations currently on the market.

Bare Essentials Fantasy Fashions
*4029 W Sahara Avenue, at S Valley View
Boulevard, West of Strip (247 4711, www.
bareessentialsvegas.com). Bus SX, 104.* **Open**
10am-7pm Mon-Sat; noon-5pm Sun. **Map** p317 X2.
Whatever your fantasy (or gender), Bare Essentials
will do you right. The camp-as-cowboys owners are
correct in their claim that they make women feel at
ease, but there are also men's essentials, costumes
and 'accessories'.

Love Jones
Hard Rock *4455 Paradise Road, at Harmon
Avenue, East of Strip (693 5007, www.hard
rockhotel.com). Bus 108.* **Open** 10am-11pm
Mon, Sun; 11am-11pm Tue-Thur; 11am-1am
Fri; 10am-1am Sat. **Map** p320 C7.
Fur-lined handcuffs, paddles, silk stockings, garter
belts and lingerie from the likes of Honey Dew and
Christie's make this a mentionable unmentionables
boutique. It also sells a few flavoured lotions, potions
and toys (but nothing electric). Hotel guests have
access to 24-hour room service.

Luggage

Dillard's and **Macy's** (for both, *see p171*)
also stock a variety of travel bags and luggage
in the lower price ranges.

Corsa Collections
Venetian (Grand Canal Shoppes) *3377 Las
Vegas Boulevard South, between Sands Avenue
& E Flamingo Road (1-866 340 9442, www.corsa
collections.com). Bus Deuce, 119, 203.* **Open**
10am-11pm Mon-Thur, Sun; 10am-midnight Fri,
Sat. **Map** p320 A6.
Handbags are this store's speciality. The designer
collection includes bags by Marc Jacobs, Michael
Kors, Longchamp, Furla, as well as luggage from
Tumi, Kipling and Swiss Army.

Shoes

There are plenty of brand-name shoe stores
scattered around the Strip, whether your taste
is for slingbacks or sneakers. The selection at
the **Grand Canal Shoppes** (*see p175*) is led
by super-chic **Jimmy Choo** (733 1802) and the
more casual **Rockport** (735 5082), while the
Fashion Show Mall (*see p177*) has smart-
casual Brit-import **Clarks** (732 1801), sports
label **Puma** (892 9988) and the all-conquering
Skechers (969 9905). Over at the **Forum
Shops** (*see p174*), you'll find Italian designer
Sergio Rossi (734 0991), the very Californian
footwear of **Donald J Pliner** (796 0900) and
The Walking Company (792 8400).

CONSUME

CONSUME

Designer Shoe Warehouse
2100 N Rainbow Boulevard, at W Lake Mead Boulevard, West Las Vegas (636 2060, www.dswshoe.com). Bus 101, 210. **Open** 10am-9pm Mon-Sat; 11am-7pm Sun.
The finest selection of discounted designer cobbling in town, with footwear stacked from floor to ceiling. While the shoes may not be this season's latest design, they're still fabulous. Accessories are available in the form of handbags and scarves.
Other locations 571 N Stephanie Street, at W Sunset Road, Henderson (997 0667).

★ New Rock Boots
804 Las Vegas Boulevard South, at Gass Avenue, Downtown (614 9464, www.newrock.com). Bus Deuce, 108. **Open** 11am-8pm Mon-Sat. **Map** p318 C3.
Cross John Fluevog's edgy style with the Doc Martens aesthetic, stir in the 1970s rock 'n' roll style of Kiss, and lo: New Rock Boots. Decorative touches such as buckles, straps, flames and skulls make the boots popular with punks, goths and bikers, but there's also a wide selection of stilettos.

FOOD & DRINK
Bakeries

Cupcakery
9680 S Eastern Avenue, at E Silverado Ranch Boulevard, Henderson (207 2253, www.the cupcakery.com). Bus 110. **Open** 8am-8pm Mon-Fri; 10am-8pm Sat; 10am-6pm Sun.
Tickle Me Pink, Boston Dream, Kir Royale… the fanciful little cakes taste as good as they sound, and with their specially designed sugar crystals, they

sparkle as much as the city. Staff can even print a digital photo on the top, and they take custom orders – see if you can coax one of the salespeople into spilling the sweet-tooth secrets of the Cupcakery's celebrity clientele.
Other locations Monte Carlo, 3770 Las Vegas Boulevard S (730 7777); 7175 W Lake Mead Boulevard, Summerlin (835 0060).

Nothing Bundt Cakes
9711 S Eastern Avenue, at E Silverado Ranch Boulevard, Henderson (314 0520, www.nothingbundtcakes.com). Bus 110. **Open** 9am-6pm Mon-Sat.
The Chocolate Chocolate Chip is a crowd-pleaser, but the carrot Bundt cake (it's a corruption of German Bund cake) is the real showstopper. Other flavours include lemon, red velvet, spice and plain chocolate.
Other locations 8320 W Sahara Avenue, at S Durango Drive, West Las Vegas (871 6301).

Candy & sweets

Las Vegas has lots of secrets, but this one hides in plain site – the 'grown-ups' playground' has a serious sweet tooth. Candy emporia have popped up in nearly every casino in town, and it's not unusual to see high-rollers, showgirls and clubgoers licking a lolly.

Lick
Mandalay Bay *3930 Las Vegas Boulevard South, at E Russell Road (207 4881). Bus Deuce, 119.* **Open** 10am-11pm daily. **Map** p317 X4.
Lick's tagline is 'What colour is your tongue?'. Customers can sample the treats and then step into a photobooth for a snapshot of their own, now brightly

Rocket Fizz.

hued licker. Setting it apart from the candy pack is an 'adult' candy section at the back of the store.

Rocket Fizz

9410 W Sahara Avenue, at S Fort Apache Road (889 4292, www.rocketfizz.com). Bus SX, 203. **Open** 10am-8pm Mon-Thur; 10am-9pm Fri, Sat; 11am-6pm Sun.

This suite of sweets offers 'the world's biggest selection of bottled soda pops', plus nostalgia-inducing vintage candy from the 1950s to the '90s.

Sugar Factory

Paris Las Vegas *3655 Las Vegas Boulevard South between E Harmon Avenue & E Flamingo Road (331 5551, www.sugarfactory.com). Bus Deuce, 202.* **Open** 10am-midnight Mon-Fri; 9am-1am Sat, Sun. **Map** p320 A7.

The sugar-shock shack of choice for candy-coloured celebrities such as the Kardashians, Britney Spears, Lindsay Lohan and the *Jersey Shore* gang, the Sugar Factory has every kind of sweet thing in stock. But its signature item is a 'couture' lollypop with a dazzling holder, in flavours like champagne, of course. They retail for upwards of $25. Which is the genius and evil of Las Vegas – on a stick.

Other locations Mirage (*see p90*); Planet Hollywood (*see p101*); MGM Grand (*see p88*).

Drinks

Las Vegas has the usual liquor stores, plus many options for wine buffs. **Envy** (*see p148*), **Picasso** (*see p143*), **André's** (*see p133*) and **Aureole** (*see p135*) each has a superb selection of wines to accompany dinner.

Lee's Discount Liquor

3480 E Flamingo Road, at S Pecos Road, East Las Vegas (458 5700, www.leesliquorlv.com). Bus 111, 202. **Open** 9am-10pm Mon-Thur; 9am-11pm Fri, Sat; 9am-9pm Sun. **Map** p317 Z3.

The enormous 'wall of vodka' is a sight worthy of a pilgrimage; old favourites, hard-to-find European wines and dirt-cheap prices make Lee's the best liquor store in town. There's a surprisingly good range of beers from around the planet and a few ciders as well.

Other locations throughout the city.

Marché Bacchus

2620 Regatta Drive, at Breakwater Drive, Summerlin (804 8008, www.marchebacchus.com). No bus. **Open** 11am-9.30pm Mon-Thur; 11am-10pm Fri, Sat; 10am-9.30pm Sun.

This fabulous little French store and restaurant (*see p154*) sells fine wines, champagnes, pâtés, cheeses and tasting kits. There are also monthly wine-tasting sessions, and outdoor seating on a terrace by the lake, where you can enjoy a glass of your favourite vintage.

Valley Cheese & Wine

1570 W Horizon Ridge Parkway, at Amador Lane, Henderson (341 8191, www.valleycheese andwine.com). No bus. **Open** 11am-8pm Mon-Sat; 11am-5pm Sun.

This gourmet wine and cheese shop supplies Las Vegas with artisanal and handcrafted wine, beer, speciality food and cheeses. Owner Bob Howald will be happy to help select wines to match your meal.

General

There isn't a major supermarket on the Strip, but all the main chains have branches within easy reach. Just east of the Strip, the branch of Safeway-owned **Vons** (1131 E Tropicana Avenue, at S Maryland Parkway, 798 8697, www.vons.com) is open 24 hours daily, and **Smith's** (2540 S Maryland Parkway, at E Sahara Avenue, 735 8928, www.smithsfood anddrug.com) is open until 1am daily. In Downtown, try **Albertsons** (1760 E Charleston Boulevard, at S Bruce Street, 366 1550, www.albertsons.com), open 6am to midnight daily.

Trader Joe's

2101 S Decatur Boulevard, at W Sahara Avenue, West Las Vegas (367 0227, www.traderjoes.com). Bus SX, 103. **Open** 8am-9pm daily.

A hip, eco- and health-conscious twist on the old-style grocery store: all products in the chain's constantly changing stock are tested to ensure that they are 'the best' (it claims). You can find gluten-, sodium- and GM-free produce as well as chocolate cookies and party foods.

Other locations throughout the city.

Whole Foods

6605 Las Vegas Boulevard South, at intersection of I-15 & I-215 (589 7711, www.wholefoods market.com). Bus SDX, 104, 117. **Open** 8am-10pm daily.

The produce and meat sections at this leading natural and organic grocer are great, but don't miss the seafood case, the deli (for wonderful cheeses and breads) and the impressive prepared foods.

Other locations 100 S Green Valley Parkway, Henderson (361 8183); 8855 W Charleston Boulevard, Summerlin (254 8655); 7250 W Lake Mead Boulevard, Summerlin (942 1500).

Specialist

Chocaholics in Vegas shouldn't miss the **Ethel M Chocolates** factory in Henderson (*see p75*), but in central Vegas there are several options. The most distinctive is Chicago-based chocolatier **Vosges Haut-Chocolat** (at the Forum Shops; 836 9866), which offers some glorious truffle concoctions.

Vosges Haut-Chocolat. *See p185.*

Otherwise, Belgian confectioner **Godiva** is at the Grand Canal Shoppes (*see p175*), the Fashion Show Mall (*see p177*) and Town Square (*see p177*).

International Marketplace

5000 S Decatur Boulevard, at W Tropicana Avenue, West Las Vegas (889 2888). Bus 103, 201. **Open** 9am-6pm Mon-Sat. **Map** p318 Y2.

This huge building is basically a warehouse containing every kind of imported edible goodie and gadget, with prices on the better side of cheap.

Rainbow's End Natural Foods

1100 E Sahara Avenue, at S Maryland Parkway, East Las Vegas (737 1338, www.rainbows endlv.info). Bus SX, 109. **Open** 9am-8pm Mon-Fri; 10am-8pm Sat; noon-5pm Sun. **Map** p317 Y2.

The closest place to the Strip to buy good quality fresh fruit also offers a broad range of herbs, vitamins and body-care items.

Siena Deli

9500 W Sahara Avenue, at S Fort Apache Road, West Las Vegas (736 8424, www.sienadeli.com). Bus SX, 203. **Open** 8am-9pm daily.

Siena's Italian owner continues to bring the best of Italian cuisine to Vegas. Prices can be steep, but the high quality is beyond doubt. Siena also stocks Italian cookware.

GALLERIES

Let's face it: the majority of Las Vegas-bound travellers did not choose the city for its cultural attractions. Yet the self-proclaimed entertainment capital of the world does have a lively visual-arts scene, much of it concentrated in the **18b Arts District** (*see p68*) near Downtown. The economic crisis of the late-2000s made art – and

the art market – a low priority, and the scene took several critical blows. Despite this, there is plenty of art to be seen – if you know where to look. While some of the major properties display fantastic art (among them the **Bellagio**, in its own art gallery, *see p53*), other incredible works exist in out of the way – or unexpected – places, such as the **Marjorie Barrick Museum** (*see p74*) on the University of Las Vegas campus and the **Emergency Arts Center** (*see p66*), in Downtown.

The monthly Downtown open-air festival **First Friday** (*see p42*), began more than a decade ago as a celebration of the local arts scene, has since grown into more of a raucous, freewheeling party. But it's still a good way to catch a glimpse of Las Vegas art (and Las Vegans) you might not otherwise see.

Below are the city's best commerical galleries.

The Arts Factory

107 E Charleston Boulevard, at S 1st Street, Downtown (383 3133, www.theartsfactory.com). Bus SDX, 108, 206. **Open** 9am-6pm daily; later evening hours for special events and First Friday. **Map** p319 C3.

Located smack in the centre of the 18b Arts District, the cavernous Arts Factory – a former warehouse – is home to more than 20 commercial-art tenants. Inside you'll find the 25-year-old Contemporary Arts Center (382 3886, www.lasvegascac.org), which showcases exhibitions of working artists, as well as studios, a bar and eatery, and a store (with items created by co-owner Debra Heiser's design company, www.heiserdesign.com). Exhibitions change monthly, and if you want a sneak peek at what's coming up, visit on Preview Thursday, which, of course, falls on the day before each month's First Friday.

Brett Wesley Gallery

1112 S Casino Boulevard, at E Charleston Boulevard, Downtown (433 4433, www.brett wesleygallery.com). Bus SDX, 108, 206. **Open** 1-7pm Wed-Sat; and by appt. **Map** p319 C2.

This relative newcomer to the Arts District hasn't wasted any time in making its presence known. Located in a stunning building at the heart of the district, Brett Wesley showcases a variety of artists and styles, from photography to surrealism. The gallery also holds lectures, artist receptions and special viewings, and Wesley will take a personal interest in helping you develop your collection.

Trifecta Gallery

Arts Factory, 107 E Charleston Boulevard #135, at S 1st Street, Downtown (366 7001, www.trifectagallery.com). Bus SDX, 108, 206. **Open** 11am-5pm Mon-Fri (until 10pm 1st Fri of mth); 11am-3pm Sat, Sun. **Map** p319 C3.

Tiny Trifecta is the labour of love of Las Vegas artist Marty Walsh, whose masterful, nostalgic paintings memorialise mid-century modern appliances and other artefacts. She also has an ingenious curatorial eye, and alternates showings of her own work with pieces by talented emerging painters. With many of the shows held here regularly selling out, Trifecta the perfect place for serious art collectors on a budget.

GIFTS & SOUVENIRS
Las Vegas souvenirs

As the cash-spending hordes schlep through the malls buying stuff you can pick up in any US city, savvy shoppers go off the beaten track for local souvenirs with more charisma. If you're after something specific to Las Vegas, the Strip is dotted with tatty shops selling everything from snow domes (it's the desert, folks!) to dice clocks, and more gambling mementos than you could shake a croupier's rake at. For unique works of art, try Dale Chihuly's gallery at the Bellagio.

★ Bonanza
2440 Las Vegas Boulevard South, at W Sahara Avenue (385 7359, www.worldslargestgift shop.com). Bus Deuce, SX, 108. **Open** 8am-midnight daily. **Map** p319 C4.
Bonanza's huge sign declares it to be the 'world's largest gift store'; certainly, it's hard to imagine one much bigger. The store sells everything from postcards to placemats, Elvis shot glasses to dice clocks, playing cards to earrings. Harkening back to the days of Route 66 gift shops, there's also plenty of American Indian turquoise and silver jewellery. *Photo p188.*

Dale Chihuly
Bellagio (Via Fiore) *3600 Las Vegas Boulevard South, at W Flamingo Road (693 7995, www. bellagio.com). Bus Deuce, 202.* **Open** 10am-11pm Mon-Wed, Sun; 10am-midnight Thur-Sat. **Map** p320 A7.

It's fitting that glass sculptor Dale Chihuly should open his first signature gallery inside the Bellagio: his largest sculpture, with more than 2,000 pieces of glass, hangs from the ceiling of the hotel lobby. While mainly focusing on affordable Chihuly glass editions, which sell like hot cakes, the store also has some more elaborate (and expensive) pieces.

★ Gamblers General Store
800 S Main Street, at S Commerce Street, Downtown (382 9903, www.gamblersgeneral store.com). Bus Deuce, 108, 206. **Open** 9am-5pm daily. **Map** p318 C2.
This well-stocked shop is packed with gift ideas for that special gambler in your life. There's gambling-related merchandise here to suit all budgets, from a single casino chip costing a couple of coins to vintage video poker machines. Along with the collectibles are pretty much everything you need to play any of the casino games, including a library of 'how to' gaming books.

Rainbow Feather Dyeing Company
1036 S Main Street, at W Charleston Boulevard, Downtown (598 0988, www.rainbowfeather co.com). Bus Deuce, 108, 206. **Open** 9am-4pm Mon-Fri; 9am-1pm Sat. **Map** p319 C2.
Master feather-crafter Bill Girard sells big, beautiful, colourful and handmade boas to everyone from showgirls to Cirque du Soleil at his unassuming store in the emerging Arts District.

Cigars

Casa Fuente
Caesars Palace (Forum Shops) *3500 Las Vegas Boulevard South, at E Flamingo Road (731 5051, www.cigarfamily.com). Bus Deuce, 202.* **Open** 10am-11pm Mon-Thur, Sun; 10am-midnight Fri, Sat. **Map** p320 A7.
The first store from the Arturo Fuente brand is halfway between a shop and a cigar bar. The

CONSUME

Trifecta Gallery.

Bonanza. *See p187.*

CONSUME

enormous walk-in humidor holds cigars from around the world. It also stocks a huge array of cigar-smoking accessories.

Havana Cigar Bar
3900 Paradise Road, between E Flamingo Road & E Twain Avenue, East of Strip (892 9555, www.havanasmoke.com). Bus 108, 203. **Open** 10am-midnight Mon-Thur; 10am-1am Fri; 2pm-1am Sat; 2-11pm Sun. **Map** p320 C7.
Aficionados swear this cigar and wine bar is the best place in town to sit down, and enjoy the pleasure of a fine cigar and a good glass of wine. Its range of accessories is as strong as that of its cigars.

★ Las Vegas Cigar Company
2510 E Sunset Road, at S Eastern Avenue (262 6100, www.lvcigar.com). Bus 110, 212. **Open** 9am-6pm Mon-Sat. **Map** p317 A8.
The Las Vegas Cigar Company's established varieties of cigar are hand-rolled daily in-house, using Cuban-seed tobacco imported from Ecuador and the Dominican Republic.

Sex & erotica

The best of the adult bookstores, the **Rancho Adult Entertainment Center** (4820 N Rancho Drive, at W Lone Mountain Drive, North-west Las Vegas, 645 6104), is open 24-7. The staff are friendly and they welcome female shoppers.

Adult Superstore
3850 W Tropicana Avenue, at S Valley View Boulevard, West of Strip (798 0144, www.vegas adultsuperstore.com). Bus 201. **Open** 24hrs daily. **Map** p317 X3.

There are four branches of this locals' favourite, but this is the biggest of them. The magazine and video sections are devoted to every fetish and fantasy that's legal in Nevada, and there's an unequalled selection of toys, fetish gear and sexy food items. **Other locations** throughout the city.

Love Boutique
3275 Industrial Road, at W Desert Inn Road, West of Strip (731 5655, www.loveboutiqueonline. com). Bus 119, 203. **Open** 10am-midnight Mon, Thur-Sun; 10am-6pm Tue, Wed. **Map** p320 A6.
Located next to the Déjà Vu strip club, Love sells an extensive collection of lingerie and novelty gift items. Kick off a bachelor/bachelorette party here. **Other locations** throughout the city.

Paradise Electro Stimulations
1509 W Oakey Boulevard, at S Western Avenue (474 2991, www.peselectro.com). Bus 119. **Open** 10am-6pm Mon-Fri. **Map** p319 B3.
'The Studio' is known for its electric muscle-stimulation devices: dildos, plugs and sheaths, all composed of clear plastic and attachable to an electrical impulse control unit that stimulates the user from the inside out, 'harmonising with the body's own electrical impulses'. If you say so.

HEALTH & BEAUTY
Complementary medicine

Bodyworks Massage Therapy
5025 S Eastern Avenue, between E Tropicana & E Hacienda Avenues, East Las Vegas (736 8887). Bus 110, 201. **Open** by appointment only. **Map** p317 Z4.

For more than ten years, Bodyworks' masseurs and masseuses have been kneading, prodding and pounding, with treatments including Swedish deep tissue and Chinese mix, as well as hot-stone therapies, muds and salts.

T&T Ginseng
4115 Spring Mountain Road, between S Arville Street & Wynn Road, West Las Vegas (368 3898). Bus 104, 203. **Open** 10am-8pm daily. **Map** p317 X2.
At this fascinating store and Chinese herbal pharmacy in Las Vegas's Chinatown, diagnosis and treatment are handled with ancient wisdom and extreme care. An oriental medical doctor and herbalist are on duty every day.

Worton's Palmistry Studios
4644 W Charleston Boulevard, at S Decatur Boulevard, West Las Vegas (386 0121). Bus 103, 206. **Open** by appointment. **No credit cards.**
The first licensed psychic in Las Vegas, Worton's has been offering professional palmistry and astrology readings since 1958.

Hairdressers & barbers

A Robert Cromeans Salon
Mandalay Bay (Mandalay Place) *3950 Las Vegas Boulevard South, at W Hacienda Avenue (632 6130, www.robertcromeans.com). Bus Deuce, 119.* **Open** 10am-6pm Mon, Sun; 9am-7pm Tue, Thur, Fri; 9am-5pm Wed. **Map** p320 A9.
The prices at crazy coiffeur Cromeans' trendy salon are about the same as his California salons: in other words, eye-watering.

Globe Salon
900 Las Vegas Boulevard South, between W Charleston Boulevard and E Bonneville Avenue, Downtown (938 4247, www.globesalon.com). Bus Deuce & all BTC-bound buses. **Open** 11am-7.30pm Tue-Thur; 9am-5pm Fri, Sat. **Map** p318 C2.
This Elle network award-winning hair-and-skin care salon is run by Vegas native and 'hairstylist to the hip' Staci Linklater, who oversees a team of professionals in a mod-style Downtown space.

Opticians

Frame Fixer (3961 W Charleston Boulevard, at S Valley View Boulevard, West Las Vegas, 735 7879) does fast, friendly and gentle repairs.

Lunettes
Paris Las Vegas *3655 Las Vegas Boulevard South, at E Flamingo Road (946 7000, www.parislasvegas.com). Bus Deuce, 202.* **Open** 9am-11pm daily. **Map** p320 A7.
Shades are a must in a city that sees an average of 320 days of sun per year. Lunettes sells products by designers including Gucci, Oliver Peoples, Cartier and Kia Yomoto.

Oculus
Caesars Palace (Appian Way Shops) *3570 Las Vegas Boulevard South, at E Flamingo Road (731 4850, www.oculusltd.com). Bus Deuce, 202.* **Open** 10am-8pm Mon-Thur, Sun; 10am-9pm Fri, Sat. **Map** p320 A7.
This outpost of Dr Ed Malik's stylish Eyes & Optics boutique offers an excellent selection of frames from designers such as Oliver Peoples and Movado, plus eye examinations, repairs and sunglasses. The optician is also available for prescription emergencies.

Pharmacies

You'll find drugstores all over the city. There's a 24-hour branch of **Walgreens** (www.walgreens.com) near the MGM Grand on the Strip (3765 Las Vegas Boulevard South, 739 9645). There's another 24-7 branch in Downtown (495 E Fremont Street, at S 4th Street, 385 1284), though the pharmacy is open limited hours (9am-5pm daily).

Shops

The major department stores (*see p171-172*) stock all the big-name brands. Canadian giant **MAC** has a store (369 8770) in the Forum Shops.

Aveda
Fashion Show Mall *3200 Las Vegas Boulevard South, at Spring Mountain Road (733 6660, www.aveda.com). Bus Deuce, 203.* **Open** 10am-9pm Mon-Sat; 11am-7pm Sun. **Map** p319, p320 B6.
Divine-smelling, all-natural hair care, skin care and beauty products. The signature lip balm is a must. **Other locations** Town Square (*see p177*; 270 2860); Aveda Institute, 4856 S Eastern Avenue, at E Tropicana Avenue, East Las Vegas (459 2900).

Fresh
Caesars Palace (Forum Shops) *3500 Las Vegas Boulevard South, at E Flamingo Road (631 5000, www.fresh.com). Bus Deuce, 202.* **Open** 10am-11pm Mon-Thur, Sun; 10am-midnight Fri, Sat. **Map** p320 A7.
Clean gets tasty with Fresh bath products, made with sugar, milk, soya and even saké. The line also includes some great perfumes and basic cosmetics in natural-looking hues for all skin tones.

Kiehl's
Caesars Palace (Forum Shops) *3500 Las Vegas Boulevard South, at E Flamingo Road (784 0025, www.kiehls.com). Bus Deuce, 202.* **Open** 10am-11pm Mon-Thur, Sun; 10am-midnight Fri, Sat. **Map** p320 A7.

CONSUME

The simplicity of the skin- and hair-care products sold at Kiehl's is part of their appeal, as is the company's commitment never to test on animals. It sells lotions and potions for all skin and hair types, created with the entire family in mind.

Sephora

Venetian (Grand Canal Shoppes) *3377 Las Vegas Boulevard South, between Sands Avenue & E Flamingo Road (735 3896, www.sephora.com). Bus Deuce, 119, 203.* **Open** 10am-11pm Mon-Thur, Sun; 10am-midnight Fri, Sat. **Map** p319 B6.
The most comprehensive cosmetics emporium in town contains stock from Dior and Yves Saint Laurent, hip offerings from Smashbox, Nars, Paul & Joe, and an impressive and good-value own-brand range. Test out the goods in the application areas or let a pro get to work on you.
Other locations Miracle Mile (*see p175*; 737 0550); Forum Shops (*see p174*; 228 3535).

Spas & salons

The odds are that you didn't travel to Las Vegas to consult a nutritionist, improve your sleeping habits or (shudder) detox. There's only one thing that most visitors want from a spa in Sin City: pleasure. Many hotel-casinos have spas these days; those listed below are among the best in the city. *See also p191* **Rejuventation Stations**.

Planet Hollywood Spa by Mandara

Planet Hollywood *3667 Las Vegas Boulevard South, between E Harmon & E Flamingo Roads (785 5772, www.mandaraspa.com). Bus Deuce, 202.* **Open** 7am-7pm daily. **Daily pass** $25. **Map** p320 A7.
With its variety of resurfacing facials, miracle lip and eye therapies and scalp massages, the Planet Hollywood spa will have you ready for your 15 minutes of fame. If you really want to be pampered like an A-lister, book the signature Mandara massage, a blend of Japanese shiatsu, Hawaiian lomi lomi, and Swedish and Balinese massage techniques, performed by two experienced therapists. Lights, camera, relax.
Other locations Paris Spa by Mandara (Paris Las Vegas, 3655 Las Vegas Boulevard S, 946 4366); Glow, a Mandara Spa (Tropicana, 3801 Las Vegas Boulevard S, 739 2680).

Qua Baths & Spa

Caesars Palace *3570 Las Vegas Boulevard South, at W Flamingo Road (731 7822, www. quabathsandspa.com). Bus Deuce, 202.* **Open** 6am-8pm daily. **Daily pass** $45; free with spa services over $75. **Map** p320 A7.
Housed in the Augustus Tower, Caesars' luxurious spa is themed after Roman baths. Within tubs of mineral-rich waters, a Laconium sauna (inspired by ancient Roman steam baths) and an arctic ice

room (heated floors and benches under falling snow), therapists practise ritualistic therapies. Take Qua's Mystic Journey and enjoy a coconut-argan oil rub along the spine, followed by a ginger-lime sugar scrub, more oil, and a blanket of warm towels. When in Rome…

★ Red Rock Spa

Red Rock *11011 W Charleston Boulevard, at I-215 (797 7878, www.redrocklasvegas.com), West Las Vegas. Bus SX.* **Open** 6am-7pm daily. **Daily pass** *Hotel guests* free. *Visitors* $35; free with spa services.
This modern retreat is frequented by local socialites as much for its proximity to their homes as for its sleek aesthetic. Situated next to the lush pool, the treatment suites appear to float on water. After a hike, order a Champagne Pedicure and Caviar Creams: this champagne cocktail for you and your feet includes 80 minutes of deep exfoliation, soothing masques, moisturising caviar lotion and menthol foot balm massage, plus, of course, a glass of champagne. Cheers!

Spa at Wynn

Wynn Las Vegas *3131 Las Vegas Boulevard South, between E Desert Inn Road & Sands Avenue (770 3900, www.wynnlasvegas.com). Bus Deuce, 108, 203.* **Open** 9am-7pm daily. **Daily pass** $25; free with salon services over $75. **Map** p319 B6.
Reserve one of the 45 treatment rooms inside this Asian-inspired retreat and indulge in a bamboo-lemongrass body scrub, a saké body treatment or a shiatsu massage. The Good Luck Ritual is based on feng shui, with a 50-minute heated Thai herb massage, a moisturising hand and foot massage, and a wild-lime botanical scalp treatment. Hotel guests are able to use the lavish spa facilities without booking a salon session; non-guests can only use the spa by booking a salon treatment (Mon-Thur only).

Tattoos & piercings

Hart & Huntington Tattoo Company

Hard Rock *4455 Paradise Road, at E Harmon Avenue, East of Strip (216 5360, www.hartandhuntingtontattoo.com). Bus 108.* **Open** 10am-1am daily. **Map** p320 C7.
Motocross legend Carey Hart and club promoter John Huntington (the man behind the original Pimp 'n' Ho Costume Ball) relocated their hip tattoo parlour from the Palms to the Hard Rock. For a time, the pair also had their own TV show, *Inked*. Huntington has since sold the shop to Hart, but the patrons hardly seem to care.

★ Pussykat Tattoo Parlor

4972 S Maryland Parkway, at E Tropicana Avenue, University District (597 1549, www. pussykat-tattoos.com). Bus 109, 201. **Open** hours vary. **Map** p317 Y3.

Rejuvenation Stations

Decadent spa treatments to soothe body and soul.

Sahra Spa & Hammam.

You come to Vegas to play hard, so when it's time to wind down it's nice to know you're in good hands at the city's finest spas – where you can erase the ravages of excess. For our money, these are the pick of the bunch.

If you're looking to flush the system, try the **Canyon Ranch SpaClub** at the Palazzo (414 3600, www.canyonranch.com/las vegas). Its Aquavana experience uses combinations of water treatments to rid the body of toxins and relax the muscles. Alternate between hot and cold treatments in the Finnish sauna (a dry-heat sauna) and the Igloo (cool air with Arctic mist) – just two of the nine aquathermal environments. Afterwards, meditate in the Wave Room, or chill out with some fresh fruit in the Conservatory. Canyon Ranch also offers more than 100 different body treatments – the largest selection in Vegas.

Vegas vacations aren't typically associated with rituals of purification, yet that's exactly what you'll get if you visit **Sahra Spa & Hammam** (Cosmopolitan, 698 7171, www.cosmopolitanlasvegas. com), a traditional Turkish-style bathhouse. Detoxification, steam treatments and a cooling bath are the cornerstones of hammam treatments; this one concludes with a full-body massage. For extra indulgence, try the Hammam Soap Ritual, a luxurious scrub that re-energises every cell on the surface of your body.

What better place to get a tune-up than at the **Reliquary Spa & Salon** at the Hard Rock (693 5520, www.hardrockhotel.com)? Bodily rejuvenation at the Reliquary Spa uses tuning forks, which are placed on strategic acupressure points on the body. In the Harmonic Massage, the vibrations and sounds of the tuning fork are said to reduce stress, lower blood pressure, alleviate pain, and improve movement and balance. The treatment is followed by the classic Rock Star Swedish massage.

The spa at the **Mandarin Oriental** (590 8886, www.mandarinoriental.com/lasvegas) stands out as being one of only 30 spas in the world to be awarded the coveted Forbes Five-Star Award. Modern techniques coupled with Eastern traditional therapies make for a holistic pampering experience. For a massage unlike any other, try the Oriental Harmony massage: two therapists work in perfect unison to balance you from head to toe.

Mandarin Oriental.

CONSUME

Owner/artist Dirk Vermin is a Vegas native and local legend who has dedicated his life to bettering the local subculture. His tattoo work is well known among aficionados; you will need to book ahead to see Vermin himself.

HOUSE & HOME

Antiques

Charleston Antique Mall

560 S Decatur Boulevard, at Alta Drive, West Las Vegas (228 4783, www.charlestonantique mall.com). Bus 103, 207. **Open** 10am-6pm Mon-Sat; 11am-6pm Sun.

This antique and vintage store recently moved to its new – and much larger – location. Now in 18,000sq ft premises, it stocks everything from furniture to casino artefacts. If you like the look of that tiki bar, then snap it up while you can: the good stuff goes pretty fast.

Funk House

1228 S Casino Center Boulevard, at E Colorado Avenue, Downtown (678 6278, www.thefunk houselasvegas.com). Bus Deuce, 108, 206. **Open** noon-5pm Mon-Sat. **Map** p319 C3.

Cindy Funkhouser's ever-growing collection is especially strong in late-1950s and early-'60s pieces, and there's a wide variety of glass, jewellery and toys in stock. One of the best antiques stores in town, the Funk House is also ground zero for First Friday (*see p42*).

★ Retro Vegas

1131 S Main Street, at W Charleston Boulevard, Downtown (384 2700, www.retro-vegas.com). Bus Deuce, 108, 206. **Open** 11am-6pm Mon-Sat; noon-5pm Sun. **Map** p319 C3.

What happens in Vegas doesn't have to stay in Vegas – especially if you take a piece of it home with you. This offbeat little shop traffics in Sin City's ephemera, everything from furniture to curios to vintage ashtrays.

INSIDE TRACK TATTOO YOU

What happens in Vegas, stays in Vegas – unless you have to take it home with you. Which will be the case if you visit one of Sin City's tattoo parlours. Many of the major hotels have ink shops: **Mario Barth's Starlight Tattoos** at Mirage and Mandalay Bay; **Hart & Huntington Tattoo Co** at the Hard Rock; **Club Tattoo** at Planet Hollywood. However, you can get more acreage for your ink by visiting an off-Strip site, like **Pussykat Tattoo Parlor** (*see p190*).

General

Among the best homewares stores in town is **Unicahome** (3901 W Russell Road, 616 9280, www.unicahome.com), which stocks everything from books to flatpack furniture by the likes of Tom Dixon.

Durette Studio

1007 S Main Street, at W Charleston Boulevard, Downtown (368 2601, www.durettecandito design.com). Bus Deuce, 108, 206. **Open** 9am-5pm Mon-Fri; by appt Sat.

Durette Candito's Arts District studio is Nevada's most prestigious supplier of decorative hardware, lighting and home accessories, many of which are exclusive, hand-crafted imports from some of the best clans of craftsmen around the world. Candito's architectural and interior-design skills are also superb.

MUSIC & ENTERTAINMENT

In the age of downloads, **Blockbuster** stores can still be found; use the store locator at www.blockbuster.com. Some mainstream new-release CDs are sold at massive discounts at **Best Buy** (*see p180*).

Zia Record Exchange

4225 S Eastern Avenue, at E Flamingo Road, East of Strip (735 4942, www.ziarecords.com). Bus 110, 202. **Open** 10am-midnight daily.

This Arizona transplant, now comfortably the best music store in town, buys and sells music and movies, trading with record companies as well as the man off the street. It even deals in vinyl. **Other locations** 4503 W Sahara Avenue, at Arville Street, West of the Strip (233 4942).

SPORT & FITNESS

The two best general sports stores are chains. Both **Big 5** (2797 S Maryland Parkway, at E Sahara Avenue, 734 6664, www.big5sporting goods.com) and **Sports Authority** (5120 S Fort Apache Road, at W Hacienda Avenue, 252 3660, www.sportsauthority.com) sell a wide range of clothing and equipment in multiple locations around the city. Fashion sportswear is also well represented: the Forum Shops (*see p174*) is home to **Nike** (650 8888), while the Miracle Mile Shops (*see p175*) has the only **David Z.** outside of New York (699 5661).

★ Bass Pro Shops Outdoor World

8200 Dean Martin Drive, at Blue Diamond Road, Silverton (730 5200, www.basspro.com). Bus 117, 217. **Open** 9am-9pm Mon-Sat; 9am-7pm Sun.

With a firing range, a gunsmith, an archery range and a custom tie shop (for anglers), this massive store is a lesson in retail as entertainment. The entrance, done

CONSUME

Unicahome.

out like an 1800s Adirondack hunting lodge, gives way to 165,000sq ft of sport-enthusiasts' paradise. Check out the waterfall that feeds the 40,000-gallon fish tank, the live duck habitat, or just pick out a tent.

Desert Rock Sports
8221 W Charleston Boulevard, at S Cimarron Road, West Las Vegas (254 1143, www.desert rocksportslv.com). Bus 206. **Open** *June-Sept* 10am-8pm Mon-Sat; 10am-6pm Sun. *Oct-May* 9am-8pm Mon-Sat; 10am-6pm Sun.
Super-cool climbing, hiking and camping gear for the outdoor enthusiast, as well as stuff for children and dogs. Practise your climbing moves before you hit the rocks on the indoor facility next door at Red Rock Climbing Center (8201 W Charleston Boulevard, 254 5604, www.redrockclimbingcenter.com).

McGhie's
4035 S Fort Apache Road, at W Flamingo Road, South-west Las Vegas (252 8077, www.mcghies. com). Bus 202. **Open** 10am-7pm Mon-Fri; 10am-6pm Sat; 10am-5pm Sun.

In business for 40 years, McGhie's embraced the snowboarding craze in the early 1990s, and later added mountain biking to its ski (both water and snow) goods. Rentals, plus advice on the area's better recreation areas, are also available.
Other locations 19 S Stephanie Street, at I-215, Henderson (800 3636); 16 Cottonwood, at Castalia Street, Blue Diamond (875 4820).

Pro Cyclery
7034 W Charleston Boulevard, at Antelope Way, West Las Vegas (228 9460, www.procyclery.com). Bus 206. **Open** 10am-7pm Mon-Fri; 9am-5pm Sat.
This long-term fixture on the Vegas cycling scene is a great source of gear for both hire and purchase. Experienced cyclists and novices alike are made to feel welcome.

REI
Green Valley Ranch (District) *2220 Village Walk Drive, at S Green Valley Parkway, Henderson (896 7111, www.rei.com). Bus 111.* **Open** 10am-9pm Mon-Sat; 11am-6pm Sun.
In 1938, 20 mountain climbing enthusiasts formed a cooperative so they could purchase some of the better gear available in Europe. Recreation Equipment Inc now has over two million members worldwide, and 70 store locations. This shop is great for backpacking, biking, mountain-climbing and kayaking gear.
Other locations 710 S Rampart Boulevard, at Alta Drive, North Las Vegas (951 4488).

TICKETS

Ticketmaster (474 4000, www.ticket master.com) sells tickets for many events, although the booking fees can be high. You should also check **Tix4Tonight** (1-877 849 4868, www.tix4tonight.com), which has many locations around town and frequently offers great deals on some of the best shows.

TRAVELLERS' NEEDS

For **airlines**, *see p292*; for **car hire firms**, *see p294*. If you're in need of extra suitcases to hold all that excess shopping, your best bets on the Strip are **Dillard's** (*see p171*) and **Macy's** (*see p171*), though prices are more reasonable at **Target** (4001 S Maryland Parkway, at E Flamingo Road, 732 2218, www.target.com).
If your mobile phone fails you, get a rental from Rent It Today (www.rentittoday.com), which serves the Las Vegas area. However, it may be cheaper simply to buy a phone from a store such as **Best Buy** (*see p180*). For more on phones, *see p298*.
If your laptop fails, try the **Best Buy Geek Squad** (*see p180*), available 24 hours a day. Mac users should try one of the **Apple stores** (*see p180*).

CONSUME

Arts & Entertainment

Casino Entertainment

Give 'em that old razzle dazzle.

Las Vegas proudly calls itself 'the entertainment capital of the world', and arguably it is – depending on how you define 'entertainment'. If you think of it under the wide rubric of 'diversion', then perhaps the city has earned its crown. But the live entertainment on offer here represents a narrow band of the performance spectrum. Even the new is almost inevitably the old, recycled, remixed – repackaged for a crowd that craves the comfort of unchallenging familiarity. If it was a hit on radio or TV from the 1960s to the '90s, don't be surprised if you find a version of it somewhere on the Strip, or touring cyclically (if not cynically) through one of its concert venues.

THE ENTERTAINMENT SCENE

During the last years of the 20th century and early years of the 21st, Las Vegas entertainment was turned on its head. The tired old revues that had defined the city for years were ushered out of the door, replaced by big-budget, high-concept pieces of populist performance art delivered by Cirque du Soleil (of whom more in a moment). A generation of tired comics and hoarse singers was replaced by still-popular stand-ups and musicians who remained on speaking terms with the charts. And the grinning showgirls were gradually pensioned off, in favour of dancers prepared to show a little more than their feathers. (The 'adult' reviews here, both male and female, are hardly as naughty as they are purported to be – for a real 'anything goes, everything shows' experience, you have to go a few blocks off the Strip to see the strippers.)

After such a dramatic shift in priorities, Las Vegas has lately been content simply to consolidate. Indeed, when it comes to entertainment, the city remains an impersonator rather than an innovator. The musical headliners are big names who won't frighten your parents (Celine Dion, Donny & Marie, Rod Stewart). And after Cirque du Soleil's first show, *Mystère*, broke box-office records, every casino on the Strip wanted one just like it – hence its current dominance of the show scene. Heaven only knows what Sinatra and Elvis would make of it all…

INFORMATION AND TICKETS

Although most of the shows listed in this section are expected to run for the shelf life of this guide, others open and close all the time. For the most up-to-date information, check 'Neon' in Friday's *Las Vegas Review-Journal*, free magazines such as *What's On*, the town's three alternative weeklies and www.vegas.com. In any given week, there are also a few big-name acts working short engagements in the city, either filling in for vacationing headliners or working in auditoria that only deal with temporary bookings (such as the **Hollywood Theatre** at the MGM Grand, *see p88*).

You're always best off buying tickets at the hotel-casino's own box office, either in person, by phone or online. If you get stuck, try **Ticketmaster** (*see p193*), but prepare to pay over the odds. If you book by phone or online, pick up the tickets at the 'will call' window. Try to book as far ahead as possible for the big shows. However, even if the show has sold out, it's worth calling the box office, especially midweek, to check for cancellations. You can also find half-price tickets to some shows at **Tix4Tonight** (1-877 849 4868, www.tix4tonight.com) in the Fashion Show Mall (*see p177*), and the Showcase Mall and Hawaiian Marketplace on the Strip; booths open at noon daily.

Shows are expensive in Las Vegas. The cheapest tickets for most big shows go for upwards of $50, and the best seats are routinely priced at three-figure sums. Some quoted prices include tax, others don't; many shows include a drink in their prices. However, there are bargains to be found. Many shows offer discounts with coupons found on flyers or in magazines. If you're a heavy gambler, you might even get comped into a show in the casino in which you've been playing. Some shows, especially those with a degree of nudity, come with age restrictions; always check if you have kids in tow.

For music venues and nightclubs, *see p219-228*.

THE SHOWS

Las Vegas's first stage productions were known as 'floor shows'. When Sophie Tucker performed at the El Rancho and Jimmy Durante played the Flamingo in the 1940s and '50s, they were preceded by a line of girls, a comic or a magician, and a speciality act (a juggler, say).

Entertainment in the city changed radically when the Stardust premièred *Lido de Paris* in 1958. The fabulous spectacle played to packed houses and set the template for productions such as *Folies Bergère* and **Jubilee!** (*see p204*); the latter is the only remaining, if dated, show of its type in Las Vegas.

There are still plenty of production shows on display, though they've moved on a little bit since the tits-and-feathers heyday. **Cirque du Soleil** now has no fewer than eight shows here, but many other big-budget shows have been tried and tested elsewhere before being picked up by the casino moguls. **Jersey Boys**, for example, made millions on Broadway before shipping out to the desert, and later proved a hit in London's West End as well.

Elsewhere, magicians still draw the crowds: even with Siegfried & Roy off the scene, there's still plenty of choice. Other options include celebrity impersonator shows, in which lookalikes sing or lip-synch in imitation of pop-culture heroes and heroines, and adult revues, featuring a parade of hardbodies taking it off for crowds of women and (more often) men. And many casinos carry on the time-honoured tradition of booking star headliners, with full-timers such as **Rita Rudner** joined by semi-resident performers such as **Elton John**, who, with his Million Dollar Piano, appears at Caesars Palace for some 50 shows a year, and regular guests like **Jay Leno**.

THE BEST SHOWS

For big illusions on a small stage
David Copperfield. *See p200.*

For naughty but nice
Pin Up. *See p198.*

For 'joust' a good time
Tournament of Kings. *See p206.*

For music history brought to life
Million Dollar Quartet. *See p205.*

For thought-provoking laughs
Blue Man Group. *See p203.*

But if you only have time for one show…
O. *See p205.*

ADULT REVUES

Zumanity

New York New York *3790 Las Vegas Boulevard South, at W Tropicana Avenue (1-866 606 7111, 740 6815, www.zumanity.com). Bus Deuce, 201.* **Shows** 7.30pm, 10pm Mon, Tue, Fri-Sun. **Tickets** $69-$125. No under-18s. **Map** p320 A8.
The idea of asking Cirque du Soleil to compile its own adult revue was an unexpected one. In parts, *Zumanity* pulls it off, most notably the more comic stretches and the two-women-in-a-fish-tank section towards the start of the show. A little too often it seems unsure whether it's better off trying to dazzle or arouse the audience, but those on the love seats (or, as the box office coyly calls them, 'duo sofas') seem to go upstairs happily enough. The Vienna-inspired jewel-box cabaret theatre, all sensual curves and touchable textures, may inspire your own per-formance later.

Male revues

Ladies, why let the guys have all the fun in Vegas when there are chiselled male specimens gyrating for your pleasure? Equal parts sensuality and humour, these male revues make for the perfect bachelorette, birthday or divorce party setting. Be warned: the performers won't let you just sit back and enjoy it; arriving inebriated and uninhibited ensures a much better time.

American Storm

Planet Hollywood *3667 Las Vegas Boulevard South, between E Harmon Avenue & E Flamingo Road (701 7778, www.american-storm.com). Bus Deuce, 202.* **Shows** 10pm Fri; 11.30pm Sat. **Tickets** $49.50-$58.65. No under-18s. **Map** p317 X3.

Divas Las Vegas: Adele.

Chippendales

Rio *3700 W Flamingo Road, at S Valley View Boulevard, West of Strip (1-855 234 7469, 777 2782, www.chippendales.com). Bus 202.* **Shows** 8pm Mon-Wed, Sun; 8pm, 10.30pm Thur-Sat. **Tickets** from $49.95. No under-18s. **Map** p317 X3.

Thunder From Down Under

Excalibur *3850 Las Vegas Boulevard South, at W Tropicana Avenue (1-800 933 1334, 597 7600, www.thunderfromdownunder.com). Bus Deuce, 201.* **Shows** 9pm Mon-Wed; 9pm, 11pm Thur, Sat, Sun; 7pm, 9pm, 11pm Fri. **Tickets** $50.95-$60.95. No under-18s. **Map** p317 X3.

Female revues

Each of these revues has some distinguishing characteristic, but at the (soft) core, each one is all about waiting for the big reveal.

Crazy Girls

Riviera *2901 Las Vegas Boulevard South, between E Sahara Avenue & E Desert Inn Road (1-877 892 7469, 794 9433, www.riviera hotel.com). Bus Deuce, 108, 203.* **Shows** 9.30pm Mon, Wed-Sun. **Tickets** $44.95-$66. No under-18s. **Map** p319 B5.

'Girls! Girls! Crazy girls!' goes the infernally catchy theme song. Well, crazy they ain't, and, if local legend is to be believed, the butts displayed in bronze outside the Riviera by way of advertisement – touching them has become a rite of passage, and the patinaed statue has the shiny patches to prove it – aren't all female. Regardless, this low-budget tit-fest, which has been around for 25 years, is a giggle: about as arousing as a kick in the teeth, granted, but lovers of Vegas camp will be in heaven.

Fantasy

Luxor *3900 Las Vegas Boulevard South, at W Hacienda Avenue (1-800 557 7428, 262 4400, www.luxor.com). Bus Deuce, 119, 201.* **Shows** 10.30pm daily. **Tickets** $39-$52. No under-18s. **Map** p320 A9.

Fantasy stages and interprets an array of top-shelf seduction scenarios. Charismatic host Sean Cooper keeps energy and anticipation running high with his comedic impersonations, singing and dancing, but you may find that you've seen this all before, and less rigidly, in your dreams.

★ Pin Up

Stratosphere *2000 Las Vegas Boulevard South, at W St Louis Avenue (1-800 998 6937, 380 7777, www.stratospherehotel.com). Bus Deuce, 108.* **Shows** 10.30pm Mon, Thur-Sun. **Tickets** $49.99-$59.99. No under-21s. **Map** p319 C4.

Although it's more nice than naughty, the Stratosphere's new show has been titillating audiences since its April 2013 debut. Led by 2011 *Playboy* Playmate of the Year Clair Sinclair, *Pin Up* is a homage to the Bettie Page-era centrefolds of a gentler, less in-your-face time. Backed by a band, Sinclair and Co make for a swinging show, and truth be told, we'd watch her in any type of clothes.

X Burlesque

Flamingo *3555 Las Vegas Boulevard South, at E Flamingo Road (1-855 234 7469, 777 2782, www.xburlesque.com). Bus Deuce, 202.* **Shows** 10pm daily. **Tickets** $61.55-$94.90. No under-18s. **Map** p320 A7.

The pretty birds of *X Burlesque* share a hotel, if not a stage, with squeaky-clean Donny & Marie. The half-dozen dancers play with fanciful props, and the old-school mid-show comics try to keep your attention while the dancers exchange one skimpy costume for the next.

CELEBRITY IMPERSONATORS

Divas Las Vegas

The Quad *3535 Las Vegas Boulevard South, between Sands Avenue & E Flamingo Road (1-855 234 7469, 777 2782, www.thequadlv.com). Bus Deuce, 108, 204.* **Shows** 10pm Mon-Thur, Sat, Sun. **Tickets** $39-$79. **Map** p319 B5.

Glamour boy Frank Marino, the long-reigning Queen of the Strip – with more than 25 years of performing in high heels and higher hair – thoroughly enjoys being a girl. And so does his cast of top-notch female impersonators, who present an eye-popping parade of top-shelf pop-culture doppelgängers: the Madonna, Beyoncé and Britney bits are snatched from their latest tours; the Celine Dion act is so artfully exact it will make you appreciate anew just how much Celine puts into being Celine.

ARTS & ENTERTAINMENT

Gordie Brown

Golden Nugget *129 E Fremont Street, at S Casino Center Boulevard (1-866 946 5336, www.goldennugget.com). Bus Deuce & all BTC-bound buses.* **Shows** 7.30pm Tue-Sat. **Tickets** $34.99. No under-16s. **Map** p318 C1.

Stallone, Eastwood and Nicholson; Dylan, Pavarotti and Elvis… Only a very few high-profile entertainers escape the attentions of this energetic singer/comic/actor/impressionist, a former political cartoonist from Canada who made his Vegas name at the Golden Nugget. Some have accused Brown of trying too hard and sacrificing himself to his characters, but it's a likeable enough show.

Legends in Concert

Flamingo *3555 Las Vegas Boulevard South, at E Flamingo Road (1-855 234 7469, 777 2782, www.legendsinconcert.com). Bus Deuce, 202.* **Shows** 7pm, 9.30pm daily. **Tickets** from $49.95; $26.85 reductions. **Map** p320 A7.

Sorry you missed Elvis? Still mourning the loss of Michael Jackson? Wish performers like Britney Spears, Lady Gaga and Barbra Streisand didn't charge $500 a ticket? Worry not: you'll find them all here in this long-running tribute show. Unlike other shows of this type, these performers – backed by a fine band and surrounded by showgirls – actually sing, usually doing several numbers or a medley of top hits.

The Rat Pack is Back

Rio *3700 W Flamingo Road, at S Valley View Boulevard, West of Strip (1-855 234 7469, 777 2782, www.riolasvegas.com). Bus 202.* **Shows** 7pm daily. **Tickets** from $49.95. **Map** p317 X3.

For those who miss the Vegas of yore, when it was a town for grown-ups – before the pool parties, candy, bijou shops and digital slot machines – here's a tribute to the era when Frank, Dino, Sammy and Joey reigned supreme. A re-creation of their classic act from the Copa Room at the Sands – complete with a 12-piece band, and all the off-colour jokes and locker-room razzing you remember.

Terry Fator

Mirage *3400 Las Vegas Boulevard South, between Spring Mountain & W Flamingo roads (1-800 963 9634, 792 7777, www.mirage.com). Bus Deuce, 203.* **Shows** 7.30pm. **Tickets** $54.99-$149.99. No under-5s. **Map** p319, p320 A6.

Replacing the late and much-loved impressionist Danny Gans was no small order. Fortunately for ventriloquist Terry Fator and the Mirage, Fator has a similar family-friendly appeal, plus a national fan base from his wins on the *America's Got Talent* TV show. And Fator (and his cast of puppet personas) can do comic and musical impressions too – he's particularly good at razzing such fellow Strip draws as Garth Brooks and Cher – all without moving his lips.

Véronic Voices

Bally's *3645 Las Vegas Boulevard South, at E Flamingo Road (1-855 234 7469, 777 2782, www.ballyslasvegas.com). Bus Deuce, 202.* **Shows** 9.30pm Thur; 7.30pm Fri, Sat. **Tickets** $60-$120. **Map** p320 A7.

Less of an impersonator and more of a vocalist extraordinaire, Canada's Véronic DiClaire manages to hit all the right notes in *Voices*, her new show at Bally's. Whether performing songs by Lady Gaga or Celine Dion (who, incidentally, gave the singer a leg up in showbiz by inviting her to open on her 2008 tour), Véronic pulls off flawless renditions of an enormous range of singers and styles.

COMEDIANS

Carrot Top

Luxor *3900 Las Vegas Boulevard South, at W Hacienda Avenue (1-800 557 7428, 262 4400, www.luxor.com). Bus Deuce, 119, 201.* **Shows** 8.30pm Mon-Wed, Sun. **Tickets** $49.95-$65.95. No under-18s. **Map** p320 A9.

Carrot Top is inescapable in Las Vegas – his freckled face, topped with blazing ginger hair, leers out from billboards and bus sides around the city. And even if you think he's too juvenile, it's guaranteed that if he coaxes you into the theatre, one way or another, you're going to laugh. Once you get past the 'zany prop comic' stigma, it's easy to see why his popularity has endured. Lightning-quick, with an ADHD attention span, inventing visual puns by the truckload, Carrot Top combines subtle political, social and cultural commentary with

Rita Rudner. See p200.

ARTS & ENTERTAINMENT

music, video and – yes – those famous props for a comedic concoction like no other in town.

George Wallace

Flamingo *3555 Las Vegas Boulevard South, at E Flamingo Road (1-855 234 7469, 777 2782, www.georgewallace.net). Bus Deuce, 202.* **Shows** 10pm Tue-Sat. **Tickets** $54.95-$82.45. No under-5s. **Map** p320 A7.

George Wallace's evenly paced, conversational style, with up-to-the-second topical comedy and social criticism, makes audiences think as well as laugh. Named one of Comedy Central's 100 greatest stand-ups of all time, Wallace veers between 'Yo' mama' jokes, comic bewilderment at the English language and audience interaction; and you never know who (Jerry Seinfeld, Chris Tucker) might show up. Don't be surprised to find him mingling on the casino floor after the show.

Rita Rudner

Venetian *3355 Las Vegas Boulevard South, between Sands Avenue & E Flamingo Road (1-866 641 7469, 414 9000, www.venetian. com). Bus Deuce, 119, 203.* **Shows** (limited performances) 8.30pm, dates vary. **Tickets** $59-$109. No under-7s. **Map** p320 A6.

In the mood for comedy that's not too blue-blooded, blue-collar or just plain blue? The former chorus girl's adult but pointedly clean brand of observational material is witty without being wanton, classy instead of crass. You'll be hard-pressed to find anyone with better bits on relationships, family and shopping, nor will you find a more earnest, likeable performer on the Strip. After years as a mainstay at Harrah's, she's now, appropriately, in the more elegant environs of the Venetian. When Rudner's not performing, the Venetian hosts a number of other great comedians on this stage, including David Spade, Tim Allen and Jim Belushi. *Photo p199.*

MAGICIANS

Criss Angel: Believe

Luxor *3900 Las Vegas Boulevard South, at W Hacienda Avenue (1-800 557 7428, 262 4400, www.luxor.com). Bus Deuce, 119, 201.* **Shows** 7pm, 9.30pm Tue, Fri, Sat; 7pm Wed, Thur. **Tickets** from $59. **Map** p320 A9.

After a blizzard of hype – Cirque invested $100 million – TV illusionist Criss Angel's show still stands on its own at the Luxor, and remains the most controversial act in town, drawing mixed reviews. Framed by the most beautiful proscenium on the Strip – a gilded steampunk fantasia – Angel runs through an erratically paced routine of vanishing tricks and anticlimactic set pieces, all with a faux-Goth flair straight out of a New Jersey strip mall. If you don't get comps or dramatically discounted tickets, you will have to suspend your disbelief at how Angel made your money disappear.

★ David Copperfield

MGM Grand *3799 Las Vegas Boulevard South, at E Tropicana Avenue (1-877 660 0660, 531 3826, www.mgmgrand.com). Bus Deuce, 201.* **Shows** 7pm, 9.30pm Mon-Fri, Sun; 4pm, 7pm, 9.30pm Sat. **Tickets** $69.99-$109.99. **Map** p320 A8.

Arguably the best-known magician working today, David Copperfield remains one of the best shows in Las Vegas as far as illusionists go. Copperfield's feats are renowned: passing through the Great Wall of China; levitating a 45-ton railway car; escaping flames, Niagara Falls and Alcatraz… Granted, you won't see these stunts in MGM's intimate Hollywood Theatre. What you will see, however, is Copperfield – master of his trade – up-close and personal.

Mac King

Harrah's *3475 Las Vegas Boulevard South, between Sands Avenue & E Flamingo Road (1-855 234 7469, 777 2782, www.harrahslas vegas.com). Bus Deuce, 202.* **Shows** 1pm, 3pm Tue-Sat. **Tickets** $32.95-$43.95. No under-5s. **Map** p320 A6.

One of the real gems of Vegas's family entertainment roster is also one of its cheapest shows. Sure, there are no big bangs or grand illusions here: the budget extends to a pack of cards, some rope, a box of Fig Newtons and a silly suit. But King's warm manner, gentle humour and casually dazzling tricks keep the audience hooked. Look for discount coupons in the local magazines, but even if you don't find them, this is well worth full price.

Criss Angel: Believe.

Elvis Hasn't Left the Building

Long live the King!

Pete Vallee.

After Elvis's untimely death in 1977, Presley impersonators swamped Las Vegas. These ersatz Elvises – (Elvi?) – would perform on any stage, jump from aeroplanes and throw out the first pitch at ballgames. Statisticians reported more Elvises in Nevada than in the King's home state of Tennessee.

More than three-and-a-half decades after Presley's death – and the subsequent resurgence of his likeness in Vegas – he's now conspicuous by his absence here. The Elvis-a-Rama Museum on Industrial Road closed its doors in 2006, and most Elvis impersonators have left town. And just last year, in 2012, Cirque du Soleil replaced its short-lived *Viva Elvis* at Aria with *Zarkana*.

But even though the King is no longer omnipresent, he's by no means gone. You just have to look a little harder to find him.

For starters, check out *Million Dollar Quartet* (*see p205*), a fantastic new show at Harrah's that recounts a one-off 1956 Sun Records recording session with Carl Perkins,

Jerry Lee Lewis, Johnny Cash and Elvis. In addition to *Quartet*, Harrah's is good for other Elvis sightings, specifically 'Big Elvis', which is the alter ego of Pete Vallee, a longtime Las Vegas Presley impersonator, who performs several times per day most weekdays in the Piano Bar at Harrah's (*see p97*). Vallee, who in recent years topped the scale at nearly 1,000 pounds (we said 'Big Elvis', right?) before dropping back to a belt-tightening 480 pounds, covers all of the King's hits in a voice that sounds as if it was cloned from Elvis's.

The city's flashiest Elvis is Trent Carlini, who fashions himself after the younger, thinner Elvis, but with a generous amount of Vegas-style rhinestones. The show, at the LVH (*see p113*), includes music from Presley's rockabilly beginnings in the 1950s to the comeback songs of the late '60s.

The LVH is also home to the annual Elvis Festival (www.lasvegaselvisfestival.com) in July. And other Elvis impersonators compete Downtown in May at the Fremont Street Experience, for the Las Vegas Ultimate Elvis Tribute Artist Contest (www.elvis.com).

True Elvis fans, meanwhile, can live out the ultimate fantasy and have the King consecrate their marriage. The Viva Las Vegas (*see p241*) and Graceland (see p240) wedding chapels both offer Elvis packages that include low-key performances, 'Blue Hawaii' themes and other commemorative tchotchkes. Remember: the more you pay, the younger and thinner your Elvis will be. You'll also have to pay extra for one who actually performs the ceremony, and doesn't just show up with a boom box to belt out a couple songs.

Getting hitched with the King.

Human Nature.

Nathan Burton
Planet Hollywood *3667 Las Vegas Boulevard South, between E Harmon Avenue & E Flamingo Road (1-800 715 9219, www.nathanburton.com). Bus Deuce, 202.* **Shows** 4pm Tue-Sun. **Tickets** $34-$44; $17-$22 reductions. **Map** p320 A7.
Nathan Burton is as much comic as he is magician, and many of his tricks utilise props and contraptions that he has perfected over his career. In fact, many of his tricks were developed from pranks he played as a kid. Burton and his bikini-clad showgirl assistants add goofy new twists to these and other time-honoured tricks. A well-spent afternoon, indeed.

★ Penn & Teller
Rio *3700 W Flamingo Road, at S Valley View Boulevard, West of Strip (1-855 234 7469, 777 2782, www.pennandteller.com). Bus 202.* **Shows** 9pm Mon-Wed, Sat, Sun. **Tickets** $75-$95. No under-5s. **Map** p317 X3.
Burly man-mountain Penn Jillette and the mute, mono-monikered Teller are the *Reservoir Dogs* to most other magicians' *Ocean's Eleven*: edgy, angry and always seemingly on the verge of going off. They've become scourges of the Magic Circle by showing the audience how tricks are done, but they deserve equal credit for the pizazz with which they pull off the illusions that they don't explain. Bonus: stick around afterwards for the inevitable autograph signings, and you may hear Teller speak.

MUSICAL HEADLINERS

Boyz II Men
Mirage *3400 Las Vegas Boulevard South, between Spring Mountain & W Flamingo roads (1-800 963 9634, 792 7777, www.mirage.com). Bus Deuce, 203.* **Shows** (limited performances) 7.30pm, dates vary. **Tickets** $39.99-$59.99. **Map** p319, p320 A6.
They may have been boys when they started their career, but this iconic R&B group is riding its success

well into manhood. The trio recently celebrated its 20th anniversary with a new album and this residency at the Mirage. Most shows are scheduled for Fridays and Saturdays, but call ahead to get specific dates.

Celine Dion
Colosseum at Caesars Palace *3570 Las Vegas Boulevard South, at W Flamingo Road (1-877 432 5463, 866 1400, www.caesarspalace.com). Bus Deuce, 202.* **Shows** (50 performances a year) 7.30pm Tue, Wed, Sat, Sun; dates vary. **Tickets** $55-$250. **Map** p320 A7.
After 'taking a break' following her five-year Vegas run with a world tour, Celine Dion returned triumphant. (Bette Midler and Cher kept the stage – which was built for Dion – warm for her.) The show, which features a 31-piece orchestra, tributes to movie music and Michael Jackson – and a duet with a hologram of herself – scales back the excess (and the French-Canadian dancer/acrobats) of her Cirque-directed spectacle, in favour of keeping the focus on Las Vegas's biggest star. Elvis who?

Donny & Marie
Flamingo *3555 Las Vegas Boulevard South, at E Flamingo Road (1-855 234 7469, 777 2782, www.flamingolasvegas.com). Bus Deuce, 202.* **Shows** 7.30pm Tue-Sat. **Tickets** from $104.50. **Map** p320 A7.
Go ahead and smirk, but the toothy Mormon brother-and-sister act fit right in on the Strip; in fact, you might even say they dominate it. Entertainers since conception, they work the Flamingo's human-scaled showroom like lifelong politicians – running on an antidepressant platform – and no one can grin, wave, point, wink, dance on tables or kiss hands like they can. There are a few duets, some Broadway, country, even cod-opera, and they work out their comic sibling rivalry with a comic dance-off. By evening's end, you'll find yourself with a lump in your throat as they roll a montage of their entire televised lives, including a galaxy of stars.

Frankie Moreno
Stratosphere *2000 Las Vegas Boulevard South, at W St Louis Avenue (1-800 998 6937, 380 7777, www.stratospherehotel.com). Bus Deuce, 108.* **Shows** 8pm Wed-Sat. **Tickets** $39.99-$49.99. **Map** p319 C4.
Local music sensation Frankie Moreno recently launched his own headlining show at the Stratosphere, and it's about time. If you're looking for the sort of musical act Vegas cut its teeth on, you won't go wrong with the piano-playing, singing Moreno and his ten-piece band. Although he can cover the classics, he has his own roster of hits that are every bit as impressive.

Human Nature
Venetian *3355 Las Vegas Boulevard South, between Sands Avenue & E Flamingo Road (1-866 641 7469, 414 9000, www.venetian.com). Bus Deuce, 119, 203.* **Shows** 7pm Mon, Thur-Sun. **Tickets** $73.45-$117.45. **Map** p319, p320 B6.
Having passed puberty, the Australian boyband wisely grew up musically, studied the Motown songbook (and style guide), and flew east to Vegas. Sponsored by Vegas resident Smokey Robinson himself, the sharp-dressed quartet currently reigns at the Sands Showroom in the Venetian with their tight, snappy revue of classic Motor City hits.

Rod Stewart
Colosseum at Caesars Palace *3570 Las Vegas Boulevard South, at W Flamingo Road (1-888 929 7849, 866 1400, www.caesarspalace.com).*
Bus Deuce, 202. **Shows** 7.30pm Wed, Sat, Sun; dates vary. **Tickets** $49-$250. **Map** p320 A7.
'Da ya think he's sexy'? Apparently a lot of people still do. Rock 'n' Roll Hall of Famer Rod Stewart kicked off 2013 with a continuation of his Las Vegas residency that's scheduled to run for at least two more years. Drawing on a collection of hits that spans more than 50 years, Stewart thrills audiences with tunes like 'Maggie May' and 'Hot Legs', while pulling out some rarities and covers sure to please the fans.

PRODUCTION SHOWS

Absinthe
Caesars Palace *3570 Las Vegas Boulevard South, at W Flamingo Road (1-800 745 3000, 866 1400, www.caesarspalace.com). Bus Deuce, 202.* **Shows** 8pm, 10pm Tue, Thur-Sat; 8pm Wed. **Tickets** $89-$114. No under-18s. **Map** p320 A7.
This pop-up show instantly became the toast of Las Vegas when it pitched its *Spiegeltent* in front of Caesars Palace at the corner of Flamingo Road. It's as if a bunch of crazy carnies colonised the Strip, with their acro-cabaret with a touch of Cirque and more than a touch of *Rocky Horror*'s sexy camp.

★ Blue Man Group
Monte Carlo *3770 Las Vegas Boulevard South, between W Harmon & W Tropicana avenues (1-800 258 3626, www.montecarlo.com). Bus Deuce, 201.* **Shows** 7pm, 9.30pm Mon-Thur, Sat; 7pm Fri, Sun. **Tickets** $64.90-$236.50. **Map** p320 A8.

Blue Man Group.

ARTS & ENTERTAINMENT

It's no surprise that Blue Man Group is such an international phenomenon: their witty, rhythmic and colourful appeal is universal – meaning no language barrier for foreign visitors – and very carefully pitched at all age groups. In their new industrial-themed theatre at the Monte Carlo, the three blue baldies cull comedy from multimedia high jinks, a festival environment from audience reactions, and music from just about everything they can get their hands on. Few performers express so much while saying so little.

Jabbawockeez

Luxor *3900 Las Vegas Boulevard South, at W Hacienda Avenue (1-800 557 7428, 262 4400, www.luxor.com). Bus Deuce, 119, 201.* **Shows** 7pm Mon, Sun; 7pm, 9.30pm Thur-Sat. **Tickets** from $55. No under-3s. **Map** p320 A9.

What happens when you filter hip hop dance, mime and seriously amped-up energy through the colour spectrum? You end up with something like *PRiSM* (an acronym for 'Painting Reality In a Spectrum of Movement'), Jabbawockeez's frenetic dance/movement show. The Season One winners of MTV's *America's Best Dance Crew* recently debuted in a specially built theatre at the Luxor. Each member is aligned with a colour – hence, the 'prism' – while they dance as if their life depended on it.

Jersey Boys

Paris Las Vegas *3655 Las Vegas Boulevard South, at E Flamingo Road (1-855 234 7469, 777 2782, www.parislasvegas.com). Bus Deuce, 202.* **Shows** 6.30pm, 9.30pm Tue; 7pm Wed-Fri, Sun; 5pm, 8.15pm Sat. **Tickets** $90.20-$184.80. **Map** p320 A7.

About all that remains of the short-lived dream of a 'Broadway West' in Las Vegas, *Jersey Boys* is a perfect show for the Strip. It might as well be nicknamed *Dreamboys*, as it traces the four-decade rise and fall of Frankie Valli and the Four Seasons through a jukebox full of hand-clapping, hip swivelling hits – 30 of them, in fact. The dancing and singing are as razor-sharp as the suits and haircuts: *Jersey Boys* makes you pine for a time when men had style.

Jubilee!

Bally's *3645 Las Vegas Boulevard South, at E Flamingo Road (1-855 234 7469, 777 2782, www.ballyslasvegas.com). Bus Deuce, 202.* **Shows** 7.30pm, 10.30pm Mon-Thur, Sat, Sun. **Tickets** $57.50-$117.50. No under-18s. **Map** p320 A7.

If you enjoyed the movie *Showgirls*, then *Jubilee!* is a must-see, as this is the over-the-topless spectacular that inspired the set pieces in that cult classic. *Jubilee!*'s staging of the sinking of the *Titanic* and Samson's destruction of the Philistines in the temple are beyond lame – rather, they're lamé. But the production numbers in this long-running camp folly, which feature endless parades of beauties wearing nothing more than outlandishly coloured (hot pink

and tangerine predominate) feathers, headdresses and rhinestones (and chorus boys in hilarious studded leather codpieces), make it one of a kind – and, somewhat sadly, the last of its kind.

Kà

MGM Grand *3799 Las Vegas Boulevard South, at E Tropicana Avenue (1-877 660 0660, 531 3826, www.mgmgrand.com). Bus Deuce, 201.* **Shows** 7pm Tue-Sat. **Tickets** $69-$150; half-price 5-11s. No under-5s. **Map** p320 A8.

The stage is the star of this Cirque spectacular, which is like a cross between videogames and Japanese manga comics, with an IMAX movie screen. Having pushed the boat out for *O* (literally, in a couple of scenes), Cirque du Soleil had to work hard to top it in this multi-million-dollar extravaganza, in which the colossal stage platform rotates, revolves and stands on end, conjuring ocean depths, arctic cliffs and desert islands. Set in an ornate theatre that calls to mind a Jules Verne steampunk fantasia, *Kà* differs from other Vegas-based Cirque shows in that it has a plot (about twins struggling to reunite). The story gets a bit lost in an array of ever more breathtaking routines; yet for all the excess, the most touching moment in the piece is a section involving hand-shadows, the simplest of theatrical effects.

★ Love

Mirage *3400 Las Vegas Boulevard South, between Spring Mountain & W Flamingo roads (1-800 963 9634, 792 7777, www.mirage.com). Bus Deuce, 203.* **Shows** 7pm, 9.30pm Mon, Thur-Sun. **Tickets** $79-$180. No under-5s. **Map** p319, p320 A6.

This could have been horrific, a parade of paperback writers coming together in Sgt Pepper's yellow submarine to help Jude get back, or something. Sure, Cirque du Soleil's Beatles show is a little too literal with the lyrics in places, but from its spectacular opening until its cheesy climax, *Love* is mostly great fun, packed with Cirque's trademark acrobatics and punctuated with playful humour. Oh, and the music's never sounded better.

Menopause: The Musical

Luxor *3900 Las Vegas Boulevard South, at W Hacienda Avenue (1-800 557 7428, 262 4400, www.luxor.com). Bus Deuce, 119, 201.* **Shows** 5.30pm Mon, Wed-Sun; 8pm Tue. **Tickets** $54.95-$70. No under-14s. **Map** p320 A9.

The *Menopause* musical juggernaut finds a home in a city known for its own frequent hot flushes. Set in the lingerie department of Bloomingdale's, *Menopause* unites not only its four stars, but also women everywhere who are tackling 'the change', head-on through dialogue and two dozen pop parodies. Women under 45 and men of all ages should stay as far away as possible.

Kà.

★ Million Dollar Quartet

Harrah's *3475 Las Vegas Boulevard South, between Sands Avenue & E Flamingo Road (1-855 234 7469, 777 2782, www.harrahslasvegas.com). Bus Deuce, 202.* **Shows** 7pm Mon-Wed, Fri, Sun; 5.30pm, 8pm Thur. **Tickets** $60.50-$84.70. No under-5s. **Map** p320 A6.

This new show at Harrah's has been giving attendees quite a bang for their buck since its debut in early 2013. The story of one legendary Sun Records jam session by four unforgettable musicians – Carl Perkins, Elvis Presley, Johnny Cash and Jerry Lee Lewis – on a December night in 1956 features songs that gave then-nascent rock 'n' roll its backbone: 'Whole Lotta Shakin' Goin' On', 'Walk the Line', 'Blue Suede Shoes'... Musicals of this calibre are rarely seen on the Strip nowadays.

Michael Jackson One

Mandalay Bay *3950 Las Vegas Boulevard South, at W Hacienda Avenue (1-877 632 7400, www.mandalaybay.com). Bus Deuce, 119.* **Shows** 7.30pm, 10pm Mon-Wed, Sat. **Tickets** $69-$150; No under-5s. **Map** p320 A9.

Undeterred by the disappointment that was *Viva Elvis*, Cirque du Soleil pushed ahead with another single-star show in *Michael Jackson One*. Part tribute, part remembrance, part spooky hologram, *One* feels like a Cirque show in only the loosest sense. Thunderously loud and thin on the imaginative acrobatics and evocative content that Cirque does best, *MJ One* is suggested for ardent Jackson fans only.

Mystère

Treasure Island *3300 Las Vegas Boulevard South, at Spring Mountain Road (1-800 392 1999, 894 7722, www.treasureisland.com). Bus Deuce, 203.* **Shows** 7pm, 9.30pm Mon-Wed, Sat, Sun. **Tickets** $75.90-$130.90. **Map** p319, p320 A6.

The first Cirque du Soleil show to reach Vegas, *Mystère* holds up very well next to the more spectacular and expensive siblings that have joined it. The

reason? It doesn't take itself too seriously, and plays for slapsticky laughs as much as it does for astonishment (*taiko* drumming, *bunraku* puppetry, dazzling gymnastic exhibitions). The design is showing its age a little, but otherwise, this long-runner is in rude health. As with all Cirque shows, you'd do well to arrive early, as the pre-show clowning with the audience is charming.

★ O

Bellagio *3600 Las Vegas Boulevard South, at W Flamingo Road (1-888 488 7111, 693 8866, www.bellagio.com). Bus Deuce, 202.* **Shows** 7.30pm, 10pm Wed-Sun. **Tickets** $93.50-$155. No under-5s. **Map** p320 A7.

It's been surpassed in the extravagance stakes by *Kà* (*see p204*), but some – including us – say this is still the best Cirque du Soleil production in town, and one of the best shows on the Strip. *O* – a pun on *eau* – is a spectacle of Fellini-esque tableaux coupled with acrobatic feats performed by 70-plus swimmers, divers, aerialists, contortionists and clowns in, on, above and around a pool/stage containing 1.5 million gallons of water. None of which goes any way towards describing just how beautiful it all is. If you only see one Cirque show... *Photo p206.*

Le Rêve

Wynn Las Vegas *3131 Las Vegas Boulevard South, between E Desert Inn Road & Sands Avenue (1-888 320 7110, 770 9966, www.wynnlasvegas.com). Bus Deuce, 108, 203.* **Shows** 7pm, 9.30pm Mon, Tue, Fri-Sun. **Tickets** $105-$195. **Map** p319, p320 B6.

Named after mogul Steve Wynn's favourite Picasso painting, this big-budget spectacular features diving, acrobatics and amazing choreography, all performed in an aqua-theatre with intimate, in-the-round seating and an ever-changing circular pool that creates towering fountains and fathomless depths. With sexy, swimsuit-clad aquatic acrobat/dancers, out-of-the-box aesthetics and an independent vision, it's pretty to watch, but it fades from memory as fast as a dream itself. But in the baking desert of the Strip, this show is like entering a pleasant humidifier for 90 minutes, and the emotionally evocative scent of chlorine is what really lingers long after the show ends.

Rock of Ages

Venetian *3355 Las Vegas Boulevard South, between Sands Avenue & E Flamingo Road (1-866 641 7469, 414 9000, www.venetian.com). Bus Deuce, 119, 203.* **Shows** 8pm Tue-Fri, Sun; 7pm, 10pm Sat. **Tickets** $69-$167. No under-5s. **Map** p319, p320 B6.

This Broadway hit turned movie flop is reanimated at the Venetian with considerably more life than Tom Cruise displayed in its big-screen version. *Rock*, which follows the story of some fame-seeking, discontented youth at an LA rock 'n' roll club in the late 1980s, is good for some nostalgic tunes, but hasn't got much going on on the story front. However, if you didn't like the '80s the first time, it will be torture.

Tony n' Tina's Wedding

Bally's *3645 Las Vegas Boulevard South, at E Flamingo Road (1-855 234 7469, 777 2782, www.ballyslasvegas.com). Bus Deuce, 202.* **Shows** 7.30pm, 10.30pm Mon-Thur, Sat. **Tickets** $90.49-$119.12. **Map** p320 A7.

In this inventive, interactive dinner-show – sort of a live-action *Jersey Shore* – ticket-holders become wedding guests taking in the nuptials and reception of an Italian-American couple coping with comically stereotypical families, a pregnant maid of honour, a drunk priest and more. The set-up is just hokey enough to make you want to brush up

on your singing and dance moves (think 'YMCA'). But once dinner is served (an Italian buffet, naturally), you'll want to hightail it like a groom on the business end of a shotgun.

Tournament of Kings

Excalibur *3850 Las Vegas Boulevard South, at W Tropicana Avenue (1-800 933 1334, 597 7600, www.excalibur.com). Bus Deuce, 201.* **Shows** 7pm Mon-Wed, Fri, Sat. **Tickets** $59 ($44.35 without dinner). **Map** p320 A8.

The phrase 'dinner and a show' takes on new meaning at this year-round indoor olde worlde fayre. Kids and those with time-period fetishes will dig the jousting knights, dancing maidens and galloping horses, as King Arthur and company re-create a vaguely medieval bygone era with fine-tuned costumes, dialogue and mannerisms. One meal *sans* utensils is cool and all, but you may find you prefer to dive knife-and-fork-first into any number of casino buffets.

V: The Ultimate Variety Show

Planet Hollywood (Miracle Mile) *3663 Las Vegas Boulevard South, between E Harmon Avenue & E Flamingo Road (1-866 932 1818, 260 7200, www.vtheshow.com). Bus Deuce, 202.* **Shows** 7pm, 8.30pm daily. **Tickets** $69.99-$89.99; half-price 2-12s. **Map** p320 A7.

The V Theater features an ever-rotating array of shows during the day and evening hours, from '60s tributes and hypnotists to pole-dancing classes and pet acrobatics. And then there's *V: The Ultimate Variety Show*, which mashes them all up together in a blender of comedy, magic, music, juggling and daredevil stunts. You never know who or what's going to be on the bill, but you can be assured that

O. *See p205.*

Tournament of Kings.

it will be fast-paced and family-friendly, though the action can get a little schizoid at times.

Zarkana

Aria at CityCenter *3730 Las Vegas Boulevard, at E Harmon Avenue (1-877 253 5847, www. arialasvegas.com). Bus Deuce.* **Shows** 7pm, 9.30pm Mon, Tue, Fri-Sun. **Tickets** $69-$180. **Map** p320 A8.

This new Cirque theatre, formerly the home of the short-lived and disappointing *Viva Elvis*, is now home to a more traditional Cirque-like show: *Zarkana*. With a score by Elton John protégé Nick Littlemore, the show tells the story of a resurrected circus led by the ringmaster, Zark. A little bit spooky, somewhat surreal and totally spectacular, *Zarkana* offers all the aerial acrobatics you expect from a Cirque production and an enchanting soundtrack to boot.

COMEDY CLUBS

Comics are as much a Vegas staple as magicians, showgirls and second-mortgage-inducing blackjack losses. In addition to marquee funnymen such as **Jerry Seinfeld** and **Jay Leno**, who make regular pilgrimages to Vegas's biggest showrooms, and acts such as **Rita Rudner** (*see p200*) and **George Wallace** (*see p200*), who have regular residencies here, the city boasts a number of pretty good comedy clubs. Shows typically run for about 80 minutes and feature two or three stand-ups plus an MC.

Brad Garrett's Comedy Club

MGM Grand *3799 Las Vegas Boulevard South, at E Tropicana Avenue (1-877 660 0660, 531 3826, www.mgmgrand.com). Bus Deuce, 201.*

Shows 8pm daily. **Tickets** $46.40-$68.40 (without Garrett); $68.40-$90.40 (with Garrett). No under-21s. **Map** p320 A8.

Garrett, best known for his co-starring role on the sitcom *Everybody Loves Raymond*, is the big draw at this laugh factory located downstairs at the MGM Grand (or, 'the basement', as he calls it). The 6ft 8in comedy giant adds a bit of star power to the 'three comics and a mic' routine at this cosy room. Performers tend to be in residence for a week at a time, and there's surprisingly little repetition of acts.

Improv at Harrah's

Harrah's *3475 Las Vegas Boulevard South, between Sands Avenue & E Flamingo Road (1-855 234 7469, 777 2782, www.harrahsla svegas.com). Bus Deuce, 202.* **Shows** 8.30pm, 10.30pm Tue-Sun. **Tickets** $37.45-$55.95. No under-21s. **Map** p320 A6.

After more than 50 years in the funny business, the jokes here are still pretty fresh. The comedy isn't improv at all – it's actually straightforward stand-up, delivered by a weekly-changing roster of three comics.

Riviera Comedy Club

Riviera *2901 Las Vegas Boulevard, between E Sahara Avenue & E Desert Inn Road (1-877 892 7469, 794 9433, www. rivierahotel.com). Bus Deuce, 108, 203.* **Shows** 8.30pm daily. **Tickets** $19.99. No under-18s. **Map** p319 B5.

The Riviera's comedy club does pretty much what you might expect, booking two solid acts per night in a fairly dreary room. The line-ups change weekly. Get tickets at the Riv's box office to secure the under-$20 price.

SHOWROOMS

Many hotel-casinos have smallish showrooms that host touring productions, concerts and other special events. Prices vary by performer and location: tickets for big-name acts at Strip venues (David Copperfield at the MGM, say) will set you back around $100, while past-their-prime hitmakers can often be seen for a mere $20 or so.

The best showroom on the Strip is the **Hollywood Theatre** at the **MGM Grand** (*see p88*), a cosy, 740-seat room that hosts a strong selection of performers as well as the aforementioned David Copperfield among its roster of regular guests. There are also strong selections of name-brand entertainment at theatres within several locals' casinos, chiefly the 800-seater **Orleans** (*see p127*), the larger **Sam's Town** (*see p130*) and the more intimate **Suncoast** (*see p130*). For larger venues that host big-name bands and other one-night stands, *see pp225-228*.

Children

There's still plenty for young fun seekers in today's Las Vegas.

The rebranding of Treasure Island says a lot about the target audience for 21st-century Las Vegas. The resort spent a lot of money sexing up its wholesome past as the family-friendly Treasure Island; in the process, it got rid of the free pirate show, a must-see back in the family-oriented days of the '90s. Oh, there is still a show and it's still free, but the stars are now the scantily clad, silicone-enhanced Sirens of TI. As with most Las Vegas attractions today, kids might enjoy the show, but it's not designed with their enjoyment in mind.

ARTS & ENTERTAINMENT

CHILD-FRIENDLY ENTERTAINMENT

Although Vegas has focused on entertaining adults of late, where there's a gap in the market, someone in Las Vegas will be only too happy to fill it, which is why there are still plenty of child-friendly amusements in the city. Video arcades and rollercoasters line the Strip; and even without Siegfried & Roy, animals remain perhaps the ultimate all-ages crowd-pleaser. Most of the major shopping malls offer an array of amusements alongside the stores. And in the showrooms, the old staples – magicians, impersonators and variety acts – still thrive. With Cirque du Soleil alone now offering eight different shows (though one of them, *Zumanity*, is unsuitable for kids; another, Criss Angel's magic act, *Believe*, is too loud and potentially frightening), there's no shortage of entertainment options.

A free outdoor Strip show that's more suitable for youngsters than the Sirens of TI is the reimagined volcano at the nearby

Mirage (*see p90*), designed by the fire-and-water techno-magicians that created the Bellagio fountains. Set to a heart-pounding worldbeat score by former Grateful Dead drummer Mickey Hart, the Mirage's magic mountain blows its fiery top every night beginning at 6pm and does it all over again every hour on the hour until 11pm.

There are also plenty of choices if you want to take in a movie or go bowling, especially if you're prepared to leave the Strip. Las Vegas has more bowling lanes per capita than any place on earth, and they all seem to have the latest high-tech stuff and gimmicks (cosmic bowling, anyone?). Even the upscale Red Rock Casino has a 72-lane centre. And for something completely different, try the **Las Vegas Springs Preserve** (*see p71*), a 180-acre eco-park.

THE LAW

State law forbids under-21s from lingering on casino floors. Children are allowed to pass through casino areas when accompanied by an adult, but they cannot remain by gaming tables or machines. If they do, a security guard is likely to ask them – politely, but firmly – to leave the casino. Parents are not permitted to bet when they have youngsters in tow.

A Clark County curfew dictates that unaccompanied under-18s are not allowed on the Strip after 9pm on weekends and holidays. Off the Strip, the curfew is 10pm, or midnight on Fridays and Saturdays and during school holidays. Teenagers have the roughest time because, until they're 21, they can't go into bars, nor most clubs or showrooms.

THE BEST KIDS' STUFF

For earth
Las Vegas Springs Preserve. *See p71.*

For wind
The **Roller Coaster** at New York New York. *See p51.*

For fire
The volcano at the **Mirage**. *See p90.*

WHERE TO STAY

Many hotel-casinos on the Strip have an arcade and/or a cinema to help keep kids entertained. Additionally, almost every hotel has a pool that, in warmer weather (also known as 'much of the year'), can be any parent's lifesaver. That said, some resorts are more family-friendly than others: the best are **Circus Circus** (*see p106*), **Excalibur** (*see p106*), and **Mandalay Bay** (*see p86*), all of which are owned by MGM Mirage. **New York New York** (*see p100*) gets a gold star for its efforts to keep the kids happy. The gambling-free **Four Seasons Las Vegas** (*see p109*) doesn't offer flashy entertainments, but the service is child-friendly, and the hotel is attached to the attraction-filled Mandalay Bay.

Off the Strip, the **Stratosphere** (*see p109*) and **Palms** (*see p114*) have good childcare facilities, as do a number of the locals' casinos, particularly **Boulder Station** (*see p128*), **Santa Fe Station** (*see p130*), **Sunset Station** (*see p130*) and **Texas Station** (*see p131*). Out at the **Westin Lake Las Vegas** (*see p131*), great family amenities include water activities such as fishing, swimming and kayaking. For more on the city's accommodation, *see pp78-131*.

EATING & DRINKING

As in most towns, the best family restaurants are heavily themed and often quite loud. The **Rainforest Café** in the MGM Grand (*see p88*; 891 8580, www.rainforestcafe.com, open 8am-11pm Mon-Thur, Sun; 8am-midnight Fri & Sat) is filled with fake foliage, life-size robotic animals and large aquariums with (real) fish. There's even the odd 'thunderstorm'. Mid-Strip food and fun can be found at the **Miracle Mile Shops** (*see p175*) next to Planet Hollywood. At the Cosmopolitan, take the kids to **Holsteins** (698 7940, www.holsteinslv.com) for outta-this-world burgers and milkshakes.

SIGHTSEEING
Animal & water attractions

The off-Strip location of **Southern Nevada Zoological Park** (*see p71*) requires quite a trip. However, if you sample the animal habitats along the Strip, you can at least get a taste of nature.

Siegfried & Roy may not perform any more, but the duo's **Secret Garden** is still open for business at the Mirage (*see p54*). Check out the lions, tigers and other cats before adjourning to the **Dolphin Habitat**. However, the best animal attraction is Mandalay Bay's **Shark Reef** (*see p51*): it features more than 100 species of fish and reptiles. At the touch pool, kids can get their hands wet touching sharks, rays and horseshoe crabs.

Over at the Mystic Falls Park at **Sam's Town** (*see p130*), a four-times-daily laser and water show, **Sunset Stampede**, tells the story of the Western pioneer experience.

Adventuredome. *See p210.*

ARTS & ENTERTAINMENT

Arcades & rides

Most major casinos have games arcades. Some consist of little more than a room with a dozen old video games, but others boast superlative arcades and even fairground attractions. Those at both the **Excalibur** (*see p106*) and **Circus Circus** (where the games surround a central ring with circus acts; *see p106*) are decent, but the best are the **Coney Island Emporium** (*see p50*) at New York New York.

Of the theme parks in the city, the indoor **Adventuredome** (*see p57*) at Circus Circus rules the roost, yet it's never so busy that you'll spend the bulk of your time in queues. The Canyon Blaster is a short but furious double-loop, double-corkscrew rollercoaster; other exciting rides include the head-rushing Inverter and the Rim Runner water flume (yes, you will get wet). There are half a dozen low-intensity rides for the little ones, plus carnival games, miniature golf and the Xtreme Zone, where you can test your mettle with rock climbing and bungee jumping.

ARTS & ENTERTAINMENT

Boundless Bouncing

Tons of fun for children with excess energy.

Got kids bouncing off the hotel room walls after being cooped up too long indoors? Take them some place where bouncing is – literally – encouraged. At **BounceU** (1000 Stephanie Place, at Patrick Lane, 735 5867, www.bounce u.com), you can turn the young ones loose and let them burn off that excess energy, rather than hop from bed to bed in your room. BounceU is just off I-515 and Russell Road in Henderson, which makes it easily accessible from Downtown or the Strip.

Send the kids padding up the stairs of the giant rubber slide, or challenge them to scale the plastic climbing wall over and over again. Other activities include bouncy castles, plastic basketball, climbing towers made of rope and an inflated boxing ring where they can strap on humongous padded gloves and vent their boredom on each other – instead of you. It's all brilliant, exhausting, fun.

BounceU has afternoon hours for 'open bounce' (3.30-5.30pm Mon, Wed-Fri; ages three and up; $8 per child), during which parents can sit and recharge, enjoying a book or magazine while the younger generation make the most of their plastic bouncy kingdom.

Friday nights are reserved for Cosmic Bounce (7.30-9pm; ages five and over), which includes pizza and free bounce time; adults can sneak away to grab a bite at the nearby Galleria Mall or one of the many dining establishments on adjacent Stephanie Street.

Or just take them during the afternoon, wear 'em out, and haul them back to the hotel where you can drop them off with a sitter while you proceed to enjoy a childfree evening. Usually works for us.

Other rides in town range from ridiculous to heart stopping. The **Roller Coaster** (*see p51*), which twists and loops through New York New York, is harrowing, but the real screams come further north at the Stratosphere, which hosts four monstrous thrill rides some 1,000 feet above the Strip: **X-Scream**, the **Big Shot, Insanity: the Ride** and **SkyJump** (for all, *see p57*).

The **Forum Shops** (*see p174*) at Caesars Palace has free animatronic shows in the mall – the 'ancient' statues come to life – and an IMAX 3-D ride called Race For Atlantis. Off the Strip, **Wet 'n' Wild** (*see p70*) is a good summer option, while the **Las Vegas Mini Gran Prix** (1401 N Rainbow Boulevard, at US 95, 259 7000, www.lvmgp.com) features an indoor arcade, miniature rollercoaster and four go-karting tracks, where the size and speed of the vehicles match the age and skill of young drivers.

Height and weather restrictions apply for many thrill rides in Las Vegas.

Educational attractions

Aside from the **Las Vegas Springs Preserve** (*see p71*), there's the **Discovery Children's Museum** (*see p68*).

Parks

Sunset Park (E Sunset Road & S Eastern Avenue), **Lorenzi Park** (W Washington Avenue & N Rancho Drive) and **Floyd Lamb State Park** (Tule Springs Road, off US 95 north of Las Vegas) are a trio of large, grassy parks with lakes and volleyball courts; Sunset and Lorenzi Parks also have tennis facilities. For details on all parks, call 455 8200.

ARTS & ENTERTAINMENT

Aside from the stand-alone **UA Showcase 8** (*see p214*) movie theatre on the Strip, many off-Strip casinos have in-house cinemas, with those at the **Orleans** and the **Palms** (*see p114*) closest to the Strip. Many of the Station casinos have movie theatres; **Sam's Town** (*see p130*), another locals' casino, counts an 18-screen multiplex among its selling points.

Most shows on the Strip are adult-oriented, whether in terms of explicit content or complex themes; tickets for those that are suitable for children, such as Cirque du Soleil's original, fabulous *Mystère* (*see p205*), the exotic and aquatic *O* (*see p205*), and Beatles-themed *Love* (*see p204*), can cost more than $100. However, there are some bargains: comedy magician Mac King (*see p200*) produces the expected rabbits and doves – and unexpected laughs – in his shows, which have cross-generational appeal and are conveniently staged in the afternoons.

RESOURCES

Babysitting & children's supplies

Several agencies in Las Vegas offer licensed babysitters who have been cleared through the sheriff's department and by the FBI. Every hotel worth its salt can arrange babysitting services; many even offer on-site babysitters. Many hotels can also arrange the delivery of children's supplies (strollers, cots, car seats, even video games); if yours can't, try **Care.com** (www.care.com).

Nurseries & activity centres

Although few of the large Strip resorts have nurseries, many of the town's neighbourhood hotel-casinos do run some kind of childcare centre. Most such operations require written consent from the parents and may ask you to leave valid ID; they may also insist that the child is potty trained. Most centres have a three-hour time limit, and only the person who drops off the children can collect them. You don't have to be an overnight guest at the hotel, but you do have to remain on the premises while your child is in the nursery.

In addition to **Kids Quest** (*see p71*), the **Kids Tyme** facilities at the Orleans (*see p127*) and the **Suncoast** (*see p130*) have licensed supervisors to entertain kids with movies, toys and crafts. Each has a five-hour limit.

Kids Quest

Various locations (www.kidsquest.com).
Open *Summer* 11am-12.30am Mon-Thur; 11am-2am Fri; 10am-2am Sat; 10am-1am Sun. *Winter* 11am-11pm Mon-Thur; 11am-1am Fri; 10am-1am Sat; 10am-11pm Sun. **Rates** $8-$9.50/hr.

Kids Quest has all manner of attractions, including a Barbie area, a big cliff and jungle area and, of course, computer games. Children aged from six weeks to 12 years can be dropped off for up to three and a half hours, but parents must remain on site. Kids Quests are located at Santa Fe and Sunset (for both, *see p139*), Boulder (*see p128)* and Texas Stations (*see p131*), as well as at Red Rock Resort (*see p126*).

ESCAPES & EXCURSIONS

Don't miss the assortment of natural and man-made attractions just outside town. **Hoover Dam**, **Valley of Fire State Park**, **Red Rock Canyon** and **Bonnie Springs/ Old Nevada** are all great for exploring with children (for all, *see pp244-269*). Further afield, children love the Desperado rollercoaster and other rides at Buffalo Bill's resort in **Primm**.

Film

Watch films from the pool.

With Las Vegas slowly but surely attaining the status of an honorary suburb of LA, it was only a matter of time before the city immersed itself completely in the glitzy twin worlds of film and fame. In the past, Vegas occasionally served as a location for movies, many of them iconic. But in the last decade, with its popularity speedily soaring among the Hollywood jet set, the city has found itself creeping into more and more feature films and TV shows, its instantly recognisable profile rising even faster than the condo towers on Las Vegas Boulevard.

For moviemakers, Vegas is now more attractive than it has ever been. But for moviegoers, it's a different story. Although the city is based on alluring distractions, and cinema is hardly its top priority, it's not hard to find the big-ticket Hollywood blockbusters in one of the city's enormous multiplexes, most of which are housed in off-Strip casinos. But of these, only Cinemark's **Century Suncoast 16** has shown any commitment to non-mainstream fare, leaving the non-casino-tied **Regal Village Square 18** as Vegas's main independent/foreign cinema destination.

That said, inroads are being made. The city's cinematic calendar is pepped up by a variety of movie-related events, from one-night marathons to the multi-day **Las Vegas Film Festival** (www.lvfilmfest.com). Of late, some properties in the city have also realised the mutual benefits of combining water and cinema, including the **Cosmopolitan** (*see p85*), which hosts a summer 'Dive-In' movie series where guests can watch popular films new and old on the hotel's four-storey screen while lounging in the fourth floor pool. **Wet 'n' Wild** (*see p70*) also got in the act, hosting a similar series for waterlogged visitors.

INFORMATION AND TICKETS

The *Las Vegas Review-Journal's* Friday 'Neon' supplement, and the free alt-weeklies *Seven* and *Las Vegas Weekly* all provide cinema schedule information. On your mobile phone, the Fandango app is a godsend, as is **Moviefone** (222 3456, www.moviefone.com). Knowing your zip code beforehand will help you select the closest multiplex. Online, head to www.lasvegas.mrmovietimes.com for details of what's on.

Tickets can be bought from box offices, or by phone and online through **Fandango** (1-800 326 3264, www.fandango.com).

MOVIE THEATRES

A score of movie houses populates the Vegas Valley. Those listed here are among the most notable and/or accessible.

AMC Town Square 18

Town Square *6587 Las Vegas Boulevard South, at the intersection of I-15 & I-215 (362 7283, www.amctheatres.com). Bus SDX, 104, 117.* **Tickets** *Regular screens* $10.50; $7 reductions; $8 before 6pm. *3D screenings* $3.50 extra.

AMC recently took over the screens at Town Square's popular cinema. Don't expect anything different than you'd see on any other screens around the city, but the theatre is nice and comfortable. There's a second AMC location, Rainbow 10 Promenade, in the north-west corner of the city (2321 N Rainbow Boulevard, at W Smoke Ranch Road, 636 2869).

Brenden Las Vegas 14

Palms *4321 W Flamingo Road, at S Valley View Boulevard, West of Strip (507 4849, www.brendentheatres.com). Bus 104, 202.* **Tickets** *Regular screens* $10.50; $7 reductions; $8 before 6pm. *3D screenings* $3.50 extra.

Essential Las Vegas Films

This city was made for the movies.

Viva Las Vegas

CASINO
MARTIN SCORSESE (1995)

How Vegas became a money machine for the mob but was lost to the 'yokels'. *Casino* begins with an operatic flourish – a falling man plunging into neon hell – and never slackens. No Scorsese movie better captures his mouthy sense of class war and cultural outsiderness. And Sharon Stone gives the performance of her lifetime as blonde hustlerette Ginger.

FEAR & LOATHING IN LAS VEGAS
MARCEL CARNE (1998)

The stakes were huge for Terry Gilliam: deliver Vegas's most notorious bit of bizarreitude faithfully. Johnny Depp uncorked a pre-*Pirates* mumbler as the Hunter S Thompson surrogate, while Benicio Del Toro gained 45 pounds to channel his companion, Dr Gonzo. Were drugs even necessary on this set?

LEAVING LAS VEGAS
MIKE FIGGIS (1995)

Watching Nicolas Cage's Oscar-winning performance as resigned-to-death alcoholic Ben Sanderson is like a smack to the head. Something of a misunderstood masterpiece, Figgis's film is frequently described as a romantic drama, when it's actually an existential plumbing of the soul. A rare case where the strength of the film rivals the (John O'Brien) novel that inspired it.

OCEAN'S 11
LEWIS MILESTONE (1960)

Which one? Those in the know understand the numeral refers to the Rat Pack original, not the 2001 Steven Soderbergh remake. His adaptation of the original whimsical crime caper may technically be a better film – but Vegas ain't nothing without Frankie, Dino, Sammy and, well, Peter Lawford.

SHOWGIRLS
PAUL VERHOEVEN (1995)

That pole needed cleaning anyway, so thanks. The knives were out for Paul Verhoeven's tits-heavy spectacular. Stinky garbage or a trove of trash manna? Neither: *Showgirls* plays more like an aerobicised parody of sex and love. Don't call it intentional, but thank pervy screenwriter Joe Eszterhas for all the inane trampdom on reality TV these days.

VIVA LAS VEGAS
GEORGE SIDNEY (1963)

As with many things Vegas-related, 'essential' doesn't have to mean 'great'. But this star vehicle for Presley isn't all that bad either. Elvis plays Lucky Jackson, a not-so-fortunate racecar driver trying to raise money to replace his car's engine. The film spawned Elvis's cover of the title song and his own entanglement with Vegas. Also, Ann-Margret!

IMAX $17; $14 reductions, and before 6pm.
Map p317 X3.
Countless consumer awards and regular high-profile premières pay tribute to the Brenden Palms' central role in the Vegas movie-going experience. That said, blockbusters usually dominate, with one major feature usually configured for the sole IMAX screen.

★ Century Orleans 18

Orleans *4500 W Tropicana Avenue, between S Decatur & S Valley View boulevards, West of Strip (889 1220, www.cinemark.com). Bus 103, 104, 201.* **Tickets** $10.75; $7 reductions; $8 before 6pm. *3D screenings* $13.75; $11.25 before 6pm. **Map** p317 X3.
This 18-screener at the Orleans ushered Las Vegas into the multiplex era with such amenities as stadium seating and THX-equipped auditoria. Although it isn't as chic as its chief competitor, the nearby Brenden Las Vegas 14 at the Palms (*see p114*), it has remained one of the valley's most loved movie theatres. Every so often, the roster includes a major studio-sanctioned art flick.

Century Suncoast 16

Suncoast *9090 Alta Drive, at N Rampart Boulevard, North-west Las Vegas (869 1880, www.cinemark.com). Bus 206.* **Tickets** $10.50; $7 reductions; $8.50 before 6pm. *3D screenings* $3.50 extra.
The 16-screen theatre at the Suncoast is a popular choice among Summerlin residents, while Vegas cineastes willing to make the trek also enjoy the CineArts series, which includes anywhere from one to three independent and foreign films. Cinemark also runs a number of other movie theatres in the city, all based in casinos and all specialising in mainstream fare. Among them are the Century 18 Sam's Town, the Century Stadium 16 Rancho Santa Fe and the Century 16 South Point. See the website for details.

★ Galaxy Luxury+

4500 E Sunset Road, between N Green Valley Parkway & Mountain Vista Street, Henderson (442 0244, www.galaxytheatres.com). Bus 212. **Tickets** $11; $7.50 reductions; $8.50 before 6pm. *3D screenings* $3 extra.
Fancy a beer with your film? This Galaxy theatre will do you one better: you can enjoy your brew in the comfort of a huge reclining chair. This brand-new movie house (which took over the space of a long-closed theatre) serves beer and wine, and features large, plush seats you'll probably have to be prised out of once the show's over. Plus, the screens are enormous, the sound is incredible, and the tickets priced the same as everywhere else. Yes, it's quite a way from the Strip and you'll need to get your ticket ahead of time, but you'll be glad that you did.

Regal Cinemas

Aliante Stadium 16 *7300 N Aliante Parkway, at I-215, North Las Vegas. Bus 119.*
Boulder Station 11 *4111 Boulder Highway, at E Desert Inn Road, East Las Vegas. Bus BHX, 203.*
Colonnade 14 *8880 S Eastern Avenue, at E Pebble Road, Green Valley. Bus 110.*
Fiesta Henderson Stadium 12 *777 W Lake Mead Parkway, at I-515, Henderson. Bus HDX, 217.*
Green Valley Ranch 10 *2300 Paseo Verde Drive, at S Green Valley Parkway, Henderson. Bus 111.*
Red Rock Resort 16 *11011 W Charleston Boulevard, at I-215, West Las Vegas. Bus SX.*
Sunset Station 13 *1301-A W Sunset Road, between N Stephanie Street & I-515, Henderson. Bus 115, 212.*
Texas Station 18 *2101 N Texas Star Lane, at N Rancho Drive, between W Lake Mead Boulevard & Vegas Drive, North Las Vegas. Bus 106, 210.*
Village Square 18 *9400 W Sahara Avenue, at S Fort Apache Road, North-west Las Vegas. Bus SX, 203.*
All venues *221 2283, www.regmovies.com.* **Admission** $11; $8 reductions; $8.50 before 6pm. Additional fees for 3D screenings.
The Regal theatres are among the busiest in town, partly due to their locations in the popular Station Casinos, but also thanks to the variety of programming. The best by far is the cinephile-favoured Village Square 18-screener, which shows as many as five non-mainstream films (plus concert simulcasts) at any given time.

UA Showcase 8

Showcase Mall, 3769 Las Vegas Boulevard South, at E Tropicana Avenue (221 2283, www.reg movies.com). Bus Deuce, 201. **Admission** $11; $8 reductions; $8.50 before 6pm. Additional fees for 3D screenings. **Map** p320 A8.
You can catch the latest blockbuster at the only movie theatre on the Strip, but don't expect lots of locals, nor any great luxury or cutting-edge cinema technology at this ageing multiplex just north of the MGM Grand. Parking in the Showcase garage is free with validation; if, that is, you can get past the parking lot that is Las Vegas Boulevard.

West Wind Las Vegas 5 Drive-In

4150 W Carey Avenue, at N Rancho Drive, North-west Las Vegas (646 3565). **Tickets** $6.75; $1 under-11s; $4.75 Tue. **No credit cards**.
This 50-year-old institution has survived several changes in ownership and the increasing popularity of indoor multiplexes, leaving it as Vegas's only remaining drive-in. It's ideal for traditionalists and cheapskates who favour bringing their own drinks and snacks, though lights emanating from the surrounding sprawl have affected visibility. Five screens offer double features of current releases; sound is available through your FM radio.

Gay & Lesbian

Vegas is coming out with a vengeance.

You'd be forgiven for thinking that the original Sin City would be a natural playground for gays. After all, what other city in America can claim such a judgement-free, libertarian attitude, especially when it comes to late-night revelry? However, for years, the opposite has been the case. It's hard to say who has squandered the potential of Las Vegas as a gay destination: the city itself or its own homosexual populace. The city missed a lucrative opportunity when Nevada declined to legalise gay marriage; it's now going to have to play catch-up with a host of other states as a same-sex wedding

destination. Nevertheless, the scene has recently been coming out in a big way, and visitors have been the main beneficiaries. Hotels such as Wynn (*see p93*) and Paris Las Vegas (*see p91*) have made concerted efforts to market themselves to the international gay community.

ARTS & ENTERTAINMENT

THE GAY SCENE

Downtown, the Neonopolis is now home to **Krave** (*see p217*), the town's first gay megaclub; the **Blue Moon Resort** (2651 Westwood Drive, 784 4500, www.bluemoon lv.com), a gay-oriented lodge with swimming pool, spa services and other amenities, is a fun and friendly place to meet other men visiting Vegas.

The local scene is also starting to look up, if gradually. The majority of gay venues reside in two dominant LGBT hubs where tourists and locals mingle freely: the so-called **Fruit Loop**, the streets around the intersection of Paradise Road and E Harmon Avenue, and **Commercial Center**, up on Sahara Avenue. Gay bars dot the valley, from old stagers such as **Snick's Place** to newer venues such as **Piranha**. The city's **Pride** event has grown enough to take over Downtown for a weekend. Unlike most US cities, which hold their Pride in midsummer, Vegas tries to avoid the blasting heat with a later parade and festival.

LESBIAN LAS VEGAS

There aren't any lesbian bars in Vegas, and women make up a very small constituent of the city's gay nightlife. However, gay bars – and even some casinos – are devoting an increasing number of nights to female-tilted events. **FreeZone** (*see p217*), the town's

unofficial lesbian hangout, throws the popular Lick Her Bust party every Tuesday; and **8½** (*see p218*) welcomes the ladies to Orchid on Wednesdays. Alternatively, **Betty's Outrageous Adventures** (www.bettysout.com) is a social group that brings lesbians together for everything from movie nights to camping trips. Most events are all-inclusive, though some are women-only.

BARS

As well as the gay bars below, a few places self-identify as 'alternative', essentially proclaiming themselves as gay-friendly operations.

Backdoor Lounge

1415 E Charleston Boulevard, at S 15th Street, Downtown (385 2018). Bus 206. **Open** 24hrs daily. **Admission** $5 Fri, Sat. **Map** p318 E3.
The Backdoor caters to Latino guys and their admirers. It's like any other Vegas bar during the week, but plays things up for the weekend with dance parties, drag shows and beauty contests.

Badlands Saloon

Commercial Center, 953 E Sahara Avenue, between S 6th Street & S Maryland Parkway, East of Strip (792 9262). Bus SX, 109. **Open** 24hrs daily. **No credit cards. Map** p317 Y2.

Time Out Las Vegas **215**

INSIDE TRACK VEGAS PRIDE

As Las Vegas's gay community expands, so does its annual **Pride Parade** (*see p40*). In September 2012, following a week of parties and get-togethers, the event celebrated its 15th anniversary with a crowd that drew nearly 35,000 people and featured kick-off speeches from comediennes Joan Rivers, Kathy Griffin and Margaret Cho. For information, visit www.lasvegaspride.org.

The smaller of the city's two Western gay bars, Badlands is an intimate space patronised in the main by men over 30 and Commercial Center loyalists. A game of pool will set you back a mere quarter, making it the cheapest in Vegas (if not the whole state).

Buffalo
Paradise Plaza, 4640 Paradise Road, between E Harmon & E Tropicana avenues, East of Strip (733 8355). Bus 108. **Open** 24hrs daily. **Map** p320 C8.
The true Fruit Loop alternative, Buffalo is the destination for leather and bear enthusiasts, though they don't always represent the majority of the bar's patrons. There's no diva posturing or twinky snobbery here, just cheap drinks and chatty customers.

Charlie's Las Vegas
5012 Arville Street, at W Tropicana Avenue, South-west Las Vegas (876 1844, www.charlieslasvegas.com). Bus 104, 201. **Open** 24hrs Mon-Sat.
Gay country fans and followers of the Nevada Gay Rodeo Association head to this Western-themed bar with a large space for both line-dancing and socialising. The place attracts both men and women, especially on Tuesdays for Drag Queen Bingo and Nothing But Country Thursdays, where a cowboy hat or going shirtless gets you half-price drinks.

Escape Lounge
4213 W Sahara Avenue, at Arville Street, West of Strip (364 1167). Bus SX, 104. **Open** 24hrs daily.
Escape is the closest thing to a gay sports bar in Vegas. Expect disco and top-40 tunes to be playing over the game. Escape has one of the warmest vibes on the local scene, and it's fun even if you're not a sports buff, .

Fun Hog Ranch
495 E Twain Avenue, between Paradise Road & Palos Verdes Street, East of Strip (791 7001, www.funhogranchlv.com). Bus 108, 109, 203. **Open** 24hrs daily. **Map** p319, p320 C6.
The delightfully and evocatively named Fun Hog is rowdy and rustically decorated. It's a 'come as you are' place, with fetish and leatherwear encouraged.

Las Vegas Eagle
3430 E Tropicana Avenue, at S Pecos Road, East Las Vegas (458 8662). Bus 111, 201. **Open** 24hrs daily. **Map** p318 Z3.
The Eagle is a favourite among older men and the Levi's/leather crowd. Expect strong drinks and a loud environment, though, sadly, the underwear parties are no more.

Las Vegas Lounge
900 E Karen Avenue, between Paradise Road & S Maryland Parkway, East of Strip (737 9350). Bus 108, 203. **Open** 24hrs daily. **Map** p317 Y3.
Everyone on the Vegas scene has a story about how they went into the seemingly nondescript Las Vegas Lounge and suddenly realised that they were at a tranny bar – the only such establishment in the state of Nevada. You'll find all the colours of the homo rainbow here; transsexual and cross-dressing go-go dancers perform more or less nightly.

Snick's Place
1402 S 3rd Street, between Las Vegas Boulevard S & S Casino Center Boulevard, Stratosphere Area (385 9298, www.snicksplace.com). Bus Deuce, 108. **Open** 24hrs daily. **No credit cards.** **Map** p319 C3.
Ask longtime gay Las Vegans where they first began meeting other similarly inclined men, and they'll probably mention Snick's, the oldest LGBT watering hole in town. Sure, it's seen better days, but it still retains a loyal following.

★ Spotlight Lounge
Commercial Center, 957 E Sahara Avenue, between S 6th Street & S Maryland Parkway, East of Strip (431 9775, www.spotlightlounge.com). Bus SX, 109. **Open** 24hrs daily. **No credit cards.** **Map** p317 Y2.
Recently renovated from top to bottom, Commercial Center's most beloved neighbourhood bar, Spotlight, is favoured for its down-to-earth guys, regular liquor busts and free-pizza nights. A firm favourite among the leather crowd.

NIGHTCLUBS

Casino-housed clubs often host LGBT promotions – check the free gay publications and alternative weeklies for ads. Online, check out the popular concierge service GayLV (www.gaylv.com). At the time of writing a brand-new club, **Affair** (3765 Las Vegas Boulevard South, between Harmon & E Tropicana avenues, 900 1251, www.affairlasvegas.com) was set to open. The space is huge, with 25,000ft devoted to dancing and DJs, and the promise of 'a performance-based nightlife experience'.

Of course, you'll also find gay revellers in most of the city's popular nightlife joints. For more, *see p219-228*.

Flex Lounge

4371 W Charleston Boulevard, at S Arville Street, West Las Vegas (385 3539, www. flexlasvegas.com). Bus 103, 104, 206. **Open** 24hrs daily.

This enduring venue attracts a very diverse crowd from various parts of the gay community. The drag revues on Fridays ('flamBOYance', www. flamboyanceshow.com) and Saturdays are the most popular events, but there's something going on here most nights.

FreeZone

610 E Naples Drive, at Paradise Road, East of Strip (794 2300, www.freezonelv.com). Bus 108. **Open** 24hrs daily. **Map** p320 C8.

If the line at Piranha is too long, then this is the next best Fruit Loop option. Thursday's boys' night party continue to be a draw; weekends are reserved for the Queens of Las Vegas, the city's longest-running drag show. Lick Her Bust on

Tuesdays is a ladies' affair, but you'll find the lesbian community well represented on any night.

GoodTimes

1775 E Tropicana Avenue, at Spencer Street, University District (736 9494, www.goodtimes lv.com). Bus 201. **Open** 24hrs daily. **Map** p317 Y3.

GoodTimes has always been renowned for its youth-oriented Monday-night liquor bust. But competition from Piranha has motivated management to abolish the cover and adopt a $1 well and draft beer promotion. Attendance is smaller during the rest of the week.

★ Krave Massive

Neonopolis, 450 E Fremont Street, at Las Vegas Boulevard (677 1740, www.kravemassive.com). Bus Deuce & all BTC-bound buses. **Open** 9pm-4am Thur-Sat. **Map** p318 D1.

See below **Massive Attack**.

Massive Attack

Downtown Las Vegas now home to world's largest gay nightclub.

Downtown's open-air mall Neonopolis has had its share of ups and downs, but it's unlikely anyone ever imagined the shopping and entertainment complex would eventually house the world's biggest gay nightclub. Popular club Krave, which was originally located on the Strip next to Planet Hollywood, rolled out its red carpet at the Downtown space in June 2013. And the new Krave isn't just larger than the old one; it's, well… massive.

Spread out over 80,000 square feet in what used to house Neonopolis's 14-screen multiplex, **Krave Massive** (*see above*) contains several dance rooms catering to different tastes, including Top 40, country & western, Latin, and hip hop, served by three separate bars. But Krave

Massive isn't aiming to be just a gigantic dancehall. The complex will also eventually – an opening date is yet to be set – host a performing arts space, a martini bar, a gay-centric comedy club, a retail store and, according to the company, the country's only LGBT movie theatre.

Krave's management aren't the only ones who believe in the financial viability of a huge homo hotspot. Tony Hsieh, Zappos.com's founder and head of Vegas's revitalising Downtown Project (*see p66*), has a small stake in the project, and Caesars Entertainment has taken a more active role, describing its partnership with Krave Massive as underscoring Caesars' desire to 'bring exemplary LGBT entertainment experiences to Las Vegas'.

★ Piranha & 8½

*4633 Paradise Road, between E Harmon & E
Tropicana avenues, East of Strip (791 0100,
www.piranhalasvegas.com). Bus 108.* **Open** from
10pm-6am daily. **Map** p320 C8.

Done out with velvet curtains, a marble-topped bar
and gigantic piranha aquariums, the $5-million
Piranha dance hall and connecting 8¼ Lounge is gay
Vegas's most beautiful nightlife palace. Go-go boys
and girls are on display in Piranha, while guests take
over the stage in 8¼; the Skybox VIP rooms give welcome respite from the usual crowds. Cocktails can
be expensive and low on booze, but it's easy to see
why this complex is a hit.

SHOPS

Get Booked

*Paradise Plaza, 4640 Paradise Road, between E
Harmon & E Tropicana avenues, East of Strip
(737 7780, www.getbooked.com). Bus 108.* **Open**
10am-midnight daily. **Map** p320 C8.

Located in the Fruit Loop, this was the last remaining
general gay retail shop in Las Vegas – until Krave
Massive announced plans to open its own retail space
Downtown. Get Booked divides its offerings between
all the usual merchandise (T-shirts, books, greeting
cards, CDs, gifts) and the naughty stuff (videos,
DVDs, underwear, lubricants, adult magazines).

CRUISING

Thanks to hook-up apps such as Grindr and
Scruff, the most popular non-nightclub cruising
spots are now virtual. Gay.com usually has two
and sometimes three chatrooms filled with
randy surfers 'looking around', as the blushed
parlance goes. Also popular are manhunt.net
and adam4adam.com, which run (often explicit)
user profiles for those in the city or visiting
soon, while cruisingforsex.com surveys high-
traffic peek-a-boo and public-sex spots. Even
lasvegas.craigslist.com has become a cruising
HQ; you can post or search ads on pages
devoted to men seeking men, casual encounter
and erotic services.

In addition to the venues below, it's worth
checking out the adult stores and the area
around Commercial Center.

Entourage Vegas

*Commercial Center, 953 E Sahara Avenue,
between S 6th Street & S Maryland Parkway, East
Las Vegas (650 9193, www.entouragevegas.com).
Bus SX, 109.* **Open** 24hrs daily. **Admission** $22
locker; $25 dressing room; $28 TV room. **Map**
p317 Y2.

If hotel spas seem a little chaste, you can rely on this
Greek-themed facility (formerly Apollo Spa) for a
more bacchanalian experience. The closest thing to
a bathhouse in the city, Entourage offers all the standard spa accoutrements (heated pool, sauna, steam
room, jacuzzis, workout equipment), plus an internet
café, community video room, private booths with
video feeds and an on-staff masseur.

Hawk's Gym

*Commercial Center, 953 E Sahara Avenue,
between S 6th Street & S Maryland Parkway, East
of Strip (731 4295, www.hawksgym.com). Bus SX,
109.* **Open** 24hrs daily. **Admission** $7; locker
$15; private dressing room $25. **Map** p317 Y2.

There is workout equipment here, of course. But
with rooms such as the Cockpit and a blackout
promo night (where, as the advertisement states,
'you almost have to feel your way around'), it's clear
that Hawk's is no 24-Hour Fitness. Fetish wear is
'greatly encouraged'.

Get Booked.

Nightlife

DJs rule the world… or Vegas at least.

In terms of quality, quantity and diversity, there are few cities in the US with a nightlife scene to rival that of Las Vegas. This is the city where people come to party – whether at music venues, the many bars and lounges, or, specifically, the fabulous and trendy nightclubs that dot the Strip and beyond.

Nightlife entertainment, as with all Vegas entertainment, is cyclical. Hot attractions work until they don't anymore, and then they're replaced by something else. This is especially true for nightclubs, which in the past couple of years have worked overtime to reinvent themselves. In addition to several new, high-profile clubs, Vegas is recasting itself as DJ central ('the new Ibiza' goes the oversaturated comparison). World-famous DJs are taking up residency for yearlong stints or more at places like MGM Grand's fabulous new **Hakkasan** (*see p221*).

And while this is the late-night scene in Sin City, over the last decade Vegas has been figuring out more ways to wrest a bang for its buck – by making sure the party never stops. Witness the preponderance of 'daylife' – daytime poolside parties that begin when the sun comes up (well, often 10am) and continue long into the evening (*see p223* **We Love the Daylife**).

Las Vegas's long-time reputation as the last stop for any musical performer worth their salt is far in the past. Sure, there's not much jazz or blues here. But when you combine the rock, pop, hip hop and country megastars appearing at major casino venues with the ever-increasing gigs in Downtown bars and clubs, it's clear that Sin City is doubling down on its musical image.

Clubs

THE SCENE

When the DJ trend really took hold depends on whom you ask, though many point to Paul Oakenfold's three-year gig at Rain, beginning in 2008. But the date of origin is less important than today's results: DJs are the new Vegas royalty; crowd magnets that reign over the hordes from behind velvet-roped VIP areas.

The success of the Light Group, which runs more than half a dozen venues, and the Angel Management Group, which operates nearly a dozen spots, has resulted in many clubs run in very similar fashion. There are advantages: the firms command enough bargaining power to retain big-name residents (such as Kaskade at the Cosmopolitan's **Marquee** (*see p223*), or on another level, *Jersey Shore*'s Pauly D, who spins

at **Haze** (*see p222*) and other clubs, and clubbers know they can expect certain standards of service. But at the same time, door policies, DJ programming and even venue design have become standardised.

If you're looking for less-mainstream sounds, whether drum 'n' bass, trance or garage rock, a number of weekly promotions at local bars draw their own scenes. Most notable among them is the **Beauty Bar** (*see p164*), where you might find DJs spinning anything from indie rock to vintage soul.

INFORMATION AND TICKETS

For information on what's on, check the free weekly magazines *Seven, Las Vegas Weekly* or *CityLife*. While some venues don't offer advance ticket sales, most of them allow patrons to reserve a table in advance if they're willing to

The Act.

fork out for bottle service. It's also a good idea to speak to your hotel concierge before settling on a venue: they may be able to offer guest list privileges to clubs affiliated with the hotel. Searching out a local party promoter online can often be beneficial; just make sure you understand what you're paying for before forking over any cash.

Men: your power is in your wallets, not in your numbers. Large groups of guys are rarely admitted to clubs; conversely, women still get preferential treatment, often not even having to pay the cover charge. Admission prices listed below are for visitors, and can vary depending on the night; locals with Nevada ID usually pay less. And if you're under 21, forget it: the bouncers here are expert at checking IDs.

★ 1 Oak

Mirage *3400 Las Vegas Boulevard South, at Spring Mountain Road, West of Strip (791 7111, www.lightgroup.com).* **Open** 10.30pm-close Tue, Thur, Fri, Sat. **Admission** $30. **Map** p319, p320 A6.

In its effort to remain relevant in the face of its newer, bigger, hipper competitors on the Strip, the Mirage couldn't have done any better than the opening of this West Coast branch of New York hotspot, 1 Oak. Since its debut in the spring of 2013, the club has hosted a veritable *Who's Who* of A-listers: performers and attendees alike. Guest musicians like Flo Rida, Snoop Dog and Kayne West have all graced its stage, while others, like the ever-controversial Chris Brown, have merely partied down here. Want to see and be seen? No need to look elsewhere.

★ The Act

Palazzo *3327 Las Vegas Boulevard South, between Sands Avenue & E Flamingo Road, (607 0222, www.theactlv.com).* **Bus** Deuce, *119, 203.* **Open** 10.30pm-4am Wed, Fri; 10.30pm-6am Sat. **Admission** $40 men; $20 women. **Map** p319, p320 B6.

Performance art meets period piece meets burlesque. If you can wrap your head around this unusual combination, you'll have a rough idea of what you will find at unique and edgy the Act, one of the Strip's newest clubs located in the Shoppes at the Palazzo. The brainchild of nightclub designer Simon Hammerstein (creator of the Box in London and New York), The Act is a funky mind-melt, intended to be experienced instead of just witnessed.

The Bank

Bellagio *3600 Las Vegas Boulevard South, at W Flamingo Road, (693 8300, www.thebanklas vegas.com).* **Bus** Deuce, *202.* **Open** 10.30pm-4am Thur-Sun. **Admission** $40 men; $30 women. **Map** p320 A7.

Maybe they should have just called the Bank something more direct, like ATM Machine, or Your Entire Wallet. The upscale club, which features a mix of expensive-sounding hip hop and rock from its resident DJs, has a capacity of 1,000, and that number or more are packed in when one of the frequent celebrity guest hosts is in the house.

Body English

Hard Rock *4455 Paradise Road, at E Harmon Avenue, East of Strip (693 5555, www.body english.com).* **Bus** *108.* **Open** 10pm-4am Fri-Sun. **Admission** $30 men; $20 women. **Map** p320 C7.

Hard Rock nightspot Body English was retooled in late 2012 following a four-year hiatus, much to the delight of its ardent fans. 'Fans' is the operative word here. Visitors to Body English usually fall into one of two camps: love it or hate it. This probably has as much to do with expectations as anything else. The smallish club is not like many of the larger spots you'll find on the Strip, which is fine – it's not on the Strip. But if you're looking for a smaller – and naughtier – experience, this might be right up your alley.

Chateau

Paris *3655 Las Vegas Boulevard South, at E Flamingo Road (776 7777, www.chateau nights.com). Bus Deuce, 202.* **Open** 10pm-4.30am Tue, Fri-Sun. **Admission** $30 men; $20 women. **Map** p320 A7.

Located on the second floor of Paris Las Vegas, the entrance to Chateau Nightclub & Gardens reveals all the expected nightlife amenities, along with attractive outdoor options: a balcony with a view of the Strip and the Bellagio fountain show, which is a rare attraction for clubs in Las Vegas. The sister club of Planet Hollywood's Gallery, Chateau shares its roster of celebrity DJs, reality-show hosts and UFC celeb-brawlers.

Eclipse

Mandalay Bay *3950 Las Vegas Boulevard South, at W Hacienda Avenue (588 5656, www.daylightvegas.com/eclipse). Bus Deuce, 119.* **Open** 10pm-3am Wed (in season). **Admission** $30. **Map** p320 A9.

Follow along closely, because this gets confusing: hotels created 'daylife' poolside parties so the partying wouldn't have to stop. After all, who wants to hit a nightclub at 2pm? So what's the next logical step? Turn a brand-new daylife pool venue into a nighttime pool nightclub after dark. Such is the case with Eclipse, Mandalay Bay's pool/club that goes by the name Daylight while the sun is shining and becomes Eclipse when the moon rises. A large pool abuts the stage, with ample room (the space is 50,000sq ft) for dancing and cabanas on either side. Six LED screens provide patrons good views of some of the hottest spinners in the biz, which so far have included Axwell, Skrillex and Nicky Romero, among others.

★ Gallery

Planet Hollywood *3665 Las Vegas Boulevard South, between E Harmon Avenue & E Flamingo Road (818 3700, www.gallerylv.com). Bus Deuce, 202.* **Open** 10.30pm-4am Mon, Thur-Sat. **Admission** $30. **Map** p320 A9.

Lovers of fine art and the fine female form unite! Both are on display at the appropriately named Gallery Nightclub, located in Planet Hollywood in the middle of the Las Vegas Strip. OK, so the 'artwork' isn't likely to inspire any heated discussions among art history majors, but the vibe is plenty hot nonetheless: case in point, Thursday night's Good Girls Gone Bad, which is bound to create inspiration of one kind or another.

★ Hakkasan

MGM Grand *3799 Las Vegas Boulevard South, at E Tropicana Avenue (891 3838, www.hakkasanlv.com). Bus Deuce, 201.* **Open** 10pm-close Thur-Sun. **Admission** from $40 men; $30 women. **Map** p320 A8.

You really can't compare any other nightclubs in Las Vegas with MGM's newly opened, gigantic Hakkasan because that would be, well, impossible. With multiple levels and room for about 7,000 revellers, Hakkasan puts the 'mega' in megaclub. To fill this aeroplane-hangar-like space when the club opened in the spring of 2013, MGM execs signed on

ARTS & ENTERTAINMENT

Gallery.

some of the hottest DJs, including Calvin Harris, DJ Tiesto, Steve Aoki and Deadmau5 for residencies. The strategy has worked. All 80,000sq ft of space is packed – from the Ling Ling Lounge to the main dancefloor – and for good reason.

Haze

Aria, CityCenter *3730 Las Vegas Boulevard South, at W Harmon Avenue (693 8300, www.hazelasvegas.com). Bus Deuce.* **Open** 10.30pm-4am Thur-Sat. **Admission** $40 men; $30 women. **Map** p320 A8.

Expect your recollection of the night before to be a little, well, hazy after a good night at Haze in CityCenter's Aria casino-hotel. The music runs the gauntlet, with guest hosts ranging from Missy Elliott to *Jersey Shore* demi-celeb Pauly D. A queue of black-clad beauties indicates you are near the entrance to the bi-level, subterranean space with a Manhattan feel to it. With booths overlooking the dancefloor, the club is designed to feel close, intimate and voyeuristic.

Hyde

Bellagio *3600 Las Vegas Boulevard South, at W Flamingo Road (693 8700, www.hyde bellagio.com). Bus Deuce, 202.* **Open** 5pm-1am Mon, Wed, Thur, Sun; 5pm-4am Tue, Fri, Sat. **Admission** $40 men; $30 women. **Map** p320 A7.

A unique venue that overlooks Bellagio's fountains, Hyde is something of a rarity among the Vegas nightclub set. The club's floor-to-ceiling windows offer a picturesque view of the dancing water, and in the comparatively early evening hours (5-11pm), the vibe is loungey and small-plate dishes from Bellagio restaurant Circo are served. As the evening wanes and the night heats up, prepare for a parade of beautiful-people VIPs gyrating to beautiful sounds.

LAX

Luxor *3900 Las Vegas Boulevard South, at W Hacienda Avenue (262 4529, www.laxthe nightclub.com). Bus Deuce, 119, 201.* **Open** 10pm-4am Wed-Sat. **Admission** $30 men; $20 women. **Map** p320 A9.

It would hardly be surprising if someone discovered a secret portal directly from Las Vegas's McCarran International Airport to LAX. Not the Los Angeles airport – the nightclub at the Luxor casino-resort. It's that crowded. Such demi-celebs as Snooki from reality show *Jersey Shore* keep packing them in to the club, which has a gothic feel, deep within the Strip's famous pyramid.

Light

Mandalay Bay *3950 Las Vegas Boulevard South, at W Hacienda Avenue (632 7777, www.thelight lasvegas.com). Bus Deuce, 119.* **Open** 11pm-4am Fri, Sat. **Admission** from $40 men; $20 women. **Map** p320 A9.

This club of the same name used to be located inside Bellagio, before operators the Light Group teamed with Cirque du Soleil (in that company's first-ever nightclub venture) and moved the show down the road to Mandalay. Tiered balconies surround an intimate dancefloor, while DJs spin from

Hakkasan. See p221.

ARTS & ENTERTAINMENT

a small, elevated stage smack in the middle of it. For added effect, Cirque performers wow the crowd, crawling across sprawling walls of LED screens or swinging from the ceiling like the proverbial residents of an asylum. We mean that in a good way.

Marquee

Cosmopolitan *3708 Las Vegas Boulevard South, at W Harmon Avenue (333 9000, www.marqueelasvegas.com). Bus Deuce.* **Open** 10pm-5am Mon, Thur; 9.30pm-5am Fri, Sat. **Admission** $50 men; $30 women. **Map** p320 A7.

The first Vegas club to integrate nightlife and 'daylife', Marquee established itself as an instant favourite with visitors and locals, with three dis-

tinctly atmospheric rooms, including the Library, a chilled space stocked with hundreds of Vegas-centric books; the main room, with an ear-melting sound system; and the lower-level Boom Box, a separate club-within-a-club. If you can't wait until night descends to get your party on, queue up for Marquee's Dayclub, which is open 10am to sunset every day (seasonally).

Moon

Palms *4321 W Flamingo Road, at S Valley View Boulevard (942 6832, www.palms.com/ nightlife/moon). Bus 104, 202.* **Open** 10.30pm-4am Tue, Thur-Sat. **Admission** $30. **Map** p317 X3.

In space, no one can hear you scream. However, they sure can see you dance, at least if they happen

---

We Love the Daylife

Poolside concerts and parties pick up where the nightlife leaves off.

Sometimes – and this is especially true in Vegas – you just don't want the party to stop. The evening is swinging, the music is thumping, the drink is flowing, and the members of the opposite sex... well, let's just say they never looked so good.

But even in a town where the action never stops the sun eventually rises, which usually has a way of casting a pall over even the most raging party. More than a decade ago, the money-mad masterminds of Las Vegas realised this didn't have to be so. 'How much better it would be', they must have thought, 'if we could keep the party going 24 hours a day'. Instead of ending the party when the light breaks, how about rebranding it and changing the venue – at least during the summer months, anyway? And so was born the concept of 'daylife'.

First on the scene was the Hard Rock, with its now-legendary **Sunday Rehab** pool parties (693 5555, www.rehablv.com), which have just celebrated their tenth season. Swim-up blackjack, DJs and celebs, frozen drinks and hard, hard bodies; there's a reason people return to Rehab year after year.

It didn't take long for other properties to recognise a good thing when they saw it. Within a few years, everybody was doing it.

Wet Republic at the MGM Grand (891 3563, www.wetrepublic.com), for example, isn't so much a pool party as a pool landmark. There are five pools, two of them saltwater; the hottest DJs imported

by way of Hakkasan (*see p221*); and a South Beach vibe that keeps on grooving. What else do you need?

Despite being in one of the newest hotels, and therefore one of the newer daylife entrants, the Cosmo (698 7000, www.cosmopolitanlas vegas.com) was an early adopter in blending nighttime activities seamlessly with those during the day.

Over at the Venetian, **Tao Beach** (388 8588, www.taobeach.com), part of the Tao nightclub/restaurant/pool party triumverate, has an Indonesia-escape theme. Chill out in one of the air-conditioned cabanas while sampling plates from Tao's menu, or skip straight to the exotic cocktails.

Who says work can't be fun? Kick back on one the chaise lounges at **Liquid Day Club & Lounge** (Aria, 693 8300, www. arialasvegas.com) – the pool area is Wi-Fi ready – and log on to your office email. Your boss will be none the wiser.

No swimsuit? No problem! Tan those 'sun-don't-shine' spots on your body at the Mirage's European-style day club, **Bare** (791 7442, www.barepoollv.com). Nab one of the day beds or reserve a cabana, while you groove to a Bare DJ.

Filed under the 'everything old is new again' category, is Mandalay's ingenious new spot, **Daylight** (632 7777, www.daylight vegas.com). This brand-new pool doubles as the Eclipse (*see p221*) at night, and during the day packs them in as Daylight.

Ahh, Vegas... Life here's a beach, isn't it?

Rain.

to be looking through Moon's retractable roof. The club's space-age design has a retro feel, but its location 53 storeys up in the Palms' Fantasy Tower offers incredible views from its two balconies and bead-curtained, floor-to-ceiling windows. The music can be a bit of a mixed bag, ranging from top-40 remixes to hip hop/rock mash-ups and occasional house nights.

Pure
Caesars Palace *3570 Las Vegas Boulevard South, at W Flamingo Road (731 7873, www.purethenightclub.com). Bus Deuce, 202.* **Open** 10pm-4am Tue, Fri-Sun. **Admission** $30. **Map** p320 A7.
Soon after opening in 2005, Pure became the hottest megaclub in Las Vegas, and it's remained so several years down the line. Its multiple levels, including a massive terrace overlooking the Strip, are always packed with patrons vying for a glimpse of Hollywood celebrities hosting parties in the labyrinthine venue.

Rain
Palms *4321 W Flamingo Road, at S Valley View Boulevard (942 6832, www.palms.com/nightlife/rain). Bus 104, 202.* **Open** 11pm-4am Fri, Sat. **Admission** $25. **Map** p317 X3.
One of the first Las Vegas clubs built in an oversized, industrial style, back in 2001, Rain closed for several months in late 2012 for a much-needed makeover. Now, facelift in place, Rain is back to doing what it does best: with non-stop dance music

and eyebrow-searing pyrotechnics best witnessed from one of the upstairs private cabanas overlooking all the action.

Surrender
Encore *3131 Las Vegas Boulevard South, between E Desert Inn Road & Sands Avenue (770 3300, www.surrendernightclub. com). Bus Deuce, 108, 203.* **Open** 10.30pm-4am Wed, Fri, Sat. **Admission** from $40. **Map** p319, p320 B6.
Surrender is more of an intimate night-nook than a full-blown nightclub – which is just fine with everyone who finds their way here. From the 90ft snake, coiled and embedded into the wall behind the bar, to the dimly lit cabanas outside next to the pool, Surrender is that kind of place that makes you want to give it all up.

Tao
Venetian *3355 Las Vegas Boulevard South, between Sands Avenue & E Flamingo Road, (388 8588, www.taolasvegas.com). Bus Deuce, 119, 203.* **Open** 10pm-5am Thur-Sat. **Admission** $30. **Map** p319, p320 B6.
This NYC import rivals Pure as the favourite party-spot of celebs visiting Vegas. And who can blame them? The Zen- and Buddhist-themed decor is intoxicating, and the multiple lounges and VIP areas lend an air of exclusivity to the venue. Other attractions include an adjacent gourmet Asian fusion restaurant, a cosy Strip-facing patio, a rooftop pool party in summer, gorgeous bathing

ladies (really) and some of the town's hottest house DJs, though music is more mainstream at weekends.

Tryst

Wynn Las Vegas *3131 Las Vegas Boulevard South, between E Desert Inn Road & Sands Avenue (770 7300, www.trystlasvegas.com). Bus Deuce, 108, 203.* **Open** 10.30pm-4am Thur-Sat. **Admission** $30. **Map** p319, p320 B6.

Descend the stairs and follow a passage through a womb-like hallway into a dark, sensual space – plush, velvety and supremely inviting. The dancefloor extends outside to overlook a private lagoon and a 94ft waterfall, with waterside bottle service and corset-wearing servers. A VIP nook with bookshelf-lined walls completes the space. Sounds like the perfect place for a… well, the name says it all.

XS

Encore *3131 Las Vegas Boulevard South, between E Desert Inn Road & Sands Avenue, (770 0097, www.xslasvegas.com). Bus Deuce, 108, 203.* **Open** 10.30pm-4am Mon, Sun; 9.30pm-4am Fri, Sat; . **Admission** $30 men; $20 women. **Map** p319 B5.

Steve Wynn doesn't do things by halves, and the opulent gold-plated nightclub at his newest casino-hotel sets a new standard of luxe. The 13,000sq ft indoor-outdoor space is gilded with rotating gold chandeliers, golden moulds of cocktail waitresses and balconies surrounding the huge dancefloor. The effect is Donald Trump's dream nightclub. Still, all that shimmering opulence might be a little hard on the eyes, but the patrons sure aren't. Book your spot well in advance if you want to have a look.

Music

Big-name stars passing through town tend to perform at the sizeable concert halls and clubs inside the Strip's resorts. Smaller bands and local groups may play less glamorous venues, but the crowds are no less enthusiastic. Hotel-casinos are realising and capitalising on this. The Cosmopolitan, for instance, hosted a two-week concert series at the **Boulevard Pool** that featured groups all playing California's Coachella festival. Over at the Hard Rock, **Vinyl** – a new, smaller alternative to the Joint – hosts indie acts and comedians most nights.

INFORMATION AND TICKETS

The free weekly papers have gig information, or check online at www.vegas.com or www.yourlocalscene.com. Most small rock and jazz venues are restricted to those aged 21 and over; age restrictions vary at larger-scale casino venues .

Tickets can generally be bought directly from venues and/or through **Ticketmaster** (*see p193*), and prices vary wildly. Shows in bars rarely come with a cover of more than $10, and many are free. But tickets for shows at the bigger casino venues can run into three figures, with no price too high for some shows by big names at the **MGM Grand Garden Arena**.

CASINO VENUES

Don't let the rather safe programme of music offered at the Colosseum in Caesars Palace put you off Vegas's grand casino venues. The

ARTS & ENTERTAINMENT

XS.

MGM Grand, Mandalay Bay, Hard Rock, Palms and Cosmopolitan all house credible concert venues that showcase touring acts in most genres on an almost nightly basis.

★ Boulevard Pool

Cosmopolitan *3708 Las Vegas Boulevard South, at W Hacienda Avenue (698 7000, www.cosmopolitanlasvegas.com). Bus Deuce.* **Tickets** $25-$200. **Map** p320 A7.

The Cosmopolitan started hosting live musical acts at Marquee before it realised what a gem it had in the Boulevard Pool. The logistics took some retooling, but the hotel-casino now features regular bands on a specially designed stage that overlooks its fourth-floor open-air pool. The music is varied – Hot Chip, Gary Clark Jr, MGMT – and the sound system (and experience) is beyond superb. Enjoy top-notch music overlooking the Strip, and don't worry about the view: the bands are broadcast on to a four-storey screen adjacent to the pool. Best Las Vegas music experience, hands-down.

House of Blues

Mandalay Bay *3950 Las Vegas Boulevard South, at W Hacienda Avenue (632 7600, www.houseof blues.com). Bus Deuce, 119.* **Tickets** from $20. **Map** p320 A9.

Though this is just one of several folk-art-filled locations across the US, the House of Blues' exciting mix of up-and-coming and established artists makes it feel like a home-grown champion. The multi-level main floor is surrounded by three bars and tiered balcony seating. Acts range from Carlos Santana, who did a residency here, to kitschy cover bands to indie stalwarts like the Flaming Lips. Sundays feature the popular Gospel Brunch.

Joint

Hard Rock *4455 Paradise Road, at E Harmon Avenue, East of Strip (693 5000 information, 1-800 745 3000 tickets, www.thejointlasvegas.com). Bus 108.* **Tickets** from $30. **Map** p320 C7.

Renovated and expanded by 1,000 seats in 2009 – the capacity is 4,000 – the Joint remains a popular mid-sized rock venue in Las Vegas, although its cracks are starting to show. There used to be a time when its stage was the only home in Vegas for rock music. Everyone from the Rolling Stones to Paul McCartney to the Killers played there. Now it's the resident home for '80s hair-metal group Motley Crue, with occasional shows thrown in by bands as diverse as Nine Inch Nails and the Pet Shop Boys.

Mandalay Bay Beach

Mandalay Bay *3950 Las Vegas Boulevard South, at W Hacienda Avenue (632 7777 information, 1-800 745 3000 tickets, www.mandalaybay.com). Bus Deuce, 119.* **Tickets** from $35. **Map** p320 A9.

Las Vegas's clement weather makes Mandalay Bay's man-made beach ideal for outdoor gigs, and

its summer concert series draws in a variety of crowd-pleasing favourites from the present, such as Ziggy Marley and Daughtry, as well as themed concerts featuring ageing artists of the past (Flock of Seagulls, Bow Wow Wow, Sugar Ray).

Mandalay Bay Events Center

Mandalay Bay *3950 Las Vegas Boulevard South, at W Hacienda Avenue (632 7777 information, 1-800 745 3000 tickets, www.mandalaybay.com). Bus Deuce, 119.* **Tickets** from $30.50. **Map** p320 A9.

Though this massive arena isn't specifically a music venue per se (it also hosts trade fairs, boxing matches and awards ceremonies), it draws some of the biggest international musical acts, from Iron Maiden to Brad Paisley and Selena Gomez. Getting in and out of the Events Center (and, for that matter, the casino) becomes a logistical nightmare during big crowd-pullers, so plan accordingly.

MGM Grand Garden Arena

MGM Grand *3799 Las Vegas Boulevard South, at E Tropicana Avenue (891 7777 information, 1-877 880 0880 tickets, www.mgmgrand.com). Bus Deuce, 201.* **Tickets** from $40. **Map** p320 A8.

This massive arena showcases the world's rock and pop royalty, from Black Sabbath to Beyoncé, tas well as events such as the Billboard Music Awards, mixed martial arts competitions and pre-season NBA match-ups. If you enjoy entertainment spectacles with 15,000 other people, the Grand Garden is the place for you. Still, it's unlikely you'll catch Drake, Justin Timberlake or Bon Jovi playing elsewhere in Vegas.

Pearl

Palms *4321 W Flamingo Road, at S Valley View Boulevard, West of Strip (942 7777 information, 944 3200 tickets, www.palmspearl.com). Bus 104, 202.* **Tickets** from $25. **Map** p317 X3.

Upon opening, the Palms appeared very keen to steal the Hard Rock's thunder: first with its boutique accommodation, then with its numerous rooftop clubs and finally with this music venue, which stages many big-name acts. With a capacity ranging from 1,100 (seated) to 2,500 (standing), the Pearl comes with an intimacy rarely found in a venue of this size, whether you're watching Marc Anthony, Journey or Jeff Beck.

★ Vinyl

Hard Rock *4455 Paradise Road, at E Harmon Avenue, East of Strip (693 5000 information, 1-800 745 3000 tickets, www.hardrockhotel.com). Bus 108.* **Tickets** Free-$98. **Map** p320 C7.

Looking for a more intimate – and diverse – experience than the acts at the Joint? You'd do well to check out the Hard Rock's newer club, Vinyl. Opened in 2012, this 650-seater hosts everything under the sun, from heavy metal mariachi act Metalachi to Courtney

Essential Las Vegas Albums

The brightest stars have lit up the Vegas stage – and made a record.

LIVE AT THE SANDS
THE RAT PACK (1963)

Recorded at the Copa Room in the Sands Hotel – site of the Rat Pack's famous 'summits' – this collection contains pretty much all the essential songs by Frankie, Dino and Sammy Davis Jr: 'Luck Be a Lady', 'The Lady Is a Tramp', 'I Only Have Eyes for You' and more, plus the comedic dialogue the Pack was known for.

I AM... YOURS: AN
INTIMATE PERFORMANCE
AT WYNN LAS VEGAS
BEYONCÉ (2009)

This small-stage show was a once-in-a-lifetime experience for those who were there. For the rest of us, there's this recording: a sonic rendering of Beyoncé at her best, taking us through her entire career, from Destiny's Child to 'Single Ladies'.

LIVE IN LAS VEGAS
TOM JONES (1969)

We could just as easily have picked Wayne Newton's *Mr. Las Vegas!*, another recording by a onetime Vegas mainstay who has since finished with this city. Jones wins out for vocal showmanship alone, Both performers had long runs here and these albums – from early in their Vegas careers – demonstrate why.

ELVIS IN PERSON AT THE
INTERNATIONAL HOTEL
ELVIS PRESLEY (1970)

Elvis was no stranger to Vegas when this album was recorded, although he had yet to become completely enmeshed in it. We find him at the International (later the Hilton, now the LVH), site of his iconic run of sold-out shows. Opening with 'Blue Suede Shows' and tracking some of his greatest hits, this is classic live Elvis.

THE LAS VEGAS STORY
THE GUN CLUB (1984)

Not a Vegas soundtrack in name alone, the psychobilly LA group behind this album had been writing twitchy, country-tinged tunes shot full of punk attitude for several years by the time it was released. Full of nervous, skittish energy trapped under an endless desert sky, *The Las Vegas Story* thrums and throbs like the city itself.

HEAVEN OR LAS VEGAS
COCTEAU TWINS (1990)

Vegas will always mean the suit-and-martini Rat Pack era to some; or the spectacle of the late 1970s, with Elvis or Liberace. For others, though, it will always be a fever dream – a trippy, surreal, disconnected experience. This is as true now as it was when *Heaven or Las Vegas* was made, as it was for Hunter S Thompson. This album is for them.

ARTS & ENTERTAINMENT

Love to local crooners. Shows are often free, and if you're not in the mood for music, check out bad-boy comedian Andrew Dice Clay, whose shtick is sure to offend even the most hardened sensibilities.

NON-CASINO VENUES

What with the emergence of bands like the Killers and Imagine Dragons, the uninitiated might be forgiven for assuming that the local music scene in Vegas is thriving. In truth, while it's not dead, its acts have always had to compete against a host of other entertainment. Finding venues willing to host smaller bands has always been a problem. Why feature music when video-poker machines make so much more money?

But that may be changing, thanks to Downtown's revitalisation. The opening of the **Beauty Bar** (*see p164*), which stages frequent indie rock shows alongside its DJ nights, coincided with plans for the Fremont East Entertainment District, which has grown almost exponentially. The Beat Coffeehouse frequently features music – often impressive locals on its open-mic nights.

★ Beat Coffeehouse & Records

520 E Fremont Street, at 6th Street, Downtown (385 2328, www.thebeatlv.com). Bus Deuce & all

Bunkhouse Saloon.

BTC-bound buses. **Open** 7am-midnight Mon-Fri; 9am-midnight Sat; 9am-5pm Sun. *Shows* times vary. **Admission** free-$10. **Map** p318 D1.

Part coffeehouse, eaterie, bar, vinyl record store and music venue, the Beat is Las Vegas's epicentre for all (anti-establishment) things Downtown. Local musicians play on the stage-less floor at the front of the store, while their fans and friends spill out on to the sidewalk of Fremont Street. Cheap food and strong coffee is available during the day; after 7pm even cheaper beer is served.

Bunkhouse Saloon

124 S 11th Street, at S Fremont Street, Downtown (384 4536, www.bunkhouselv.com). Bus 108, 207. **Open** 24hrs daily. *Shows* times vary. **Admission** free-$15. **Map** p318 E2.

This former country bar closed in the summer of 2013 for a makeover. While that wasn't welcome news to Bunkhouse fans, who liked the taxidermy-and-cowboy decor, the management promised the redo wouldn't sacrifice BH's charm. It's still too early to tell, but as long as the Bunkhouse keeps up the steady diet of fabulous music nightly, we'll be OK with it.

Cheyenne Saloon

3103 N Rancho Drive, at W Cheyenne Avenue, North-west Las Vegas (645 4139). Bus 106, 218. **Open** 24hrs daily. **Admission** free-$13.

If you're looking for hard rock, you could do worse than to make the trip out here for some cheap beer and loud music. The stage is sizeable, the sound system is impressively robust, and the sunken dance floor is an unexpected touch that makes this rough-edged strip-mall dive a local favourite.

★ Double Down Saloon

4640 Paradise Road, at E Naples Drive, East of the Strip (791 5775, www.doubledownsaloon.com). Bus 108. **Admission** free. **Open** 24hrs daily.

Dive-y atmosphere, free admission and live punk bands make the Double Down one of the coolest venues in Vegas. Bands that have graced its stage include acts like TSOL, Dickies and the Supersuckers. It's also known for its jukebox filled with ska, surf, psychobilly and punk tunes, as well as tasty alcoholic concoctions such as Ass Juice.

JAZZ, BLUES & ACOUSTIC MUSIC

Given the fact that Las Vegas is widely perceived to have an overabundance of lounge acts, its jazz scene is surprisingly slight. Most casino lounges have been overrun by pop cover-bands ; those that haven't offer the kind of light jazz of which only Kenny G would be proud. Still, there are a few standard-bearers: the **Bootlegger Bistro** (*see p154*) welcomes renowned jazz pianist Guy Mancuso on Tuesdays through Thursdays, as well as other acts throughout the week.

Performing Arts

Move away from the Strip for a different kind of show.

Theatre in Las Vegas is dominated by the extended-engagement productions on the Strip: much larger than life, and always condensed for tourist audiences who are presumed not to speak English, and certainly not to be in the market for three hours of Brecht. You'll find little in the way of intricate storylines or even two-act structures in these bank-busting shows, but the levels of talent and professionalism can make for an engrossing spectacle.

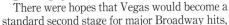

There were hopes that Vegas would become a standard second stage for major Broadway hits, but less-than-stellar sales saw the arrival and departure of *Avenue Q, Hairspray, The Producers*, Monty Python's *Spamalot* and *Mamma Mia!* (which lasted five years at Mandalay Bay). In their place are the established Cirque and Cirque-esque spectacles, and dependable acts such as Celine Dion, and Donny and Marie Osmond. (For these and other casino-based shows, *see p78-131*.)

The big news for lovers of classical music is the opening of the **Smith Center** (*see below*) in 2012. Set in 60 acres of parkland called Symphony Park, the centre has hosted serious theatre and is the new home of the Las Vegas Philharmonic.

ARTS & ENTERTAINMENT

MAJOR VENUES
Smith Center for the Performing Arts
361 Symphony Park Avenue, at S Grand Central Parkway, Downtown (749 2012, www.thesmith center.com). Bus SDX & all BTC-bound buses. See p231 **The Next Stage**.

INFORMATION & TICKETS
Las Vegas Weekly and the 'Neon' supplement in Friday's *Las Vegas Review-Journal* carry classical music, theatre and dance listings. For advance tickets, which aren't always necessary, contact the theatres directly rather than an outside agent such as Ticketmaster.

CLASSICAL MUSIC
It used to be that the University of Las Vegas (895 2787, http://pac.unlv.edu) was key to classical music in Vegas. While the university still plays a crucial role, providing a home for the **Charles Vanda Master Series** as well as a new chamber music programme, some of the activity has moved Downtown to the **Smith Center for the Performing Arts** (*see above*). The Las Vegas Philharmonic,

for example, which used to call UNLV home, now performs at the Smith Center.

Las Vegas Philharmonic
Smith Center for the Performing Arts, for listings see left (258 5438 information, 749 2000 tickets, www.lvphil.com). **Tickets** $25-$94. **Map** p318 C2.
Since its beginnings in 1998, Las Vegas's resident orchestra has gradually gained recognition under music director Harold Weller. The Phil is celebrating its 15th season, and its repertoire has remained largely highbrow, with new works occasionally commissioned from contemporary composers. Aside from the concerts at Smith Center, the Phil also performs pop classics to family audiences in annual recitals timed to coincide with holidays such as Independence Day.

DANCE COMPANIES
Nevada Ballet Theatre
243 2623, www.nevadaballet.org. **Tickets** vary.
Associated with UNLV, the Nevada Ballet Theatre remains Las Vegas's only fully professional ballet company and training academy, favouring classical

works and other time-tested pieces likely to entertain even complete neophytes. However, artistic director James Canfield, formerly of the Joffrey Ballet, is spearheading a push to present new work and forms in the hope of attracting new audiences. Shows are held at different venues around the city, with many landing at the Smith Center for the Performing Arts (see p229).

UNLV Dance Theatre
4505 S Maryland Parkway, between E Flamingo Road & E Tropicana Avenue, University District (895 3827, dance.unlv.edu). Bus 109, 202. **Tickets** free-$25. **Map** p317 Y3.

UNLV's dance programme features a mix of performances by faculty, students and guest artists. Classical ballet and modern works are both represented, with productions held at the Artemus Ham Concert Hall and the Judy Bayley Theatre.

THEATRE

Off-Strip community theatre in Las Vegas lives very much in the shadow of the big-ticket blockbusters, but it's there if you know where to look. Companies such as **Super Summer Theatre** and the well-established **Las Vegas Little Theatre** stage high-quality productions; the LVLT has both a 155-capacity main stage and the smaller Fischer Black Box at its disposal, and occasionally even rents the latter to outside companies. For more alternative fare, a number of fringy, ambitious production companies come and go, among them **Onyx Theatre** and Downtown's **Cockroach Theatre Company**.

Tucked away within the sizeable **UNLV** campus is a thriving and forward-thinking theatre department. Major productions play in the 550-seat **Judy Bayley Theatre**; smaller shows are staged at the more intimate **Paul Harris Theatre** and the **Black Box**, which is also used for student productions and many of the more low-key productions put together by the **Nevada Conservatory Theatre**. Alongside the university's theatre programme, UNLV's Department of Dance is responsible for many of the more worthwhile dance performances, both from UNLV students and visiting troupes.

The city's library system contains three modern, comfortable spaces. The theatres at **Summerlin Library** (1771 Inner Circle, West Las Vegas, 507 3860, www.lvccld.org) and **West Las Vegas Library** (951 W Lake Mead Boulevard, North Las Vegas, 507 3980, www.lvccld.org) both have proscenium stages and seat roughly 300; the auditorium at **Clark County Library** (see p297) features a thrust stage and seats 400. Details of performances can be found at www.lvccld.org.

THEATRE COMPANIES & SMALLER VENUES

Cockroach Theatre Company
Art Square Theatre, 1025 S 1st Street, at W Charleston Boulevard, Downtown (818 3422, www.cockroachtheatre.com). Bus Deuce, 108, 206. **Tickets** $10-$20. **Map** p318 C3.

This nomadic theatre group has been staging offbeat productions since 2002. Their roaming ways recently came to a stop after settling in this space in Downtown's arts district. Recent productions included Bekah Brunstetter's *You May Go Now* and Arthur Miller's *Death of a Salesman*.

Las Vegas Academy Theatre
315 S 7th Street, at Bridger Avenue, Downtown (799 7800, www.lvacademytheatre.org). Bus Deuce & all BTC-bound buses. **Tickets** $7-$25. **Map** p318 D2.

The site of the city's first high school was nearly razed in the early 1990s. Instead, it found new life as the Las Vegas Academy of the Arts, a high school devoted to performing and visual disciplines. The LVA's Academy Theatre hosts impressive shows in a variety of genres: recent seasons included productions of *Sweeney Todd*, *Cats*, *Miss Saigon* and *The Grapes of Wrath*. These kids are far better than they should be.

Las Vegas Little Theatre
3920 Schiff Drive, at Spring Mountain Road & S Valley View Boulevard, South-west Las Vegas (362 7996, www.lvlt.org). Bus 104, 203. **Tickets** $15-$24; $14-$21 reductions. **Map** p317 X3.

Las Vegas's oldest community theatre company regularly hosts sell-out productions at its main stage and the Fischer Black Box. The companion Insomniac Project occasionally features less-mainstream works; fledgling companies also sometimes rent the building for their productions and to hold workshops.

★ Onyx Theatre
Commercial Center, 953 E Sahara Avenue, between S 6th Street & S Maryland Parkway (732 7225, www.onyxtheatre.com). Bus SX, 109. **Tickets** $10-$25. **Map** p317 Y2.

Another member of Vegas's growing underground theatre scene, Onyx hosts productions in a variety of styles, from burlesque and improv to traditional stagings such as an excellent recent production of *The Glass Menagerie*. If you're looking for something quirky and wonderful, seek this company out.

Rainbow Company
Charleston Heights Arts Center, 801 S Brush Street, at W Charleston Boulevard, Summerlin (229 6553, www.rainbowcompany.org). **Tickets** $7; $3-$5 reductions.

This youth-theatre group stages about a half-dozen family-friendly productions each year. Shows are staged at the Charleston Heights Arts Center.

★ Super Summer Theatre
Spring Mountain Ranch State Park, Red Rock Canyon (594 7529, www.supersummertheatre. org). No bus. **Tickets** $12-$20.
Super Summer Theatre is staged in the coolest place in town – quite literally. On a summer evening, the temperature at the outdoor stage in Red Rock Canyon is a good 20 degrees below that of the sweltering city. Complete with looming rock walls and flittering bats, this outdoor amphitheatre is an appealingly novel place to catch a musical production – the 20-minute sunset drive from the city is as moving and dramatic as anything onstage. The season runs from June to August (bring your bug spray and, yes, a sweater) and usually features three or four populist shows performed in rotation; most of the leading performers are veterans of Strip revues. Patrons rent chairs or spread out on blankets with picnic baskets; get

there early for a good spot. Tickets are available from the UNLV ticket centre (*see below*).

UNLV Theatre Department
4505 S Maryland Parkway, between E Flamingo Road & E Tropicana Avenue, University District (895 3011, www.unlv.edu/theatre). Bus 109, 202. **Tickets** $25-$35. **Map** p317 Y3.
Together with the Nevada Conservatory Theatre, a an ambitious crew that includes seasoned pros from all over the world as collaborators, UNLV presents a large spread of productions in spring and autumn in the Judy Bayley Theatre. Great productions can also be found in the Paul Harris Theatre and the Black Box, where the MFA playwriting programme workshops pieces by students and faculty. An annual series of student-penned one-act plays in spring and autumn typically yields some memorable stuff.

The Next Stage
The Smith Center injects some cultural cachet into Sin City.

Perhaps it began with the fine-dining explosion in the 1990s. You could certainly say the Bellagio sped it along. One by one the feather-and-boa shows packed up, and were replaced largely by Cirque du Soleil productions and other sophisticated entertainments. Fast-forward a decade into the new century and witness the arrival of CityCenter and hotels like Aria and the Cosmopolitan. What next, hotels without casinos? Wait...

Las Vegas, it seems, has been – gulp! – growing up. This once anything-goes, completely permissive frontier town is gaining some cultural sophistication. Don't believe it? Then look no further than Downtown's Smith Center for the Performing Arts.

Located just across the street from the new city hall, the Smith Center (*see p229*) is the first venue of its kind in Las Vegas. Designed to put Vegas on the same cultural playing field as similarly sized cities, the Smith Center has done that and then some. Since opening in March 2012, the 2,050-seat theatre has hosted major touring productions ranging from *The Color Purple* to *Wicked*, and a lot more in between.

In addition to the larger theatre, Smith Center also has two 250-seaters, the Cabaret Jazz Theater, an intimate space for music and other performances overlooking Symphony Park, and a studio theatre, frequently home to performances by the Nevada Ballet Theatre (*see p229*).

In addition to the centre's larger Broadway shows in the 2013 season, such as *Les Misérables*, *Evita* and *The Book of Mormon*, music from artists as varied as Willie Nelson, Buddy Guy and the Kronos Quartet is the norm here. Throw in the occasional eclectic speaker (actor Alan Alda, for example), and you have an line-up that appeals to a broad audience. What's not to love?

For a city that values its entertainment value, the Smith Center is long overdue. It's hard to imagine Bugsy Siegel ever envisioned Las Vegas visitors sitting down to chamber music – this isn't your grandpappy's cigar-chompin', fistful-of-dollars wagering, showgirl-grabbing cowtown anymore.

Sport & Fitness

A sporting chance.

Far be it from us to detract from the enjoyment of betting on your team – a predictably popular pastime in this town – but getting your heart rate pumping from sideline enthusiasm doesn't count as exercise. Happily, the word 'sports' isn't always followed by the word 'book' in Las Vegas: there are plenty of opportunities in and around the city for watching and taking part in an array of games. That said, Vegas remains the largest US city without either a major-league team or a major-league-quality sporting arena.

THE POLITICS OF SPORT

During his tenure, Mayor Oscar Goodman appeared determined to bring a major-league team to the city, and he didn't seem fussy about which sport got here first. In 2005, he wooed the Florida Marlins baseball team; the following year, in the wake of Hurricane Katrina, the suddenly homeless New Orleans Saints of the NFL seemed another possibility. And in 2007, Vegas even managed to host the NBA All-Star Game. But neither the Marlins nor the Saints made the leap, and NBA commissioner David Stern then announced that basketball wouldn't be returning to Sin City unless or until a major-league-calibre arena is built.

THE FIGHTING SPIRIT

For now, the only options for spectators not keen on auto racing are minor-league or college sports. And there's always – always – **mixed martial arts** (MMA), which also goes by the name 'ultimate fighting': the no-holds-barred cage-match bashes that have caught on big-time worldwide. The violent sport/spectacle has made Vegas its unofficial home, and many of its major bouts are broadcast from here.

GETTING ACTIVE

The choices are broader if you're keen to get active. Bowling, tennis, swimming, cycling and horse riding are all popular options, and Vegas is packed with excellent health clubs and spas. And despite being in the middle of the desert, the city is dotted with world-class golf courses. Further out, **Red Rock Canyon** (*see p348*) is good for hiking, cycling and rock climbing, and **Lake Mead** (*see p246*) is great for fishing and

even scuba diving. Indeed, one of the many peculiarities about Las Vegas is that you can go water skiing (on Lake Mead) and snow skiing (at Mount Charleston) on the same day and still be back at the hotel for dinner, at least if you're prepared to get up miserably early and don't mind returning home exhausted.

Outside the inferno-like summer months, the climate here is pleasant and sunny. Be sure to drink plenty of water and load up on sunscreen. In summer, plan outdoor activities for early in the day to avoid the midday sun.

SPECTATOR SPORTS

Auto racing

With two paved ovals, a dirt course and a drag strip, the 1,500-acre **Las Vegas Motor Speedway** (7000 Las Vegas Boulevard North, 644 4444, www.lvms.com) reverberates with events throughout the year, among them the VW frenzy that is October's **Bugorama**. The biggest is the **NASCAR 400 Nextel Cup** race in March, which draws more than 150,000 fans to Las Vegas (and, irony of ironies, creates huge traffic jams to and from the event).

Baseball

The AAA affiliate of the **New York Mets**, the **Las Vegas 51s** (www.lv51.com), plays 72 games between April and September at **Cashman Field** (850 Las Vegas Boulevard North, at Washington Avenue, Downtown, 386 7100). Although the 51s is among the most consistently successful teams in the

---

INSIDE TRACK
CALLING ALL ALIENS

The Las Vegas 51s are named after Nevada's mysterious and legendary alien home base, Area 51 (*see pp256-257*).

Pacific Coast League, the 10,000-seat stadium is generally about half-full, and tickets ($8-$13) are usually available on the gate. The ballpark opens in March with an exhibition game featuring major-league stars.

Basketball

If this weren't Vegas, you might get away with saying the **UNLV Runnin' Rebels** (www.unlvrebels.com) are the only game in town. The stars of the HBO Sports documentary film *Runnin' Rebels of UNLV*, the Las Vegas university team, coached by Dave Rice, made it to the Sweet 16 of the NCAA tournament in 2012, following their last appearance in 2007. There hasn't been this much excitement around the team since the days when Jerry Tarkanian, aka Tark the Shark, led them to the NCAA title in 1990. Between November and March, games are played at the **Thomas & Mack Center** (E Tropicana Avenue & Swenson Street); call 739 3267 for tickets, which cost $15-$30.

The **Lady Rebels**, UNLV's women's basketball team ($9 a game), play at the **Cox Pavilion** (739 3267, www.unlvrebels.com), next door to the Thomas & Mack. The team has been posting as many wins as the men of late.

Boxing

With blood, sweat and spit, boxing draws the richest of the rich and the poorest of the poor, just like Vegas itself. The hotels used regularly for big bouts are **Mandalay Bay** (*see p86*, which also hosts numerous 'ultimate fighting' events), the **MGM Grand** (*see p88*) and **Caesars Palace** (*see p83*). Call each hotel or Ticketmaster (1-800 745 3000) ahead of the fight for tickets, which can cost several thousand dollars but nonetheless often sell out quickly.

Football

The **UNLV Rebels** college team plays under coach Bobby Hauck at **Sam Boyd Stadium** (Boulder Highway & Russell Road, 739 3267, www.unlvrebels.com) between September and December. Tickets, on sale from July, cost $15-$30. Sam Boyd Stadium also hosts the **Maaco Bowl Las Vegas**

(www.lvbowl.com), which features the best of the Mountain West Conference.

Golf

Because of its year-round golf-friendly climate and resort ambience, the Las Vegas area is home to more than 40 golf courses – including Las Vegas National, site of Tiger Woods' first PGA victory, and backdrop to scenes from *Casino*. The area annually hosts many PGA tournaments and other high-calibre events. For more information on local golf tournaments visit the **Southern Nevada Golf Association** (458 4653, www.snga.org). For golf courses, *see p236*.

Ice hockey

The city's resident team, the **Las Vegas Wranglers** (284 7777, www.lasvegas wranglers.com), takes to the ice between October and April at the 9,000-seat **Orleans Arena** (*see p127*). Competing in the West division of the National Conference, the team had been a feeder club for the NHL's Calgary Flames and then the Phoenix Coyotes, before becoming an independent club in 2011. At $18.75-$40, tickets are worth their weight in body slams, ice brawls and speeding-puck action; the crowd's enthusiasm is even hotter than the temperatures outside.

Cycling in Red Rock Canyon.
See p224.

Mixed martial arts/ ultimate fighting

Vegas is a frequent host and headquarters for the MMA/UFC craze, which is on the verge of surpassing boxing as a big-ticket draw, and is pulling a younger and considerably rowdier crowd. Big bouts, which are often broadcast live via pay-per-view cable, take place at **Mandalay Bay** (*see p86*) and the Garden Arena at the **MGM Grand** (*see p88*). Visit www.ufc.com and www.mmafighting.com for scheduled events; call either hotel or Ticketmaster (1-800 745 3000) ahead of the fight for tickets.

Rodeo

Every December, the **National Finals Rodeo** (*see p42*) sweeps into town, packing the Thomas & Mack Center with riders who make riding a bucking bronco look as easy as sitting on a carousel horse. See www.nfrexperience. com for details of events. The relatively new **South Point Equestrian Center** (796 7111, www.southpointeventscenter.com) hosts events year-round.

In October, the best professional bull riders in the world come to the Thomas & Mack to compete in the **Built For Tough Professional Bull Riders Finals**. For tickets, call 1-866 727 7469 or see www.pbrnow.com.

Tennis

Home to world-famous tennis pros Andre Agassi and Steffi Graf, Las Vegas is the site of many professional tennis tourneys. Several casino resorts have tennis facilities, and there are four good public courts, including the **Darling Tennis Center** (7901 W Washington Avenue, 229 2100, www.darling tenniscenter.net).

ACTIVE SPORTS
Auto racing

If you'd like to get out of the stands and into the car, contact **Dream Racing** (*see p235* **Get Your Motor Runnin'**) or the **Richard Petty Driving Experience** (1-800 237 3889, www. drivepetty.com). At the Richard Petty Experience, you can sit in the passenger seat ($99-$159) or behind the wheel ($449-$3,200), while Dream Racing focuses on your skills as an actual driver.

Bowling

A number of casinos have huge, 24-hour alleys, among them the **Suncoast** (64 lanes; *see p130*), **Sam's Town** (56 lanes; *see p130*) and the **Red**

Rock (72 lanes, with a VIP section; *see p126*). There are also alleys with slightly more limited hours at the **Gold Coast** (70 lanes; *see p129*), the **Orleans** (70 lanes; *see p127*) and **Santa Fe Station** (60 lanes; *see p130*). **Strike Zone** at **Sunset Station** (72 lanes; *see p130*) is a little more modern. For all, call ahead before making a special trip: local bowling leagues take over entire alleys on selected nights, and some alleys are open only to over-21s at night.

Cycling

Looking around Vegas, you'd think that the only cyclists are Mormon missionaries. Don't be put off: although thee urban areas are incredibly auto-centric, there are thrilling cycle trails surrounding the city, even if you have to drive to get there.

McGhie's Ski Bike & Board (4035 S Fort Apache Road, between W Flamingo Road & W Saddle Avenue, 252 8077, www.mcghies.com) rents out road and mountain bikes (from $40 a day), and can arrange group tours.

Possible routes include the eight-mile off-road **Cottonwood Valley Loop** near Red Rock Canyon (head west on Highway 160 and look for a dirt road six miles past the junction with Highway 159) and the **River Mountain Peak**, a ten-mile trek between Las Vegas and Henderson (drive along US93/95 to Equestrian Drive and turn east).

Fishing

Lake Mead (*see p246*) is stocked with half a million rainbow trout annually, and also contains black and striped bass; the upper Overton Arm of the lake is good for crappie, bluegill and catfish. **Lake Mohave** is also good for rainbow trout. In the city, check out **Lorenzi Park** (Rancho Drive & Washington Avenue), **Sunset Park** (Sunset Road & Eastern Avenue) or **Floyd Lamb State Park** (*see p250*).

To fish from any Nevada shore, you'll need a Nevada fishing licence; a special stamp is required for trout fishing. To fish from a boat on Lake Mead, you'll also need a stamp from Arizona, as the two states share jurisdiction of the lake. For details on all aspects of fishing in Nevada, contact the **Nevada Division of Wildlife** (486 5127, www.ndow.org), ask at a ranger station for the current hotspots or consult **Fish Incorporated** (565 8396, www.fishincorporated.com).

Golf

Las Vegas has about half the courses it needs to meet demand; call several weeks ahead and show up with a three-figure sum if you want to

Get Your Motor Runnin'

Extreme adventures are all the rage in Vegas.

Just the anticipation of visiting Las Vegas is enough to make you feel as if you're firing on all six cylinders. Once you get here, it's time to go into overdrive. People come to Vegas for a variety of reasons: shows, food, gambling, shopping, weather... But increasing numbers are heading here for another reason as well: extreme adventures.

Take **Dream Racing** (605 2010, www.dreamracing.com), for example. Located at the Las Vegas Speedway, this experience allows you test your reflexes while tearing round the track at insanely high speeds in racing or street cars. This is no ride-along, go-kart-type fantasy, either. Drivers choose from such iconic autos as the Lamborghini LP 570-4, a Porsche 911 Carrera S, or (our favourite) the Ferrari 458 Italia.

But don't think you're just going to hop into one of these expensive motors and drive away. Dream Racing is all about the proper experience, which begins with detailed instruction from one of the track's pro racers. (Lesson no.1: everything you thought you knew about driving is wrong.)

After an intense crash course in race-car driving, you'll be given a chance to warm up on one of the state-of-the-art simulators. Once the instructor thinks you have it down, you head out and get in a car for the real deal.

Strap on a helmet (equipped with a two-way mic) and your instructor will get into the passenger seat beside you. Then you hit the track for anywhere from five to seven laps of high-speed mania. The instructor coaches you along the way, but operating one of these vehicles – as fast as you can without a safety net – is sure to set your heart racing.

If you aren't into cars, no worries: Vegas offers a variety of other adventures. Gun enthusiasts will have a blast at **Battlefield Vegas** (*see p61*), where guests are armed and turned loose to reenact historical battles like Hamburger Hill in the Vietnam War or D-Day clashes. Those looking for a modern assault milieu can choose from experiences such as S.W.A.T. or Heavy Strike, all with era-appropriate weaponry.

Not feeling the thrill yet? Head over to **Sky Combat Ace** (1-888 494 5850, www.skycombatace.com) where, instead of operating a car, you get to fly a plane. Choose the Adrenaline Rush package for some honest-to-goodness aerial dogfighting and flying manoeuvres like loops and Cuban 8s.

Or maybe you want to lose control without being in control. If that's the case, head straight for the Stratosphere where, at the top of the tower, you'll find a number of rides, including the heart-stopping **SkyJump** (*see p57*). Take the elevator to the 108th floor, slide into a jumpsuit and then saunter over to the platform edge. Be forewarned: that last step – at 850 feet – is a doozy.

With so many choices, it's enough to make a daredevil's head spin. Which is appropriate, since Las Vegas is all about extremes.

ARTS & ENTERTAINMENT

Dream Racing.

Royal Links.

play on any of the best. **Las Vegas Preferred Tee-Times** (1-877 255 7277, www.lvptt.com) can arrange reservations at a number of courses. Rates are cheaper in the heat of summer and later in the afternoon. Most courses are open from 7am to dusk; one exception is the par-three **Cloud Nine** course at Angel Park (254 4653, www.angelpark.com), where nine of the 12 holes are floodlit. Sharpen up your game at **Butch Harmon's School of Golf** at the Rio Secco Golf Club (1-888 867 3226, www.butchharmon.com).

Bali Hai Golf Club

5160 Las Vegas Boulevard South, at W Russell Road, South of Strip (450 8191, www.balihai golfclub.com). Bus SDX, 104. **Green fees** *June-Aug* $175-$195; $125-$150 twilight. *Sept-May* $265-$325; $189-$229 twilight. **Map** p320 A9.
This challenging par-71 track includes seven acres of water features, 2,500 palm trees, Augusta white sand and more than 100,000 tropical plants.

Craig Ranch Golf Course

628 W Craig Road, between N Martin Luther King Boulevard & Losee Road, North Las Vegas (642 9700). No bus. **Green fees** $19-$35; $5-$16 juniors.
Established in 1962, Las Vegas's first public course is a favourite with locals, thanks in part to the fabulously low prices.

Desert Pines Golf Club

3415 E Bonanza Road, at N Pecos Road, East Las Vegas (450 8170, www.golfdesertpines.com). Bus 111, 215. **Green fees** *June-Aug* $69-$79; $39-$49 twilight. *Sept-May* $99-$129; $69-$79 twilight. **Map** p317 Z1.
The public course at Desert Pines has been recognised as one of the premier upscale courses in the country by *Golf Digest*, with a tight, 6,810-yard, par-71 layout, tree-lined fairways and nine holes on water. The climate-controlled practice facility is the best in Las Vegas.

Legacy Golf Club

130 Par Excellence Drive, at Green Valley Parkway, Henderson (897 2187, www.thelegacy gc.com). Bus 111. **Green fees** *June-Sept* $75-$90; $55 twilight. *Oct-May* $100-$155; $75-$85 twilight.
This handsome, 7,233-yard, par-72 course is host each year to US Open qualifying, but is also a popular choice with the public.

Royal Links

5995 E Vegas Valley Drive, east of S Nellis Boulevard, East Las Vegas (450 8181, www.royal linksgolfclub.com). No bus. **Green fees** *June-Aug* $95-$155; $75-$85 twilight. *Sept-May* $175-$275; $135-$175 twilight.
The Royal Links course is modelled on 11 different courses used for the Open championship; there's a replica of the Postage Stamp at Troon and the Road Hole at St Andrew's.

TPC Las Vegas

9851 Canyon Run Drive, at N Town Center Drive, Summerlin (256 2000, www.tpc.com). **Green fees** *June-Aug* $125-$150; $75 twilight. *Sept-May* $225-$275; $170-$190 twilight.
Recognised by *Golf Digest* as one of its 'Best Places to Play', this 6,772-yard course that fronts the beautiful Red Rock Canyon was co-designed by Bobby Weed and Ray Floyd.

Gyms & sports centres

Most major hotel-casinos have some sort of fitness facility on the premises.

Las Vegas Athletic Club

2655 S Maryland Parkway, at Karen Avenue, East Las Vegas (734 5822, www.lvac.com). Bus 109, 204. **Open** 24hrs daily. **Rates** $15/day; $35/wk. **Map** p317 Y2.
All six Vegas branches have pools, saunas, jacuzzis, Nautilus, free weights and dozens of classes, plus childcare services. Most locations are open 24 hours. **Other locations** throughout the city.

24 Hour Fitness

2605 S Eastern Avenue, at E Sahara Avenue, East Las Vegas (641 2222, www.24hour fitness.com). Bus SX, 110. **Open** 24hrs daily. **Rates** $15/day. **Map** p317 Z2.

In addition to gym facilities, 24 Hour has a kids' club and rock climbing. Larger branches also have pools and basketball courts. The latest branch is at the Molasky Building in Downtown (100 City Parkway). **Other locations** throughout the city.

Hiking

The **Sierra Club** (732 7750, www.sierraclub. com) organises hikes around Red Rock Canyon, Mount Charleston and the Lake Mead area.

Horse riding

See p250.

Hunting & shooting

Call the **Nevada Division of Wildlife** (486 5127, www.ndow.org) for information on hunting dove, quail and waterfowl in the Lake Mead area, and details of seasonal hunting of deer, elk, antelope and bighorn sheep.

The **American Shooters Supply & Gun Club** (3440 Arville Street, between W Desert Inn & Spring Mountain roads, 719 5000, www.americanshooters.com) is a 50-yard indoor range. Meanwhile, the **Gun Store** (2900 E Tropicana Avenue, between McLeod & Harrison drives, 454 1110, www.thegunstorelasvegas.com) offers more shooting options, from M16s to machine guns. **Battlefield Vegas** (*see p61*) also offers indoor and outdoor ranges.

Pool & billiards

Cue Club

953 E Sahara Avenue, at S Maryland Parkway, East of Strip (735 2884, www.lvcueclub.com). Bus SX, 109. **Open** 24hrs daily. **Map** p317 Y2. Vegas's largest pool hall.

Rafting & kayaking

See p247 **Rolling on the River**.

Rock climbing

If you don't fancy trekking to Red Rock Canyon (*see p248*), you can practise at the **Nevada Climbing Center** (3065 E Patrick Lane, between S Eastern Avenue & S Pecos Road, 898 8192, www.nvclimbing.com) or **Red Rock Climbing Center** (8201 W Charleston Boulevard, at South Cimarron Road, 254 5604, www.redrockclimbingcenter.com).

Scuba & skin diving

For diving at Lake Mead, *see p247*.

Snow sports

The mountains are closer (and snowier) than you think. Just 47 miles away, the **Las Vegas Ski & Snowboard Resort** (385 2754, 593 9500 snow conditions, www.skilasvegas.com) at Lee Canyon on Mount Charleston (*see p250*) offers action for all abilities, and has a half-pipe and terrain park. In good years, the season runs from November to April, with the park open 10am-4pm.

A three-hour drive from Vegas on I-15 and SR 145 is the two-mountain, all-abilities **Brian Head Ski Resort** in Utah (1-866 930 1010, www.brianhead.com). The resort offers mountain biking and hiking in the summer.

Swimming

Almost every hotel and motel in Las Vegas has a pool, although most are leisure-oriented and not ideal for high-speed lap swimming. Open seasonally from early morning until twilight, the poshest hotel pools on the Strip include **Caesars Palace** (*see p83*), the vast **MGM Grand** (*see p88*), the **Rio** (*see p115*) and **Mandalay Bay** (*see p86*). Many have sections given over to topless sunbathing. Downtown, the pool at the **Golden Nugget** (*see p121*) has an integrated shark tank. Most hotel pools are available only to guests at the resort (or, in some cases, at an affiliated property), but many of them are open to all comers for summer pool parties (*see p223* **We Love the Daylife**).

Tennis

It's becoming more difficult to find a tennis court on the Strip – unsurprising, given the price of land. However, some hotels still maintain courts. At **Bally's**, **Flamingo**, **Las Vegas Hilton**, **Paris**, **Plaza** and **Riviera** guests have priority, but they're also open to the public. **Bally's** (*see p95*) has eight courts, twice as many as the **Flamingo** (*see p96*). You can also play at some sports centres and parks, such as the **Darling Tennis Center** (*see p234*; free-$5.50/hr).

Water-skiing

Behind the Hoover Dam, huge **Lake Mead** (*see p246*) offers great water-skiing. **Invert Sports** at Lake Mead Marina (1-888 205 7119, www.invertsports.com) hires out the necessary equipment, and organises trips and lessons in water-skiing, tubing and wakeboarding.

Weddings

Goin' to the chapel…

Nevada authorities never saw fit to enforce a waiting period on couples wanting to apply for a marriage licence. So when the soon-to-be-betrothed realised that they'd have to wait a whole three days for a marriage licence in California (thanks to the Gin Law, enacted in 1912 to dissuade drunken lovers from taking the plunge), whirlwind elopements to Vegas quickly became the fashion. Hollywood celebrities such as Betty Grable and Rita Hayworth began the trend, but legions of ordinary couples soon followed. The lenient state laws continue to draw impatient sweethearts, keen to get spliced without a moment's delay: the world's top destination for lovers, Las Vegas hosts around 120,000 weddings each year.

WEDDINGS VEGAS-STYLE

In the early days, weddings were performed in hotel rooms or, more often, by a justice of the peace at the county clerk's office. The first wedding chapel to provide a one-stop service centre was founded by the Reverend JD Foster in 1933. But the wedding business didn't really take off until the '40s, when diminutive white steeples started popping up along Las Vegas Boulevard. The industry suffered from the general slump that befell the city in the 1970s, but it bounced back with the glittering '90s renaissance, as hotel-casinos began to provide increasingly luxurious alternatives to the independent chapels that still dream south of Downtown.

In the past, couples were attracted by two main attributes to a Vegas marriage: the casual modernity of an instant wedding and the price. Today, though, the once-trendy thing-to-do has become a tradition of sorts, with a unique all-American romance of its own. And it's still pretty cheap. On the Strip, you can get married in your car, atop the Eiffel Tower or on a gondola. Or you could head north towards Downtown to one of the town's old-school independent chapels, where Elvis himself (sort of) could preside over the ceremony.

A basic package wedding at an independent Downtown chapel can cost as little as $75. However, this price excludes a number of crucial services ('donation' to the minister, tip for the limo driver, flowers and so on), all of which can result in a heftier bill than anticipated. Set charges tend to be rather higher at resort chapels, but the packages include more options and extras. Call around before making your decision. And whether your cultural touchstone for the experience is Joan Didion's comic essay 'Marrying Absurd' or the episode of *Friends* in which Ross and Rachel get spliced after getting drunk in their hotel room, the lavish and loopy – or lavishly loopy – Vegas wedding of your dreams can be yours.

HOW TO DO IT

Before taking the plunge, both bride and groom will need a marriage licence. The happy couple should present themselves at the **Marriage Bureau** (201 E Clark Avenue, at S Casino Center Boulevard, Downtown, 455 0000, www.clark countynv.gov) with $60 in cash and valid photo ID; the office is open a hard-working 8am to midnight every day. To save time, download the marriage licence application form from the website and fill it out before you arrive. You'll need to be able to prove that you are who you say you are and that you're at least 18 years of age; US citizens will need their social security numbers, while foreigners should bring ID in English. If either of you have been married before, you'll need to give the date and time the marriage ended, although you won't need to produce any certificates.

Once you've got a marriage licence, you'll need to hold the wedding ceremony within a year. It must be conducted in the state of Nevada by a licensed person, who will present you with a marriage certificate once the deed has been done. The quickest and cheapest option is to walk the two blocks from the bureau to the **Commissioner of Civil Marriage** (1st floor, 309 S 3rd Street, at Bridger Avenue, Downtown, 455 3474, open 2-6pm Mon-Thur, Sun; 8am-10pm Fri, Sat). Bring a witness and you can finish the job for the bargain price of $50 (cash only; they don't give change). But with so many more charismatic chapels within walking or drive-through distance, it's best to look around.

You may not need a reservation at many of the city's freestanding chapels. However, it's always best to make one in advance in order to avoid queues or disappointment, especially at weekends or other busy times (Valentine's Day, for example). The whole procedure could all be over in no time at all, but some ceremonies are more time-consuming; it all depends on how much fuss you want to make (and how much you're willing to spend).

Non-US citizens will need certified copies of both the marriage licence and the marriage certificate for their union to be recognised at home. Both are available at nominal cost from the Marriage Bureau and the office of the Commissioner of Civil Marriage respectively, at the time or thereafter by post. Non-US citizens may also require an apostille in order that their marriage is recognised as legally binding in their home country. This is easily obtainable (for a small fee) from the Notary Division of the Secretary of State; further details are available on the Marriage Bureau's website.

WEDDING CHAPELS
Hotel-chapel weddings

Resort chapels are more formal than Downtown ones; couples should plan on booking ahead.

Artisan
1501 W Sahara Avenue, at Highland Drive, West of Strip (1-800 554 4092, 214 4000, www.theartisanhotel.com). Bus SX, 108. **Map** p319 A4.
Antiques and gilt-framed prints make the Artisan an elegant, funky and very un-Vegas spot for a wedding. The Gothic chapel is delightfully spooky, and the bar and the dining hall are perfect for a chic reception.

Bellagio
3600 Las Vegas Boulevard South, at W Flamingo Road (1-888 987 6667, 693 7111, www.bellagio. com). Bus Deuce, 202. **Map** p320 A7.
Whether you choose the grand South Chapel or the intimate East Chapel, Bellagio offers a Vegas take on old-fashioned European opulence. The Deluxe package starts at $2,000; the Cosa Bella is a cool $25,000.

THE BEST WEDDINGS

For classic Vegas romance
Little Church of the West. *See p240.*

For a simulated marriage
Cosmopolitan. *See below.*

For only-in-Vegas speed
A drive-through wedding. *See p241.*

★ Cosmopolitan
3708 Las Vegas Boulevard South, between W Harmon Avenue & W Flamingo Road (1-855 455 1055, 698 7640, www.cosmopolitanlasvegas.com). Bus Deuce **Map** p320 A7.
Not planning on a Vegas wedding? Well, you never know… But if you want the experience without the commitment, visit the Cosmo's Pop-Up Wedding Chapel. Have fun with packages like Hitched in a Hurry or On a Whim. Or, for the truly serious, seal your fate with a legally binding ceremony.

Excalibur
3850 Las Vegas Boulevard South, at W Tropicana Avenue (1-877 750 5464, 597 7777, www. excalibur.com). Bus Deuce, 201. **Map** p320 A8.
Get dressed up in ermine-trimmed Renaissance garb to marry in the Excalibur's 'fairytale' chapel.

Flamingo
3555 Las Vegas Boulevard South, at E Flamingo Road (1-800 933 7993, 733 3111, www.flamingo lasvegas.com). Bus Deuce, 202. **Map** p320 A7.
Apparently, Bugsy Siegel's private suite was torn down to make room for the Flamingo Garden chapel, which remains one of the most elegant and old-school Strip-resort settings in which to marry.

Paris Las Vegas
3655 Las Vegas Boulevard South, at E Flamingo Road (1-877 650 5021, 946 7000, www.paris lasvegas.com). Bus Deuce, 202. **Map** p320 A7.
Whether you marry in the 90-capacity Chapelle du Paradis or atop the Eiffel Tower, this is one way to say you got married in Paris and Las Vegas. For $69.99, bag yourself a risqué wedding-cake topper.

Venetian
3355 Las Vegas Boulevard South, between Sands Avenue & E Flamingo Road (1-866 548 1807, 414 4280, www.venetianweddings.com). Bus Deuce, 119, 203. **Map** p319, p320 B6.
There's a traditional chapel here, but you can also say 'I do' on a gondola afloat a faux-canal in faux-Venice or on a footbridge under the blue faux-sky painted with faux-clouds. It's more charming than it sounds, though you'll pay for it: weddings range from $2,000 to $16,500.

INSIDE TRACK
GAY CEREMONIES

Although gay and lesbian couples aren't eligible for marriage licences, there are options in the city, although a little advance planning is necessary. Many chapels, both standalone operations and casino-based facilities, offer 'commitment ceremonies' for same-sex couples. However, they generally won't call it a wedding, and other chapels simply don't stage lesbian and gay ceremonies at all. Always call ahead.

Independent weddings

A Christian Pastor 2 U

378 7000, www.spiritofprophecy.org.
Pastor Rick and his family offer an evangelical Christian wedding service, which is something of a novelty in Vegas. The pastor is willing to travel to Cathedral Rock, Mount Charleston or elsewhere to conduct the ceremony; prices start at $349.

Chapel of the Flowers

1717 Las Vegas Boulevard South, at E Oakey Boulevard, the Strip (1-800 843 2410, 735 4331, www.littlechapel.com). Bus Deuce. **Open** 7am-8pm Mon-Thur; 7am-9pm Fri, Sat. **Map** p319 C4.
There are actually three chapels at this well-kept, popular facility, along with a florist and a photography studio. The chapel even offers couples the opportunity to broadcast weddings live on the internet, so the folks at home can share the joyful occasion. Prices start at $195; $3,755 will buy you a wedding on the floor of the Grand Canyon, with helicopter flights included.

Cupid's Wedding Chapel

827 Las Vegas Boulevard South, at Hoover Avenue, Downtown (1-800 543 2933, 598 4444, www.cupidswedding.com). Bus Deuce, 108, 206. **Open** 10am-6pm Mon-Thur, Sun; 10am-1am Fri, Sat. **Map** p318 C3.
This chapel's classic heart-shaped sign is one of the most striking beacons in the vicinity. Staff can be a little rude, but with packages starting at $179 (for the You Send Me Wedding), who's complaining?

Graceland Wedding Chapel

619 Las Vegas Boulevard South, at E Bonneville Avenue, Downtown (1-800 824 5732, 382 0091, www.gracelandchapel.com). Bus Deuce & all BTC-bound buses. **Open** 9am-11pm daily. **Map** p318 C2.
Rose bushes on the patio and a dove motif on the stained-glass windows complete the tidy air of this 'Elvistablishment', where options run from $199 to $499 (for the Famous Dueling Elvis package). The King will perform at any ceremony but he can only officiate at renewals.

★ Little Church of the West

4617 Las Vegas Boulevard South, at Russell Road, the Strip (1-800 821 2452, 739 7971, www.little churchlv.com). Bus Deuce. **Open** 10am-midnight daily. **Map** p318 E3.
Voted the city's best chapel for years by the *Las Vegas Review-Journal*, the quaint Little Church is in the National Registry of Historical Places. Zsa Zsa Gabor wed here; hopefully, your marriage will last longer.

Little White Wedding Chapel

1301 Las Vegas Boulevard South, at Park Paseo, Downtown (1-800 545 8111, 382 5943, www.a littlewhitechapel.com). Bus Deuce, 206. **Open** 8am-2am Mon-Thur, Sun; 24hrs Fri, Sat. **Map** p319 C3.
There are five chapels at this Vegas classic, where Frank Sinatra married Mia Farrow in 1966. The drive-through Tunnel of Love was designed for those with physical handicaps, but it's now popular with anyone after a quickie wedding in true only-in-Vegas style.

Mon Bel Ami

607 Las Vegas Boulevard South, at E Bonneville Avenue, Downtown (1-866 503 4400, 388 4445, www.monbelami.com). Bus Deuce & all BTC-bound buses. **Open** 10am-10pm daily. **Map** p318 C2.
This well-landscaped and inviting chapel schedules its ceremonies a full hour apart. Hair and make-up artists, a manicurist and a massage therapist are among the services. The Le Petite package starts at $199; the Crème de la Crème costs $1,599.

A Special Memory Wedding Chapel

800 S 4th Street, at Gass Avenue, Downtown (1-800 962 7798, 384 2211, www.aspecial memory.com). Bus Deuce & all BTC-bound buses. **Open** 8am-10pm Mon-Thur, Sun; 8am-midnight Fri, Sat. **Map** p318 C2.
The inside of this three-chapel facility is bright and inviting; it even looks like a real church, albeit one with a lot of lights. Ceremonies in the chapels cost anywhere from $199 to $1,095. Grand Canyon, Valley of Fire and Red Rock packages are also available.

Sweethearts Wedding Chapel

1155 Las Vegas Boulevard South, at Park Paseo, Downtown (1-800 444 2932, 385 7785, www.sweetheartschapel.com). Bus Deuce, 206. **Open** 11am-8pm daily. **Map** p319 C3.
This modest chapel seats 35 and has a bridal boutique on site. The $759 special includes a wedding gown, a headpiece, an underskirt, shoes and a tux.

★ Vegas Adventure Wedding Chapel

1600 Las Vegas Boulevard South, at E Wyoming Avenue, the Strip (1-888 463 1399, 270 2522, www.vegasadventureweddings.com). Bus Deuce. **Open** 10am-8pm daily. **Map** p319 C3.
This outfit essentially has two settings: traditional and not so traditional. You can get married in the chapel, where all weddings are scheduled at least an

hour apart, or at an outdoor location, including the Valley of Fire or a lakeside ceremony at nearby Lake Jacqueline. Or there's the 'Stoner Wedding with Chong', a ceremony officiated by a Chong (of Cheech & Chong) impersonator, complete with faux doobie.

Vegas Weddings
320 S 3rd Street, between Bridger & Lewis avenues, Downtown (1-800 823 4095, 933 3464, www.702 wedding.com). Bus Deuce & all BTC-bound buses. **Open** 8am-midnight daily. **Map** p318 C2.
This two-chapel venue is perfect for walk-ins: it's one of the closest to the Marriage Bureau. Packages start at $199, with the Indulge package at $2,099; outdoor options include Lake Mead and the Grand Canyon. Staff can broadcast weddings live on the internet.

Viva Las Vegas Chapel
1205 Las Vegas Boulevard South, at Park Paseo, Downtown (1-800 574 4450, 384 0771,
www.vivalasvegasweddings.com). Bus Deuce, 206. **Open** 9am-8pm Mon-Thur, Sun; 9am-10pm Fri, Sat. **Map** p319 C3.
Known for its themed weddings, which range from sci-fi to western via the obligatory Elvis-slanted ceremony, Viva Las Vegas has more sets than some movie studios. Same-sex commitment ceremonies are treated with care.

Wee Kirk o' the Heather
231 Las Vegas Boulevard South, at Bridger Avenue, Downtown (1-800 843 5266, 382 9830, www.weekirk.com). Bus Deuce & all BTC-bound buses. **Open** 10am-8pm Mon-Thur, Sun; 9am-9pm Fri, Sat. **Map** p318 D2.
This tiny chapel has been going since 1940 and is one of the oldest still in operation. Done out to resemble a toy version of a Scottish church, it's also one of the cutest. Prices range from $87 to $1,212.12 – for the Ulimate 12-12-12 package.

Weddings on Wheels

Regrets? I've had a few.

Two recently acquainted people stumble down Las Vegas Boulevard with a yard of margarita in one hand and ads for in-room strippers in the other. Making out under the Eiffel Tower, inspiration strikes. The pair decide, after craps and blackjack and maybe another drink, to go full-on Vegas (baby!) and get hitched. A short ride to the Marriage Bureau ensues, followed by the filling out of applications, each party glancing over the other's shoulder to learn their partner's surname.

Turning in their forms, they glance around the tiny office and privately make bets as to which of the other swaying couples will 'make it'. The night clerk doesn't bother to check a most-wanted list for bi-coastal bigamist killers stopping off from the desert leg of a cross-country rampage and, instead, turns the form into a licence.

So, where to go? How about the famous Little Church of the West? Perhaps one of the chapels whose signage inadvertently advertises random celebrity couplings, such as Joan Collins and Michael Jordan? Or maybe they could be married by Elvis? Yes! But, dammit, you have to book an Elvis in advance, and time seems short. Then one of them remembers you can get married in

Vegas without even leaving your car – at the Little White Wedding Chapel, for instance . They drive up, roll down the window and greet an internet-ordained minister leaning out to exchange electroplated wedding bands for cash.

The ceremony is pleasant enough but unlikely to be remembered in its entirety. A few items survive the haze: the wedding photo (the happy couple show off their rings from the front seats), and a congratulatory gift pack from the chapel containing, among other things, a heart-shaped key ring and coupons for deodorant.

Las Vegas is beautiful in the morning, but with daylight comes sobriety, and a reminder that night is only night but daytime is Real Life. The legally bound strangers emerge from a Downtown motel, dry-mouthed and slightly confused, and take a long look at each other. Or a short one. Back in their respective home towns, they initiate divorce proceedings, surprised and disappointed to learn that there isn't a drive-through for that too, and, upon imparting their now-famous-among-friends Vegas story, are often asked: 'So, did you get fries with that?'

Escapes & Excursions

Escapes & Excursions

Out of the casino and into the desert.

Man cannot live on free cocktails and enormous buffets alone. After a while, iridescent sun will become more attractive than fluorescent striplights, and fresh air will appeal more than cranked-to-the-max air-conditioning; even if, as is the case in summer, the temperatures outside are well into three figures. Happily, the roads leading out of Las Vegas offer some terrific escape routes, with opportunities for some great trips. Within 50 miles of the city, you'll find desert parks (Red Rock Canyon, Valley of Fire), boating and fishing (on Lake Mead), man-made marvels (Hoover Dam) and

even skiing (Mount Charleston). Further afield is the world-class natural stunner that is the Grand Canyon in Arizona; the wilderness of the California desert, with Death Valley, the US's largest national park; the singular attractions of Reno in Nevada, and the stupendous rock formations of southern Utah.

Day Trips
HEADING EAST
The Hoover Dam

The bare facts are staggering enough. It's 726 feet high. At its base, it's 660 feet thick; at its crest, it's 1,244 feet wide. It weighs 6.6 million tons. The building of it used enough concrete to pave a highway between San Francisco and New York. Its reservoir is 110 miles long and around 500 feet deep, and can hold enough water to cover the entire state of Nevada six inches deep. So far, so impressive. But then you actually catch sight of the **Hoover Dam**, and you can scarcely believe your eyes.

Without the Hoover Dam (née Boulder Dam, but renamed in 1947 for President Herbert Hoover, under whose administration the project was begun), much of the Southwest would not exist. The dam controls the Colorado River, providing electricity and water to nearly 20 million people in Nevada, California and Arizona, and makes it possible for cities and farmland to flourish in one of the driest, hottest and most inhospitable regions of the world.

In the early 20th century, the sheer power of the Colorado River made the building of the Hoover Dam both necessary and terrifying. Black Canyon was chosen as the location for

the project, which was overseen by the Bureau of Reclamation and came with four main aims: flood prevention, silt control, water storage and electrical-energy generation.

Building it was a mammoth task. The Colorado had to be temporarily diverted so the dam wall could be constructed. The concrete would have taken 100 years to set if left under normal conditions, so the cooling process was sped up by pumping ice-cold water through a network of pipes laid into each block of concrete. Vast pipes some 30 feet in diameter, known as penstocks, were lowered from an overhead cableway 800 feet above the canyon floor and squeezed into tunnels blasted out of the side walls. An army of 16,400 workers – remember, the project was built at the height of the Depression – laboured day and night for four years, finishing in February 1935… two years ahead of schedule.

The dam straddles the border between Arizona and Nevada. The skinny, perennially congested **Highway 93** passes over the top, although traffic was significantly eased with the October 2010 opening of the four-lane **Hoover Dam Bypass** a quarter of a mile south of the dam. Officially named the Mike O'Callaghan-Pat Tillman Memorial Bridge (after former Nevada governor Mike O'Callaghan, who died in 2004, and professional footballer Pat Tillman who left his career to enlist in the army after 9/11, and

Day Trips

To Death Valley
& Reno

Nellis Air Force Base

Desert National Wildlife Refuge

N E V A D A

95

93

15

93

Spring Mountains National Recreation Area

156

157

158

△ Mount Charleston (11,918ft) (p250)

Towards Utah

Overton

169

Visitor Centre

Valley of Fire State Park (p248)

169

Overton Beach

Echo Bay

167

NORTHSHORE SCENIC DRIVE

Lake Mead (p246)

Temple Bay

A R I Z O N A

Callville Bay

93

Lake Mead National Recreation Area

Las Vegas Bay

Hoover Dam (p244)

166

Lake Mead Marina

Visitor Centre

Boulder City (p246)

167

95

To Laughlin

147

146

Floyd Lamb State Park (p250)

Las Vegas Beltway

93

LAS VEGAS

See p317

515

95

Henderson

93

95

15

To Jean

Goodsprings

To Los Angeles

95

215

159

Scenic Loop

Visitor Centre

Blue Diamond

Bonnie Springs Old Nevada

Red Rock Canyon National Park (p248)

Spring Mountain State Park

160

15 miles

20 km

© Copyright Time Out Group 2013

CALIFORNIA

0

0

was killed by friendly fire in Afghanistan), it is nearly 2,000 feet long, with a 1,060-foot twin-rib concrete arch. The $240 million bridge spans the Black Canyon and connects the Arizona and Nevada approach highways nearly 900 feet above the Colorado River. Even if you've seen the Hoover Dam before, this spectacular new bridge calls for another visit. You can walk across it: there's a sidewalk entrance on the north side of the bridge.

The 459-car parking garage (parking $7; there are free lots on the Arizona side of the bridge) and the visitors' centre are on the Nevada side of the border. The latter is something of a necessary evil, through which the bulk of the 'Discovery' tour is conducted. Booking isn't required, but early arrival is recommended to beat both crowds and traffic. (The 'Hard Hat' tours, which took visitors closer to the action, were suspended post 9/11 and seem unlikely to resume.)

The **tour** ($11, $9 reductions, free under-3s) is a mixed bag. The films are informative, but the waiting in line is frustrating and the way in which visitors are herded in and out of cinemas and galleries, while no fault of the knowledgeable, enthusiastic staff – it's to do with the hamfisted design of the centre itself – is an irritation. But in between the movie and the exhibition, you'll get to see inside the dam, specifically a long hall that contains eight huge generators.

Back outside, note a few interesting features on or near the dam. Chief among them are a pair of 30-foot sculptures, the *Winged Figures of the Republic*, flanking a flagpole above a terrazzo floor inlaid with a celestial map; it marks Franklin D Roosevelt's dedication of the dam in September 1935. The white mark on the shoreline indicates the flood level in 1983, when Lake Mead rose to within seven feet of the top. But while these are nice diversions, they won't be what you remember. That'll be the sheer size of the place, one of the greatest man-made constructions on the planet.

GETTING THERE
To reach the Hoover Dam from Las Vegas, take US 93 south for 32 miles. You'll pass through Boulder City en route.

TOURIST INFORMATION
For information on tours, call 1-866 730 9097 or 494 2517, or see www.usbr.gov/lc/hooverdam. The **visitors' centre** is open 9am to 6pm daily; tours end at 5.15pm.

Boulder City

Driving down Highway 93 from Vegas, you'll pass some small motels, the odd restaurant and a few stalls selling Mexican pottery and other handicrafts. Only slowly do you realise that something's missing. Built in 1931 to house the workers at the dam, **Boulder City** is one of only two towns in Nevada where gambling is illegal (the other is tiny Panaca, in Lincoln County).

Triangular in shape, Boulder City was the first 'model city' in the US, built according to progressive planning theories. The Bureau of Reclamation, government buildings and a park sit at the apex of the triangle, with the workers' houses radiating down from there. It was never intended to be a permanent settlement, but it got a second wind during World War II and is now flourishing. There's more on the area at the **Boulder City/Hoover Dam Museum** (294 1988, www.bcmha.org, $1-$2) within the Boulder Dam Hotel.

WHERE TO STAY, EAT & DRINK
Boulder City is small-town Americana, and a good eating option in that vein is **Milo's Best Cellars** (538 Nevada Highway, 293 9540, www.miloswinebar.com), which has a nice, lightish menu. Those who prefer the grain to the grape are directed to the **Boulder Dam Brewing Company** (453 Nevada Highway, 243 2739, www.boulderdambrewing.com).

If the atmosphere appeals, stay at the historic **Boulder Dam Hotel** (1305 Arizona Street, 293 3510, www.boulderdamhotel.com, doubles $80-$140); it counts Howard Hughes among its former guests. In the basement, **Matteo's Underground Lounge** (293 0098, www.matteodining.com) stages regular shows by local bands.

GETTING THERE
Boulder City is 25 miles south of Vegas (seven miles west of Hoover Dam) on US 93. To see the historic district, turn off at the business loop, which rejoins US 93 on the far side of the town.

TOURIST INFORMATION
In the Boulder Dam Hotel, the **Chamber of Commerce** (293 2034, www.bouldercity chamberofcommerce.com) has maps and local information.

Lake Mead

Around ten million visitors come to Lake Mead's 550 miles of shoreline each year to sail, fish, swim, water-ski, camp and generally enjoy watery pleasures in the desert. Wholly artificial, the lake was created when the Colorado was blocked by the Hoover Dam. It's an incongruous sight, a large blue splodge surrounded by barren mountains and canyon-tops.

The lake is the centrepiece of the huge **Lake Mead National Recreation Area**, which also includes Lake Mohave to the south (formed

Rolling on the River

Go kayaking on the Colorado for stunning views of the Hoover Dam.

Lake Mead, the reservoir that sprawls off the Colorado, is man-made, as, of course, is the Hoover Dam, which diverts water into it. Amid such man-made monsters so close to a city defined by artifice, it's easy to forget that the Colorado River itself is a living, breathing watercourse. But so it goes and so it flows, winding its way down through the south-west towards the Gulf of California. You can join it for a while.

One of several firms that operates kayaking trips on the Colorado, Desert Adventures (293 5026, www.kayaklas vegas.com) offers visitors unique views of the Hoover Dam from the water below. Sign up for one of their half-day kayaking tour ($159 per person) and you'll set off from close to the dam's base; from here, you'll cruise eight miles downriver in the company of a guide, stopping for a packed lunch en route.

It can get windy down on the surface, but the dam and the width of the river both help mitigate against whitewater. It's perfect for novices, not least because it's surprisingly easy to learn. The views are amazing and the exercise bracing. And after the awful traffic approaching the dam, all that open space will come as a glorious relief.

Hoover Dam and the Colorado River Bridge.

when the Colorado River was stemmed again in 1953 by the Davis Dam) and the desert east to the edge of Grand Canyon National Park (*see p251*) and north to Overton. There's a $10 permit fee per car (or $5 per person), which grants seven days' access to the whole area.

Lakeside Scenic Drive (Highway 146) and Northshore Scenic Drive (Highway 167) skirt the western and northern sides of Lake Mead for nearly 60 miles. The route isn't very scenic, but it's the access road for the concession-operated marinas along the Nevada shoreline, several of which have been closed or forced to relocate due to continually dropping water levels at Lake Mead. All have small ranger stations, grocery stores and some form of restaurant; some also have swimming beaches (without lifeguards), picnic sites, motels, showers and gas stations. **Lake Mead Marina** on Boulder Beach (293 3484, www.riverlakes.com), which had to be relocated three miles south (and closer to Boulder City) in 2008 due to lowering water levels, and the **Las Vegas Boat Harbor** (293 1191, www.lasvegasboatharbor.com) are the largest, closest and busiest marinas;

further north are the **Callville Bay Marina** (565 8958, www.callvillebay.com) and **Echo Bay Resort** (394 4000).

The best way to explore the lake is by boat. There are numerous secluded coves, sandy beaches and narrow canyons accessible only by water, and the warm, clear lake is ideal for swimming: the water temperature averages 78°F (26°C) in spring, summer and autumn. You can hire a boat from the marinas; expect small fishing boats to cost around $20-$40 for two hours or $60-$120 per day, with large ski boats roughly three times the price. Alternatively, take a cruise on the *Desert Princess* paddlesteamer ($26-$61.50), run by **Lake Mead Cruises** (293 6180, www.lakemeadcruises.com).

Lake Mead offers some of the best year-round sport **fishing** in the country, but it's also one of the country's top freshwater **scuba diving** destinations. Visibility averages 30 feet and can reach double that in winter, better enabling divers to see the dramatic drop-offs and boat wrecks. The most popular location is **Scuba Park**, adjacent to Lake Mead Marina.

You can rent equipment for around $35 a day from **American Cactus Divers** (3985 E Sunset Road, Henderson, 433 3483, www.diving.net/amcactus.html).

WHERE TO STAY, EAT & DRINK

For an eaterie on the water try the **Las Vegas Boat Harbor House Café** (293 3081). Lodging is available at **Echo Bay** (394 4000, rates $60-$115) and the **North Shore Inn** (397 6000, rates $85-$135). There are campgrounds (293 8990, rates $10) at many marinas. Close by is upscale **Lake Las Vegas** (*see p75*).

GETTING THERE

The visitors' centre is 27 miles south of Vegas on Highway 93, at the junction with Lakeshore Scenic Drive (Highway 146). To reach Las Vegas Bay, Boulder Beach and Lake Mead marinas, bypassing the visitors' centre, take Boulder Highway south from Vegas and turn left at Lake Mead Drive (Highway 146), or take I-15/US 93 north to exit 45 in North Las Vegas and turn on to Lake Mead Boulevard east (Highway 147). Both routes join the shore road.

TOURIST INFORMATION

Consult the NPS website (www.nps.gov/lame). The **Alan Bible Visitor Center** (293 8990, 9am-4.30pm Wed-Sun) on US 93 has maps and details on activities. There are also information stations at Boulder Beach, Echo Bay, Callville Bay, Las Vegas Bay and Temple Bar.

Valley of Fire State Park

An hour north-east of Las Vegas lies a natural marvel that's every bit as spectacular as the resorts on the Strip. Bounded by the grey limestone Muddy Mountains to the south and west, **Valley of Fire** was the first state park in Nevada, and is still one of its most breathtaking.

The main attractions are the red sandstone formations, created from sand dunes deposited 135 to 150 million years ago and sculpted by wind and water into bizarre, anthropomorphic shapes: look for **Elephant Rock** and **Seven Sisters** along Highway 169, the east–west road through the park. A two-mile loop road runs past some of the most dramatic rock formations.

The park is easily explored in a day. Hiking is permitted, but there are few marked trails, and all are very short. Get advice on hiking and a trails map from the visitors' centre (*see right*). The road north from the centre offers a panoramic view of multicoloured sandstone at **Rainbow Vista** and ends at the White Domes picnic area. An easy trail from Rainbow Vista leads to spectacular rocks at **Fire Canyon**,

from where you can see the spot where Captain Kirk met his doom in *Star Trek: Generations*.

Atlatl Rock, on the scenic loop road, has a number of petroglyphs, while others are visible on the short trail to **Mouse's Tank**, a natural water basin used in the 1890s as a hideout by a renegade Indian known as Mouse. Visit the **Lost City Museum** in Overton (397 2193, www.nevadaweb.com/lostcity/), eight miles north of the park, to learn about the Indian inhabitants, from the ancient Basketmaker people and the Puebloans (Anasazi) to the Paiute, whose descendants still live in southern Nevada.

Summer highs top 110°F (43°C); as such, the best times to visit are spring and autumn. If you're lucky, you may spy a desert tortoise (Nevada's state reptile) and you're sure to see antelope ground squirrels (aka chipmunks). Don't feed or pet them: they're suspected of carrying the fleas that transmit bubonic plague.

GETTING THERE

Head north on I-15 for 33 miles to Highway 169: it's 17 miles to the park's western entrance. You can also enter the park from Lake Mead, off Northshore Scenic Drive (*see 247*).

TOURIST INFORMATION

Advice on hiking and a trails map are available from the **visitors' centre** (397 2088, http://parks.nv.gov/vf.htm), which also has displays on the area's geology, ecology and human history. Signposted along Highway 169, it's open 8.30am-4.30pm daily. Park entrance is $10.

HEADING WEST

Red Rock Canyon & around

A mere 20 miles from the gaming tables of Vegas is one of Nevada's most beautiful outdoor areas. The cool, deep-cut canyons of the **Red Rock Canyon National Conservation Area** make it a popular hiking spot year-round, while climbers come here from all over to enjoy some of the best rock climbing in the US.

Part of the Spring Mountains, Red Rock Canyon has as its centrepiece a nearly sheer escarpment of Aztec sandstone, the remnant of ancient sand dunes that covered the area 180 million years ago. Roughly 65 million years ago, the Keystone Thrust Fault pushed older grey limestone over younger sandstone, reversing the normal layering and resulting in today's dramatic landscape. The red and cream Calico Hills are more rounded, as they're not protected from erosion by a higher limestone layer.

Attracted by the water, Native Americans have used Red Rock Canyon since about 3500 BC: evidence remains in the form of rock art (etched petroglyphs and painted pictographs), as well as artefacts such as arrowheads and ceramics. More than 45 mammal species also inhabit the park, among them mountain lions, coyotes, kangaroo rats, mule deer and the near-mythical desert bighorn sheep, but you'll be lucky to spot any. The most visible animals are the non-native burros (donkeys), around 50 of which live around Red Rock Canyon. Observe from a distance and never feed them (it's illegal and dangerous).

Stop first at the visitors' centre (clearly signed) for information and a map, before exploring the one-way, 13-mile scenic drive (also popular with cyclists) through the canyon. The road gives access to numerous hiking trails and three picnic sites. Some trails are not marked clearly and require some scrambling; so take a topographic map (available at the visitors' centre) and a compass.

A good introduction to the Calico Hills at the start of the drive is the two-and-a-half-mile **Calico Tank** trail from Sandstone Quarry. Just above the tank is a fine view (smog permitting) of the valley and the Strip's casino monoliths. Other good, short summer hikes include **Ice Box Canyon** and **Pine Creek Canyon**. For further details of the scores of other trails, pick up a copy of the BLM's trail leaflet. Guided hikes are led by park staff at the weekends and some weekdays, and by the Sierra Club (732 7750, www.nevada.sierraclub.org).

Red Rock is popular with rock climbers. Stop at **Desert Rock Sports** (*see p193*) for gear and some practice on the indoor wall, before calling in at the visitors' centre. There's further detail in these guides: Joanne Urioste's *The Red Rocks of Southern Nevada* and *The Red Book Supplement*, as well as *Red Rock Odyssey* by DeAngelo and Thiry (all Verex Press, www.verexpress.com, $21.95, $19.95, $24.95), and Todd Swain's *Rock Climbing: Red Rocks* (Falcon Press, www.falcon. com, $30). Alternatively, get to know the Old West like an old Westerner with **Cowboy Trail Rides** (387 2457, www.cowboytrailrides.com), which can saddle you up and take you on a tour of Red Rock. Rides ($99-$250) are accompanied by a guide; first-timers are welcome and booking is required.

If you'd prefer something less physical, head further west on Highway 159 to the green oasis of **Spring Mountain State Park**, at the base of the dramatic Wilson Cliffs. Admission to the park includes entrance to the New England-style ranch house, where the $7-$12 day-use fee is payable (875 4141, http://parks.nv.gov/ smr.htm, 10am-4pm daily, Nov-Mar; 10am-5pm daily, Apr, May, Sept, Oct; 11am-7pm daily, June-Aug). Stroll around the buildings in the fenced grounds and picnic on a grassy meadow. There are walking tours year-round, and open-air theatre and concerts in summer.

Bonnie Springs Old Nevada

1 Gun Fighter Lane, off Highway 159 (875 4191, www.bonniesprings.com). No bus. **Open** *May-Oct* 10.30am-6pm daily. *Nov-Apr* 10.30am-5pm daily. **Admission** $20/car. **Credit** MC, V.
South on Highway 159 sits this mock Wild West town, with a melodrama and hanging staged daily

Red Rock Canyon.

(times vary by season). It's rather dilapidated but good fun; visitors can take a horse ride ($30), and there's also a free petting zoo, a restaurant and a motel (875 4400, rates $85-$165).

GETTING THERE

To reach the visitors' centre, head west on Charleston Boulevard (Highway 159) for 20 miles. If you're staying near the southern end of the Strip, drive south on I-15, take Highway 160 (towards Pahrump), then turn right on to Highway 159, passing Bonnie Springs and Spring Mountain en route to Red Rock Canyon.

TOURIST INFORMATION

The Red Rock Canyon visitors' centre (515 5350, www.nv.blm.gov/redrockcanyon) offers information, maps and a chance to pay the $7-per-car fee. The centre is open daily from 8am to 4.30pm; however, the scenic drive itself is open longer hours (6am-8pm Apr-Sept; 6am-7pm Oct, Mar; 6am-5pm Nov-Feb).

Mount Charleston & around

It's true: you can jet-ski near Las Vegas in the morning and snow-ski in the afternoon. A mere 45 minutes north-west of the city lies the Spring Mountain Recreation Area, more commonly known as **Mount Charleston**. It's part of the massive Spring Mountain Range, dominated by Charleston Peak, the highest point in southern Nevada at 11,918 feet. In the winter, you can ski and snowboard at Lee Canyon; in summer, hike the forested slopes, far cooler than the city. There are also picnic sites and several campgrounds in the area.

Watch the vegetation change as you climb into the mountains, moving from creosote, bursage and Joshua trees on the lower slopes to piñon and Utah juniper, through ponderosa pine and mountain mahogany, and finally to gnarled bristlecone pines where the tree-line peters out at 10,000 feet. Due to the isolation of the range, around 30 species of flora and fauna are unique to this 'sky island'.

There are two roads into the area, both off US 95. Nearest to Las Vegas is Highway 157 (Kyle Canyon Road), which ascends prettily through winding canyons and wooded slopes to the **Resort at Mount Charlton** (*see right*), a rustic-style lodge with a huge lobby warmed by an open fireplace. The road continues west for another few miles, past a small park office (872 5486, closed Mon & Tue in winter), terminating at **Mount Charleston Lodge** (*see p251*). Here, you'll find a 24-hour bar, restaurant, riding stables and some delightful log cabins.

From the Mount Charleston Hotel, Highway 158 (Deer Creek Highway) heads north to the junction with Highway 156 (Lee Canyon Road).

Seven miles along Highway 158, the short Desert View Trail leads to a spectacular view of the valley and the mountains. At the junction with Highway 156, turn left for the ski area, usually open November to April. The elevation here is 8,500 feet, with three chairlifts leading up another 1,000 feet to 13 slopes. (For more on skiing in the area, *see p237*.) Drive back to US 95 on Highway 158 for a fine view of the desert below.

The US Forest Service prefers hikers to stick to designated trails, but there are numerous unmarked hikes around Mount Charleston (take a compass and a trail guidebook). The six-mile **Bristlecone Trail** provides worthwhile views of limestone cliffs and bristlecone pines; the short trail to **Mary Jane Falls** is both more strenuous and more rewarding, with hikers climbing 900 feet to a waterfall. The mother of all hikes, though, is the 18-mile round trip to **Mount Charleston Peak**, a difficult and demanding trail that's not clear of snow until as late as July. From the summit you can enjoy a stunning view of southern Nevada, eastern California and southern Utah. For all hikes, you'll need warm clothing and water.

On your way to Mount Charleston, stop off at **Floyd Lamb Park**; it's the former site of Tule Springs Ranch, where prospective divorcees waited out their six-week residency requirement in the 1940s and '50s. Located 15 miles from the city (though now surrounded by sprawl), its lawns, cottonwoods and four lakes make it a popular picnicking and fishing spot. It's best to avoid weekends if you don't like crowds. During the week, it's serene; not even the swankiest Strip hotels can match the peacocks that wander around the white ranch buildings. There's no camping, though: the park, for which admission costs $6 (229 8100, www.lasvegasnevada.gov), is solely a day-use facility.

Further away is the **Desert National Wildlife Refuge** (879 6110, www.fws.gov/refuge/desert), established in 1936 to protect the desert bighorn sheep and its habitat. A gravel road leads to a self-service information centre, where you can pick up a leaflet on the refuge and stroll around the ponds of Corn Creek Springs. The western half of the refuge is used by the Nellis Air Force Range as a bombing area and is closed to the public, while the rest is a nature reserve, accessible by two unmaintained dirt roads: you'll need a high-clearance or four-wheel-drive vehicle in order to gain access to them. Summer is the best time to spot the elusive bighorn sheep; the wildflowers are usually in bloom from March to May.

WHERE TO STAY, EAT & DRINK

Accommodation and eating options on Mount Charleston are few and far between. The **Resort at Mount Charleston** (1-888 559 1888,

872 5500, www.mtcharlestonresort.com) has a cavernous dining room and 57 rooms (doubles $89-$170), though a better bet is the characterful **Mount Charleston Lodge** (1-800 955 1314, 872 5408, www.mtcharlestonlodge.com), where the cosy log cabins ($200-$375) come with desks and offer wonderful views down over the landscape. The restaurant serves solid American fare, and doubles as a bar in the evening. There are also several camping areas; midweek, you can often find a spot by driving in, though weekends book up early in season.

GETTING THERE

Take US 95 north from Downtown for about 35 miles to reach Highway 157; Highway 156 is about 12 miles further on. In winter, you'll need snow chains on the mountain roads.

The Grand Canyon, Arizona

Of Arizona's two major towns, sprawling Phoenix has little to offer the visitor except sun and golf, while the more characterful Tucson is too far away to visit comfortably in a couple of days. It's no surprise, then, that most visitors to Arizona from Las Vegas head as directly east as the roads allow, towards one of the world's great natural wonders: the Grand Canyon. You'll have seen pictures, TV footage, maybe even an IMAX film on a larger-than-life-size screen. Yet nothing will prepare you for your first glimpse of the epic, breathtaking, unknowable Grand Canyon.

Grand Canyon National Park sprawls across a length of 277 miles, most of which is difficult to reach and rarely visited; just a tiny portion is accessible from the **South Rim**, where most visitors congregate. The canyon is misnamed: it's not just one rip in the earth, but a series of canyons surrounding the central gorge cut by the Colorado River, a staggering 5,000 feet from top to bottom. At an average elevation of 7,000 feet, the South Rim isn't unbearably hot in summer, but temperatures a mile further down at the bottom can edge beyond 110°F (43°C). The best months to visit are April, May, September and October, avoiding the relatively rainy (and tourist-packed) summer months and the snowbound winters.

Entrance to the park costs $25 per car ($12 per person for pedestrians, cyclists and motorcycles), valid for seven days. Although it's possible to make a see-it-and-scram trip in one long day, we recommend that you stay at least two nights, allowing time to explore the village, spin around the rim drives, take in the lookout points and venture into the canyon itself.

EN ROUTE TO THE SOUTH RIM

Some 150 miles west of the South Rim, the Grand Canyon forms the northern boundary of the Hualapai Indian Reservation. Although it's not as spectacular as the South Rim, the western canyon is closer to Las Vegas and will give you a taste of the grandeur to be found further east.

Roughly an hour south-east of Las Vegas, there's the option of a detour to a high-concept, high-budget attraction within the reservation. Opened in 2007, the **Grand Canyon Skywalk** (1-877 716 9378, 1-702 220 8372, www.grand canyonskywalk.com, *photo p252*) is a free-standing glass bridge that extends directly over the canyon, giving visitors the opportunity to stand 4,000 feet above the earth and look down into it. So far so good, until you take into account the breathtaking $81.95 admission fee – all individuals are required to purchase a Legacy pass (1-888 868 9378, www.grandcanyon west.com) to enter the reservation plus pay the additional cost for the Skywalk – and the fact that cameras aren't allowed on the damn thing.

If money is no object and you have a photographic memory, then head to Skywalk by taking a left off US 93 on to Pierce Ferry Road, 40 miles south of the Hoover Dam, and then turning right on to Diamond Bar Road 28 miles later. From here, it's a simple drive to the reservation's other attractions, such as rafting tours (**Hualapai River Runners** 1-928 769 2636), camping and helicopter rides. The tribal headquarters are further south in **Peach Springs**, where the **Hualapai Lodge** (900 Route 66, 1-928 769 2230) provides lodging and dining facilities along with permits for sightseeing, fishing and camping. For further details, see www.bestgrandcanyondestinations.com.

If you choose to pass on the walk and continue along US 93, you'll hit **Kingman**. From here, you have a choice. If you're in a hurry, take speedy I-40 east. But if you've a little more time and a little more romance about your person, head along what is now the longest surviving portion of the iconic Route 66. Much of the 2,448-mile Mother Road,

INSIDE TRACK ARIZONA TIME

Note that Arizona observes Mountain Standard Time year-round, without daylight saving time in summer. This means that from the first Sunday in November until the second Sunday in March, Arizona is one hour ahead of Las Vegas, but is effectively in the same time zone for the remainder of the year.

ESCAPES & EXCURSIONS

Grand Canyon National Park. *See p251.*

which originally linked Chicago with Santa Monica, has been bypassed or replaced by major highways. But this portion survives, just about. In Kingman, swing by the **Powerhouse Route 66 Museum** (120 W Andy Devine Avenue, 1-928 753 9889, www.gokingman.com), before driving west through dusty **Hackberry**, the aforementioned Peach Springs and on to **Seligman**, where you can reconnect with I-40.

Continuing west along I-40 will bring you to **Williams**, 60 miles south of the National Park. Some use the town as a staging post en route to the canyon, the entrance to which is 60 miles due north along Route 64 or along a picturesque, narrow-gauge steam railway (*see p254*). Others, though, prefer the larger **Flagstaff**, 35 miles east. Situated at the base of the **San Francisco Peaks**, the highest mountains in Arizona, this pleasant railroad and university town has motels, restaurants, cafés and a brewpub, as well as the **Lowell Observatory** (www.lowell.edu), from which Pluto was first spotted in 1930. For more information, contact the Chamber of Commerce (101 W Route 66, 1-928 774 4505, www.flagstaffchamber.com).

THE SOUTH RIM

The majority of the annual five million visitors to Grand Canyon National Park head for the **South Rim** and the restaurants, shops and sights of **Grand Canyon Village**, on the edge of the canyon. Inevitably, it's crowded, but it remains remarkably untouristy; or, in some cases, pleasantly retro-touristy. It's also closer to the Colorado River than the North Rim and affords much better views into the canyon.

If you have sufficient patience to avoid driving straight to the rim, park your car and take a free shuttle bus to the **Canyon View Information Plaza**, where you'll find a

visitors' centre and bookstore (open 8am-5pm daily). Pick up a variety of literature from here, offering comprehensive information on sights, transportation, facilities and activities, and ask the rangers for tips on hikes. Stroll to **Mather Point** for your first gob-smacking view of the canyon, before riding the shuttle bus from Information Plaza into Grand Canyon Village.

Grand Canyon Village

Travellers have been coming to gawp at the Grand Canyon since the 19th century, and Grand Canyon Village remains proud of its history. The village is dotted with historic buildings, many of them built by pioneering female architect Mary Colter for the Fred Harvey Travel Company. Pick up a leaflet and take the self-guided walking tour around the village's historic district, starting at the **Santa Fe Railway Station** (1909), the terminus for the **Grand Canyon Railway** (*see p254*). Across the road on the canyon's edge is the luxurious **El Tovar Hotel**, a wooden structure in hunting-lodge style that cost a cool $250,000 to build in 1905. Next to it is the **Hopi House**, designed by Colter in 1904 as a showroom for Indian handicrafts. Colter modelled the building on a terraced Hopi dwelling, using local stone and wood, and employing Hopi builders. Nearby is **Verkamps**, completed in 1906 and one of the canyon's oldest continuously operating stores.

Walking west from the hotel along the Rim Trail, you'll pass the modern **Kachina** and **Thunderbird** lodges, and the pioneer-style, stone-and-log **Bright Angel Lodge**, designed by Colter in 1935. If you're here in winter, warm your hands at the fabulous 'geological' fireplace, the design of which mimics the layers of rock in the Grand Canyon. The hearth is made from stone from the bed of the Colorado River; at the top of the chimney breast sits a layer of Kaibab limestone.

Just beyond Bright Angel Lodge is the **Bucky O'Neill Cabin**, which dates from the 1890s and is the oldest surviving building on the rim, and the **Lookout Studio** (Colter, 1914), which now houses a gift shop. Perched on the edge of the precipice, the studio was designed as an observation building from which visitors could view the canyon. Colter didn't want the building to detract from its surroundings, and created a stone structure that merges with the surrounding rock. From a distance, the structure is almost invisible.

The nearby **Kolb Studio** was built by pioneering photographers Ellsworth and Emery Kolb, who started snapping mule riders here in 1902. The lack of water on the rim meant the brothers were required to hike halfway down the canyon to their developing tent at Indian Gardens to process the photos, then clamber back to the top before the mules returned. (To this day, all water at the South Rim is pumped up from inside the canyon; look for the trans-canyon pipeline on the Bright Angel Trail.) The Kolbs were also the first to film a boat trip down the Colorado, in 1912. The studio houses a bookstore and gallery, and has displays on the brothers' work. Beyond here is the head of the Bright Angel Trail (see p256).

Along the South Rim

Two roads lead west and east from the village along the canyon rim, each providing very different views into the canyon. You can also walk along the edge of the rim on the 12-mile, pedestrian-only **Rim Trail**. The village section of the trail is paved; elsewhere it can get rocky.

The eight-mile **Hermit Road** is closed to private vehicles. Instead, visitors are encouraged to take the shuttle bus that departs from the western edge of the village to **Hermit's Rest**, built by Mary Colter as a refreshment stop in 1914. The building, now in use as a gift shop, is deliberately primitive in style, and designed to blend with its natural surroundings (fortunately, a Swiss chalet design was rejected). From here, you can set off on the Hermit Trail (see p256) into the canyon.

The shuttle bus stops at various observation points on its way west. Among them is the spectacular **Abyss**, where the Great Mohave Wall drops 3,000 feet to the Tonto Platform above the Colorado River. On its return, the bus stops only at Mohave Point and **Hopi Point**. If you're planning to watch the sunset, check the time of the last bus before you leave to avoid a long, dark walk back to the village.

Along the East Rim, **Desert View Drive** runs 25 miles in the opposite direction as far as the park's eastern entrance. On the way, the road passes several excellent lookout points,

with access to the **South Kaibab** and **Grandview Trails** (for both, see p256). Near the end of the drive, there's an 800-year-old ruin of an Anasazi pueblo and the **Tusayan Museum**, which provides somewhat scanty information on the history and culture of the canyon's Native American inhabitants.

The drive finishes at **Desert View**, which offers the clearest views of the Colorado River. This is also the location of the **Watchtower**, a circular, 70-foot (21-metre) tower regarded as Colter's masterpiece. A remarkable re-creation of the ancient Indian towers Colter had seen at Mesa Verde and Canyon de Chelly, its ground-floor room is modelled after a kiva (or sacred ceremonial chamber), while the roof provides a panoramic view of the Grand Canyon, the Painted Desert and the San Francisco Peaks, 40 miles to the south. The centrepiece is the **Hopi Room**, decorated with vivid Hopi designs depicting various gods and legends.

To learn more about the geology, history and archaeology of the South Rim, join one of the National Park Service's ranger-guided walks or activities. Check the park's website or ask at the visitors' centre for a programme schedule.

Where to eat & drink

There are three restaurants, two self-service cafés and a takeaway snack bar in the Grand Canyon Village, all open daily. The splendid, dark wooden dining room (with its large Indian murals) at the **El Tovar Hotel** is very popular: you can take your chances at breakfast and lunch, but must book for dinner (1-928 638 2631); hotel guests take priority over non-guests.

Nearby are the less formal **Bright Angel Restaurant** and the **Arizona Room** steakhouse (closed Jan, Feb). **Maswik Lodge** has a sports bar and an inexpensive but rather institutional cafeteria; there's a larger cafeteria at **Yavapai Lodge**. Wherever you dine, have a drink in the lounge at the El Tovar, decorated by the ubiquitous Colter. There are also snack bars at **Hermit's Rest** and **Desert View Marketplace**, and a deli at Market Plaza.

Where to stay

There's plenty of accommodation in Grand Canyon Village, but demand is high: book as far ahead as you can (we're talking months, not weeks). That said, there are sometimes rooms available for walk-in visitors at Yavapai and Maswik Lodges, occasionally even in high season. Book through **Xanterra Parks & Resorts** (1-888 297 2757, 1-303 297 2757 outside US, www.grandcanyonlodges.com). Usually, the more expensive rooms at the hotels and lodges listed below come with a canyon view.

ESCAPES & EXCURSIONS

Complete with a grand lobby adorned with stuffed animal heads, the **El Tovar Hotel** (doubles $178-$426), offers the most splendid lodging in the village. Try to get a room with a spacious private balcony overlooking the rim. Other options are the 1930s **Bright Angel Lodge** (doubles $81-$340) and the more modern, motel-style **Kachina** and **Thunderbird Lodge** (doubles $173-$184), also on the edge of the canyon. **Maswik Lodge** (doubles $92-$173) and **Yavapai Lodge** (doubles $114-$163) are located in a pine forest a short walk away.

There are also two campsites at the South Rim, run by the National Park Service. There are more than 300 pitches at the **Mather Campground**, but booking is recommended from March to mid November (1-928 638 7851, www.recreation.gov). Outside these times, campsites are available on a walk-up basis, and the standard $18 fee drops by $3. Roughly 25 miles east of Grand Canyon Village, **Desert View Campground** is open from mid May to mid October on a walk-up basis ($12).

A few miles south of Grand Canyon Village, just outside the park, is **Tusayan**. At the National Geographic Visitor Center, there's a supremely superfluous IMAX cinema and a rather more useful parking fee pay-station, which will mean you don't have to queue on entry. Among the basic motels are the **Red Feather Lodge** (1-800 538-2345, 1-928 638 2414, www.redfeatherlodge.com, doubles $120-$160), the **Best Western Squire Inn** (1-800 622 6966, 1-928 638 2681, www.grandcanyon squire.com, doubles $200-$250) and a **Holiday Inn Express** (1-888 465 4329, 1-928 638 3000, www.hiexpress.com, doubles $200-$220). A free shuttle-bus service runs between Tusayan and the village. There are also plenty of motels in Flagstaff and Williams.

For lodging options in the canyon, *see p257*.

Getting there

By air

Several companies offer scheduled flights from the Las Vegas area to Grand Canyon Airport at Tusayan. Among them are **Air Vegas** (1-800 940 2550, 1-702 501 8470, www.airvegas.com), which operates several flights a day from the airport in North Las Vegas; a return flight costs $210. For details of sightseeing flights over the Grand Canyon, *see p257*.

By bus

Bus service between Flagstaff, Williams and Grand Canyon Village is offered by **Open Road** (1-855 563-8830, 1-602 997-6474, www.openroad tours.com), which charges $95 round trip adult; $55 children between Flagstaff and the Grand Canyon.

Greyhound (*see p292*) runs bus services from Las Vegas to Flagstaff (6hrs; $117-$145 return).

By car

To reach the South Rim, head south-east on US 93 to I-40 east, then turn left (north) on to Highway 64 at Williams. It's 290 miles from Vegas and the journey takes about five hours. As an alternative, drive to Williams and board the Grand Canyon Railway (*see below*).

By rail

The **Grand Canyon Railway** (1-800 843 8724, 1-928 773 1976, www.thetrain.com) runs train services from the depot in Williams to the old **Santa Fe Station** in the heart of Grand Canyon Village. Trains leave Williams at 9.30am and depart from the Grand Canyon at 3.30pm. There are various 'classes' of service in an assortment of historic carriages, and characters in costume entertain passengers en route. The trip takes 2hrs 15mins; tickets, which exclude the park fee, cost $70-$190 ($40-$110 children, who are not allowed in the Observation Dome or luxury coaches).

Getting around

To encourage a more serene appreciation of nature, the park service has limited private-vehicle access in some areas and is expanding pedestrian and bicycle routes around the South Rim. The bus shuttles are a pleasant and workable alternative to private transport.

By bus

A free shuttle-bus service operates on three interconnecting routes around the South Rim: the **Village Route**, serving Canyon View Information Plaza and the main village destinations; the **Hermit's Rest Route**, along the rim from the west side of the village to Hermit's Rest; and the **Kaibab Trail Route**, from Canyon View to Yaki Point. A route for visitors needing mobility assistance operates from Canyon View to Mather Point.

By car

Canyon View Information Plaza, Mather Point, Yaki Point Road and Hermit Road are not accessible to private vehicles.

By coach

Choose from various Xanterra-run sightseeing trips around the canyon rim, including the **Hermit's Rest Tour** ($26 per person, children under 16 free when accompanied by paying adult), the **Desert View Tour** ($45), and popular 90-minute **Sunrise** and **Sunset** tours ($20.50). For reservations, call 1-888 297 2757; alternatively, visit the desks at Bright Angel, Maswik and Yavapai Lodges, or at Canyon View Information Plaza.

Grand Canyon.

By taxi
A 24hr taxi service is available on 1-928 638 2822.

THE NORTH RIM

From the South Rim, you can see lightning forks hit the **North Rim** ten miles across the canyon. However, to reach it, you'll have to hike down to the bottom and back up again, drive 220 miles all the way around the canyon, or catch the daily shuttle bus. The North Rim is 1,000 feet higher than the South Rim and is only open from mid May to mid October. It has fewer facilities and, thus, fewer visitors than the South Rim, which is why many longtime visitors prefer it up here; the tranquil atmosphere can still evoke what it may have been like to visit the canyon in the early days. That said, you should book ahead for lodging, which is at a premium during busy seasons. Facilities include a visitors' centre, a grocery, a camping shop and a post office.

Where to stay, eat & drink

Run by Forever Resorts, the **Grand Canyon Lodge** (1-877 386-4383, www.grandcanyon lodgenorth.com) is the only lodging inside the park at the North Rim. Cabins cost $121-$187; there's also a dining room and a campsite (Jan-mid Apr 1-928 645 6865; mid May-mid Oct 1-928 638 2611), as well as the Grand Canyon chuck-wagon cookout experience (June-Sept, $22-$35), for which booking is advisable. There are also lodging and eating facilities at **Kaibab Lodge** (1-928 638 2389, www.kaibablodge.com, cabins $85-$155) and **Jacob Lake Inn** (1-928 643 7232, www.jacoblake.com, doubles $89-$138), respectively 18 and 45 miles north of the park.

Getting there

By bus
The only public transport to the North Rim is the **Trans Canyon Shuttle** bus service, (www.trans-canyonshuttle.com), which leaves the South Rim at 1.30pm daily and makes the return ride at 7am (mid May-mid Oct only). The journey takes about 4hrs 30mins and costs $80 ($160 round trip). Call 1-877 638 2820 for details.

By car
From Las Vegas, head north on I-15, then east on Hwy 9, Hwy 59 and US 89A to **Jacob Lake**. The park entrance is 30 miles south of Jacob Lake on Hwy 67; the rim is a further 14 miles. At a distance of 263 miles, the North Rim is nearer to Las Vegas than the South Rim, but the journey takes longer.

EXPLORING THE CANYON
Hiking

However limited your time may be, try to hike at least part of the way into the canyon. As jaw-dropping as the views undoubtedly are from the rim, the gulf is almost too huge to allow a full appreciation of this unique environment. Really, you need to get closer: to soak up the stunning colours of the cliffs, to identify the different geological layers of rock, and to see the turbulent brown waters and hear the roar of the Colorado River. The basic rule of hiking into the canyon is that it takes twice as long to hike up as down; if you have three hours, turn around after an hour.

Although the upper trails teem with crowds, remember that you're not at a theme park. The

Hiking in the Grand Canyon.

extremes of terrain and climate are dangerous: always seek and heed advice from rangers, and ensure you're in decent physical shape and properly equipped. Note, too, that overnight hikes (and camping stays) require a backcountry permit, which is issued on a strictly limited basis. Always try to apply for one in advance via the website; you can take your chances on the day and turn up at the **Backcountry Information Center** at 8am, but you may find yourself with a lengthy wait.

Hikers should note that mule riders have priority on the Bright Angel, South Kaibab and North Kaibab trails. Stop walking when the mules approach, and follow any instructions given by the rider leading the tour.

Backcountry Information Center

Grand Canyon National Park, PO Box 129, Grand Canyon, AZ 86023 (1-928 638 7875, 1-5pm Mon-Fri; www.nps.gov/grca). **Open** *mid May-mid Oct* (walk-in visitors) 8am-noon, 1-5pm daily. **Rates** *Permit* $12 by foot, $25 by vehicle, per night. **No credit cards**.

Apply here for a backcountry permit, required for all overnight camping trips except those that involve designated camp sites (where fees range from $10-$23 per night). Applications open four months prior to the month in which you plan to hike; for example, applications for hiking trips in May are processed from 1 January. Apply as early as possible.

Bright Angel Trail

Grand Canyon Village to Plateau Point. **Round trip** 19.2 miles. **Duration** 2 days.

This popular trail follows the line of a wide geological fault, which shifted the layering of the rock strata; as you descend, you'll notice that the layers on the left are much higher than those on the right. Water is usually available (May-Sept) at the rest houses 1.5 miles and three miles from the trailhead. They're good day-hike destinations but can get crowded. Experienced hikers could head for the campground at Indian Gardens (4.5 miles); the tall cottonwoods here, planted in the early 1900s, can be seen from the rim. From Indian Gardens, continue to Plateau Point (6.1 miles) for a view into the river gorge.

Grandview Trail

Grandview Point to Horseshoe Mesa. **Round trip** 6.4 miles. **Duration** 1 day.

This unmaintained trail is steep and should only be attempted by experienced hikers. There's no water en route, but there are toilet facilities at Horseshoe Mesa, the site of an abandoned mining works.

Hermit Trail

Hermit's Rest to Colorado River. **Round trip** 18.4 miles. **Duration** 2-3 days.

This difficult trail passes Hermit Gorge, Santa Maria Spring and the Redwall Formation en route to the Colorado River and is recommended for experienced desert hikers only. A precipitous side trail leads for 1.5 miles to Dripping Springs. There is no drinking water on the trail; spring water must be treated.

North Kaibab Trail

North Rim to Colorado River Bridge. **Round trip** 29.2 miles. **Duration** 3-4 days.

The North Kaibab trail starts about 1.5 miles from Grand Canyon Lodge on the North Rim and begins with a beautiful but steep hike through the trees. The Supai Tunnel (1.8 miles) is an ideal day hike with a great view of the canyon, plus water and toilet facilities. There is little shade beyond this point. More experienced hikers might make it to Roaring Springs, but should not attempt to go further than this and back in one day. Beyond Roaring Springs, the trail continues to Phantom Ranch (13.8 miles) and the Colorado River Bridge (14.6 miles).

South Kaibab Trail

Yaki Point to Phantom Ranch. **Round trip** 12.6 miles. **Duration** 2 days.

This trail, which starts five miles east of Grand Canyon Village, is shorter but steeper than Bright Angel trail, dropping 5,000ft (1,500m) in six miles. The route follows a series of ridge lines, crossing the Colorado at the Kaibab Suspension Bridge on its way to Phantom Ranch. There is no campground or drinking water en route; hike to the tree-dotted plateau of Cedar Ridge (1.5 miles) if you're short of time.

Mule rides

Mule rides into the canyon are operated by **Xanterra** (*see p253*), and booking is essential. The three-hour day trip ($122.81 per person) takes you 3,200 feet down the **Abyss Overlook**. On the one-night ride ($523.43 per person), you'll go down the **Bright Angel Trail**, eat lunch at **Indian Garden**, then proceed over the Colorado River on a suspension bridge, and stay overnight in a cabin at **Phantom Ranch** (*see right*). You can even defy saddle-soreness with a three-day trip, which includes two nights at Phantom Ranch ($714.46 per person). All rates include accommodation and food.

Plane & helicopter rides

Plane and helicopter rides over the rim are a major cause of air and noise pollution in the canyon, reducing visibility and disturbing the area's natural tranquillity. Rides are not available from within the park. However, if you must get a bird's-eye view, various outfits operate services out of Grand Canyon Airport in Tusayan. Plane rides start from around $100-$145; helicopter rides are more expensive. For flights departing from Las Vegas, *see p254*.
Grand Canyon Airlines *1-866 235 9422, www.grandcanyonairlines.com.*
Papillon Grand Canyon Helicopters *1-888 635 7272, 1-702 736 7243, www.papillon.com.*

River rafting

Follow in the wake of one-armed explorer Major John Wesley Powell, who in 1869 became the first man to navigate the length of the Colorado River by boat, by taking a river trip through the rapids of the Grand Canyon. It's a major undertaking: you'll need at least eight days to travel the 277 miles downriver from Lees Ferry at the far eastern end of the Grand Canyon to Pearce Ferry on Lake Mead, and you'll have to book months in advance. A list of approved operators is on the NPS's Grand Canyon website.

You can take a shorter trip by hiking in or out of the canyon. Firms such as **Canyoneers**

(1-800 525 0924, 1-928 526 0924, www.canyoneers.com) also offer shorter trips that start or finish at **Bright Angel Beach** near Phantom Ranch. Trips such as these entail less time on the river, and you'll also have to hike in or out of the canyon at the beginning or end of your trip.

For whitewater trips from **Diamond Creek** in Grand Canyon West, roughly a four-hour drive from the South Rim, *see p251*.

Staying in the canyon

Phantom Ranch, down at the bottom of the canyon, was designed by Mary Colter in 1922 and is a welcome oasis after the rigours of a strenuous hike. Hikers who stay here do not need backcountry permits, but will need to book months in advance: the dorms ($46.33 bed) are usually filled to capacity. Duffel service (where your pack is carried by mule) is an additional $66.79 each way. Non-guests can eat here, but must book meals in advance ($20.88 breakfast, $12.66 packed lunch, $28.39-$44.05 dinner).

There are campsites at **Indian Gardens**, **Bright Angel** (next to Phantom Ranch) and **Cottonwood Springs** (May-Oct, accessible from the North Rim on the North Kaibab Trail). You'll need a backcountry permit to stay at any of them; *see p256*.

TOURIST INFORMATION

For general information, call the **National Park Service** on 1-928 638 7888. Alternatively, check the detail-packed if slightly convoluted website at www.nps.gov/grca, which has information on accommodation, hiking and backcountry permits, plus maps of the area.
Arizona Office of Tourism *1-866 275 5816, www.arizonaguide.com.*

California

The relationship between Nevada and southern California has always been an uneasy one. Nevadans view their near-neighbours with wariness, while California natives look back with downright suspicion. And yet the traffic between the two states has never been greater. The route between the two states takes the driver through pioneer country, traversed in the 19th century by migrants heading westwards, celebrated in the 20th century in Hollywood Westerns, and now offering 21st-century trippers a dramatic landscape. Don't forget that parts of southern California are uninhabited and often scorching. Take suitable precautions when driving and hiking (*see p258* **Inside Track**).

ALONG I-15

You can throw the dice one last time at a pair of mini-gambling resorts along I-15, south of Las Vegas but before the border with California. **Jean**, the closest of the pair to Vegas, is home to the MGM-owned **Gold Strike** (1-800 634 1359, 477 5000, www.goldstrikejean.com), a pretty basic casino-hotel if you're looking for a place to stay, or you can visit the ghost town of **Goodsprings**, which hit the headlines in 1942 when Clark Gable waited for news of the plane crash that killed his wife, Carole Lombard.

Right on the Nevada–California border, **Primm** is a three-resort cluster of more modern aspect. The success of **Whiskey Pete's**, the Primm family's first casino-hotel, was so great that they followed it with two more, **Primm Valley** and **Buffalo Bill's** (1-888 774 6668, www.primmvalleyresorts.com for all three). However, the main reason to pull in here is the presence of **Fashion Outlets Las Vegas** (874 1400, www.fashionoutletlasvegas.com), a better-than-you'd-expect outlet mall that features a number of familiar brands that aren't present at either Vegas outlet enterprise.

Continuing south, I-15 passes through stunning scenery along the northern boundary of **Mojave National Preserve** (*see below*). The small town of **Baker**, 90 miles south of Vegas, makes a convenient gateway to this wilderness, and is home to the world's tallest thermometer, which measures 134 feet top to toe. West, the I-15 continues through stark desert for 60 miles until it reaches **Barstow**, a bleak town notable primarily for its location on historic Route 66. Beyond the high-desert hicktown of **Hesperia**, I-15 takes you through the pine-capped wilderness of the San Bernardino Mountains until it hits the Los Angeles sprawl.

MOJAVE NATIONAL PRESERVE

Covering a gigantic rectangle bordered by I-15 to the north and I-40 to the south, the 2,500-square-mile **Mojave National Preserve** is a Cinderella park: it has no honeypot attractions, low visitorship and few facilities, and is really best approached as a giant desert sampler. The meeting point of three of the four types of North American desert (Mojave, Great Basin and Sonoran), it contains a variety of terrains, features and ecosystems, including the human.

Because its protected status is relatively recent, historical relics of inhabitants and would-be conquerors, from early man right through to 20th-century ranchers, dot the landscape. Spanish explorers, western pioneers and routefinders, soldiers, navvies and settlers passed this way, leaving behind roads and railroads still in use today. The best times to

visit are spring or autumn; it's brutally hot from mid May to mid September, often over 110°F (43°C). Whenever you visit, admission is free.

Mojave National Preserve has been developed only minimally: there are just four paved roads and three marked trails, and gas and lodging are available only on its borders. You can see plenty by car and on short walks, but those with four-wheel-drive vehicles will find it an off-road paradise. The numerous unpaved roads include the 140-mile east–west Mojave Road, a Native American track developed by successive users.

If you're coming from Vegas along I-15, be sure to fill up with both gas and drinking water at the town of Baker. If you've only a few hours, a 67-mile triangular drive from Baker, via the Kelbaker Road, Kelso–Cima Road and Cima Road, to rejoin I-15 at the end of the trek, is a good introduction to the sights.

You'll pass the reddish humps of over 30 young volcanic cones before reaching **Kelso**; once a major passenger stop on the Union Pacific Railroad, it was named after a local railroad worker when his name was the first one pulled from a hat by colleagues looking to christen the site. The grand, Spanish Mission-style depot, built in 1924 and closed in 1985, has been converted into a visitors' centre. From here, you can detour to the 500-foot (150-metre) Kelso sand dunes by heading south on the Kelbaker Road and turning right after about seven miles on to a signed dirt road.

Back in Kelso, turn left towards **Cima**, passing the 7,000-foot (2,150-metre) Providence Mountains (currently closed to visitors) en route. At Cima, you can take Cima Road towards I-15 past the gently swelling Cima Dome, which has the largest stand of Joshua trees in the world. Alternatively, head along Morning Star Mine

Mojave National Preserve.

Road to Nipton Road up the Ivanpah Valley, then either take a left to I-15 or a right to tiny **Nipton**, at the preserve's northern edge. Here you'll find a railroad crossing, a town hall and the charming **Hotel Nipton** (*see below*).

An interesting diversion from I-40 is a stretch of the old Route 66, featuring the kind of bleak desert landscapes beloved of cinematographers and the similarly iconic Americana of photogenic **Amboy**. To the east, 66 crosses I-40 and dips back into the preserve to **Goffs**, a lonely spot despite its status as 'the Desert Tortoise Capital of the World'. Further south is **Joshua Tree National Park** (www.nps.gov/jotr), worth a look in its own right.

Where to stay & eat

Lodgings within the park are limited to a pair of campgrounds. **Mid-Hills** is usually cooler than **Hole-in-the-Wall** (www.nps.gov/moja/planyourvisit/campgrounds.htm), and always much prettier. You'll need to drive some reliable but not always comfortable dirt roads to get here; Hole-in-the-Wall is accessible on blacktop from I-40. The fee at each is $12, and pitches are distributed on a first-come, first-served basis.

On the edge of the park, **Baker** has a clutch of basic non-chain motels as well as the rammed and rated **Mad Greek Diner** (1-760 733 4354), where both Greek and American fast food is served to motorists. However, the pick of the park-side lodging options is the **Hotel Nipton** (1-760 856 2335, www.nipton.com, rates vary by season), a century-old hotel in splendid desert isolation (except, that is, for its Wi-Fi access). If the main building is full, stay in one of the eco-cabins scattered behind the main building. Also here is the **Whistle Stop Oasis** (1-760 856 1045, 707 Nipton Road), a basic-looking shack where Bill Sarbello's food (especially the burgers) is better than it has any right to be.

Getting there

By car

Baker is 90 miles south of Las Vegas on I-15. Nipton is located on Hwy 164, accessible via I-15 or Hwy 95, 63 miles south of Las Vegas. To reach Joshua Tree, take Kelbaker Road through the Mojave National Preserve and head south via Amboy until you reach Twentynine Palms; it's 130 miles from Baker.

Tourist information

Mojave National Preserve: Kelso Depot Visitor Center *Kelbaker Road, Kelso (1-760 252 6108, www.nps.gov/moja).* **Open** 9am-5pm daily.
Mojave National Preserve: Hole-in-the-Wall Information Center *Essex & Black Canyon roads, north of I-40 (1-760 928 2572, www.nps.gov/moja).* **Open** *May-Sept* 10am-4pm Fri-Sun. *Oct-Apr* 9am-4pm Wed-Sun.

DEATH VALLEY NATIONAL PARK

Enlarged and redesignated a national park under the 1994 Desert Protection Act, Death Valley is now the largest national park outside Alaska, covering more than 5,156 square miles. It's also, famously, one of the hottest places on the planet. The park's website calmly offers that 'Death Valley is generally sunny, dry and clear throughout the year'. True, but the word 'generally' masks a multitude of curiosities. Air temperatures regularly top 120°F (49°C) in July and August; fearsome by anyone's standards.

However, while the park is usually parched, receiving fewer than two inches of rain in an average year, it's not immune from water. In August 2004, terrifying flash floods hit Death Valley, killing two tourists and destroying parts of Highway 190. Reconstruction of the road was completed a couple of years later, but the same thing could happen again at any time.

Get your bearings at the **Death Valley Visitor Center** (*see below*) at **Furnace Creek**, where you'll find an excellent bookshop, decent exhibits, a useful orientation film and helpful staff. Stop in for advice on current weather and road conditions (some tracks are accessible only to four-wheel-drive vehicles), pay your fee of $20 per car and take the opportunity to fill up at one of the park's three expensive gas stations.

However, if you've entered the park on Highway 190 from Las Vegas, you'll pass two of the most amazing sights en route to Furnace Creek, and it may save time to stop at them before hitting the visitors' centre. Roughly 13 miles off the main road and standing 5,475 feet above sea level, **Dante's View** is a great place from which to survey the park's otherworldly landscape. And three miles south of Furnace Creek lies **Zabriskie Point**, famed for the eponymous 1970 Antonioni film but recognisable by its ragged, rumpled appearance.

There's more to see further south of Furnace Creek. At **Golden Canyon**, there's a simple two-mile round-trip hike that's best walked in the late afternoon sunlight, when you'll see how the canyon got its name. Continuing south, the landscape gets plainer. Nine miles down the road is the **Devil's Golf Course**, a striking, scrappy landscape formed by salt crystallising and expanding; a few miles further is bleak, eerie **Badwater**, just two miles as the crow flies from Dante's View but more than 5,000 feet lower. Indeed, this is the lowest point in the Western Hemisphere, 282 feet below sea level. Unexpectedly, it's only 85 miles from the highest point in the lower 48 states, the 14,494-foot Mount Whitney in the Sierra Nevada. An annual 'ultramarathon' race – covering 135 miles (www.badwater.com) – is held between the two, though it no longer extends all the way to Whitney's summit.

Heading north from Furnace Creek offers a greater variety of sights. The remains of the **Harmony Borax Works** have been casually converted into a short trail; there's a similarly simple walk, less historic but more aesthetically pleasing, at nearby **Salt Creek**. Following the road around to the left will lead you past the eerie **Devil's Cornfield** and the frolic-friendly **Sand Dunes**, which rise and dip in 100-foot (30-metre) increments, and on to the small settlement at **Stovepipe Wells**. Taking a right and driving 36 miles will lead you to the luxurious **Scotty's Castle**; built in the 1920s for Chicago millionaire Albert Johnson, it was named after Walter Scott, his eccentric chancer of a friend. Rangers tell the story on 50-minute tours (usually hourly, 9am-5pm, $11 adults; $6-$9 reductions).

It's often too hot to hike, but there are plenty of trails in Death Valley, short and long. The options include the 14-mile round trip to the 11,000-foot (3,300-metre) summit of **Telescope Peak**, a good summer hike (the higher you climb, the cooler it gets). Starting at Mahogany Flat campground, you climb 3,000 feet for some spectacular views of Mount Whitney. In winter, only experienced climbers with ice axes and crampons should attempt it.

Where to stay & eat

Set into the hillside above Furnace Creek Wash, the **Furnace Creek Inn** (1-760 786 2345, www.furnacecreekresort.com, closed mid May-mid Oct, doubles $265-$455) was built in the 1930s, and retains a cultured dignity reminiscent of the era from which it emerged. The rooms are charming and well equipped, the landscaped gardens are picture-perfect and the pool is a delight. The inn's restaurant, where the upscale Californian food is far better than you might expect, is the best eating option in the area.

The nearby **Furnace Creek Ranch** (1-760 786 2345, www.furnacecreekresort.com, $138-$219) has 200 motel-style rooms and cabins, as well as a pool, tennis courts and the world's lowest golf course, plus a pretty basic restaurant and bar. The 83-room **Stovepipe Wells Village** (1-760 786 2387, www.escapetodeathvalley.com, doubles $80-$145) also has food on offer, but few other amenities. Four of the park's nine campgrounds are free, with the others costing between $12 and $18 a night. The most central, and the only one for which reservations are taken, is at **Furnace Creek** (1-877 444 6777, 1-760 786 2441, www.recreation.gov).

Getting there

By car

From Vegas, head south on I-15 towards LA, exit on to Blue Diamond Road (at Silverton), then head west on Hwy 160 over the Spring Mountains. A few miles after Pahrump, take Bell Vista Road to Death Valley Junction and Hwy 190 into the park (120 miles). (Returning to Vegas via Death Valley Junction, note that Bell Vista Road is labelled State Line Road.) Alternatively, take US 95 to Beatty and then head south on Hwy 374.

Tourist information

Death Valley Visitor Center *Furnace Creek, Death Valley National Park (1-760 786 3200, www.nps.gov/deva).* **Open** 8am-5pm daily.
Scotty's Castle Visitor Center *Scotty's Castle, Death Valley National Park (1-760 786 2392, www.nps.gov/deva).* **Open** *Summer* 9am-4.30pm daily. *Winter* 8.30am-5pm daily.

Nevada

Those who claim that there's plenty more to Nevada outside Las Vegas are overstating their case a little. Those who aver that there's plenty more *of* Nevada outside Las Vegas, on the other hand, are right on the money. Although the state is the seventh largest in the Union, almost three-quarters of its residents live within 40 miles of Las Vegas, with half the remainder in the Reno-Sparks urban area. That leaves an awful lot of not very much.

The under-visited **Valley of Fire State Park** (*see p248*) is stunning. The drive north-west from Vegas to **Reno** on I-95 offers a desert landscape alternately bleak and beautiful under skies as big as you'll ever see. The smattering of towns along it are scruffy but fascinating, all in thrall to the prospectors and chancers who established them a century ago. And then there's the **Extraterrestrial Highway**, named after the many extraordinary tales of UFO sightings and other sinister goings-on at the Nevada Test Site's mysterious and infamous Area 51.

Opera in a Ghost Town

Tiny Death Valley Junction is home to a unique kind of opera house.

Death Valley Junction is not your archetypal ghost town. It was settled not by travelling pioneers or gold-hungry prospectors but by the Pacific Coast Borax Company, which built it in the mid 1920s to house company workers. When they left, the town crumbled, until a fortysomething ballet dancer arrived from New York in 1967, took over a derelict community hall and began to fashion from it her own American dream.

Renovating the building as the Amargosa Opera House, Marta Becket turned coffee-cans into spotlights and filled the room with garden chairs. She even painted an audience on the walls, which made performing in an empty hall, as she often did, easier to bear. Eventually word spread, and people travelled to see both Becket's

theatre and her self-devised, folk art-ish performance pieces. In the early 1980s, Becket finally bought the property. Audiences, fascinated by this tale of devotion and self-imposed isolation, continued to come.

Tom Willett, Becket's longtime partner, died of a stroke in 2005, but the octogenarian Becket has continued without him, staging shows every Saturday night. There's nowhere quite like it.

Amargosa Opera House
Death Valley Junction, intersection of SR 190 & SR 127, just E of Death Valley National Park (1-760 852 4441, www. amargosa-opera-house.com). **Tickets** $15 adults; $12 children. Booking essential.

ESCAPES & EXCURSIONS

Death Valley. *See p259.*

THE ROAD TO RENO

US 95 leaves the lights of Las Vegas behind in a hurry. As the road roars out through the city's north-western corner, the landscape visible from the driver's seat empties from urban sprawl into endless desert. Get used to the view. You'll have seen a lot like it by the time your 450-mile ride from Vegas to Reno is complete. Soon, you'll be rolling past **Mount Charleston** (*see p250*). On the right sits **Nellis Air Force Range**, a vast tract of desert that, with an area of 5,200 square miles, is slightly larger than the state of Connecticut.

From 1951 until 1995, the US government, which owns more than 80 per cent of the land in Nevada, used the **Nevada Test Site**, which is flanked on three sides by the Nellis Range, to test atomic weapons, both above ground and beneath it. Day-long tours of the site, which leave from the **Atomic Testing Museum** in Las Vegas (itself worth a visit; *see p58*), are available to those prescient enough to book two months ahead and prepared to supply all manner of information to pass security screenings. For details, see www.nv.doe.gov or call 295 3521.

Shortly after Indian Springs, you'll leave Clark County and enter Nye County. At 18,147 square miles, it's the third largest county in the US, but it's also one of the emptiest: the 2008 census tagged the population at 44,375. At **Amargosa Valley**, close to the junction of US 95 and SR 373 (leading towards Death Valley), an unprepossessing cluster of buildings houses a bar, a gas station and a brothel, making it perhaps America's ultimate (male) travellers' rest area. Across the road sits a bar; nearby, on SR 373, sits Jackass Airport, named for the animal rather than the idiocy of the local pilots. And that's more or less it.

For years, the government has planned to use **Yucca Mountain**, just north of Amargosa Valley, as the repository for the country's spent nuclear waste. The Department of Energy even set a date for the site's opening: 31 March 2017. However, Nevada senator (and, as of 2013, Senate majority leader) Harry Reid has insisted that the plan will never come to pass; this one looks set to run and run. Tours of the mountain, which sits inside the Nevada Test Site, are available to those who book well in advance; visit www.ocrwm.doe.gov.

Head 30 miles north-west of Amargosa Valley and you'll find **Beatty**, established – as were so many towns at the turn of the 20th century – by prospectors ambitious to make their fortunes. When word got around that Ed Cross and Frank 'Shorty' Harris had discovered a goldmine in the hills, hundreds of hopefuls descended on the area, leading Walter Beatty to set up a town on his homestead. The volunteer-run **Beatty Museum** (417 Main Street, 1-775 553 2303, www.beattymuseum.org) offers exhibits and anecdotes about these early days.

Beatty is now a ramshackle collection of casinos and bars, but at least it's still alive, which is more than can be said for nearby **Rhyolite**. An archetypal gold rush town, it sprung up after gold was found in August 1904. The first lots were sold in February 1905; by 1908, 10,000 locals were served by schools, hospitals, 50 bars, an opera house and a red-light district. But by 1910, all but a few hundred had moved on to the next boomtown, leaving the town to crumble. Today, a handful of buildings sit in various states of disrepair, weather-beaten and neglected, but refusing to vanish; hand-drawn street signs remind visitors that these tracks were once busy thoroughfares. It's a fascinating, melancholy place. To reach it, take SR 374 south from Beatty (towards Death

Valley) for about four miles, then take a right. Also here is the **Goldwell Open Air Museum** (870 9946, www.goldwell museum.org), a haunting spot that comprises half a dozen works by Belgian artists who settled in the area 20 years ago. Look out for Albert Szukalski's sculpture *The Last Supper*, although, to be honest, it's pretty hard to miss.

Some 50 miles north of Beatty sits **Goldfield**, another former mining town whose population surged from nothing to 10,000 between 1902 (when gold was discovered here) and 1907, and then doubled in the following three years. It didn't last, but Goldfield refused to die: a population of 500 makes it a sizeable settlement for this part of the world. If several grand stone buildings, including the Goldfield Hotel, the courthouse and the imposing former fire station, are poignant reminders of the town's heyday, the Mozart Club bar offers evidence that not everybody got lucky.

It's 26 miles from here to **Tonopah**, on US 95 at about the halfway point between Vegas and Reno. Jim Butler found silver here in 1900; over the next 15 years, almost $150 million of ore was dug from the small mines that dot the area. The **Central Nevada Museum** (1900 Logan Field Road, 1-775 482 9676, www.tonopahnevada.com, closed Mon & Tue) details this history, though you might be better off heading for the century-old buildings at the **Tonopah Historic Mining Park** (520 McCulloch Avenue, 1-775 482 9274, www.tonopahhistoricminingpark.com, closed Mon & Tue Nov to Feb, $5).

From here, the landscape gets plainer. Settlements seem further apart – the next town of any note, **Hawthorne**, is 100 miles down the road – and there's little to engage the senses save the freedom of an open road. Until, that is, a few miles after Hawthorne, when you find US 95 narrowing and curving – quite a shock after 300 miles of mainly straight highway – as it forces its way around a sizeable body of water.

In prehistoric times, **Walker Lake** covered much of western Nevada. These days, though still 20 miles long, it's in decline: with the Walker River diverted for irrigation purposes, the lake has dropped 100 feet since 1930. While not spectacularly beautiful, the lake and the park that frames it are popular spots for swimming, boating and camping.

Past **Schurz**, a town every bit as unbecoming as its name, there are several routes to Reno. The quickest is to take US 95 north to Fallon, then pick up US 50 and Alternate US 50 to the surprisingly picturesque I-80, and head west on the Interstate into Reno. A slightly slower, slightly more scenic option is to head west on Alternate US 95 at Schurz, via the pleasant town of **Yerington** and the enjoyably green **Fort Churchill Historic**

State Park in Silver Springs (1-775 577 2345, www.parks.nv.gov/fc.htm, admission $7), and then pick up I-80 to Reno near Fernley. The slowest option is to take this latter route as far as Silver Springs, then take US 50, SR 341 and US 395 into Reno via **Virginia City** (*see p266*). Our advice? Take the speedy run into Reno, but return to Vegas via Virginia City.

Where to stay, eat & drink

In Tonopah, the large **Tonopah Station** casino (1137 Erie Street, 1-866 611 9777, www.tonopah station.com) has a slot gaming area, rooms, a restaurant and a wonderful collection of old chrome slot machines in the basement. **El Marques** (348 N Main Street, 1-775 482 3885) serves decent, good-value Mexican food.

Hawthorne has a number of motels and one casino, the **El Capitan** (540 F Street, 1-775 945 3321, www.northernstarcasinos.com).

Tourist information

For information about **Tonopah**, contact the Chamber of Commerce at 301 Brougher Avenue (1-775 482 3859, www.tonopahnevada.com).

RENO

Popular culture flags the differences between Nevada's largest cities. In song, Las Vegas is the town that set Elvis's soul on fire; Reno is where Johnny Cash shot a man just to watch him die. On film, Vegas looks glamorous, stealing scenes from every actor dumb enough to compete with it. The finest Reno movie is Paul Thomas Anderson's *Hard Eight* (aka *Sydney*), a bleak tale set in the shadows of the town's gaming industry.

To visitors, Reno can't compete with Las Vegas. The casinos are smaller and shabbier, the lights less dazzling, the dining not as varied and the entertainment decidedly wearier. But to suggest that Reno is Vegas in miniature is to do it a disservice: after all, it's never attempted to compete with its glossier, more glamorous rival. Reno hardly sees itself as a gambling town at all; rather, it's a pretty little city with numerous and varied attractions, one of which is casinos.

Reno long ago made a deliberate decision not to become Las Vegas. In the 1950s, the city fathers passed a law that limited gambling to downtown Reno, then sat back and let Vegas explode in popularity, population and wealth. The 25-year law expired in 1978; since then, just enough (but not too many) casinos have opened, attracting just enough (but not too many) gamblers. At the same time, Reno has diversified its economy and tourism marketing focus, growing at a controlled pace.

Burn It Up

Burning Man has become a mega-event.

To say the Burning Man Festival isn't really like most other events in Nevada is to say that Las Vegas isn't really like most other cities. Each year, in the week leading up to Labor Day, more than 50,000 people gather in the isolated Black Rock Desert to build a temporary, self-contained city; the physical, spiritual and symbolic centre of which is a 50-foot effigy that's set aflame at the end of the event. What goes on beforehand defies both belief and easy description: the event will be unlike anything you've ever experienced before. Self-expression is prized above all else, with self-reliance second; temperatures can range from 32°F to 104°F (0°C to 40°C). Either way, for one week you'll be part of the world's most eccentric, creative and fascinating community. Tickets frequently sell out well in advance of the event, so plan ahead. For more, see www.burningman.com.

Locals are proud of their town and disparaging about their putative rival; there's little love lost between Renoites and Las Vegans. In truth, gambling aside, the two cities have as little in common as San Francisco and Los Angeles. Where Vegas is an anything-goes, 24-7 kind of town, Reno is slower, prettier and more conservative. The flow of the Truckee River through downtown is attractive; if the Riverwalk that's been built around it doesn't differ wildly from the formula that's been applied in countless other American cities (a few shops, a handful of restaurants), it's no less pleasant for its lack of originality.

Reno also benefits from the variety of its seasons. Winter can be cold, but you won't hear a word of complaint from the skiers who jam the slopes of the 20-plus resorts within an hour of town. Summer, meanwhile, is usually balmy, with outdoor events galore. The biggest is **Hot August Nights** (www.hotaugustnights.net), a 1950s-themed mix of classic cars and rock 'n' roll, but **Street Vibrations** in September (www.roadshowsreno.com), the Harley-Davidson equivalent, keeps pace with it.

Sightseeing

The **Nevada Museum of Art** (160 W Liberty Street, 1-775 329 3333, www.nevadaart.org, closed Mon & Tue, $10), housed in a striking black building, has a strong permanent

collection, the majority of pieces from the last century, plus temporary shows: check online for details.

The **National Automobile Museum** (10 S Lake Street, 1-775 333 9300, www.auto museum.org, $10) is the best museum in Reno, and one of the finest in the state. The building holds more than 200 cars spanning a timeframe of more than a century, from an 1892 Philion Road Carriage – imagine a throne stuck on top of an outsized perambulator – to altogether less dignified Ed Roth Kustom creations. The cars, including 1940s Lincolns, a 1930s Mercedes and a divine 1957 Cadillac, are all beautifully maintained.

Reno's other attractions sit on the University of Nevada campus. At the **Fleischmann Planetarium** (1650 N Virginia Street, 1-775 784 4811, www.planetarium.unr.edu), star shows run alongside 70mm nature films. A stone's throw away at the **Nevada Historical Society** (1650 N Virginia Street, 1-775 688 1190, http://museums.nevadaculture.org), there's a fine primer on the history of the state and a good bookstore.

Casinos

Though there are a handful of casinos out of the centre, notably the monstrous **Grand Sierra Resort** (formerly the Reno Hilton; 2500 E 2nd Street, at US 395, 1-775 789 2000, www.grandsierraresort.com) and the colourful **Peppermill** (2707 S Virginia Street, at W Grove Street, 1-866 821 9996, www.peppermill reno.com), Reno's gambling is mostly downtown. Some of the names in lights will be familiar, among them the characterless **Harrah's** (219 N Center Street, at E 2nd Street, 1-775 786 3232, www.harrahsreno.com) and the family-friendly **Circus Circus** (500 N Sierra Street, at W 5th Street, 1-800 648 5010, www.circusreno.com).

Other casinos, though, are unique to Reno. The **Eldorado** (345 N Virginia Street, at W 4th Street, 1-800 879 8879, www.eldoradoreno.com) is the most pleasant operation, while the upscale **Silver Legacy** (407 N Virginia Street, at W 4th Street, 1-800 687 8733, www.silverlegacyreno.com) boasts a lobby filled with treasures from Tiffany's. It's in contrast to the basic **Club Cal-Neva** (38 E 2nd Street, at N Virginia Street, 1-877 777 7303, www.clubcalneva.com).

Where to eat & drink

Stay in or near a casino, as almost all visitors to Reno do, and you'll probably eat a number of your meals there. Of the downtown spots, the Eldorado and Harrah's offer the best dining; try Roxy's at the former and the Steak House at the latter. The Cal-Neva Virginian attracts the bargain-hunters. Out of the centre, the Grand Sierra and the Peppermill are among the strongest for food: the Peppermill's buffet is Reno's best and its White Orchid offers the finest dining in town. For all, *see p264*.

Outside the casinos, you can find fine and messy Mexican food at **Bertha Miranda's** (336 Mill Street, at Lake Street, 1-775 786 9697, www.berthamirandas.com), heavy traditional Basque scran at **Louis' Basque Corner** (301 E 4th Street, at Evans Avenue, 1-775 323 7203, www.louisbasquecorner.com) and splendid

coffee and more at **Java Jungle** (246 W 1st Street, at S Arlington Avenue, 1-775 329 4484, www.javajunglevino.com). You can sink microbrews at the attractive, slightly tucked-away **Silver Peak** (124 Wonder Street, at Holcomb Avenue, 1-775 324 1864, www.silverpeakbrewery.com), which serves upscale bar food.

Where to stay

Roughly 25,000 rooms are available in Reno, running the pricing gamut from dirt-cheap to sky-high. Prices peak in August (it's worth booking) but are cheap in winter: you can often get a room in one of the downtown casinos or motels for under $30. Note that rooms in casinos that have a sister Vegas hotel won't necessarily be in an identical mould.

Tourist information

Reno's visitor centre is in the lobby of the **National Bowling Stadium**. Alternatively, phone the information line at the Reno-Sparks CVA (1-800 367 7366, www.visitrenotahoe.com).

AROUND RENO
Carson City

As state capitals go, **Carson City**, 30 miles south of Reno on US 395, is not one of the more demonstrative. Still, what it lacks in pomposity it makes up for in quaintness, albeit a quaintness balanced by a string of casinos on Carson Street, the town's main drag, and also US 395.

Cynics suggest that the real balance of power in Nevada is held by the casino owners in Las Vegas, but the politicos of Carson City can still pack a punch when they need to. The centres of

Reno.

their activity are the **Nevada State Capitol** (N Carson Street, at Musser Street), a handsome domed structure dated 1871, and the **State Legislature**, a dreary building erected nearby a century later. The Kit Carson Trail, a two-mile walk detailed on a map available from the Chamber of Commerce (1900 S Carson Street, 1-775 882 1565, www.carsoncitychamber.com), offers a decent overview of the town's history.

Most of these buildings are closed to the public, but one that isn't is the suitably grand old US Mint Building at 600 N Carson Street, which for the last 60 years has served as the eclectic **Nevada State Museum** (1-775 687 4810, www.nevadaculture.org). The state's historic railroad comes under the microscope at the **Nevada State Railroad Museum** (2180 S Carson Street, 1-775 687 6953, www.nsrm-friends.org). Rides on old trains are offered most weekends outside winter. Still, the few casinos aside, there's not much nightlife here, and Carson City is best taken in during a day trip from Reno or Lake Tahoe.

Virginia City

A pleasant half-hour drive from Reno (south on US 395 for eight miles, then east on SR 341 for another eight miles) will take you to one of the most authentic historic mining towns in the West, where the discovery of gold and silver in nearby mines on the land of Henry Comstock sparked a furious bonanza in the 1860s. Of course, **Virginia City** is now also one of the most touristy towns in the West, its thin main drag soaked with themed bars, tatty museums – try the **Way It Was Museum** (118 N C Street, 1-775 847 0766, www.visitvirginiacity.org), which looks like the Smithsonian next to some of its neighbours – photo studios and other less easily categorisable attractions (for example, the Delta Saloon's 'Suicide Table').

That said, provided you avoid summer weekends, when C Street can get claustrophobic with tourists, it's great fun. If you take the time to wander off the main drag, it's even a little bit more than that. The Walking Tour, available from the town's visitor centre, takes in the town's most fascinating buildings, among them the regenerated **Piper's Opera House** (12 N B Street, 1-775 847 0433). Visitors should note that many of the town's sights close during the viciously chilly winters.

Eating and drinking options in Virginia City are hardly varied, but you can wash down your sandwich or burger with a beer or a Coke in any number of establishments. There aren't too many places to stay, reflecting Virginia City's status as a day-tripper's paradise; in fact, you're best off driving back to Reno to find a bed for the night. And if you've got time, take the long

way round – south on SR 341, then west on US 50 and back north on US 395 – in order to stop in at the magnificent **Chocolate Nugget** candy factory (56 SR 341, 1-775 849 0841) and pick up a couple of bags of sugar-rush.

Lake Tahoe

After you've driven through miles of desert, Reno's verdant trim comes as a pleasant surprise. But it's as nothing compared to **Lake Tahoe**, which sits on the California border, a 45-minute drive from Reno (south on US 395 for eight miles, then west on SR 431 for 25 miles). Some 22 miles long and 12 miles wide, it's one of the world's most beautiful alpine lakes.

Tahoe's two main settlements are at either end of the lake, both within a few miles of the state line. **Incline Village**'s population of 9,952 is swelled in winter by skiers (the slopes of **Mount Rose-Ski Tahoe** and **Diamond Peak** are nearby, with **Northstar-at-Tahoe** and the well-regarded **Squaw Valley USA** just across the state line), and in summer by hikers and people here for outdoor sports. Three miles west, in **Crystal Bay**, on the state line, are a handful of casinos; the best of them is the **Cal-Neva** (1-800 225 6382, www.calnevaresort.com).

South Lake Tahoe, meanwhile, also has its casinos, temptingly positioned on the Nevada edge of the state line. Among those offering accommodation are the **Montbleu** (formerly Caesars Tahoe; 1-888 829 7630, www.montbleuresort.com), **Harrah's** (1-800 427 7247, www.harrahslaketahoe.com), and its relation **Harveys** (1-775 588 6611, www.harveystahoe.com). On the California side sit restaurants, bars and motels. Skiers flock here in winter – **Heavenly**, **Sierra-at-Tahoe** and **Kirkwood** are the nearest slopes – while summer brings a more demure holidaymaker.

THE EXTRATERRESTRIAL HIGHWAY & AREA 51

Of course, you won't see anything. No one ever does. And if you're thinking about walking into the desert for a closer look, think again: you may find yourself greeted by employees of the US government wielding the kind of weaponry that'll encourage you to turn around in a hurry.

Still, SR 375 continues to draw tourists year-round. A few are here to plane-spot the military aircraft that roar overhead. A handful are on their way north to Ely. But the reason most people are ploughing up and down SR 375 is its now-official nickname, and what reputedly rests just a few miles west of the road.

If you've taken US 95 north to Reno, you'll already have skirted the western edge of the

Extraterrestrial Highway.

Nellis Air Force Range (*see p262*). Well, if you take SR 375, a plain-as-day desert road that links US 93 with US 6 in central Nevada, you'll be edging along its eastern perimeter. No one gave this much thought until the 1980s, when physicist Bob Lazar, in a series of interviews with local news gadfly George Knapp, claimed he had worked at Papoose Lake inside the range on alien spaceships. He also gave details – scant, but enough to light the touchpaper of conspiracy theorists – of the previously unknown dry-bedded Groom Lake, allegedly a test site for top-secret new military aircraft and, more contentiously, the centre of government investigations into alien life. After the numbered grid square in which the base sits on maps of the test site, it's become known as **Area 51**; as a result of its notoriety, SR 375 has been nicknamed the **Extraterrestrial Highway**.

The US government refuses to acknowledge the existence of Area 51. Rumours persist that the notoriety of the base forced the government to move its operations from here to Utah during the 1990s. Either way, sightings of UFOs near the road are predictably common, and just as predictably difficult to substantiate.

Take care: someone is watching your movements. Don't cross into the military zone: you'll be arrested, questioned and fined. Armed guards are authorised to use 'deadly force' on trespassers. The border is not marked on maps and is often hard to detect: it's defined by orange posts, some topped with silver globes, and occasional 'restricted area' signs but no fence.

The only town on SR 375 is **Rachel**, a scruffy collection of houses and huts that's home to a little under 100 people. This number is swelled by tourists staying at the **Little A'Le'Inn**, a slightly scruffy motel-bar-restaurant combo stocked with cheaply made, dearly priced alien ephemera and staffed by chatty people unafraid of engaging customers in a conversation about politics (tip: if you're a Democrat, keep your mouth shut).

Since 1995, when the military annexed more land, the only view of Area 51 is from **Tikaboo Peak**, 26 miles from the base. You get superb views of the desert, but even with binoculars, all you'll see of the base is a few distant buildings. It's a strenuous hike, best done in summer and early in the morning, before heat haze distorts the view. The best route is via a dirt road off US 93 at milepost 32.2, south of Alamo. It's just over 22 miles to Badger Spring and then a two-hour hike to the summit, but it's easy to get lost.

Where to stay, eat & drink

The aforementioned **Little A'Le'Inn** (1-775 729 2515, www.aleinn.com) has seven rooms in run-down trailers: you get a shared bathroom, a communal kitchen-cum-living room and UFO photos. The bar serves beer and burgers.

Getting there

By car
Take US 93 north for 107 miles to the junction with SR 375, aka the Extraterrestrial Highway. Rachel is 36 miles north-west of the junction. When driving, watch not so much for aliens but wandering cows: much of the road is an open range, and collisions occur regularly.

Utah

Utah will come as a culture shock after Las Vegas. In the Mormon-dominated state, it can be hard just to find a bar that serves alcohol here, or a restaurant that stays open past 9pm. But southern Utah is a unique place, not to say a spectacular one. National Park follows National Recreation Area follows National Monument, and hulking rock formations give way to vistas by turns peculiar and pretty. Zion National Park is a bit of both.

ZION NATIONAL PARK

A few hours north from Las Vegas, Zion National Park is a glorious introduction to the canyon country of south-east Utah. Zion's 2,000-foot (600-metre) cliffs and towering rock formations were discovered by early Mormon travellers in the 1880s. Originally called Mukuntuweap (roughly 'like a quiver', a description of the canyon's shape), its name was changed to Zion when it became a national park in 1919. With more than 2.5 million visitors annually, Zion is busy all year. However, it's best avoided in winter, when snow and ice make the trails tough to negotiate, and summer, when temperatures top 110°F (43°C).

The main entrance to the park is in the south, near the pretty town of **Springdale** (admission $25 per car, valid for seven days). Just beyond the entrance are the park's two campgrounds (*see p269*) and visitors' centre (staff are wonderfully helpful), with the tidy new **Zion Human History Museum** a further half-mile inside the gates. From April to October, when parts of the park are off-limits to cars, visitors should leave their cars at the south entrance or in Springdale, then take a free bus into the park. The rest of the park is open to private cars, but vehicles wider than 7ft 10in (2.39m) or higher than 10ft 4in (3.15m) must be escorted through the Zion–Mount Carmel tunnel ($25 per vehicle), which can lead to delays.

The majority of the park's sights and trails are accessible or visible from the six-mile dead-end **scenic drive**, which starts at the main entrance and winds through the Virgin River gorge. (It's one of the aforementioned sections of the park that's closed to private cars from April to October.) The names of the vividly coloured Navajo sandstone rock formations along the drive echo the first visitors' religious sensibilities: the **Great White Throne**, **Angel's Landing**, the **Three Patriarchs**, the **Pulpit** and the **Temple of Sinawava**. Scan the sheer rock faces and you may see the ant-like figures of climbers; routes are detailed in Eric Bjornstad's *Desert Rock: Rock Climbs in the National Parks* (Falcon Press, www.falcon.com), an excellent resource for any traveller wanting to go climbing in this part of the world.

There are plenty of hiking trails off the scenic drive. The busiest are the short, easy routes along the valley floor, such as **Weeping Rock** (0.5 miles, 30 minutes) and the **Riverside Walk** (two miles, one and a half hours), but the best views are at the end of the **Watchman Trail** (two and a half miles, two hours) and the five-mile, four-hour trail to and from **Angel's Landing**. Don't even attempt the latter if you're afraid of heights: the last half-mile follows a steep, narrow ridge fitted with chains.

Perhaps the most spectacular hike is through the 16-mile **Narrows**, with canyon walls up to 2,000 feet high and at times only 20-30 feet apart. Be prepared to wade (or swim) through cold water and check conditions at the visitors' centre: there can be flash floods in summer. For hikers travelling from the top down, a permit is required (fee based on group size: 1-2 people $10; 3-7 $15; 8-12 $20). For all hikes leaving from the bottom and heading up, as far as Big Springs, there is no permit fee through the Narrows.

East from Springdale and the scenic drive, you'll travel along the twisting **Zion–Mount Carmel Highway**, an engineering miracle when it was built in 1930. The impressive route leads through two long, narrow tunnels, passing scenery that is completely different from the landscapes of Zion Canyon. This is slickrock country: vast white, orange and pink rock formations, eroded into domes and buttes and marked with criss-cross patterns, loom next to the road. You can't miss the huge white monolith of **Checkerboard Mesa**.

Kolob Canyons, which is located in the park's north-western corner, has its own entrance (at exit 40 off I-15) and visitors' centre, from where a stunning five-mile drive leads into the red-rock **Finger Canyons**. There are also two hiking trails to embark on from here; the

Zion National Park.

longer trail culminates at **Kolob Arch**, which, at 310 feet, is possibly the world's largest natural arch.

Where to eat & drink

Inside the park, the **Red Rock Grill** at **Zion Lodge** (*see below*) is open for breakfast, lunch and dinner. Reservations are recommended for the latter, especially in summer; call 1-435 772 7760.

Springdale has plenty of cafés and restaurants, but – this is Utah, folks – a shortage of bars. The closest you'll find is the **Bit & Spur** (1212 Zion Park Boulevard, 1-435 772 3498, www.bitandspur.com, main courses $17-$26), a Mexican-slanted restaurant with outdoor seating. **Oscar's Café** (948 Zion Park Boulevard, 1-435 772 3232, www.cafeoscars.com, main courses $10-$18) serves sturdy burgers, a vegetarian and vegan menu, Mexican dishes and other straightforward treats, while the family-friendly **Wildcat Willie's Ranch Grill & Saloon** at the Bumbleberry Inn (897 Zion Park Boulevard, 1-435 772 0115, www.wildcatwillies.com) has a nice line in breakfasts.

Where to stay

Within the park sits the rustic-style **Zion Lodge** (1-888 297 2757, www.zionlodge.com), built in 1925 by the Union Pacific Railroad. Accommodation at the lodge includes six suites, 40 cabins and 75 motel-style rooms; prices range from $160 to $200 depending on the time of year and availability; you'll need to book well in advance between April and October.

There are also two campgrounds inside the park. The **Watchman Campground** is open all year (rates $16-$20); reservations are taken from March to early November (1-877 444 6777, www.nps.gov), with pitches allocated on a first-come, first-served basis at other times. The **South Campground** is open only from March to October and operates on a walk-up basis only (rates $16). Group campgrounds are also available to organised groups of nine to 40 people by booking in advance (1-877 444 6777, www.nps.gov, rates $3 per person).

There are many places to stay in Springdale, including the 40-room **Cliffrose Lodge & Gardens** (281 Zion Park Boulevard, 1-800 243 8824, www.cliffroselodge.com, doubles $159-$399) and, perhaps most appealingly, the **Desert Pearl Inn** (707 Zion Park Boulevard, 1-888 828 0898, www.desertpearl.com, doubles $143-$300). For details of other options, contact the **Zion Canyon Visitors' Center**; note that not all of the town's hotels and motels are open in winter.

Getting there

To reach the park (164 miles from Vegas), take I-15 north, watching your speed once you leave Nevada (and being particularly careful in Arizona, where the police aren't slow to stop speeding cars). Head through the pleasant Mormon town of St George and turn right at exit 16 on to Highway 9 to Springdale. To visit the Kolob Canyons area, continue for 25 miles on I-15 until you reach exit 40.

Tourist information

Kolob Canyons Visitors' Center *3752 E Kolob Canyon Road, New Harmony (1-435 586 9548, www.nps.gov/zion).* **Open** *Spring-early summer, autumn* 8am-5pm daily. *Summer* 8am-6pm daily. *Winter* 8am-4pm daily.

Zion Canyon Visitors' Center Springdale *1-435 772 0170/3256, www.nps.gov/zion).* **Open** *Spring-early summer, autumn* 7am-6pm daily. *Summer* 7am-8pm daily. *Winter* 8am-4.30pm daily.

Zion Canyon Visitors Bureau *1-888 518 7070, www.zionpark.com.*

BEYOND ZION

At **Mount Carmel Junction**, east of the park, Highway 9 joins up with US 89 for access to the rest of Utah and Arizona, and scenery that is arguably even more spectacular and other-worldly than in Zion.

Heading north on US 89 and then east on SR 12 takes you to **Bryce Canyon National Park** (1-435 834 5322, www.nps.gov/brca), where the landscape of vast rock hoodoos is breathtakingly odd. It's dramatically snow-cloaked in winter but mild during the summer months, making it ideal for the casual hiker. Try the Tower Bridge Trail, a three-mile round-trip through some extraordinary scenery, or venture out on to the Rim Trail, which affords astonishing views of this peculiar landscape. Admission to the park is $25 for private vehicles, a pass that's valid for seven days. The website above has details on accommodation.

Travelling north up Highway 12 from Zion, through **Dixie National Forest**, brings you to the **Capitol Reef National Park** (1-435 425 3791, www.nps.gov/care). While it's by no means as spectacular as its neighbours, and doesn't offer anything like the variety of hikes that you'll find at Bryce Canyon or Zion, it's geologically fascinating and worth a brief diversion if you're heading this way.

Alternatively, leave Zion on US 89 south towards the Grand Canyon.

In Context

History

Lighting up the desert was a gamble that has paid off in spades.

TEXT: WILL FULFORD-JONES

Around 25,000 years ago, at the tail end of the last ice age, the large valley in which Las Vegas now sits was partly under water. Glaciers were retreating from the mountains that ring the Las Vegas Valley; the glacial run-off fed a vast lake, 20 miles wide and thousands of feet deep.

The Strip was built at what was once the deepest part of the lake. The lake's outlet was a river known now as the Las Vegas Wash; it flowed for only 40 miles, but was larger than any other river in the western United States. At its mouth, the Wash was swallowed by the monster waterway that had been carving the Grand Canyon for a couple of hundred million years, later named the Colorado River.

Palaeo-Indians lived in caves near the lake's shoreline, which receded as the climate changed gradually from cold and wet to warm and dry. The first Las Vegans shared the tule marsh at the edge of the lake with prehistoric horses, giant ground sloths, American camels and massive condors, and hunted big Pleistocene mammals (woolly mammoth, bison, mastodon and caribou) as early as 13,000 BC. Little is known about these early inhabitants. However, from 5,000 years ago, a clearer picture of the local prehistoric people begins to emerge.

FROM HUNTER GATHERERS TO FARMERS

Hunter-gatherers known as Archaic Indians introduced a culture that evolved over four millennia. The area they occupied was by then desert, although spring water bubbled to the surface and flowed down the Las Vegas Wash (now a creek) to the canyon-carving Colorado River. Even so, it wasn't until the first centuries AD that signs of civilisation sprang up in and around Nevada's southern desert. By AD 500, they had evolved into an organised people: hunting with bows and arrows, making pottery, mining salt and trading with their neighbours.

Three centuries later, the Anasazi tribe was cultivating beans and corn in irrigated fields, living in 100-room pueblos, fashioning artistic pots and mining turquoise. Mysteriously, they disappeared from the area around 1150: perhaps due to disease, drought, overpopulation or war, though no one really knows for sure. A large Anasazi village was discovered in 1924; parts of it are now preserved at the Lost City Museum in Overton, north-east of Las Vegas.

Southern Paiutes, hunter-gatherers more like Archaic Indians than the Anasazi, claimed the abandoned territory, but they never achieved the advanced elements of their predecessors' society. For the next 700 years, the Paiutes remained semi-nomadic, establishing base camps of movable 'wickiups' (similar to tepees), cultivating squash and corn at the springs and creeks, and travelling seasonally to hunt and harvest wild foods. A frequent stopover on their travels was the Big Spring, the centre of a lush riparian habitat. Now known as the Las Vegas Springs Preserve, it opened as a park, visitor attraction and educational facility in 2007.

MEXICANS AND MORMONS

The first white men to enter the region, arriving in the early 19th century, were Mexican traders, who travelled along the Old Spanish Trail blazed by Franciscan friars to connect Spanish-Catholic missions scattered between New Mexico and the California coast. In 1830, three decades before the Civil War, Antonio Armijo set out from Santa Fe to trade goods along the trail. An experienced scout in his party by the name of Rafael Rivera found a short cut via the Big Spring, and became the first non-native to set foot on the land. He named the area Las Vegas, or 'the Meadows'.

By the time John C Fremont, a surveyor and cartographer for the Army Topographical Corps, passed through the Las Vegas Valley in 1845, the Old Spanish Trail had become the most travelled route through the Southwest. With Big Spring providing the only fresh water within a day's march, the area had become a popular camping spot. Having settled at the shore of the Great Salt Lake a few hundred miles further north-east, Latter-Day Saints also regularly passed through Las Vegas on their way to Los Angeles. Indeed, by the early 1850s, Mormon pioneer parties, wagon trains and mail carriers travelling between central Utah and southern California stopped at Big Spring with such frequency that Church elders decided to colonise the area.

In 1855, a party of Mormon missionaries was dispatched from Salt Lake City to establish a community at Las Vegas that would serve the travellers on the trail and convert the Paiute people. The missionaries erected a fort, dug irrigation ditches, cultivated crops and even managed to befriend some Indians. But the rigours of domesticating a vast desert proved beyond them. Crops failed and rations were meagre. Timber had to be hauled from the nearest mountainsides, 20 miles away.

Even so, the mission might have succeeded had the colonists not located deposits of lead nearby. The discovery attracted miners from Salt Lake City, whose need for food, lumber and shelter taxed the colonists' already inadequate supplies to breaking point. Despite the miners' vociferous objections, the colonists petitioned Salt Lake City to be recalled, and the mission was abandoned in 1858. A small remnant of the Mormon fort survives as the oldest standing structure in Las Vegas.

IN CONTEXT

Take Me to the Moon

The best-laid plans can fail to come to fruition.

If you hadn't noticed, Las Vegas is all about excess. You won't be able to move in the city without bumping into the world's largest this, the world's most luxurious that or the world's most expensive other thing. But for all the visions of grandeur that come to fruition, there are twice as many delusions that never make it past the planning stage.

Some of these plans are good ideas that, for whatever reason, can't find the financing or the favours required for lift-off. Some are heavy on hype yet light on logic, tossed out by hucksters hoping to make a quick buck. Others are so absurd that they don't stand a chance. And still others are such hopeless pipe dreams that even normally respectful TV reporters can't help sniggering between the lines.

Perhaps the biggest and most symbolically foolish of these fantasies was Moon, a 250-acre, $5-billion, 10,000-room lunar-themed mega-resort announced with much fanfare in 2002. Michael Henderson, the pitchman for this lunacy, poured every imaginable amenity into his plans, probably figuring he might as well throw it all against the wall and see what stuck. But despite the promise of a zero-gravity simulator and a 'crater wave pool', Moon disappeared almost immediately from the local radar screen. From the start, it had as much chance of being built in Las Vegas as it did of opening on the moon itself.

Following behind Moon in terms of unrealised scope are the various figments of the imagination that have dogged the old El Rancho property. After plans for the $1-billion Starship Orion hotel-casino were lost in space in 1996, several ill-conceived incarnations of Countryland USA (1997-99) came and went. The lot was subsequently slated for casinos modelled on London, one of three such proposals down the years, and San Francisco, a theme favoured

at various times by no fewer than four teams of Vegas developers. Both fell by the wayside, and plans for the 4,000-room, Miami Beach-themed Fontainebleau on the site are still on hold.

Some developers simply don't seem to have done their research. Desert Kingdom (1994) was the name of a proposed hotel planned for 34 vacant acres next to the Desert Inn and aimed purely at high rollers. The plans called for 3,500 rooms, which was only about 3,000 rooms in excess of the number of high rollers around at the time; the project was quietly but quickly cancelled. Just up the Strip in 1999, promoter extraordinaire Bob Stupak floated a proposal for the Boat, a 1,200-cabin, *Titanic*-themed hotel and time-share complex complete with an iceberg-shaped mall. Naturally, it sank without a trace.

Other failed adventures have come with celebrity endorsements. The World Wrestling Federation bought Debbie Reynolds' hotel-casino (originally the Paddlewheel, now the Greek Isles) for $10.6 million in 1998 and pinned its hopes on a $100-million, 1,000-room resort with a wrestling theme. They sold it a year later. The site now occupied by the Palms was once tagged as the home of Desert Winds (1993), an $87-million, 400-room fantasy themed after the ill-starred musical Jackson family, and for Sound Stage, a 1,000-room project launched by Black Entertainment Television in 1997. Other off-the-wall plans that never left the drawing board included casinos themed after Bugsy Siegel (1998), Elvis Presley (1999 and 2006) and even Gen X (2000). But none were quite as absurd as Winter Wonderland, a chilly casino centred around a climate-controlled dome where it snowed every day. Only in Vegas? Happily not.

OD GASS AND HELEN STEWART

Soon after the Mormons abandoned Las Vegas, prospectors picked up where the lead miners left off and discovered that the ore averaged a rich $650 per ton in silver. A small mining boomtown mushroomed in the desert around Big Spring. Miners who arrived too late to get in on the action fanned out from the settlement and found gold along the Colorado River, about 50 miles south-east of Las Vegas.

One of the gold-seekers, Octavius Decatur Gass, saw a more enticing opportunity: homesteading the well-watered valley. Craftily, Gass appropriated the Mormon fort in 1865, using the lumber to build a ranch house and utility shop. He dug irrigation canals, planted grain, vegetables and fruit trees, and ran cattle on a chunk of land known as Las Vegas Ranch. Over the next ten years, Gass expanded his land and water holdings, assumed civic duties and helped other homesteaders get established.

However, Gass's ambition eventually got the better of him. In financial trouble by the 1870s, he took a loan from Archibald Stewart, a rich rancher from the mining boomtown of Pioche. When, in 1881, Gass couldn't repay the loan, Stewart foreclosed on it and took over the Las Vegas Ranch, expanding the property until he was shot dead in 1884 after an argument with a ranch hand from a neighbouring spread. Stewart's wife Helen ran the ranch for the next 20 years, buying up more acreage, making a living in the livestock business, and running a resort for nearby ranchers and a campground for travellers on the Mormon Trail.

The San Pedro, Los Angeles & Salt Lake Railroad arrived in 1903, its planned route running through the heart of the ranch. Thanks to its strategic location and plentiful water, Las Vegas had been designated a division point for crew changes, a service stop for through trains and, eventually, a site for maintenance shops. Ready to retire, Mrs Stewart sold most of her 2,000-acre site for $55,000, but deeded ten acres to the Paiutes, who'd been reduced to living on the edge of town through government largesse. For this and other civic-minded deeds, Stewart is considered the First Lady of Las Vegas.

In preparation for the land sale, Stewart hired JT McWilliams to survey her property. The canny McWilliams discovered and immediately claimed 80 untitled acres just west of the big ranch, planned a town site and began selling lots to a steadfast group of Las Vegas 'sooners' (the earliest speculators on the scene). In late 1904, two railroad construction crews, one from the north-east and one from the south-west, converged on Las Vegas Valley. And then, in January 1905, a golden spike was driven into a tie near Jean, Nevada, 23 miles south of Las Vegas, ceremonially completing the railroad.

GAMBLING ON PROSPERITY

McWilliams's settlement, known as Ragtown, was one of a long line of boomtowns that had been erupting across Nevada over the preceding 50 years. On the day the first train travelled through Big Spring on its route between Salt Lake City and Los Angeles, Ragtown's saloons, banks and tent hotels teemed with settlers, speculators, tradesmen and itinerants. But the San Pedro, Los Angeles & Salt Lake Railroad had other plans for the settlement. It organised a subsidiary, Las Vegas Land & Water, to build its own town.

Officials laid out the town site, scraped the scrub from 40 square blocks and staked 1,200 lots. The new town site of Las Vegas received national publicity, and demand for the land was high, with prospective buyers coming by train from Los Angeles ($16 return) and Salt Lake City ($20). Competition for locations proved so overwhelming that the railroad scheduled an auction, pitting eager settlers against Los Angeles real-estate speculators and East Coast investors. All were gambling on the prosperity of yet another western railroad boomtown.

The auction was held on 15 May 1905 at the intersection of Main and Fremont streets. The bidding quickly inflated the price of choice lots to more than double their listed values. The locals over in Ragtown grumbled about the railroad tactic of encouraging out-of-town investors to heat up the prices. But when it was over, nearly 1,000 lots had been sold for the grand total of $265,000, which was $195,000 more than the railroad had paid for the entire Las Vegas Ranch only three years earlier.

The proud new property owners immediately searched out the stakes marking the boundaries of their lots and erected makeshift shelters on them. Ragtowners rolled their possessions over to the new Las Vegas on horse- and ox-drawn wagons. What remained of the first town site burned to the ground four months later, and the first Las Vegas building boom followed.

SETTLING IN

In stereotypical western fashion, the first structures to go up were saloons and brothels, built in the designated nightlife and red light district on Block 16 between Ogden and Stewart streets, and 1st and 2nd streets (now the parking lot at Binion's). Hotels, restaurants, banks and shops were erected along Fremont Street; railroad and town administrative offices, a school, a post office and two churches surrounded the core. The railroad company built the infrastructure: gravel streets and plank sidewalks, water service and sporadic electricity. Houses went up along the residential streets of the eight-block-long and five-block-wide town; supplies arrived daily by train. By New Year's Day 1906, some 1,500 pioneers were calling Las Vegas home. However, the initial boom was short-lived. Barely a year passed before the railroad town managers showed their true colours, concerned first with operating the main line and last with servicing the town. Their refusal to extend pipes beyond the town site stunted growth, forcing the rural dwellers to dig wells and tap into the aquifer. Fires, conflicts and the usual growing pains of a young settlement slowed the influx of new residents, reducing both property values and optimism. The heat, dust and isolation contributed to the consensus of discomfort.

A rare bit of good news arrived in 1909, when the Nevada Legislature created Clark County in the south of the state (it was named after William Clark, the chairman of the San Pedro, Los Angeles & Salt Lake Railroad) and named Las Vegas as its seat of government. Two years later, the railroad gave the town a boost when it opened a shop designed to help maintain the steam locomotives, passenger coaches and freight cars along the line. Hundreds of jobs were created at a single stroke; by the time the shop was fully staffed, the population of Las Vegas had doubled to 3,000. Telephone service arrived, with the first phone (taking, of course, the number '1') installed at the cigar counter in the lobby of the Hotel Nevada (now the Golden Gate). And in 1915, big town generators began supplying electricity to residents 24 hours a day.

But for the next 15 years, everything went downhill. The railroad found itself losing business to car and truck traffic, and workers were laid off. Union Pacific bought up the San Pedro, Los Angeles & Salt Lake Railroad, relegating it to the status of a small siding on a vast nationwide network. Measures brought in by Union Pacific severely inhibited the town's growth; when it then closed the railroad maintenance shops, locals were driven to leave town in search of work. Las Vegas would have disappeared by the late 1920s if it hadn't been for a monumental federal dam-building project gearing up nearby.

THE HOOVER DAM

The 1,450-mile Colorado River had been gouging great canyons and watering lush valleys for aeons, when the US government decided to harness its flow in the service of irrigation, electricity, flood control and recreation. The Bureau of Reclamation began to consider damming the Colorado in 1907, narrowing down the choice of locations for the dam to two canyons east of Las Vegas. In 1930, six years after the site for it had been selected, Congress appropriated the $165 million necessary to build the Boulder Dam.

Anticipation of the dam project began to fuel noticeable growth in the railroad town. By the time construction began in 1931 (the name change, from the Boulder Dam to the Hoover Dam, was announced

Vegas Vic, the Neon Cowboy

'Still a frontier town.'

This tag line, dreamed up in the 1940s by the J Walter Thompson Agency in Los Angeles, in order to promote a dusty little gambling town halfway between the City of Angels and the City of Saints (Salt Lake City), was an appealing one. The fact that Las Vegas had never actually been a frontier town – watering hole and railroad stop would be more accurate – was no bar to the creation of a quintessential cowpoke to go along with the Chamber of Commerce's PR campaign. Thus was born Vegas Vic, a long and lanky cartoon with a strong chin and a welcoming glint in his squinty eye. Decked out in dude-ranch finery, a cigarette dangling from his lips, Vic beckoned the weary traveller to fun and sun in the desert.

However, Vic would likely be forgotten if not for his incarnation as that most powerful of Vegas icons: the neon sign. Translated by the Young Electric Sign Company into 48 feet of metal and glass, Vegas Vic became the unofficial mayor of Fremont Street when he was installed on the façade of the Pioneer Club in 1947 (the current version dates from 1951). Motors moved Vic's arm, his thumb out like some sort of demented hitchhiker, while a hidden loudspeaker boomed out, every few minutes or so, a welcome to the rubes: 'Howdy, Podner!'

Vic's monotonous greeting got on everyone's nerves after a few years, most famously actor Lee Marvin's. While in town working on a Western, Marvin leaned out of his hotel window, across the street at the Mint, and shot poor Vic full of arrows. It seems Vic's voice was interfering with a particularly heavy hangover. Vic was soon silenced; a few years later, when the mechanism in his arm gave out, the Pioneer Club's owners didn't bother to fix it.

They didn't need to. By then, Vic, in his gaudy wide-brimmed hat,

yellow-checked shirt, red kerchief and blue jeans, was a signature part of Downtown. It's a measure of his fame that when the Fremont Street Experience canopy was built in 1995, he wasn't removed but merely lowered a few feet, giving him the appearance of a giant stuck in a low-ceilinged room. Long before then, though, he'd been joined on Glitter Gulch by Vegas Vicky, a neon cowgirl with entirely different assets.

Sadly, Vic and Vicky were doomed to enjoy each other only from afar: they literally work different sides of the street. Vic now presides over the Pioneer Club in name only, the casino having long since been replaced by a souvenir shop, while Vicky crowns the Girls of Glitter Gulch strip joint. Vic and Vicky might not be remnants of an 'Old West' Vegas that never was, but they're cherished relics of the honky-tonk town of the last century, at the moment when the final frontier of glitz, glamour and gambling was about to be crossed forever.

at the inauguration ceremony), a long-distance phone service, a federal highway linking Salt Lake City to Los Angeles and regular air-passenger services had arrived. The population soared to 5,000, with thousands more passing through Las Vegas en route to the soon-to-be-tamed river.

Even today, the building of the Hoover Dam is mind-boggling in its immensity. The nearest power plant was 200 miles away in southern California; wires had to be strung all the way from it in order to supply electricity. Some 5,000 workers had to be hired, and an entire town (Boulder City) was built to house them and their families. Most dauntingly of all, the mighty Colorado River itself had to be diverted simply for the project to begin. It took 16 months to hack four diversion tunnels through the canyon walls before the river could be routed around the construction site. Only then could work begin on what would eventually become one of the man-made wonders of the world.

Some five million buckets of concrete were poured into the dam over a two-year period. When it was completed in 1935, Hoover Dam stood 656 feet (200 metres) wide at its base, 49 feet (15 metres) thick at its crest, 1,358 feet (414 metres) across and 794 feet (242 metres) tall. After the diversion tunnels were closed, it took a further three years to fill Lake Mead. At 109 miles long, reaching a depth of 545 feet (166 metres), it's the largest man-made lake in North America. The legacy of the dam has been monumental, endowing Las Vegas with the power and the water it needed to fulfil its early promise.

THE NEW BOOM

In 1931, another event occurred that was to have long-lasting implications for Las Vegas: the statewide legalisation of wide-open casino gambling. Backroom illegal gambling had long been the norm for the libertine frontier state of Nevada. But when legislators gave gambling their blessing (along with easy divorces, no-wait marriages, prostitution and championship boxing matches), the transformation of Las Vegas from a railroad company town into a casino company town began in earnest.

Casino operators migrated in droves to the only state in the union where they could ply their trade without risking arrest; vice-starved visitors followed. The bars and casinos moved a block, from the shadows of Ogden Street to the more inviting Fremont Street. The ladies of the night stayed behind at Block 16, but lights began to brighten the gambling joints along Fremont, soon nicknamed 'Glitter Gulch'.

> *'While the masters of the underworld were making a decent wage all over the US, they looked upon Las Vegas as the Promised Land.'*

Las Vegas also enjoyed widespread publicity from the building of the dam. By 1935, when 20,000 people saw Franklin D Roosevelt preside over the Hoover Dam dedication ceremony, word was beginning to get around that this little town by the dam was a slice of the authentic Wild West, with legal casinos, legal prostitution and legal everything else. Temptation led to prosperity, which in turn led to construction. Three new casinos were built at the start of the 1940s: the El Cortez in Downtown, and the Last Frontier and El Rancho on the Los Angeles Highway, a stretch of road that would eventually come to be known as the Strip.

With the nation preparing for World War II, the federal government took over a million acres north of Las Vegas for use as a training school for military pilots and gunners. Between 1940 and 1945, the Las Vegas Aerial Gunnery School trained thousands of pilots, navigators, bombers and gunners, then shipped them to the fronts in Europe or the Pacific. The school eventually expanded to three million acres. And in 1942, Basic Magnesium, one of the largest metal-processing factories in the country, was built halfway between Las Vegas and Boulder City. At the peak of production, 10,000 workers were processing millions of tons of magnesium, a newly exploited metal used in the manufacture of bomb casings, aeroplane components and flares. To house them, an entire town was built: Henderson, Las Vegas's first next-door neighbour. During the war years, its population doubled from 8,500 to 17,000.

THE MOB AND THE BOMB

As much as the war brought economic benefits to Las Vegas, it also gave a boost to organised crime throughout the US, as the black market in scarce consumer goods resulted in handsome profits for those savvy enough to sell them. But while the masters of the underworld were making a decent wage all over the US, they looked upon Las Vegas as the Promised Land. Flush with cash from bootlegging during Prohibition and black-market trading during the war, gangsters from all over the country stood poised to invade Nevada with money, management and muscle. All they needed was someone to raise a torch and show them the way. Enter Benjamin 'Bugsy' Siegel: tall, handsome and fearless, and partnered by the most powerful criminal bosses in the country.

Siegel elbowed into and bowed out of several casinos during the early 1940s, until he finally settled on the Flamingo. He insinuated himself into the management (which, contrary to popular myth, already existed), then so terrorised the team that they fled for their lives and left him with the unfinished joint. Siege knew nothing about building a casino; construction ran $4 million over budget. Less than six months after the doors opened in December 1946, Siegel was assassinated in his girlfriend's Beverly Hills mansion.

Thus began 20 years of the Italian-Jewish crime syndicate's presence in Las Vegas, and ten years of the biggest hotel-building boom the country had ever seen. Black money from top Mob bosses, along with their fronts, pawns, soldiers and workers, poured in from the underworld

power centres of New York, New England, Cleveland, Chicago, Kansas City, New Orleans, Miami and Havana. Between 1951 and 1958, 11 major hotel-casinos opened in Las Vegas, nine on the Strip and two Downtown. All but one was financed by dirty cash.

Eventually, a full 25 years after gambling was legalised in Nevada, the state and federal governments woke up to the questionable histories of the people who were in charge of the largest industry in Vegas. In every other state in the US, they were considered criminals; in Vegas, they'd successfully bought power, influence and respectability. The war between the police and the gangsters began, but it was overshadowed by an event that cast the town in a very strange light.

When the federal government went looking for a vast tract of uninhabited land on which to perfect its nuclear weapons, it found one at the Las Vegas Aerial Gunnery School. Just 70 miles north-west of the city, the Nevada Test Site went on to host roughly 120 above-ground nuclear test explosions, about one a month for a decade. Thousands of guinea-pig soldiers were deployed near the explosions, purposefully exposed to the shockwaves so medical teams could measure the effects of the radiation.

A few locals worried about which way the wind blew. However, most of the 65,000 Las Vegans seemed to revel in the notoriety that radiated from the tests. The boosters had a ball, marketing everything from 'atom burgers' to pictures of Miss Atomic Blast, and the openings of several casinos were scheduled to coincide with blasts. People had picnics atop the tallest buildings in town, looking across at the mushroom clouds. The Nuclear Test Ban treaty in 1962 drove the explosions underground, where 600 tests were held in the following three decades. But the reputation remained.

THE DIATRIBE

The Mob, the bombs, the gambling and the general naughtiness of Las Vegas attracted plenty of heat from the rest of the United States, most of it magnified

IN CONTEXT

by the media. A steamroller of criticism levelled the town's reputation, turning it into a national scandal. Known as 'the Diatribe', this systematic attack remains the greatest ever public castigation of an American city. The assault coloured Las Vegas's image for 30 years.

At the same time, though, people flocked to the town, proving the old rule about all publicity being good publicity. These pilgrims found that a strange thing happened at the Nevada state line: criminals who crossed it were suddenly accorded the status of legitimate businessmen, while the good citizens of the rest of the country suddenly became naughty boys and girls. These were the glamour years, when you didn't go out in Las Vegas after dark if you weren't wearing a suit or a cocktail dress. Crap shooters rolled the bones elbow-to-elbow with hit men. Mafia pit bosses had the 'power of the pencil' to hand out free rooms, food and beverages at their discretion, and the comps flowed as easily as the champagne.

During this period, Frank Sinatra, Dean Martin and Sammy Davis Jr performed in the Copa Room at the Sands, then invaded lounges around town. Joining the likes of Shecky Greene, Buddy Hackett and Louis Prima on stage, the Rat Pack became iconic fixtures of the new, high-rollin' Vegas. Many locals and visitors who were around from the early 1950s to the mid '60s still pine for these lost years.

The end of the Diatribe can be traced back to the arrival of multi-millionaire Howard Hughes. Smuggled under cover into town in November 1966, the tycoon settled into the ninth floor of the Desert Inn, from where he cultivated his eccentricities and planned his assault on the city. When the management at the Desert Inn threatened him with eviction, reputedly because they wanted to reserve his penthouse for high rollers, he dug $13 million from his bank account and bought the hotel. Over the next few years, Hughes went on to spend $300 million in the city, buying five casinos (including the Sands), an airport, an airline and the KLAS TV station, the latter purely so he could control the all-night programming he obsessively watched.

The publicity generated by his spending spree turned around the town's reputation: no longer was it run by the Mob. Between 1968 and 1973, another dozen casinos opened, many of them run by respected companies that had previously been careful not to touch the crime-riddled town with a bargepole. It took a little while for various task forces to hound the old gangsters into oblivion; one scandal after another erupted at the older casinos at which the Mob was still entrenched. But eventually, in the mid 1980s, the city's casinos were free of any discernible Mob involvement.

BIGGER, BETTER, MORE FANTASTIC

In November 1989, a maverick 47-year-old businessman by the name of Steve Wynn opened a $650-million pleasure palace in the heart of the Strip. The size, elegance and price tag of the Mirage stunned the old guard in Las Vegas. But the enthusiasm with which the public greeted it, and the $1-million-a-day profits that resulted, galvanised the industry, and changed both the look and the culture of Las Vegas. The old casinos, with their scruffy buffets and lounges, were soon replaced by sophisticated resorts, complete with impressive restaurants, high-budget shows and plush lounges. A new breed of visitor, more moneyed than at any point since the 1960s, came to see them.

There was plenty to see. The Excalibur, a family-friendly, medieval-themed casino-resort, opened in 1990, followed in 1993 by the pyramidal Luxor, the pirate-technic Treasure Island and the 5,005-room MGM Grand. The Hard Rock brought some glamour back to the town when it opened in 1995; the 1,257-foot Stratosphere Tower, the opulent Monte Carlo and the pop art New York New York all opened between April 1996 and January 1997. Another wave of construction crested in October 1998 with the opening of the $1.6-billion Bellagio, then the most expensive hotel ever built. The $1-billion Mandalay Bay, all hipness and whimsy, followed six months later, with the $1.5-billion Venetian and the $760-million Paris Las Vegas making their debuts in September 1999, and a year later, came the Aladdin.

The Rat Pack outside the Sands.

were all levelled, to be replaced by the Bellagio, a parking lot, the Venetian, Mandalay Bay and the new Aladdin (now Planet Hollywood) respectively. Implosions in 2001 and 2004 finally levelled the Desert Inn; on its site now stands Wynn Las Vegas, which in 2005 became the first major casino to arrive on the Strip in a half-decade. And in 2007, nearly 50 years after it opened, the Stardust was blown up. The beloved Sahara is next – it closed in 2011 and is currently being replaced by SLS, a new luxury resort expected to open in 2014.

21ST-CENTURY VEGAS

Despite the fact that the town already has more than 150,000 hotel rooms and 19 of the 30 largest hotels on earth, Las Vegas continues to grow – this despite a global economic crisis that nearly brought construction on proposed projects like Echelon (on the old Stardust site) and Plaza Las Vegas (where the New Frontier used to be) to a standstill. Other large casino projects, like Fontainebleau, began but weren't finished. Today, the 68-storey Fontainebleau sits empty and unfinished on the north end of the Strip. After a slight blip post-9/11, visitor numbers in Las Vegas have now reached record levels. An astonishing 37 million people, around ten per cent of them from abroad, visited the city in 2009, spending billions in the process. Many people check out Sin City once just to see what all the fuss is about, but millions more become regulars, attracted by the agreeable climate, the big-budget shows, the swanky hotels, the increasingly excellent food, the fashionable nightlife and, of course, the chance of instant riches.

Indeed, many have relocated to the world's greatest boomtown. Las Vegas is the largest American city to have been founded in the 20th century, and was also its fastest growing major metropolitan area for more than a decade. The city celebrated its 100th birthday in 2005, marking a century during which it developed from a desolate railroad town to the glamour capital of the world. Heaven only knows what the next ten decades will bring.

The biggest thing – literally – ever to hit Las Vegas is the CityCenter complex, a $10-billion city within a city, and a high-style confluence of casinos, resort hotels, condos and time-share units, and high-end shopping, dining and entertainment. Owned by MGM Mirage and located between the Monte Carlo and Bellagio (its own internal monorail links the properties), it is the largest and most expensive private construction project in history. Eight world-class 'starchitects' designed the components of the project, which include Aria Resort & Casino, Vdara Hotel & Spa, Mandarin Oriental Las Vegas, Veer Towers and the Crystals retail and entertainment district. Adjacent to CityCenter is the Cosmopolitan, which opened in 2011 and quickly became the liveliest place in town.

While these major casinos went up, others came tumbling down. The building boom of the 1990s was accompanied by the spectacular implosion of a number of key casinos. Between October 1993 and April 1998, the Dunes, the Landmark, the Sands, the Hacienda and the old Aladdin

IN CONTEXT

Key Events

c800 Anasazi civilisation begins to develop in the southern Nevada desert.
c1150 The semi-nomadic southern Paiute tribe claim territory abandoned by the Anasazi.
1830 Rafael Rivera discovers a short cut via Big Spring while on the trading route from Santa Fe. He names the area Las Vegas.
1845 The surveyor John C Fremont visits the Las Vegas Valley.
1855-58 Mormon missionaries from Salt Lake City establish a short-lived community at Las Vegas. Lead is discovered in the area.
c1858 Silver ore and gold are discovered, prompting the growth of a mining boomtown.
1865 The old Mormon fort is appropriated by OD Gass and redeveloped as the Las Vegas Ranch.
1881 The Las Vegas Ranch is taken over by Archibald Stewart.
1903 Helen Stewart sells most of the Las Vegas Ranch to the San Pedro, Los Angeles & Salt Lake Railroad. JT McWilliams claims 80 acres of land west of the Las Vegas Ranch and subdivides it as lots for a planned town site, known as Ragtown.
1905 The Salt Lake City to Los Angeles railroad is completed at Jean, Nevada. A subsidiary of the railroad company auctions 1,000 lots for a new town site across the tracks from Ragtown. Four months later, Ragtown burns down.
1905 The new town of Las Vegas begins to develop with a nightlife district on Block 16 (today's Downtown).
1924 Two canyons east of Las Vegas are chosen as the site of an ambitious new project to dam the Colorado River.
1931 Gambling is legalised in Nevada, prompting an influx of casino operators into Las Vegas. Construction begins on the Hoover Dam, with Boulder City established to house the workers.
1935 President Roosevelt and 20,000 others attend the Hoover Dam dedication ceremony.

1940s Three major casinos are built: El Cortez, El Rancho and the Last Frontier.
1946 Construction of Benjamin 'Bugsy' Siegel's Flamingo casino.
1947 Bugsy Siegel is shot dead in Beverly Hills. For the next 20 years, the Mob dominates gambling in Las Vegas.
1951-58 Eleven hotel-casinos open in Vegas; ten are funded by the Mob.
1951-62 Around 120 nuclear bombs are detonated over the Nevada Test Site.
1960-61 The Rat Pack perform in the Copa Room at the Sands casino.
1962 First Limited Nuclear Test Ban Treaty prohibits atmospheric nuclear explosions.
1962-92 800 nuclear devices detonated underground at the Nevada Test Site.
1966 Millionaire Howard Hughes takes up residence at the Desert Inn, buying up six casinos and stimulating a boom.
1990-2000 Myriad new resorts are built on the Strip and beyond it. The town undergoes a new lease of life and the population of Clark County soars.
2003 Celine Dion opens '…A New Day' at the custom-built Colosseum at Caesar's Palace. The show changes the face of entertainment in Las Vegas.
2004 Hard Rock Hotel launches its Sunday pool party called Rehab, launching the 'daylife' craze.
2005 Ultimate Fighting becomes a major draw, along with NASCAR and televised poker championships.
2005 The city celebrates its centenary; Steve Wynn opens Wynn Las Vegas.
2007 The Stardust is demolished.
2010 MGM Mirage's 67-acre CityCenter complex opens. Two beloved off-Strip cultural institutions – the Las Vegas Art Museum and the Liberace Museum – close their doors.
2011 The Cosmopolitan opens next door to CityCenter. The Sahara closes. Carolyn Goodman, wife of Oscar, is elected mayor.
2013 Wildfires rage for two weeks just outside Vegas, following a heatwave.

Architecture

Vegas's serious new structures are being built to last.

The Las Vegas Strip has always been a movie set of sorts. With each new era, relics of the greatest hits in oasis-style hospitality make way for a fresh backdrop and new stars. Just as the mid-century modernist Dunes was imploded for the sake of the opulent Bellagio, so the Treasure Island that helped launch the theme-happy family era in Vegas was repackaged into the younger, sexier TI. The trend in Las Vegas has always been for disposable or mutable architecture; this is a city more likely to tear down its laurels than rest on them. Along the Strip, it's survival not so much of the fittest but of the tallest, the biggest and the boldest.

But times are changing. The next era in Vegas architecture seems set to throw things off cycle. While some of the town's history will inevitably vanish, what's going up – high up – are attractions that are more dense, more metropolitan and even a little more green. For a change, they're also being built to last.

CITYCENTER

The most significant exponent of the new era in Vegas construction, and the most expensive privately funded development in the US, is MGM Mirage's $11-billion **CityCenter** complex of buildings, which sprang up on the 76 acres between the Bellagio and the Monte Carlo. A city within a city rising from the middle of the Strip, CityCenter suddenly dominated the skyline. The addition of 'starchitect'-designed Aria, Vdara, Mandarin Oriental, Veers Towers – and the star-crossed Harmon, which is in danger of being demolished without ever opening, because of faulty construction – changed the gravitational centre of Las Vegas.

CityCenter opened in stages, beginning in December 2009 with Pelli Clarke Pelli's 60-storey, 4,004-room hotel-casino **Aria** (*see p81*). A striking addition to the new skyline is Helmut Jahn's two 37-storey Veer Towers, twin oblongs that lean a startling five degrees in opposite directions. Other world-class architects contributed buildings to the complex, including Rafael Vinoly (the condo-hotel **Vdara**, *see p111*); London's Foster & Partners (the star-crossed Harmon Hotel & Spa, which was never completed); Kohn Pederson Fox (**Mandarin Oriental**, *see p110*); and Daniel Libeskind (the strikingly spiky, museum-like **Crystals** high-end shopping centre, *see p173*). A unifying theme is conspicuous by its absence; instead, CityCenter is a model of large-scale contemporary urban architecture, with a number of sleek towers and eco-friendly credentials. Next door to CityCenter, there's the even newer **Cosmopolitan** (*see p85*), which opened in 2011 and attracts a younger, more urbane crowd. It was designed by Arquitectonica with an unusual vertical orientation – the casino, clubs, entertainment venues, restaurants and retail are played out on three floors rather than the usual single-storey sprawl.

ECONOMIC WOES HIT DEVELOPMENTS

There were big plans for more of this mini-metropolitan movement at the northern end of the Strip, where Echelon Place

Vdara

Vdara.

started going up on the old Stardust casino lot. But construction on that massive project, which called for four hotels, came to a sudden halt in 2010, leaving a half-finished framework as a dire symbol of the economic collapse that affected Las Vegas more than perhaps any other US city. In 2013, Boyd sold its interest in the property to Malaysian gaming giant the Genting Group. Genting announced plans to build a $2-billion resort on the site. The Asian-themed hotel-casino, which is expected to break ground in 2014, is projected to have 3,500 rooms and include a replica of the Great Wall of China.

Another dream deferred is a casino-resort project called the Fontainebleau. Former Mandalay Resorts boss Glenn Schaeffer proposed what would have been one of the most architecturally significant resorts in modern Vegas; its 25-acre, 68-storey, 3,889-room design was inspired by the style of Morris Lapidus (who designed the original in Miami Beach in the 1950s). Construction ceased due to bankruptcy in 2009; the casino-hotel's furnishings were sold to Downtown's Plaza Hotel & Casino for its refurbishment. For now, the property sits unfinished, its future uncertain.

Las Vegas is unsentimental about getting rid of what's not working – in other words, not making as much money as it once did – and that means literally blowing up old buildings to make way for new, potentially more lucrative structures. The latest landmark to meet this fate is the venerable Rat Pack roost, the Sahara casino and hotel, which closed its doors in 2010, just shy of its 60th birthday. But rather than implode the Sahara, the fate of so many other properties, it is now being removed piecemeal to make way for the high-end SLS, which is expected to open in 2014.

BRIGHT SPOTS

Some bright spots have emerged despite the money crunch: the City of Las Vegas (with help from Newland Communities) has been developing its own urban core on a long-barren Downtown railroad lot formerly known as the 61 Acres but now renamed Union Park. Marquee projects here include the Frank Gehry-designed **Lou Ruvo Center for Brain Health**, which opened in 2009 – the typically twisty steel-clad structure appears to be melting in the Vegas heat — and David Schwarz's more conservatively styled **Smith Center for the Performing Arts**, which began providing a much-needed home for non-casino culture in the Vegas valley when it opened in May 2012. They were recently joined by a new **City Hall** – a largely glass and steel building that looks as if it's somehow poised for take-off. Other projects on and around the site include a couple of boutique hotels and the proposed 57-storey World Jewelry Center, although its future is not altogether certain. On adjacent land, the vast **World Market Center** continues to change shape and dominates its corner of the cityscape, with seven buildings devoted to hospitality and the home-furnishings trade, including the Las Vegas Design Center, which is open to the public.

The old Las Vegas City Hall has been taken over by the giant internet shoes-and-accessories website Zappos.com, which has imported hundreds of energetic young hipsters to Las Vegas – their presence is already having an influence on the culture of Downtown Las Vegas. This influence is readily apparent in the skyrocketing popularity of condominiums Downtown. Consider the **Juhl**, a high-, medium- and low-rise, mixed-use building just a couple of blocks off Las Vegas Boulevard on E Bonneville Avenue. The building had the misfortune of opening amid the economic crash in 2009, but it's now a hot commodity. Other high-rise condos have appeared all around Las Vegas: steel and glass and concrete structures in desirable locations that look as if they're built to last and that people might want to actually inhabit long-term, as opposed to the dreary two-storey apartment complexes that otherwise dot the valley.

The cityscape isn't only developing aesthetically: Las Vegas has also finally got out of the starting blocks in the green movement. Around 20 projects in the area have been approved for the US Green Building Council's LEED certification, among them a sustainable TV campus (Vegas PBS) and a neighbourhood of luxury holiday homes (Enchantment Way). Even CityCenter is getting in on the act, the largest project to be LEED-certified. But the granddaddy of all green projects is the **Las Vegas Springs Preserve** (*see p71*), a central park with seven LEED Platinum structures that are both built to be sustainable and designed to teach sustainability to visitors.

With such high-profile projects in the pipeline, Vegas is taking on a more refined appearance. But those who hanker after the decadent ol' days will still find plenty to dazzle. The 64-storey gold-and-white **Trump International Hotel & Tower** (*see p110*) opened in 2008– notably without a casino – across the Boulevard from Steve Wynn's bronze-and-tan **Wynn Las Vegas** (*see p93*), standing taller, gaudier and somehow even shinier than its neighbour. Wynn named his building's sibling **Encore**; the adjacent 2,000-room tower opened in 2008 and featured even more lavish decor, with a butterfly motif. Meanwhile, Wynn's competitive neighbour Sheldon Adelson played his **Palazzo** (*see p92*) card in the same year, opening a 3,000-room tower resort to complement his Venetian casino-resort.

IN CONTEXT

IN CONTEXT

THE EARLY DAYS

Although Las Vegas has been a popular resort town for more than half a century, the way in which its hotels are designed has altered hugely down the years, as much thanks to social change as by any direct design imperative. The old Vegas was a Mafia-controlled demi-monde, where men gambled wearing jackets and ties, watched by women clad in diamonds and ballgowns. Back then, gambling was illegal in much of the US. But now that it's permitted in 48 of the 50 states, and now that the industry is controlled not by the Mob but by big business, the town has reinvented itself.

From World War II onwards, when the town's expansion began to take hold, Las Vegas developed its own distinctive style, a dazzlingly vulgar cocktail of expressionist modern architecture and monumental neon signs that illuminated stretches of desert on Las Vegas Boulevard. A key figure in this development was Wayne McAllister, a pioneering southern Californian architect whose influence over modern Vegas is perhaps greater than that of any other designer. It was McAllister who built the cowboy-flavoured El Rancho, the first themed resort on what's known as the Strip, back in 1941. A decade later, he constructed the original Sands, the Rat Pack's casino of choice, and also had a hand in the Desert Inn.

The town's smaller hotels were, if anything, even more exotic, and in some cases positively space-age. Many were products of the automotive age, built to dazzle and attract passing drivers. At the original Mirage, built in 1952, swimmers could be seen through portholes on the street-front side of the pool; indeed, the motel became better known as the Glass Pool Inn, as it was rechristened more than three decades after it opened. In 1961, Paul Revere Williams' La Concha Motel drew attention for its zinging concrete lobby, the design of which aped the form of a shell.

Modern Vegas has upped the scale and sophistication of its resorts, adding shops and amusements to create vast complexes replicating the kind of walk-through fantasies popularised by Disney. The kaleidoscope of neon that was once the city's trademark has been dwarfed by themed resorts approximating all kinds of cities, countries and (the key word here) experiences. As a result, little remains from the 1950s and '60s. As the town unsentimentally continues to cut ties with its past, most of the properties mentioned in the preceding pair of paragraphs have been destroyed in the name of progress. The sole survivor is the old La Concha lobby, salvaged in 2007 and scheduled to be rebuilt Downtown by the Neon Museum (*see p64* **A Paean to Neon**).

ENTERTAINMENT ARCHITECTURE

The earliest gambling joints on what became the Strip had a western flavour. The El Rancho, which opened in 1941, and the Last Frontier, which followed a year later, took as their themes nostalgia for the Old West. A few years down the line, Benjamin 'Bugsy' Siegel helped

Caesars Palace.

create the **Flamingo** (*see p96*) in 1946, an LA Moderne-style tropical paradise. With variations, this style reigned during the adults-only, post-war years. But when Jay Sarno built his instantly sensational, pseudo-Roman **Caesars Palace** (*see p83*) in 1966, and followed it two years later with the camp **Circus Circus** (*see p106*), the die was cast.

After a relatively quiet few years, the stakes in the theming game escalated with the work of Steve Wynn, without whom Vegas would look very different. In 1989, Wynn opened the South Seas-themed **Mirage** (*see p90*), which melded the upmarket stylings of Siegel's Flamingo with the fantasy of Caesars and the mass appeal of Circus Circus, and became the Strip's first mega-resort. Then, four years later, the entrepreneur delivered the Caribbean-inspired **Treasure Island** (*see p104*) just next door. The same period saw the construction of the riotous, candy-coloured **Excalibur** (1990; *see p106*), the agreeably preposterous **Luxor** (1993; see p98) and the ugly but enormous **MGM Grand** (1993; *see p88*). However, it was Wynn's duo that really reversed the downward spiral of Las Vegas of the early 1980s.

Casino bosses have since gone in for even more extravagant design. Where once the properties were signed by fizzing neon, the theming is now so wild that the casinos introduce themselves. The Egyptian-themed exterior of the Luxor is, from street level, a vast black glass pyramid guarded by a squatting sphinx; the hotel, casino and sign are integrated into one structure, so the building itself is the sign. **New York New York** (*see p100*) represented theming at its most fully realised when it opened four years later with a mini-Grand Central Station, a half-size Statue of Liberty and 12 jaunty, 1:3-scale skyscrapers mimicking the Manhattan skyline. And in 1999, **Paris Las Vegas** (*see p91*) dropped a half-size replica of the Eiffel Tower on to the Strip. It looks tongue-in-cheek – and it is – but the attempts at authenticity are touching; although the tower is welded together, cosmetic rivets have been positioned in the appropriate places.

Paris Las Vegas is one of several resorts that have taken their cues from across the Atlantic. For casino moguls – and, arguably, for middle Americans who make up the greater part of Vegas's custom – Europe equals sophistication. With that in mind, it's no surprise that two of the Strip's most luxurious and expensive resorts have carefully realised European themes.

The first to open was the $1.6-billion **Bellagio** (*see p82*), an Italianate theme park for high-rolling grown-ups built by Wynn in 1998. The property is fronted by an eight-acre imitation of Lake Como; inside, marble is conspicuous in both the lobbies and the rooms. The basic trefoil tower structure is hardly innovative, but there are imaginative moments within, among them the glass anemones by sculptor Dale Chihuly on the lobby ceiling, the extravagant conservatory and the lake's dancing fountains. The Sands, meanwhile, was replaced in 1999 by the **Venetian** (*see p92*), which links the Rialto bridge to the Doge's Palace and piazza San Marco.

Other developments in Vegas's casinos have come with the expansion of its shopping scene from negligible to extensive. One of Las Vegas's most stunning themed environments, the **Forum Shops** (1993; *see p174*) at Caesars Palace, set a trend that's since been emulated at Paris Las Vegas, the Venetian and Planet Hollywood. This cod-Roman shopping street, complete with trompe l'oeil sky (and lighting that simulates the transition from dawn to dusk), showed casino moguls that malls could be money-spinners, and also introduced convincing aged walls and styrofoam sculptures to a city that had previously been quite happy with cheerfully silly evocation. The mall's expansion in 2004 brought another only-in-Vegas innovation: spiral escalators.

AFTER DARK

Aiming for younger, more upscale and more urbane customers, the gaming kings of Las Vegas have hired some of the world's top architects and designers to create swanky new restaurants,

IN CONTEXT

nightclubs and lounges inside their casinos. It's here that you'll find some of the city's more exciting design touches. Not all are original, granted; some restaurants have been described as 'New York-style', while a few nightclubs are keen to play up their European origins or their retro fittings. But there's vibrancy here, not to mention excess.

The **Palms** resort (*see p114*), which opened in 2001, has been at the forefront of the movement towards a cooler kind of ostentation. Three of its venues deliver it in spades: **Rain** (*see p224*), a nightclub and concert venue with a lounge, an elevated dancefloor and (the Vegas touch) light fixtures that shoot fire; **Ghostbar** (*see p164*), where the similarly retro edge would make Austin Powers feel at home; and the **N9ne** steakhouse (*see p152*), where coloured lights wash the ceiling. Other casinos have been getting in on the act, most recently the Beatles-themed, Cirque du Soleil-created **Revolution** lounge (*see p161*) at the Mirage.

Not every ode to modernity sits on the Strip. At 3rd and Ogden streets in Downtown, the owners of the currently-closed Lady Luck casino have opened a handsome locals' favourite called **Triple George** (*see p153*), complete with an adjoining, brick-walled piano bar. Completed in 2007, the Fremont East Entertainment District benefitted from wider, more pedestrian-friendly sidewalks and retro signage, with smartly designed venues such as the **Downtown Cocktail Room** (*see p165*) and the **Griffin** (*see p165*) teasing a hip, metropolitan vibe out of some gritty old structures. And all without a single slot machine in sight.

NON-RESORT ARCHITECTURE

Attention was first drawn to the city's public architecture in the late 1980s with Charles Hunsberger's ambitious and controversial library-building programme. Using a range of architects with a view to making each of the nine libraries adventurous and unique, the programme was an attempt to create, without precedent, a Las Vegas 'high' architectural style. Characterised by earthen forms, variegated concrete

and sandy stone, pyramids, cones and »dry desert landscaping, the libraries can be seen as an effort to reflect and adapt to the harsh environment of the Mojave desert; the Sahara West Library & Las Vegas Arts Museum, the West Charleston Library and the Summerlin Library & Performing Arts Center are perhaps the best examples. This trend reached its extreme with the Clark County Government Center (600 S Grand Central Parkway). Other lively buildings also welcome visitors, and perhaps even inspire them. The tech-savvy **Lied Library** (*see p297*) at UNLV, for example, is a concrete, steel and glass structure with towering east windows and a massive, inviting lobby. And the first structure visitors are likely to notice is the sleek Terminal D at McCarran International Airport. Having announced its authority with steel and glass, the terminal incorporates both past (Googie-style graphics, vintage passenger planes) and contemporary (exposed steel trusses, hangar-high ceilings, large glass windows). While you're here, look out for the airport's award-winning new control tower, a robot-like structure crowned with what (intentionally) looks like a policeman's cap.

One of the most visible additions is Downtown's Lloyd D George Federal Courthouse (333 Las Vegas Boulevard South). Designed by Dwarsky & Associates of LA, with a keen emphasis on security in the wake of the 1995 Oklahoma City bombing, the plaza is raised above street level, and the building itself has a blast-resistant wall of windows facing Las Vegas Boulevard. Nearby is the Regional Justice Center, an award-winning complex designed by Tate Snyder Kimsey that consolidated the operations of the municipal, justice and state supreme courts into 'one user-friendly courthouse'. One of these more friendly uses is the Marriage License Bureau, which has its own entrance, as well as a small courtyard and canopy of trees for happy snappers.

Yet despite growing aspirations, these public buildings represent only a few bright points in an architectural desert.

Non-resort Las Vegas is still defined by endless one- and two-storey stucco-and-Spanish-tile tract houses and monotonous shopping centres, convenience stores and fast-food restaurants. There's little evidence of planning, just an ugly chequerboard of 'leapfrog' development spreading in all directions.

Downtown is re-emerging as a residential district, especially within the historic 160-home John S Park neighbourhood, east of Las Vegas Boulevard South and north of Charleston Boulevard. However, on the whole, living close to the centre is still seen as undesirable in a city where roads have not yet become permanently gridlocked. Affluent and middle-class families prefer residential enclaves built around golf courses and artificial lakes on the edge

Hoover Dam.

of the valley; on the Strip, high-rise condos such as Turnberry Place at the north end, and Park Towers at the south, appeal largely to jet-setters here for six weeks a year. One of the latest such statements comes in the shape of the two sleek Panorama Towers, perched near the Strip alongside Interstate 15.

Supplementing its gated neighbourhoods, Las Vegas has gone one step further – as usual – with 'master-planned' communities, town-sized swathes of privately owned land on which management companies create entire societies (housing in several price brackets, business and commercial districts, retirement complexes, schools, parks – even hospitals). Residents sign up to the community's rules and, in theory, settle back to enjoy their suburban utopia.

The most carefully planned of such communities was **Summerlin** (see p70). With its abundance of parks, sports fields, tennis courts and trails, not to mention its proximity to Red Rock Canyon, it's favoured by outdoorsy urbanites and disdained by those who thrive on an independent lifestyle. (You want to paint your house green? Forget it.) People have continued to buy into what has become the new American Dream; similar planned communities include Seven Hills and Anthem, both in Henderson, and Aliante in North Las Vegas. However, the latest breed, among them Inspirada near Anthem and Kyle Canyon in the north-west, have at least attempted to incorporate 'new urbanism' to counteract ills such as the lack of pedestrian destinations.

Of all the structures here, there's one you absolutely can't miss. The quirk? It's not a building, not in Las Vegas and not designed by an architect. Conceived by engineer John Savage and built as part of Roosevelt's public-works programme, the monumental **Hoover Dam** (see p244) on the Colorado River is a marvel of human ingenuity. Utterly utilitarian, with art deco touches, it has the grandeur and permanence missing from most buildings in Vegas. What's more, completed in 1935, it's older than almost anywhere else in the city.

IN CONTEXT

Essential Information

Getting Around

ARRIVING & LEAVING

By air

Las Vegas's **McCarran International Airport** (261 5211, www.mccarran.com) is just five minutes from the south end of the Strip, which makes the trip from airport to hotel relatively painless. The airport itself is clean and modern, and takes first (and last) tilt at the tourist dollar with halls of slot machines and video poker.

There are hundreds of internal flights to Las Vegas each week. However, direct international flights are limited; from the UK, for example, only Virgin Atlantic (from London Gatwick) and British Airways (from London Heathrow) fly direct. Most flights to and from Europe require passengers to change at an East Coast airport or at LAX.

Public bus routes 108 and 109 run north from the airport: the 108 heads up Swenson Avenue and stops at the LVH, while the 109 goes along Maryland Parkway. Shuttle buses run by **Bell Trans** (739 7990, www.bell-trans.com), **Grayline** (1-800 472 9546, www.grayline.com) and **Ritz** (889 4242, www.shuttlelasvegas.com) run to the Strip and Downtown 24 hours a day. Expect to pay $7 for transport to a Strip hotel, slightly more to Downtown.

Taxis can be found outside the arrivals hall. There's a $1.80 surcharge on all fares originating at McCarran; bearing that in mind, expect to pay $15-$25 to get to most hotels on the Strip, or $22-$27 to Downtown (plus tip).

Airlines

Air Canada 1-888 247 2262, aircanada.com

Alaska Air 1-800 426 0333, www.alaskaair.com.

American Airlines 1-800 433 7300, www.aa.com.

British Airways 0844 493 0787, www.britishairways.com.

Delta domestic 1-800 221 1212, international 1-800 241 4141, www.delta.com.

Jet Blue 1-800 538 2583, www.jetblue.com.

Southwest 1-800 435 9792, www.southwest.com.

United Airlines domestic 1-800 864 8331, international 1-800 538 2929, www.united.com.

US Airways domestic 1-800 428 4322, international 1-800 622 1015, www.usairways.com.

Virgin Atlantic UK: 0844 209 7777. US: 1-800 862 8621, www.virginatlantic.com.

By road

The main roads leaving the city are the **I-15**, which runs south-west towards LA and north-east towards Salt Lake City, and the **US93** and **US95**, which head respectively, north into Nevada and south into Arizona and California. For details of car hire, see p294.

Greyhound buses (1-800 231 2222, www.greyhound.com) arrive at the bus station on 200 Main Street, just by the Plaza. The ride from LA ($60 one-way) takes between five and eight hours. Reservations are not required.

PUBLIC TRANSPORT

The bus network is run by the Regional Transportation Commission of Southern Nevada (RTC). The Bonneville Transit Center (BTC) is the transfer point for many routes. For a system map, see p314.

Bonneville Transit Center (BTC)
101 E Bonneville Avenue, Downtown (228 7433, www.rtc southernnevada.com). Bus Deuce & all BTC-bound buses. **Open** 7am-5.30pm daily. **Map** p318 D1.

RCT fares & tickets

Most routes cost $2 or $1 for over-62s and 6-17s and the disabled, but only with a Reduced Fare Photo Identification Card

(available from the DTC). The exception is the Deuce route along the Strip, which costs $6 for a two-hour pass or $8 for a 24-hour pass. $20 gets you a 3-Day All Access Pass. Use exact change. Transfers are free, if you ask for one when you pay. A 30-day system pass costs $65.

RCT routes

Buses run 24-7 on the Deuce route along Las Vegas Boulevard, and roughly 5.30am-1.30am elsewhere. The buses are safe and relatively comprehensive in their coverage of the city. Bus stops are marked by signs with the blue, white and gold RTC Transit logo; most have shelters.

The most useful bus for tourists is the **Deuce**: named as it's a double-decker bus, it travels the length of Las Vegas Boulevard from the DTC in the north to just by I-215 in the south, stopping in front of all major casinos. Deuces are often busy, especially at night.

Most bus routes run along the length of a single street, some with a quick turnaround at either end of the route. Buses with a route number beginning in '1' generally run north–south; those starting '2' run east–west. Below is a list of some key routes.

BHX	Boulder Highway Express
Deuce	Las Vegas Boulevard
SDX	Strip & Downtown Express
SX	Sahara Avenue Express
103	Decatur Boulevard
105	Martin Luther King Boulevard/Industrial Road
106	Rancho Drive
107	Boulder Highway
108	Paradise Road
109	Maryland Parkway
110	Eastern Avenue

113	Las Vegas Boulevard (north of BTC only)
201	Tropicana Avenue
202	Flamingo Road
203	Spring Mountain Road/Twain Avenue
206	Charleston Boulevard
207	Alta Drive/Stewart Avenue
208	Washington Boulevard

Many bus routes, among them the Deuce, 105, 108, 109, 113 and 207, stop at the BTC. Throughout the listings in this book, we've used the shorthand 'BTC-bound buses' to refer to these buses.

Monorails & shuttle buses

After teething problems, the **Las Vegas Monorail** is now running a reliable service along Paradise Road and then behind the Strip. However, it hasn't displaced the numerous hotel buses and monorails.

Las Vegas Monorail
699 8200, www.lvmonorail.com.
The pricey and not wholly convenient Las Vegas Monorail runs from **Sahara Avenue** to the **MGM Grand**, stopping at the **LVH**, the **Las Vegas Convention Center**, **Harrah's**, the **Flamingo** and **Bally's**. The service runs 7am-midnight Mon, 7am-2am Tue-Thur, 7am-3am Fri-Sun. The journey time from end to end is usually around 15 minutes. Single-ride tickets cost $5 and one-day passes go for $12; three-day passes for $28.

Other monorails
Free, 24hr monorails, separate to the Las Vegas Monorail, link the **Mirage** and **TI**; and **Excalibur**, the **Luxor** and **Mandalay Bay**. For all of them, it's often quicker to walk. A free monorail connects the **CityCenter** complex with the adjacent **Monte Carlo** and **Bellagio** resorts.

Free shuttle buses
A shuttle bus connects the **Rio** with **Harrah's** on the Strip, just south of **Planet Hollywood** (formerly the Aladdin). Nearby, the **Palms** lays on a shuttle to and from the **Fashion Show Mall**

and the **Forum Shops**. The **Hard Rock** runs a shuttle that loops around from the hotel to the **Forum Shops**, **Planet Hollywood** and **the MGM Grand**. Shuttle buses link **Sam's Town** to Downtown and the Strip, and the **South Point** and the Strip. And there are free shuttle buses linking **Green Valley Ranch**, **Red Rock**, **Palace Station** and **Sunset Station** to both the Strip and McCarran Airport.

BUS TOURS

Gray Line Tours *1-800 472 9546, www.graylinelasvegas.com.*
Gray Line offers a handful of Vegas-based bus tours, including an evening city tour (3.5hrs, $59), plus trips out to the Grand Canyon (14hrs, $175), and a half-day jag to Lake Mead and the Hoover Dam (4.5hrs, $65). Discounts are often available by booking in advance online.

TAXIS & LIMOS

There are **taxi ranks** outside most hotels; restaurants and bars will be happy to call a cab for you. Technically, you're not allowed to hail a taxi from the street and most won't stop if you try, but it's usually OK to approach an empty cab with its light on if it has stopped in traffic. Meters start at $3.30, and increase by $2.60 per mile. If you have a complaint, note the cab number and call the **Nevada Taxicab Authority** (486 6532, www.taxi.state.nv.us). For lost property, *see p297*.

Limousines are a flash and popular way of getting around. The rides vary from the basic black stretch ($50/hr) to huge SUVs with hot tubs, disco balls and the like ($115/hr). Many limos are available for hire outside hotels and the airport. Limo drivers are not allowed to solicit passengers, but you are perfectly at liberty to approach them for a ride.

Cab companies

Desert *386 9102.*

Whittlesea Blue Cab *384 6111.*

Yellow-Checker-Star (YCS)
873 2000, www.ycstrans.com.

Limousine companies

Bell Trans *739 7990, www.bell-trans.com.*

Las Vegas Limo *888 4848, www.lasvegaslimo.com.*

Presidential *731 5577, www.presidentiallimolv.com.*

DRIVING

If you're based on the Strip, a mix of buses, taxis, monorails and feet will get you to most places. However, automobile rental is affordable in Vegas; a car is recommended if you're staying away from the Strip or are keen to visit off-Strip attractions, and essential if you're planning to visit any out-of-town destinations.

The Las Vegas streets get very congested in the morning and evening rush hours (7-9am, 4-6pm), as well as at weekends, when traffic is horrific in tourist areas after 4pm. The Strip is slow-going most of the time and turns into a virtual car park when the town is busy.

The nearby parallel streets – Industrial Road and Frank Sinatra Drive to the west, Paradise Road to the east – move faster, and provide access to several casinos. For north–south journeys longer than a block or two, it's often worth taking I-15, which runs parallel to the Strip. If you're trying to get east–west across town, take the Desert Inn arterial, a mini-expressway that runs under the Strip and over I-15 (though there are no junctions at either).

I-15 intersects with the east–west US 95 north-west of Downtown. US 95 connects to the 53-mile beltway (I-215) at the edges of the valley, which leads commuters around the region. Because Las Vegas is constantly tearing itself down and rebuilding itself, there's usually a great deal of road construction going on on I-15; for road conditions, call 1-877 687 6237 or see www.nevada dot.com/traveler/roads.

Speed limits vary in Nevada. In general, the speed limit on freeways is 65mph; on the highway, it's either 65mph or 70mph. Limits on main urban thoroughfares (such as Tropicana Avenue) are 45mph; elsewhere, limits are 25mph, 30mph or 35mph. Look for signs in construction zones and near schools, which often enforce a reduced limit.

Unless otherwise specified, you can turn right on a red light, after stopping, if the street is clear. U-turns are not only legal (unless

ESSENTIAL INFORMATION

specified) but often a positive necessity given the length of the blocks. In case of a car accident, call 911; do not move the cars involved in the accident until the police ask you to do so.

In Nevada, you can be arrested for driving under the influence if your blood alcohol level is 0.08 or higher (or 0.02 for under-21s). If you're pulled over, the police can give you a drink-driving test on the spot. If you refuse, you'll be taken to jail for a blood test, which will be taken by force if necessary.

Gas is far cheaper than in Europe, but pricey for the US. There are gas stations by Circus Circus and across from Mandalay Bay; stations abound on (among others) Paradise Road, Maryland Parkway, Tropicana Avenue and Flamingo Road. For mechanics and full-service gas stations, see 'Automobile repair' in the *Yellow Pages*.

The **American Automobile Association (AAA)** provides maps, guidebooks and other useful information. They're free if you're a member or belong to an affiliated organisation, such as the British AA. The main Vegas office, open 8.30am-5.30pm during the week, is at 3312 W Charleston Boulevard; call them on 415 2200 or see www.aaa.com for more details.

Car hire

Most car-hire agencies are at or near the airport. Call around for the best rate, booking well in advance if you're planning to visit over a holiday weekend or for a major convention. When business renters are scarce, though, you should get a good rate, and maybe – if you ask nicely – an upgrade.

Almost every firm requires a credit card and matching driver's licence; few will rent to under-25s. Prices won't include tax, liability insurance or collision damage waiver (CDW); US residents may be covered on their home policy, but foreign residents will need to buy extra insurance. UK travellers should note that while rental deals struck with the UK offices of the major firms include insurance, it's often cheaper to rent the car from the US office and rely for insurance on the good-value, year-long policy available from www.insurance4carhire.com.

Alamo *US: 1-800 462 5266, 263 8411, www.alamo.com. UK: 0871 384 1086, www.alamo.co.uk.*

Avis *US: 1-800 331 1212, 531 1500, www.avis.com. UK: 0844 581 0147, www.avis.co.uk.*

Budget *US: 1-800 527 0700, 736 1212, www.budget.com. UK: 0844 544 3439, www.budget.co.uk.*

Dollar *US: 1-800 800 3665, www.dollar.com. UK: 0808 234 752, www.dollar.co.uk.*

Enterprise *US: 1-800 800 227, 365 6662, www.enterprise.com. UK: 0800 800 227, www. enterprise.co.uk.*

Hertz *US: 1-800 654 3131, 220 9700, www.hertz.com. UK: 0843 309 3099, www.hertz.co.uk.*

National *US: 1-800 227 7368, 263 8411. UK: 0870 400 4581. Both: www.nationalcar.com.*

Thrifty *US: 1-800 847 4389, 896 7600, www.thrifty.com. UK: 01494 751 500, www.thrifty.co.uk.*

Motorcycle rental

Eaglerider *876 8687, www.eaglerider.com.*

Harley-Davidson of Southern Nevada *431 8500, www.lvhd.com.*

Parking

Most hotel-casinos have valet parking, which is convenient, safe and free (apart from the $2-$5 tip on your way out). If you see a sign saying the valet car park is full and you're in a luxury car, stay put: chances are the valets will find a spot for you. Hotel guests also get preferential treatment; when the attendant asks to see your room key, $5-$10 will often substitute. Self-parking is free and abundant in the multilevel parking structures at every Vegas resort (Downtown casinos require a validation stamp), but the convenience of lots is variable.

CYCLING

In a word: don't. Some try and get away with cycling on the Strip on weekend nights, when traffic has slowed to a crawl. But it's dicey even then; and at other times, the drivers on the three- and four-lane roads in the city simply aren't looking for cyclists: you're taking your life in your hands.

HELICOPTER

Plane and helicopter rides over the rim of the Grand Canyon are a major cause of air and noise pollution. But if you care to disregard the concerns of Las Vegas locals and Grand Canyon environmentalists, then **Sundance** is Nevada's best regarded helicopter tour operator. City tours run from $85-$110, with trips to the Grand Canyon starting at around $375. Other by air options for the Grand Canyon include **Grand Canyon Airlines** and **Papillon Grand Canyon Helicopters** (for both, *see p257*).

Sundance Helicopters
1-800 653 1881, 736 0606, www.helicoptour.com, www.sundancehelicopters.com.

WALKING

Pedestrians are rarely seen off the Strip in Vegas, and even there they face danger from carefree and often careless drivers. The bridges on the Strip help, but it's still tricky. Jaywalking is so potentially deadly that police often issue citations. Laws, and physics, favour the driver: never put yourself in the path of cars that have the green light.

The safest places to cross are the overhead pedestrian bridges at several key Strip locations, bridges that (of course) guide you past the entrances of the casinos on each corner. You can find them at Tropicana Avenue, at Flamingo Road, and at Spring Mountain Road near Wynn Las Vegas. Where there are no bridges, closely follow all traffic signals and check both directions twice before stepping into the street.

It's possible to take short-cuts from one Strip hotel to the next, but you're likely to get trapped in a maze of service roads. Use our maps to guide you and don't underestimate the distances between resorts: the Strip is longer than it looks, and walking it end to end will take at least 90 minutes and almost certainly longer. And always factor in plenty of time to get out of the resort in which you've been staying, dining, gambling or partying: you may be as much as a 15-minute walk from the main exit.

Resources A-Z

TRAVEL ADVICE

For up-to-date information on travel to a specific country – including the latest on safety and security, health issues, local laws and customs – contact your home country government's department of foreign affairs. Most have websites with useful advice for would-be travellers.

AUSTRALIA
www.smartraveller.gov.au

CANADA
www.voyage.gc.ca

NEW ZEALAND
www.safetravel.govt.nz

REPUBLIC OF IRELAND
foreignaffairs.gov.ie

UK
www.fco.gov.uk/travel

USA
www.state.gov/travel

ADDRESSES

Addresses follow the standard US format. The room and/or suite number usually appears after the street address (where applicable), followed by the city name and the zip code. Note that Las Vegas Boulevard South is the official name of the Strip. For more on orientation, *see p49* **Getting Your Bearings**.

AGE RESTRICTIONS

Admission to nude clubs 18.
Admission to topless clubs 21.
Buying/drinking alcohol 21.
Driving 16.
Gambling 21.
Marriage 16 (with parental consent) or 18 (without).
Sex 16 (heterosexual) or 18 (homosexual).

ATTITUDE & ETIQUETTE

During the warmer months, shorts and T-shirts are accepted wear along the Strip as well as in most casinos, though dressing up to a minimum of smart-casual has become the norm. Some lounges and nightclubs have dress codes (sports shoes, T-shirts and jeans may be prohibited), and dining in some high-end restaurants can be formal.

BUSINESS

Conventions & conferences

Mandalay Bay (*see p86*) is another also a popular venue for hosting conventions.
Las Vegas Convention Center
3150 Paradise Road, at Convention Center Drive, East of Strip (892 0711, www.lvcva.com). Bus 108, 213. **Map** p319 C5.

Sands Expo & Convention Center
210 Sands Avenue, at Koval Lane, East of Strip (733 5556, www.sandsexpo.com). Bus 203, 213. **Map** p320 B6.

Couriers & shippers

Many hotels have business centres with courier services.

DHL *1-800 225 5345, www.dhl.com.*
FedEx *1-800 463 3339, www.fedex.com.*
UPS *1-800 742 5877/ www.ups.com.*

Office services

Bit by Bit *474 6311, www.bit-by-bit.com.*
Rents laptops, desktop computers and other electronics. Call ahead to arrange delivery.
FedEx Kinko's *395 Hughes Center Drive, at Paradise Road, East of Strip (951 2400, http://fedex.kinkos.com). Bus 108, 213.* **Open** 24hrs daily. **Map** p320 C7.
The prominent chain of copy shops has five branches in the Las Vegas area; this is one of two that are open 24hrs. Services include printing, shipping and internet access.

Useful organisations

For the **Las Vegas Chamber of Commerce** and the **Las Vegas CVA**, For both, *see p299*.

CONSUMER

For complaints about casinos, contact the **Gaming Control Board** (486 2000, www.gaming.nv.gov). For general enquiries and complaints, contact the privately operated **Better Business**

Bureau (320 4500, http://southern nevada.bbb.org, which receives and investigates complaints, or the Consumer Affairs Division of the **Nevada Department of Business & Industry** (486 7355, www.fyiconsumer.org).

CUSTOMS

Travellers arriving in Vegas on an indirect international flight will go through customs and immigration at the airport in which they change planes. This involves reclaiming baggage at the transfer airport, taking it through customs and then checking it in again. Connection times should take account of this.

On US flights, non-US citizens are given two forms – one for immigration, one for customs – which must be filled in and handed in at the appropriate desk on landing. Foreign visitors can import the following items duty-free: 200 cigarettes or 50 cigars (not Cuban; over-18s only) or 2kg of smoking tobacco; one litre of wine or spirits (over-21s only); and up to $100 in gifts ($800 for returning Americans). You must declare and maybe forfeit plants and foods. Check www.cbp.gov/xp/cgov/travel before travelling.

DISABLED

Vegas is a disabled-friendly city. Strip resorts are fully wheelchair-accessible, from pools, spas and restrooms to gambling facilities; things are a little harder in the older Downtown properties. A few casinos offer games for sight- and hearing-impaired players. Disabled parking is found almost everywhere; buses and many taxis are adapted to take wheelchairs (though be sure to ask when you book).

ESSENTIAL INFORMATION

The **Southern Nevada Center for Independent Living** (889 4216, www.sncil.org) offers advice, information, transport and equipment loans (including wheelchairs) for disabled people. The **Society of Accessible Travel and Hospitality** (1-212 447 7284, www.sath.org) can provide advice for disabled people planning trips to all corners of the US.

DRUGS

The use of illegal drugs, including clubbing drugs such as ecstasy, is quite prevalent in Vegas. Dealers will approach you all over town, but take care. And always watch your drinks: illicit drugs are sometimes slipped into unattended glasses. The local authorities have a strict zero-tolerance policy on drug use and trafficking. If you're implicated in a drug sale or purchase, you will be arrested and charged, and if convicted could receive a maximum sentence of five to ten years in jail.

ELECTRICITY

The US uses a 110-120V, 60-cycle AC voltage. Except for dual-voltage flat-pin shavers, most foreign visitors will need to run appliances through an adaptor. Most US TVs and DVDs use a different frequency from those in Europe.

EMBASSIES & CONSULATES

The nearest foreign consulates to Las Vegas are in Los Angeles.

Australia *Suite 3150, Century Plaza Towers, 2029 Century Park East, Los Angeles, CA 90067 (1-310 229 4800, www.losangeles.consulate. gov.au.* **Open** 9am-5pm Mon-Fri.
Canada *9th Floor, 550 S Hope Street, Los Angeles, CA 90071 (1-213 346 2700, www.canada international.gc.ca/los_angeles.* **Open** 8.30am-4.30pm Mon-Fri.
New Zealand *Suite 600E, 2425 Olympic Boulevard, Santa Monica, CA 90404 (1-310 566 6555, www.nzcgla.com).* **Open** 8.30am-4.30pm Mon-Fri.
Republic of Ireland *Suite 3350, 100 Pine Street, San Francisco, CA 94111 (1-415 392 4214, www. consulateofirelandsanfrancisco.org).* **Open** 9am-12.30pm Mon, Wed, Fri.
South Africa *Suite 600, 6300 Wilshire Boulevard, Los Angeles, CA 90048 (1-323 651 0902, www.link2southafrica.com).* **Open** 9am-noon Mon-Fri.

United Kingdom *Suite 1200, 11766 Wilshire Boulevard, Los Angeles, CA 90025 (1-310 481 0031, 24hr emergencies 1-877 514 1233).* **Open** 8am-4.30pm Mon-Fri.

EMERGENCIES

In an emergency, dial **911** (free from public phones) and state the nature of the problem.

GAY & LESBIAN

Q-Vegas (www.qvegas.com) is the leading media resource for the GLBT community. You can pick up the monthly magazine or download it from the website.

Gay and Lesbian Community Center of Southern Nevada *401 S Maryland Parkway, at Lewis Avenue, Downtown (733 9800, www.thecenterlv.com).* **Open** 10am-10pm Mon-Fri .
A nonprofit gathering place and information clearinghouse that holds meetings and support groups.

HEALTH

Doctors are available around the clock in emergency rooms and at some UMC Quick Care locations, and by appointment during regular hours. AM-PM Doc (1-888 267 6362, www.ampmdoc.com) also offers in-room service.
 Most hospitals accept major insurance plans, but – unless it's an emergency – you should call ahead to check. Large hotels have access to on-call doctors, at a cost.

Accident & emergency

All the hospitals below have a 24-hour ER, although only **Sunrise** and **UMC** have out-and-out trauma centres. The UMC is the only hospital that by law must treat all patients. The ER entrance is on the corner of Hasting and Rose Streets.

Desert Springs Hospital *2075 E Flamingo Road, at Burnham Street, East Las Vegas (733 8800, www. desertspringshospital.net). Bus 202.*
North Vista Hospital *1409 E Lake Mead Boulevard, between Las Vegas Boulevard North & N Eastern Avenue, North Las Vegas (649 7711, www.northvistahospital.com). Bus 113, 210.*
St Rose Dominican Hospital *102 E Lake Mead Drive at Boulder Highway, Henderson (564 2622, www.strosehospitals.org). Bus 107, 212.*

Summerlin Hospital Medical Center *657 N Town Center Drive, at Hualapai Way, North-west Las Vegas (233 7000, www.summerlin hospital.org). No bus.*
Sunrise Hospital & Medical Center *3186 S Maryland Parkway, between E Sahara Avenue & E Desert Inn Road, East Las Vegas (731 8000, www.sunrise hospital.com). Bus 109.*
University Medical Center *1800 W Charleston Boulevard, at Shadow Lane, West Las Vegas (383 2000, www.umcsn.com). Bus 206.*
Valley Hospital Medical Center *620 Shadow Lane, off W Charleston Boulevard, West Las Vegas (388 4000, www.valleyhospital.net). Bus 206.*

Contraception & abortion

Planned Parenthood *3220 W Charleston Boulevard, between S Rancho Drive & S Valley View Boulevard, West Las Vegas (878 7776, www. pprm.org). Bus 206.* **Open** (appointment only) 9am-5pm Mon,Wed; 11am-7pm, Tue, Thur.; 9am-4pm Fri; 9am-2pm Sat.; 10am-3pm Sun.
This non-profit organisation can supply contraception (including the morning-after pill), treat STDs, perform abortions and test for AIDS (results take a week). **Other location** 3300 E Flamingo Road #25 (547 9888).

Dentists

The **Nevada Dental Association** (1-800 962 6710, 255 4211, www. nvda.org) will make referrals to registered local dentists.

Hospitals

See p296 **Accident & emergency**.

Pharmacies

Over-the-counter and prescription drugs are readily available all over town. For pharmacies, *see p189.*

STDs, HIV & AIDS

For information, local resources, support groups and free, confidential tests, contact **Aid for AIDS of Nevada**. For treatment of STDs and free AIDS tests, visit **Planned Parenthood** (*see p296). See also below* **Helplines**.

Aid for AIDS of Nevada (AFAN) *Suite 170, 701 Shadow Lane, West*

of Strip (382 2326, www.afaniv.org).
Bus 206. **Open** 7am-5pm Mon-Fri.

HELPLINES

For information on what to do in
an emergency, *see above*. See also
above **Health**.

Alcoholics Anonymous *598 1888.*
Gamblers Anonymous *529 0202.*
Narcotics Anonymous *369 3362.*
Poison Control Center *732 4989.*
Rape Crisis *366 1640.*
Suicide Prevention *486 8225.*

ID

You'll need to prove your age with a
photo ID (passport, driver's licence
or state ID card) when buying
tobacco and alcohol, gambling, and
entering strip clubs and nightclubs.

INSURANCE

Non US nationals should arrange
comprehensive insurance, including
medical insurance, before departure;
US citizens should consider doing
the same. Medical centres will ask
for details of your insurance
company and your policy number;
keep them with you at all times.

INTERNET

Most hotels have high-speed
connections wired into every room
(around $10 per day); some have
wireless access. Savvy laptoppers
can link to free Wi-Fi at 12 branches
of the **Coffee Bean & Tea Leaf**,
among them in the Miracle Mile
Shops (*see p175*; 696 0564), at the
Venetian (*see p92*; 650 0734) and in
the University District (4550 S
Maryland Parkway, between E
Flamingo Road & E Tropicana
Avenue (944 5029). There's also free
wireless in the **Fashion Show
Mall** (*see p177*) and in the city's
libraries (*see below*).

For those without a laptop, the
pickings are slimmer. A few
convenience stores have terminals,
but prices are high. Public libraries
(*see below*) offer free, time-limited
access; **FedEx Kinko's** (*see p295*)
has paid-for access; and the display
computers in the Apple Store serve
as an unofficial internet café.

LEFT LUGGAGE

Hotel bell desks are happy to
look after bags for up to 12 hours.
Lockers are available in McCarran
Airport; expect to pay $2-$3/hr or
$8-$12/day.

LEGAL HELP

If you're arrested, call your
insurance firm, your consulate or the
Lawyer Referral Service on 382 0504.
If you do not have a lawyer, the
court will appoint one for you.

LIBRARIES

There are public libraries thoughout
the Las Vegas-Clark County Library
District (www.lvccld.org). Most are
open 10am-7pm, Mon-Thur; 10am-
6pm Fri-Sun.

Clark County Library *1401 E
Flamingo Road, at S Maryland
Parkway, University District (507
3400). Bus 109, 202.* **Map** p317 Y3.
Lied Library *4505 S Maryland
Parkway, between E Flamingo Road
& E Tropicana Avenue, University
District (895 2255, www.library.
nevada.edu). Bus 109.* **Map** p317 Y3.

LOST PROPERTY

Casinos all have lost and found
departments. If you lose an item
in a cab, call the taxi firm.

McCarran International Airport
Terminal 1 (261 5134). **Open** 7am-
11pm, daily .
**RCT South Strip Transfer
Terminal** *6675 S Gillespie Street, at
I-215 (1-800 228 3911, 228 7433).
Bus Deuce, 105, 109, 212.* **Open**
7am-5.30pm Mon-Fri.

MEDIA

Daily newspapers

The **Las Vegas Review-Journal**
(www.reviewjournal.com) offers
toothless but serviceable coverage of
local and national stories. 'Neon', the
R-J's pull-out entertainment guide
issued each Friday, has listings for
films, shows and restaurants.

The **Las Vegas Sun**
(www.lasvegassun.com) once
offered a populist, left-leaning
alternative to the conservative
R-J, but it's now an eight-page
shadow of its former self, folded
into the *R-J* each morning; however,
despite this curious arrangement,
the papers are run separately.
The *Sun*'s news reporting has
considerably more bite than
the *R-J*'s.

As well as the city's two daily
papers, the **Los Angeles Times**
is widely available, and most Strip
hotels will also carry the **Wall
Street Journal** and the **New
York Times**.

Alternative weeklies

The newest, hippest and slickest of
the alt-weeklies is *Seven* (www.
vegasseven.com), a city magazine
with a special interest in the club
and pool-party scene, run by
Wendoh Media, which funds other
publications such as *Vegas/Rated*
(www.vrated.com), and the nightlife-
centric website Spy on Vegas
(www.spyonvegas.com). .

The *Las Vegas Weekly* (free,
www.lasvegasweekly.com) has gone
through various editorial phases, but
is now very much focused on
entertainment. Ironically, then, it's at
its best when it looks at the broader
picture of Las Vegas life.

A good deal less glossy and a
touch more political than the *Weekly*,
the relatively low-key *Las Vegas
CityLife* retains a fanbase. The
writing is solid and often excellent,
but the design is right out of 1985.

Other magazines

Numerous freebie mags, such as
Today in Las Vegas, *What's On* and
Las Vegas Magazine, are distributed
free at hotels and other tourist spots.
They're useful for show listings and
discount coupons, but the editorial is
little more than regurgitated press
releases; don't stop here if you're
after recommendations.

For gaming news, check out the
monthly *Las Vegas Advisor*, focused
on the city, or the weekly *Gaming
Today*, which has a wider remit.

MONEY

The US dollar ($) is split into 100
cents (¢). Coins run from the copper
penny (1¢) to the silver nickel (5¢),
dime (10¢), quarter (25¢), the less
common half-dollar (50¢) and the
rarely seen dollar (silver and gold).
Notes ('bills') are all the same green
colour and size, but come in
denominations of $1, $5, $10, $20, $50
and $100. Credit cards are accepted
in almost every hotel, shop and
restaurant, but do keep cash on hand
just in case (and, of course, for tips).

Banks & ATMs

ATMs are ubiquitous in Las Vegas:
you'll find them in stores, bars,
casinos and even strip clubs. ATMs
accept most major credit and debit
cards, but almost all will charge a
usage fee. You can withdraw cash
on a card without a PIN at most
casinos, though you'll be charged a
premium. It's cheaper to visit one of
the banks scattered all over town.

Bureaux de change

Some casinos have their own bank or bureau de change; all have a 24-7 cashier's cage where you can cash most US bank and travellers' cheques, and exchange most major currencies. Indeed, the casinos tend to offer better rates on currency than **American Express**. At non-casino hotels, you should be able to cash travellers' cheques at the front desk with photo ID.

American Express *Fashion Show Mall, 3200 Las Vegas Boulevard South, at Spring Mountain Road (739 8474, www.americanexpress. com). Bus Deuce, 205, 203.* **Open** 9am-9pm Mon-Fri; 10am-8pm Sat; 11am-6pm Sun. **Map** p319, p320 A6.

Lost/stolen credit cards

American Express *1-800 992 3404, travellers' cheques 1-800 221 7282, www.americanexpress.com.*
Diners Club *1-800 234 6377, www.dinersclub.com.*
Discover *1-800 347 2683, www.discovercard.com.*
MasterCard *1-800 622 7747, www.mastercard.com.*
Visa *1-800 847 2911, www.visa.com.*

Tax

Sales tax is 8.1%; food (groceries) purchased in stores are exempt. Room tax is 12%.

NATURAL HAZARDS

The most obvious hazards are the heat and sun, but summer visitors should be prepared for other severe weather: flash floods are not uncommon in July and August.

OPENING HOURS

The casinos, their bars and at least one of their restaurants or coffeeshops are open all day, every day. Many grocery stores, dry-cleaners and gas stations are also open 24-7. On a local level, however, Las Vegas keeps small-town hours. Many eateries close at 10pm; non-chain shops may shut at 6pm and won't open on Sundays. Office hours are 9am to 5pm or thereabouts.

POLICE

For emergencies, dial **911**. For non-emergencies, there's a police station at 400 E Stewart Avenue, just off Las Vegas Boulevard in Downtown (795 3111).

POSTAL SERVICES

US mailboxes are red, white and blue. Packages weighing more than 16 ounces must be taken to a post office (*see below*). For couriers and shippers, *see p295*.

Stamps are sold in shops and from machines. For your nearest post office, call 1-800 275 8777 and quote the zip code.

Main post office *1001 E Sunset Road, at Paradise Road, East of Strip (1-800 275 8777). Bus 212.* **Open** 8am-9pm Mon-Fri; 8am-4pm Sat. **Map** p317 Y4.
Downtown station *201 Las Vegas Boulevard South, between E Fremont Street & E Bonneville Avenue (1-800 275 8777). Bus Deuce & all DTC-bound buses.* **Open** 8.30am-5pm Mon-Fri. **Map** p318 D1.
Strip station *3100 Industrial Road, at Stardust Way, West of Strip (1-800 275 8777). Bus Deuce, 105.* **Open** 8.30am-5pm Mon-Fri. **Map** p319 A5.

Poste restante

General delivery mail (*poste restante*) can be collected from the Downtown station (to: General Delivery, Las Vegas, NV 89101). You'll need to show a photo ID when you collect it.

RELIGION

For your nearest **Episcopal** church, call 737 9190; and for **Methodist**, 369 7055.

Congregation Ner Tamid *55 Valley Verde Drive, Henderson (733 6292). Bus 112.* Jewish Reform.
First Baptist Church *4400 W Oakey Boulevard, West Las Vegas (821 1234). Bus 104.*
First Presbyterian Church *1515 W Charleston Boulevard, West of Strip (384 4554). Bus 206.* **Map** p319 B3.
Guardian Angel Cathedral *302 Cathedral Way, at E Desert Inn Road (735 5241). Bus Deuce.* **Map** p319 B5. Catholic.
Islamic Center of Las Vegas *3799 Edwards Avenue, North-west Las Vegas (395 7013). Bus 106.*
Temple Beth Sholom *10700 Havenwood Lane, Las Vegas (804 1333). Bus 211.*

SAFETY & SECURITY

There's less crime than you might expect in Las Vegas. Casinos have such elaborate security systems that few serious offences take place

within them, and those that do occur are hurriedly swept under the carpet for the sake of reputation. However, on the streets, pickpockets and muggers strike more often than the city would like. Be careful, especially in the seedier areas of Downtown, and follow a few simple precautions.

● Only take out what you need: leave the bulk of your money in a room safe or in a safety deposit box at the hotel.
● Keep a note of the numbers and details of your passport, driving licence, travellers' cheques, cards and insurance policies, along with the phone numbers you'll need to report their loss (*see left*).
● Take the usual precautions with your wallet or handbag, especially on buses.
● If you're threatened with a weapon, give your assailants what they want. Then immediately find a phone and call the police (**911**).

SMOKING

In 2007, smoking was banned in most establishments that serve prepared food (casinos and strip clubs were exempt). However, many businesses flouted the law, and it remains a matter for debate whether continued enforcement is possible. Smoking is ubiquitous on casino floors, though a couple have non-smoking areas. A few hotels (such as the Four Seasons) are entirely smoke-free; most others offer non-smoking rooms.

STUDY

Many local colleges feed the service and gaming industry. Those looking to learn how to become a dealer or croupier must attend one of the city's specialist dealer schools.

PCI Dealers School *90 Coronado Center Drive, Suite 140, Henderson, NV 89052 (877 4724, www.pcidealerschool.com).*

TELEPHONES
Dialling & codes

There are two area codes for Nevada: 702 for Clark County (including Las Vegas) and 775 for the rest of the state. Within Vegas, there's no need to use 702: just dial the seven-digit number. Outside the city, calls are long distance: dial 1, then the area code, then the number. The 1-800, 1-866, 1-877 and 1-888 codes denote toll-free numbers;

THE LOCAL CLIMATE

Average temperatures and monthly rainfall in Las Vegas.

	High (°C/°F)	Low (°C/°F)	Rainfall (mm/in)
Jan	14 / 57	3 / 37	15/ 0.59
Feb	17 / 63	5 / 41	18 / 0.69
Mar	21 / 69	8 / 47	15 / 0.59
Apr	26 / 78	12 / 54	4 / 0.15
May	31 / 88	17 / 63	6 / 0.24
June	37 / 99	22 / 72	2/ 0.08
July	40 / 104	26 / 78	11 / 0.44
Aug	39 / 102	25 / 77	11 / 0.45
Sept	34 / 94	21 / 69	8 / 0.31
Oct	27 / 81	14 / 57	6 / 0.24
Nov	19 / 66	7 / 44	8 / 0.31
Dec	14 / 57	3 / 37	10 / 0.40

many are accessible from outside the US, but you'll be charged for your call. Calls to 1-900 numbers will be charged at premium rates.

Most hotels charge a flat fee for calls to local and toll-free numbers. Long-distance and international calls can be pricey if direct-dialled from a hotel. You're better off using a US phonecard, whether tied to a domestic account or bought as a one-off. Drugstores and convenience stores sell them in various denominations.

Mobile phones

Vegas operates on the 1900 GSM frequency.Travellers with modern tri-band phones will have no trouble using them.

Operator services

Collect calls (reverse-charge) 0. **Local directory enquiries** 411. **National directory enquiries** 1 + [area code] + 555 1212 (if you don't know the area code, dial 0 for the operator). **International calls** 011 + [country code] + [area code] + [number]. **International country codes** UK 44; New Zealand 64; Australia 61; Germany 49; Japan 81.

TIME

Nevada operates on Pacific Standard Time, eight hours behind GMT (London). Clocks go forward by an hour in late April, and back in late October. (Note: neighbouring Arizona has no daylight saving time.)

TIPPING

Tipping is a way of life in Las Vegas. Limo drivers ($10-$25 per ride), valet parking attendants ($2-$5), cocktail waitresses ($1-$2),

housekeepers ($2-$4 a night) and even desk clerks ($10-$20 if you're looking for a better room) all ride the tip gravy train. For information on tipping in casinos, see p23.

TOURIST INFORMATION

There are many self-styled tourist offices on the Strip, but only those listed below are official..

Las Vegas Chamber of Commerce *6671 Las Vegas Boulevard. South, Suite 300 Las Vegas, NV 89119 (641 5822, www.lvchamber.com).* Bus 104, 408. **Open** 8am-5pm Mon-Fri. **Map** p320 C6. Advice, brochures, maps and a few coupons are available if you visit in person; there's also a good phone information service, and you can write in advance for a visitor pack. **Las Vegas Convention & Visitors Authority** *3150 Paradise Road, opposite Convention Center Drive, East of Strip, Las Vegas, NV 89109 (892 0711, www.visit lasvegas.com).* Bus 108, 213. **Open** 8am-5pm Mon-Fri. **Map** p319 C5. Write to the very excellent LVCVA for a visitor pack that includes lists of hotels, a brochure, a map and the regularly updated *Showguide*. In the UK, contact Cellet Travel Services for details on Vegas (020 7367 0979, www.visitlasvegas.co.uk).

VISAS & IMMIGRATION

Under the **Visa Waiver Program**, citizens of 27 countries, including the UK, Ireland, Australia and New Zealand, do not need a visa for stays in the US of less than 90 days (business or pleasure) if they have a passport valid for six months beyond the return date, a return (or open standby) ticket and permission to travel through the Electronic System

for Travel Authorization (ESTA) system (see www.cbp.gov/esta). Visitors must fill in the ESTA form and (and pay $14) at least 72 hours before travelling. Once granted, permission is valid for two years or until your passport expires.

Canadians and Mexicans do not need visas. All other travellers must have visas. Application forms can be obtained from your nearest US embassy or consulate.

UK travellers should consult the US Embassy's website at http://london.usembassy.gov or call its helpline on 09042 450100 for information.

WHEN TO GO

Though there's no off-season in Las Vegas, it's slightly quieter (and cheaper) between the Thanksgiving and Christmas holidays, and during the heat of July and August. Public holidays are always busy. If you're planning a short visit, try to avoid busy, pricey weekends. The convention schedule has a major effect on hotel prices and availability.

Climate

Las Vegas has blue skies and little rain all year round. In July and August, it can get absurdly hot during the day, with temperatures soaring to more than 110°F (43°C). Drink lots of water and wear a hat, sunglasses and sunscreen. Conversely, winter nights can dip below freezing. For average temperature and rainfall, *see left* **The Local Climate**.

Public holidays

1 Jan New Year's Day **3rd Mon in Jan** Martin Luther King Jr Holiday **3rd Mon in Feb** Presidents' Day **Mar/Apr** Easter Sunday **last Mon in May** Memorial Day **4 July** Independence Day **1st Mon in Sept** Labor Day **last Fri in Oct** Nevada Day **2nd Mon in Nov** Veterans' Day **4th Thur in Nov** Thanksgiving **25 Dec** Christmas Day.

WORK

To work, non-nationals must be sponsored by a US company and get an H-1 visa. They also have to convince immigration that no American is qualified to do the job. Contact your US embassy for details.

ESSENTIAL INFORMATION

Further Reference

BOOKS

Non-fiction

Al Alvarez *The Biggest Game in Town*
It's almost three decades old, but Alvarez's account of the World Series of Poker still fascinates.
Fred E Basten & Charles Phoenix *Fabulous Las Vegas in the 50s: Glitz, Glamour & Games*
A nostalgic full-colour collection of photographs, menus and postcards from the lost glory days of Vegas.
Susan Berman *Easy Street; Lady Las Vegas: The Inside Story Behind America's Neon Oasis*
Both written by the daughter of a Mob insider, and made all the more creepy by her murder in 1999.
Christina Binkley *Winner Takes All: Steve Wynn, Kirk Kerkorian, Gary Loveman and the Race to Own Las Vegas*
Wall Street Journal reporter takes you behind the back rooms and the eye in the sky to meet the moguls who created contemporary Las Vegas.
Jeff Burbank *License to Steal*
A detailed exposition of the legal side of Nevada gaming control and how it participated in building Las Vegas.
Norm Clarke *Norm Clarke's Vegas Confidential: Sinsational Celebrity Tales*
The dirt behind the dirt, by Vegas' premier newspaper gossip columnist.
Deke Castleman *Whale Hunt in the Desert: The Secret Las Vegas of Superhost Steve Cyr*
A fascinating glimpse into the world of the high roller, via one of the town's most powerful casino hosts.
Su Kim Chung *Las Vegas Then and Now*
Vintage photographs of Las Vegas, printed alongside images of the same locations in the 21st century. A clever idea that's executed well.
John D'Agata *About a Mountain*
A dual meditation on the US government's plan to store nuclear waste in nearby Yucca Mountain – and on the toxic darkness of Vegas itself.

Sally Denton & Roger Morris *The Money and the Power: The Making of Las Vegas and Its Hold on America*
This investigative history of how Vegas was shaped and corrupted is perhaps the best single-volume history of the city.
Pete Early *Super Casino: Inside the 'New' Las Vegas*
A fizzing journalistic account of the 1990s revolution in resort-building.
William L Fox *In the Desert of Desire*
The nature of culture and the culture of nature in Las Vegas.
Steve Friess *Gay Vegas: A Guide to the Other Side of Sin City*
Comprehensive exploration of the flip side of Las Vegas.
Jeff German *Murder in Sin City: The Death of a Las Vegas Casino Boss*
Reporter German explores the 1998 death of Ted Binion.
Mark Gottdiener, Claudia C Collins & David R Dickens *Las Vegas: The Social Production of an All-American City*
A fascinating look at the social phenomenon of Vegas, from how a city grows in the desert to what it means to live off the tourist dollar.
Rick Harrison *License to Pawn: Deals, Steals and My Life at the Gold & Silver*
True tales from the patriarch of the hit History Channel series *Pawn Stars*.
AD Hopkins & KJ Evans (eds) *The First 100: Portraits of the Men and Women Who Shaped Las Vegas*
A thought-provoking, well-written encyclopaedia.
Joan Burkhart Whitely *Young Las Vegas 1905-1931: Before the Future Found Us*
A photographic essay on the city's early years.
Paul McGuire *Lost Vegas: The Redneck Riviera, Existentialist Conversations With Strippers, and the World Series of Poker*
A vividly funny behind-the-curtain take on the adult playground.
Rick Lax *Fool Me Once: Hustlers, Hookers, Headliners, and How Not to Get Screwed in Vegas*
Clever and illuminating first-person study of deception, as personified by showgirls, call

girls, card counters, magicians and pickup artists.
Shaun Levy *Rat Pack Confidential*
A modern, funky appraisal of the Rat Pack years and beyond.
David Littlejohn, Eric Gran *The Real Las Vegas: Life Beyond the Strip*
A writing team of UC Berkeley journalism graduate students look at how real life is lived in this 24/7 service economy and shed light on its implications and repercussions.
Eric Andrès Martinez *24/7: Living It Up and Doubling Down in the New Las Vegas*
An attorney and journalist spends his $50,000 advance in this modern-day *Fear and Loathing*.
Robert D McCracken *Las Vegas: The Great American Playground*
A mix of history and commentary, and a great read to boot.
James McManus *Positively Fifth Street: Murders, Cheetahs, and Binion's World Series of Poker*
McManus was sent on assignment to cover the 2000 World Series of Poker, but ended up taking part. Great fun.
Ben Mezrich *Busting Vegas: A True Story of Monumental Excess, Sex, Love, Violence and Beating the Odds*
Another gripping tale of card counters beating the house, by the author of *Bringing Down the House*, which inspired the movie *21*.
Eugene P Moehring & Michael S Green *Las Vegas: A Centennial History*
The best of the centennial books.
Matthew O'Brien *Beneath the Neon: Life and Death in the Tunnels of Las Vegas*
Vegas's subterranean homeless encampments.
Dick Odessky *Fly on the Wall: Recollections of Las Vegas' Good Old, Bad Old Days*
Very readable first-person tales of 1950s and '60s Vegas.
Nicholas Pileggi *Casino: Love and Honour in Las Vegas*
True story of the Mob's role in Vegas that inspired the film: a crackling read.
William F Roemer *The Enforcer: Spilotro – The Chicago Mob's Man Over Las Vegas*

Vegas attorney Oscar Goodman kept Tony 'The Ant' Spilotro out of jail. Goodman later became mayor and Spilotro is dead, beaten to death and buried in an Indiana cornfield.

Hal Rothman *Neon Metropolis: How Las Vegas Started the 21st Century*
Late UNLV history professor deconstructs Las Vegas's myth.

Hal Rothman & Mike Davis (eds) *The Grit Beneath the Glitter: Tales from the Real Las Vegas*
A spotty but often fascinating collection of essays about the city.

Geoff Schumacher *Howard Hughes: Power, Paranoia & Palace Intrigue; Sun, Sin and Suburbia: An Essential History of Modern Las Vegas*
Former *CityLife* editor uncovers Hughes's fascinating history and surveys the last few decades in readable fashion.

Cathy Scott *Murder of a Mafia Daughter: The Life and Tragic Death of Susan Berman*
Journalist Cathy Scott investigates the murder of the mafia daughter-turned-author.

John L Smith *No Limit: The Rise and Fall of Bob Stupak & Las Vegas' Stratosphere Tower; Running Scared: The Life and Treacherous Times of Las Vegas Casino King Steve Wynn; Of Rats and Men: Oscar Goodman's Life from Mob Mouthpiece to Mayor of Las Vegas; Sharks in the Desert: The Founding Fathers and Current Kings of Las Vegas*
Preposterously prolific *R-J* columnist dishes the dirt on two major casino players, the current mayor and the men who shaped the town.

Nick Tosches *Dino*
Scorching biog of the Rat Packer.

Mike Tronnes (ed) *Literary Las Vegas*
A great anthology of journalism from 1952 to the late 1990s.

Robert Venturi, Steven Izenour & Denise Scott Brown *Learning from Las Vegas: The Forgotten Symbolism of Architectural Form*
Fascinating study of the auto-driven architecture of the Strip.

Mike Weatherford *Cult Vegas: The Weirdest! The Wildest! The Swingin'est Town on Earth*
Vegas-related offbeat movies, ornery characters, unforgettable trivia, all explained in gossipy detail by an *R-J* columnist.

Fiction

Larry McMurtry *Desert Rose*
The *Terms of Endearment* writer turns his attention to the portrayal of a washed-up showgirl.

P Moss *Blue Vegas*
A book of characterful short stories by P Moss, owner of Downtown's character-filled Double Down saloon.

John O'Brien *Leaving Las Vegas*
Love, loneliness and alcoholism in the city of fun. This is despair writ large.

Wendy Perriam *Sin City*
Personal drama played out against an impersonal city.

Tim Powers *Last Call*
A fantasia on the Las Vegas myth, in which Bugsy Siegel is the Fisher King and tarot cards the deck of choice at the Flamingo's poker tables.

Mario Puzo *Fools Die*
The Godfather author returns with another 'sweeping epic'.

Hunter S Thompson *Fear and Loathing in Las Vegas*
The drug-crazed classic is always worth re-reading.

Michael Ventura *The Death of Frank Sinatra*
Cracking private-eye story set among the implosions of the early 1990s.

Gambling

Gambling guides are many and varied, but a sizeable number are poorly researched and dangerously misleading. We recommend ordering material direct from renowned gambling experts Huntington Press (1-800 244 2224, www.huntingtonpress. com), which publishes all the books listed below.

Ian Andersen *Burning the Tables in Las Vegas: Keys to Success in Blackjack and in Life*
A high-stakes blackjack player reveals how he gets away with it.

Rick Garman *Las Vegas for Dummies*
Insider tips on game rules, jargon and how not to make a fool of yourself.

Bob Dancer *Video Poker for the Intelligent Beginner*
Proper strategies for video poker novices from a master. A must for players.

Max Rubin *Comp City: A Guide to Free Gambling Vacations*
A classic text on casino comps, now in its second edition. A hilarious read.

Jean Scott *The Frugal Gambler*
How to get the most from the least. A classic text.

Olaf Vancura & Ken Fuchs *Knock-Out Blackjack: The Easiest Card-Counting System Ever Devised*
This former astrophysicist's 'unbalanced' count eliminates most of the mental gymnastics of other systems. Not easy, but doable.

FILM

In addition to these movies, TV shows worth catching (either on TV or DVD) include *American Casino*, *Casino*, *CSI: Las Vegas* and *The Real World: Las Vegas*.

America's Sweethearts (2001)
Take on the rom com, filmed in Lake Las Vegas. Stars Billy Crystal.

Bugsy (1991)
Witty script (James Toback), classy direction (Barry Levinson) and great performances (Beatty, Bening).

Casino (1995)
Martin Scorsese's three-hour mishmash of gambling and the Mob, voiceovered to death.

The Cooler (2003)
Set in Vegas (but filmed mostly in Reno). William H Macy stars.

Diamonds Are Forever (1971)
Bond (Connery, this time) in Vegas. Silly gadgets abound.

Fear and Loathing in Las Vegas (1998)
This relentless adaptation of the Thompson classic was a cult movie before it was even released.

The Grand (2008)
Comedy with Woody Harrelson as an unlucky casino owner in the midst of a poker tournament.

Honeymoon in Vegas (1992)
Nicolas Cage in engagingly oddball comedy mode.

Leaving Las Vegas (1995)
This Mike Figgis masterpiece stars Cage as a self-destructive alcoholic.

Meet Me in Las Vegas (1956)
Problem gambler hooks up with Strip dancer in a familiar plot, brightened by Cyd Charisse as the dancer.

Ocean's 11 (1960)
With all the Rat Pack present, this kitschy, corny film has become the de facto video history of a romantic Vegas era. Soderbergh's 2001 *Ocean's Eleven* deploys George Clooney and chums in a surprisingly vigorous high-tech remake.

Ocean's Thirteen (2007)
The sequel to *Eleven* and *Twelve*, with the usual suspects in Vegas one more time.

ESSENTIAL INFORMATION

One From the Heart (1980)
Coppola's Las Vegas love story, flawed but still somehow winning. Tom Waits and Crystal Gayle (duetting!) provide the beautiful soundtrack.

Rain Man (1988)
Dustin Hoffman's autistic Raymond – and brother Charlie (Tom Cruise) – finds his ability to remember numbers comes in handy in Vegas.

Showgirls (1995)
Some films that are universally panned on release benefit from a later reappraisal. Paul Verhoeven's Vegas misadventure still isn't one of them.

Swingers (1996)
First feature by Doug Liman: 90 minutes learning how not to pick up girls. Vince Vaughn is still trading off the kudos.

21 (2008)
Kevin Spacey leads a crew of card-counting MIT students in this thriller based on the book *Bringing Down the House*.

Viva Las Vegas (1963)
Fun film for those nostalgic for the old, swanky Vegas and the young, svelte Elvis. Ann-Margret co-stars.

What Happens in Vegas (2008)
Ashton Kutcher and Cameron Diaz: What the 21st century has to settle for in lieu of Elvis and Ann-Margret.

The Hangover (2009)
Gross-out buddy comedy with Bradley Cooper, Ed Helms and Zach Galifianakis piecing together an epic blackout.

MUSIC

Beyoncé *I Am … Yours: An Intimate Performance at Wynn Las Vegas*
The new-era diva as up-close as you're ever going to get.

Noel Coward *Live at Las Vegas*
Astonishingly racy for its time, Sir Noel's dry wit captured during his 1955 stand at the Desert Inn.

Crystal Method *Vegas*
This techno duo studied at UNLV.

Celine Dion *A New Day: Live in Las Vegas*
The audio and visual record of Queen Celine's history making five-year stand at the Colosseum at Caesars Palace. Elvis who?

David Holmes *Ocean's Eleven*
Funky, spunky soundtrack to the Steven Soderbergh remake of the Rat Pack classic.

The Killers *Hot Fuss*
Indie-rock from Vegas; the first band from the town to make it big in aeons.

Barry Manilow *Live From Las Vegas*
Documentary DVD about Manilow's long-running stint as Elvis's successor at the Las Vegas Hilton.

Wayne Newton *Wild, Cool and Swingin'*
Back when he still had a voice.

Panic! At the Disco
A Fever You Can't Sweat Out
Theatrical indie rockers straight out of Summerlin.

Elvis Presley *Live in Las Vegas*
As Elvis got fatter, his shows got glammer. This box set is all the fat Elvis you'll ever need. Classic.

Louis Prima *Collectors Series*
Glorious, hard-swingin' lounge stuff from the 1950s.

Frank Sinatra *Sinatra at the Sands*
Classic recording of Frank backed by the Count Basie Orchestra.

Various Artists *The Rat Pack: Live at the Sands*
The definitive audio record of Dino (on top form), Sammy and the Chairman of the Board.

BLOGS & PODCASTS

www.lasvegasadvisor.com/whatsnews.cfm
Anthony Curtis offers news and tips on the Las Vegas Advisor blog.

www.lasvegassun.com/blogs/kats-report
In The Kats Report, personable journalist John Kasilometes interviews the citizens of the Strip.

http://dmckee.lvablog.com
The inside info from Dave McKee's Stiffs & Georges blog/podcast will make you feel like a Vegas local.

http://thestrippodcast.blogspot.com
Tireless journalist Steve Friess provides big scoops and Top Tourist Tips of the Week on his blog and its companion weekly podcast.

www.vegasdeluxe.com
Wondering where Robin Leach went? He's here in Vegas, schmoozing and boozing with Vegas stars and starlets.

WEBSITES

www.allvegaspoker.com
Indispensible site for Vegas poker players. Lists up-to-the-minute news about games around the city.

www.bj21.com
Head here for the invaluable monthly 'Current Blackjack News',

which details current playing conditions at every casino in the city.

www.cheapovegas.com
An excellent guide to Vegas casinos, slanted towards cash-poor travellers but with enough useful information for all.

www.crecon.com/vintagevegas
Nothing here but images of classic Las Vegas matchbooks, postcards and gambling chips. Isn't that enough?

www.dtlv.com
New site chronicling the rise of Downtown Las Vegas. Smart, witty and insightful.

www.firstfridaylasvegas.com
Information on Vegas's highly successful monthly cultural event.

www.knpr.org
Run by the local NPR affiliate, this site has a great programming archive with transcripts and audio files.

www.lasvegas.com
The official consumer website of the Las Vegas Convention & Visitors Authority has all sorts of information.

www.lasvegasadvisor.com
The online version of the gambling bible has all the latest gambling tips, advice on how to make the most of your cash, and an always-interesting 'Question of the Day' section.

www.reviewjournal.com
Your first stop for Vegas news. The weekly eNeon newsletter is a useful entertainment resource.

www.lasvegassun.com
Award-winning website, with cool interactive history features.

www.nextshooter.com/vegas
The latest news on craps in Vegas: where to play and where to avoid.

www.vegas.com
This portal includes reviews of bars and restaurants, and listings of shows, films and nightlife. Useful resource, even if the reviews read a like PR copy.

www.vegaschatter.com
A must-read site for all the goings-on around town. Its news, gossip, opinion and no-holds-barred writing make consistently enjoyable.

**www.vegastodayand
tomorrow.com**
Annoying design, but until recently this site offered good info on the city's extraordinary wave of construction.

www.wizardofodds.com
A phenomenally detailed survey of casino games, including incisive tips on where to find the best odds in Vegas. An excellent site.

Index

★ indicates a
critic's choice

1 Oak 220★
18b Arts District 68
24 Hour Fitness 237
35 Steaks + Martinis
 150★

A

A Christian Pastor 2U
 240
A Robert Cromeans
 Salon 189
A Special Memory
 Wedding Chapel 240
abortion 296
Absinthe 203
accident & emergency
 296
Act, the 220
addresses 295
adult revues 197-198
Adult Superstore 188
Adventuredome 57, 210
African American
 History Month 43
Agave 153
Age of Chivalry
 Renaissance Fair 41
age restrictions 295
Agent Provocateur 183
airlines 292
airport 292
Albertsons 185
Alexis Park 116
Alizé 150
Amargosa Opera House
 261
AMC Town Square 18
 212
America 133
American Fish 133
American Shooters
 Supply & Gun Club
 237
American Storm 197
André's 133
Andrea's 133
animal attractions
 209
antiques shops 192
Apple Store 180
Aquaknox 134
arcades 210
Architecture
 283-289
Area 51 266-267
Aria 81★
Arizona 251-257
Arizona Charlie's
 Boulder 128

Artisan 118
 wedding chapel 239
Artisan Lounge 164
Arts Factory, the 186
Aruba Hotel 119
Atelier de Joël
 Robuchon, L' 155★
ATMs 297
Atomic Liquors 164★
Atomic Testing
 Museum 59★
Aurora 158
Aureole 135
Auto Collections at the
 Quad 54
auto racing 232
Aveda 189

B

babysitting 211
baccarat 23-24
Bacchanal Buffet 156
Backcountry
 Information Center
 256
Backdoor Lounge 215
Badlands Saloon 215
Baker 258
bakeries 184
Bali Hai Golf Club 236
Bally's 95
Bank, The 220
banks 297
Bar at Times Square
 159
Bare 223
Barbers 189
Bare Essentials
 Fantasy Fashions 183
Barmasa 135
Barneys New York 181
Bars & Lounges
 158-169
 By area:
 Downtown 164-167
 Off-Strip 163-164
 Rest of the City
 167-168, 169
 Strip, The 158-163,
 169
 By type:
 gay 215-216
 lounges 169
 Features:
 the best bars 159
 cocktails 163
Barth's Starlight Tattoo
 192
Bartolotta Ristorante
 di Mare 135
baseball 232
basketball 233

Bass Pro Shops
 Outdoor World 192
Battlefield Vegas 51,
 235
Bauman Rare Books
 179
Beat Coffeehouse &
 Records 228
Beatty 262
Beatty Museum 262
Beauty Bar 164★
Bellagio 82★ 272
 wedding chapel 239
Bellagio Fountains 53★
Bellagio Gallery of Fine
 Art 53
Bertha Miranda's 265
Best Buy 180
Best Western Squire
 Inn 254
Betting *see* gambling
Big Shot, X Scream
 & Insanity: the
 Ride & Freefall 57
big six 29
bingo 24
Binion's 65
Bit & Spur 269
Black & White Party 40
blackjack (21) 24-27
Blue Man Group 203★
Boca Park Fashion
 Village 176
Bodies 50
Body English 220
Body Works Massage
 Therapy 188
Bonanza 187
Bonneville Transit
 Center 292
Bonnie Springs Old
 Nevada 249
books 300-301
bookshops 178-179
Bootlegger Bistro 154
Border Grill 135
Botero 135
bottle service 220
Bouchon 135
Boulder City 246
Boulder City/Hoover
 Dam Museum 246
Boulder Dam Brewing
 Company 246
Boulder Dam Hotel 246
Boulder Station 128
Boulevard, Le 173
Boulevard Mall 176
Boulevard Pool 226
BounceU 210
Bourbon Street Cabaret
 169
bowling 234

boxing 233
Boyz II Men 202
Brad Garrett's Comedy
 Club 207
Brenden Las Vegas 14
 212
Brett Wesley Gallery
 186
Brian Head Ski Resort
 237
Bright Angel
 Restaurant & Lodge
 252, 254
Bright Angel Trail 256
Broadacres Open Air
 Swap Meet 178
Brooks Brothers 181
Bryce Canyon National
 Park 269
Budget Suites 119
Buffalo 216
Buffalo Bill's 258
Buffalo Exchange 182
Buffet at Bellagio 156
buffets 156-157
 see also Restaurants
 & Buffets
Build-a-Bear Workshop
 180
Bunkhouse Saloon 228
Burberry 181
bureaux de change 298
Burger Bar 136
BurGR 136
Burning Man Festival
 264
bus tours 293
buses 292-293
business 295

C

C Level 181
Cabaret, Le 169
Caesars Palace 83★
California 257-260
 Along I-15 258
Death Valley National
 Park 259-260
Mojave National
 Preserve 258-259
Canyon Ranch SpaClub
 191
Capitol Reef National
 Park 269
car hire 294
Carnaval Court 169
Carnegie Deli 136
Carnival World Buffet
 156
Carriage House 118
Carrot Top 199
Carson City 265-266

INDEX

INDEX

INDEX

Maps

Escapes and Excursions

0   40   80 miles

0   100 km

© Copyright Time Out Group 2013

Pyramid Lake

Reno (p262)

Virginia City (p266)

Fallon

Lahontan Lake

Lake Tahoe (p266)

Yerington

Schurz

N E V A D A

Walker Lake

SACRAMENTO

Hawthorne

SAN FRANCISCO

Tonopah

Yosemite National Park

Mono Lake

Goldfield

MODESTO

Scotty's Junction

Rhyolite

FRESNO

Kings Canyon National Park

Death Valley National Park

Monterey

Salinas

Mt Whitney (14,494ft)

Stovepipe Wells

Furnace Creek

Badwater (-282ft)

Ballarat

C A L I F O R N I A

PACIFIC OCEAN

BAKERSFIELD

M O J A V

CANADA

Vancouver

Calgary

Seattle

Regina

Winnipeg

Québec

Montreal

Ottawa

Boston

Minneapolis

Buffalo

New York

Detroit

Pittsburg

Philadelphia

Salt Lake City

Chicago

Washington

Barsto

San Francisco

Denver

Kansas City

St Louis

Las Vegas

U S A

Memphis

Hesperia

Los Angeles

Oklahoma City

Atlanta

Charleston

San Diego

Phoenix

Dallas

San Bernardino Mtns

MEXICO

Houston

New Orleans

Miami

CUBA

LOS ANGELES

Transit | map

↑ N

Map is not to scale
Mapa no es a escala

DOWNTOWN LAS VEGAS →

Centennial Hills

Aliante

Summerlin

DOWNTOWN LAS VEGAS
For more details see

Note: Frequent Service at SHARED STOPS only on Routes 113/MAX
Nota: Servicio frecuente en las paradas compartidas en la Ruta 113/MAX.

Legend Leyenda

Frequent Service Route (highlighted in yellow)
15 minutes or better on Weekday afternoons
20 minutes or better during other daytime hours
Servicio Frecuente (resaltado en amarillo)
15 minutos o mejor en las tardes de lunes a viernes
20 minutos o mejor durante las otras horas del día

Regular Service Route
Ruta de Servicio Regular

Bonneville Transit Center (BTC)
Centro de Transporte Bonneville

Transit Center + Park & Ride
Centro de Transporte + Park & Ride

BHX	Boulder Highway Express
CX	Centennial Express
HDX	Henderson & Downtown Express
MAX	Metropolitan Area Express
	Strip & Downtown Express
S&A	Sahara Express-A (via West Charleston & East Lake Mead)
SSB	Sahara Express-B (via West Sahara & Vegas Valley)
DNX	Downtown & Veterans

— Limited Stop Routes: Rutas con Paradas Limitadas
— Resort Corridor Routes: Rutas del Corredor Turísticos
— Residential Routes: Rutas Residenciales
— Commuter Express Routes: Rutas Express

BTC
Bonneville Transit Center

Street Index

3 1170 00947 7872

STREET INDEX

Central
Las Vegas

X — W LAKE MEAD BOULEVARD

59 Texas Station

VEGAS DRIVE

W OWENS AVENUE

Y

Las Vegas Motor Speedway

604

Z

15

W WASHINGTON AVENUE

Old LV Mormon Fort Historic Park

E WASHINGTON AVENUE

EASTERN AVENUE

S PECOS ROAD

1

Lorenzi Park

Nevada State Museum

W BONANZA ROAD

Cashman Field

LV Natural History Museum

515

95

Las Vegas Springs Preserve

ALTA DRIVE

Children's Discovery Museum/ Smith Center

MAIN STREET

LAS VEGAS BOULEVARD

FREMONT STREET

Desert Pines Golf Course

Las Vegas Premium Outlets

See p319

To Arizona Charlie's

W CHARLESTON BOULEVARD

Arts Factory

See p318

159

FREMONT STREET

93

W OAKEY BOULEVARD

MAIN ST

E WYOMING AVENUE

E OAKEY BOULEVARD

S MARYLAND PARKWAY

515

2

BOULDER HWY

Stratosphere

E SAHARA AVENUE

88 90 Commercial Center

To Sam's Town & Boulder Station

589

44

Palace Station

Circus Circus

LVH

Las Vegas Country Club

S EASTERN AVENUE

95

S VALLEY VIEW BOULEVARD

15

"THE STRIP"

Riviera

Las Vegas Convention Center

E DESERT INN ROAD

To Henderson, Lake Mead, Boulder City & Laughlin

SPRING MOUNTAIN ROAD

Fashion Show Mall

Wynn Las Vegas

41

39

112

SANDHILL ROAD

57

35 118

TI

Palazzo Venetian

SANDS AVENUE

Monorail

TWAIN AVENUE

Las Vegas Hilton Country Club

3

Rio

Mirage

Harrah's Quad

PARADISE ROAD

115

Caesars Palace

Flamingo

7 99 100

Palms

102 26

Bellagio

Bally's

Paris LV

E FLAMINGO ROAD

Cosmopolitan

Planet Hollywood

114

CityCenter

HARMON AVE

UNLV

E HARMON AVENUE

Monte Carlo

New York New York

Showcase Mall

Hard Rock

43

Orleans

593

46

MGM Grand

Thomas & Mack Center

40

111

Excalibur

Hooters

E TROPICANA AVENUE

SWENSON ST

S MARYLAND PARKWAY

S EASTERN AVENUE

42

MCLEOD DRIVE

S PECOS ROAD

4

Tropicana

Luxor

Mandalay Bay

LAS VEGAS BOULEVARD SOUTH

McCarran International Airport

See p320

SANDHILL ROAD

15

604

E SUNSET ROAD

562

50

1 Casinos & Hotels pp78-131
1 Restaurants & Buffets pp132-157
1 Bars & Lounges pp158-169

0 ——— 1 mile
0 ——— 1 km

© Copyright Time Out Group 2013

To Sunset Station

Time Out Las Vegas **317**

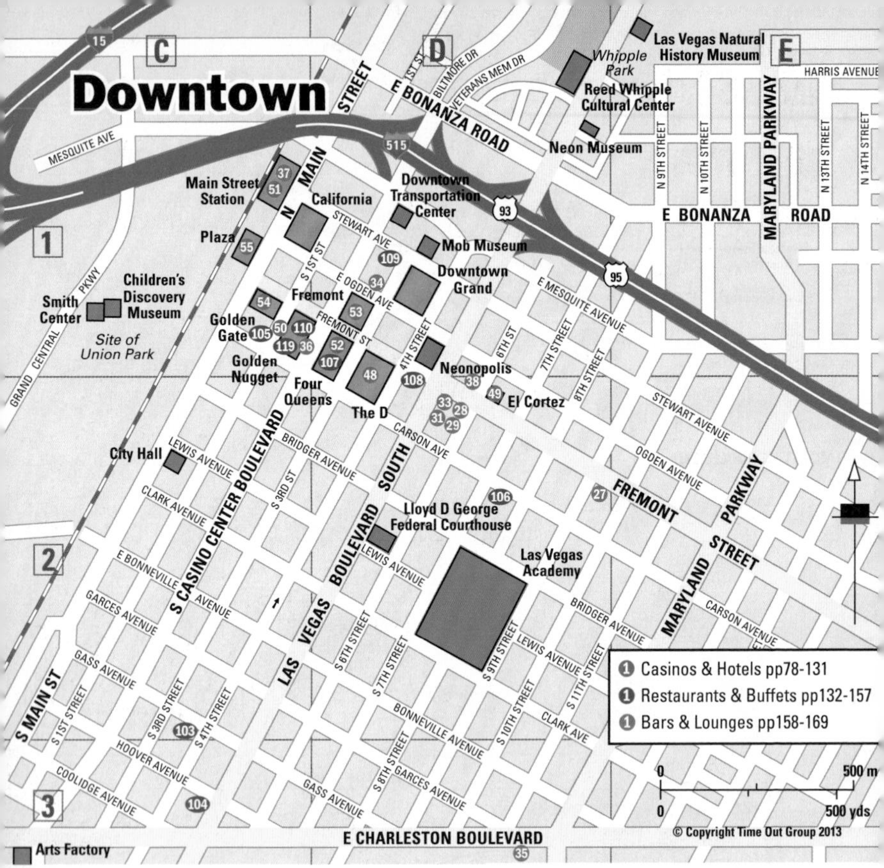
Downtown
C
D
E
1
2
3
15
515
93
95
MESQUITE AVE
N MAIN STREET
1ST ST
BILTMORE DR
VETERANS MEM DR
E BONANZA ROAD
Whipple Park
Las Vegas Natural History Museum
Reed Whipple Cultural Center
Neon Museum
HARRIS AVENUE
N 9TH STREET
N 10TH STREET
MARYLAND PARKWAY
N 13TH STREET
N 14TH STREET
E BONANZA ROAD
Main Street Station
California
Downtown Transportation Center
Plaza
STEWART AVE
Mob Museum
S 1ST ST
E OGDEN AVE
Downtown Grand
Fremont
Smith Center
Children's Discovery Museum
Site of Union Park
GRAND CENTRAL PKWY
Golden Gate
Golden Nugget
Four Queens
FREMONT ST
The D
4TH STREET
Neonopolis
El Cortez
6TH ST
7TH STREET
8TH STREET
E MESQUITE AVENUE
STEWART AVENUE
OGDEN AVENUE
CARSON AVE
City Hall
LEWIS AVENUE
BRIDGER AVENUE
S CASINO CENTER BOULEVARD
S 3RD ST
SOUTH
LAS VEGAS BOULEVARD
Lloyd D George Federal Courthouse
FREMONT STREET
MARYLAND PARKWAY
CLARK AVENUE
LEWIS AVENUE
Las Vegas Academy
E BONNEVILLE AVENUE
GARCES AVENUE
BRIDGER AVENUE
CARSON AVENUE
S 6TH STREET
S 7TH STREET
S 9TH STREET
LEWIS AVENUE
S 11TH STREET
GASS AVENUE
S MAIN ST
S 1ST STREET
S 3RD STREET
S 4TH STREET
BONNEVILLE AVENUE
S 10TH STREET
CLARK AVE
HOOVER AVENUE
COOLIDGE AVENUE
S 8TH STREET
GARCES AVENUE
GASS AVENUE
E CHARLESTON BOULEVARD
Arts Factory
Casinos & Hotels pp78-131
Restaurants & Buffets pp132-157
Bars & Lounges pp158-169
0
500 m
0
500 yds
© Copyright Time Out Group 2013

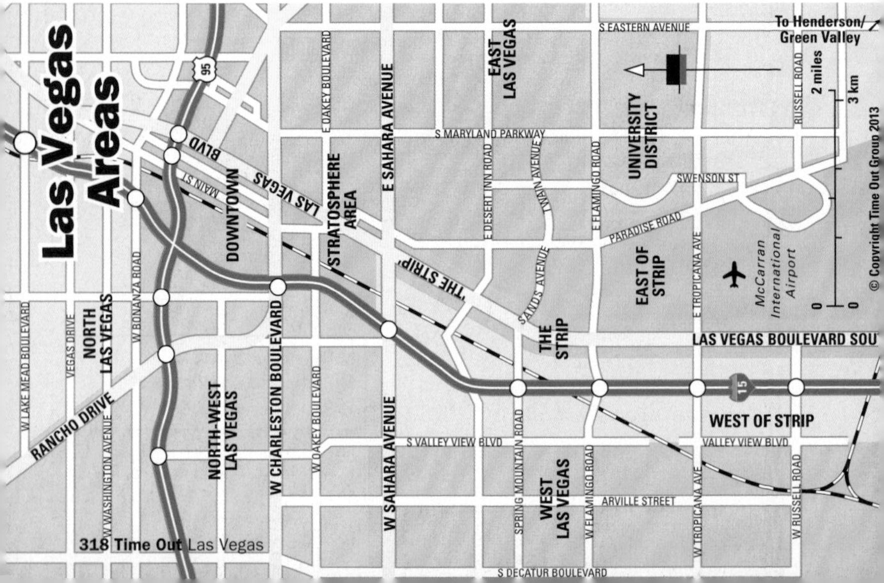
Las Vegas Areas
95
15
S EASTERN AVENUE
To Henderson/ Green Valley
E OAKEY BOULEVARD
E SAHARA AVENUE
EAST LAS VEGAS
UNIVERSITY DISTRICT
RUSSELL ROAD
2 miles
3 km
S MARYLAND PARKWAY
LAS VEGAS BLVD
N MAIN ST
DOWNTOWN
STRATOSPHERE AREA
E DESERT INN ROAD
TWAIN AVENUE
E FLAMINGO ROAD
SWENSON ST
PARADISE ROAD
THE STRIP
SANDS AVENUE
EAST OF STRIP
E TROPICANA AVE
McCarran International Airport
© Copyright Time Out Group 2013
0
0
W BONANZA ROAD
W LAKE MEAD BOULEVARD
VEGAS DRIVE
NORTH LAS VEGAS
W CHARLESTON BOULEVARD
THE STRIP
LAS VEGAS BOULEVARD SOU
RANCHO DRIVE
W WASHINGTON AVENUE
NORTH-WEST LAS VEGAS
W OAKEY BOULEVARD
W SAHARA AVENUE
SPRING MOUNTAIN ROAD
WEST OF STRIP
S VALLEY VIEW BLVD
VALLEY VIEW BLVD
WEST LAS VEGAS
W FLAMINGO ROAD
ARVILLE STREET
W TROPICANA AVE
W RUSSELL ROAD
S DECATUR BOULEVARD

The Strip
(South)

© Copyright Time Out Group 2013